RUSSELL GRANT'S
ZODIAC BABY NAMES

D0307493

RUSSELL GRANT'S
ZODIAC BABY NAMES

The complete book of Baby Names
defined by Star Sign

HAY HOUSE

Australia • Canada • Hong Kong • India
South Africa • United Kingdom • United States

First published and distributed in the United Kingdom by:
Hay House UK Ltd, 292B Kensal Rd, London W10 5BE. Tel.: (44) 20 8962 1230;
Fax: (44) 20 8962 1239. www.hayhouse.co.uk

Published and distributed in the United States of America by:
Hay House, Inc., PO Box 5100, Carlsbad, CA 92018-5100. Tel.: (1) 760 431 7695
or (800) 654 5126; Fax: (1) 760 431 6948 or (800) 650 5115. www.hayhouse.com

Published and distributed in Australia by:
Hay House Australia Ltd, 18/36 Ralph St, Alexandria NSW 2015.
Tel.: (61) 2 9669 4299; Fax: (61) 2 9669 4144. www.hayhouse.com.au

Published and distributed in the Republic of South Africa by:
Hay House SA (Pty), Ltd, PO Box 990, Witkoppen 2068.
Tel./Fax: (27) 11 467 8904. www.hayhouse.co.za

Published and distributed in India by:
Hay House Publishers India, Muskaan Complex, Plot No.3, B-2,
Vasant Kunj, New Delhi – 110 070. Tel.: (91) 11 4176 1620;
Fax: (91) 11 4176 1630. www.hayhouse.co.in

Distributed in Canada by:
Raincoast, 9050 Shaughnessy St, Vancouver, BC V6P 6E5.
Tel.: (1) 604 323 7100; Fax: (1) 604 323 2600

© Russell Grant, 2009

The moral rights of the author have been asserted.

The author of this book does not dispense medical advice or prescribe the
use of any technique as a form of treatment for physical or medical problems
without the advice of a physician, either directly or indirectly. The intent of the author
is only to offer information of a general nature to help you in your quest for emotional
and spiritual wellbeing. In the event you use any of the information in this book
for yourself, which is your constitutional right, the author and the
publisher assume no responsibility for your actions.

A catalogue record for this book is available from the British Library.

ISBN 978-1-84850-024-2

Printed in the UK by CPI Bookmarque, Croydon, CR0 4TD.

To dear Tigger, whose name says it all – with love

CONTENTS

WHAT'S IN A NAME?
and
How to select what you're looking for

I'd just finished watching a TV documentary on George V and his wife, Queen Mary of Teck, about how the British Royal Family had to change their name during the First World War due to public antipathy against their very-obviously-German surname, the formidable Saxe-Coburg-Gotha.

The Germans even had a type of bomber named Gotha, so this double whammy of the wretched Huns' nomenclature was getting to the British public's sensitivities about all things Teutonic – after all, they were the enemy. The British public suddenly became conscious that that great institution, the bastion of national devotion, pride and patriotism the Royal Family, were actually German! So what to do about it? The obvious solution was to change their name.

It just goes to show just how much the English (as opposed to the British) forget that their ancestors are likely to be Anglo-Saxons and Jutes, mostly from north German regions. The Royals bowed to the inevitable and changed their dynastic name to what sent out the most British vibration at their disposal, the most British of all castles – Windsor. The Battenbergs also relented, giving up their German-sounding name (but carrying on making nice marzipan cakes) and went for a direct English translation – Mountbatten. So you can change a name in a twinkling but thicker-than-water blood always remains the same, you're stuck with it.

A part of my love of history is etymology; finding out what is in a name and where it stemmed from. It started by being really fascinated at how the place where I lived, Middlesex, got its name. It actually means the land of the Middle Saxons; as opposed to the East Saxons (Essex), or South Saxons (Sussex) – you get the idea.

Long before astrocartography (finding the right place for you to live according to your astro chart) became popular, I was already looking at places from the Kingston and Glastonbury zodiacs to the origins of a topographical name to see how it fitted into astrology.

It occurred to me that places that had evolved from watery areas fitted well into the water planets, the Moon or Neptune, and the water signs, Scorpio, Cancer and Pisces.

Equally, those settlements with mountains, hills and dales with outlying hamlets and farmsteads were often named after clearings in woodland – neatly fitting into the earth element. Some place names have become personal names, such as Ashley.

The British Royal name change was massive. It didn't just change their ancestral history but their current and future identity and how they were seen and perceived by the public and world at large. It created a massive transformation in their PR and proved that your name is as important as the first impressions you give when you first meet someone; how you look, behave and speak are all thrown into the mix, but before you even get to that stage it is your name that sets the precedent. It will create an impression to the person who hears it. It sends out a vibration as to the kind of person you might be even before you meet, in much the same way as when you give your address people know which side of the tracks you come from.

As a New Moon Aquarian it was likely before I was even born that I would be called something eccentric, unfashionable or nouveau. In 1951, in post-war Britain, Russell (with two L's – wow!), was completely off-the-wall. In my school of 300 pupils I was the ONLY one named Russell, although there were surnamed Russells. Living with the disaster that was Russell was, of course, all that was needed for me to be bullied, made fun of and it was only when I grew older that I realised that this was a good name to have in my line of work in the public eye.

To be called Russ was always a term of endearment; Russell meant something was up; I was Rusty usually to school friends, Grant to teachers, General (after General Grant) to one school-teacher, Granty usually when involved in sport. And yet people always were more struck by my name when I became famous: 'Is that your REAL name, or did you make it up?' people wondered. No, I didn't; Mum and Dad gave it me, although Mum does admit that she wanted something just in case I became famous!

But when I looked inside the name Russell with two L's (it was usually spelt with one), I found it was good for a double Aquarian in the 1950s because it was 'different', and what are Aquarians? Different. This has become more evident with my young band of fans and followers who have recently renamed me Retro Russ as apparently I am 'dead cool' even 'wicked'. I do hope so!

Putting my etymological cap back on, I researched my own names. Russell is Old French, presumably Norman. My surname Grant comes from one of the most renowned Scottish Highland clans – and also derived originally from the French 'grande' – grand, large, maximus – in a Jupiter kind of way. Well, that was certainly me. Did this mean I was related to Michel Le Grande the French composer or some great Queen, like Mary, Queen of Scots? It appears that Grande became Grand then Grant when some Celts, Bretons presumably, connected with their British-based Celtic cousins.

The origins of these names came originally from the annals of the past and would have been how a person was recognised. In many places in Wales too many Davids would have ended up as Dai bach (little Dave or term of endearment, e.g. dear Dave), Dai fawr (big Dave), Dai Llaith (Dave the Milkman), Dai Tup (Stupid Dave), Dave Fynwy (Dave from Monmouth) and so on – and that is how surnames became known. Keeping up with the Jones was all about finding out which one first!

We all owe our names to ancestors who needed to differentiate one from the other. That is why many of us carry the names of clans, Scots and Irish, or place names, as it was easy to call someone after where they lived. Common sense, really.

But there are other names that seem senseless or even a mystery. How do you get the surname McCambridge? Because it was a Gaelic name that sounded like an English name, and so it became what it sounded like phonetically.

I would warn any parent that you must keep in your mind when naming your child that they are an individual and they have to carry their name with them for the rest of their lives. From school to marriage to form filling; spare a thought when you christen someone you love with a name like Peaches Lulu Apricot or Trixie Pixie Bell Grapefruit; they have to bear this crushing appellation for the rest of their lives. They might get used to it but imagine the first day at school, at work or anywhere else; it will be ridiculed. Take a look at the Uranian section for some true examples from New Zealand.

Of course, when we come into our own we can always change our names and that's where this splendid wee book comes into its own. Or if you are a parent who wants to give your kid, cat or pup the right vibration, then it is all in here.

I believe you can enhance your sun sign by matching the vibration of your name with the astro-essence of you. So if you are born under the sign of Libra, then a Venus or Libran name will enrich your spirit and soul and make it easy for people to relate to you, accept you and embrace your heart vibration.

If you know your own astrologicals (based on your date, time and place of birth) and have Moon in Cancer, you know that a Moon or Cancerian name is going to support your sensitivities and give you a sense of security and protection.

I have also noticed in my name experimentation – not at all scientific but more Aquarian observation – that our names are often altered by friends or family to become our pet names. Forget 'Princess' and 'Mummy's Little Soldier', they are universal and nursery names. Mainly in the macho world of men they will add a Y to a one-syllable surname – Giggs becomes Giggsy; Payne becomes Payney and so on. If that's not possible, then they will take a surname like Lawrence and shorten it to Lorro!

This makes it more cootchy, as we would say in Wales, more cosy and palsy. Tag a Y or O on to a butch name and you see it gives it a different tincture, a Bach tincture, small and nice, laddie and back to the schoolyard, which some chaps mentally never leave.

Authors and artists have pen names or noms de plume. My dear mum loves to paint and just after the war was a high-flying contracts secretary in the movie business at the world-famous Pinewood Studios just outside London. She was renowned for always having a spare corned-beef or cheese roll in her drawers (office table… just in case you thought…) and earned the nickname Scoff. This was way back in the late 1940s but 70 years later when she started to paint she became Van Scoff and signed her works of art accordingly.

Movie stars often have names thrust upon them by publicity departments, press men or moguls. Take Frances Gumm. Not exactly the name of a megastar like Judy Garland, is it, but that's her birth name. Marilyn Monroe is still a Hollywood icon and sensation and her original first name, Norma Jean, seems to have gained a new currency through the song and lyrics of others like Elton John. Again, not a real name, he was born Reginald Kenneth Dwight.

Let me share a very important piece of astrological knowledge. This book is not just for increasing the positive side of your God-given personality and potential, but to also add what you haven't got and possibly need, and it can all be done by adding to or tweaking your current name status.

A weak Mars at birth – which means the planet's natal position is challenged by other planets, sign or position – can create havoc. One of the symptoms is a bad temper, so perhaps an anger management course might well be called for. Astrologically that means enter Venus or the Moon. A good name introduced to a bad Mars will soothe the savage star, for a touch of velvet Venus or softer planets placed alongside a hairy Mars name can cool things down and bring out the more positive side: dead sexy, assertive and a go-getter.

For instance, Andrew is a perfect Mars name, but if your Mars is negatively aspected you might overdo the Mars, so we need to pacify it with some velvet Venus. Ashley is a good Venus name, so you could become Andrew Ashley or Drew Ashley or Ashley Drew; by the time you've finished you'll have fun finding a handle that you've not been saddled with but one you've worked out as being absolutely right for you.

Letters of the alphabet are also good to bring into your name. For instance A is an Aries letter and E is Venus, so you could have Andrew E. Oppenheimer.

Watch out for parental ego when choosing your child's name. After all, you are placing on your little one the name you want, not what they would necessarily go for. One dear friend of mine, Stephen Palmer, was so keen to have one of his children bearing his name that when his daughter was born she was christened Stephanie. It wasn't long before – lo and behold – his wife Jane announced she was pregnant again; it turned out to be a boy and they called him Stephen. I did suggest a change to Steven but it never happened; well, I suppose that gives them scope to call the next child Steven with a 'V'! And yet Little Stephen (which inevitably is what the child gets called when there are two or three in the same living space) was given a pet-name of Monkey! Why? Because he looked and acted like one! It still stuck some 20 years later.

Talking about Little or Big Stephen, my other half, Doug, has a brother called (you will never guess) – Russell. He also has two L's; the difference is that he was born in 1948 in Blackpool, Lancashire, and I was born in 1951 in Uxbridge, Middlesex. So I ended up being called Little Russell, even though I was very portly by then and living up to my surname! Because of my weight I became known in the Beaumont family as Tubbs – nothing to do with Miami Vice – but simply to differentiate me from their other Russell.

The American habit of calling kids Junior or giving Roman numerals such as George Hamilton I, II, III, IV looks good on paper, but in reality the child is always going to be called Junior. The Sword of Damocles hangs over their head forever more as always being less experienced, less wise and lesser than Senior. The British sitcom *Are You Being Served?* summed this up in having the owner of the Grace Brothers store known as Young Mr Grace, even though he was as old as Methuselah!

So before I let you loose on this book, please remember. When you give your baby a name, are you saddling them with something that could end up as emotional baggage or are you giving them something that makes them proudly stand out as being a strong individual?

Giving your child a name or a numeral, hoping they will be a chip off the old block or just like your mum or dad, is one thing. Of course, it's nice to put in the names of grandparents or a family name in their full appellation; that's not an issue. But far, far more importantly they are a new kid on the block and need their identity to be branded on them via a name to underline that they are a unique individual and have an exclusive vibration that is activated every time their name is called, spoken or written.

This astrological bible of names will give you everything you need to get the cosmic vibrations flowing. Each time you mention your child's name it will make their personality stronger and their traits more pronounced, so make sure it's one that does that rather than consciously trying to create a mini-you out of your own ego. Isn't it enough they have your DNA? Think about it.

HOW TO FIND THE
NAME YOU WANT

All the names are listed under their respective planets and signs. When you look at each entry you will see a list of names starting with the most relevant and followed by different spellings and variants, which are the same name but spelt in an unusual or novel way. Sometimes you will see a very popular name at the end of the list, this is often that culture's version of a global name.

Because many of the names are associated with the energy of a planet you will find those names listed under the signs the planets rule: you will see which in the heading of each chapter.

For example, a Venus name will be found under her two signs: Taurus and Libra. There is a planetary appendix which will give you the difference between the two types of Venus.

That does not mean the names listed are the same, however. Those allocated to Taurus are different from those for Libra, even though they share the same planet. As a result, of course there will be some that will cross over – that is bound to happen when one planet rules two signs. Venus is love but she comes with a different kind of loving if in Taurus or Libra; a read of the chapter header will explain this for all the signs and their planets.

I have then taken into account the element of the signs in question. This is why you find a name like George under Taurus but not under Libra: the etymology of George is earthy Taurus. Under Libra you will discover a name such as Keanu, which refers to a cool breeze and which comes under the auspice of airy Libra.

A sequence of names will be found under different signs. That is because I have taken into account the qualities of a sign and have researched each name thoroughly to find out the origin of every single insert. With the results I have then been able to allocate them to one or more of the 12 signs.

Because each planet means more than one thing (for instance, Jupiter is international travel or foreign affairs, but is also belief, worship and faith), you will find these under their respective signs. Mercury is also travel but not faith or worship, so some names tie up with both Mercury and Jupiter, which rule four signs between them.

Where a name has an uncertain or unknown origin it has been given to Scorpio or Pisces, as both are signs of mystery. Scorpio is more likely to have names where the origins will never be found, whereas Pisces tends to cover those where the root is confused or misty; in other words, some of the explanation is available but not all.

In some cases there are disputed meanings, maybe two or three or even more suggestions. Using my interest and love of both etymology (the derivation of words, in this case names) and astrology, where I have not been able to find a singular answer, I have given the name to those signs it does identify with.

This book has been a huge undertaking, and the one thing I can confirm and pride myself in is that every name has been subject to the thoroughness, scrutiny and at times pedantry that my natal Mercury in Capricorn and Saturn rising has to offer: formidable at the best of times when looking for perfection. But perfection is never, ever possible; it simply doesn't exist. However, I have got close, for I have turned every stone to gather the facts to give you the best that a book like this can offer.

You can be sure this book has been a labour of love rather than work, which is very often the best reason for doing something; time constraints can sometimes make you lose love along the way, but in time you learn to love again.

You will find most Western names correspond to the Christian faith and come from the Bible (that is supposedly why they are known as Christian names). I recently saw a television programme where a woman was having a pagan naming ceremony for her daughter Isabella: is she in for a surprise when she finds out what it means!

Some faith-based names popular in many cultures and countries have been listed with their local spellings. I have covered these names in all the languages I have been able to find a translation. This adds to the information packed in this little name-bible to bring you a publication that is comprehensive and definitive in every way.

You can use this book purely to find names and their meanings or you can choose a name according to a baby's birth sign. If you want to dig deeper and produce a name that is all-embracing you can select any of those that create the kind of vibration you are seeking in order to bring out the best in your offspring.

Of course, you can also use this book for naming your pet, your car or even YOU!

The Little Red-Headed One, Great, Large, Le Grande

CAPRICORN

22nd December to 20th January

Planet: Saturn

Day: Saturday

Stones: turquoise, garnet

Metal: lead

Colours: black, white, brown, grey

Design: checks, straight lines, squares

Trees: elm, holly, ivy, poplar, quince, pine, yew, lime

Flora: pansy, azalea, magnolia, camellia, poinsettia and any flowers that bloom during or over Christmas

Famous Capricorns: Prince Albert Victor (Duke of Clarence) • Mohammed Ali • Kirstie Alley • Elizabeth Arden • Shirley Bassey • St Bernadette • Orlando Bloom • David Bowie • Nicholas Cage • Al Capone • Jim Carrey • Paul Cezanne • Kevin Costner • Gérard Depardieu • Marlene Dietrich • Faye Dunaway • Gracie Fields • Frederico Fellini • Joe Frazier • Ava Gardner • Mel Gibson • William Gladstone • Hermann Goering • Barry Goldwater • Cary Grant • Oliver Hardy (of Laurel and!) • Sir Anthony Hopkins • Howard Hughes • St Joan of Arc • Ladybird Johnson • Jude Law • Annie Lennox • David Lloyd George • Martin Luther King • Rudyard Kipling • Ricky Martin • Ethel Merman • Isaac Newton • Richard Nixon • Aristotle Onassis • Dolly Parton • Louis Pasteur • Edgar Allen Poe • Elvis Presley • King Richard II • Helena Rubenstein • Anwar Sadat • Albert Schweitzer • Josef Stalin • Howard Stern • St Theresa • JRR Tolkein • Mary Tyler Moore • Richard Widmark • Tiger Woods • Mao Zedong.

Planetary Influences: see Saturn at the back of this book (page 431)

Boys

Aaron, Aron, Arron, Arun, Aharon, Arke, Arn, Arran • Biblical/Egyptian • *mountain of strength*

'Abbās • Arabic • *austere, severe*

'Abd-al-Hakīm • Arabic • *servant of the wise, Allah*

'Abd-al-Halīm • Arabic • *servant of the patient, Allah*

'Abd-al-Qādir • Arabic • *servant of the capable, Allah*

Abner, Avner • Biblical/Hebrew • *father of light*

Absalom, Absolon • Biblical/Hebrew • *father of peace*

Abraham, Abe, Avraham, Avrom, Abe, Avhamon • Hebrew/Aramaic • *father of the tribes or nations*

Abram • Biblical/Hebrew • *high father*

Adam, Addam, Ádhamh, Adamo, Adán, Adama • Biblical/Hebrew/Jewish • *earth*

Ádhamhnán • Irish Gaelic • *great fear*

Adie, Adaidh, Adam • Scots Gaelic • *earth*

Adina, Adin • Jewish/Hebrew • *so slender!*

Aegidus, Agid, Giles • Latin/Greek • *kid, a young goat*

'Ahmad, Ahmed • Arabic • *highly commendable*

Ailpein, Alpine, Alpin • Pictish/Scots Gaelic • *white*

Åke, Achatius, Åge • Germanic/Norse • *either ancestor or the semi-precious stone garnet*

Alan, Alain, Ailin, Ailean, Alyn, Alun, Allan, Allen • Celtic • *vague origins but likely to be a rock*

Alban, Albanus, Albie, Alby • Latin • *confused origins, perhaps Alba meaning white*

Albion • Latin/Celtic • *white or rocky cliff notionally referring to the white cliffs of Dover*

Aldous, Aldebrand, Aldemund, Alderan • Norman • *the root means old*

Algot • Norse • *gothic elf; magical powers*

Alby, Ailbhe • Irish Gaelic • *white*

Altman • Jewish/Hebrew • *old man*

Amerigo, Emmerich • Spanish/Visigothic • *a person who works hard to gain*

Aneislis • Irish Gaelic • *careful, pensive, thoughtful*

'Ammar • Arabic • *longevity*

Anisim, Onisim, Onesimos • Greek • *useful, worthwhile*

Anthony, Antony, Tony, Antain, Antaine, Anton, Antoine, Antonio, Antoni, Antonin, Antoninus, Ante, Antun, Antal, Antanas, Anthos, Antwan, Antonino, Nino, Ninny, Anthony, Antoine, Anton, Antonio, Antonius • Etruscan/Roman • *Roman family name but with confused origins*

Antiochos, Antiekhein, Antioco • to hold out against all the odds

Antip, Antipas, Antipater • just like your father!

Anwar • Arabic • *crystal clear and bright*

Antrim, Aontraim • Irish Gaelic • *county in Ulster, Great Britain meaning one wee house!*

Arkadi, Arkadios • Greek • *a man from Arcadia*

Arfon • British/Welsh • *area of Caernarfon and the ancient Britons'*

princedom of Gwynedd
**Arnold, Arnaud, Arnd, Arndt,
Arnaldo, Amwald** • Germanic •
eagle power
Arne • Norse • *eagle*
Arrigo, Enrico • Germanic/Spanish/
Italian • *power comes from the home
or family (meaning nation too)*
Arjun • Sanskrit • *white and silver*
**Arnold, Arnald, Arnaud, Arnwald,
Arn, Arnie** • Germanic/Frankish •
he rules like an eagle
Arwel • British/Welsh • *I wept over
you*
Ashley • English • *ash wood or forest*
Ashraf • Arabic • *honourable and
distinguished*
Ashok • Sanskrit • *emotionally
controlled*
Aulay, Amhladh, Amlaidh, Olaf •
Scots Gaelic/Norse • *ancestor, heir,
descendant*
Auliffe, Amhlaoibh • Irish Gaelic/
Norse • *ancestor, heir, descendant*
Axel, Absalom • Biblical/Hebrew/
Danish • *father is peace*

Bai • Chinese • *white*
Barclay, Berkeley, Berkley • Anglo-
Saxon • *birch tree or wood*
**Barnabas, Barnaby, Barney, Barny,
Barnabé, Bernebe, Barnaba,
Barna, Bernabé** • Biblical/Greek •
son of consolation
Bastien, Sébastien, Sebastián •
Greek • *venerable, wise*
Beresford • Anglo-Saxon • *the ford
in the river where the beaver lives*
Bojing • Chinese • *to win admira-
tion and respect*
**Boniface, Bonifacio, Bonifacius,
Bonifaz** • Latin • *good fate*
Boqin • Chinese • *wins or earns*

respect
**Brandon, Brandan, Branden,
Brandyn, Don, Branton** • Anglo-
Saxon • *the hill filled with a shrub
called broom*
Braxton • Anglo-Saxon • *the village
of the badger (brock)*
Brent, Brenton • British/Welsh •
holy river or hill
Brinley, Brynley • Anglo-Saxon •
burnt field or razed meadow
Brodie, Brody • Scots Gaelic • *a
castle or fortress*
Bruno • Germanic • *brown*
Bryn • British/Welsh • *hill*
Burnett, Burnet • Norman •
*brown complexion or hair, toasted
colouring; razed or burned fields
after harvest*
Buxton, Buchestanes, Bucstones •
Anglo-Saxon • *stones that rock and
roll*

Cadfan • British/Welsh • *summit of
the battle*
Cain, Kane, Cane • Jewish/Hebrew •
a craftsman
Caius • Latin • *a man of the earth*
**Calvin, Cal, Cathal, Calbhach,
Calvagh** • Latin/Irish Gaelic • *bald*
Calogero • Greek • *the older the
better*
**Cameron, Camron, Kamerson,
Kamran, Camsron** • Scots Gaelic •
crooked nose
Campbell, Cambell, Cambeul •
Scots Gaelic • *crooked mouth*
Caolán, Kelan, Keelan • Irish Gaelic
• *slender, slim, trim*
Carson • American/English • *a
Christian, follower of Jesus Christ*
Ceallach, Kelly • Irish Gaelic • *fair-
haired or monk church monastery*

Chauncey, Chauncy • English • *the chancellor*

Cheng • Chinese • *accomplished*

Chongkun • Chinese • *second brother mountain*

Christhard • German • *as brave and strong as Christ*

Christmas, Noël • English/French • *the nativity of Jesus Christ*

Cian, Kian, Keene • Irish Gaelic • *old or ancient*

Ciarán, Kieron, Cieran, Kieran, Kieren, Keiran • Irish Gaelic • *black*

Cinnéidigh, Kennedy • Irish Gaelic • *ugly head*

Clark, Clarke, Clarkson • English • *a clerk as in penpusher*

Cleveland • English • *a tribe from the hills (Cleveland Hills, North Riding of Yorkshire)*

Clive • English • *the man who lives in a cave or cliff*

Cosmo, Kosmas, Cosimo, Kosmos • Greek • *there is beauty in order*

Craig, Creag • Scots Gaelic • *rock*

Crónán, Cronin • Irish Celtic • *dark, swarthy complexion*

Cuimín, Comyn • Irish Gaelic • *bent, doubled-over, crooked*

Da • Chinese • *attain, accomplish, achieve*

Dale • English • *a valley dweller*

Dalton, Daleton • Anglo-Saxon • *the village in the valley*

Damon, Daman, Damaso • Greek • *a man full of self-control or a man who tames*

Daniel, Dan, Danny, Danyal, Deiniol, Daniele, Daniil, Taneli, Dannie • Biblical/Hebrew/Jewish • *God is my judge*

Darragh, Dair, Dáire, Darach,

Daragh, Darach, Dara • Irish Gaelic • *son of oak*

Darius, Dareios, Darayavahush, Darayamiy • Greek/Persian • *he who possesses, looks after the good and wellness of all*

Dayaram • Sanskrit • *as kind and tender as Rama, the perfect man/divinity*

Delun • Chinese • *virtuous respected*

Dickon, Richard, Dick, Dicky, Dickie • Germanic/Norman • *strong, brave and powerful*

Didier, Desiderius • Latin • *longing for*

Diego, Didacus, Santiago • Spanish • *supplanter, a cuckoo in the nest! Edging out someone to take their place against their will*

Dingxiang • Chinese • *stable fortune*

Dominic, Dominick, Dom, Dominique, Domingo, Dominicus, Dominus • Latin/Roman Catholic • *Lord, as in St Dominic, founder of the Dominican order*

Donagh, Donnchadh, Donough, Donncha, Duncan, Donn, Don • Irish Gaelic • *brown noble chieftain*

Dong • Chinese • *east/winter*

Donovon, Donovan, Donndubhan, Donndubhain • brown, dark black-haired chief

Dositheos, Dosifei • Greek • *God-given*

Douglas, Doug, Dougie, Duggie, Dubhglas • black stream or pool

Doyle, Dubhghaill, Dubhghall, Dùghall, Dougal, Dugal, Dugald • Scots Gaelic • *black, dark, stranger*

Duane, Dubhán, Dwane, Dwayne, Dwain, Dubhain • dark, black

Dubhdara • Irish Gaelic • *black oak*

Duncan, Donnchadh • Celtic •

brown chief or noble leader
Dunstan • English/Roman Catholic
• *dark stone*
Dwyer, Duibhuidhir • Irish Gaelic
• *personal name meaning brown,
black, tawny, dark yellow; maybe
sensible and wise*

Ebenezer • Biblical/Hebrew/Jewish
• *stone of help, memorial stone*
Edsel, Etzel • Germanic • *nobleman
or father*
**Edward, Ed, Eddie, Eideard,
Eudard, Edvard, Édouard,
Eduardo, Duarte, Edoardo, Edvard,
Eduard, Eetu, Ned, Ted, Neddy,
Teddy, Ewart, Eadbhárd, Eadweard**
• Anglo-Saxon • *a person who
guards his riches, blessed with wealth*
Ehrenfried, Arnfried • Germanic •
*peace with honour or person who,
like the eagle, has power, but uses it
as a deterrent*
Eilif • Scandinavian • *one alone, for
always, evermore, eternal life*
Eldon, Elsdon, Elladun • Anglo-
Saxon • *Ella's Hill in County
Durham*
Elof • Scandinavian • *the single
descendant/heir*
Enoch • Biblical/Hebrew/Jewish •
experienced and wise
Enrique, Heinrich, Henry •
Visigothic/Germanic • *power comes
from the home or family (meaning
nation too)*
Erhard, Erhardt • Germanic •
*honoured because of his strength
and fortitude*
Eric, Erik, Erick, Erich, Einnrik, Eirik
• Norse • *one ruler or king alone, no
other*
Ernest, Ern, Ernie, Ernst, Ernesto •

German • *serious in all things and
will fight to the death; means busi-
ness to the point of obsession*
Errol, Erol, Erroll, Eryl • Scottish •
*Scots surname from a place name in
Perthshire*
Ethan • Biblical/Hebrew/Jewish •
longevity, strong and firm
Euan, Éoghan, Ewan, Ewen, Evan •
Gaelic • *yew tree*
Ewald, Ewawalt • Germanic • *a
wise and just ruler; powerful leader,
lawful ruler, judge*
Ezra, Esdras • Biblical/Jewish/
Hebrew • *help!*

Fādil • Arabic • *generous, respected
and conscientious*
Fakhri • Arabic • *diligent, high
achiever, gets where he wants on
merit*
Faraj • Arabic • *solves worries and
grief*
Fawzi • Arabic • *victorious and
triumphant, reaching the pinnacle*
Feichín, Fiach • Irish Gaelic • *raven*
Fiachra, Fiach • Irish Gaelic • *King
of the Hunt, King of the Ravens*
Fikri • Arabic • *intellectual and
contemplative*
Firoz • Arabic • *champion and
successful*
Flint, Fflint • English • *hard rock*
Floyd, Lloyd, Llwyd • English/
British Welsh • *grey*
**Fraser, Frazer, Frazier, Frisselle,
Fresel, Freseliere, Frasier** • Norman
French/Scots English • *from a
family name with no known origin*
Frost, Freosan • Anglo-Saxon •
*a person who looks icy, cold, snowy
white hair or beard*

Galen, Galenus, Galene • Latin/ Greek • *calmness*

Garbhán, Garvan • Irish Gaelic • *rough, cruel, wicked*

Garfield • Anglo-Saxon • *a person who lives near a field shaped like a pyramid or triangle*

Garnet, Grenate, Granatum • Norman/Latin • *either a dealer in pomegranates or the precious stone*

Garrick, Garrigue • Languedoc French • *an open stretch of limestone prairie*

Gennaro, Januarius, Janus • Latin • *the month of January; from Janus, the god who could look forward and back*

George, Georgie, Geordie, Seoirse, Seòras, Deòrsa, Siors, Siorus, Siorys, Georg, Jörg, Jurgen, Joris, Joren, Jurg, Jørgen, Jorn, Göran, Jöran, Örjan, Georges, Jorge, Jordi, Giorgio, Georgi, Yuri, Yegor, Yura, Jerzy, Jiri, Juraj, Jure, Yrjo, Gyorgy, Jurgis, Juris, Georgos, Geergain, Georgios • Greek/Latin/Norman • *farmer or someone who works on the land*

Geraint, Gerontios, Geronitius, Gerontos • British/Welsh • *old man*

Gerasim, Gerasimos • Greek • *honoured old man*

Gereon • Greek • *old man*

Gerhard, Gerhardt, Geert, Gert • Germanic • *strong, dedicated swordsman*

Gideon • Hebrew/Jewish • *he who cuts someone down to size*

Giles, Gyles, Aegidius, Aigidios, Gilles, Aegidus, Gide, Gil • Latin/ Greek/English • *kid, a young goat*

Gladstone, Glaedstan • Anglo-Saxon • *the stone where the red kite lands*

Glen, Glenn, Gleann • Scots Gaelic • *valley*

Glyn, Glynn • British/Welsh • *valley*

Gopal • Sanskrit • *cowherd and the king of the earth*

Göran, Örjan, Jöran, Jörn • Scandinavian/Serbo-Croat • *man from the mountains*

Gordon • Scottish • *unknown origins could spring from place name in Aberdeenshire or similar in Normandy*

Gotam • Sanskrit • *ox, symbol of wealth*

Graham, Graeme, Grahame, Grandham, Granham • Anglo-Saxon • *a person from a gravelly place; originally Grantham, Lincolnshire*

Gray, Grey, Graig, Riabhach • Gaelic/Anglo-Saxon • *grey hair, grey beard, grey clothes*

Grwn • British/Welsh • *ridge, embankment*

Gunther, Gunter, Gunnar, Gunder, Gunne, Gunni • Germanic • *the army brings strife and lays the land waste*

Gustav, Gustave, Gus, Gustaf, Gösta, Gustavus, Gustavo • Scandinavian • *staff or supporter of the*

Gwalchmai • British/Welsh • *plain of the hawks or ospreys*

Gwynedd • British/Welsh • *a moun-tainous Welsh princedom*

Haakon, Håkon, Hagen, Håkan • Norse/Germanic • *high-born son, relative, like a house/fort, stockade*

Hale, Halh • Anglo-Saxon • *a person who lives off the beaten track; perhaps a hermit*

Hall, Heall, Halle, Halldor, Hallstein, Halstein, Halsten, Hallsten • rock

Halvard, Halvor, Hallvard, Hallvor, Halvar • Scandinavian • *defender like a rock*

Hamilton • Anglo-Saxon • *a flat-topped hill or mound, like Cape Town's mountain*

Hari • Sanskrit • *pet name for Vishnu or Krishna, preservation of the universe*

Harlan, Harland, Harley • English/American • *grey rock or fields where the hares run*

Hartmann, • Germanic • *hard man!*

Hārūn, Aaron • Arabic • *mountain of strength*

Hawk, Hauk, Hawke, Hafoc • Anglo-Saxon/English • *hawk, bird of prey*

Haydn, Heiden, Heidano, Hayden, Haydon • Germanic • *heathen or pagan*

Haytham • Arabic • *young eagle*

Heath • English • *scrubland*

Heber, Éibhear • Irish Gaelic/Biblical/Jewish/Hebrew • *an enclave, a ghetto*

Hector, Hektor, Ekhain, Eachann, Eachdonn • Greek/Scots Gaelic • *restrained, holds himself back/Brown horse*

Henry, Henri, Harry, Anraí, Einrí, Eanraig, Heinrich, Henrik, Henrike, Hinrich, Hendrik, Enrique, Enric, Henrique, Enrico, Henryk, Hal, Jindrich, Heikki, Henrikas, Henning, Harris, Harry, Henry, Harry, Hank, Hawkin • Germanic • *power comes from the home or family (meaning nation too)*

Hikmat • Arabic • *wise*

Hongqi • Chinese • *red flag or banner*

Hywel, Hywell, Howell • British/Welsh • *conspicuous by his eminence*

Iago, Jacob, James • Biblical • *supplanter, a cuckoo in the nest! Edging out someone to take their place against their will*

Ib, Jepp, Jacob • Scandinavian • *supplanter, a cuckoo in the nest! Edging out someone to take their place against their will*

Ibrāhīm, Abraham • Arabic • *father of the tribes or nations*

Idwal, Iudwal • British/Welsh • *master of the ramparts and turrets*

Igor, Ivor, Ifor, Yherr • Russian/Scandinavian • *the army with archers who shoot with bows of yew*

Ingram, Engelram • Norman/Norse • *Norman family name after the Viking fertility god, Ing, and his pet Raven*

Ira • Hebrew/Jewish • *vigilant, observant, watchful*

Islwyn, Isllwyn • British/Welsh • *below the grove of trees*

Italo, Italus • Latin • *father of Romulus and Remus, founders of Rome*

Ivar, Iver • Scandinavian • *archer warrior whose bow is made of yew*

Ivo, Yves, Ivon • Germanic • *yew tree*

Ivor, Ifor, Yherr, Iobhar, Íomhar • Scandinavian/Norse • *the army with archers who shoot with bows of yew*

Jabez • Biblical/Jewish/Hebrew • *I bear him with sorrow, sorrowful*

Jada • Biblical/Hebrew/Jewish • *he knows*

James, Iacomus, Jago, Jaime, Jamie, Jim, Jamey, Jimmy, Jimmie, Séamas, Séamus, Seumas,

Seumus, Hamish, Jaume, Jacques, Jaume, Jaimes, Giacomo, Jameson, Jamieson, Jamey, Jamee, Jami, Jaimie, Jem, Jacobus • Biblical/Latin • *supplanter, a cuckoo in the nest! Edging out someone to take their place against their will*

Jared, Jarred, Jarod, Jarrod • Biblical • *descent*

Janero, Gennaro, Januarius • Latin • *month of January after the Roman god Janus*

Jeremiah, Jeremy, Jerry, Jem, Gerry, Jeremias • Biblical/Hebrew/Jewish • *appointed by God*

Jeremy, Jem, Jeremiah • English • *appointed by God*

Jerker, Jerk, Erik • Scandinavian • *one ruler or king alone, no other*

Jesús, Joshua • aramaic/Jewish • *saviour*

Jlanyu • Chinese • *building the universe*

Jim, Jimmy, James • English • *supplanter, a cuckoo in the nest! Edging out someone to take their place against their will*

Jingguo • Chinese • *building the nation*

Jitendra, Jitender, Jitinder • Sanskrit • *all-powerful, all-mighty, in control*

Job, Joby, Jobey • Biblical/Jewish/Hebrew • *persecuted*

Jock, Jocky, Jack • Scots • *nickname for a Scotsman*

Jörg, George, Jurgen, Jørgen, Georgianus, Jörn • Scandinavian • *farmer or someone who works on the land*

Joyce, Josce, Josse, Joducus, Ioduc, Joss • Breton Celtic • *lord*

Kalidas • Sanskrit • *servant of Kali*

Kay, Caius, Gaius • Latin • *a man of the earth*

Keane, Kean, Cian • Irish Gaelic • *old or ancient*

Keanu • Hawaiian • *cool breeze from the mountains*

Keenan, Cianain, Cian, Cianin • Irish Gaelic • *descendant of Cian, old and ancient*

Keiller, Keilor, Keiller • Canadian/English • *Scots surname from a place in Perthshire*

Keir, Kerr, Kjarr • Norse • *a person who lives in marshes covered in shrubs and brushwood*

Keiran, Ciarán • Irish Gaelic • *black*

Keith • British/Welsh • *wood, copse or thicket, or a man from East Lothian*

Kellen, Kelan, Cailein, Ailein, McKellern, Macailein, Maccailein • Gaelic • *slender, slim, trim or son of Alan or son of Colin*

Kelly, Ceallach, Ceallaigh • Irish/English • *fair-haired, or monk, church, monastery*

Kennedy, Cinnéidigh • Irish Gaelic • *ugly head*

Khwaja • Persian • *the master*

Kieran, Ciarán • Irish Gaelic • *black*

Korbinian, Corvus, Hraban • Latin/Frankish • *raven*

Krishna, Kishen, Kistna • Sanskrit • *black, dark, intense*

Kyran, Kieran, Ciarán • modern/Irish Gaelic • *black*

Landon, Langdon, Langdun • Anglo-Saxon • *the long hill*

Laurence, Lawrence, Larry, Laurentius, Laurentum, Laurie, Lawrie, Labhrás, Labhrainn,

Lorenz, Laurens, Lars, Laurent, Lorencio, Llorenc, Laurenco, Lorenzo, Lawson, Lavrentios, Lavrenti, Laurencjusz, Wawrzyniec, Vavrinec, Lovrenc, Lauri, Lasse, Lassi, Lorinc, Laz, Lenz, Lavrenti • Latin • *man from Laurentum, the capital of the Latins*

Leland, Layland, Leyland • Anglo-Saxon • *land that is used for growing crops over years and left fallow for one*

Léopold, Luitpold, Leopoldo • Germanic/Bavarian • *bold man*

Leslie, Les, Leascuilinn, Lesslyn • Scots Gaelic • *the place where holly grows*

Li • Chinese • *profit, business acumen and respectable*

Liaqat • Persian • *dignified, noble, wise and clever*

Linden, Linde, Lyndon, Lynden • Anglo-Saxon • *lime tree*

Linford, Lindford, Lynford • Anglo-Saxon • *the lime trees or flax plant that grow by the ford in the river*

Linton, Lynton • Anglo-Saxon • *the village by or with a lime*

Linton, Lynton • Anglo-Saxon • *the place where the lime tree or flax plants grow*

Liwei • Chinese • *profit and greatness*

Lleu, Lugg, Lughus, Lugh • British/Welsh • *dark, bright and shining*

Lloyd, Llwyd, Floyd • British/Welsh • *the grey man*

Logan • Scots Gaelic • *a family name or someone from Logan in Ayrshire*

Lomán • Irish • *bare*

Lonán, Lonain • Irish Gaelic • *blackbird*

Lorin, Loren, Lorrin, Laurence • Latin • *man from Laurentum, the capital of the Latins*

Lorne, Latharna, Lorn • Canadian/English • *Scottish place name Lorne, Argyll*

Ludger, Luitger • Friesian • *place name derived from famous monk*

Madison, Madde, Madeleine, Maud • American/English • *son of Maud or Matilda, the battleaxe*

Mahmūd • Arabic • *respected and laudable*

Maitland, Maltalent, Mautalent, Mautalant • Anglo-Saxon/Norman • *bad-tempered or from Mautalant, a barren place in Normandy*

Majdi, Magdi • Arabic • *conscientious and worthy of praise*

Mallory, Mallery, Malheure, Malerie • Norman • *unhappy or unfortunate one*

Ma'mūn • Arabic • *reliable and trusted*

Maoilíosa • Irish Gaelic • *follower of Jesus Christ*

March, Marche, Mensis • Norman • *a person who lives on the borders*

Mason, Macon, Macian • Germanic/Frankish/Anglo-Saxon • *a person who makes things with stone*

Maximilian, Maximilianus, Maximus, Max, Maximillian, Maximilien, Aemilianus • Latin/Germanic/Bavarian/Austrian

Meinhard • Germanic • *strong as a rock*

Melor • Russian • *a combination of Marx, Engels, Lenin, October, Revolution*

Melvin, Melvyn, Mel, Melvin, Melville, Melvyn, Malleville •

a man from a bad place
Merdardo • Germanic • *unknown prefix but ends with strong and hardy*
Merl, Meriel, Merle, Merula • Norman/Latin • *a blackbird*
Myrddin, Merlyn, Merlin • British/ Welsh • *sea fort or sea hill*
Miles, Michael, Milo, Myles, Maoilios • Latin • *soldier of God*
Montgomery, Montgomeric, Monty • Germanic/Norman • *the powerful man from the hill country*
Morton, Morten, Moses, Mort, Mortun • Anglo-Saxon • *village by or on moorland*
Moses, Moshe, Moïse, Moss, Moses, Mostyn, Monty • Biblical/ Hebrew/Egyptian • *born of God*
Muir, More • Scots/English • *moorland*

Na'īm • Arabic • *he who enjoys his own company; happy is his lot*
Nājib, Nāgib • Arabic • *cultured, cultivated, in a class of his own*
Nazaire, Nazarius, Nazario • Latin • *Nazareth, Jesus Christ's home town*
Ned, Edward • Anglo-Saxon • *a careful, prudent ruler who looks after his riches and possessions*
Nianzu • Chinese • *ancestors revered*
Nicomedo, Nico, Nikomedes • Greek • *to plan a victory*
Nigel, Nigellus, Nihel, Neil • Latin/English • *black as pitch or passionate, dead sexy, really desirable*
Nikita, Aniketos • Greek/Russian • *unconquered*
Nino, Giannino • Latin/Spanish • *the boy, referring to the Christ Child*
Noble, Nobilis • American English/ Norman Latin • *someone who has*

noble qualities even if not born aristocratic
Noël, Nael, Natalis, Noelle • Latin/Norman • *nativity of Christ: Christmas*
Norbert, Nordberht • Germanic • *a bright light from the north, northern lights, Aurora Borealis*
Norton, Nordtun • Anglo-Saxon • *the northern village, homestead or enclosure*

Oakley, Oakleigh • American/ English • *an oak wood or clearing in the forest*
Odhrán, Oran, Oren • Irish Gaelic • *ashen, pale*
Olaf, Olav, Anuleif, Olof, Ottwolf, Ola, Ole, Oluf, Olov, Olaus, Olai • Norse • *ancestor, heir, descendant*
Oleg, Helgi • Norse • *prosperous, the chap who created Kiev, Ukraine*
Olijimi • Nigeria • *God gave me this*
Oliver, Olivier, Olivarius, Ollie, Oleifr, Noll • Germanic/Frankish/ Norse • *olive tree*
Onisim, Anisim • Greek • *useful, worthwhile*
Örjan, Jurian, George • Scandinavian • *farmer or someone who works on the land*
Oren, Oran, Orin, Orren, Orrin • Biblical/Hebrew/Jewish • *a pine tree*
Orlando, Roland • Italian • *a person who is famous for the real estate they own; land, territory*
Otis, Ote, Ode • Germanic/Frankish • *wealthy, prosperous*
Otmar, Ottmar, Ottomar • Germanic • *famed riches*
Ove, Aghi • Norse • *frightened or in awe of a weapon of terror*
Ozzy, Oz, Ozzie • Anglo-Saxon •

shortened version of any name beginning with Os, meaning God

Parker • American/English • *a*
person who is a warden or game-
keeper in hunting park or chase
Parvaiz • Persian • *lucky, auspicious,*
successful
Patrick, Pàdraig, Pat, Paddy, Patsy,
Páraic, Patrice, Patricio, Patrizio,
Porick, Podge, Pàra, Pàdair,
Pàidean, Padrig, Paddy, Patrick,
Pat, Patrice • Latin/Irish Gaelic •
patrician
Paul, Paulus, Pol, Pål, Poul, Pall,
Pauwel, Påvel, Pablo, Pau, Paulo,
Paolo, Pavlos, Pavao, Pavle, Paavo,
Paulius, Pablo • Latin • *Roman*
family name meaning little or small
Paulino, Pablo, Paulus • Spanish/
Italian • *Roman family name*
meaning little or small
Pearce, Pierce, Perais • Norman •
the rock or stone
Peleg • Biblical/Hebrew/Jewish •
division, border or boundary
Penn • American/English • *a hill or*
pen for domestic animals
Percival, Parsifal, Parzifal,
Perceval, Peredur, Percy, Perce,
Perce, Pearce, Pierce, Percy, Piers,
Perceval, Perce • Celtic/Norman
• *Celtic name of Peredur; Peredur's*
valley
Percy, Piers, Percival, Perci,
Persiacum, Persius, Perse,
Percehaie, Percerhaie • Latin/
Gaulish • *Pierce's hedge*
Peter, Pete, Petros, Peadar, Pedr,
Piet, Pieter, Per, Petter, Par, Pierre,
Pedro, Perico, Pere, Pietro, Piero,
Pyotr, Piotr, Petr, Petar, Pekka,
Peitari, Peteris, Petras, Petrus, Petya,

Pette, Pedr • Greek • *the rock or stone*
Piaras, Piers, Pierce, Pearce • Irish/
English • *Pierce's hedge*
Pitt • Anglo-Saxon • *a man who*
lives in a pit
Placido, Placidus • Latin/Italian •
calm, quiet, placid
Potter • American English •
someone who sells
Prakash • Sanskrit • *a famous,*
radiant person
Preston, Preosttun • Anglo-Saxon
• *priest's*
Prince, Princeps • Latin/English •
royal title
Prokopios, Prokopi, Prokofi,
Prokope • Greek • *successful*
Prudenzio, Prudentius, Prudens,
Prudencio • Latin • *prudent*

Quartus • Latin • *four*
Quirinius • Latin • *governor*

Rafferty, Rabhartaigh,
Robhartaigh, Raff • Irish Gaelic •
descendant of Robhartaigh
Raghav • Sanskrit • *from name for*
Rama, descendant of Raghu
Rajendra • Sanskrit • *mighty king,*
mighty
Ramiro • Spanish/Visigothic • *a*
man famous for his advice and
counselling
Raven, Rafn, Raefn • Norse • *Odin's*
winged friend
Raymond, Ray, Raimund,
Raginmund, Raimondo, Raimundo
• Germanic/Frankish
Rayner, Rainer, Raginheri,
Raginhari, Reiner, Raniero, Ragnar,
Regner, Rainerio • Germanic/
Frankish • *adviser to the army; army*
commander

Reginald, Reg, Reggie, Reginaldus, Reynold, Reginwald • Germanic/ Norman • *advice rule*

Régis • French/Provençal • *the ruler*

Reid • Anglo-Saxon • *someone who lives in a clearing in the woods*

Reineke, Reine • Germanic • *counsellor*

Reinhard, Reinhardt, Reine • Germanic • *strong, firm advice*

Reinhold, Reinwald, Reine • Germanic • *splendid, wonderful adviser*

Reinmar, Reine • Germanic • *famous adviser, speaker*

Remus, Remo • Latin • *with Romulus, founder of Rome*

Rémy, Remigius, Remi, Remigio, Remix • Latin • *oarsman or man at the tiller*

Reuben, Reuven, Rube, Rubén • Biblical/Hebrew/Jewish • *behold, a son!*

Reynold, Reginald, Reynaud, Raginwald, Reginald, Ray, Reynard, Ragin, Renard, Ray, Rinaldo, Reinaldo, Rheinallt • Germanic/Norman • *advice rule*

Rhett, Rhet, Raedt, Raet • Dutch • *advice counsel*

Ridley, Reodleah • Anglo-Saxon • *clearing of reeds*

Riscu • African • *prosperity*

Roald, Hrod • Norse • *famous ruler, famous chief*

Robhartach, Rob • Irish Gaelic • *bringer or broker of prosperity and wealth*

Roderick, Rod, Roddy, Rodric, Rory, Ruaridh • Germanic/ Visigothic • *famous and powerful*

Rodrigo, Hrodric, Ruy • Spanish/ Visigothic • *a man with fame and power; El Cid*

Roland, Rodland, Rowland, Roly, Rowley, Rolie, Rolland, Roldan, Rolant • Germanic • *famed throughout land*

Romulus, Romolo • Latin • *one of the founders of Rome*

Rónán • Irish Gaelic • *sealion as Capricorn the seagoat*

Roscoe, Raskog • Norse

Rosendo • Visigothic • *a man on the path to fame*

Roshan • Persian/Urdu • *splendid, glorious/famous*

Ross, Rós • Gaelic • *family name from geographical term for a headland or promontory*

Rowan, Ruadhan • Gaelic/English • *descendant of Ruadhan, little red one*

Royle, Rygehyll, Royal • Anglo-Saxon • *the hill where rye is grown*

Rune, Runi, Runolf, Run • Norse • *named after the Norse magical alphabet*

Rurik, Hrodrik, Roderick • Norse • *famous ruler, the name of the man who founded Russia's Novogorod, the Big New City*

Rushdi • Arabic • *old head on young shoulders; ahead of his years*

Russell, Russ, Rous, Rousel, Russel, Rusty • Norman • *little red one*

Ryan, Riain • Irish Gaelic • *little king, descendant of Riain*

Sābir, Sabri • Arabic • *patience is a virtue, persevere*

Sacheverell, Sautechevreuil, Sachie • Norman • *surname from place name Saute Chevreuil meaning roebuck leap*

Sage, Sauge, Sapius • Anglo-Saxon

• *a herb or wise person*

Sakhr • Arabic • *solid as a rock*

Sālih • Arabic • *devout, devoted*

Salvatore, Salvator, Salvador • Latin • *saviour*

Samson, Shimshon, Shemesh, Sampson, Sansone, Sammy, Sammie • Biblical/Hebrew/Jewish • *the sun*

Samuel, Shemuel, Shaulmeel, Sam, Sammy, Sawyl • Biblical/Hebrew/Jewish • *name of God, God had heard, listen to God*

Santiago, Iago, Jacobus, James • Spanish • *supplanter, a cuckoo in the nest! Edging out someone to take their place against their will*

Satish • Sanskrit • *the fact of a matter, the true reality*

Saturday • English • *born on a Saturday, Saturn's day*

Saturnino, Saturnus, Nino • Latin • *Saturn*

Sava, Sabas, Sabbas, Saba • Greek/Jewish • *old man*

Sayyid • Arabic • *lord and master*

Scott • Gaelic • *a man from Ireland who settles in Scotland*

Séamus, Shamus, Séamas, James, Seumas • Gaelic • *supplanter, a cuckoo in the nest! Edging out someone to take their place against their will*

Seanán, Shannon , Senan • Irish • *wise, mature and ancient*

Sekar • Sanskrit • *summit, the best at what you do*

Selwyn, Selewyn, Selewine, Silvanus, Silas, Selwin • Anglo-Saxon • *prosperous, high-flying friend*

Severiano, Severus, Severo, Severinus, Sören, Severinus,

Severino, Seve • Latin • *Roman family name meaning stern, austere*

Shamshad • Persian • *tall as a box tree*

Shankar, Sankar • Sanskrit • *confers welfare, to look after*

Shabbetai, Shabbath, Shabath, Shabtai • Jewish/Hebrew • *the Sabbath*

Shan • Chinese • *mountain, symbolic of success, eternal and ambition*

Shanyuan • Chinese • *foot of the mountain*

Shaw, Sceaga, Skog • Anglo-Saxon • *a wood or copse of trees*

Shelby • Norse • *willow farm*

Sheldon • Anglo-Saxon • *steep-sided valley; embankmen*

Shen • Chinese • *intense, deep and wary*

Sheridan, Sirideain • Irish Gaelic • *descendant of Sirideain, the searcher*

Shi • Chinese • *symbolic of strength and support*

Shirong • Chinese • *reward as a result of learning*

Shiva • Sanskrit • *beautiful, timely, death and regeneration*

Shneur, Senior • Jewish/Yiddish • *senior*

Shoushan • Chinese • *longevity, mountain*

Shunyuan • Chinese • *following back to the roots or source*

Shyam • Sanskrit • *dark, black and handsome, sexy*

Siddhartha • Sanskrit • *Buddha, attainment*

Silas, Silouanus, Silvanus, Silva • Latin • *God of the Forests*

Silver, Siolfor, Seolfor • Anglo-Saxon • *the metal silver*

Silvester, Silver, Sylvester, Silvano, Silvestro, Silvestre, Sly, Slie • Latin • *a person from the woods or forest*

Simran • Sikh • *he who meditates, yogic*

Siyu • Chinese • *thinking of the planet Earth*

Stamford, Stanford, Stan • Anglo-Saxon • *where the stones are, you can ford the river*

Standish, Stanedisc, Stan • Anglo-Saxon • *the field or meadow filled with stones*

Stanilas, Stanislaus, Stanislaw, Aneislis • Slavic • *glory to the court, glorious courtier or politician*

Stanley, Stan, Stanleah • Anglo-Saxon • *the clearing filled with stones*

Steel, Style, Styal, Steele • Anglo-Saxon • *a person who works with hard metal*

Stein, Steyne, Sten, Steen, Steinn • Norse • *stone*

Stone, Stan • Anglo-Saxon • *stone*

Sture, Stura • Scandinavian • *wilful, contrary, independent spirit*

Sudhir • Sanskrit • *wise and strong*

Sultan • Arabic • *ruler, leader*

Sylvain, Silvano • Italian • *a person from the woods or forest*

Tad, Tadhg, Thaddeus, Tig, Tim, Taddeo, Teague, Teigue, Tadeo • Irish Gaelic • *poet, wise man, philosopher*

Talfryn, Tal • British/Welsh • *the top end of the hill*

Tancredo • Germanic • *thoughtful counsel*

Tarquin, Tarquinius • Etruscan • *Roman family name with no known root*

Tawfiq • Arabic • *prosperity and luck*

Télésphore, Telesforo, Telephoros • Greek • *fulfilment, completion, conclusion*

Terrell, Tyrell • Norman • *a person who is hard to pull this way or that, very fixed!*

Theobald, Peudbald, Theo, Thibault, Tiobold • Germanic • *a tribe of people known for their boldness in the face of adversity*

Thierry, Theodoric • French/Greek • *ruler of the people*

Thornton, Thorn, Tornton • Anglo-Saxon

Tiernan, Tighearnan, Tighearnach, Tierney • Irish Gaelic • *lord or chief*

Tikhon • Greek • *bullseye! Hitting the mark or target*

Timothy, Tim, Tadhg, Timmy, Timotheus, Timotheos, Timetheo, Timmy, Tiger, Timothee, Timo, Timoteo Timofei • Biblical/Latin/Greek • *honour God*

Tingguang • Chinese • *bright garden or courtyard*

Tingzhe • Chinese • *judgement or wisdom is required*

Tony, Anthony, Tone, Tönjes, Antonius, Tonio • Estruscan/Roman • *Roman family name but with confused origins*

Torsten, Torstein, Thorstein, Thorsteinn • Norse • *the god Thor with the strength of a stone*

Travis, Traverser • Norman • *someone who worked collecting tolls on the roads or highways, crossing roads*

Tremaine, Tremayne, Tremen • British/Welsh/Kernow • *Cornish for homestead and stone*

Tristram, Tristam, Trystram, Tristan, Trystan, Tristram, Dristan, Drystan • British/Welsh • *riotous,* *sad, sorrowful, chaos*

Tucker, Tucian • Anglo-Saxon/ American English • *surname originally meaning to tease and torment*

Turner • English • *a person who makes objects by turning them on a lathe or wheel*

Tybalt, Theobald • Germanic • *a tribe of people known for their boldness in the face of adversity*

Tyler, Tylor, Ty, Tye, Tigele, Tegula • Anglo-Saxon/Latin • *a man who covers things like a roof*

Tyrell, Tyrrell, Tirel, Terrell • Norman • *a person who is hard to pull this way or that, very fixed!*

Udo • Germanic • *riches*

Ughtred, Uhtraed • Anglo-Saxon • *dawn counsel; a person who is good and wise in the mornings*

Ùisdean, Eysteinn, Hugh, Hùisdean • Irish Gaelic • *a man who is forever unchanging like a stone*

Ulric, Wulfric, Ulrick, Ulrich, Utz • Germanic • *power and riches*

Ulysses, Odysseus, Odyssesthai, Ulick, Ulisse, Ulises • Greek/Latin • *a person who can hate and despise*

Urien, Orbogen • British/Welsh • *born with a silver spoon in his mouth; privileged*

Uttam • Sanskrit • *the ultimate*

Vadim, Vladimir • Russian/Slavic • *origins vague but could be shortened Vladimir meaning ruler*

Vasco, Velasco, Belasco, Velásquez • Spanish/Basque • *crow*

Vasu • Sanskrit • *simply the best*

Vaughan, Vaughn, Fychan, Bychan • British/Welsh • *small, little*

Veit, Wido, Guy • Germanic • *wood or wide*

Venkat • Sanskrit • *sacred mountain near Madras*

Vere, Ver, Vern, Vernon • Celtic/ Gaulish • *alder tree*

Vernon, Vere, Vern • Gaulish • *alder tree*

Vester, Silvester • Latin • *a person from the woods or forest*

Vidkun, Vidkunn • Norse • *lateral thinking, wise, experienced*

Vinay • Sanskrit • *education, intelligence, learning*

Vinayak • Sanskrit • *demonic*

Vladimir, Volodya, Valdemar, Waldemar • Slavic • *great, famous leader or ruler*

Volkmar • Germanic • *famous people*

Vumilia • Swahili • *have courage, bear patiently*

Vyacheslav, Wenceslas • Slavic/ Latin • *greater and even greater glory*

Wajīh • Arabic • *a man people want to emulate, their role model*

Waldemar, Waldo, Wald, Walker, Wealcere, Wealcan, Woldemar • Germanic • *famous ruler*

Walter, Waldhari, Wealdhere, Wat, Walt, Walther, Wolter, Valter, Gualtiero, Gwallter • Germanic

Warwick, Waerwic, Werwic • Anglo-Saxon • *industrial area by a dam or weir*

Watkin, Wat, Walter • Germanic • *commander of the army*

Weizhe • Chinese • *sagacious and wise*

Wenceslas, Ventieslav, Wenzel • Slavic • *greater and even greater glory*

Wendell, Wendel • Germanic • *a member of the Slav tribe living between the Elbe and Oder*

Wentworth, Winterwort • Anglo-Saxon • *winter enclosure or paddock*

Whitney, Whiteney • Anglo-Saxon • *the white island*

Wilberforce, Wilberfoss, Wilburgfoss, Wilbur • Anglo-Saxon/Latin • *Wilburg's ditch*

Willoughby, Weligbyr • Anglo-Saxon/Norse • *the village by the willow tree*

Windsor, Windelsora • Anglo-Saxon • *the place on the river with a windlass (special crane to move heavy weights)*

Winston, Wynnstan • Anglo-Saxon • *stone of joy*

Witold • Germanic • *ruler of the wood or wide as in open country*

Wolfram, Wolf • Germanic • *wolf raven*

Woodrow, Woody • English • *a hamlet with a row of houses*

Woody, Carpenter • English • *nickname for a carpenter or worker with wood*

Wynfor, Wyn • British/Welsh • *white, blonde, holy, blessed*

Wystan, Wigstan • Anglo-Saxon • *memorial stone where the battle was fought*

Xiu • Chinese • *graceful, cultivated*

Xue • Chinese • *studious, knowledge*

Yadav • Sanskrit • *descendant of Yadu or Krishna*

Yakim, Akim • *created by God*

Yang • Chinese • *formed, perfection*

Yaoting • Chinese • *honouring the garden or family*

Yaozu • Chinese • *honouring the ancestors and the past*

Yāsir, Yusri • Arabic • *wealthy, prosperous*

Yehiel, Jehiel • Biblical/Hebrew/Jewish

Yevgeni, Eugenios, Eugene • Russian • *well bred and high born*

Yi • Chinese • *sure and resolute*

Yilma • Ethiopian • *may he prosper*

Yingjie • Chinese • *hero, courageous, brave*

Yongnian • Chinese • *eternity, forever*

Yongrui • Chinese • *eternally or forever lucky*

Yongzheng • Chinese • *eternally; forever scrupulous and conscientious*

Yorath, Iorwerth • British/Welsh • *a handsome, beautiful Lord or Chief*

Yorick, Jorck, George • Danish/Greek • *farmer or someone who works on the land*

Yuri, Yura, Georgi • Russian/Greek • *farmer or someone who works on the land*

Yusra • Arabic • *rich, well endowed*

Yūsuf, Joseph • Arabic/Biblical • *God is my salvation*

Yves, Ive, Ivo • Germanic • *yew tree*

Zachary, Zach, Zak • Greek/English/Biblical • *God has remembered*

Zacharias, Zak, Zechariah, Zachariah, Zakaria, Zach • Biblical/Jewish/Hebrew • *God has remembered*

Zakariyya, Zakariya • Biblical/Arabic • *God has remembered*

Zane • American English • *unknown roots of British surname*

Zechariah • Biblical/Jewish/Hebrew

• *God has remembered*
Zed, Zedekiah • Biblical/Jewish/
Hebrew • *justice of Yahweh*
Zhong • steadfast and devoted
Ziyād • Arabic • *to grow and build*

Girls

Abigail, Abbie, Abby, Abbey, Abbigail, Abbiegail, Abbygail, Abigayle, Abi • Biblical/Jewish/ Hebrew • *my father is joy, father is exaltation*

Abilene, Abbie, Abby, Abbey, Abi, Lena • Biblical/Jewish/Hebrew • *an area of Palestine or the Holy Land meaning grass or grasses*

Abishag, Avishag • Biblical/Jewish/ Hebrew • *wise and educated*

Acacia, Akakia, Wattle • Greek/ Latin • *acacia wood, holy wood that had special powers as a hex against evil*

Adamina • Biblical/Hebrew/Jewish • *earth*

Adelheid, Adalheid, Aleida, Aleit, Alke, Elke, Adèle • Germanic • *noble woman, carries herself well*

Adeltraud • Germanic • *strong and noble*

Adélaide • Germanic • *noble, kind and caring*

Adèle, Adelle, Addie, Addi, Addy, Adeline, Adelina, Aline Adela, Adella, Alette • French • *noble*

Aeron, Agrona • British/Welsh • *Celtic Goddess of Battle or Agriculture*

Aeronwen • British/Welsh • *white, sacred and fair*

Afāf • Arabic • *chastity, refinement, elegance*

Africa • Latin • *the dark continent*

Agatha, Agathe, Aggie, Agata, Ågot, Águeda, Agathos • Greek • *good and honourable*

Agrippina, Agrafena • Latin/ Estruscan • *family name of old Roman family*

Ailbhe • Irish Gaelic • *white*

Alaina, Alana, Alayna, Alanna, Alannah, Alanah, Allana, Alanda, Alanis, Ailin • Gallic • *vague origins but likely to be a rock*

Alba • Latin/Germanic • *white or elfin*

Alberta, Albertina • French/ Germanic/Anglo-Saxon • *bright and noble*

Albina, Bina, Albus, Albius • Latin • *Roman family name meaning white*

Alice, Alicia, Alesha, Alisia, Alys, Alisha, Alissa, Alesha, Alisa, Alissa, Ailish, Alis, Alys • Norman

Alina, Allina • Arabic • *noble and lovely*

Aline, Adeline, Alainn • French/ Gaelic • *noble*

Alison, Allie, Ally, Aly, Alysoun, Aliyah, Aaliyah, Allison, Allyson • Norman • *noble and kind*

Allana, Alana • Gaelic • *vague origins but likely to be a rock*

Alma, Almus • Latin • *nourishing, nurturing, kind like a mother*

Alte • Jewish/Hebrew • *old woman*

Alva, Alvah, Ailbhe, Alvina • Scots Gaelic • *white*

Amalia • Latin/Germanic • *all work, no play*

Amber, Ambar • Latin/Arabic • *beautiful golden-coloured fossilised resin*

Amīna • Arabic • *peaceful, secure*

Angustias • Spanish/Roman Catholic • *Our Lady of Sufferings*

Ann, Anne, Anna, Annabel, Annette, Annetta, Anouk, Anni, Annelie, Anneli, Annella, Annabell, Annabella, Annabelle, Belle, Annie, Anna, Anneke, Anke,

Anoushka, Anouska, Arabella, Arabel Anna, Ana • Biblical/Jewish/ Hebrew • *God has favoured me*

Annalisa, Annaliesa, Annalise, Annelise, Annelies, Anneli • German • *combo of Anne and Elisabeth • God has favoured me; God is my oath*

Annunziata, Nunzia, Anunciación, Anunciata • Roman Catholic

Anthousa, Anfisa • Greek • *flower*

Antonia, Anthonia • Estruscan/ Roman • *Roman family name but with confused origins*

Antoinette, Toinette, Tonette, Antonella, Antonia, Toni, Antonina • Estruscan/Roman • *Roman family name but with confused origins*

Anuradha • Sanskrit • *Stream of Oblations, 28th asterism of Hindu astrology*

Aphra, Afra • Latin • *a woman from Africa, the dark continent*

Arianrhod • British/Welsh • *silver wheel, or silver disc, the name of the Celtic Goddess of the Moon*

Arantxa, Arancha, Aranzazu • Basque • *place name meaning thorn bush*

Aretha, Arete • Greek/American English • *excellent*

Arlette • Germanic/Norman • *uncertain roots but possibly eagle*

Armelle, Artmael • Breton Celtic • *a female chief who is a steady as a rock*

Asenath • Biblical/Egyptian • *she is Daddy's little princess*

Asha • Sanskrit • *hope*

Ashley, Ashleigh, Ashlee, Ashlie, Ashly, Lee, Leigh • Anglo-Saxon • *ash wood or forest*

Aslög, Asslaug, Åslaug • Swedish • *God-consecrated*

Ashlyn, Ashlynne, Ashlynn, Ashlynne, Ash, Lyn • Anglo-Saxon/ British Welsh • *ash tree by the lake*

Asmā, Asmah • Arabic • *prestigious*

Ashton • Anglo-Saxon • *the village with an ash tree*

Aspen, Aespe • Anglo-Saxon • *the aspen tree*

Athene, Athena, Athina, Athenai • Greek • *Greek Goddess of Wisdom and protector of the city of Athens*

Audra, Audrey, Audrie, Audry, Audrina • Anglo-Saxon • *strength and noble of character*

Aurelia, Auriol • Latin • *Roman family name meaning golden*

Aurelie • Latin/French • *Roman family name meaning golden*

Azalea, Azalia, Azeleos, Azania, Azaria, Azelia • Greek • *azalea: flower that flourishes in dry soil*

Bailey • English • *the bailiff!*

Bathsheba, Sheba, Bathsheeva • Biblical/Jewish/Hebrew • *daughter of the oath*

Béibhin, Béibhinn, Bébhionn, Bébinn • Irish Gaelic • *white lady, fair lady*

Beige, Fawn • American English • *colour of undyed woollen cloth*

Beile, Beyle, Beylke • Jewish/ Yiddish/Slavic • *white, pale, beautiful*

Bernadette, Bernine, Berneen, Bernadetta, Benedetta, Bettina • Germanic

Bernardine, Bernadine, Bernarda • Roman Catholic • *strong and hardy like a bear*

Bernita • Germanic • *strong and hardy like a bear*

Bess, Bessie, Bet, Beth, Elizabeth,

Elisabeth, Bethan, Betsy, Betty, Bette, Bettina, Buffy, Beitidh, Elisheba • Hebrew/Greek • *God is my oath or God is my abundance*

Bethlehem, Belem • Biblical/Jewish/Hebrew • *where Jesus was born*

Beverley, Beverly, Bev • Anglo-Saxon • *the stream of the beavers*

Berwen • British Welsh • *fair or white-headed*

Bethan, Beth • British/Welsh • *God is my oath or God is my abundance*

Bianca, Blanca • Italian/Spanish • *white*

Bibi • Persian • *lady of the house*

Bina, Albina, Devorah, Deborah, Binah, Bine, Binke • Jewish/Hebrew/Yiddish • *bee or understanding*

Bláithín, Bláthnat, Blanid, Bianaid • Irish Gaelic • *flower*

Blanche, Bianca, Blanca • pure white, blonde

Blodyn, Blodeyn, Blod • British/Welsh • *flower*

Blodwedd, Blodeuwedd, Blod • British/Welsh • *flower face*

Bodil, Bothild, Botilda • Norse • *compensation for the battle*

Borghild • Norwegian • *fortified for the battle*

Brady, Braidy • Irish Gaelic • *descendant of Bradach, one of Bradach's bunch*

Branwen, Bronwen, Brangwen • British/Welsh • *raven or beast that is holy, sacred and white*

Brandy, Brandyewijn • Dutch/Anglo-Saxon • *distilled wine or the hill filled with a shrub called broom*

Brayne, Broyn, Brayndel • Jewish/Yiddish • *brown*

Breanna, Brianna, Breanne • Irish Celtic • *high or royal born, noble*

Brenna, Braonan • American English/Irish Gaelic • *descendant of Braonan, moist, droplet of water*

Briar, Briony, Bryony, Bryonia • Anglo-Saxon/Greek • *a thorny plant or shrub*

Bridget, Briget, Bridgid, Brigid, Biddy, Bride, Bridy, Bridie, Bridey, Brigitte, Britt, Brighid, Birgit, Brigette, Birgitta, Brigitta, Bedelia, Bríd, Breda, Breeda, Bree, Bríghe, Brídín, Bri, Brighida, Berit, Britta, Birgitte, Birthe, Birte, Ffraid • Irish Gaelic • *the exalted one*

Brie, Bracia, Bree • Latin/Australian English • *marshland rather than soft cheese*

Brittany, Britney • Latin • *the Celtic-speaking province of north-west France, so-called due to the influx of Celts from Cornwall when the Romans invaded, and who transferred Britannia, their name for the island, across to this part of France*

Brónach, Bronagh • Irish Gaelic • *sad and sorrowful*

Brooklyn, Lyn, Breukelen • Dutch • *a district of New York City when it was New Amsterdam under Dutch control, and meaning broken land*

Brunella • Germanic • *brown*

Caileigh, Kayley, Kayleigh, Caleigh, Caollaidhe • Irish Gaelic • *a descendant of Caollaidhe, the prefix meaning a slender man*

Calico • Indian • *a light cotton fabric from Calicut, a port in Kerala state*

Cameo, Cammeo • Italian/Oriental • *carving of a silhouette on a mineral such as ivory*

Camilla, Milla, Millie, Milly, Camille, Camila • Latin/French • *Roman family name; perfection*

Candice, Candace, Canditia, Candy, Candi • Latin/Ethiopian • *pure and sincere; whiter than white*

Canna • Latin/English Australian • *reed; bright flowers that grow in warm climes like Oz*

Caoilfhionn, Caoilainn, Keelin, Caolffionn • Irish Gaelic • *slender and white maiden*

Caprice, Capriccio, Capra • Italian • *hedgehog hair and as intransigent as a goat*

Carey, Ciardha, Carrie • English/ Irish Gaelic • *pure and descendant of Ciardha*

Carmel, Carmella, Carmelina, Camelita, Carmen, Carmine, Carmela • Roman Catholic • *Our Lady of Carmel, the mountain where early Christians lived as hermits and later became the Carmelite order of monks*

Casey, Casy, KC, Kacey, Kaci, Kacie • Irish Gaelic • *a watchman; keeps guard in war*

Cassandra, Cassie, Kassie, Cass, Cassy, Cassidy • Greek mythology • *a woman who could see into the future but no one ever believed her*

Cecilia, Cécile, Cecily, Cecelia, Cissie, Cissey, Sessy, Sissi, Sissy, Cecille, Cecilie, Cacille, Cacilia, Caecilia, Cicely • Latin/English • *old Roman family name Caecilius, from the Latin for blind*

Ceinwen • British/Welsh • *lovely, beautiful, sacred and white*

Celia, Célie, Caelia, Caelum, Celina • Latin • *Roman family name meaning heaven*

Céleste, Celestine, Celestina, Celia, Celine, Marcelline, Caelius, Caelia, Caelestis • Latin • *Roman family name meaning heaven*

Céline, Caelina, Marceline, Marcelline, Caelius, Celina • Latin/French • *Roman family name meaning heaven*

Celyn • British/Welsh • *holly*

Chandra • Sanskrit • *the moon*

Chandrakanta • Sanskrit • *night, time of the moon*

Chanel, Chanelle, Shanelle • French/modern • *in honour of Gabrielle CoCo Chanel, founder of the perfume house*

Chantal, Chantelle, Shantell • French • *in honour of St Jeanne-Françoise, a woman of great charity and virtue who married the Baron de Chantal; when he died she adopted a severe religious life following St Francis of Sales*

Charna, Cherna, Charnke, Charnele, Charnelle, Chernke, Chernele • Jewish/Yiddish • *dark, black*

Chausika • Swahili • *of the night*

Chelsea, Kelsey, Chelsey, Chelsie • Anglo-Saxon • *the chalk landing place in Chelsea, Middlesex*

Cherish, Cherir • Norman • *to treasure something priceless or invaluable*

Cherith, Cheryth • Biblical • *a dry riverbed at a place called Cherith*

Chevonne, Siobhán, Shivaun • English/American/Irish Gaelic • *God is gracious or gift of God*

Cheyenne, Sahiyena • French Canadian • *an Indian tribe from Dakota*

Chiara, Clare, Claire, Clara, Ciara,

Kiarah, Kiara, Kiera, Clair, Clarette, Clarinda, Clarrie, Clarus • Latin/ Italian • *bright, famous, crystal-clear*

Chloe, Chloris, Cloris, Khloris, Khloe • Greek • *another name for the Goddess of Fertility, Demeter or Ceres*

Christine, Christiana, Chris, Chrissy, Christianne, Christina, Cristina, Kristina, Chriselda, Chrissie, Christa, Christabel, Christabella, Christabelle, Cristobel, Christobel, Christelle, Christella, Christel, Christene, Christeen, Cristina, Cairistine, Cairistiòna, Crystin • Scots Gaelic/ Latin • *follower of Christ*

Christian, Christiane, Christiana, Anna, Christie, Christy, Kristy, Christina, Chris, Tina, Cristiona, Cairistiòna, Stineag, Cairistine, Crystin, Kristin, Kristina, Kerstin, Kirsten, Krzystyna, Kirsti, Kirsty, Krisztiana, Krisztina • Scots Gaelic/ Latin • *follower of Christ*

Chrystal, Crystal, Chrystalla, Chrystellina, Khyros, Khrysos • Greek • *gold*

Ciannait • Irish Gaelic • *ancient one*

Ciara • Irish Gaelic • *black one*

Cilla, Priscilla, Pricus, Prissy • Biblical/Latin • *Roman family name meaning ancient, old*

Cinnamon, Kinnamon • Greek/ Jewish • *brown-coloured spice*

Ciorstaidh, Ciostag, Kirsty, Kirstie, Chirsty, Curstaidh, Curstag • Scots Gaelic/Scandinavian/Latin • *follower of Christ*

Clare, Claire, Clara, Chiara, Klara, Kiara, Clara, Kiarah • Latin/English • *bright, famous, crystal-clear*

Clarice, Claritia • Latin/French/ English • *bright, famous, crystal clear*

Clarissa, Clarisa, Clarice, Clarrisse, Clarisse, Claris, Clarissa, Cáitir • Latin • *bright, famous, crystal-clear*

Claudia, Claudine, Claude, Claudinia, Claudette, Klavdia • Latin • *from the old Roman family name Claudius*

Clematis, Klematis, Clem, Clemmie • Greek • *climbing plant or vine meaning twig or branch*

Cleopatra, Cleo, Clio, Kleos, Kleio, Kleopatra • Greek/Ptolemaic • *glory to father*

Clova, Clove, Clover, Clavus, Clafre • Latin/French • *the spice that when dried looks like a nail*

Cody, Codi, Codie, Codee, Codey, Cuidightheach • Irish Gaelic/ American English • *descendant of Cuidightheach, a helpful and caring person*

Consilia, Conseja • Roman Catholic • *Mary of good counsel and advice*

Consolata, Consuelo • Roman Catholic • *Maria Consolata, 'Mary of Solace'*

Constance, Connie, Konnie, Constantia, Konstanze, Contanze • Latin • *constancy; steadfast and faithful*

Corazón • Roman Catholic • *sacred heart, the heart of Jesus*

Cosima • Greek • *world order, means beauty*

Crescentia, Kreszenz • Latin/ Bavarian • *growing, flourishing as in the waxing crescent moon; a positive omen*

Cruz • Roman Catholic • *cross, meaning Mary, Christ's mother, in agony at the foot of the cross; her* *son's crucifixion*

Crystal, Chrystalle, Chrystall, Krystallos, Krystal, Kristel, Krystle • Greek • *ice*

Cynthia, Kynthia, Kynthos, Cyndy, Cindy, Sindy, Cinzia • Greek • *Mount Kynthos on the island of Delos is the birthplace of Artemis, the Goddess of the Moon and the Hunt*

Dahlia, Dale, Dalia, Dalya, Dahl, Dale • Swedish • *named after botanist Anders Dahl from Sweden*

Dáireann, Doreen, Dorind, Dorinda, Dorean • Irish Gaelic • *vague origins but maybe the daughter of Finn*

Daiyu • Chinese • *black jade*

Dale • Anglo-Saxon • *a valley dweller*

Dana, Ana • Irish Gaelic • *name of an ancient Celtic fertility goddess, especially in Ireland*

Danae • Greek mythology • *her great grandfather founded the Greek tribe of Danai or Argives; she was raped by Zeus/Jupiter when he appeared to her as a shower of gold; she gave birth to the hero Perseus*

Dawn, Aurora, Dawne, Duha, Dagung • Anglo-Saxon • *daybreak!*

Deborah, Debra, Debbie, Debora, Debrah, Deb, Debbi, Debby, Debi, Debs, Devorah, Dvoire • Biblical/Hebrew/Jewish • *bee as in buzz, buzz!*

Deirbhile, Dervilla, Derfile, Deirbhail • Irish Gaelic • *daughter of Fal or the poet*

Deirdre, Deidre • Irish Gaelic • *woman*

Della, Adela • French • *noble*

Demi, Demetria • Greek • *follower*

of the goddess Demeter

Deryn • British/Welsh • *blackbird*

Desdemona, Dysdaimon, Mona • Greek/Latin • *unfortunate stars*

Destiny, Destinata, Destry, Destinie, Destiney, Destinee • Latin/Norman • *power of fate*

Devin, Damhan, Damhain • Irish Gaelic • *descendant of Damhan, connected to the fawn or deer*

Dharma, Karma, Nirvana, Samsara • Sanskrit • *custom, tradition or decree from on high*

Digna • Latin • *worthy*

Diketi • Swahili/Kenyan • *small*

Dimity, Dimitos • Irish/Greek • *a light cotton fabric from Italy meaning two double warp thread!*

Dinah, Dina • Biblical/Hebrew/Jewish • *judgement*

Dolores, Deloris, Delores, Doloris, Lola, Lolita, Dolly • Roman Catholic • *Our Lady of the Seven Sorrows of the Virgin*

Dolly, Dorothy, Dolores, Dora • English/Greek • *gift from God*

Dominica, Dominique, Dominga • Latin/Roman Catholic • *Lord, as in St Dominic, founder of the Dominican order*

Domitilla, Domitius • Latin • *a Roman imperial family name*

Donatella, Donatus • Latin • *given by God*

Dongmei • Chinese • *winter plum*

Donla, Dunnflaith • brown lady

Dorothea, Dorothy, Dorothee, Dorothie, Dot, Dottie, Dotty, Dodie, Dolly, Dorofei, Dorotheos, Dorete, Dee • Greek • *gift from God*

Dreda, Etheldreda • Anglo-Saxon • *noble and strong*

Drusilla, Drausus, Drasus • Latin •

from the old Roman family name
Du'ā • Arabic • *prayer and worship*
Durga • Sanskrit • *out of bounds, off limits, inaccessible*
Dvoire, Devorah • Jewish/Yiddish • *bee*

Earla, Erla, Earlina, Erline, Earline, Earlene, Earleen • American/English • *a noble person*
Edda, Hedda • Germanic/Icelandic • *elder younger!*
Ernestine, Ernestina, Earnestine, Earnestina • *serious in all things and will fight to the death; means business to the point of obsession*
Ebba, Eadburga • Anglo-Saxon • *prosperity, fortress*
Ebony, Ebenos, Ebenius • Greek/Latin/American English • *a very black wood*
Edith, Eden, Edun, Edon, Edie, Edyth, Edythe, Eadgyth • Anglo-Saxon • *prosperity, riches and strife or war, possibly she who gains her wealth through the booty of war*
Edwina, Edwardina • Anglo-Saxon • *a person who guards her riches, blessed with wealth*
Ehrentraud, Arntraut • Germanic • *with strength goes honour, or she has the strength of an eagle*
Eiddwen, Eiddunwen • British/Welsh • *fond, passionate, desire, holy, white, fair*
Eilwen, Aelwen • British/Welsh • *white, sacred, fair brow*
Eira • British/Welsh • *snow*
Eirian • British/Welsh • *silvery bright, beautiful*
Eirlys • British/Welsh • *snowdrop*
Eirwen • British/Welsh • *pure as snow*

Elfriede, Adalfrid, Elfreda • Germanic • *peace is noble*
Elke, Adelheide • Germanic • *noble woman, carries herself well*
Elizabeth, Elisabeth, Elisheba, Elise, Eliza, Elisa, Elsa, Liza, Lisa, Liz, Beth, Bet, Bess, Lisbet, Lisbeth, Lysbeth, Elsie, Bessie, Bessy, Betty, Betsy, Tetty, Libby, Lizzie, Lizzy, Buffy, Eilis, Ealasaid, Elisabet, Elisabete, Elisabetta, Elisavet, Yelizaveta, Elzbieta, Alzbeta, Elizabeta, Erzsebet, Elspeth, Elita, Elire • American English • *elite person, upper class, VIP*
Elkan, Elkie, Elkanah • Jewish/Hebrew • *possessed by God*
Elma • English American • *combo of Elizabeth and Mary*
Elspeth, Elsbeth, Elspie, Elsie, Elspet, Elizabeth • Scots English/Biblical • *God is my oath*
Elva, Alva • Scots Gaelic • *white*
Élise, Elyse, Elysia, Alicia, Elisabeth • Biblical/French • *God is my oath*
Emelia, Amelia, Emilia • Latin/Italian • *old Roman family name meaning rival, competitor*
Emily, Aemilia, Aemilius, Émilie • Latin • *old Roman family name meaning rival, competitor*
Encarnación, Incarnatio • Roman Catholic • *incarnation of Jesus Christ*
Erica, Ericka, Erika • Norse • *one ruler or king alone, no other*
Ermengard, Ermgard, Irmgard, Irmengard, Irmingard • Germanic • *this entire enclosure is mine*
Ernesta, Ernestina, Erna, Ernestina • German • *serious in all things and will fight to the death; means business to the point of obsession*
Esmé, Esmee, Esmie, Aestimare,

Aestimatus, Edme • Latin • *priceless, highly prized and valued*

Ethel • Anglo-Saxon • *noble*

Eugenia, Eugenios, Eugenius, Eugenie • Greek • *well bred and high born*

Evangeline, Evangelina • Greek/Latin/French • *good tidings from the gospel*

Evette, Yvette • English/French • *yew tree*

Evonne, Yvonne • English/French • *yew tree*

Eydl, Edel • Jewish/Yiddish • *noble*

Fabia, Fabienne, Fabiola • Latin • *old Roman family name meaning a bean*

Fadilā • Arabic • *a moral, ethical, virtuous woman*

Faith • English • *she who trusts in God, faithful follower*

Fawziyya • Arabic • *accomplished and successful woman*

Fayrūz • Arabic • *turquoise, birthstone of Capricorn*

Fenella, Fionnuala, Finella, Finola • Scots Gaelic • *white, fair, shoulders*

Fennel, Faeniculum, Faenum • Latin • *grass turned into a spice*

Fidda, Fizza • Arabic • *silver*

Fiesta, Festa • Latin/Spanish • *celebration, particularly over a baby's birth*

Fikriyya • Arabic • *pensive, contemplative, intelligent, intellectual*

Fíona, Fionn, Ffion, Ffion, Fina • Irish Gaelic • *vine*

Fiona, Fionn, Ffion • Scots Gaelic/British Welsh • *white, fair*

Finola, Fionnuala, Fionola, Nuala, Finuala, Fionnguala, Fenella, Finella, Finola • Scots Gaelic •

white, fair, shoulders

Flavia, Favius, Flavie • Latin • *old Roman family name meaning yellow-haired*

Flora, Floris, Flo, Florence, Floella, Florrie, Ffloraidh • Latin • *old Roman family name meaning flower*

Frauke • German • *a lady from northern Germany*

Freda, Frederica, Freddie, Frieda, Elfreda, Winifred, Frederika, Friede, Friederike • *peace*

Frume, Fromm • Jewish/Yiddish • *pious, devout and virtuous*

Fulvia, Fulvius • Latin • *an old Roman family name meaning dark, dusky, exotic*

Gabrielle, Gabriella, Gabi, Gaby, Gabby, Gabriel, Gabriele, Gabriela • Biblical/Hebrew/Jewish • *woman of God*

Gail, Gael, Abigail, Gaelle, Gaile, Gale, Gayle • Biblical/Jewish/Hebrew • *shortened version of Abigail • my father is joy, father is exaltation*

Gaia, Ge • Greek • *goddess of the Earth, mum of Saturn*

Galina, Gala, Galene • Greek • *calm*

Garnet, Grenate, Granatum • Norman/Latin • *either a dealer in pomegranates or the precious stone*

Gauri, Gowri • Sanskrit • *white*

Gemma, Jemma • Italian • *precious jewel*

Genette, Jeanette • Biblical/English/Latin • *God is gracious or gift of God*

Geneva, Geneve, Ginevra • French • *after the Swiss city or can be variant of Jennifer or short form of Geneviève*

Genevieve, Jennifer, Genoveffa, Ginevra • Celtic • *a female chief or leader of the tribe of people*

Genista, Genesta • Latin • *the shrub plant called broom, a bright yellow hue*

Georgina, Georgena, Georgette, Georgene, Georgia, Jorja, Georgiana, Georgie, Georgina, Georgine, Georene • Greek/Latin/Norman • *farmer or someone who works on the land*

Gerd, Gerda, Gärd, Garo • Norse • *goddess of fertility, protection as in a fort or castle*

Ghāda • Arabic • *young, graceful, refined woman*

Giachetta • Biblical/Latin • *LADY James! Supplanter, a cuckoo in the nest! Edging out someone to take their place against their will*

Gillian, Gill, Jill, Gillyflower, Gillaine, Jillian, Jilly, Gilly • Latin • *from Julius, a Roman family name*

Ginny, Virginia, Jane, Jaine, Jane, Ginnie, Jinny • Biblical/English/Latin • *pet name for Virginia or Jane*

Giovanna • Biblical/English/Latin • *LADY John! God is gracious or gift of God*

Giuletta, Giulia • Latin/Italian • *from Julius, an old Roman name*

Giuseppina • Biblical/Italian • *God is my salvation*

Gladys, Gwladys, Gwladus • British Welsh/Latin • *uncertain origins but said to be a local form of Claudia from the old Roman family name Claudius*

Glenn, Glen, Glenna, Glennette, Glenette • Scots Gaelic • *valley*

Glenys, Glynis, Glennis, Glenis, Glenice, Glenise, Glennys, Glynnis • British/Welsh • *pure and holy*

Godiva • Anglo-Saxon/Latin • *God's gift*

Gormlaith, Gormflaith • Irish Gaelic • *a splendid, illustrious woman or princess*

Grace, Gracie, Gratia, Grazia, Graziella, Gracia , Graciela • Latin • *grace*

Greer, Grier • Greek/Scots English • *from a Scottish surname, Gregor • watchful*

Griselda, Grizelda, Grizel, Grishild • Germanic • *grey battle*

Gro, Groa, Gruach • Norse/Celtic • *evolving/old woman*

Guadalupe • Roman Catholic • *site of a convent with the famous image of the Virgin Mary*

Gudrun, Guro • Norse • *magical, enchanted, a witch or wise woman*

Gunnborg • Norse • *a fort or castle ready for attack*

Gunnvor, Gunvor, Gunver • Norse • *cautious and prepared for battle*

Gwen, Gwendolen, Gwendoline, Gwenllian, Gwendolin, Gwendolyne, Gwendolyn, Gwenfrewi • British/Welsh • *white*

Gwendolen, Gwendoline • British/Welsh • *white or silver sacred ring*

Gwenllian • British/Welsh • *fair, white complexion*

Gwerful, Gwairmul • British/Welsh • *shy, modest, compromising*

Gwyneira • British/Welsh • *pure as snow*

Gwyneth, Gwynedd, Gwynneth, Gwenith, Gwynaeth • British/Welsh • *happiness or named after the British Welsh princedom of Gwynedd based on Snowdonia area where the ancient Brits (Welsh) fought the*

Anglo-Saxons in guerrilla warfare

Hadya • Arabic • *a woman with inner peace*

Hafza • Arabic • *devoted to the Koran*

Haidee, Aidoios • Greek/literary • *name of a character in Lord Byron's Don Juan; meaning modest*

Hailey, Hayley, Hallie, Haylee, Hailee, Haley, Haleigh, Hegleah • Anglo-Saxon • *meaning a clearing for*

Hāla • Arabic • *ring or halo around the Moon*

Hannah, Hanne, Johanna, Hanna • Biblical/Jewish/Hebrew • *God has favoured me*

Hansine • Germanic • *God is gracious or gift of God*

Hazel, Haesel • Anglo-Saxon • *the hazel tree, for the Celts a magic tree*

Heather, Hather • English • *moorland plant in rich purple hues*

Heaven, Heofon • American English/Anglo-Saxon • *where good people go after this life*

Hecate • Greek • *Goddess of Magic and Enchantment*

Heidi, Adelheid, Adélaide, Heide • Germanic • *noble woman, carries herself well*

Heledd, Hyledd • British Welsh/Celtic mythology • *not entirely sure of its root but it is the name of a princess whose name is at the heart of a lament for her brother's death*

Helen, Helena, Hélène, Elena, Elen, Elin • Greek/English • *ray of sunshine, sunbeam, sunny; another analogy is it means torch of the moon*

Helga, Heilag, Hella • Norse • *successful, prosperity, wealth*

Helme, Friedhelm, Helma • Germanic • *well-protected man who comes in peace*

Hephzibah, Hepzibah, Hepsie, Effie • Biblical • *my delight is in her (my newborn daughter)*

Hermine • Germanic • *a female soldier*

Hiba • Arabic • *a gift or prize from God*

Hikmat • Arabic • *wisdom*

Hilda, Hylda, Hilde, Elda • Germanic • *battleaxe*

Hildegard, Hildegarde • Germanic • *battlefield*

Hillevi • Danish • *safe and protected in war!*

Holly, Hollie, Holi, Holeg, Holin • Anglo-Saxon • *the holly, shrub or tree*

Honor, Honour, Honora, Honorah, Honoria, Honoré, Honorine, Honorina, Norine, Noreen • Norman/Latin • *an honoured woman*

Hope, Hopa • Anglo-Saxon • *Christians' belief in the resurrection and life everlasting*

Horatia • Etruscan • *Roman family name with no certain root*

Hortense, Hortensia, Hortensius, Hortus • French/Latin • *old Roman family name meaning garden*

Huidai • Chinese • *sagacious black*

Huifen • Chinese • *wise and fragrant*

Huizhong • Chinese • *wise devotion*

Huda • Arabic • *a woman who is wise and judicious counsellor or adviser; agony aunt*

Íde, Ita • Irish Gaelic • *unknown origins, possibly related to thirst*

Ida • Germanic/Frankish/Norman

• *worker*

Ihāb • Arabic • *a gift from God*

Ilse, Ilsa, Elisabeth • Germanic/ Biblical • *God is my oath*

In'ām • Arabic • *a gift given or bestowed by God*

Inés, Inez, Agnès • Spanish/Greek • *pure and holy*

Irma, Erma, Ermen, Irmgard, Irmtraud, Irmen, Irmengard, Ermengard, Irmgard, Irmingard, Irmentrud, Ermentrud, Irmentraud • all and nothing less

Isabel, Isobel, Isa, Isabella, Isabelle, Isobelle, Isobella, Izzy, Izzie, Sibéal, Iseabail, Ishbel, Isbel, Elizabeth • Spanish/Biblical/ Hebrew/Jewish • *God is my oath*

Ismene • Greek mythology • *Greek tragedy!*

I'tidāl • Arabic • *everything in moderation*

Ivy, Ifig • Anglo-Saxon • *ivy: the climbing plant called the survivor*

Jacalyn, Jacqueline, Jackalyn, Jaclyn • Biblical/Latin/English • *supplanter, a cuckoo in the nest! Edging out someone to take their place against their will*

Jacqueline, Jackalyn, Jacalyn, Jacqualine, Jacqueline, Jacquelyn, Jacquelyne, Jacquiline, Jacaline, Jacuelline, Jacqueline, Jacklyn, Jaclyn, Jacki, Jackie, Jacky, Jacqui, Jacquie, Jaqui, Jaki, Jakki, Jacquelyn, Jacquelynn, Jacquetta, Giachetta • Biblical/Latin/French • *supplanter, a cuckoo in the nest! Edging out someone to take their place against their will*

Jada, Yada • Biblical/Hebrew/Jewish • *he knows*

Jaime, Jame, Jamesina, Jamie, Jamey, Jamee, Jami, Jaimie, Jaimee • Biblical/Latin/Spanish • *supplanter, a cuckoo in the nest! Edging out someone to take their place against their will*

Jalīla, Galīla • Arabic • *exalted on high*

Jamila, Gamila • Arabic • *graceful as well as beautiful*

Jana, Yana, Jan • Biblical/English/ Latin • *God is gracious or gift of God*

Jane, Jeanne, Jehanne, Jaine, Jayne, Jain, Jean, Joan, Janie, Janey, Joanna, Jaynie, Síne, Siân, Johanna, Hanne, Hansine, Johanne, Janja, Jannja, Sheena Jensine, Jonna, Jeanne, Juanna, Juana, Giovanna, Gianna, Hana, Jana, Janeen, Janelle, Jaynia • Biblical/French/Latin • *God is gracious or gift of God*

Janet, Jannet, Janett, Janette, Jan, Janetta, Janeta, Seònaid, Shona, Seona • Biblical/English/Latin

Janice, Janis, Janise, Jannice, Jan • Biblical/French/Latin • *God is gracious or gift of God*

Jan, Janna • Biblical/English • *God is gracious or gift of God*

Jasmine, Jasmyn, Jazmin, Jazmine, Yasmīn, Yasmine, Jasmina, Yasmina, Jaslyn, Jaslynne • Persian/Norman • *evergreen shrub or vine with glorious fragrance*

Jean, Joan, Jane, Jeanne, Jehanne, Jehanna, Jeane, Jeana, Gina, Jeanna, Jeane, Jeanetta, Jeanette, Jeanie, Jeanine, Jeannette, Jeanne, Jeanett, Jenette, Jennet, Jenet, Ginett, Ginnette, Ginetta, Ginnetta, Jeannie, Jeannine, Jeannique, Jannike • Biblical/

French • *God is gracious or gift of God*

Jerrie, Jerry, Geri, Gerry • Biblical/English • *appointed by God*

Jetta, Jaiet, Gagates • Latin/Norman • *jet, fossilised wood or coal: a black stone from Gagai (a city in Lycia, Asia Minor, now Turkey)*

Jewel, Jouel, Iocus • Latin/Norman • *rare stone that is a plaything, a delight to the eyes*

Jill, Jillian, Gillian, Gill, Jilly, Gilly, Jillie • Latin • *from Julius, a Roman family name*

Jing • Chinese • *stillness, contemplation or luxurious, comfort*

Joan, Ionna, Iohanna, Joanna, Johanna, Joanne, Johanne, Joanie, Joni, Siobhán, Chevanne, Siubhan, Jane, Shevaune, Chevaune, Shona, Shevanne, Joann, Seonag • Biblical/Norman • *God is gracious or gift of God*

Jocasta, Jacasta • literary Greek • *mother of Oedipus, tragic figure in classical mythology*

Joelle, Joël • Biblical/Hebrew/Jewish/French • *God*

Joely, Jolene, Jolie, Jollie, Joleen, Jolie, Joli, Jol • Norse/French • *pretty one; also gay and festive; yuletide*

Johanna, Johna, Johannah, Johanne, Joanna, Joanne, Jo, Jannike • Biblical/Latin • *God is gracious or gift of God*

Jonina • modern English/Biblical/English • *God is gracious or gift of God*

Jonquil, Jonquille, Junco, Juncus • French/English/Spanish • *plant: reed*

Joy, Joie, Gaudia • Latin/French • *joyful in the lord*

Joyce, Josce, Josse, Joducos, Joducus, Iodoc, Joss • Breton Celtic • *lord*

Juan • Chinese • *gracious*

Juanita, Janita, Janita • Spanish • *God is gracious or gift of God*

Julia, Juli, Julie, Giulia, Julietta, Guilietta, Juliet, Juliette, Guiliette, Juliana, Julianus, Julianna, Julianne, Julián, Juliane, Julieann, Julien, Julieanne, Julienne Jools, Julia, Jules, Juleen, Julianne • Latin • *a Roman family name*

Juniper, Jennifer, Rothem, Juniperus • Biblical/Hebrew/Jewish/Latin

Juno, Úna • Irish Gaelic/Roman/English • *uncertain roots; starvation or lamb*

Justina, Justine • Latin • *a Roman family name*

Kailash • Sanskrit • *mountain home of Kubera, the god of wealth*

Kanti • Sanskrit • *as beautiful as the moon*

Karma • Sanskrit • *action, seen as bringing upon oneself inevitable results, good or bad, either in this life or in a reincarnation*

Kausalya • Sanskrit • *a member of the Kosala family of people*

Kay, Kaye • Latin • *a man of the earth*

Kayla, Kayley, Kaylah • American English • *a descendant of Caollaidhe, the prefix meaning a slender man*

Kayley, Kayleigh, Kayly, Kaylie, Kayli, Kaylee, Kaileley, Kailey, Kaily, Kalie, Kalee, Kaleigh, Cayleigh, Caileigh, Caleigh Caileigh, Kayley, Kayleigh, Caleigh,

Caollaidhe, Kailey, Kayley, Kaley, Keely, Keeley, Kayley, Keighley • Irish Gaelic • *from Caollaidhe, meaning a slender man, or from Caoilfhionn, meaning slim and white and pale*

Kiera, Keira • Norse • *a person who lives in marshes covered in shrubs and brushwood*

Keisha, Nkisa • West African • *favourite daughter*

Kendra, Kendrick • British/Welsh/ Scots Gaelic • *a sacred place high on a hill or son of Henry or royal power*

Kennedy, Cinnéidigh • Irish Gaelic • *ugly head*

Kenzie • English/Scots Gaelic/ Biblical • *the cassia tree or shortened MacKenzie*

Keturah • Biblical/Hebrew/Jewish • *incense, the strong perfume from frankincense used to purify in sacred places*

Kezia, Cassia, Kizzie, Kizzy, Keziah, Kenzie • Biblical/Hebrew/Jewish • *the cassia tree, known as the bark of cinnamon in the USA and Canada*

Kimberley, Kim, Kimberly, Kimberlie, Kimberlee, Kimberleigh, Kimberli, Kymberley, Kym • Anglo-Saxon/American English • *etymology is a personal name such as Kimma's wood or clearing. But gained popularity after the South African town of Kimberley where the British took on the Boers*

Kirsten, Christine, Kristine, Kerstin • Danish/Norwegian/English/ Latin • *follower of Christ*

Kirstie, Kirstin, Kirsty, Kirstie, Christine, Chirsty, Ciorstaidh, Ciorstag, Curstaidh, Curstag • Scots English/Latin • *follower of Christ*

Klara, Clara • German/Latin • *bright, famous, crystal clear*

Kreszenz, Crescentia • Latin/ Bavarian • *growing like the moon*

Kris, Kristina, Kristina, Kristen • Swedish/Czech/Latin • *follower of Christ*

Krista, Christa • German/Latin • *follower of Christ*

Kristel, Krystal, Chrystal • German/ Greek • *gold*

Kristie, Christie, Kirstie, Kristina, Kristy • American English/Latin • *follower of Christ*

Kristina, Kristine, Christine, Christina, Kristeen, Kristene, Kerstin, Kirsten, Tina • Swedish/ Czech/Latin • *follower of Christ*

Kumari • Sanskrit • *daughter or princess*

Kyla • Gaelic • *narrow in geographical terms; a region in Ayrshire*

Kyra, Kyria, Kira • Greek • *lady*

Leila, Laila, Layla, Leyla • Arabic • *a beautiful dark woman, as enchanting as the night, intoxicating to the senses*

La Keisha • African American • *the favourite daughter*

Lakshmi • Sanskrit • *lucky in matters of luck, money and beauty*

Lamyā • Arabic • *a woman with fulsome brown lips*

Lana, Alana, Alanah, Lanna, Svetlana • American English • *vague origins but likely to mean a rock*

Larch, Larche, Larix • American English/German/Latin • *sacred tree to the Shaman*

Lark, Lawerce • North American/ Australian/English/Anglo-Saxon • *dawn song*

Laverne, Lavern • American English/Gaulish • *alder tree*

Leah, Léa, Lia, Azalea, Lee, Leia • Biblical/Hebrew/Jewish • *weary*

Leigh, Lee • Anglo-Saxon • *a clearing in the wood*

Leila, Laila, Layla, Leyla, Lela, Lila • Arabic • *a beautiful dark woman, as enchanting as the night, intoxicating to the sense*

Leocardia, Leukados • Latin • *clear and bright as crystal*

Lesley, Lesslyn • Scots Gaelic • *the place where holly grows*

Li • Chinese • *upright*

Líadan • Irish Gaelic • *grey*

Libby, Elizabeth • English • *God is my oath*

Liese, Elisabeth • German • *God is my oath*

Lijuan • Chinese • *beautiful and graceful*

Lili, Lilli, Elisabeth • German • *God is my oath*

Lilian, Lilly, Lily, Lili, Lillian, Lilium, Lily, Lillie, Lilly, Lili, Lilli • Latin/ Norman • *pet name for Elizabeth, God is my oath, or from the flower lily, known as the flower for the pure*

Lindall, Lindale, Linda, Lindell, Lindal • Anglo-Saxon • *valley where the flax grows*

Linden, Linda, Lindie • Anglo-Saxon • *lime tree*

Linnéa, Linnaea • Swedish • *name honouring botanist Carl von Linne*

Lisa, Liza, Elyse, Lise, Liese, Élise, Elisabeth • French/German • *God is my oath*

Lisette, Lise, Elisabeth, Lysette, Lise, Lys, Liz, Lis, Elisbet, Liza, Eliza, Lisa, Lizzie, Lizzy, Lizi, Elizabeth • English/French • *God is my oath*

Livia, Livius • Latin • *Roman family name Livius, uncertain origin but maybe means a hue of the colour blue*

Lola, Dolores • Roman Catholic • *Our Lady of the Seven Sorrows of the Virgin*

Lolicia, Lola, Delicia • American English/Roman Catholic • *Our Lady of the Seven Sorrows of the Virgin*

Lolita, Lola, Lolita • Roman Catholic • *Our Lady of the Seven Sorrows of the Virgin*

Lone, Abelone, Magdelone • Danish • *Mary Magdelene aka Mary of Magdala, woman healed of evil spirits*

Lucretia, Lucrece, Lucrezia, Lucretius • Latin • *Roman family name, Lucretius, with no known origins*

Lujayn • Arabic • *silver*

Luli • Chinese • *dewy jasmine*

Lyudmila, Lyuda, Ludmil • Slavic • *a tribe of kind people, a family of gracious folks*

Madeleine, Madelaine, Magdalene, Magdala, Madelene, Madlyn, Madelyn, Madalene, Madaline, Madoline, Magdalen, Maddie, Maddy, Maddalena • Biblical/French • *Mary Magdelene aka Mary of Magdala, woman healed of evil spirits*

Madīha • Arabic • *praiseworthy, commendable*

Madison, Maddison, Mady, Maddie • American/English • *son of Maud or Matilda, the battleaxe*

Madrona, Matrona • Jewish • *from the name Matron, a wish for the baby girl to become a mother herself*

Magda, Magdalene, Magadelena,

Lena • Biblical/Slavic/German • *Mary Magdelene aka Mary of Magdala, woman healed of evil spirits*

Maitland, Maltalent, Mautalent • Anglo-Saxon/Norman • *bad-tempered or from Mautalant, a barren place in France*

Mallory, Malerie, Mallery • Norman • *unhappy or unfortunate one*

Manala • Arabic • *to acquire, to attain, to own*

Manuela • Biblical/Spanish • *God is with us or amongst us*

Maoilosa • Irish Gaelic • *follower of Jesus Christ*

Mara, Naomi • Biblical/Jewish/Hebrew • *bitter*

Marietta, Mariella, María, Mairéad, Margaret, Mariette, Maretta • Biblical/Italian • *Mary Magdelene aka Mary of Magdala, woman healed of evil spirits*

Marina, Marinus, Marius, Marna • Latin • *Roman family name, clouded meaning but associated with someone of or from the sea*

Marla, Marlene, Magdalene • modern • *Mary Magdelene aka Mary of Magdala, woman healed of evil spirits*

Marlene, Maria, Magdalena • German • *Mary Magdelene aka Mary of Magdala, woman healed of evil spirits*

Marna, Marnie • Swedish/Latin • *Roman family name; clouded meaning but associated with someone of or from the sea*

Marsha • Anglo-Saxon • *a person who lives on marshy ground or fenland*

Marwa • Arabic • *a fragrant plant and shiny pebble*

May, Mae, Maybelle, Maybella • Anglo-Saxon • *the magical hawthorn tree which is also known as may; the month of May*

Maysa, Mayyas • Arabic • *a woman with a graceful but proud gait*

Medea, Medesthai • Greek mythology • *a Colchian princess in 'Jason and the Golden Fleece'; means to contemplate and reflect*

Mehetabel, Mehitabel • Biblical/Jewish/Hebrew • *God makes happy*

Mehjibin • Persian • *she has a face that is as beautiful as the temples of the moon*

Mei • Chinese • *plum winter endurance*

Meifen, Meixiang • Chinese • *plum fragrance*

Meihui • Chinese • *beautiful wisdom*

Meilin • Chinese • *plum jade*

Meixiu • Chinese • *beautiful grace*

Mélanie, Melania, Melaina, Melany, Melony, Mellony, Meloney, Melloney, Melas • Latin/Greek/Norman • *black, dark*

Melissa, Melita, Melitta Lissa, Melissa, Lyssa Lita, Melita, Melitta • Greek • *honey bee*

Meredith, Meredydd • British/Welsh • *unknown prefix plus lord*

Merle, Meriel, Merula • Norman/Latin • *a blackbird*

Michaela, Mikayla, Mica, Micah • Biblical/Hebrew/Jewish/English • *who is like God?*

Michele, Michelle, Michel, Chelle, Shell, Micheline • Biblical/Hebrew/Jewish/English • *who is like God?*

Milla, Camilla, Camille • Latin/French • *Roman family name meaning perfection*

Millena, Milenna • Czech • *grace and favour*

Millicent, Milesende, Amalswinth, Millie, Milly, Mills • Germanic/Frankish/Norman • *strength, labour, work*

Modesta, Modestus • Latin • *personal name, meaning cautious and restrained*

Mona, Muadhnait, Monos, Muadh • Irish Gaelic • *noble*

Monica, Monere, Monique, Monika • Latin/Phoenician • *cautious counsel, to advise or warn*

Montserrat • Catalan • *the Lady of Montserrat, a Benedictine monastery near Barcelona*

Morven, Morvern, Mhorbhairne, Morbheinn • Scots • *area of north Argyll or big peak*

Myfanwy, Myf • British/Welsh • *your lady, your woman*

Myra, Myrrha, Mary, Miranda, Mairéad • Latin • *anagram of Mary meaning myrrh; the embalming spice*

Myrtle, Myrtille, Myrtilla, Myrta • Greek/Latin/Norman • *a tree with fragrant leaves; it means perfumed*

Nabīla • Arabic • *upper-crust woman*

Nada • Arabic • *she is like the morning dew and generous with it*

Nahla • Arabic • *she is as refreshing as a drink of water, she quenches my thirst*

Na'īma • Arabic • *a woman who is contented and happy*

Najāh, Nagāh • Arabic • *a woman who is progressive and successful*

Najiba, Nagiba • Arabic • *cultured, cultivated and a cut above the rest*

Najwa, Nagwa • Arabic • *secrets abound, a woman who is discreet and confidential, keeper of secrets*

Nan, Nancy, Nanette, Ann • Biblical/Jewish/Hebrew • *pet form of Ann, of uncertain origins: God has favoured me*

Nancy, Nan, Ann, Annis, Agnes, Nancie, Nanci, Nance • Biblical/Jewish/Hebrew • *pet form of Ann, of uncertain origins: God has favoured me*

Nanette, Nan • Biblical/Jewish/Hebrew/French • *pet form of Ann, of uncertain origins: God has favoured me*

Nasrīn • Persian/Arabic • *wild rose/a star set in the constellation of the Eagle and the Lyre*

Nastasia, Anastasia • Greek/Russian • *short form of Anastasia, resurrection*

Natalia, Natalya, Natalie, Natasha • Latin/Russian • *the birth of Jesus Christ or reborn with faith*

Natalie, Nathalie, Natalia • Latin/French • *the birth of Jesus Christ or reborn with faith*

Natasha, Natalia, Noel • Latin/Russian • *the birth of Jesus Christ or reborn with faith*

Nazaret, Nazareth • Roman Catholic • *Jesus Christ's native village*

Nerina, Nerine, Nereus • Greek/Latin • *sea god/family name Nero or Nerio*

Nerys • British/Welsh • *lady*

Nesta, Nester, Nostos, Agnès • British Welsh/Greek • *pure and holy*

Ngaio • New Zealand Maori • *a clever tribe or people*

Nia, Nyah • Swahili • *with a purpose*

Nieves • Roman Catholic • *Our*

Lady of the Snows
Nigella • Latin • *black as pitch*
Ninel • Russian • *Lenin, spelt backwards!*
Ning • Chinese • *tranquillity*
Noelle • Latin/Norman • *nativity of Christ: Christmas; particularly a child born during the 12 days of Christmas*
Nola, Fionnuala • Irish Gaelic • *descended from Nolan or champion chariot fighter*
Nóra, Honora, Norah, Nonie • Irish Gaelic/Latin • *an honoured woman*
Noreen, Nóirín, Norene, Norine, Honoria • Irish Gaelic/Latin • *an honoured woman*
Nuala, Fionnuala, Nola • *fair hair down to her bonny shoulders*
Nuha • Arabic • *a woman who is clever, intellectual and cerebrally bright*
Nuo • Chinese • *graceful*
Nyamekye • Ghanian • *given by God*

Olympe, Olympia • Greek • *a woman from Olympus, the mountain of the Gods*
Odile, Odila, Ottilie, Ottoline • Germanic • *prosperous and wealthy*
Olga, Helgi • Norse • *prosperous*
Olive, Olivia, Oliff, Oliffe, Oliva • Latin • *olive tree, a symbol of peace and abundance*
Olivia, Olive, Oliva • literary invention/Latin • *William Shakespeare named Olivia as the rich heiress in* The Tempest
Olwen, Olwin, Olwyn • *footprint, path, white, sacred*
Olufemi • Nigerian • *God loves me*
Ophelia, Ophelos • Italian/Greek •

• help!
Oralie, Aurelie, Aurelia, Oralee • Latin/French • *Roman family name meaning golden*
Orna, Odharnait • Irish Gaelic • *sallow complexion*
Ornella, Ornelia, Ornetta, Ornello • Tuscan • *the flowering ash tree*
Ottilie, Odile, Odila • Germanic • *prosperous and wealthy*
Ottoline • Germanic • *prosperous and wealthy*

Pandora, Dora, Pandoran • Greek mythology • *all and every gift; alluding to Pandora's box that she was told never to open, when she did, she allowed everything evil and bad out, leaving the fairy Hope as the only thing left inside*
Pansy, Pensee • Norman • *flower whose name means 'thought'*
Paris, Parisii • Latin/Celtic • *member of the Parisii tribe, origins unknown*
Parvati • Sanskrit • *daughter of the mountains*
Patience, Pati • Latin • *to suffer, a virtue*
Patrice, Patricia • Latin/French/ Irish Gaelic • *patrician*
Patricia, Patrice, Pat, Tricia, Trisha, Trish, Patty, Pattie, Patti, Patsy, Patrizia, Paudeen, Páidín • Latin/ Irish Gaelic • *patrician*
Paula, Paola • Latin/Italian/English • *Roman family name meaning little or small*
Paulette, Paula, Paulina, Paola • Latin • *Roman family name meaning little or small*
Pauline, Paulina • Latin/French • *Roman family name meaning little or small*

Perdita, Perdie, Purdee, Purdy, Perditus • Latin/literary invention • *William Shakespeare invented the name from the Latin 'lost' as one of his characters in* The Winter's Tale

Pernilla, Pella, Pernille, Petronel, Petronilla • Latin/Greek/Swedish • *a stone or someone who lives in the country*

Petronel, Petronella, Petronilla, Petronius • Latin • *a Roman family name Petronius that could be connected to St Peter*

Petra, Peta, Piera, Peta, Petra • Greek • *rock or stone*

Phoebe, Phoibos, Phoebus • Latin/Greek • *bright: Goddess of the Moon*

Pia, Pius • Italian • *pious*

Pierce, Pearce, Perse, Pierette, Peta • Greek • *the rock or stone*

Pilar • Roman Catholic • *Our Lady of the Pillar; appearance of the Virgin on a pillar at Zaragossa*

Portia, Porcia, Porcius, Porcus, Porsha • Latin • *Roman family name of Porcus, meaning pig*

Presentación • Roman Catholic/Spanish • *presentation of the Virgin at the Temple in Jerusalem*

Prisca, Priscilla, Priscus • Biblical/Latin • *Roman family name meaning ancient or old*

Priscilla, Cilla, Prissy, Priscus • Biblical/Latin • *Roman family name meaning ancient or old*

Prunella, Ella, Pru, Prue • Latin • *pruna: plum*

Purificación • Roman Catholic/Spanish • *Feast of the Purification when Virgin purges of the uncleanliness associated with childbirth*

Purnima • Sanskrit • *full moon*

Qingge • Chinese • *crystal house*

Qingling • Chinese • *celebrating understanding*

Qingzhao • Chinese • *clear understanding, crystal illumination*

Radegund, Radegunde • Germanic • *a counsellor, adviser in times of trouble*

Radha • Sanskrit • *success!*

Raelene, Rae • Germanic/Frankish/English Australian • *adviser to the army; army commander*

Rafferty, Rabhartaigh, Robhartach • Irish Gaelic • *descendant of Robhartaigh*

Ragna • Norse • *advice from the gods*

Ragnborg, Ramborg • Norse • *decisions and protection from the gods*

Ragnhild, Raghnallt, Regina, Raghnaid • Norse • *seek counsel from the gods*

Raimunde, Raimund, Raimonda • Germanic/Frankish • *adviser to the army; army commander*

Rajani, Rajni • Sanskrit • *something of the night… as dark as night*

Rajni • Sanskrit • *queen of the night*

Ramona • Catalan/Visigothic • *adviser, protector*

Randa • Arabic • *a desert-bound sweet perfumed tree*

Rathnait, Ronit • Irish Gaelic • *a woman of grace and prosperity*

Raven, Rafn, Raefn, Ravenna • Anglo-Saxon/Norse • *Odin's winged friend, the raven*

Ravenna • Italian • *an Italian city, someone from Ravenna, the capital of Roman mosaic*

Reagan, Regan, Riagain • Irish Gaelic/English • *descendant of*

*Riagain, the impulsive or impatient
one*
**Renée, Reenie, Rena, Renatus,
Renata, Serena, Rina** • Latin •
reborn; resurrected
Renata, Renée, René, Renate •
Latin • *reborn*
Rhetta • Dutch • *advice, counsel*
Rida • Arabic • *one who has God's
(Allah's) approval*
**Riley, Rileigh, Ryley, Reilly,
Rygelegh, Roghallach** • Anglo-
Saxon/Irish Gaelic • *a field where
the rye crop has been cleared*
Rīm • Arabic • *white antelope*
Ritz, Ritzy • American English •
posh hotel name
Rocio • Roman Catholic • *Our Lady
of the Dews, or tears shed for the
wickedness of the world*
Rowen, Ruadhan • Gaelic/English •
descendant of Ruadhan, little red one
**Roxanne, Roxane, Roxana,
Roxanna, Roxy, Rozanne** • Latin/
Greek/Persian • *dawn*
Roxy • American English • *flashy,
glitzy but just a little nouvelle riche!*
Ruomei • Chinese • *like a plum*
Ruqayya • Arabic • *talisman, lucky
charm, magic spell, moving upwards,
advancing/ascending*
Ryanne, Ryan, Riain • Irish Gaelic/
English • *little king, descendant of
Riain*

Sabāh • Arabic • *morning*
Sabriyya • Arabic • *a woman who is
patient, persevering and dedicated*
Safā • Arabic • *a pure, chaste woman
who is sincere and goodly*
Sahar • Arabic • *morning has
broken, dawn*
Salha • Arabic • *devoted and*

dedicated
Salma • Arabic • *a person who looks
after those she loves; a protector*
Salomé, Shalom • Greek/Hebrew/
Aramaic • *peace*
Salwa • Arabic • *she who consoles
others and gives a shoulder to cry on*
Samantha, Sam, Sammy, Sammi •
Biblical/Hebrew/Jewish
Sandhya • Sanskrit • *twilight of the
gods, devout, ritualistic*
Sarala • Sanskrit • *as straight as the
pine and honest as the day is long*
Saraswati • Sanskrit • *filled with
waters of knowledge of the arts,
learning and academia*
Saskia, Sachs • Dutch/Germanic •
Saxon (the tribe)
Saturday • Latin • *Saturn's day*
Savannah, Savanna • American
English/Spanish • *treeless plane*
Seanach • English/Norman French
• *old, wise and venerable*
Selina, Selena, Selene, Slie, Sly •
Greek • *goddess of the moon*
Senga • Gaelic • *slender*
Serenissima • Italian/Venetian •
serene
Sévérine, Severina, Severa • Latin •
Roman family name, austere, severe
Shae, Shea, Shay, Séaghdha • Irish
Gaelic • *descendant of Séaghdha*
Shahīra • Arabic • *destiny for fame
and fortune*
Shamshad • Persian • *like a box tree
she is lean, tall and elegant*
Shan • Chinese • *a woman who
bears herself elegantly; like royalty or
a model*
**Shannon, Shantelle, Shan,
Seanain, Seanán** • Irish Gaelic •
wise, mature and ancient
Shana, Sian, Shanae, Shania,

Shanee, Siani, Siân • American English/British Welsh

Shane • Irish Gaelic/English • *supplanter, a cuckoo in the nest! Edging out someone to take their place against their will*

Shannagh, Shannah, Seanaigh, Seanach • Irish Gaelic • *surname; descendant of Seanach*

Shanta • Sanskrit • *she who finds inner peace through yoga or meditation*

Shanti • Sanskrit • *she who finds tranquillity and serenity through yoga*

Sharifa • Arabic • *a woman who is eminent in her field and honourable to the nth degree*

Sharmila • Sanskrit/Hindi • *she who is selfless, modest and protective*

Shaughan, Shaun, Shaughn, Shawn • Irish Gaelic/English • *supplanter, a cuckoo in the nest!*

Silver, Silvette, Argentia, Silvestra • Latin • *a person from the woods or forest*

Sinéad, Janet, Jeanette, Seònaid, Shona, Seona • English/Scots Gaelic • *God is gracious or gift of God*

Siobhán, Joan, Jehanne, Shevaun, Chevonne, Chevaun, Chevaunne, Shevaunne, Jehanne, Joan • English/Norman French/Biblical/Irish Gaelic • *God is gracious or gift of God*

Sioned, Janet • English/British Welsh • *God is gracious or gift of God*

Sissy, Sisi, Sissey, Sissie, Elisabeth • Jewish/Hebrew/Bavarian • *God is my oath*

Sissel, Cecily • Scandinavian/ English • *old Roman family name Caecilius, from the Latin, meaning blind*

Sita • Sanskrit • *she ploughs a straight furrow; symbolic of all wifely virtures and goddess of nature*

Sixten • Swedish • *victory stone*

Slane, Slaney • Irish Gaelic • *descendant of Sluaghadhan*

Sloan, Sluaghhadain • Irish Gaelic • *a descendant of Sluaghadh, the tribe who go on raids and quick attacks*

Sloane, Sloan • English • *after Sloane Square in London, name given to a 'Sloane ranger'*

Sofia, Sophia, Sofya, Sofie, Sophie, Sofie, Sophy • Greek • *wisdom*

Sonia, Sonya, Sonje • Greek • *wisdom*

Song • Chinese • *pine tree*

Sorrel, Sorrell, Sorell, Sorel, Sur • Norman/German/Frankish • *the herb sorrel with its sour leaves*

Solange, Sollemnia, Sollemna • Latin • *solemn*

Soledad, Sol • Roman Catholic • *Our Lady of Solitude*

Solveig, Solvig, Solvej • Norse • *strength through the family or home*

Song • Chinese • *pine tree*

Sri • Sanskrit • *a royal personage who radiates the light of goodness, beauty and wealth*

Sroel, Israel • Jewish/Yiddish • *one who strives with God*

Sultana • Arabic • *empress, queen*

Sujata • Sanskrit • *excellent character or born of nobility*

Sumati • Sanskrit • *good thoughts, devout in prayer*

Summer, Haf, Sumor • Anglo-Saxon • *someone born in the summer*

months (southern hemisphere)
Sunita • Sanskrit • *she's a good girl who gives wise advice*
Shushila • Sanskrit • *she has a lovely nature and is so placid too*
Swanhild, Swanhilda, Swanhilde, Svanhild • Saxon • *she glides through conflict (battle) like a swan*
Sylvestra, Silvestra • Latin • *a person from the woods or forest*
Sylvia, Silvia, Sylvie, Silvia, Sylvia, Sylve, Sylvius • Latin/English/French/Italian • *someone who loves or inhabits the woods or forest*

Tacey, Tace, Tacita • Latin/English • *to be silent*
Talia, Talya, Natalya, Thalia • Latin/Russian • *the birth of Jesus Christ or reborn with faith*
Tanya, Tania, Tanja • Latin • *Sabine Roman family name*
Tara, Teamhair, Tarra, Taree • Irish Gaelic • *a hill that was the seat of the high kings of Ireland*
Tara • Sanskrit • *a shining star who carries the troubles of the world on her shoulders*
Tasha, Natasha • Latin • *the birth of Jesus Christ or reborn with faith*
Tatiana, Tanya, Tatyana, Tatianus, Tatius • Latin/Russian • *Sabine Roman family name, Tatius, of vague origins*
Tempe, Temnein • Greek • *a valley in Greece; the legendary home of the Muses, the nine goddesses of the arts and sciences*
Terri, Terry, Theresa, Terryl • Latin/Irish Gaelic • *from the Roman Family name Terentius and Irish for someone who takes the initiative*
Thalia, Talia, Thallein • Greek • *one of the nine Muses; the goddess of comedy whose name means to prosper comedically*
Thanā • Arabic • *a woman ready to praise and be praised; everything she does deserves praise*
Thecia, Theokleia • Greek • *glory of God*
Theda, Teud, Theodosia • Latin • *people, tribe or race*
Themba • Zulu • *trusted*
Theodora, Dora, Teodora, Feodora • Greek • *God-given or giving to God or God's gift*
Theodosia, Dosy, Theodosis • Greek • *God-given*
Theokleia, Thecia, Tekla • Greek • *glory of God*
Thurayya, Surayya • Arabic • *coping with sorrow and sadness*
Tia, Laetitia, Lucretia, Tiana, Tiara • Spanish/Portuguese • *aunty or short form of any name ending in -tia*
Tierra • American Spanish • *land, earth, terra firma*
Tiffany, Theophania, Theosphainein • English/Greek • *Epiphany: God will appear*
Ting • Chinese • *graceful*
Tita • Latin • *old Roman name, unknown origins*
Toni, Tonia, Tonia, Tonya, Antonia, Antoinette • Estruscan/Roman
Treasa, Trean • Irish Gaelic • *a woman of intense, immense strength*
Trista, Trysta • American English/British Welsh • *rowdy, rebellious, blue, melancholic, chaotic*
Tyler, Tigele, Tegula, Tylor • Anglo-Saxon/Latin • *a man who covers structure with fabric, stone or slate*

Ulrike, Ulrika, Ulla • Germanic/Anglo-Saxon • *from riches come*

power; power and riches; wolf power
Uma • Sanskrit • *turmeric or flax;*
messenger of the gods
'Umayma • Arabic • *little mother*
Úna, Unity, Oona, Oonagh, Euna
• Irish Gaelic • *uncertain roots;*
starvation or lamb
Ursula, Ursa, Urchi, Ersoula • Latin
• *she-bear*
Usha • Sanskrit • *Goddess of the*
Dawn
Ute, Uda • Germanic • *heritage,*
roots, belonging

Valérie, Valeria, Valère, Val •
French/Latin • *old Roman name*
Valerius meaning healthy, robust and
strong
Vera, Verus • Slavic • *a woman with*
faith
Verna, Verona, Verena • American
English/Gaulish • *alder tree*
Vesta, Hestia • Latin • *Roman*
goddess of the hearth; hestia is the
same in the Greek pantheon
Vienna, Wien, Vindo, Vianna •
Celtic • *white*
Vimala • Sanskrit • *a peerless person,*
pure as crystal
Virginia, Verginius, Ginny, Ginnie,
Virginie • Latin • *Roman family*
name Vergilius but confusion reigned
when the spelling was changed to
Virgilius, which means the maiden
or virga as in stick
Virtudes • Roman Catholic/Spanish
• *seven Christian virtues*
Vivienne, Vivien, Viv, Vi, Vivi,
Vivienne, Vivianne, Béibhinn
• Latin/Norman • *Roman name*
Vivianus meaning life
Vivien, Vivian, Vivienne, Béibhinn
• Celtic/Irish Gaelic/Arthurian

Legend • *white or fair lady*

Wafā • Arabic • *a faithful, loyal,*
devoted woman
Walburg, Walburga • Germanic •
she rules over a stronghold or fort
Waltraud, Waltrud, Waltrude •
Germanic • *rules with great strength*
Wanda, Wenda, Wendelin •
Germanic/Polish/Slavic • *a member*
of the Slav tribe living between the
Elbe and Oder
Wen • Chinese • *refinement*
Whitney, Whitley, Witney,
Whitleah, Whiteney • Anglo-Saxon
Wilma, Wilhelmina, Billie,
Wilmette, Wilmetta • Anglo-Saxon
• *she is famous for her willpower and*
strength of character
Winifred, Winfred, Win, Winnie,
Wynnfrith, Gwenfrewi, Winfriede,
Winfried • Germanic
Wynne, Wynn, Wine • British
Welsh/Anglo-Saxon • *a friend and/*
or one who is blessed and sacred

Xiaofan • Chinese • *rather ordinary*
or ordinary dawn
Xiaoli • Chinese • *morning jasmine*
Xiaowen • Chinese • *morning clouds*
Xingjuan • Chinese • *getting more*
graceful every day
Xue • Chinese • *white and pure as*
the driven snow
Xueman • Chinese • *snowy, cool*
composure and grace

Ya • Chinese • *grace*
Yael, Jael • Biblical/Hebrew/Jewish
• *a wild goat*
Yana, Jana • Biblical/English/Latin •
God is gracious or gift of God
Yanlin • Chinese • *forest of swallows,*

also Beijing, Chinese capital
Yanmei • Chinese • *swallow plum*
Yarrow, Yarrowe, Gearwe •
Anglo-Saxon/English
Yelena, Helen, Helena • Russian/
Greek • *ray of sunshine, sunbeam,
sunny; another meaning is torch of
the moon*
Yelisaveta, Elisabeth • Hebrew/
Jewish • *God is my oath*
Yevgenia, Eugenios • Russian/
Greek • *well bred and high born*
Ying • Chinese • *a clever girl*
Yingtai • Chinese • *terrace of flowers*
Yue • Chinese • *moon*
Yun • Chinese • *cloud*
Yusra • a woman who attracts
wealth, prosperity and good things
Yves, Eve • French/Germanic • *yew
tree*
Yvette, Yves • French/Germanic •
yew tree
Yvonne, Yvon, Yves • French/
Germanic • *yew tree*

Zélie, Célie, Celia, Zaylie, Zaylee, •
French/ Latin • *Roman family name
meaning heaven*
Zelah • Biblical/Hebrew/Jewish •
*literal meaning is 'side'; one of the 14
cities of the tribe of Benjamin*
Zelda, Griselda, Grizelda •
Germanic • *grey battle*
Zhaohui • Chinese • *crystal wisdom*
Zhu • Chinese • *bamboo: a lucky
plant, symbol of happiness, wealth
and health*
Zillah • Biblical/Hebrew/Jewish •
shade
Zindzi • South African • *stability*
Zinnia • German • *a flower from
Mexico named after botanist JG Zinn*
Zongying • Chinese • *heroine,
someone others look up to; a role
model*
Zula • South African/Zulu •
someone from the Zulu tribe

AQUARIUS
21st January to 19th February

Planets: Uranus and Saturn

Day: Saturday

Stone: amethyst

Metals: uranium and lead

Colours: rainbow spectrum, sky blue, metallic

Design: speckled and freckled, stars 'n' stripes, gingham, polka dots and all unconventional shapes

Trees: pine, alder, rowan, mountain ash, holly, ivy

Flora: violet, snowdrop, orchid, blue cornflower and alpine plants

Celebrities: Queen Anne • Jennifer Aniston • Sir Francis Bacon • Tallulah Bankhead • John Barrymore • Jack Benny • Humphrey Bogart • Eva Braun • George Burns • Robert Burns • Lord Byron • Eddie Cantor • Princess Caroline of Monaco • Lewis Carroll • Carol Channing • Stockard Channing • Anton Chekov • Ronald Coleman • Alice Cooper • Charles Darwin • Geena Davis • James Dean • Ellen DeGeneres • Charles Dickens • Matt Dillon • Christian Dior • Thomas Edison • King Farouk • Mia Farrow • Fredrico Fellini • Bridget Fonda • Clark Gable • Zsa Zsa Gabor • Peter Gabriel • Galileo Galilei • Russell Grant • Gene Hackman • King Henry VII • James Joyce • Carol King • Mario Lanza • Jack Lemmon • Abraham Lincoln • Charles Lindbergh • Douglas MacArthur • Harold MacMillan • Édouard Manet • Adolph Manjou • Bob Marley • Queen Mary I • W Somerset Maugham • John McEnroe • Jeanne Moreau • Wolfgang Amadeus Mozart • Paul Newman • Jack Nicklaus • Kim Novak • Boris Pasternak • Anna Pavlova • Ronald Reagan • Vanessa Redgrave • Burt Reynolds • Franklin D Roosevelt • Gypsy Rose Lee • John Ruskin • Babe Ruth • Franz Schubert • Jane Seymour • Cybill Shepherd • Gertrude Stein • Justin Timberlake • John Travolta • Lana Turner • Jules Verne • Robert Wagner • Kaiser Wilhelm II • Oprah Winfrey • Virginia Woolf.

Planetary Influences: see Saturn and Uranus at the back of this book (pages 431 and 435)

Boys

'**Abbās** • Arabic • *austere, severe*

Abner, Avner • Biblical/Hebrew • *father of light*

Abraham, Abe, Avraham, Avrom, Abe, Avhamon • Hebrew/Aramaic • *father of the tribes or nations*

'**Ahmad, Ahmed** • Arabic • *highly commendable*

Aitor • Basque • *founder of the Basques, local hero*

Aldous, Aldebrand, Aldemund, Alderan • Norman • *the root means old*

Algot • Norse • *elf and gothic*

Alfred, Alfie, Alf, Aelfraed, Alfredo • Anglo-Saxon • *supernatural, faerie counsel help*

Alger, Algie, Aelfgaer • Anglo-Saxon • *an old enchanted, noble spear with magical powers possibly from a sacred location*

Aloysius, Alois, Alwisi, Alaois • Provençal/Latin/Germanic • *all-wise, all-seeing*

Altman • Jewish/Hebrew • *old man*

Alvar, Alfhere, Álvaro • Anglo-Saxon/Visigothic/Spanish • *army with faerie fighters, very Lord of the Rings!*

Alvin, Aelfwine, Athelwine • Anglo-Saxon • *elfin, noble or faerie friend*

Alwyn, Aylwin, Alvin • British/Welsh/Anglo-Saxon • *he who has faerie friends*

Ambrose, Ambroise, Ambrosius, Ambrois, Ambroix, Ambrogio, Ambrosio, Ambrosios, Ambros, Emrys, Ambros, Ambrogio, Ambrozy, Ambroz • Latin • *immortal, eternal*

Amerigo, Emmerich • Spanish/Visigothic • *a person who works hard to gain power*

Amilcare • Phoenician/Italian • *friend of the God Melkar*

Armitabh • Sanskrit • *eternal splendour*

'**Ammar** • Arabic • *longevity*

Amnon • Biblical/Jewish/Hebrew • *faithful, loyal*

Åmund, Agmund • Norse • *living on the edge, seeks protection*

Anil • Sanskrit • *air and wind*

Anselm, Anselmo • Germanic • *divine face, divine protection (helmet)*

Antshel, Anshel, Amshel • Jewish/Yiddish • *angel*

Arduino, Hartwinn • Germanic • *best friend*

Arrigo, Enrico • Germanic/Spanish/Italian • *power comes from the home or family (meaning nation too)*

Arjun • Sanskrit • *white and silver*

Armani, Armanno, Hariman • Lombardic/Italian/Germanic • *freeman*

Arran • English • *island making up County of Buteshire*

Asdrubale, Asrubaal • Phoenician/Italian • *give aid to the lord or receive it*

Asher • Jewish/Hebrew • *auspicious, born happy under a lucky star*

Ashish • Sanskrit • *prayer, wish or blessing*

Ashraf • Arabic • *honourable and distinguished*

Åsmund, Assmund • protected by the gods

Athan, Athanase, Athanasius, Afanasi, Athanasios, Athanatos •

Latin/Greek • *eternal life*
Aubrey, Aubry, Alberic, Albric,
Aelfric, Aubrey, Alberic, Albericus
• Germanic/Anglo-Saxon/Latin • *he*
who has the power of the faeries
Averill, Eoforhild, Alfred • Norman/
Anglo-Saxon • *supernatural, faerie*
favours
Avery • Norman/Anglo-Saxon •
supernatural, faerie favours
'Azīz • Arabic • *unconquerable,*
adored

Balder • Norse • *ruler or chief*
prince, said to be pure and beautiful
Baldwin, Maldwyn, Baudouin •
English • *a bold and brave friend*
Barak • Jewish/Hebrew • *a bolt of*
lightning
Barnabas, Barnaby, Barney, Barny,
Barnabé, Bernebe, Barnaba,
Barna, Bernabé • Biblical/Greek •
son of consolation
Bastien, Sébastien, Sebastián •
Greek • *venerable, wise*
Benjamin, Ben, Benny, Bennie,
Benjamim, Benjie, Benji, Benjy,
Venyamin, Binyamin, Benno,
Bendik • Hebrew/Jewish • *son of my*
right hand, my right-hand man
Bertram, Bertie, Bert, Bertrand,
Beltrán, Beltran, Burt, Albert •
German • *bright*
Bingwen • Chinese •
clever/cultivated
Blaise, Blaize, Blas • Latin/French •
to limp, limping
Blakeney • English • *he from the*
black island
Bo • Chinese • *waves*
Bolin • Chinese • *my elder brother*
the rain
Booker • English • *a man who*

bleaches the laundry
Börries, Liborius • German/Celtic •
to be free!
Bran • British/Welsh • *raven*
Brendan, Brendon, Breandán,
Brendanus • Latin • *prince, heir*
Brice, Bryce • Gaulish/Celtic •
speckled
Brizio, Brictius, Fabrizio • Gaulish
• *speckled*
Brychan • British/Welsh • *speckled*
Bud, Buddy • American/English •
a friend
Burgess • Anglo-Saxon • *a man who*
is on a town council

Caleb, Kaleb • Hebrew/Jewish • *he*
who rages like a dog, needs anger
management!
Carlos, Carolus, Charles • Spanish/
Latin • *freeman*
Carlton • English • *the place of the*
free men
Casey, KC, Casy, Kacy, Kacey, Kasey
• Irish Gaelic • *a watchman; keeps*
guard in war
Caxton, Kakktun, Kokkton • Anglo-
Saxon/Norse • *a lump of land for an*
enclosure or straggled-out settlement;
disordered
Cedric • literary name • *invented by*
Sir Walter Scott
Charles, Carl, Karl, Carlo, Carlos,
Séarlas, Teàrlach, Siarl, Karel,
Carel, Charel, Carles, Karol, Carol,
Kaarle, Karoly, Karolis, Charlie,
Charley • Germanic • *a freeman*
Chas, Chaz, Chuck, Chuckie,
Chukkie • American/English •
clipped name
Charlton, Chas, Chaz, Chuck,
Chuckie, Chukkie • English • *the*
place where the free men live

Chenglei • Chinese • *greatness to come*

Chongkun • Chinese • *second brother mountain*

Chonglin • Chinese • *second brother unicorn*

Cian, Kian, Keene • Irish Gaelic • *old or ancient*

Claus, Klaus, Niklaus • German • *the people are victorious*

Cleon • African American • *invented name*

Cody, Cuidightheact, Macoda • Irish Gaelic • *descendant of Oda, a helpful soul*

Coinneach, Kenneth • Scots Gaelic • *handsome, beautiful, sexy*

Conrad, Konrad, Corrado • Germanic • *one who gives forthright and candid advice*

Constantine, Constanz, Costin, Constantin, Cystenian, Constant • Latin • *constant, steadfast, loyal, devoted*

Corbin, Corbinian • Anglo-Saxon/Norman • *crow*

Cosmo, Kosmas, Cosimo, Kosmos • Greek • *there is beauty in order*

Crawford • Anglo-Saxon • *ford where the crows gather at the river*

Cuthbert, Bert, Cuddy, Cuddie, Cuithbeart • Anglo-Saxon • *a man well known for what he does, his personality or wit*

Dai, Dei • British/Welsh • *this chap shines forth*

Daley, Dalaigh, Dalach, Daly • Irish Gaelic • *altogether now! A gathering or a moot*

Damon, Daman, Damaso • Greek • *a man full of self-control or a man who tames*

Dante, Durante • Latin • *strong and steadfast, personal name originally*

Darius, Dareios, Darayavahush, Darayamiy • Greek/Persian • *he who possesses, looks after the good and wellness of all*

Darwin, Deorwine • Anglo-Saxon • *dear, good, bosom buddy*

Davis, Davies • American/English • *in honour of Jefferson Davis leader of the Dixie states*

Delbert, Del, Delmar • Caribbean English • *invented name*

Diarmuid, Dermot, Diarmuit, Diarmit • unsure but perhaps without envy

Dieter • Germanic • *the army of the people*

Dietfried • Germanic • *people of peace or peaceful people*

Dietmar, Theodemar, Theodemaris • Germanic • *famous people or person*

Dietrich, Diederick, Terry • Germanic • *people power or powerful person*

Dietwald • Germanic • *powerful people, ruling tribe*

Disgleirio • modern Welsh • *bright and dazzling*

Dónal, Domhnall, Donall • Irish Gaelic • *ruler of the world*

Donald, Don, Donny, Donnie, Donnell, Dolly, Dhomhnuill, Domhnall • Scots Gaelic • *world ruler*

Dong • Chinese • *east/winter*

Dorian, Dorien, Dorieus, Dorianus, Doron • literary name • *Oscar Wilde's invention for The Portrait of Dorian Gray; a Greek connection for the people who settled in southern Greece*

Dunstan • English/Roman Catholic • *dark stone*

Dustin, Dusty, Thorstein • Norse • *Thor, God of Thunder's stone*

Duyi • Chinese • *independent and at one*

Ernest, Earnest, Eornost • Germanic • *a very serious, tenacious person who never gives up*

Edwin, Edwyn, Eardwine • Anglo-Saxon • *a wealthy, prosperous friend*

Eilif • Scandinavian • *one alone, for always, evermore, eternal life*

Éimhín • Irish Gaelic • *speedy, fast, swift, prompt, quick*

Eladio, Helladio • Greek • *a man from Greece*

Elmo, Erasmus • Germanic • *magic helmet*

Emrys, Ambrose • British Welsh • *immortal, eternal*

Englebert, Engelbrecht • Germanic • *bright angel*

Enlai • Chinese • *favours foreseen*

Enoch • Biblical/Hebrew/Jewish • *experienced and wise*

Enos • Biblical/Hebrew/Jewish • *mankind*

Ernest, Ern, Ernie, Ernst, Ernesto • German • *serious in all things and will fight to the death; means business to the point of obsession*

Erwin, Irwin • Germanic • *a good, loyal and honoured*

Esmé, Aestimare, Aestimatus • Latin • *truly esteemed and highly valued*

Ethan • Biblical/Hebrew/Jewish • *longevity, strong and firm*

Eunan, Ádhamhnán, Adomnae, Ádhamh • Irish • *he's a right little horror! Strikes fear in my heart*

Eutrope, Eutropios, Eutropos, Eutropio • Greek • *what a nice polite boy and so clever*

Ewald, Ewawalt • Germanic • *a wise and just ruler; powerful leader, lawful ruler, judge*

Eyolf • Scandinavian • *lucky wolf, like a gift or talisman*

Fabio, Fabius • Latin • *Roman family name who were powerful during the republic*

Fabrizio, Fabrice, Fabricius, Fabricio • Italian/Etruscan • *Roman family name; one noted for his incorruptibility*

Fādil • Arabic • *generous, respected and conscientious*

Fahīm • Arabic • *a man of deep understanding and wisdom*

Fakhri • Arabic • *diligent, high achiever, gets where he wants on merit*

Falk, Falke, Yehoshua • German/Yiddish • *hawk or falcon*

Farīd • Arabic • *unique, beyond compare*

Farūq, Farouk • Arabic • *clever, intuitive and wise*

Fathi • Arabic • *conqueror or freedom giver*

Feichín, Fiach • Irish Gaelic • *raven*

Feng • Chinese • *sharp, cutting wind*

Fiachna, Fiach • Irish • *raven hunt chase*

Fiachra, Fiach • Irish • *King of the Hunt, King of the Ravens*

Fidel, Fidelis • Latin • *faithful to the end*

Fihr • Arabic • *fusion*

Fikri • Arabic • *intellectual and contemplative*

Firdos • Arabic • *paradise*

Firmin, Firminus, Firmino, Fermin
• Latin • *he who cannot be moved; firm*

Fitzroy, Fitz • Norman/English • *often the bastard son of the king*

Flint, Fflint • English • *hard rock*

Frank, Franklin, Frankie • Germanic • *a loyal and free man or from the Frankish tribe*

Frost, Freosan • Anglo-Saxon • *person who looks icy, cold, snowy white hair or beard*

Fry, Frig, Freo, Frio • Anglo-Saxon/Norse • *either freeman or a small man*

Fulgenzio, Fulgentius, Fulgens, Fulgencio • Latin • *shining*

Gallagher, Gallchobhar • Irish Gaelic • *foreign ally, helpful stranger*

Gaylord, Gaillard, Gay, Gaye • Norman • *a dandy or popinjay*

Gebhard, Gebbert, Geert, Gerd • German • *gifted with strength*

Geming • Chinese • *radical revolution*

Gennaro, Januarius, Janus • Latin • *the month of January, from Janus, the god who could look forward and back*

Geoffrey, Jeffrey, Jeff, Geoffroi, Geoff, Godofredo, Sieffre • Germanic/Frankish/Lombardic • *a stranger in your own land or foreigner who pledges allegiance*

Germaine, Jermaine, Germanus, Germain • French/Latin • *brother*

Germain, Germanus • Latin • *brother*

German, Germanus • Latin • *brother in God*

Ghayth • Arabic • *rain*

Gilbert, Gib, Gibb, Gilberto

• Germanic/Frankish/Roman Catholic • *he who pledges or sacrifices his life for greater things*

Gideon • Hebrew/Jewish • *he who cuts someone down to size*

Gino, Giorgino, Luigino • Latin • *clipped name of any full name that ends in 'gino'*

Gladstone, Glaedstan • Anglo-Saxon • *the stone where the red kite lands*

Gladwin • Anglo-Saxon • *an optimistic, positive friend*

Glaw • British/Welsh • *rain*

Gobind • Sikh • *name of one of the pantheon of Sikh gurus*

Godwin, Godwine, Win • Anglo-Saxon • *God is my friend*

Goito, Goyo, Goya, Gregorio • Spanish • *watchful*

Goodwin, Godwine • Anglo-Saxon • *not to be confused with Godwin; it means a good friend*

Göran, Örjan, Jöran, Jörn • Scandinavian/Serbo-Croat • *man from the mountains*

Gratien, Gratianus, Gratus, Graciano, Gratianus • Latin • *most pleasing*

Grazian, Gratianus, Gratus • Latin • *a very nice man*

Geraint, Gerontios, Geronitius, Gerontos • British/Welsh • *old man*

Gérard, Jed, Ged, Jerrold, Gerry, Jerry, Gerrard, Geraud, Gerardo, Geraud, Gearóid, Gerald, Geraldo, Gerallt • Germanic/Frankish • *a brave, strong man with a spear as his weapon*

Gereon • Greek • *old man*

Gerhard, Gerhardt, Geert, Gert • Germanic • *strong, dedicated swordsman*

Gregory, Gregorios, Gregor, Greg, Gregg, Greig, Greagoir, Griogair, Grigor, Joris, Greger, Gregers, Grégoire, Gregorio, Grigori, Grzegorz, Rehor, Grgur, Reijo, Gergely, Grigor • Greek • *watchful*

Guang • Chinese • *light*

Gumersindo • Spanish/Visigothic • *path of man*

Guoliang • Chinese • *where you are there is kindness*

Guowei • Chinese • *status quo*

Guni • Hebrew/Jewish • *rainbow-coloured*

Gwalchmai • British/Welsh • *plain of the hawks or ospreys*

Gwilym, Gwilim, Gwillym, William • British Welsh • *his helmet gives him magical protection and the will to win*

Gwynedd • British/Welsh • *happiness or named after the British Welsh princedom of Gwynedd, based on Snowdonia area where the ancient Brits (Welsh) fought the Anglo-Saxons in guerrilla warfare*

Habīb • Arabic • *beloved, adored*

Hādi • Arabic • *mentor, guru, reflective and spiritual*

Hakeem, Hakīm • Arabic • *wise and sagacious*

Hale, Halh • Anglo-Saxon • *a person who lives off the beaten track; perhaps a hermit*

Hall, Heall, Halle, Halldor, Hallstein, Halstein, Halsten, Hallsten • *rock*

Halldor • Norse • *rock, name of God of Thunder*

Hari • Sanskrit • *pet name for Vishnu or Krishna*

Hartwin • Germanic • *a faithful friend*

Harvard, Hereward, Hervard • American/English • *the vigilant soldier, the army guard*

Hāsim • Arabic • *decisive, incisive and quick*

Hawk, Hauk, Hawke, Hafoc • Anglo-Saxon/English • *like a hawk, bird of prey*

Haydn, Heiden, Heidano, Hayden, Haydon • Germanic • *heathen or pagan*

Haytham • Arabic • *young eagle*

Heber, Éibhear • Irish Gaelic/Biblical/Jewish/Hebrew • *an enclave, a ghetto*

Henning • Scandinavian • *clipped form of Henrik and Johannes*

Herbert, Bert, Herebeorht, Herb, Herbie, Heribert • German • *a famous army that carries all before it; a shining light*

Hildebrecht • Germanic • *bright light in the battle*

Hjalmar • Norse • *magic helmet that protects the wearer*

Holger, Hogge • Norse • *a warlike island-dweller with a sharp weapon*

Hopcyn, Hopkin, Hob, Robert • British/Welsh • *famous and bright*

Hubert, Hugbert, Huppert, Hupprecht, Hobart • Germanic • *brilliant heart and famed mind*

Hugh, Huw, Hugues, Hugo, Aodh, Hughie, Hewie, Huey, Hewie, Hughie, Huwie • Germanic/Frankish • *heart, mind and spirit*

Hugo, Hugh • Germanic/Frankish/Latin • *heart, mind and spirit*

Huojin • Chinese • *fire metal*

Husām • Arabic • *sword, sabre, rapier*

Ibrāhīm, Abraham • Arabic • *father of the tribes or nations*

Illtud, Iltyd • British/Welsh • *a multitude or congregation of people/ the public*

Indra • Sanskrit • *God of the Sky and Lord of Rain*

Ingemar, Ingmar • Norse • *famous, well known to God*

Ingram, Engelram • Norman/Norse • *Norman family name after the Viking fertility god, Ing, and his pet raven*

Innes, Aonghas, Inis • Scots Gaelic • *an island or man from Innes in Moray*

Iorwerth, Iolo, Iolyn, Yorath • British/Welsh • *a handsome, beautiful lord or chief*

Ira • Hebrew/Jewish • *vigilant, observant, watchful*

Irwin, Erwyn, Irwyn, Everwyn • *a good, loyal and honoured friend*

Isidore, Izzy, Izzie, Isidoros, Isidor, Isidro, Isidoro • Greek/Egyptian • *a gift from the goddess Isis, deity of magic and life*

Itamar • Biblical/Jewish/Hebrew • *island of palms*

Jacob, Iago, Jakob, Jaap, Jacques, Jacobo, Giacobbe, Yakov, Jakub, Jakov, Jaako, Jacobus, Yaakov, Jacques, Jacob, James, Jacobus, Akev, Iacobus, Iakobos • Biblical/ Hebrew/Jewish • *grabbed by the heel!*

Jamshed • Muslim/Parsis • *king and founder of Persopolis*

Janmuhammad • Persian • *breath of Muhammed*

Jarod, Jarrod, Gerald • English • *he who rules with a spear*

Jarrett, Garrett • Irish/English • *he who rules with a spear*

Jarvis, Jervis • Germanic/Frankish/ English • *unknown origin; possibly a man with a spear or something pointed*

Javier, Xavier • Roman Catholic/ Basque • *the new house*

Janero, Gennaro, Januarius • Latin • *month of January*

Jeffrey, Geoffrey, Jeff, Geoff, Jefferson, Jeffery, Jeffry, Jep • *a stranger in your own land or foreigner who pledges allegiance*

Jerold, Jerrold, Gerald, Jerry, Gerry • English • *he who rules with a spear*

Jerrard, Gerrard, Gerard • American/English • *he who rules with a spear*

Jianguo • Chinese • *patriotic*

Jianyu • Chinese • *building the universe*

Jing • Chinese • *a boy born in the capital city Beijing or regional capital*

Jingguo • Chinese • *building the nation*

Jūda, Gūda • Arabic • *goodness and kindness transcend all*

Junjie • Chinese • *beautiful, brilliant*

Karam, Karīm • Arabic • *generous, magnimous, philanthropic*

Karl, Charles, Karlmann • Germanic • *freeman*

Keanu • Hawaiian • *cool breeze from the mountains*

Keelan, Keelahan, Ceileachain • British/Welsh/ Irish Gaelic • *companion or friend; descendant of Keelahan*

Kenneth, Ken, Cinaed, Cainnech, Coinneach, Kennith, Kenny, Cenydd, Canice, Canicius,

Cainneach • Latin/ English/Gaelic • *handsome, gorgeous, pleasing to the eye and rather adorable!*

Kendrick, Kenrick, Cenric, Ceneric, Cynwrig, Maceanrig, Cyneric • British/Welsh/Scots Gaelic • *a sacred place high on a hill, or son of Henry or royal power*

Kenelm, Cenehelm • Anglo-Saxon • *he who is a bold and assertive warrior protected by his magic helmet*

Khalil • Arabic • *best friend*

Kimberley, Kimberly, Kim, Kym • Anglo-Saxon/American English • *after the South African town of Kimberley where the British took on the Boer; especially 15th February*

Kolya, Nikolai • Russian • *victory over or with the people*

Konrad, Conrad, Kurt • Germanic • *bold counsel*

Konstantin, Constantinus • Latin • *constant, steadfast, loyal, devoted*

Koppel, Jacob • Jewish/Yiddish • *grabbed by the heel!*

Korbinian, Corvus, Hraban • Latin/Frankish

Lakshman, Laxman • Sanskrit • *the mark of God; most auspicious*

Lark, Lawerce • Anglo-Saxon/ Australian/North American • *the lark, the bird*

Leander, Leandro, Leandros, Leander, Leandros, Leonaner, Lee, Léandre • Greek • *lion man, man with the strength of a lion*

Lei • Chinese • *thunder*

Léger, Luitger, Leodegar, Leo • Germanic • *a tribe of people with spears*

Lennox, Levenach, Lenox • Scots Gaelic • *the place of the elm trees*

Leslie, Les, Leascuilinn, Lesslyn • Scots Gaelic • *the place where holly grows*

Levi, Levy • Hebrew/Jewish • *making a connection*

Li • Chinese • *profit, business acumen and respectable*

Liam, Ulliam, William • Irish Gaelic/Norman • *willpower, with a helmet, possibly magic, to give divine protection*

Liang • Chinese • *bright, luminous, radiant*

Liaqat • Persian • *dignified, noble wise and clever*

Lindsay, Lindissi • Anglo-Saxon • *old Saxon kingdom whose root means Lelli's island*

Liwei • Chinese • *profit and greatness*

Lleu, Lugg, Lughus, Lugh • British/ Welsh • *dark, bright and shining*

Lonán, Lonain • Irish Gaelic • *blackbird*

Lucian, Lucianus, Lucius, Lucien, Luciano, Lucio, Lux • Latin • *light*

Lughaidh, Lewis, Lewie, Louis, Louie • Irish Gaelic • *bright and shiny*

Lyle, De L'isle • Norman/Gaelic • *someone from the isles or marshy land*

Macharia • Kenya • *lasting friend*

Mackenzie, Maccoinnich, Coinneach, Makenzie, Makensie, Mckenzie, Mack • English/Scots Gaelic • *handsome, gorgeous, pleasing to the eye and altogether rather adorable!*

Mahavir • Sanskrit • *great hero, founder of the Jain religion*

Mahendra, Mahinder, Mohinder
• Sanskrit • *Great Indra, first great Buddhist missionary*

Māhir • Arabic • *clever, dexterous, skilful*

Mājid • Arabic • *brighter than a star*

Manfred, Manffred, Mainfred, Manfried, Manfredo • Germanic • *man of peace*

Manley, Manly • Anglo-Saxon • *common land, for all men*

Marat • Russian/French • *named after a Swiss-born French revolutionary, Jean-Paul Marat*

Maximilian, Maximilianus, Maximus, Max, Maximillian, Maximilien, Aemilianus • Latin/Germanic/Bavarian/Austrian • *a great person through industry and hard work*

Māzin • Arabic • *origin confused, might come from rain clouds*

Meinhard • Germanic • *strong as a rock*

Meinrad • Germanic • *unswayed, determined counsellor*

Melor • Russian • *a combination of Marx, Engels, Lenin, October, Revolution*

Merl, Meriel, Merle, Merula • Norman/Latin • *blackbird*

Merrill • Breton Celtic • *bright sea*

Meshulam, Meshullam • Biblical/Jewish/Hebrew • *a generous friend*

Methodius, Mefodi • Greek • *following the path or road, spiritual as much as a traveller*

Minsheng • Chinese • *vox pop*

Mohammed, Muhammed, Mohammad, Mohamed, Muhammad, Muhammed, Mo • praiseworthy and possessing the finest perfect qualities

Mordecai, Motke, Motl, Marduk • Biblical/Persian • *he who worships Marduk, the god of magic and water*

Motke, Mordecai, Motl • Biblical/Jewish/Yiddish • *he who worships Marduk, the god of magic and water*

Muhammed • Arabic • *sacred qualities, scrupulous*

Mukhtār • Arabic • *preferred to all others*

Mungo, Munghu, Munga, Fychi, • British/Welsh • *carissimus amicus meaning dearest friend; pet name of St Kentigern*

Munīr • Arabic • *shining, dazzling, glorious*

Mustafa, Mustapha • pure, the chosen one

Nadīm • Arabic • *best friend, companion you share your social life with*

Naʿīm • Arabic • *he who enjoys his own company; happy is his lot*

Nājib, Nāgib • Arabic • *cultured, cultivated, in a class of his own*

Narayan, Narain • Sanskrit • *destiny of man; son of creation*

Naresh • Sanskrit • *ruler of men*

Narottam • Sanskrit • *best of men*

Nāsir, Nazir • Arabic • *a good ally and friend; helping and supportive*

Neal, Neil, Neale, Nigel, Niall • Irish Gaelic/English • *passionate, champion, winner, dead sexy, really desirable; some say it means a man who cannot commit*

Nelson, Nell, Neil • English • *passionate, champion, winner, dead sexy, really desirable; some say it means a man who cannot commit*

Neo, Neos • modern Greek • *new*

Neville, Neuville • Norman • *a new*

place or new village

Newton, Newt, Neowe • Anglo-Saxon • *a new village or new homestead*

Nicasio, Nikasios • victorious

Nicholas, Nikolaos, Nicolás, Nickolas, Nick, Nik, Nico, Nicky, Nioclás, Neacal, Nikolaus, Niklaus, Nicolaas, Nikolaas, Niklaas, Niels, Nils, Nicolao, Nicolau, Nicola, Niccolo, Nicolo, Nikolai, Mikolaj, Mikolas, Mikulas, Nikola, Nikolaj, Niilo, Miktos, Mykolas, Nik, Niklas, Nels, Neacal, Nikelaos • Greek/English • *victory for or over the people*

Nicol, Nicholl, Nicola, Nichola, Nichol, Nicole • English • *victory for or over the people*

Nicodemus, Nikodemos, Nicodème, Nico, Nicodim, Nicodemo • Greek/Latin • *victory for or over the people*

Nigel, Nigellus, Nihel, Neil • Latin/English • *black as pitch or passionate, dead sexy, really desirable; maybe a commitment phobe*

Norbert, Nordberht • Germanic • *a bright light from the north, northern lights, Aurora Borealis*

Norton, Nordtun • Anglo-Saxon • *the northern village, homestead or enclosure*

Nūr • Arabic • *luminous*

Odd, Oddbjörn • Norse • *the sharp point of a weapon*

Oded • Jewish/Hebrew • *he who encourages or persuades, compelling*

Oleg, Helgi • Norse • *prosperous, the chap who created Kiev, Ukraine*

Oren, Oran, Orin, Orren, Orrin • Biblical/Hebrew/Jewish • *a pine tree*

Orville • literary invention • *Lord Orville, created by Fanny Burney in her novel* Evelina

Oswin, Oswine, Oz • Anglo-Saxon • *God is my friend*

Ottokar, Odovacar • Germanic • *being watchful and observant brings riches*

Ozzy, Oz, Ozzie • Anglo-Saxon • *clipped version of any name beginning with Os, meaning God*

Parnell, Parnel • Irish/English • *named after Irish republican Charles Parnell*

Peng • Chinese • *a mythological bird*

Pengfei • Chinese • *flight of the peng*

Peter, Pete, Petros, Peadar, Pedr, Piet, Pieter, Per, Petter, Par, Pierre, Pedro, Perico, Pere, Pietro, Piero, Pyotr, Piotr, Petr, Petar, Pekka, Peitari, Peteris, Petras, Petrus, Petya, Pette, Pedr, Pier • Greek • *the rock or stone*

Philip, Phil, Phillipos, Phileinhippos, Pip, Pilib, Filib, Philipp, Filip, Philippe, Phillip, Felipe, Felip, Filipe, Filippo, Filip, Vilppu, Fulop, Filipes, Philipp, Pino • Greek • *friend or lover of horses*

Pitt • Anglo-Saxon • *a man who lives in a pit*

Porfirio, Porphyrios, Porphyrius, Porphyra, Porfirio • Greek • *the colour purple*

Pravin • Sanskrit • *dexterous, clever and skilful*

Prokhoros, Prokhor • Greek • *very artistic, chief of a troupe of singers, dancers, actors*

Qi • Chinese • *enlightened, wonderment and intellectual*

Qianfan • Chinese • *thousand sails*
Qiqiang • *enlightenment and strength*

Ra'd • Arabic • *thunder*
Rafīq • Arabic • *friend, companion who is gentle and kind*
Raghīd • Arabic • *freedom-loving and devil-may-care*
Raghnall, Raonull, Rannal, Ronald • Norse • *wise, decisive chief or an oracle of the gods or kings*
Ragnvald • Norse • *an oracle of the gods or kings*
Rajiv • Sanskrit • *striped and/or the blue lotus*
Ramiro • Spanish/Visigothic • *a man famous for his advice and counselling*
Ramón, Raimundo, Raymond • Catalan/Germanic • *adviser, protector*
Ramsay, Ramsa, Ramsey • Anglo-Saxon • *island of wild garlic*
Ranjit • Sanskrit • *charming, coloured, rainbow*
Ranulf, Reginulf, Ran, Reginulf • Norse • *adviser or counsellor to wolves*
Rashād, Rashīd • Arabic • *spiritual or religious wisdom*
Raúl, Ralph • Spanish • *wolf counsel*
Raven, Rafn, Raefn • Anglo-Saxon/Norse • *Odin's winged friend, the Raven*
Reagan, Regan, Riagain • Irish Gaelic/English • *descendant of Riagain, the impulsive or impatient one*
Reineke, Reine • Germanic • *counsellor*
Reinhard, Reinhardt, Reine • Germanic • *strong, firm advice*

Reinhold, Reinwald, Reine • Germanic • *splendid, wonderful adviser*
Reinmar, Reine • Germanic • *famous adviser, speaker*
Reuel • Biblical/Jewish/Hebrew • *friend of God*
Reynold, Reginald, Reynaud, Raginwald, Reginald, Ray, Reynard, Ragin, Renard, Ray, Rinaldo, Reinaldo, Rheinallt • Germanic/Norman • *advice rule*
Rhett, Rhet, Raedt, Raet • Dutch • *advice, counsel*
Roald, Hrod • Norse • *famous ruler, famous chief*
Rodney, Rod, Roddy • Anglo-Saxon • *famous island; a person from there*
Roland, Rodland, Rowland, Roly, Rowley, Rolie, Rolland, Roldan, Rolant • Germanic • *famed throughout the land*
Rolf, Rodwulf, Rudolf, Rollo, Rodolfo • Germanic • *famed wolf*
Rollo, Roul, Rolf • Norman • *famed wolf*
Ronald, Ron, Ronnie, Ronny, Roni, Ranald, Randal, Rognvald • Norse • *adviser to the gods or king*
Rosendo • Visigothic • *a man on the path to fame*
Roshan • Persian/Urdu • *splendid glorious/famous*
Ru • Chinese • *Confucian scholar*
Rudolf, Rudolphus, Rodwulf, Rolf, Rudolph, Rudy, Rudi, Rodolphe, Rudy, Rudolf, Rodolf, Hrodwolf, Rodolpho • Germanic • *famed wolf*
Rune, Runi, Runolf, Run • Norse • *named after the Norse magical alphabet*
Rurik, Hrodrik, Roderick • Norse • *famous ruler, the name of the man*

who founded Russia's Novogorod, the Big New City

Rushdi • Arabic • *old head on young shoulders; ahead of his years*

Safdar • Arabic • *a man who breaks ranks; loose cannon*

Safwat • Arabic • *choice and best*

Sage, Sauge, Sapius • Anglo-Saxon • *a herb or wise person*

Samant • Sanskrit • *universal, the whole thing*

Sāmi • Arabic • *elevated*

Sanjeev • Sanskrit • *reviving, resuscitating*

Saturday • English • *born on a Saturday, Saturn's day*

Saturnino, Saturnus, Nino • Latin • *Saturn*

Scevola, Scaevola, Scaevus • left-handed

Séaghdha • Irish Gaelic • *like a hawk, fine and goodly*

Sekar • Sanskrit • *summit, the best at what you do*

Selwyn, Selewyn, Selewine, Silvanus, Silas, Selwin • Anglo-Saxon • *prosperous, high-flying friend*

Seth, Set • Egyptian/Greek • *dazzling God of Chaos and Deserts*

Severiano, Severus, Severo, Severinus, Sören, Severinus, Severino, Seve • Latin • *Roman family name meaning stern, austere*

Sgàire, Skari • Scots Gaelic/Norse • *a seabird that mews like a cat!*

Shah • Muslim/Persian/Sufi • *king, god, lord, emperor, divine*

Sharīf • Arabic • *eminent in his field*

Shining • Chinese • *let the world be at peace*

Sidney, Sydney • Anglo-Saxon •

an ait, a small island in a river or a wide river meadow

Silver, Siolfor, Seolfor • Anglo-Saxon • *the metal silver*

Simran • Sikh • *he who meditates, yogic*

Siyu • Chinese • *thinking of the planet Earth*

Solomon, Shlomo, Sol, Solly, Saloman • Biblical/Hebrew/Jewish • *peace*

Somerled, Sumarlid, Summerlad, Somhairle, Sorley • Scots Gaelic/Norse • *summer traveller (southern hemisphere)*

Somhairle • Irish Gaelic/Norse • *summer traveller (southern hemisphere)*

Sondre, Sindri • Norse/Norwegian • *no known origins but in Norse mythology a magical dwarf*

Spike • English • *a nickname for a person whose hair sticks up like a permanent bad-hair day*

Stanilas, Stanislaus, Stanislaw, Aneislis, Stanislav • Slavic • *glory to the court, glorious courtier or politician*

Sterling, Sterrling • Anglo-Saxon • *little star*

Stian, Stigand, Kris, Stig • wanderer

Stirling, Ystrefelyn • British/Welsh/Anglo-Saxon • *Melyn's tribe or people*

Storm • American English • *thunderstorm*

Sture, Stura • Scandinavian/Swedish • *wilful, contrary, independent spirit*

Subhash • Sanskrit • *eloquent and articulate*

Sudhir • Sanskrit • *wise and strong*

Suleimān, Sulaymān • Biblical/

Arabic • *peace*
Sumantra • Sanskrit • *a person who is well versed in the classics*
Sverre, Sverri, Sverra • Norse/Norwegian • *spinning, swirling about*

Tad, Tadhg, Thaddeus, Tig, Tim, Taddeo, Teague, Teigue, Tadeo • Irish Gaelic • *poet, wise man, philosopher*
Talāl • Arabic • *morning dew or fine rain*
Taliesin, Tal • British/Welsh • *bright, shiny brow*
Tammaro • Germanic • *clever; famous mind*
Tancredo • Germanic • *thoughtful counsel*
Tao • Chinese • *great waves*
Teàrlach, Toirdhealbhach • Irish Gaelic • *a man who takes the initiative, starts things*
Tegan, Teg • British/Welsh • *a rather lovely or beautiful person*
Tempest, Tempeste, Tempestas • Latin • *nickname for a person with a tempestuous temperament*
Tengfei • Chinese • *soaring high*
Terence, Terentius, Terry, Toirdhealbhach, Tel, Terrance, Terrence • Latin/Irish Gaelic • *from the Roman family name Terentius and Irish for someone who takes the initiative*
Terrell, Tyrell • Norman • *a person who is hard to pull this way or that, very fixed!*
Thelonius, Till, Tillo • Germanic/Dutch • *the people*
Theophilus, Theosphilos, Theo, Théophile, Teofilo • Biblical/Greek • *God's friend or friend of God*

Thierry, Theodoric • French/Greek • *ruler of the people*
Till, Dietrich • Germanic • *the people*
Tingfeng • Chinese • *thunderbolt or lightning peak*
Tingzhe • Chinese • *judgement or wisdom is required*
Tiordhealbhach, Tárlach, Traolach, Turlough • Irish • *instigator, initiator*
Tor, Thor, Tord • Norse • *the god Thor*
Torbjörn, Thorbjörn, Torben, Torbern • old Norse • *god Thor with the strength of a bear*
Torcall, Torquil • Norse • *the sacrificial or sacred cauldron of Thor, the God of Thunder*
Tore, Ture • Norse • *a man like the god Thor*
Tormod, Torrmod • Norse • *a man with the courage of Thor, the God of Thunder*
Torolf, Torulf, Torolv • Norse • *god Thor with the strength of a wolf*
Torsten, Torstein, Thorstein, Thorsteinn • Norse • *the god Thor with the strength of a stone*
Torvald, Thorwald • Norse • *ruler with the power of Thor*
Tory, Torir, Thor, Thori, Thorir • Norse/Danish • *Thor*
Tristan, Trystan, Tristram, Tristam, Trystram, Tristram, Dristan, Drystan • British/Welsh • *rowdy, rebellious, blue, melancholic, chaotic*
Tuathal, Toal • Irish Gaelic • *chief of the clan or tribe*
Tudur, Tudor, Tudyr, Teutorix • British/Welsh • *king or chief of the tribe*
Ty, Tyler, Tyrone, Tye, Tyrese • American English • *clipped*

Tyrell, Tyrrell, Tirel, Terrell • a person who is hard to pull this way or that, very fixed!

Ughtred, Uhtraed • Anglo-Saxon • *dawn counsel; a person who is good and wise in the mornings*
Ugo, Hugo, Hugh • Germanic • *heart, mind and spirit*
Ùisdean, Eysteinn, Hugh, Hùisdean • Irish Gaelic • *a man who is forever unchanging like a stone*
Ulysses, Odysseus, Odyssesthai, Ulick, Ulisse, Ulises • Greek/Latin • *a person who hates*
Umashankar • Sanskrit • *union of two people*
Urban, Urbanus • Latin • *a person who lives in the city*
'Usmān, 'Uthmān • Arabic • *bustard (a bird!)*
Uttam • Sanskrit • *the ultimate*
Uwe • Germanic/Norse • *sharp blade, in awe*

Val, Valentin, Valentine, Valentinius, Valens, Velten, Valentino, Valentinus, Ualan, Uailean, Folant • Latin • *flourishing, blooming, blossoming: Valentine's Day is 14th February*
Valéry, Val • Germanic • *foreign power*
Vasco, Velasco, Belasco, Velásquez • Spanish/Basque • *crow*
Vere, Ver, Vern, Vernon • Celtic/Gaulish • *alder tree*
Vermil • African American • *modern creation*
Vernon, Vere, Vern • Gaulish • *alder tree*
Vidkun, Vidkunn • Norse • *lateral*

thinking, wise, experienced
Vinay • Sanskrit • *education, intelligence, learning*
Vlas, Blasius, Blaesus, Blaise, Vlasi • Latin • *area of the throat, perhaps person with a lisp; St Blaise rules the throat and his feast day is 3rd February*
Volkmar • Germanic • *famous people*
Voshon • African American • *modern made-up name*

Wasīm, Wazim • Arabic • *what a stunner! Beautiful to look at, delightful to know*
Weizhe • Chinese • *sagacious and wise*
Wendice • African American • *invented name*
Willard, Will Wilheard • Anglo-Saxon • *a person with tremendous willpower, powerful in every way*
William, Wilhelm, Will, Bill, Willy, Willie, Billy, Willis, Wilmot, Ulliam, Uilleam, Gwilym, Willem, Willi, Vilhelm, Vilhjalm, Guillaume, Guillermo, Guillem, Guilherme, Guglielmo, Vilem, Viljem, Vilmos, Vilhelmas, Vilhelms, Wim • Germanic/Norman
Willibrand • Germanic • *will and flaming sword*
Wilmer, Wilmaer • Anglo-Saxon • *he is famous for his willpower and strength of character*
Wilmot, Willmott, William • Germanic/Norman • *pet name for William*
Winfred, Wyn, Win, Wynnfrith, Winfried • Germanic • *a kind, peace-loving friend*
Windsor, Windelsora • Anglo-Saxon • *the place on the river with*

a windlass (special crane to move heavy weights)

Wolfram, Wolf • Germanic • *wolf, raven*

Worede • Ethiopian • *came from above*

Wuzhou • Chinese • *five continents*

Wynne, Wyn, Wine, Wynn • British Welsh/Anglo-Saxon • *a friend and/ or one who is blessed and sacred*

Xavier, Javier, Etcheberria, Xaver • Roman Catholic/Basque • *the new house*

Xayvion • African American • *made up name*

Xiang • Chinese • *circling in the air*

Xin • Chinese • *new*

Xue • Chinese • *studious, knowledge*

Yakov, Yaakov, Jacob, Yankel • Biblical/Hebrew/Jewish • *grabbed by the heel!*

Ya'qūb, Jacob • Arabic/Biblical • *grabbed by the heel!*

Ye • Chinese • *bright*

Yefim, Euphemios • Russian/Greek • *eloquent, articulate speaker*

Yingpei • Chinese • *to be admired*

Yongliang • Chinese • *forever light and bright*

Yorath, Iorwerth • British/Welsh • *a handsome, beautiful lord or chief*

You • Chinese • *friend*

Zāhir • Arabic • *radiant, bright, luminous*

Zamir • Arabic • *ideas, mental thoughts*

Zemin • Chinese • *favoured people*

Zhen • Chinese • *astonishment, surprise*

Zhengzhong • Chinese • *loyal and trustworthy*

Zhiqiang • Chinese • *strength of will*

Girls

Abishag, Avishag • Biblical/Jewish/Hebrew • *wise and educated*

Acacia, Akakia, Wattle • Greek/Latin • *acacia wood, holy wood that had special powers as a hex against evil*

Aegle, Aglaia • Greek • *splendid radiance*

Aileen, Eileen, Ailie • Irish Gaelic • *desired by others*

Ailsa, Ealasaid, Alfsigesey • Norse • *elfin victory, supernatural powers*

Áine • Irish • *as bright and radiant as the Queen of the Faeries*

Aingeal • Irish • *angel*

Aisling, Aislin, Aislinn • *she who has visionary dreams*

Alaina, Alana, Alayna, Alanna, Alannah, Alanah, Allana, Alanda, Alanis, Ailin • Gaelic • *vague origins but likely to be a rock*

Alba • Latin/Germanic • *white or elfin*

Alberta, Albertina • French/Germanic/Anglo-Saxon • *bright and noble*

Alfreda, Freddie, Fred • Anglo-Saxon • *supernatural, faerie counsel help*

Aloisa, Aloisia • Latin/Germanic • *all-seeing wisdom*

Allana, Alana Gaelic • vague origins but likely to be a rock

Aloisia • Provençal/Latin/Germanic • *all-wise, all-seeing*

Alte • Jewish/Hebrew • *old woman*

Althena • modern • *a combo of Althea and Athene*

Alyssa, Alissa • Greek mythology • *frenzied, hysterical*

Amal • Arabic • *hope, expectation, anticipation*

Amaryllis, Amaryssein • Greek • *to sparkle*

Amethyst • Greek/English • *birthstone of Aquarius; meaning not drunk!*

Amice, Amity, Amita, Amicitia • Latin • *friendship*

Ángeles • Spanish/Roman Catholic • *Our Lady of the Angels*

Angelica, Angélique, Angelika • Latin • *a girl of the angels*

Anitra • literary invention • *created by Henrik Ibsen as the name of an Arabic Princess in* Peer Gynt

Antigone • Greek • *contrary, the antithesis, born against the odds or contrary to conditions*

Aparición • Roman Catholic • *Christ's appearance to the disciples after Easter's resurrection*

Araceli • Spanish/Latin American • *the sky is an altar to God*

Arianrhod • British/Welsh • *silver wheel*

Aretha, Arete • Greek/American English • *excellent*

Armani • Lombardic/Italian/Germanic • *freeman*

Armelle, Artmael • Breton Celtic • *a female chief who is a steady as a rock*

Asha • Sanskrit • *hope*

Ashanti • Ghanian • *tribe from Ghana*

Ashley, Ashleigh, Ashlee, Ashlie, Ashly, Lee, Leigh • Anglo-Saxon • *ash wood or forest*

Aisling, Aishling • Irish Gaelic • *a dream, vision or premonition*

Ashlyn, Ashlynne, Ashlynn, Ashlynne, Ash, Lyn • Anglo-Saxon/British Welsh • *ash tree by the lake*

Asmā • Arabic • *prestigious*

Aster • Ethiopian • *star*

Ashton • Anglo-Saxon • *the village with an ash tree*

Assumpta, Assunta, Asunción • Latin • *the assumption of the Virgin Mary into heaven*

Astra, Estelle, Aster, Stella , Astrum • Greek/Latin • *star*

Athene, Athena, Athina, Athenai • Greek • *Greek Goddess of Wisdom and protector of the city of Athens*

Attracta, Athracht • Latin • *she is like a magnet, she draws people to her*

Aubree • Germanic/Anglo-Saxon/Latin • *she who has the power of the faeries*

Ava, Avaline, Aveline, Avelina, Evelyn, Eveline, Avila, Avis, Avice • Greek • *desired*

Aveline, Eibhlín, Ailbhilin, Ellin, Eileen • French/Irish Gaelic • *desired by others*

Avery • Norman/Anglo-Saxon • *supernatural, faerie favours*

Bahiyya • Arabic • *a beautiful, radiant, dazzling woman*

Bathsheba, Sheba, Bathsheeva • Biblical/Jewish/Hebrew • *daughter of the oath*

Beathag • Irish Gaelic • *life*

Belaynesh • Ethiopian • *you are above all*

Bertha, Berthe, Berta • Germanic • *bright and famous*

Billie • Germanic/Norman • *her helmet gives her magical protection and the will to win*

Blaise, Blaize • Latin/French • *to limp, limping*

Blythe, Blithe • Anglo-Saxon • *a*

sanguine spirit

Bobbie, Roberta • Germanic • *famous and bright*

Branwen, Bronwen, Brangwen • British/Welsh • *raven or beast that is holy, sacred and white*

Brenna, Braonan • American English/Irish Gaelic • *descendant of Braonan; moist, droplet of water*

Bronte • Greek • *thunder*

Candelaria • Spanish/Roman Catholic • *Candlemas, the purification of the Virgin Mary*

Cara, Kara • Italian/Irish Gaelic • *beloved friend*

Careen • literary invention • *one of Scarlett O'Hara's sisters in* Gone with the Wind

Carla, Carlene, Charlene, Charlotte, Carlotta, Charlotta, Carleen, Carlin, Carlina, Carlyn, Carlynne, Carline, Carolina, Caroline, Carly, Karly, Carley, Carola, Carlie, Carli, Carolyn, Caro, Carrie, Carol, Carole, Caryl, Caryll, Sharlene, Charlie, Charley, Lotte, Lottie, Tottie • Italian/English/Germanic • *a freeman*

Casey, Casy, KC, Kacey, Kaci, Kacie • Irish Gaelic • *a watchman; keeps guard in war*

Cassandra, Cassie, Kassie, Cass, Cassy, Cassidy • Greek mythology • *a woman who could see into the future but no one ever believed her*

Celia, Célie, Caelia, Caelum, Celina • Latin • *Roman family name meaning heaven*

Céleste, Celestine, Celestina, Celia, Céline, Marcelline, Caelius, Caelia, Caelestis, Celine, Caelina, Marceline, Marcelline, Caelius,

Celina • Latin/French • *Roman family name meaning heaven*

Celyn • British/Welsh • *holly*

Charisma, Karrisma, Kharisma • Greek • *spiritual blessings*

Charity, Caridad, Caritas, Carus • Latin • *dear charity; humanitarian*

Charline, Charlene, Sharlene, Shalene • French/American English /Australian/Germanic • *a freeman*

Charlotte, Carlotta, Karlotte, Karlotta, Séarlait • French/ Germanic • *a freeman*

Chelsea, Kelsey, Chelsey, Chelsie • Anglo-Saxon • *the chalk landing place in Chelsea, Middlesex*

Cheryl, Cherry, Beryl, Cheryll, Cherryl, Cherril, Cherrill, Sheryl • modern invention, combo of Cherry and Beryl

Cheyenne, Sahiyena • French Canadian • *a Native American tribe from Dakota*

Chiara, Clare, Claire, Clara, Ciara, Kiarah, Kiara, Kiera, Clair, Clarette, Clarinda, Clarrie, Clarus • Latin/ Italian • *bright, famous, crystal clear*

Ciannait • Irish • *ancient one*

Cilla, Priscilla, Pricus, Prissy • Biblical/Latin • *Roman family name meaning ancient, old*

Clare, Claire, Clara, Chiara, Klara, Kiara, Clara, Kiarah • Latin/English • *bright, famous, crystal clear*

Clarice, Claritia • Latin/French/ English • *bright, famous, crystal clear*

Clarissa, Clarisa, Clarice, Clarrisse, Clarisse, Claris, Clarissa, Cáitir • Latin • *bright, famous, crystal clear*

Constance, Connie, Konnie, Constantia, Konstanze, Contanze • Latin • *constancy; steadfast and faithful*

Crystal, Chrystalle, Chrystall, Krystallos, Krystal, Kristel, Krystle • Greek • *ice*

Cushla • Irish Gaelic • *the beat of my heart*

Cyd, Syd, Sidney • Anglo-Saxon • *an ait, a small island in a river or a wide river meadow*

Cynthia, Kynthia, Kynthos, Cyndy, Cindy, Sindy, Cinzia • Greek • *Mount Kynthos on the island of Delos is the birth of Artemis, Goddess of the Moon and the Hunt*

Dahlia, Dale, Dalia. Dalya, Dahl, Dale • Swedish • *named after botanist Anders Dahl from Sweden*

Danika, Danica • Slavic • *morning star*

Daria • Greek/Persian • *he who possesses, looks after the good and wellness of all*

Dassa, Dassah, Hadassah, Esther • Hebrew/Persian/Jewish • *Myrtle, Star and Persian Goddess of Fertility, Love and War, Ishtar*

Delphine, Delfina, Delphina • Latin • *a woman from Delphi, the place of the oracle of the Gods*

Deryn • British/Welsh • *blackbird*

Destiny, Destinata, Destry, Destinie, Destiney, Destinee • Latin/Norman • *power of fate*

Disgleirio • British/Welsh • *bright, glittering, dazzling*

Dija, Deja • French • *already seen*

Dīma • Arabic • *monsoon, deluge*

Dixie • American English/Cajun • *someone from the American South/ Confederate states*

Donella, Donna • Scots Gaelic • *world ruler*

Dongmei • Chinese • *winter plum*
Dusty, Dustie, Dustee • Norse •
Thor, god of thunder's stone

Eira • British/Welsh • *snow*
Eirian • British/Welsh • *silvery bright, beautiful*
Eirlys • British/Welsh • *snowdrop*
Eirwen • British/Welsh • *pure as snow*
Electra, Ellettra • Greek • *brilliant*
Elfleda, Aethelflaed • Anglo-Saxon • *supernatural strength or power*
Elvina, Alvina • Anglo-Saxon • *elfin, noble or faerie friend*
Enfys, Iris • British/Welsh • *rainbow*
Ennis, Enis, Innis, Inis, Ynys • Irish Gaelic • *island*
Erdemute, Erdmuthe • Germanic • *indomitable spirit*
Ernesta, Ernestine, Erna, Ernestina • German • *serious in all things and will fight to the death; means business to the point of obsession*
Esther, Esta, Hester, Haddasah, Eistir, Ester • Hebrew/Persian/Jewish • *Myrtle, Star and Persian Goddess of Fertility, Love and War, Ishtar*
Estelle, Stella • Latin/Norman • *star*
Evelyn, Éibhleann, Aibhilin • Irish Gaelic/English • *desired by others*

Fay, Fae, Faye • English • *fairy or prescient*
Fancy, Fantasy • American English • *whim, vagary*
Fathiyya • Arabic • *liberation!*
Fawziyya • Arabic • *accomplished and successful woman*
Feige, Fayge, Feygl, Vogel, Zipporah • Jewish/Yiddish • *bird*
Fern, Fearn • Anglo-Saxon • *the*

plant that repels evil spirits
Fidda, Fizza • Arabic • *silver*
Fikriyya • Arabic • *pensive, contemplative, intelligent, intellectual*
Flair, Flairer • American English/French • *showing an individual talent*
Frauke • German • *a lady from northern Germany*

Gae, Gay, Gaye • English • *bright, jolly, cherry, sanguine*
Gaia, Ge • Greek • *Goddess of the Earth, mum of Saturn and Uranus*
Galia • Jewish/Hebrew • *wave*
Genevieve, Jennifer, Genoveffa, Ginevra • Celtic • *a female chief or leader of the tribe of people*
Germaine, Jermaine • Latin • *brother*
Gertrude, Gert, Gertie, Gerde, Gertrud, Gerda, Gertraud, Gertraut, Gertrudis • Germanic
Gertrun • Germanic • *magic spear*
Ghislain, Ghislaine, Giselle, Gisil • Germanic/Frankish
Gigi • French • *pet name for Giselle* • *to pledge or promise something or someone to confirm an alliance*
Giselle, Gisil, Gisella, Gisela, Gigi • Germanic/Frankish • *pledge, to pledge or promise something or someone to confirm an alliance*
Glaw • British/Welsh • *rain*
Gormlaith, Gormflaith • Irish Gaelic • *a splendid, illustrious woman or princess*
Gro, Groa, Gruach • Norse/Celtic • *evolving/old woman*
Gudrun, Guro • Norse • *magical, enchanted, a witch or wise woman*
Gumersinda • Spanish/Visigothic • *the path of man or woman*

Gwendolen, Gwendoline • British/ Welsh • *white or silver sacred ring*

Gwyneth, Gwynedd, Gwynneth, Gwenith, Gwynaeth • British/Welsh • *happiness or named after the British Welsh princedom of Gwynedd, based on Snowdonia area where the ancient Brits (Welsh) fought the Anglo-Saxons in guerrilla warfare*

Hadassah, Dassah, Esther • Hebrew/Persian/Jewish • *Myrtle, Star and Persian Goddess of Fertility, Love and War, Ishtar*

Harmony, Harmonie • English • *concord, unity, friendship*

Harriet, Henriette, Henrietta, Hattie, Hennie, Hettie • German/ French/English • *a famous army that carries all before it; a shining light*

Hazel, Haesel • Anglo-Saxon • *the hazel tree, for the Celts a magic tree*

Heather, Hather • English • *moorland plant in rich purple hues*

Hecate • Greek • *Goddess of Magic and Enchantment*

Heike • Germanic • *a famous army that carries all before it; a shining light*

Helmina, Wilhelmina, Helmine • Germanic • *her helmet gives her magical protection and the will to win*

Henrietta, Henriette, Enriqueta • German/French/Spanish • *a famous army that carries all before it; a shining light*

Hikmat • Arabic • *wisdom*

Hilary, Hillary, Hilarie, Hilly, Hilario • Latin • *hilarious!*

Hildebrande • Germanic • *flaming sword into battle*

Holly, Hollie, Holi, Holeg, Holin • Anglo-Saxon • *the holly tree*

Huguette, Huette- Germanic/ Frankish/French • heart, mind and spirit

Huifen • Chinese • *wise and fragrant*

Huiling • Chinese • *wise jade wind chime*

Huda • Arabic • *a woman who is wise and judicious counsellor or adviser; agony aunt*

Ianthe, Violet, Flower, Ionanthos, Iolanthe • Greek • *a beautiful deep purple flower*

Ilene, Eileen • Norman French/ modern English • *desired by others*

Iola, Iole • Greek • *violet, the flower*

Iona, Nonie • Latin/Gaelic • *sacred island in Hebrides in north Britain*

Ione, Nonie • English • *Ionian Islands*

Iris • Greek • *Goddess of the Rainbow*

Irma, Erma, Ermen, Irmgard, Irmtraud, Irmen, Irmengard, Ermengard, Irmgard, Irmingard, Irmentrud, Ermentrud, Irmentraud • all and nothing less

Isadora, Isidoro, Izzy • Greek/ Egyptian • *a gift from the goddess Isis, deity of magic and life*

Isla • Scots • *name of Hebridean island in north Britain*

Ivy, Ifig • Anglo-Saxon • *ivy: the climbing plant known as the survivor*

Jacoba • Biblical/Hebrew/Jewish • *grabbed by the heel!*

Jada, Yada • Biblical/Hebrew/Jewish • *he knows*

Jaswinder • Sikh • *the thunderbolt*

Jāthibiyya, Gāzbiyya • Arabic •

charm personified
Jay, Jaye, Jai • English • *named after the letter 'J', short and snappy*
Jemima • Biblical/Hebrew/Jewish • *dove; as bright as day*
Jinghua • Chinese • *what a splendid situation!*
Joely, Jolene, Jolie, Jollie, Joleen, Jolie, Joli, Jol • Norse/French • *pretty one; also gay and festive; yuletide*
Jordan, Hayarden, Jordana • Hebrew/Jewish • *flowing down*
Jyoti • Sanskrit • *light of mind, light of freedom, light of paradise*

Kaneesha • African American • *modern invention*
Karla, Carla • Scandinavian/English/Germanic • *a freeman*
Karlene, Karleen, Carlene, Carleen • American English • *a freeman*
Karlotte, Karlotta, Carlottam Charlotte • German/Slavic • *a freeman*
Karita, Caritas, Caritas, Charity • Swedish/Latin • *dear charity; humanitarian*
Karola, Carolyn, Karoline, Karolina, Carolina, Carola, Karoline • Scandinavian/English/Germanic • *a freeman*
Kausalya • Sanskrit • *a member of the Kosala family of people*
Keelin, Kylin, Cianian, Cilan • British/Welsh/Gaelic • *companion or friend*
Kelly, Kelley, Kellie, Ceallach • Irish Gaelic • *bright-headed, quick-tempered*
Keren, Kerenhappuch, Keran, Kerin, Kerrin, Keron, Kerena, Kerina • Biblical/Hebrew/Jewish

• *ray of light or eye painted in the shape of a horn*
Kestrel, Cresserelle, Cressele • Norman/English • *bird of prey; from the Norman French: a rattle*
Kimberley, Kim, Kimberly, Kimberlie, Kimberlee, Kimberleigh, Kimberli, Kymberley, Kym • Anglo-Saxon/American English • *etymology is a personal name such as Kimma's wood or clearing. But gained popularity after the South African town of Kimberley where the British took on the Boers; especially 15th February*
Klara, Clara • German/Latin • *bright, famous, crystal-clear*
Kumari • Sanskrit • *daughter or princess*
Kylie, Kyley, Kylee, Kyleigh, Kyla, Kelly • Australian/Aborigine • *boomerang is said to be the ethnic meaning but it seems more likely to be an invention of Kyle and Kelly*

Lan • Chinese • *orchid*
Lana, Alana, Alanah, Lanna, Svetlana • American English • *vague origins but likely to mean a rock*
Lani, Leilani • Polynesian/Hawaiian • *sky, heaven*
Lanfen • Chinese • *perfumed orchid*
Laoise, Leesha, Luigseach • Irish Gaelic • *unsure origins but most possibly Lug, Goddess of Light/ someone from County Laoise*
Larch, Larche, Larix • American English/German/Latin • *sacred tree to the shaman*
Laverne, Lavern • American English/ Gaulish • *alder tree*
Lesley, Lesslyn • Scots Gaelic • *the*

place where holly grows

Liberty, Liberta, Libertas • English/ Norman/Latin • *freedom*

Lidwina, Liduina, Luzdivina • Germanic • *friendly people*

Lilac, Lilak, Nilak • Persian/Arabic • *blue or hues of blue*

Liling • Chinese • *beautiful jade wind chime*

Lindsey, Linsey, Linsy, Linzi, Linzie, Lynsey • Anglo-Saxon • *old Saxon kingdom whose root means Lelli's island*

Linnéa, Linnaea • Swedish • *name honouring botanist Carl von Linne*

Livia, Livius • Latin • *Roman family name Livius, uncertain origin but maybe means a hue of the colour blue*

Lleucu, Leucu, Lughaidh, Lugh, Lucy, Lucía, Lugh, Lugus • British Welsh/Latin • *light*

Lottie, Lotte, Charlotte • French/ Germanic • *a freeman*

Lottelore • modern • *combo of Lotte (Charlotte) and Lore (Eleanore)*

Lourdes, Lurdes • Roman Catholic • *a French place of pilgrimage where a young girl had visions of the Virgin*

Lucía, Lucilla, Lucy, Lucie, Luce, Lucetta, Luciana • Latin • *light*

Lucien, Lucienne • Latin • *light*

Lucilla, Lucille, Lucy, Lucille, Lucy, Luci • Latin • *light*

Lucinda, Lucía, Sinda, Cindy, Sindy, Lucy, Lucinde • Latin • *light*

Lucie, Lucy, Lucinda, Luíseach, Lucía, Lucinde, Liùsaidh • Norman/ Latin • *light*

Lujayn • Arabic • *silver*

Luz, Lux, Luzdivina • Roman Catholic • *Our Lady of Light; referring to the Virgin*

Lyssa, Alyssa, Lissa • Greek mythology • *frenzied and hysterical*

Lyudmila, Lyuda, Ludmil • Slavic • *a tribe of kind people, a family of gracious folks*

Mackenzie, Mackenzee, Makenzie, Makensie, Makensey, Mckenzie, Coinneach, MacCoinnich, Mickenzie • English/Gaelic • *hand- some, gorgeous, pleasing to the eye and rather adorable!*

Madeleine, Madelaine, Magdalene, Magdala, Madelene, Madlyn, Madelyn, Madalene, Madaline, Madoline, Magdalen, Maddie, Maddy, Maddalena • Biblical/French • *Mary Magdelene aka Mary of Magdala, woman healed of evil spirits*

Madīha • Arabic • *praiseworthy, commendable*

Magda, Magdalene, Magadelena, Lena • Biblical/Slavic/German • *Mary Magdelene aka Mary of Magdala, woman healed of evil spirits*

Mahāsin • Arabic • *charming and admirable qualities*

Malak • Arabic • *angel*

Malvina, Malamhin, Maggi, Maggie, Malamhin • literary inven- tion • *name created by poet James McPherson meaning smooth brow in Gaelic*

Manara • Arabic • *she sends out a radiant light like a pharo (lighthouse)*

María de los Ángeles, Mary-Ange • Spanish • *Mary of the Angels*

Marietta, Mariella, María, Mairéad, Margaret, Mariette, Maretta • Biblical/Italian • *Mary Magdelene aka Mary of Magdala, woman*

healed of evil spirits
Marilee, Marylee, Marylou,
Marilene, Marilla, Marioa •
American English • *invented names*
all based on Mary or Maria
Marisa, Maria, Marissa • modern
name • *rooted in Mary*
Marla, Marlene, Magdalene •
modern • *Mary Magdelene aka*
Mary of Magdala, woman healed of
evil spirits
Marlene, Maria, Magdalena •
German • *Mary Magdelene aka*
Mary of Magdala, woman healed of
evil spirits
Maura, Mavra • Latin • *Moor, as in*
Arab
May, Mae, Maybelle, Maybella
• Anglo-Saxon • *the magical*
hawthorn tree which is also known
as may; the month of May
Meg, Mag, Magg, Meggie, Madge
• English/Greek • *clipped name for*
Margaret: pearl
Mei • Chinese • *plum winter*
endurance
Meifeng • Chinese • *beautiful wind*
Meihui • Chinese • *beautiful wisdom*
Mercia, Mercy, Mecedes, Merces
• Latin • *showing compassion for*
others' plight
Merle, Meriel, Merula • Norman/
Latin • *a blackbird*
Mertice • African American •
modern invention
Meryl, Mary • American English
Breton Celtic • *bright sea*
Milagros • Roman Catholic • *Our*
Lady of Miracles
Mina, Wilhelmina, Calumina,
Normina • Scots Gaelic • *clipped*
name for any name ending in -mina!
Minnie, Wilhelmina • Germanic/

Norman • *her helmet gives her*
magical protection and the will to
win
Mirabelle, Mirabella, Mirabellis,
Mirari, Mirabilis • Latin/French •
wonderful, glorious
Miranda, Randa, Randy, Randie,
Amanda • literary invention/Latin
• *William Shakespeare invented*
this name for his heroine in The
Tempest: *admire, wonder at or in*
awe of her loveliness
Monica, Monere, Monique,
Monika • Latin/Phoenician •
cautious counsel, to advise or warn
Morven, Morvern, Mhorbhairne,
Morbheinn • Scots • *a rea of north*
Argyll or big peak
Munira • Arabic • *radiant, bright,*
send out a light
Muriel, Muireall, Meriel, Merrill •
Breton Celtic/Scots Irish Gaelic •
bright sea
Myra, Myrrha, Mary, Miranda,
Mairéad • Latin • *anagram of Mary*
meaning myrrh; the embalming spice

Nadia, Nadya, Nadezhda, Nadine
Nadezhda, Nadya • Russian • *hope*
Nadine, Nadia • Russian/French •
hope
Nadira, Nadra • Arabic • *a woman*
who is rare and precious
Nahla • Arabic • *she is as refreshing*
as a drink of water, she quenches my
thirst
Najah, Nagah • Arabic • *a woman*
who is progressive and successful
Nanda, Ferdinanda, Hernanda •
Spanish/Italian • *clipped form of*
Ferdinanda or Hernanda
Nanna • Norse • *daring one!*
Nasrīn • Persian/Arabic • *wild rose,*

a star set in the constellation of the Eagle and the Lyre

Nastasia, Anastasia • Greek/ Russian • *clipped form of Anastasia • resurrection*

Nell, Nella, Nellie, Nelly, Eleanor, Ellen, Helen • English • *clipped name for Eleanor, Ellen or Helen*

Nerissa, Nereis • literary invention/ Greek • *sea sprite or nymph Nerissa invented by William Shakespeare for Portia's lady-in-waiting in* The Merchant of Venice

Nessa, Agnessa, Agnes, Vanessa • English • *clipped form of any name ending in -nessa!*

Nettie, Annette, Jeannette • English • *clipped form of all names ending in -nette*

Ngaio • New Zealand Maori • *a clever tribe or people*

Nia, Niamh, Neve • British Welsh/ Irish Gaelic • *beautiful and bright*

Nia, Nyah • Swahili • *with a purpose*

Niamh, Neve, Nia • Irish Gaelic • *beautiful and bright*

Nieves • Roman Catholic • *Our Lady of the Snows*

Nihāl • Arabic • *a person whose thirst is slaked*

Nina, Nena, Ninette, Ninon, Antonina • Russian • *clipped form of names that end in -nina*

Ninel • Russian • *Lenin, spelt backwards!*

Nirvana • Sanskrit • *extinction, disappearance of the individual soul into the universal*

Nita, Neats, Anita, Juanita • Spanish • *clipped form of names ending in -nita!*

Norma • artistic Italian • *Felice Romani invented the name for*

Bellini's opera

Normina • *a man from the north; Norseman or Viking*

Nuha • Arabic • *a woman who is clever, intellectual and cerebrally bright*

Nura, Nūr • Arabic • *this woman will light up your life and she has unique features too*

Olympe, Olympia • Greek • *a woman from Olympus, the mountain of the Gods*

Oighrig, Aithbhreac, Erica, Effie, Euphemia, Eithrig, Eiric, Efric • Scots Gaelic • *speckled one*

Oktyabrina • Russian • *commemorates the October revolution of 1917*

Ona, Anona, Fiona, Honor • English • *clipped name for any that end in -ona*

Oighrig, Eiric, Eithrig, Aithbhreac • Scots Gaelic • *new speckled one perhaps referring to freckles*

Onora, Nora, Honora • English • *clipped name for any name ending in -nora*

Orna, Odharnait • Irish Gaelic • *sallow complexion*

Ornella, Ornelia, Ornetta, Ornello • Tuscan • *the flowering ash tree*

Owena • British/Welsh • *born of Esos or Aesos, Celtic deity*

Padma • Sanskrit • *lotus flower, energy centres of the chakra*

Pamela, Pam, Pammy, Pamella • poetic invention • *Sir Philip Sidney, Elizabethan (First) poet, created the name*

Pandora, Dora, Pandoran • Greek mythology • *all and every gift; alluding to Pandora's box that she*

was told never to open, when she did,
she allowed everything evil and bad
out, leaving the fairy Hope as the
only thing left inside

Paris, Parisii • Latin/Celtic • *member
of the Parisii tribe, origins unknown*

Parvati • Sanskrit • *daughter of the
mountains*

Peizhi • Chinese • *admiring iris*

**Perdita, Perdie, Purdee, Purdy,
Perditus** • Latin/literary invention
• *William Shakespeare invented the
name from the Latin 'lost' as one of
his characters in* The Winter's Tale

Philippa, Phil, Philippina • Greek •
friend or lover of horses

**Philomena, Philomenus,
Philomenes, Phileinmenos,
Philoumena, Filumena, Filomena**
• Greek/Germanic • *loyal, strong
friend, platonic friendship*

Phoenix • Latin/Greek • *mythical
bird that represents rebirth or
reincarnation*

**Phyllis, Phillida, Phyllis, Phyllidos,
Phyllidis, Phyllida, Phyllicia,
Phylicia** • Greek mythology • *a
Thracian queen, Phyllis died for
love and transformed herself into
an almond tree; her name means
leaves or leaf and she is a symbol of
undying love and friendship*

Pippa, Philippa • Greek • *friend or
lover of horses*

Patribha • Sanskrit • *clever, radiant,
imaginative and precocious*

Prisca, Priscilla, Priscus • Biblical/
Latin • *Roman family name meaning
ancient or old*

Priscilla, Cilla, Prissy, Priscus •
Biblical/Latin • *Roman family name
meaning ancient or old*

Qingge • Chinese • *crystal house*

Qingling • Chinese • *celebrating
understanding*

Qingzhao • Chinese • *clear understanding, crystal illumination*

Radegund, Radegunde • Germanic
• *a counseller, adviser in times of
trouble*

Raffaella, Rafaela • Biblical •
archangel

Ragā, Rajā • Arabic • *perpetual
anticipation is good for the soul*

Ragna • Norse • *advice from the
gods*

Ragnborg, Ramborg • Norse • *decisions and protection from the gods*

Rainbow, Regnboga • Anglo-Saxon
• *rainbow*

Raisa • Slavic • *paradise, heaven*

Ramona • Catalan/Visigothic •
adviser, protector

Randa, Miranda, Randy • American
English • *clipped Miranda*

Raven, Rafn, Raefn, Ravenna •
Anglo-Saxon/Norse • *Odin's winged
friend, the Raven*

Rāwiya • Arabic • *a narrator of classical Arabic poetry and prose, and
beautiful speaker*

Reagan, Regan, Riagain • Irish
Gaelic/English • *descendant of
Riagain, the impulsive or impatient
one*

**Regina, Queenie, Raine, Régine,
Raghnailt, Ragnhild** • Latin/Roman
Catholic • *queen (of heaven)*

**Rene, Renata, Irene, Renee,
Doreen, Maureen** • English • *short
for any name ending in -reen or -rene*

Rhetta • Dutch • *advice, counsel*

**Rhoda, Rhodon, Rose, Roda,
Rodos** • Greek • *rose or someone*

from Rhodes, the island of roses
Rhona, Rona • Scots • *name of Hebridean island off northern Britain*
Ricki, Ricky, Rikki, Riki • English • *short form of any name ending in -rick*
Rike, Ulrike, Frederike • Scandinavian/German • *short form of any name ending in -rike*
Rita, Magarita • Spanish • *short form of Margarita*
Robbin, Robbie, Roberta • Germanic • *famous and bright*
Roberta, Robbie • Germanic • *famous and bright*
Robyn, Robin • Germanic • *famous and bright*
Rocio • Roman Catholic • *Our Lady of the Dews, or tears shed for the wickedness of the world*
Rong • Chinese • *macho woman; tomboy*
Ros, Roz, Rosalind, Rosamund • English • *shortened for any name beginning with Ros*
Roshanara • Persian • *her beauty is like honey to the bee, she is a magnet of loveliness*
Roxy • American English • *flashy, glitzy but just a little nouvelle riche!*
Ruda • Slavic • *ingenious*
Ruiling • Chinese • *lucky jade wind chime*
Runa • Norse • *a woman who has magical powers she uses through the runes or secret spells*
Ruqayya • Arabic • *talisman, lucky charm, magic spell, moving upwards, advancing/ascending*

Safiyya • Arabic • *the best friend anyone could have*

Sage, Sauge, Sapius • English/Norman/American English • *the herb sage that promotes wisdom*
Salha • Arabic • *devoted and dedicated*
Salma • Arabic • *a person who looks after those she loves; a protector*
Salwa • Arabic • *she who consoles others and gives a shoulder to cry on*
Samantha, Sam, Sammy, Sammi • Biblical/Hebrew/Jewish • *the name of God, God has heard, listen to God*
Samsara • Sanskrit • *just passing through, referring to life being just part of a cycle*
Sanā • Arabic • *a brilliant, radiant woman*
Saniyya • Arabic • *wonderful, dazzling woman*
Saoirse, Seersha • Irish Gaelic • *freedom, liberation*
Sappho • literary Greek • *poetess Sappho, noted for her verse honouring lesbian passion*
Sarai • Biblical/Jewish/Hebrew • *contentious*
Saraswati • Sanskrit • *filled with waters of knowledge of the arts, learning and academia*
Saskia, Sachs • Dutch/Germanic • *Saxon, the tribe*
Saturday • Latin • *Saturn's day*
Siegrun, Sigrun, Sigi • she who uses the runes or magic to gain power over her enemies
Seanach • English/Norman French • *old, wise and venerable*
Seren, Serena, Serenus • British/Welsh • *star*
Shahīra • Arabic • *destiny for fame and fortune*
Shakti • Sanskrit • *she possesses the power of the Gods*

Shakuntala • Sanskrit • *a rare bird*
**Shannon, Shantelle, Shan,
Seanain, Seanán** • Irish • *wise,
mature and ancient*
Shanta • Sanskrit • *she who
finds inner peace through yoga or
meditation*
Shanti • Sanskrit • *she who finds
tranquillity and serenity through
yoga*
Shaoqing • Chinese • *young blue*
Sharifa • Arabic • *a woman who is
eminent in her field and honourable
to the nth degree*
Silver, Silvette, Argentia, Seolfor •
Anglo-Saxon • *silver, the metal*
Sky, Skye • Gaelic • *take your pick,
the sky as in heaven or Skye as in the
north British island*
Socorro • Roman Catholic • *Our
Lady of Perpetual Succour*
**Sofia, Sophia, Sofya, Sofie, Sophie,
Sofie, Sophy** • Greek • *wisdom*
Sonia, Sonya, Sonje • Greek •
wisdom
Song • Chinese • *pine tree*
Sorcha, Clara • Gaelic • *brightness*
Solange, Sollemnia, Sollemna •
Latin • *solemn*
Soledad, Sol • Roman Catholic •
Our Lady of Solitude
Sprite, Spiritus, Esprit • American
English • *a mischievous spirit*
Star, Starr, Stella • English • *a star
(heavenly rather than celebrity)*
Stella, Stella Maris • Latin • *a star
and Star of the Seas (often used to
describe the Virgin Mary)*
Storm, Sturmdrang • American
English • *thunderstorm*
Suha • Arabic • *star*
Summer, Haf, Sumor • Anglo-Saxon
• *someone born in the summer*

months (southern hemisphere)
Sunita • Sanskrit • *she's a good girl
who gives wise advice*
Suyin • Chinese • *straight talking*
Svea • Swedish • *patriotic name for
Sweden*
Svetlana, Sveta, Photine • Slavic/
Greek • *light*
**Sybil, Sybille, Sybilla, Sibylla,
Sibilia, Sibella, Sibéal, Cybille,
Sibilla, Sibella, Cybil, Cybill** • Greek
mythology • *a woman with the
power to predict; a devotee of Apollo,
the sun god*
Sydney, Sid, Sidney • Anglo-Saxon
• *an ait, a small island in a river or
a wide river meadow*
Sylphide, Sylva, Silva, Sylpha •
Latin/French • *airborne, invisible
sylphlike spirits*

Tahiyya • Arabic • *hello!*
Tanisha • African American •
modern Invention
Tara • Sanskrit • *a shining star who
carries the troubles of the world on
her shoulders*
Teal, Teale, Teling • German/Dutch/
English • *a bird!*
Teàrlag • Irish Gaelic • *a woman
who takes the initiative, starts things*
Tempe, Temnein • Greek • *a valley
in Greece; the legendary home of the
Muses, the nine goddesses of the arts
and sciences*
Tempest, Tempeste, Tempestas
• Latin/Norman/Englisg • *nick-
name for a person with a wild
temperament*
Theda, Teud, Theodosia • Latin •
people, tribe or race
Thelma, Thelema • Greek • *to wish
or have the will*

Themba • Zulu • *trusted*

Thera, Theresa • Greek • *vague origins; could be short for Theresa or Greek isle of Thera*

Tia, Laetitia, Lucretia, Tiana, Tiara • Spanish/Portuguese • *aunty or short form of any name ending in -tia*

Tiana, Tia, Christiana, Tianna • American English • *suffix of any name ending in -tiana: e.g. Christiana*

Tiara, Tia • Greek/Latin • *half a crown! The Persians used to wear hats like the Coneheads!*

Tikvah, Tikva • Biblical/Jewish/Hebrew • *hope*

Tina, Christina • English • *short form of any name ending in -tina*

Tisha, Laetitia, Patricia, Tish, Tricia, Trisha • modern • *short form of any name ending in -tia or -cia*

Torborg, Thorbjorg • Norse • *fortified place belonging to the god Thor*

Tordis • Norse • *goddess connected to Thor*

Tori, Tory, Toria • Norse/Danish • *Thor*

Tori, Tory, Toria • English • *short form of Victoria*

Tottie, Charlotte, Lottie, Totty, Lotte, Carlotta • English • *short form of Charlotte*

Tova, Tofa, Turid, Tove, Tufa • Norse • *the god Thor made me beautiful*

Trude, Gertraud, Gertrude, Traute, Trudy, Traude • German • *short form of any name ending in -raud or -raude*

Trina, Treena, Catrina, Treena • English • *short form of any name ending in -tina*

Trista, Trysta • American English/British Welsh • *rowdy, rebellious, blue, melancholic, chaotic*

Trudy, Trudi, Trudie, Gertrude, Ermintrude, Ermentrud, Trude • English/German • *short form of any name ending in -rude*

'Um-Kalthūm • Arabic • *mother of a little cherub!*

'Umniya • Arabic • *your wish is my desire*

Vanessa, Nessa, Venessa • literary invention/Dutch • *created by Jonathan Swift from his lover's Dutch surname Vanhomrigh*

Velma • modern English/Greek • *to wish or have the will*

Verna, Verona, Verena • American English/Gaulish • *alder tree*

Vimala • Sanskrit • *a peerless person, pure as crystal*

Viola, Violet, Vi • Latin • *the flower: violet*

Violet, Violette, Violetta, Violeta, Vi • Latin/Norman • *the flower: violet*

Wafā • Arabic • *a faithful, loyal, devoted woman*

Wanda, Wenda, Wendelin • Germanic/Polish/Slavic

Wendy, Wenda, Wendi, Gwendolen • literary invention • *JM Barrie created it for his book* Peter Pan *from his own nursery name Fwendy-Wendy meaning friend*

Wenling • Chinese • *refined jade wind chime*

Whitney, Whitley, Witney, Hwitleah, Whiteney • Anglo-Saxon • *the white island*

Widād • Arabic • *an affectionate, friendly girl*

Wilhelmina, Mina, Minnie, Billie,

Wilma • Germanic/Norman • *her helmet gives her magical protection and the will to win*

Willa • Anglo-Saxon • *a person with tremendous willpower, powerful in every way*

Wilma, Wilhelmina, Billie, Wilmette, Wilmetta • Anglo-Saxon

Winifred, Winfred, Win, Winnie, Wynnfrith, Gwenfrewi, Winfriede, Winfried • Germanic • *a kind, peace-loving friend*

Wynne, Wynn, Wine • British Welsh/Anglo-Saxon

Xaveria • Roman Catholic/Basque • *the new house*

Xenia • Greek • *hospitality and a welcome to or from a stranger or foreigner*

Xiaoling • Chinese • *morning wind chime*

Xiaoqing • Chinese • *little blue*

Xiaozhi • Chinese • *little iris; long life and prosperity*

Xiurong • Chinese • *charming personality*

Xue • Chinese • *snow meaning white, pure as the driven stuff*

Xueman • Chinese • *snowy composure and grace*

Yanlin • Chinese • *forest of swallows also Beijing, Chinese capital*

Yanmei • Chinese • *swallow plum*

Yanyu • Chinese • *swallow jade*

Yu • Chinese • *jade or rain*

Yuan • Chinese • *shining peace*

Yuming • Chinese • *jade brightness*

Yun • Chinese • *cloud*

Yunru • Chinese • *charming*

Zélie, Célie, Celia, Zaylie, Zaylee, • French/Latin • *Roman family name meaning heaven*

Zenith, Samtarras • Arabic • *overhead (celestial) path*

Zéphyrine, Zephyrus, Zephyros • Latin/Greek/French • *the west wind or breeze*

Zhaohui • Chinese • *crystal wisdom*

Zhilan • Chinese • *iris orchid*

Zillah • Biblical/Hebrew/Jewish

Zinnia • German • *a flower from Mexico named after botanist JG Zinn*

Zipporah, Zip, Zippor • *little bird*

Zongying • *heroine, the others look up to; a role model*

PISCES
20th February to 20th March

Planets: Neptune and Jupiter

Day: Thursday

Stones: aquamarine and alexandrite

Metals: neptunium and tin

Colours: sea green, jade green, peacock green, technicolor, colour where no one predominates, for instance sea green: is it green or blue?

Design: diffuse and nebulous, shapes fuzzy at the edges, no strict borders, blurred boundaries, holograms that deceive the eye

Trees: elder, dogwood, coconut, mangrove, cypress, birch, palm

Flora: daffodil, water lily, water iris, tulip, mosses, ferns, seaweed all pond plants

Celebrity Pisceans: Czar Alexander III • Ursula Andress • Jim Backus • Tammy Faye Bakker • Elizabeth Barrett Browning • Drew Barrymore • Harry Belafonte • Alexander Graham Bell • Jon Bon Jovi • Sir Richard Burton • Karen Carpenter • Enrico Caruso • Johnny Cash • Michael Caine • Neville Chamberlain • Frédéric Chopin • Glenn Close • Nat 'King' Cole • Nicolaus Copernicus • Tom Courtenay • Daniel Craig • Cindy Crawford • Billy Crystal • Fats Domino • Patrick Duffy • Wyatt Earp • Albert Einstein • Yuri Gargarin • Jackie Gleason • Mikhail Gorbachev • Kelsey Grammer • Alan Greenspan • Jame Gumb (aka Buffalo Bill) • George Frideric Handel • Jean Harlow • George Harrison • Rex Harrison • Patty Hearst • King Henry II • Frankie Howerd • Victor Hugo • Quincy Jones • Edward M Kennedy • Michel Le Grande • Henry Longfellow • Rob Lowe • Percival Lowell (discovered Pluto) • Zeppo Marx • Michelangelo • Glenn Miller • Sir John Mills • Liza Minnelli • Rupert Murdoch • Vaslav Nijinsky • David Niven • Rudolf Nureyev • Irene Papas • Sam Peckinpah • Bernadette Peters • Sidney Poitier • Lynn Redgrave • Pierre Auguste Renoir • Rihanna • Nikolai Rimsky-Korsakov • Kurt Russell • Neil Sedaka • Andrés Segovia • Ariel Sharon • Nina Simone • Rudolph Steiner • John Steinbeck • Sharon Stone • Levi Strauss • Jimmy Swaggart • Elizabeth Taylor • James Taylor • Kiri Te Kanawa • Claire Trevor • Ivana Trump • Tommy Tune • Gloria Vanderbilt • George Washington • Bruce Willis • Joanne Woodward • Billy Zane.

Planetary Influences: see Neptune and Jupiter at the back of this book (pages 440 and 463)

Boys

Abbán • Irish Gaelic • *abbot*

Abbondio, Abundius, Abundans • Latin • *abundant*

Abel, Hevel • Biblical • *breath, saint for the dying*

Abid • Arabic • *worshipper*

Absalom, Absolon • Biblical/Hebrew • *father of peace*

Ádhamhnán • Irish Gaelic • *great fear*

Adrian, Adrien, Adriano, Hadrianus • Latin • *a man from Hadria which the Adriatic Sea is named*

Aeneas, Aineas, Ainein, Angus • Greek • *singing praises*

Alan, Alain, Ailin, Ailean, Alyn, Alun, Allan, Allen • Celtic • *vague origins but likely to be a rock*

Alaric, Aliric • Germanic • *a foreign power or powerful, ruling stranger perhaps invader*

Alban, Albanus, Albie, Alby • Latin • *confused origins, perhaps Alba meaning white or albion meaning Britain*

Alfio • Sicilian • *unknown root*

Alfred, Alfie, Alf, Aelfraed, Alfredo • Anglo-Saxon • *supernatural, faerie counsel, help*

Alger, Algie, Aelfgaer • Anglo-Saxon • *an old enchanted, noble spear with magical powers possibly from a sacred location*

Alirio • Spanish • *unknown origin*

Alvin, Aelfwine, Athelwine • Anglo-Saxon • *elfin, noble or faerie friend*

Alwyn, Aylwin, Alvin • British/Welsh/Anglo-Saxon • *he who has faerie friends*

Amadeus, Amédée, Gottlieb, Amedeo • Latin/Germanic • *Love God or God of Love!*

Amador, Amator • Spanish • *lover*

Amal • Arabic • *hope, longing*

Amato, Amatus, Amado • Latin • *beloved*

Ambrose, Ambroise, Ambrosius, Ambrois, Ambroix, Ambrogio, Ambrosio, Ambrosios, Ambros, Emrys, Ambros, Ambrogio, Ambrozy, Ambroz • Latin • *immortal, eternal*

Amias, Amyas • English • *unknown root*

Armitabh • Sanskrit • *eternal splendour*

Amos • Biblical/Jewish/Hebrew • *to carry the Lord like St Christopher*

Amrit • Sanskrit • *immortal, divine foods*

Anand • Sanskrit • *blissfully happy*

Angelo, Ángel, Angelos • Greek/Latin • *messenger of God*

Aniello, Agnellus • little lamb, patron saint of Naples

Anselm, Anselmo • Germanic • *divine face, divine protection (helmet)*

Anacleto, Anacletus, Anakletos, Aniceto • Latin/Greek • *invocation*

Anastasio, Anastasis • Greek • *resurrection*

Anthony, Antony, Tony, Antain, Antaine, Anton, Antoine, Antonio, Antoni, Antonin, Antoninus, Ante, Antun, Antal, Antanas, Anthos, Antwan, Antonino, Nino, Ninny, Anthony, Antoine, Anton, Antonio, Antonius • Etruscan/Roman • *Roman family name but with confused origins*

Antshel, Anshel, Amshel • Jewish/

Yiddish • *angel*

Arthur, Arturo, Artair, Arthur, Artorius, Art • British Welsh/Celtic mythology • *unknown origins possibly bear man*

Arran • English • *island in the Firth of Clyde in north-west Britain making up County of Buteshire*

Arvind • Sanskrit • *lotus*

Arwel • British/Welsh • *I wept over you*

Asa • Biblical/Hebrew/Jewish • *doctor, one who heals*

Asdrubale, Asrubaal • Phoenician/Italian • *give aid to the lord or receive it*

Asher • Jewish/Hebrew • *auspicious, born happy under a lucky star*

Ashish • Sanskrit • *prayer, wish or blessing*

Åsmund, Assmund • protected by the gods

Athan, Athanase, Athanasius, Afanasi, Athanasios, Athanatos • Latin/Greek • *eternal life*

'Ātif • Arabic • *compassionate and sympathetic*

Aubrey, Aubry, Alberic, Albric, Aelfric, Aubrey, Alberic, Albericus • Germanic/Anglo-Saxon/Latin • *he who has the power of the faeries*

Augustine, Augustus, Austin • *great, the max, magnificent, nobody does it better*

Augustus, Auguste, Gus, Augustín, Augustine, Agostino, Augusto, Avgust, Agustin, Aghaistin, Aibhistin, Augustijn, Agusti, Agostinho, Agostino, Avgustin, Tauno, Agoston, Augustinas, Augere • Latin • *great, the max, magnificent, expansive, nobody does it better*

Averill, Eoforhild, Alfred • Norman/Anglo-Saxon • *supernatural, faerie favours*

Avery • Norman/Anglo-Saxon • *supernatural, faerie favours*

Averki, Aberkios • Greek • *unknown root*

Axel, Absalom • Biblical/Hebrew/Danish • *father is peace*

Ayman • Arabic • *blessed be, wealthy*

Azriel • Jewish/Hebrew • *God helps*

Balder • Norse • *ruler or chief prince, said to be pure and beautiful*

Baldev • Sanskrit • *God of Strength and playboy!*

Baptiste, Baptist, Bautista • Biblical • *John the Baptist*

Barak • Arabic • *blessing*

Barnabas, Barnaby, Barney, Barny, Barnabé, Bernebe, Barnaba, Barna, Bernabé • Biblical/Greek • *son of consolation*

Barrymore • American English • *no known origins*

Bartholomew, Barton, Bart, Barthélemy, Bartholomaus, Bartolomé • Biblical/Jewish/Hebrew • *son of Tolmai from Galilee*

Baruch • Biblical/Jewish/Hebrew • *blessed*

Beatus, Beat • Swiss • *blessed*

Beau • French • *beautiful and bonny boy*

Bellarmino • Roman Catholic/Jesuit • *named after Italian saint Roberto Bellarmino*

Bem • Nigerian • *peace*

Benedict, Bennett, Benneit, Benedikt, Bendt, Bent, Benoît, Benito, Benet, Bento, Benedetto, Benedikt, Benedykt, Pentii, Benedek, Bendikts, Beynish,

Benes, Benedictus, Benneit • Latin • *blessed*

Bilal, Bilil • Arabic • *moist*

Blaise, Błaize, Blas • Latin/French • *to limp, limping*

Blakeney • English • *he from the black island*

Bo • Chinese • *waves*

Bohai • Chinese • *my elder brother is the sea*

Boleslav • Russian • *distinctly large and rather glorious*

Boniface, Bonifacio, Bonifacius, Bonifaz • Latin • *good fate*

Brent, Brenton • British/Welsh • *holy river or hill as in River Brent that flows through Middlesex*

Brewster • English • *a man who brews, a brewer*

Buck • American/English • *cowboy, stag or doe*

Burkhard • Germanic • *safe harbour, strong protection*

Caerwyn, Carwyn, Caradog, Caradoc • British/Welsh • *sacred love*

Cai, Kay • British/Welsh • *rejoice!*

Cainneach, Kenny • Irish Celtic • *handsome, beautiful, founder of Kilkenny*

Callum, Colm, Calum, Columba, Cole, Colmán, Colum • Latin/Scots Gaelic • *dove*

Caoimhín, Kevin • Irish Gaelic • *beloved, beautiful, enchanting*

Caolite • Irish Gaelic • *origins vague linked to legendary sprinter Mac Ronain*

Carson • American/English • *a Christian, follower of Jesus Christ*

Ceallach, Kelly • Irish Gaelic • *fair-haired or monk church monastery*

Cecil, Cesil • Latin/English • *old Roman family name Caecilius, from the Latin, meaning blind*

Ceri, Kerry • British/Welsh/Irish Gaelic • *unknown origin, maybe the dark one*

Chongan • Chinese • *second brother of peace*

Chonglin • Chinese • *second brother unicorn*

Christopher, Chris, Christian, Crìsdean, Karsten, Christiaan, Carsten, Christer, Chretien, Cristiano, Krysztian, Krisztian, Christie, Christy, Kristy, Kristopher, Christopha, Kristopha, Críostóir, Christoph, Christofoor, Kristafoor, Kristoffer, Christophe, Cristobál, Cristofol, Cristovao, Cristoforo, Krzysztof, Krystof, Hristo, Risto, Kristof, Kristaps, Kit, Kester • Greek • *the man who bears Jesus Christ*

Christhard • German • *as brave and strong as Christ*

Christian, Carsten, Christer, Kristian, Criosd, Crìsdean • Latin • *follower of Christ*

Cillian, Killian, Kilian • Irish Gaelic • *fight or church*

Claude, Claud, Claudius, Claudio • Latin • *a lame man*

Claver, Klaver • Roman Catholic/Catalan • *honouring St Pere Claver*

Cledwyn • British/Welsh • *a man who might be rough and ready on the outside but on the inside he is holy, spiritual and soft*

Clem, Clément, Clemmie, Cliamain, Clemente • Latin • *merciful, gentle, compassionate*

Coinneach, Kenneth • Scots Gaelic • *handsome, beautiful, sexy*

Colby, Colton • American/English/

Norse • *a man who makes charcoal or who has dark looks*

Colombe, Columba, Callum, Colmán, Colm, Colum, Columbano • Latin • *dove*

Colin, Collin, Coll, Nicholas, Cailean • English/Scots Gaelic • *dove*

Cormac, Cormag • Irish/Scots Gaelic • *origins vague*

Cugat, Cucuphas • Catalan • *unknown origin*

Cynddelw • British/Welsh • *he who worships holy and sacred images, pagan or Christian*

Dai, Dei • British/Welsh • *this chap shines forth*

Dalmazio, Dalmatius, Dalmacio • Latin • *a person from Dalmatia in the Adriatic*

Damián, Damianos, Damien, Demyan • Greek • *vague roots but could be 'to kill'*

Daniel, Dan, Danny, Danyal, Deiniol, Daniele, Daniil, Taneli, Dannie • Biblical/Hebrew/Jewish • *God is my judge*

Daren, Darren, Darien, Darius, Darin, Darron, Daron • American/English • *unknown origins*

Darnell, Darnel • Norman • *not entirely known origins but possibly a type of grass or shrub*

David, Dave, Davy, Dewi, Dafydd, Dai, Davie, Davey, Dàibhidh, Davide, Taavi, Daw, Dawson, Dawūd, Dewi, Dewydd, David, Dai • Biblical/Hebrew • *vague origins but possibly from a baby word meaning darling one, especially 1st March*

Dayaram • Sanskrit • *as kind and tender as Rama, the perfect man/divinity*

Dean, Dino, Deane, Dene Denu, Decanus, Dane • Anglo-Saxon • *a man who served as dean in a Christian church or cathedral sense*

Declan, Deaglán • Irish Celtic • *unknown origins*

Delun • Chinese • *virtuous, respected*

Deming • Chinese • *virtuous, bright*

Demid, Diomedes • Greek • *wisdom of Zeus/Jupiter*

Dennis, Denis, Denys, Den, Dionysios, Denny, Dioniso, Dionizy, Denes, Dionysius • Greek/French • *named after the god Dionysius*

Derek, Dereck, Derrick, Deryck, Del, Dirk, Theodoric • German/Dutch • *god's gift*

Desiderio, Desiderius, Desiderium • Latin • *longing*

Devdan • Sanskrit • *gift of the gods*

Devdas • Sanskrit • *servant of the gods*

Devin, Damhain • Irish Gaelic/American English • *descendant of the Damhan; fawn, deer*

Dewey, Dewy • British/Welsh/American/English • *possibly the English spelling of Dewi, which means David, darling one*

Dexter, Dex, Dexy • Anglo-Saxon/Latin • *a female dyer/laundress or right-handed*

Didier, Desiderius • Latin • *longing for*

Dietfried • Germanic • *people of peace or peaceful people*

Dieudonné • French • *God-given*

Diggory, Digory • Norman • *vague roots, possibly means lost or gone astray*

Dilwyn • British/Welsh • *fair, blonde, white, blessed, sacred, holy*

Dion, Dionis, Diodoros, Diogenes • French/Latin • *gift from Zeus or Jupiter*

Dionysus, Bacchus • Greek • *Dionysus, God of Wine, Orgies and Partying*

Dominic, Dominick, Dom, Dominique, Domingo, Dominicus, Dominus • Latin/Roman Catholic • *Lord, as in St Dominic, founder of the Dominican order*

Donat, Donato, Donatus, Donatien, Donatianus • *given by God*

Donghai • Chinese • *eastern sea*

Doran, Deoradhain, Deoradh • *traveller, such as pilgrim or stranger*

Dorotheos, Dorofei • Greek • *gift of God*

Dositheos, Dosifei • Greek • *God-given*

Doyle, Dubhghaill, Dubhghall, Dùghall, Dougal, Dugal, Dugald • Scots Gaelic • *black, dark, stranger*

Drogo, Dorogo, Drog • Norman/Slavic • *ghost or spirit; dear one*

Duald, Dubhaltach, Dubhfholtach • Irish • *black-haired*

Duane, Dubhán, Dwane, Dwayne, Dwain, Dubhain • *dark, black*

Duff, Dubh • Irish Gaelic • *dark- or black-haired man*

Dwight, Diot, Dionysa • English • *a woman (that's right: female!) who worships the God of Orgies*

Dylan, Dillon, Dyllon • British/Welsh • *sea*

Eden, Edan • Hebrew/Jewish • *Garden of Eden, a place of sheer pleasure*

Ehud • Jewish/Hebrew • *compassionate and pleasant*

Éibhear • *origin unknown but name of the son of Mil, leader of Gaels that conquered Ireland*

Eilif • Scandinavian • *one alone, for always, evermore, eternal life*

Elias, Eli • Biblical/Greek • *Yahweh is God*

Eliezer, Eleazar, Eli • Jewish/Hebrew • *God's help*

Elijah, Eliezer, Elisha, Eli, Eliyahu, Eli • Jewish/Hebrew • *Yahweh is God*

Elliott, Eliott, Elliot, Elias, Elijah • English • *Yahweh is God*

Elkanah, Elkan • Jewish/Hebrew • *possessed by God*

Ellair, Ceallair, Cellarius, Cella, Ellar • Scots Gaelic • *a person who works in pub or monastery as a steward*

Elpidio, Elpidius, Elpidios • Latin/Greek • *hope*

Elvis, Elwyn, Elwin, Elian, Allan • American/English • *unknown origins although there was a Hibernian St Elvis in the 6th century*

Elwyn, Alyn • British/Welsh • *white, fair, blessed, sacred and holy*

Emmanuel, Emanuel, Manny, Immanuel • Biblical/Hebrew/Jewish • *God is with us or amongst us*

Emeterio, Emeterius, Hemiterius • Greek/Latin • *roots unknown; especially 3rd March*

Emidio • Latin • *vague origin, patron saint of Ascoli Piceno*

Emlyn, Aemilianus, Aemilius, Aemulus • British/Welsh/Latin • *vague roots, possibly means a rival*

Emrys, Ambrose • British/Welsh • *immortal, eternal*

Erastus, Rastus • Biblical/Greek • *beloved*

Erin, Éirinn • Irish • *romantic name poets give to Ireland*

Ermenegilde, Hermengildo • French/Visigothic • *a total sacrifice*

Eusebio, Eusebios, Eusebes • Greek • *revered, pious*

Eustace, Eustakhios, Euistathios, Eustache, Eustaquio • Greek/French • *confused roots; could mean juicy, tasty grapes!*

Evan, Iefan, Ieuan, Ifan • British/Welsh • *John, Johannes; God is gracious or gift of God*

Ewald, Ewawalt • Germanic • *a wise and just ruler; powerful leader, lawful ruler, judge*

Eyolf • Scandinavian • *lucky wolf, like a gift or talisman*

Ezekiel, Zeke • Biblical/Jewish/Hebrew • *God gives me strength*

Ezra, Esdras • Biblical/Jewish/Hebrew • *help!*

Fabrizio, Fabrice, Fabricius, Fabricio • Italian/Etruscan • *Roman family name, one noted for his incorruptibility*

Fādi • Arabic • *redeemer, saviour, God*

Fardorgh, Feardocha • Irish Gaelic • *dark man*

Faysal, Feisal • a man or judge who knows the difference between good and bad, right and wrong

Ferapont, Therapon • Greek • *he who worships*

Ferdinand, Ferdinando, Ferdi, Ferdie, Fernand, Fernando, Ferdinando, Hernando, Fernán, Hernán • Spanish • *a man at peace wherever he is; always ready and prepared to travel*

Filat, Feofilakt, Theophylaktos • Greek • *protected by God*

Firdos • Arabic • *paradise*

Fishl, Fish, Fisch • Jewish/Yiddish • *simply fish!*

Florian, Florentius, Florenti, Florencio • Latin • *flowery and romantic*

Fraser, Frazer, Frazier, Frisselle, Fresel, Freseliere, Frasier • Norman French/Scots English • *Scots family name with no known origins*

Frédéric, Frederick, Frederik, Fritz, Fred, Phredd, Freddie, Fredick, Fredric, Friedrich, Frerik, Freek, Fredrik, Federico, Frederico, Fryderyk, Bedrich, Rieti, Frigyes • Germanic/Frankish

Fridtjof • Norse • *quiet, like a thief in the night*

Friedemann • German • *man of peace*

Fürchtegott • German • *fear God*

Gabriel, Gabby, Gaby, Gabriele • Biblical/Hebrew/Jewish • *man of God*

Gamaliel • Jewish/Hebrew • *benefit of God*

Ganesh • Sanskrit • *Lord of the Hosts*

Gennadi • Russian • *roots unknown; name of orthodox saint*

Gareth • Welsh/British • *unknown origins, possibly linked to Geraint*

Gavin, Gawain, Gauvain • Celtic • *unknown root*

Gerasim, Gerasimos • Greek • *saint of the Eastern Orthodox Church; honoured old man*

Gervaise, Gervase, Jervaise, Jervais, Gervais, Gervas, Gervasio • Germanic/Frankish • *unknown origin; possibly a man with a spear*

or something pointed

German, Germanus • Latin •
brother in God

Gethin, Gethen, Cethin • British/
Welsh • *dark, dusky, exotic*

Gilbert, Gib, Gibb, Gilberto
• Germanic/Frankish/Roman
Catholic • *he who pledges or sacri-
fices his life for greater things*

Gjord, Gyrd, Jul • Norse • *God of
Peace*

Gleb, Gudeif • Norse/Russian • *he
who lives his life like a god or saint;
heir of God*

Gobind • Sikh • *name of one of the
pantheon of Sikh gurus*

**Godfrey, Godefroy, Gofraidh,
Godfrid, Godfred** • Germanic/
Frankish • *God of Peace*

Godwin, Godwine, Win • Anglo-
Saxon • *God is my friend*

Gomer • Biblical/Jewish/Hebrew •
complete and wholesome

Gordon • Scottish • *unknown
origins could spring from place
name in Aberdeenshire or similar in
Normandy*

Goronwy, Gronw • British/Welsh
• *uncertain origin but by legend an
adulterous murderer*

Gottfried, Götz • Germanic • *God of
Peace, God bring me peace*

Gotthard • Germanic • *God give me
strength*

Gotthelf • Germanic • *God help me*

Gotthold, Gottwald • Germanic •
wonderful (lovely) God

Gottlieb, Theophilus • Germanic •
love God

Gottlob • Germanic • *praise God*

Grant, Grand, Grande • Anglo-
Saxon/Norman • *a large, portly
person*

Grayson, Greifi, Greyve • Norse/
English • *son of a steward, a
publican*

Guangli • Chinese • *lighting up
virtue and propriety*

Guoliang • Chinese • *where you are
there is kindness*

Gwyn, Gwynn, Wyn • British/Welsh
• *white, holy, sacred and blond*

Gwynfor • British/Welsh • *a large,
grand man who is sacred, holy,
blessed and fair*

Habacuc, Habakkuk • Biblical/
Jewish/Hebrew • *embrace, a kiss*

Habīb • Arabic • *beloved, adored*

Habimana • Rwandan • *there is God*

Hādi • Arabic • *mentor, guru, reflective and spiritual*

Hai • Chinese • *the sea*

Hamdi • Arabic • *praise be, grateful*

**Handel, Hans, Hans, Hansel,
Johannes** • Germanic • *God is
gracious or gift of God*

Hannibal, Haanbaal • Phoenician
• *I give the Lord grace and favour or
he gives it to me*

Hari • Sanskrit • *pet name for Vishnu
or Krishna, preservation of the
universe*

Harinder • Sikh • *Hari (Vishnu) and
Indra, the supreme God*

Harlan, Harland, Harley • English/
American • *grey rock or fields where
the hares run*

Hartley, Hartleigh • Anglo-Saxon •
*the clearing where the deer feed and
gather*

Hāshim • Arabic • *crusher, breaks
bread*

Hassan, Hasan • Arabic • *a beautiful
and beneficent man*

Heddwyn • British/Welsh • *tranquil*

and peaceful white, fair and sacred
Heilyn, Ynheilio • British/Welsh •
steward, keeper of the cellars
Hemming, Heming • Norse •
*chameleon-like, changes shape to
camouflage*
Heng • Chinese • *eternal, forever*
**Hermenigild, Hermengildo,
Emengildo** • Spanish/Visigothic • *a
total sacrifice*
Hernán, Fernando, Hernando •
Spanish • *a man at peace wherever
he is; always ready and prepared to
travel*
**Hershel, Herschel, Hirsch, Heshel,
Heshi** • Jewish/Yiddish • *a hart, deer
or stag*
Hieronymus, Hieronymos, Jérôme
• Latin/Greek • *I bear a holy name*
Hillel • Jewish/Hebrew • *praise him!*
Hirsh, Hirsch • Jewish/Yiddish • *a
hart, deer or stag*
Hishām • Arabic • *crusher (as in
sacred bread) and giver*
Homer, Homeros • Greek • *possibly
a hostage*
Horace, Horatius, Horatio •
Etruscan • *Roman family name with
no certain root*
Horatio, Horatius, Horace •
Etruscan • *Roman family name with
no certain root*
Hosea • African American •
salvation
**Hugh, Huw, Hugues, Hugo, Aodh,
Hughie, Hewie, Huey, Hewie,
Hughie, Huwie** • Germanic/
Frankish • *heart, mind and spirit*
Hugo, Hugh • Germanic/Frankish/
Latin • *heart, mind and spirit*
Hussein, Husayn • Arabic • *exqui-
site, precious, beautiful*
Hyacinth, Hyakinthos • Greek/

English • *love and passion*
Hyam • Jewish/Hebrew • *a person
who prays for the ill or dying for their
recovery*

Ian, Iain, John • Scots Gaelic •
Biblical • *God is gracious or gift of
God*
**Ianto, Ifan, Ieuan, Iohannes, John,
Iefan, Ioan** • British/Welsh • *God is
gracious or gift of God*
Iarlaithe, Jarlath • Irish • *vague
origins but maybe chief, leader*
Idris • British/Welsh • *a passionate,
loving lord or lord of passion and
desire*
Idrīs • Arabic • *sacred and true,
prophet*
Ifor, Ivor • British/Welsh • *no known
origin*
Igal • Biblical/Jewish/Hebrew •
redeemer
**Ignazio, Ignatius, Ignus, Ignace,
Ignaz, Egnatius, Ignati, Ignacio**
• Latin/Estruscan • *Roman family
name with confused roots*
Ihsān • Arabic • *charitable, giver*
Ilya, Elias, Elijah • Greek/Biblical •
meaning Yahweh is God
Imām • Arabic • *leader and piety*
Indalecio, Indoletius • Latin •
unknown origin
Ingemar, Ingmar • Norse • *famous,
well known to God*
Inigo • Spanish/Basque • *Roman
family name with confused roots*
**Innocenzo, Innocentius, Innocens,
Innokenti, Inocencio** • *innocent,
childlike; many saints and popes
named this*
Iosif, Osip, Joseph • Biblical/Jewish/
Hebrew • *God will add another*
Irvine, Irvin, Erwin, Irving, Israel •

British/Welsh • *fresh, clear water*
**Isaac, Zak, Zac, Zack, Ike, Izaak,
Isak** • Biblical • *unsure roots, probably the hireling or the laugh of a baby*
Isaiah, Izzy, Isaïe • Biblical/Jewish/Hebrew • *God is salvation*
'Isām • Arabic • *protection, keeper of the faith*
Iser, Iserl, Issur • Jewish/Yiddish • *he who strives with God*
Ishmael, Ismā'īl • Arabic • *receiver of the divine spirit; listen to God*
'Ismat • Arabic • *innocent and without sin*
Israel, Jacob • Biblical/Jewish/Hebrew • *he who strives with God*
Ivan, John, Ewan • Russian • *God is gracious or gift of God*

Jabez • Biblical/Jewish/Hebrew • *I bear him with sorrow, sorrowful*
Jābir, Gābir, Jabr, Gabr • Arabic • *compassionate, comforter*
Jack, John, Jankin, Jan, Jehan, James, Jacques, Jock, Jake, Jak, Jac, Jackie, Jackson, Jacky, Jackin • English • *God is gracious or gift of God*
Jada • Biblical/Hebrew/Jewish • *he knows*
Jamāl, Gamāl • Arabic • *beautiful, lovely, with poise*
Jagannath • Sanskrit • *Lord of the World Vishnu, as in sacred Puri*
Jagdish • Sanskrit • *ruler of the world, Brahma, Vishnu and Shiva*
Jahangir • Persian • *he's got the whole world in his hands*
Jake, Jack • English • *God is gracious or gift of God*
Jan, John, Johannes • Germanic/Slavic • *God is gracious or gift of God*

Janmuhammad • Persian • *breath of Muhammed*
Jason, Jayson, Iason • Greek • *healer or he who heals*
Javan, Jevon, Jeavon, Jeevon • Biblical/Hebrew/Jewish • *wine*
Javed • Persian • *eternal*
Jawdat, Gawdat • Arabic • *kindness personified and supreme*
Jean, Jehan, Gene • French • *God is gracious or gift of God*
Jed, Jedidiah, Ged • Biblical/Hebrew/Jewish • *beloved of God*
Jenkin, Jankin, Siencyn • British/Welsh • *God is gracious or gift of God*
Jens, Jons, Johann • Scandinavian • *God is gracious or gift of God*
Jeffrey, Geoffrey, Jeff, Geoff, Jefferson, Jeffery, Jeffry, Jep • Anglo-Saxon • *a stranger in your own land or foreigner who pledges allegiance*
Jeremiah, Jeremy, Jerry, Jem, Gerry, Jeremias • Biblical/Hebrew/Jewish • *appointed by God*
Jeremy, Jem, Jeremiah • Biblical/English • *appointed by God*
Jérôme, Hieronymos, Jerry, Jerrie, Jeri, Jerónimo, Geronimo, Hierosonoma • Greek
Jesús, Joshua • Aramaic/Jewish • *saviour*
Jinān • Arabic • *beautiful gardens, paradise*
Jinhai • Chinese • *golden sea*
Jinjing • Chinese • *golden mirror*
Joe, Jo, Joey • English • *God will add another*
Joachim, Jo, Johoiachin, Joaquin, Jochim, Jochem, Jochen, Joakim, Jokum • Biblical • *created by God*
Job, Joby, Jobey •

Biblical/Jewish/Hebrew
Jody, Jude • American/English •
uncertain root possibly from Jude;
praise
Joël, Yahel • Biblical/Hebrew/Jewish
• *God*
John, Iohannes, Johannes,
Ioannes, Johannán, Johanan, Eóin,
Seán, Ian, Iain, Seathan, Ieuan,
Siôn, Johann, Johannes, Jan, Jens,
Johan, Jons, Jon, Jan, Johan, Jean,
Juan, Joan, Joao, Giovanni, Gianni,
Ioannis, Iannis, Ivan, Juhani, Jussi,
Hannu, Janos, Janis, Johnnie,
Johnny, Jack, Hank, Jonathan,
Johnathan, Jonny, Jon, Johnson,
Juwan, Johnston, Johnstone,
Jones • Biblical/English/Latin • *God*
is gracious or gift of God
Jonathan, Jon, Jonn, Johnny,
Johnnie, Jonathen, Jonathon •
Biblical • *God has given*
Jordan, Judd, Hayarden • Hebrew/
Jewish • *flowing down*
Joseph, Jo, Joey, Jose, Josef, Yosef,
Joe, Jo, Seosamh, Ioseph, Josef,
Jozef, Josep, Giuseppe, Iosif, Josip,
Jooseppi • Biblical/Hebrew/Jewish
• *God shall add another son*
Joshua, Josh • Biblical/Hebrew/
Jewish • *God is my salvation*
Josiah, Josh • Biblical/Hebrew/
Jewish • *God heals*
Jozsef, Osip, Jazeps, Juozapas •
Biblical/Jewish/Hebrew • *God will*
add another son
Jūda, Gūda • Arabic • *goodness and*
kindness transcend all
Judah, Judas • Biblical/Hebrew/
Jewish • *praise*
Jude, Judas • Biblical/Greek • *praise*
Judge, Dayan • Norman/Latin/
Hebrew/Jewish • *a rabbinic judge or*

legal judge
Julián, Jules, Julianus, Julius,
Julyan, Jolyon, Julien, Julio, Jools
• Latin
Junaid • Muslim/Sufi • *in honour of*
a holy mystic
Justin, Justyn, Justinus, Justus,
Iestyn • Latin/English • *a Roman*
name of unsure origins

Kamil, Camillus • Latin • *order of*
monks who nursed the sick
Karam, Karīm • Arabic • *generous,*
magnimous, philanthropic
Kasi • Sanskrit • *radiant; Varanasi or*
Benares, sacred city on the Ganges
Kelly, Ceallach, Ceallaigh •
Irish/English • *fair-haired or monk,*
church, monastery
Kelsey, Ceolsige • Anglo-Saxon •
ship of victory
Kendall, Kendal, Kendale, Kendel,
Kendell, Kendle, Kendyl, Cynddelw
• Anglo-Saxon/British/Welsh •
someone who worships Celtic deities
or a place in Westmorland, Kendal
named after River Kent
Kendrick, Kenrick, Cenric, Ceneric,
Cynwrig, Maceanrig, Cyneric •
British/Welsh/Scots Gaelic • *a*
sacred place high on a hill or son of
Henry or royal power
Kerry, Ceri • English/British/Welsh •
after the Celtic Goddess of Poetry
Kevin, Caioimhin, Keven, Kevan,
Kevyn, Caoimhean • English/
Irish Gaelic • *beloved, beautiful,*
enchanting
Khayrat • Arabic • *good deed, kind*
actions
Khayri • Arabic • *charitable,*
merciful, good
Kjell, Keld, Kjetil, Kjeld, Ketill, Ketil

• sacred kettle or cauldron

Kirk, Kirkja • Norse • *a church or someone who lives near one*

Kilment, Clément, Clemens • Latin • *merciful*

Krishna, Kishen, Kistna • Sanskrit • *black, dark, intense*

Lachlan, Lachlann, Lochlann, Lochlan, Lachie, Lockie, Loughlin, Lochlainn, Lochlainn, Lachlan, Laughlin, Loughlin • Scots Gaelic • *a man from the land of the lochs or Norway*

Lakshman, Laxman • Sanskrit • *the mark of God; most auspicious*

Lal • Sanskrit/Prakrit • *dear, sweet, darling one; king*

Lamont, Lagman, Logmad • Norse • *a man of the law; legal person*

Lancelot, Lance • British/Welsh/Celtic • *unknown origin*

Lazarus, Laz, Lazare, Eleazar, Lazaros, Lazar • Biblical/Greek/Aramaic/Hebrew • *God is my helper*

Leannán, Lennan, Lennon • Irish Gaelic • *fairy lover, fairy darling*

Leberecht • Protestant German • *live your life properly, give it to God*

Lemuel • Hebrew/Jewish • *devoted to God*

Lennon, Leannain • Irish Gaelic • *fairy lover, fairy darling*

Ling • Chinese • *compassionate and understanding*

Lleu, Lugg, Lughus, Lugh • British/Welsh • *dark, bright and shining*

Loyal, Leial, Legalis • Norman/Latin • *keep it legal*

Ludger, Luitger • Friesian • *place name derived from famous monk*

Lyall, Lisle, Liulf • Norse • *vague origins, wolf*

Lycerius, Licerio • Latin • *possibly light or wolf*

Lyle, De L'isle • Norman/Gaelic • *someone from the isles or marshy land*

Madhukar • Sanskrit • *the bee, sweet as honey*

Mahavir • Sanskrit • *great hero, founder of the Jain religion*

Mahendra, Mahinder, Mohinder • Sanskrit • *Great Indra, first great Buddhist missionary*

Mahmūd • Arabic • *respected and laudable*

Mainchín, Mannix • Irish • *monk*

Makarios, Macaire, Macario, Makari • Greek • *blessed one*

Malachi, Malachy, Maoileachlainn • Biblical/Irish Gaelic • *my messenger or follower of St Seachnall or St Secundinus*

Malcolm, Maelcoluim, Maelcoluim • Scots Gaelic • *follower of St Columba, the dove*

Manfred, Manffred, Mainfred, Manfried, Manfredo • Germanic • *man of peace*

Manuel, Emmanuel • Biblical/Spanish • *God is with us or amongst us*

Maoilíosa • Irish Gaelic • *follower of Jesus Christ*

March, Marche, Mensis • Norman • *a person who lives on the borders, the Marches or born in the month of March; named after God of War and Sex, Mars*

Marius • Latin • *Roman family name; clouded meaning but associated with someone of or from the sea*

Masterman • Anglo-Saxon • *a butler*

Mathias, Matthias, Matthaeus, Matthäus, Mattathia • Biblical/ Greek/Jewish/Aramaic/Latin • *gift of God*

Matthew, Matt, Mathew, Mattathia, Maitiu, Matthias, Maitias, Mata, Matha, Matthäus, Matthijs, Mads, Mathies, Mats, Mathieu, Mateo, Mateu, Mateus, Matteo, Mattia, Matvei, Mateusz, Maciej, Matej, Matyas, Matija, Matti, Matyas, Mate, Mattanah, Mattaniah, Mattathah, Mattatha, Mattathiah, Mattathias • Biblical/Hebrew/Jewish/English

Maurice, Moris, Morris, Mo, Maurus, Moritz, Maurizio, Mauricius, Mavriki, Mauricio, Maurits, • Latin • *a dark swarthy person as in a Moor from Arabia*

Mauro • Latin • *a Moor as in Arab; early followers of St Benedictine*

Māzin • Arabic • *origin confused, might come from rain clouds*

Menahem, Mendel, Menachem • Jewish/Yiddish/Germanic • *comforter*

Mendel, Mandel, Menahem, Mandy • Jewish/Yiddish/Germanic

Merdardo • Germanic • *unknown beginning but ends with strong and hardy*

Meredith, Meredydd, Maredudd, Meredudd • uncertain beginning but ends with Lord

Myrddin, Merlyn, Merlin • British/ Welsh • *sea fort or sea hill*

Merrill • Breton Celtic • *bright sea*

Methodius, Mefodi • Greek • *following the path or road, spiritual as much as a traveller*

Meurig, Mauricius, Mouric, Meuric, Maurice • British/Welsh • *a dark*

swarthy person as in a Moor from Arabia

Michael, Micah, Micheal, Meical, Mihangel, Machiel, Mikael, Mikkel, Michel, Miguel, Miquel, Michele, Mikhail, Michal, Mihovil, Mihajlo, Mihael, Mikko, Mihaly, Mike, Mick, Micky, Mikey, Mickey, Meical • Biblical/Hebrew/Jewish/English • *who is like God?*

Michelangelo • Bibilical • *angel*

Mihangel, Michael • British/Welsh • *Michael the Archangel*

Miles, Michael, Milo, Myles, Maoilios • Latin • *soldier of God*

Mingli • Chinese • *lighting up propriety*

Minzhe • Chinese • *sensitive, wise*

Misha, Micha, Mikhail • Russian • *he who is like God*

Mitchell, Michael, Michel, Mitch • Norman/English • *he who is like God*

Mitrofan, Metrophanes • Greek • *vision of the mother Mary*

Mitya, Dmitri • Russian • *follower of the goddess*

Modesto, Modest • Latin • *modest*

Montmorency, Montmaurentius, Monty • Roman/Gaulish/Norman • *the dark hill, possibly linked to Moors or Arabs*

Mordecai, Motke, Motl, Marduk • Biblical/Persian • *he who worships the God of Magic and Water, Marduk*

Morgan, Morgannwg, Morcant • British/Welsh • *vague beginning but ends with ending, completion, full circle*

Morris, Maurice, Mo, Miuris • English/Latin • *a dark swarthy person as in a Moor from Arabia*

Mortimer, Mortemer, Muiriartach •
Norman • *dead sea or stagnant lake*
**Moses, Moshe, Moïse, Moss,
Moses, Mostyn, Monty** • Biblical/
Hebrew/Egyptian • *born of God*
Motke, Mordecai, Motl • Biblical/
Jewish/Yiddish • *he who worships
the God of Magic and Water,
Marduk*
Muhammed • Arabic • *sacred quali-
ties, scrupulous*
Muirgheas, Maurice, Muiris • Irish
Gaelic • *sea choice or choice of seas*
**Muirisartach, Muicheachtach,
Mortime, Murtyr** • *seaman, sailor*
Muhsin • Arabic • *good to others,
compassionate*
Mun'im • Arabic • *charitable, donor*
Murchadh, Murrough • Irish Gaelic
• *sea battle or war*
Murdo, Murdoch, Muireadhach •
Scots Gaelic • *Lord of the Sea*
Mu'tasim • Arabic • *trust in God or
the Lord*
Myron • Greek • *the embalming
spice, myrrh*

Nādir • Arabic • *rare, priceless,
precious*
Nahman, Nahum, Naum • Jewish •
comforter
Nā'il • Arabic • *he who cannot lose,
always comes up smelling of roses*
Nāji, Nāgi • Arabic • *rescued and
saved*
Naoise • Irish • *vague; in legend the
lover of Deirdre was Naoise*
Napoleon, Napoleone • Italian •
*unsure origin; may mean sons of the
mist or the Naples Lion*
**Narcissus, Narkissos, Narcisse,
Narciso** • Greek/Latin • *linked with
the daffodil but unsure origins*

Narendra • Sanskrit • *shaman,
witchdoctor, doctor king*
Nataraj • Sanskrit • *Lord of the
Dance*
Nathan, Nat, Jonathan, Nathen •
Biblical/Hebrew/Jewish • *God has
given*
**Nathaniel, Nat, Nathanael,
Natanaele** • Biblical/Greek/English
• *God has given*
Nazaire, Nazarius, Nazario • Latin •
Nazareth, Jesus Christ's home town
Neopmuk • Czech • *someone
from the town of Pomuk; St John of
Pomuk, patron saint of Bohemia,
especially 20th March*
Nerio, Nereus • Greek • *sea god*
Nestor, Nestore • Greek • *personal
name of King of Pylos, in legend one
of the Greeks (bearing gifts!) at Troy*
Niall, Neal, Neale, Nile, Niles, Neil
• Gaelic • *passionate, champion,
winner, dead sexy, really desirable;
some say it means a cloudy man*
Niaz • Persian • *prayer, gift, sacrifice*
Nikita, Aniketos • Greek/Russian
• *unconquered; name of Orthodox
saint*
Ninian, Ninianus, Ninnyaw •
British/Welsh • *unsure origins*
Nino, Giannino • Latin/Spanish •
the boy, referring to the Christ Child
Nizār • Arabic • *confused origin;
might mean small or little one*
Njord, Nerthus • Norse • *Norse God
of Sea and Fertility*
Noah, Nahum, Noë • Biblical/
English • *to rest*
Nolasco • Latin • *personal name
honouring the man who rescued the
Christians from the Moslems during
the Crusade*
Norbert, Nordberht • Germanic • *a*

bright light from the north, northern lights (Aurora Borealis)
Nyabera • Kenyan • *the good one*

Obadiah, Abdullah • Biblical/ Hebrew/Jewish • *servant of God*
Obed • Hebrew/Jewish • *God's servant*
Ocean • modern English • *the ocean*
Oisín, Ossian, Osheen • Irish Gaelic • *stag*
Olijimi • Nigerian • *God gave me this*
Onofre • Egyptian • *a man who opens up to God*
Ophelos, Ofelos • Greek • *help!*
Osbert, Osbeorht • Anglo-Saxon • *illuminated by God, famous for his devotion*
Oscar, Oskar • Irish • *friend of wild-life, especially deer and stags*
Osian, Oisín, Ossian, Oisein • Gaelic • *stag*
Osmond, Osmund, Oz • Anglo-Saxon • *God is my protector*
Oswald, Osweald, Oz, Ozzy, Osvaldo • Anglo-Saxon • *my ruler is God or God rules*
Oswin, Oswine, Oz • Anglo-Saxon • *God is my friend*
Ove, Aghi • Norse • *frightened or in awe of a weapon of terror*
Ozzy, Oz, Ozzie • Anglo-Saxon • *clipped version of any name begin-ning with Os, meaning God*

Paderau • modern Welsh • *a rosary*
Padma • Sanskrit • *lotus position, the chakra*
Palmer • English • *a pilgrim who'd been to the Holy Land and returned with a palm branch*
Palmiro, Palmiere • Latin/Spanish • *a pilgrim who brought back a palm*

from the Holy Land
Paris, Parisii • Latin/Celtic • *member of the Parisii tribe, origins unknown*
Pascal, Paschalis, Pascha, Pasquale, Pascual • Latin/French • *pascal lamb; Easter time*
Pàrlan, Párthalán • Gaelic • *uncer-tain origin may be linked to Irish for Bartholomew*
Pelayo, Pelagios, Pelagius, Pelagos • Greek • *the wide and open seas*
Pepe, Pepito, Joseph, José • Spanish • *God is my salvation*
Peregrine, Peregrinus, Perry, Pellegrino • Latin • *stranger, wanderer, foreigner*
Pesah, Pesach, Pascal • Hebrew/ Jewish • *Passover*
Philbert, Filaberht, Philibert, Filbert • Greek/Germanic/Frankish • *dear, beloved*
Phoenix, Phoinix • Latin/Greek • *mythical bird that represents rebirth or reincarnation*
Pontius, Ponzio, Poncio • Latin • *family name, origin unknown*
Porfirio, Porphyrios, Porphyrius, Porphyra, Porfirio • Greek • *the colour purple*
Pradbodh • Sanskrit • *springtime; awakening of nature, flowers*
Prasad • Sanskrit • *by the grace of God, gifts from the deity to the worshippers*
Primitivo, Primitivus • Latin • *the first, earliest saints or martyrs*
Primo, Primus • Latin • *numero uno, number one!*
Prokhoros, Prokhor • Greek • *very artistic, chief of a troupe of singers, dancers, actors*
Pryderi • British/Welsh • *a carer, someone who is anxious*

Purushottam • Sanskrit • *divine being*

Qāsim • Arabic • *giver*
Qi • Chinese • *enlightened, wonderment and intellectual*
Qianfan • Chinese • *thousand sails*
Qingshan • Chinese • *celebrating goodness*
Qiqiang • Chinese • *enlightenment and strength*
Qiu • Chinese • *autumn or fall (southern hemisphere)*
Quirce, Quiricus • Latin • *name of a three-year-old child martyred with his mother in Tarsus AD 304*
Qusay • Arabic • *vague origin but could mean someone who comes from a long way away*

Ra'fat • Arabic • *mercy, compassion, forgiveness*
Rajanikant • Sanskrit • *beloved of the night*
Rajiv • Sanskrit • *striped and/or the blue lotus*
Ram, Rama, Ramu, Ramakrishna, Ramgopal, Ramnarayan • Sanskrit • *nice, lovely, kind*
Ramesh • Sanskrit • *night-time tranquillity and serenity; sleep*
Raphael, Rafael, Rafa, Rapha, Raffaele • Biblical/Jewish/Hebrew • *God has healed*
Rashād, Rashīd • Arabic • *spiritual or religious wisdom*
Rastus, Erastus • Biblical/Greek • *beloved*
Ra'ūf • Arabic • *caring and compassionate*
Rearden, Ríordan, Rordan, Ríoghbhardán • English/Irish Gaelic • *wee poet king*

Rémy, Remigius, Remi, Remigio, Remix • Latin • *oarsman or man at the tiller*
Renato, Renatus • Latin • *reborn*
René, Renatus, Renato • Latin • *reborn; resurrected*
Rida • Arabic • *affirmation, validation by God (Allah); contented*
Ríordan, Rearden, Ríoghbhardán • Irish • *poet king or king of the poets*
Rocco, Rokko, Roc, Rokko, Rocky, Rok, Rocky, Roche, Roch, Roque • Germanic • *rest*
Rogelio, Rogelius, Rogellus • Latin • *unknown origin, maybe request*
Rohan • Sanskrit • *ascension, healing, medicine*
Romeo, Romaeus • Latin • *a pilgrim who has visited Rome*
Rónán • Irish Gaelic • *sealion*
Roscoe, Raskog • Norse • *the wood where the doe and deer gather*
Ru • Chinese • *Confucian scholar*
Rune, Runi, Runolf, Run • Norse • *named after the Norse magical alphabet*

Sachdev • Sanskrit • *truth of God, totally honest*
Salāh • Arabic • *righteous and devout religiously*
Sālih • Arabic • *devout, devoted*
Salvatore, Salvator, Salvador, Sal • Latin
Samīr, Sameer • Arabic • *confidant at night, a night conversation*
Samuel, Shemuel, Shaulmeel, Sam, Sammy, Sawyl • Biblical/Hebrew/Jewish • *name of God, God has heard, listen to God*
Sancho, Sanctus • Latin/Spanish • *holy*
Sanford, Stanford, Stamford •

Anglo-Saxon
Santos • Roman Catholic • *saints*
Saul • Biblical/Hebrew/Latin • *asked for, prayed for, yearned for*
Seathan, Jean, Jehan • Scots Gaelic/French/Biblical/English/Latin
Serge, Sergio, Sergius • Latin/Etruscan • *old Roman family name of unsure roots*
Sergei, Serzha • Russian/Etruscan • *old Roman name of vague roots*
Sgàire, Skari • Scots Gaelic/Norse • *a seabird that mews like a cat!*
Shafīq • Arabic • *compassionate*
Shah • Muslim/Persian/Sufi • *king, God, lord, emperor, divine mystic*
Shamīm • Arabic • *a very precious fragrant person*
Shankar, Sankar • Sanskrit • *confers welfare, to look after*
Shen • Chinese • *intense, deep and wary*
Shining • Chinese • *let the world be at peace*
Shiva • Sanskrit • *beautiful, timely, death and regeneration*
Shukri • Arabic • *giving thanks*
Shyam • Sanskrit • *dark, black and handsome, sexy*
Simran • Sikh • *he who meditates, yogic*
Sirideán • Irish Gaelic • *unsure roots; likely to be someone who seeks*
Skipper, Schipper • Dutch/Scandinavian • *boss, ship's captain or someone who skips across ships*
Sly • American English • *a person who is full of guile and basically sly as a fox!*
Solomon, Shlomo, Sol, Solly, Saloman • Biblical/Hebrew/Jewish • *peace*

Sondre, Sindri • Norse/Norwegian • *no known origins but in Norse mythology a magical dwarf*
Spiridion • Greek/Latin • *soul*
Srikant • Sanskrit • *beloved of Sri, Goddess of Light, Beauty and Wealth*
Sriram • Sanskrit • *devotee or worshipper of the Lord Rama*
Stacey, Eustace • English/Greek • *confused roots; could mean juicy, tasty grapes!*
Stafford • Anglo-Saxon • *the river ford good for landing*
Stuart, Stewart, Stu, Stew • French • *primarily a surname given to a person who served as a steward in a big house, manor or palace*
Suleimān, Sulaymān • Biblical/Arabic • *peace*
Swapan • Sanskrit • *sleep, perchance to dream*
Svyatoslav, Syvantoslav • Slavic • *sacred glory*

Tad, Tadhg, Thaddeus, Tig, Tim, Taddeo, Teague, Teigue, Tadeo • Irish Gaelic • *poet, wise man, philosopher*
Tāha • Arabic • *opening letters of the 20th sura in the Koran*
Tao • Chinese • *great waves*
Taqi • Arabic • *God-fearing*
Tara • Sanskrit • *shining light for the saviour; carrying the Lord*
Tavares • African American • *unknown origin*
Tarquin, Tarquinius • Etruscan • *Roman family name with no known root*
Tarun, Taroon • Sanskrit • *dawn, the early sun, young, tender growth of love and romance*
Tasgall, Taskill, Asketill • Norse •

the sacred pot or cauldron
Tate • English • *a personal name from medieval times, no known root*
Tegan, Teg • British/Welsh • *a rather lovely or beautiful person*
Télésphore, Telesforo, Telephoros • Greek • *fulfilment, completion, conclusion*
Teodosio • Greek • *God-given*
Thaddeus, Labbaeus, Theodoras, Theodotos, Thad, Tad • Biblical/Aramaic/Greek • *given by God or God's gift*
Theo, Théodore, Theobald, Theodor, Teodoro • Greek • *God*
Theo, Ted, Teddy, Theodor, Theodoor, Teodor, Teodoro, Feodor, Fyodr, Teuvo, Tivador, Todor, Teodors, Theodoric, Tiobad, Ted, Teddy, Edward, Theodos, Theodosios, Teodosio, Todos, Theodoros • Greek • *God-given or giving to God or God's*
Timothy, Tim, Tadhg, Timmy, Timotheus, Timotheos, Timetheo, Timmy, Tiger, Timothee, Timo, Timoteo, Timofei • Biblical/Latin/Greek • *honour God*
Tirso, Thyrsos • Oriental • *follower of Dionysus (Bacchus)*
Titus, Tito, Tiziano, Titianus, Titian • Latin • *old Roman name, unknown origins*
Tobias, Tobiah, Tobijah, Toby • Biblical/Hebrew/Greek • *God is good*
Tochukwa • Nigerian • *praise God*
Tony, Anthony, Tone, Tönjes, Antonius, Tonio • Estruscan/Roman • *Roman family name but with confused origins*
Torcall, Torquil • Norse • *the sacrificial or sacred cauldron of Thor, the*

God of Thunder
Toribio, Turibius • Latin/Spanish • *unknown roots, very local Iberian name*
Toussaint • French • *tous les saints; a child who has the blessings of all the saints*
Traugott • Germanic • *trust in God*
Tulsi • Sanskrit • *the herb, basil; so holy; is also a goddess*
Tyson, Ty, Tison • Greek/Norman • *girl's name for Dionysius (yes, this is the boy's list!), God of Wine or meaning a hot-tempered person*

Ugo, Hugo, Hugh • Germanic • *heart, mind and spirit*
Uzziah, Uziah • Biblical/Jewish/Hebrew • *power of Yahweh*
Uzziel, Uziel • Biblical/Jewish/Hebrew • *power of God*

Vadim, Vladimir • Russian • *origin unknown*
Vanya, Ivan • Russian • *God is gracious or gift of God*
Vergil, Virgil • Latin • *family name with confused origins; could refer to Virgo the maiden or virga as in stick*
Virgil, Vergilius, Virgilius, Vergil, Virgilio, Vigil • Latin • *Roman family name Vergilius but confusion reigned when the spelling was changed to Virgilius, which means the maiden or virga as in stick*
Vissarion, Bessarion • Greek • *origins vague*

Wade, Wadan, Wada, Gewaed • Anglo-Saxon • *a ford, as in river, to wade across*
Wahīb • Arabic • *philanthropist, giver, donor, benefactor*

Wā'il • Arabic • *reverts to the faith* (*Islam*)

Wencheng • Chinese • *refined, elegant and accomplished*

Wenyan • Chinese • *refined, chic, chaste and gifted*

Whitney, Whiteney • Anglo-Saxon • *the white island*

Wilfrid, Wilfrit, Walfrid, Wilfrey, Wilf, Wilfried, Vilfred • Germanic • *the will for peace*

Willoughby, Weligbyr • Anglo-Saxon/Norse • *the village by the willow tree*

Wolfgang, Wolf, Volf • Germanic • *where the wolf goes*

Wynfor, Wyn • British/Welsh • *white, blonde, holy, blessed*

Wynne, Wyn, Wine, Wynn • British Welsh/Anglo-Saxon

Xiu • Chinese • *graceful, cultivated*

Xolani • Xhosa South Africa • *please forgive*

Yahya, John • Arabic/Biblical • *God is gracious or gift of God*

Yakim, Akim • *created by God*

Yashpal • Sanskrit • *cherishes splendour*

Yasīn • Arabic • *opening letters of the 36th sura of the Koran*

Yehiel, Jehiel • Biblical/Hebrew/Jewish • *God lives*

Yigael • Jewish/Hebrew • *he shall be redeemed*

Yitzhak, Isaac • Jewish/Hebrew • *unsure roots, probably the hireling or the laugh of a baby*

Yongnian • Chinese • *eternity, forever*

Yongrui • Chinese • *eternally or forever lucky*

Yongzheng • Chinese • *eternally; forever scrupulous and conscientious*

Yoram • Biblical/Jewish/Hebrew • *Yahweh is high*

Yorath, Iorwerth • British/Welsh • *a handsome, beautiful lord or chief*

Yosef, Joseph, Yūsuf • Jewish/Hebrew/Arabic • *God is my salvation*

Yuan, Juan, John • Manx Gaelic • *God is gracious or gift of God*

Yūnis, Younis, Jonah • Arabic/Biblical • *dove*

Yūsuf, Joseph • Arabic/Biblical • *God is my salvation*

Zachary, Zach, Zak • Greek/English/Biblical • *God has remembered*

Zacharias, Zak, Zechariah, Zachariah, Zakaria, Zach • Biblical/Jewish/Hebrew • *God has remembered*

Zadok • Biblical/Jewish/Hebrew • *just or righteous*

Zakariyya, Zakariya • Biblical/Arabic • *God has remembered*

Zane • American English • *unknown roots of British surname*

Zeb, Zebedee, Zebulun • Biblical/Hebrew/Greek • *gift of Jehovah*

Zebadiah, Zabdi, Zabadiah, Zebedee • Biblical/Hebrew/Jewish • *living with, to dwell, Yahweh has given*

Zabulun, Zabulon, Zebulon, Zabal • Biblical/Hebrew/Jewish • *exaltation*

Zechariah • Biblical/Jewish/Hebrew • *God has remembered*

Zed, Zedekiah • Biblical/Jewish/Hebrew • *justice of Yahweh*

Zeke, Ezekiel • Biblical/Jewish/

Hebrew • *God gives me strength*
Zeno, Zenon • Greek • *Zeus or Jupiter*
Zenodoros • Greek • *gift of Zeus/Jupiter*

Zephaniah, Zep • Biblical/Jewish/ Hebrew • *hidden by God*
Zian • Chinese • *peaceful soul*

Girls

Abīr • Arabic • *fragrant*

Abital, Avital • Biblical/Jewish/ Hebrew • *dewy and moist*

Abla • Arabic • *voluptuous*

Acacia, Akakia, Wattle • Greek/ Latin • *acacia wood, holy wood that had special powers as a hex against evil*

Addolorata • Italian • *Our Lady (Virgin Mary) of Sorrows*

Adria, Adrianne, Adrienne, Adrianna, Adriana, Adrienne • Latin • *person from Hadria after which the Adriatic Sea is named*

Aeronwen • British/Welsh • *white, sacred and fair*

Afāf • Arabic • *chasity, refinement, elegance*

Africa • Latin • *the dark continent*

Agnès, Aggie, Aigneis, Inés, Agnese, Agnessa, Agnieszka, Anezka, Aune, Agnese, Agne, Annis, Annys, Annice, Aigneis, Agnethe, Agnetis, Agnete, Ågot • Greek • *pure and holy*

Aileen, Eileen, Ailie • Irish Gaelic • *desired by others*

Aimee, Aimi • French • *beloved one*

Áine • Irish • *as bright, as radiant as the Queen of the Faeries*

Aingeal • Irish • *angel*

Aisling, Aislin, Aislinn • *she who has visionary dreams*

Alaina, Alana, Alayna, Alanna, Alannah, Alanah, Allana, Alanda, Alanis, Ailin • Gaelic • *vague origins but likely to be a rock*

Alba • Latin/Germanic • *white or elfin*

Alfreda, Freddie, Fred • Anglo- Saxon • *supernatural, faerie counsel, help*

Aloisa, Aloisia • Latin/Germanic • *all-seeing wisdom*

Allana, Alana • Gaelic • *vague origins but likely to be a rock*

Aloisia • Provençal/Latin/Germanic • *all-wise, all-seeing*

Althea, Althaia • Greek • *uncertain origin*

Amāni • Arabic • *desire, passion*

Amparo • Roman Catholic/Spanish • *may the Virgin Mary protect me and all Christians*

Amrit • Sanskrit • *divine, immortal, good enough to eat*

Amy, Amie, Aimie, Aimee • Norman • *beloved*

Anais, Ana, Anya • Biblical/Catalan/ Provençal • *God has favoured me*

Anastasis, Anastasia • Greek/ Russian • *resurrection*

Angel, Ángela, Angelina, Angeline, Angie, Ange, Angelos • Greek • *messenger of God*

Angela, Angelita • Latin/Greek • *messenger of God*

Ángeles • Spanish/Roman Catholic • *Our Lady of the Angels*

Angelica, Angélique, Angelika • Latin • *a girl of the angels*

Angosto • Spanish/Galician/Roman Catholic • *Our lady of Angosto, a place where the Virgin appeared*

Angustias • Spanish/Roman Catholic • *Our Lady of Sufferings*

Anita, Ana • Spanish/ Biblical • *God has favoured me*

Anitra • literary invention • *created by Henrik Ibsen as the name of an Arabic princess in* Peer Gynt

Ann, Anne, Anna, Annabel, Annette, Annetta, Anouk, Anni,

Annelie, Anneli, Annella, Annabell, Annabella, Annabelle, Belle, Annie, Anna, Anneke, Anke, Anoushka, Anouska, Arabella, Arabel Anna, Ana • Biblical/Jewish/Hebrew • *God has favoured me*

Annalisa, Annaliesa, Annalise, Annelise, Annelies, Anneli • German • *combo of Anne and Elisabeth; God has favoured me and God is my oath*

Anneka, Anika, Annika, Anna, Anniken • German/Dutch • *God has favoured me*

Annemarie, Annmarie, Annamarie, Annamaria • modern • *combo of Anne and Maria; God has favoured me*

Anona, Annona • Latin • *unsure root but possibly corn supply*

Antonia, Anthonia • Estruscan/Roman • *Roman family name but with confused origins*

Antoinette, Toinette, Tonette, Antonella, Antonia, Toni, Antonina • Estruscan/Roman • *Roman family name but with confused origins*

Anuradha • Sanskrit • *Stream of Oblations, 28th asterism of Hindu astrology*

Anwen, Annwen • British/Welsh • *blessed and beautiful*

Anwyl, Annwyl • British/Welsh • *beloved, darling, dear*

Aparición • Roman Catholic • *Christ's appearance to the disciples after Easter's resurrection*

Aphra, Afra • Latin • *a woman from Africa, the dark continent*

Araceli • Spanish/Latin American • *the sky is an altar to God*

Aranrhod • British/Welsh • *huge, big, round, plump and humped!*

Ariadne, Arianna, Ariana, Arianne • Greek/Cretean • *most holy*

Arlene, Arleen, Arline, Marlene, Charlene • American English • *unknown origin*

Arlette • Germanic/Norman • *uncertain roots but possibly eagle*

Åsa, Ase • Norse • *God*

Asha • Sanskrit • *hope*

Aisling, Aishling • Irish Gaelic • *a dream, vision or premonition*

Aslög, Asslaug, Åslaug • Swedish • *God-consecrated*

Aubree • Germanic/Anglo-Saxon/Latin • *she who has the power of the faeries*

Ava, Avaline, Aveline, Avelina, Evelyn, Eveline, Avila, Avis, Avice • Greek • *desired*

Aveline, Eibhlín, Ailbhilin, Ellin, Eileen • French/Irish Gaelic • *desired by others*

Avery • Norman/Anglo-Saxon • *supernatural, faerie favours*

Avis, Aveza • Germanic/Norman • *unknown root*

'Awātif • Arabic • *affectionate and tender*

Bay, Baie, Baca, Bacca • Latin/Norman • *bay tree*

Beata, Beate • Swiss • *blessed*

Beatrice, Beatrix, Bea, Bee, Beattie, Beatriz, Beitiris, Betrys, Viatrix, Viator, Beatus • blessed through life

Becca, Beck, Becky, Bekki, Rébecca • Biblical/Jewish/Aramaic • *unknown origins; many suggestions, from cattle stall to snare*

Benedicta, Benedicte, Benita • Latin • *blessed*

Bess, Bessie, Bet, Beth, Elizabeth, Elisabeth, Bethan, Betsy, Betty,

Bette, Bettina, Buffy, Beitidh, Elisheba • Hebrew/Greek • *God is my oath or God is my abundance*

Bethan, Beth • British/Welsh • *God is my oath or God is my abundance*

Blaise, Blaize • Latin/French • *to limp, limping*

Blodwen, Blodwyn, Blod • British/Welsh • *sacred, holy flowers*

Branwen, Bronwen, Brangwen • British/Welsh • *raven or beast that is holy, sacred and white*

Brenna, Braonan • American English/Irish Gaelic • *descendant of Braonan; personal name moist, droplet of water*

Bridget, Briget, Bridgid, Brigid, Biddy, Bride, Bridy, Bridie, Bridey, Brigitte, Britt, Brighid, Birgit, Brigette, Birgitta, Brigitta, Bedelia, Bríd, Breda, Breeda, Bree, Brighe, Brídín, Bri, Brighida, Berit, Britta, Birgitte, Birthe, Birte, Ffraid • Irish Gaelic • *the exalted one*

Brónach, Bronagh • Irish Gaelic • *sad and sorrowful*

Bushra • Arabic • *happy news, glad tidings and fine omen*

Calaminag, Calumina, Columbine, Columba • Scots Gaelic • *dove*

Calista, Callie, Callie, Calixta, Calixtus • Latin • *cup as in a Christian chalice or holy grail*

Caoimhe, Keeva • Irish Gaelic • *full of grace, very lovely and so tender*

Caris, Charis, Karis, Carissa • Greek • *grace*

Carmel, Carmella, Carmelina, Camelita, Carmen, Carmine, Carmela • Roman Catholic • *Our Lady of Carmel, the mountain where early Christians lived as hermits and later became the Carmelite order of monks*

Casilda • Spanish • *unsure origins; an 11th-century Moorish saint, she lived in Toledo*

Cassandra, Cassie, Kassie, Cass, Cassy, Cassidy • Greek mythology • *a woman who could see into the future but no one ever believed her*

Cecilia, Cécile, Cecily, Cecelia, Cissie, Cissey, Sessy, Sissi, Sissy, Cecille, Cecilie, Cacille, Cacilia, Caecilia, Cicely • Latin/English • *old Roman family name Caecilius, from the Latin, meaning blind*

Ceinwen • British/Welsh • *lovely, beautiful, sacred and white*

Ceri, Kerry • British/Welsh • *romantic, holy and beautiful*

Ceridwen, Ceridwynn, Ceri • British/Welsh • *goddess of poetry*

Chalice • Latin • *cup as in a Christian chalice or holy grail*

Chanel, Chanelle, Shanelle • French/Modern • *in honour of Gabrielle CoCo Chanel, founder of the perfume house*

Chantal, Chantelle, Shantell • French • *in honour of St Jeanne-Françoise, a woman of great charity and virtue who married the Baron de Chantal; when he died she adopted a severe religious life following St Francis of Sales*

Chardonnay • modern French/English • *a variety of grape that makes the wine Chardonnay*

Charis, Karis, Caris, Clarissa, Charisse • Greek • *grace*

Charisma, Karrisma, Kharisma • Greek • *spiritual blessings*

Charity, Caridad, Caritas, Carus • Latin • *dear charity; humanitarian*

Cherie, Cheri, Cherie, Cheree, Sheree, Querida • French • *darling*

Chevonne, Siobhán, Shivaun • English/American/Irish Gaelic • *God is gracious or gift of God*

Chorine, Choreen, Corinne, Corinna • French • *chorus or dancing girl*

Chunhua • Chinese • *spring flower*

Christine, Christiana, Chris, Chrissy, Christianne, Christina, Cristina, Kristina, Chriselda, Chrissie, Christa, Christabel, Christabella, Christabelle, Cristobel, Christobel, Christelle, Christella, Christel, Christene, Christeen, Cristina, Cairistine, Cairistiòna, Crystin • Scots Gaelic/Latin • *follower of Christ*

Christian, Christiane, Christiana, Anna, Christie, Christy, Kristy, Christina, Chris, Tina, Cristiona, Cairistiòna, Stineag, Cairistine, Crystin, Kristin, Kristina, Kerstin, Kirsten, Krzystyna, Kirsti, Kirsty, Krisztiana, Krisztina • Scots Gaelic/Latin • *follower of Christ*

Ciorstaidh, Ciostag, Kirsty, Kirstie, Chirsty, Curstaidh, Curstag • Scots Gaelic/Scandinavian/Latin • *follower of Christ*

Clelia, Cloelia • Latin • *a heroine part true, part fantasy; she was a hostage who escaped back to Rome by swimming the River Tiber*

Clémentine, Clem, Clemmie • Latin/French • *merciful, gentle, compassionate*

Clemency, Clemencie, Clementis • Latin • *leniency and mercy*

Cody, Codi, Codie, Codee, Codey, Cuidightheach • Irish Gaelic/American English • *descendant of*

Cuidightheach, a helpful and caring person

Columbina, Columbine, Bina, Binnie, Colimbina, Colombe • Latin • *dove*

Coral, Corallia, Coralie, Corallium • Latin/Jewish • *beautiful pink underwater mineral found in reefs in warm waters*

Corazón • Roman Catholic • *sacred heart, the heart of Jesus Christ*

Cruz • Roman Catholic • *cross, meaning Mary, Christ's mother, in agony at the foot of the cross; her son's crucifixion*

Dagmar • Slavic/Danish • *combo of peace, day, dear, maiden*

Dáireann, Doreen, Dorind, Dorinda, Dorean • Irish Gaelic • *vague origins but maybe the daughter of Finn*

Damayanti • Sankrit • *she has a hold over men, she can sedate them*

Damhnait, Davnat, Damh • *fawn, stag or deer*

Daniella, Danielle, Danya, Daniele, Daniela • Biblical/Hebrew/Jewish

Danya, Donya • American English/Biblical/Hebrew/Jewish • *God is my judge*

Dareen, Darrene • American/English • *unknown origins*

Davina, Davida, Davena, Davinia • Biblical/Hebrew • *vague origins but possibly from a baby word meaning darling one*

Deirbhile, Dervilla, Derfile, Deirbhail • Irish • *daughter of Fal or the poet*

Delice, Delyse, Delicia, Delysia, Delicae, Delicius, Delite, Delicia • Latin • *angel delight!*

Delilah, Delila • Biblical • *uncertain origins*

Delmar, Delma, Fidelma, Delamar • Spanish American • *of the sea*

Delwyn • British/Welsh • *pretty, love, pure, sacred*

Dena, Dina • Anglo-Saxon

Denise, Denese, Denice, Deneze, Deniece, Dionysia • Greek • *Dionysus, God of Wine, Orgies and Partying*

Deòiridh, Dorcas • Gaelic • *pilgrim*

Desiree, Desire • Latin • *longed for!*

Devin, Damhan, Damhain • Irish Gaelic • *descendant of Damhan, connected to the fawn or deer*

Dietlind • Germanic • *tender, soft and kind; people love her*

Dilwen • British/Welsh • *white, fair, true, genuine and sacred*

Dija, Deja • French • *already seen*

Dīma • Arabic • *monsoon, deluge*

Diva, Divine • Italian • *goddess!*

Dolores, Deloris, Delores, Doloris, Lola, Lolita, Dolly • Roman Catholic • *Our Lady of the Seven Sorrows of the Virgin*

Dolly, Dorothy, Dolores, Dora • English/Greek • *gift from God*

Dominica, Dominique, Dominga • Latin/Roman Catholic • *Lord, as in St Dominic, founder of the Dominican order*

Donatella, Donatus • Latin • *given by God*

Dorcas, Tabitha, Deòiridh • Greek • *fawn, doe, gazelle, antelope*

Dorothea, Dorothy, Dorothee, Dorothie, Dot, Dottie, Dotty, Dodie, Dolly, Dorofei, Dorotheos, Dorete, Dee • Greek • *gift from God*

Du'ā • Arabic • *prayer and worship*

Dulcie, Dowse, Dulcia, Dulcis • Latin • *sweet*

Dylanne • British/Welsh • *sea*

Dymphna, Damhnait, Dympna • Irish/Flemish • *uncertain origins; fawn or deer*

Echo, Ekho • Greek • *a word that has come to mean a nymph who pined after the beautiful boy Narcissus, who was only interested in himself; as a result she was left with nothing but her voice*

Eglantine, Aiglent • English • *sweetbriar*

Eiddwen, Eiddunwen • British/Welsh • *fond, passionate, desire, holy, white, fair*

Eileen, Aileen, Eibhlín, Eilín • Norman French • *desired by others*

Eilwen, Aelwen • British/Welsh • *white, sacred, fair brow*

Eimear, Émer, Eimh • Irish Gaelic • *vague origins but comes from the word for swift, the bird, describing a person who is fast and quick*

Eleri • British/Welsh • *unknown root; might be a river name*

Elreen, Eirene, Irène • Greek • *peace*

Elaine, Helen, Elain, Elayne, Eliana • British/Welsh • *hind, fawn, doe*

Elfriede, Adalfrid, Elfreda • Germanic • *peace is noble*

Elizabeth, Elisabeth, Elisheba, Elise, Eliza, Elisa, Elsa, Liza, Lisa, Liz, Beth, Bet, Bess, Lisbet, Lisbeth, Lysbeth, Elsie, Bessie, Bessy, Betty, Betsy, Tetty, Libby, Lizzie, Lizzy, Buffy, Eilis, Ealasaid, Elisabet, Elisabete, Elisabetta, Elisavet, Yelizaveta, Elzbieta, Alzbeta, Elizabeta, Erzsebet, Elspeth, Eliza • Biblical/Hebrew/Jewish • *God is my oath*

Elisha, Eleesha • Jewish/Hebrew • *Yahweh is God*

Elkan, Elkie, Elkanah • Jewish/ Hebrew • *possessed by God*

Ellis • Biblical/Greek • *Yahweh is God*

Elma • American English • *combo of Elizabeth and Mary*

Éloise, Héloïse, Elouise • Germanic/ Frankish • *uncertain origin*

Elspeth, Elsbeth, Elspie, Elsie, Elspet, Elizabeth • Scots English/ Biblical • *God is my oath*

Eluned, Eiluned, Luned, Lunet, Lunete, Eilun • British/Welsh • *icon, image*

Elvina, Alvina • Anglo-Saxon • *elfin, noble or faerie friend*

Élise, Elyse, Elysia, Alicia, Elisabeth • Biblical/French • *God is my oath*

Emeny, Emonie, Ismene • Germanic/Greek mythology • *uncertain roots*

Encarnación, Incarnatio • Roman Catholic • *incarnation of Jesus Christ*

Engracia, Enkrates, Encratis, Encratia, Gratia • Latin • *grace*

Enid • British/Welsh • *unknown root*

Ennis, Enis, Innis, Inis, Ynys • Irish Gaelic • *island*

Ermengild, Ermengildo, Irmengild • French/Visigothic

Ermintrude, Trude, Trudy • Germanic/Frankish • *you are my entire world, my beloved*

Esperanza, Sperantia • Latin • *hope*

Evadne • Greek • *well, good, fine, but the final suffix is confused in origin*

Evelyn, Éibhleann, Aibhilin • Irish Gaelic/English • *desired by others*

Fadīla • Arabic • *a moral, ethical, virtuous woman*

Faith • English • *she who trusts in God, faithful follower*

Fakhriyya • Arabic • *this woman is glorious and expects nothing for nothing; everything is unconditional*

Fang • Chinese • *fragrant*

Farida • Arabic • *a gem, a precious stone*

Fathiyya • Arabic • *liberation!*

Fātima • Arabic/Muslim/Roman Catholic • *abstainer from all bad or wicked things; mother*

Fay, Fae, Faye • English • *fairy or prescient*

Fiedhelm, Fedelma, Fidelma • Irish • *unknown origin but name given to a beautiful Irish Bouddicca*

Fenfang • Chinese • *perfumed, aromatic*

Fern, Fearn • Anglo-Saxon • *the plant that repels evil spirits*

Fifi, Joséphine • French/Biblical/ Hebrew/Jewish • *short name for Joséphine, meaning God is my salvation*

Freda, Frederica, Freddie, Frieda, Elfreda, Winifred, Frederika, Friede, Friederike • *peace*

Friedelinde • Germanic • *soft, tender, gentle and peaceful*

Frume, Fromm • Jewish/Yiddish • *pious, devout and virtuous*

Fulvia, Fulvius • Latin • *an old Roman family name meaning dark, dusky, exotic*

Gabrielle, Gabriella, Gabi, Gaby, Gabby, Gabriel, Gabriele, Gabriela • Biblical/Hebrew/Jewish • *person of God*

Galia • Jewish/Hebrew • *wave*

Garnet, Grenate, Granatum • Norman/Latin • *either a dealer in pomegranates or the precious stone*

Gemma, Jemma • Italian • *precious jewel*

Genette, Jeanette • Biblical/English/Latin • *God is gracious or gift of God*

Ghāda • Arabic • *young, graceful, refined woman*

Ghadīr • Arabic • *stream, brook, watercourse*

Ghufrān • Arabic • *forgiveness*

Gilda • Germanic • *sacrifice*

Ginny, Jane, Ginnie, Jinny • Biblical/English/Latin • *pet name for Virginia or Jane; God is gracious or gift of God*

Gioconda, Jucunda • Latin • *happy, jovial, jocund*

Giovanna • Biblical/English/Latin • *LADY John! God is gracious or gift of God*

Gislög, Gisillaug, Gislaug • Norse • *sacred hostage*

Giuseppina • Biblical/Italian • *LADY Joseph! God is my salvation*

Gladys, Gwladys, Gwladus • British/Welsh • *uncertain origin, but said to be a local form of Claudia*

Glenda, Gwenda • British/Welsh • *good, clean, pure and holy*

Glenys, Glynis, Glennis, Glenis, Glenice, Glenise, Glennys, Glynnis • British/Welsh • *pure and holy*

Godiva • Anglo-Saxon/Latin • *God's gift*

Gormlaith, Gormflaith • Irish Gaelic • *a splendid, illustrious woman or princess*

Grace, Gracie, Gratia, Grazia, Graziella, Gracia , Graciela • Latin • *grace*

Gráinne, Grania, Granya • Irish Gaelic • *unknown roots but possibly Goddess of the Harvest*

Greta, Gretta, Greet, Gretchen, Margaretta, Margareta, Grete, Margarette, Margarethe • Greek/Norman/English • *pearl*

Griet, Margriet • North Germanic • *pearl*

Guadalupe • Roman Catholic • *site of a convent with the famous image of the Virgin Mary*

Gudrun, Guro • Norse • *magical, enchanted, a witch or wise woman*

Gumersinda • Spanish/Visigothic • *the path of man or woman*

Gwenda • British/Welsh • *a good, holy, pure woman*

Gwendolen, Gwendoline • British/Welsh • *white or silver sacred ring*

Gwenfrewi • British/Welsh • *time for reconciliation*

Gwerful, Gwairmul • British/Welsh • *shy, modest, compromising*

Gwenyth, Gwenith • British/Welsh • *wheat, romantic word for the pick of the crop!*

Habība • Arabic • *beloved one*

Habibunah • Swahili • *our beloved*

Hadīl • Arabic • *a woman with a voice like the cooing of doves; soft, lovely voice*

Hadya • Arabic • *a woman with inner peace*

Hafza • Arabic • *devoted to the Koran*

Hāgar, Hājar • Arabic • *uncertain origins*

Haidee, Aidoios • Greek/literary • *Lord Byron called a character in* Don Juan *Haidee, meaning modest*

Hailey, Hayley, Hallie, Haylee, Hailee, Haley, Haleigh, Hegleah • Anglo-Saxon • *meaning a clearing for hay*

Hannah, Hanne, Johanna, Hanna
• Biblical/Jewish/Hebrew • *God has favoured me*

Hanān • Arabic • *as tender as a woman's heart*

Hansine • Germanic • *God is gracious or gift of God*

Hayfā • Arabic • *slender, delicate flower*

Heaven, Heofon • American English/Anglo-Saxon • *where God is and good people go after this life*

Hecate • Greek • *Goddess of Magic and Enchantment*

Heledd, Hyledd • British Welsh/Celtic mythology • *not entirely sure of its root but it is the name of a princess whose name is at the heart of a lament for her brother's death*

Héloïse, Éloise • Germanic/Frankish • *uncertain origins*

Herlinda • Germanic • *a compassionate army*

Hiba • Arabic • *a gift or prize from God*

Hind, Hinde • Arabic • *no known origin*

Honey, Honeg, Honig • Anglo-Saxon • *sweet nectar, someone who is sweet*

Hope, Hopa • Anglo-Saxon • *Christians' belief in the resurrection and life everlasting*

Horatia • Etruscan • *Roman family name with no certain root*

Hualing • Chinese • *flourishing fuling (herb used in oriental medicine)*

Huguette, Huette • Germanic/Frankish/French • *heart, mind and spirit*

Huian • Chinese • *kindness, peace*

Huifang • Chinese • *kind and fragrant*

Huifen • Chinese • *wise and fragrant*

Huizhong • Chinese • *wise devotion*

Huda • Arabic • *a woman who is wise and judicious counsellor or adviser; agony aunt*

Hulda, Huldah • *sweet, lovable, adorable*

Hyacinth, Jacinth, Jacinthe, Jacintha, Hyakinthos • Greek/English • *love and passion*

Ianthe, Violet, Flower, Ionanthos, Iolanthe • Greek • *a beautiful deep purple flower*

Íde, Ita • Irish • *unknown origin, possibly referring to thirst*

Ihāb • Arabic • *a gift from God*

Ihsān • Arabic • *charity, generosity*

Ilene, Eileen • Norman French/modern English • *desired by others*

Ilse, Ilsa, Elisabeth • Germanic/Biblical • *God is my oath*

Imān • Arabic • *faith, belief*

In'ām • Arabic • *a gift given or bestowed by God*

Inés, Inez, Agnès • Spanish/Greek • *pure and holy*

Iolanda, Yolanda • Germanic/Frankish • *unknown origins*

Iola, Iole • Greek • *violet, the flower*

Iona, Nonie • Latin/Gaelic • *sacred island in Hebrides in north Britain*

Ione, Nonie • English • *Ionian islands*

Irène, Eirene, Irina, Ira, Arina • Greek • *peace*

Isabel, Isobel, Isa, Isabella, Isabelle, Isobelle, Isobella, Izzy, Izzie, Sibéal, Iseabail, Ishbel, Isbel, Elizabeth • Spanish/Biblical/Hebrew/Jewish • *God is my oath*

Isadora, Isidoro, Izzy • Greek/Egyptian • *a gift from the goddess*

Isis, deity of magic and life
Isolde, Isolda, Iseult, Esyllt •
Arthurian mythology/British Welsh
• *a beautiful Irish Princess*
Isla • Scots • *name of Hebridean
island in north Britain*
'Ismat • Arabic • *she who is without
sin, perfection*
Ismene • Greek mythology • *Greek
tragedy!*

Jacinta, Hyacinth, Jacinthe •
Greek/Spanish/French • *love and
passion*
Jada, Yada • Biblical/Hebrew/Jewish
• *he knows*
Jaleesa • African American • *no
known origin*
Jamila, Gamila • Arabic • *graceful as
well as beautiful*
Jana, Yana, Jan • Biblical/English/
Latin • *God is gracious or gift of God*
Janaki • Sanskrit • *vague origin*
**Jane, Jeanne, Jehanne, Jaine,
Jayne, Jain, Jean, Joan, Janie,
Janey, Joanna, Jaynie, Síne,
Siân, Johanna, Hanne, Hansine,
Johanne, Janja, Jannja, Sheena
Jensine, Jonna, Jeanne, Juanna,
Juana, Giovanna, Gianna, Hana,
Jana, Janeen, Janelle, Jaynia** •
Biblical/French/Latin • *God is
gracious or gift of God*
**Janet, Jannet, Janett, Janette, Jan,
Janetta, Janeta, Seònaid, Shona,
Seona** • Biblical/English/Latin •
God is gracious or gift of God
Janice, Janis, Janise, Jannice, Jan
• Biblical/French/Latin • *God is
gracious or gift of God*
Jan, Janna • Biblical/English • *God
is gracious or gift of God*
Jasmine, Jasmyn, Jazmin, Jazmine,

**Yasmīn, Yasmine, Jasmina,
Yasmina, Jaslyn, Jaslynne** •
Persian/Norman • *evergreen shrub
or vine with glorious fragrance*
Jawāhir, Gawāhir • Arabic • *a
dazzling jewel*
**Jean, Joan, Jane, Jeanne, Jehanne,
Jehanna, Jeane, Jeana, Gina,
Jeanna, Jeane, Jeanetta, Jeanette,
Jeanie, Jeanine, Jeannette,
Jeanne, Jeanett, Jenette, Jennet,
Jenet, Ginett, Ginnette, Ginetta,
Ginnetta, Jeannie, Jeannine,
Jeannique, Jannike** • Biblical/
French • *God is gracious or gift of
God*
Jemima • Biblical/Hebrew/Jewish •
dove; as bright as day
Jerrie, Jerry, Geri, Gerry • Biblical/
English • *appointed by God*
Jiao • Chinese • *lovely, dainty*
Jinana • Arabic • *a woman as
beautiful and mystical as the Garden
of Eden*
Jingfei • Chinese • *forever fragrant*
**Jo, Joe, Joanna, Joanne, Jody,
Josephine, Josie, Josey** • Biblical/
Greek • *God is gracious or gift of
God*
**Joan, Ionna, Iohanna, Joanna,
Johanna, Joanne, Johanne, Joanie,
Joni, Siobhán, Chevanne, Siubhan,
Jane, Shevaune, Chevaune,
Shona, Shevanne, Joann, Seonag**
• Biblical/Norman • *God is gracious
or gift of God*
Jocasta • literary Greek • *mother
of Oedipus, tragic figure in classical
mythology*
Joelle, Joël • Biblical/Hebrew/
Jewish/French • *God*
**Johanna, Johna, Johannah,
Johanne, Joanna, Joanne, Jo,**

Jannike • Biblical/Latin • *God is gracious or gift of God*

Jonina • modern English/Biblical • *God is gracious or gift of God*

Josefa, Yosefa • Bibilical/Hebrew/ Jewish • *God will provide me with another son*

Joséphine, Josefine, Josephina, Josefina, Jo, Josie, Jozie, Josette, Fifi, Posy, Josefa, Jozefa, Josée, Josiane, Seosaimhín, Josianne, Josiane • Biblical/French • *God will provide me with another son*

Joy, Joie, Gaudia • Latin/French • *joyful in the Lord*

Juan • Chinese • *gracious*

Juanita, Janita, Janita • Spanish • *God is gracious or gift of God*

Juno, Úna • Irish Gaelic/Roman/ English • *uncertain roots; starvation or lamb*

Jyoti • Sanskrit • *light of mind, light of freedom, light of paradise*

Kalpana • Sanskrit • *filled with fantasy*

Kanta • Sanskrit • *you are desirable because you are so lovely*

Karenza, Carenza • British/Welsh/ Kernow • *love, loving to be loved*

Karita, Caritas, Caritas, Charity • Swedish/Latin • *dear charity; humanitarian*

Karma • Sanskrit • *action, seen as bringing upon oneself inevitable results, good or bad, either in this life or in a reincarnation*

Keila • African American • *refuge*

Kerry, Keri, Ceri • English/British/ Welsh/Irish Gaelic • *after the Celtic Goddess of Poetry*

Keturah • Biblical/Hebrew/Jewish • *incense, the strong perfume from*

frankincense used to purify in sacred places

Khayriyya • *a woman with a charitable heart*

Kirsten, Christine, Kristine, Kerstin • Danish/Norwegian/English/ Latin • *follower of Christ*

Kirstie, Kirstin, Kirsty, Kirstie, Christine, Chirsty, Ciorstaidh, Ciorstag, Curstaidh, Curstag • Scots English/Latin • *follower of Christ*

Kris, Kristina, Kristina, Kristen • Swedish/Czech/Latin • *follower of Christ*

Krista, Christa • German/Latin • *follower of Christ*

Kristie, Christie, Kirstie, Kristina, Kristy • American English/Latin • *follower of Christ*

Kristina, Kristine, Christine, Christina, Kristeen, Kristene, Kerstin, Kirsten, Tina • Swedish/ Czech/Latin • *follower of Christ*

Kumari • Sanskrit • *daughter or princess*

Leila, Laila, Layla, Leyla • Arabic • *a beautiful dark woman, as enchanting as the night, intoxicating to the senses*

Lakshmi • Sanskrit • *lucky girl in matters of luck, money and beauty*

Lalita • Sanskrit • *this girl is as playful as a kitten; affectionate and amorous*

Lamyā • Arabic • *a woman with fulsome brown lips*

Lana, Alana, Alanah, Lanna, Svetlana • American English • *vague origins but likely to mean a rock*

Lanying • Chinese • *lustrous indigo*

Laoise, Leesha, Luigseach • Irish

Gaelic • *unsure origins but most possibly Lug, Goddess of Light; someone from County Laoise*

Lara, Larissa, Larrisah • Russian/Greek • *unsure meaning, perhaps someone from a town near Thessaloniki, in northern Greece*

Larch, Larche, Larix • American English/German/Latin • *sacred tree to the shaman*

Larissa, Lara, Larry • Russian/Greek • *unsure meaning, perhaps someone from a town near Thessaloniki, in northern Greece*

Lata • Sanskrit • *she is as supple as a tendril*

Lawāhiz • Arabic • *shy glances, whispered secrets*

Layla • Arabic • *a beautiful dark woman, as enchanting as the night, intoxicating to the senses*

Leda • Greek mythology • *Queen of Sparta who was raped by Zeus/Jupiter in the shape of a swan*

Leela, Lila • Sanskrit • *very sexy*

Leila, Laila, Layla, Leyla, Lela, Lila • Arabic • *a beautiful dark woman, as enchanting as the night, intoxicating to the senses*

Leonora, Eleonora, Léonore, Elenonore, Eleanore, Lenora, Lennora, Lennorah, Lenorah, Lena • Germanic/Frankish/Provençal • *prefix means foreign or stranger, the suffix is unknown*

Libby, Elizabeth • English • *God is my oath*

Libe, Liebe • Jewish/Yiddish/German • *love or darling*

Liese, Elisabeth • German • *God is my oath*

Lifen • Chinese • *beautiful fragrance*

Lijuan • Chinese • *beautiful and graceful*

Lili, Lilli, Elisabeth • German • *God is my oath*

Lilian, Lilly, Lily, Lili, Lillian, Lilium, Lily, Lillie, Lilly, Lili, Lilli • Latin/Norman • *flower that is associated with purity and resurrection*

Lilith, Lily • Biblical/Jewish/Hebrew • *screech owl, nightmare or night monster*

Līna • Arabic • *a woman with the figure of a palm tree*

Linda, Belinda, Lynda, Lindie, Lindy, Lyn, Lynn, Lynne, Linden, Lin, Lyn, Lynne, Linnet, Lindsey, Lenda • Spanish/Visigothic/Germanic • *pretty, passive, tender and soft*

Lindsey, Linsey, Linsy, Linzi, Linzie, Lynsey • Anglo-Saxon • *Old Saxon kingdom whose root means Lelli's island*

Lisa, Liza, Elyse, Lise, Liese, Élise, Elisabeth • French/German • *God is my oath*

Lisette, Lise, Elisabeth, Lysette, Lise, Lys, Liz, Lis, Elisbet, Liza, Eliza, Lisa, Lizzie, Lizzy, Lizi, Elizabeth • English/French • *God is my oath*

Livia, Livius • Latin • *Roman family name Livius, uncertain origin but maybe means a hue of the colour blue*

Lois • Biblical • *uncertain origins*

Lola, Dolores • Roman Catholic • *Our Lady of the Seven Sorrows of the Virgin*

Lolicia, Lola, Delicia • American English/Roman Catholic • *Our Lady of the Seven Sorrows of the Virgin*

Lolita, Lola, Lolita • Roman Catholic • *Our Lady of the Seven Sorrows of the Virgin*

Lone, Abelone, Magdelone • Danish
• *Mary Magdelene aka Mary of*
Magdala, woman healed of evil spirits
Lourdes, Lurdes • Roman Catholic
• *a French place of pilgrimage where*
a young girl had visions of the Virgin
Lubna • Arabic • *storax tree that has*
sweet, honey-like sap, used to make
perfume and incense; a fragrant,
perfumed, honey-tasting woman as
intoxicating as incense
Lyn, Lynn, Lynne, Line • French •
uncertain origin
Lynette, Lynette, Linnet, Linotte,
Linnette, Linette • Spanish/French
• *pretty, passive, tender and soft*

Madeleine, Madelaine,
Magdalene, Magdala, Madelene,
Madlyn, Madelyn, Madalene,
Madaline, Madoline, Magdalen,
Maddie, Maddy, Maddalena •
Biblical/French • *Mary Magdelene*
aka Mary of Magdala, woman
healed of evil spirits
Madhu • Sanskrit • *she is as sweet as*
honey and younger than springtime
Madhur • Sanskrit • *sweetie!*
Maeve, Meadhbh, Mave, Meave,
Medh, Mab, Medb • Irish
mythology • *intoxicating!*
Mahalia, Mahali, Mahalah • Biblical
• *no known root*
Mair, Meir, Mary, Mari • British/
Welsh • *a drop of the sea*
Malfada • Spanish/Visigothic • *no*
certain root
Magali, Magalie • Provençal • *pearl*
Magda, Magdalene, Magadelena,
Lena • Biblical/Slavic/German
• *Mary Magdalene aka Mary of*
Magdala, woman healed of evil
spirits

Maggie, Margaret, Magaidh • Scots
Gaelic/Greek/Latin/Norman • *pearl*
Maha • Arabic • *oryx, an antelope*
with large, beautiful eyes
Mahalia, Mahalah, Mahali •
Biblical/Jewish/Hebrew/Aramaic
• *unsure; either tender or marrow*
– perhaps tender down to her
marrow!
Mai, Maria, Margit • Scandinavian •
combo of Maria/Mary and Margaret
Maia, Maya, Mya • Latin • *Roman*
goddess of youth, life, rebirth, love
and sexuality
Mairenn, Muireann • Irish Gaelic •
as fair as the sea
Maisie, Margaret, Mairéad, Maisy •
Greek/Scots Gaelic/English • *pearl*
Malati • Sanskrit • *she is like the*
jasmine, she is even more beautiful
at night
Marja, Maria • Dutch/Finnish/
Estonian • *a drop of the sea*
Malak • Arabic • *angel*
Mallory, Malerie, Mallery • Norman
• *unhappy or unfortunate one*
Mame, Mamie, Margaret, Mary
• American English • *short for*
Margaret or Mary
Manda, Amanda, Mandy, Mandi,
Mandie • *she is fit to be adored and*
amoured
Manon, Marie • Biblical/French •
pet name for Marie
Manuela • Biblical/Spanish • *God is*
with us or amongst us
Maoilosa • Irish Gaelic • *follower of*
Jesus Christ
Mareta, Märta, Merete • Danish • *a*
drop of the sea
Margaret, Margeurite, Margarita,
Margarites, Margaron, Pearl,
Marina, Margery, Marjory,

Marjorie, Magarette, Margaretta, Meg, Peg, Madge, Marge, Maggie, Meg, Meggie, Peggy, Peggie, Peggi, Margie, May, Daisy, Mairéad, Mairghead, Mared, Marged, Marget, Mererid, Margaretha, Margareta, Margarethe, Margrit, Margret, Meta, Margriet, Margrethe, Marit, Merete, Mereta, Mette, Margeurite, Margarita, Margarida, Margherita, Margareta, Malgorzata, Marketa, Marketta, Margrieta, Margarita, Margaretha, Margherita, Margrethe, Margit, Maighread, Maretta, Mared, Marged • Greek • *pearl*

Margot, Margaux, Marguerite, Margarete, Margit • Greek/Latin/ Norman • *pearl*

Margery, Marjorie, Marjorie, Margery, Marjory, Marjie, Margaret, Margery, Margie, Marjy, Marji, Marga, Marge, Marsaili • Greek/English • *pearl*

Maria, Mary, Ria, Marie, Mariah, Máiri, Marieta, Mariam, Miriam, Mariella, Marietta, Maris, Marea, Marie, Manon • Biblical/Jewish/ Hebrew/Latin/Christian • *a drop of the sea*

María José • Roman Catholic • *combo of Mary the Virgin and Joseph the father*

Mariam, Miriam, Mariamne • Biblical/Jewish/Hebrew/Christian

María de los Ángeles, Mary-Ange • Spanish • *Mary of the Angels*

Marietta, Mariella, María, Mairéad, Margaret, Mariette, Maretta • Biblical/Italian • *Mary Magdelene aka Mary of Magdala, woman healed of evil spirits*

Marika, Maria • Biblical/Slavic • *a drop of the sea*

Marilee, Marylee, Marylou, Marilene, Marilla, Marioa • American English/Biblical/Jewish/ Hebrew/Latin/Christian • *names all based on Mary or Maria; a drop of the sea*

Marina, Marinus, Marius, Marna • Latin • *Roman family name; clouded meaning but associated with someone of or from the sea*

Maris, Stella Maris • *modern name; uncertain root but from Maria or Mary, meaning Star of the Sea*

Marisa, Maria, Marissa • *modern name based on Mary; a drop of the sea*

Marla, Marlene, Magdalene • modern • *Mary Magdelene aka Mary of Magdala, woman healed of evil spirits*

Marlene, Maria, Magdalena • German • *Mary Magdelene aka Mary of Magdala, woman healed of evil spirits*

Marna, Marnie • Swedish/Latin • *Roman family name; clouded meaning but associated with someone of or from the sea*

Martirio • Roman Catholic/Spanish • *to be a martyr*

Mary, Marie, Maria, Miriam, May, Molly, Máire, Mair, Moira, Maura, Mairia, Màiri, Màili, Mari, Marja, Mariya, Marya, Marija, Marica, Masha, Miriam, Maryam, Moire • Biblical/French/English • *a drop of the sea*

Maura, Mary • Irish/Celtic/Latin • *a drop of the sea*

May • English • *pet name for Mary and Margaret*

Maysa, Mayyas • Arabic • *a woman with a graceful but proud gait*

Meadhbh, Medb, Maeve, Mave, Meave • intoxicating woman; she who makes men drunk

Meg • English/Greek • *short name for Margaret; pearl*

Mercedes • Roman Catholic • *Our Lady of Mercies, alluding to the Virgin Mary*

Meena, Meenaskshi • Sanskrit • *Pisces the fish*

Meg, Margaret, Mag, Magg, Maggie, Megan, Meggie • Greek/Latin/English • *pearl*

Megan, Meg, Meghan, Meaghan, Meagan, Marged, Margaret • Greek/Gaelic • *pearl*

Mehetabel, Mehitabel • Biblical/Jewish/Hebrew • *God makes happy*

Meirong • Chinese • *beautiful soul and personality*

Meixiu • Chinese • *beautiful grace*

Mélanie, Melania, Melaina, Melany, Melony, Mellony, Meloney, Melloney, Melas • Latin/Greek/Norman • *black, dark*

Melinda, Melanie, Lucinda • modern • *combo of Mélanie and Lucinda*

Mercedes, Merche, Mercy, Mary • Spanish • *Mary of Mercies*

Mercia, Mercy, Mecedes, Merces • Latin • *showing compassion for others' plight*

Meredith, Meredydd • British/Welsh • *unknown prefix plus lord*

Merete, Margareta, Mereta, Mette, Meta • Greek/Latin/Danish • *pearl*

Meryl, Mary • American English/Breton Celtic • *bright sea*

Mia, Maria • Swedish/Danish/Biblical • *a drop of the sea*

Michaela, Mikayla, Mica, Micah • Biblical/Hebrew/Jewish/English • *who is like God?*

Michele, Michelle, Michel, Chelle, Shell, Micheline • Biblical/Hebrew/Jewish/English

Mignon, Mignonette, Minette • French • *little darling, cutie, sweetie*

Milagros • Roman Catholic • *Our Lady of Miracles*

Millena, Milenna • Czech • *grace and favour*

Mimi, María, Mary • Italian • *pet name for Maria or Mary*

Mingzhu • Chinese • *bright pearl*

Miriam, Maryam, Mary, Maria, Maiamne, Myriam, Mirjam • Biblical/Jewish/Hebrew • *uncertain origin but is the root of Mary and Maria*

Misty, Mistie • English • *obscure or vague*

Mitzi, Maria • Biblical/French/Bavarian • *a drop of the sea*

Mohini • Sanskrit • *a woman who is enchanting and bewitching*

Moira, Moyra, Maura, Máire, Mary, Moya • Irish Gaelic/French/Biblical/English • *a drop of the sea*

Molly, Mollie, Mary, Mally • Biblical/French/English • *a drop of the sea*

Montserrat • Catalan • *the Lady of Montserrat, a Benedictine monastery near Barcelona*

Morag, Mór, Móirín, Moreen • Irish Scots Gaelic • *great, large, huge*

Morgan, Morgana • British/Welsh • *vague beginning but ends with ending, completion, full circle*

Morna, Muirne • Scots Gaelic • *beloved*

Muhsina • Arabic • *a charitable,*

kind and compassionate woman

Muireann, Muirinn • Irish Gaelic •
as fair as the sea

Muirgheal • Irish Celtic • as bright
as the sea

Muna • Arabic • sexy, desirable and
gives out hope and optimism

Murdag, Murdann, Murdina • Scots
Gaelic • Lord of the Sea

Muriel, Muireall, Meriel, Merrill •
Breton Celtic/Scots Irish Gaelic •
bright sea

**Myra, Myrrha, Mary, Miranda,
Mairéad** • Latin • anagram of Mary
meaning myrrh; the embalming spice

Myriam, Miriam • Biblical/French
• uncertain origins but is the root of
Mary and Maria

Myrna, Muirne, Morna • Irish
Gaelic • beloved

Myrtle, Myrtille, Myrtilla, Myrta •
Latin/Norman/Greek • a tree with
fragrant leaves; in Greek it means
perfumed

Nabīla • Arabic • upper-crust
woman

**Nadia, Nadya, Nadezhda, Nadine
Nadezhda, Nadya** • Russian • hope

Nadine, Nadia • Russian/French •
hope

Nadira, Nadra • Arabic • a woman
who is rare and precious

Nadiyya • Arabic • a woman who is
as fresh and moist as morning dew

Nahla • Arabic • she is as refreshing
as a drink of water, she quenches my
thirst

Najāt, Nagāt • Arabic • a woman
who has been saved, rescued or
redeemed, or helps others to confess

Najiba, Nagiba • Arabic • cultured,
cultivated and a cut above the rest

Najwa, Nagwa • Arabic • secrets
abound, a woman who is discreet
and confidential, keeper of secrets

Nan, Nancy, Nanette, Ann •
Biblical/Jewish/Hebrew • pet form
of Ann, of uncertain origins; God has
favoured me

**Nancy, Nan, Ann, Annis, Agnes,
Nancie, Nanci, Nance** • Biblical/
Jewish/Hebrew • pet form of Ann, of
uncertain origin; God has favoured
me

Nanette, Nan • Biblical/Jewish/
Hebrew/French • pet form of Ann, of
uncertain origin; God has favoured
me

Naomh • Irish • holy, saintly

Narelle, Narellan • Australian
Aborigine • no known root, apart
from a town called Narellan

Nastasia, Anastasia • Greek/
Russian • short form of Anastasia;
resurrection

Natalia, Natalya, Natalie, Natasha
• Latin/Russian • the birth of Jesus
Christ or reborn with faith

Natalie, Nathalie, Natalia • Latin/
French • the birth of Jesus Christ or
reborn with faith

Natasha, Natalia, Noel • Latin/
Russian • the birth of Jesus Christ or
reborn with faith

**Nerida, Nerys, Phillida, Phyllis,
Nerissa, Nereis** • British Welsh/
Greek • sea nymph or lady

Nerina, Nerine, Nereus • Greek/
Latin • sea god/family name Nero
or Nerio

Nerissa, Nereis • literary inven-
tion/Greek • sea sprite or nymph;
Nerissa was invented by William
Shakespeare for Portia's lady-in-
waiting in The Merchant of Venice

Nessa, Neassa, Neasa, Ness • Irish Gaelic • *unknown meaning but the name of a character in Irish legend*

Nesta, Nester, Nostos, Agnès • British Welsh/Greek • *pure and holy*

Netta, Nettie • Gaelic/English • *confused origins; perhaps passionate in all she does, a champion*

Ngaire, Nyree • New Zealand Maori • *unknown origin*

Nihād • Arabic • *ground that resembles a female's breasts and contours*

Nihāl • Arabic • *a person whose thirst is slaked*

Ning • Chinese • *tranquillity*

Nirvana • Sanskrit • *extinction, disappearance of the individual soul into the universal*

Nuo • Chinese • *graceful*

Nyamekye • Ghanaian • *given by God*

Nyree, Ngaire • New Zealand English • *unknown origin*

Oceana • modern English • *the ocean*

Oksana, Oxana • Russian • *praise God*

Olive, Olivia, Oliff, Oliffe, Oliva • Latin • *olive tree, a symbol of peace and abundance*

Olwen, Olwin, Olwyn • *footprint, path, white, sacred*

Olufemi • Nigerian • *God loves me*

Ophelia, Ophelos • Italian/Greek • *help!*

Ofra, Ophrah, Ophra • Biblical/Jewish/Hebrew • *fawn, as in deer*

Oprah, Orpah, Ophrah • American English • *uncertain origin*

Oriana, Aurum, Oriane • Spanish/Norman • *uncertain roots but may mean gold*

Órla, Ona, Anona, Fíona, Honor, Orfhlaith, Orflaith, Orlaith • Irish Gaelic • *golden lady or princess*

Paderau • British/Welsh • *Lady of the Rosary, alludes to the Virgin Mary*

Padma • Sanskrit • *lotus flower, energy centres of the chakra*

Padmavati • Sanskrit • *full of lotus flowers*

Padmini • Sanskrit • *lotus pond or lake*

Paleley, Sudan • *sweet*

Paloma, Palumba • Latin • *dove*

Pamela, Pam, Pammy, Pamella • poetic invention • *Sir Philip Sidney and Queen Elizabeth I created the name*

Pandora, Dora, Pandoran • Greek mythology • *all and every gift; alluding to Pandora's box that she was told never to open, when she did, she allowed everything evil and bad out, leaving the fairy Hope as the only thing left inside*

Paraskeue, Praskovya • Greek • *Good Friday, the Friday before Easter Sunday*

Parthenope, Parthenosops • Greek mythology • *maiden as in the goddess Athene in her form and face; one of the sirens, who lured men to her with their enchanting, bewitching voices was named Parthenope*

Pascale, Pascuala • Latin/French • *pascal lamb; Easter time*

Patience, Pati • Latin • *to suffer, a virtue*

Paz • Roman Catholic • *Our Lady of Peace*

Pearl, Perle, Peninnah, Perla • Jewish/Hebrew • *pearl*

Peg, Peggy, Peggi, Margaret, Meg, Pegeen, Peigín, Peig, Peigi • Greek/ Latin/Norman • *pearl*

Pélagie, Pelagia, Pelagios, Pelagos, Pelageya • Greek • *open sea*

Penelope, Pen, Penelops, Penny, Penni • Greek • *uncertain origin but 'duck' is one suggestion*

Peninnah, Pen, Pearl, Perle, Peninna, Penina • Biblical/Hebrew/ Jewish/Latin • *coral or pearl, beautiful pink underwater mineral found in warm water*

Petula, Pet, Petulare • Latin/ Christian • *to ask or plead humbly for mercy or forgiveness*

Phoenix • Latin/Greek • *mythical bird that represents rebirth or reincarnation*

Phyllis, Phillida, Phyllis, Phyllidos, Phyllidis, Phyllida, Phyllicia, Phylicia • Greek mythology • *a Thracian Queen, Phyllis died for love and transformed herself into an almond tree; her name means leaves or leaf and she is a symbol of undying love and friendship*

Pia, Pius • Italian • *pious*

Piedad • Roman Catholic • *Our Lady of Piety*

Pilar • Roman Catholic • *Our Lady of the Pillar; appearance of the Virgin on a pillar at Zaragossa*

Polly, Poll, Pollie • Biblical/French/ English • *a drop of the sea*

Poppy, Popaeg, Papaver • Latin/ Anglo-Saxon • *the flower*

Posy, Posey, Josephine, Poesy • Biblical/English • *God will provide me with another son*

Priya • Sanskrit • *beloved one*

Psyche, Psykhe • Greek • *butterfly, spirit and soul*

Purificación • Roman Catholic/ Spanish • *Feast of the Purification, when Virgin purges of the uncleanliness associated with childbirth*

Qing • Chinese • *navy blue*

Radegund, Radegunde • Germanic • *a counsellor, adviser in times of trouble*

Radwa • Arabic • *an area in the holy city of Mecca*

Raffaella, Rafaela • Biblical • *archangel, God has healed*

Ragā, Rajā • Arabic • *perpetual anticipation is good for the soul*

Rāgya, Rājya • Arabic • *seventh month of the Muslim calendar*

Rhamantus, Rhamanta • British/ Welsh • *romantic*

Raisa • Slavic • *paradise, heaven*

Rajani, Rajni • Sanskrit • *something of the night, as dark as night*

Rajni • Sanskrit • *Queen of the Night*

Rakaya • Tunisian • *sweet*

Rakeisha • African • *no known root*

Rathnait, Ronit • Irish Gaelic • *a woman of grace and prosperity*

Rati • Sanskrit • *she desires; gives sexual pleasure and carnal knowledge*

Rāwiya • Arabic • *a narrator of classical Arabic poetry and prose and beautiful speaker*

Rébecca, Rebekah, Beathag, Becca, Becks, Bex, Becky, Becki, Rella, Rebekka, Reba • Biblical/ Jewish/Hebrew/Aramaic • *shadowy or vague origins possibly connected to 'cattle stall' but doubtful*

Renée, Reenie, Rena, Renatus, Renata, Serena, Rina • Latin • *reborn, resurrected*

Remedios • Roman Catholic • *Our Lady of the Remedies; through prayer the Virgin heals*

Renata, Renée, René, Renate • Latin • *reborn*

Renxiang • Chinese • *lucky fragrance*

Rhoda, Rhodon, Rose, Roda, Rodos • Greek • *rose or someone from the island of roses, Rhodes*

Rhona, Rona • Scots • *name of Hebridean island off northern Britain*

Ria, Maria • German • *a drop of the sea*

Rida • Arabic • *one who has God's (Allah's) approval*

Rio • Portuguese/Spanish • *river*

Rocio • Roman Catholic • *Our Lady of the Dews, or tears shed for the wickedness of the world*

Romy, Rosemarie, Rosemary, Romey, Rosmarinus • German/Latin • *sea dew*

Roni, Ronnie • Latin/English • *shortened Veronica; true image*

Rosaire, Rosario • Roman Catholic • *Our Lady of the Rosary*

Rosalind, Rosaleen, Rosalyn, Roslind, Rosaline, Rosalin, Rosalynne, Rosalynn • Germanic/Frankish • *horse, tender and soft, passive and weak*

Rosemary, Rosemarie, Rosie, Roschen, Rosmarie, Rosmarinus • Latin • *sea dew*

Rou • Chinese • *mild and gentle*

Runa • Norse • *a woman who has magical powers she uses through the runes or secret spells*

Rupinder • Sanskrit • *beauty beyond compare*

Ruqayya • Arabic • *talisman, lucky charm, magic spell, moving upwards, advancing/ascending*

Ruth, Ruthi, Ruthie, Rut, Rutt, Roo • Biblical/Jewish/English • *unknown roots but in English: compassion*

Sabina, Sabine • Latin • *from the Sabine women who were kidnapped by the Romans*

Sadhbh, Syve, Sive, Sabia • Irish Gaelic • *sweet as honey*

Safā • Arabic • *a pure, chaste woman who is sincere and goodly*

Sage, Sauge, Sapius • English/Norman/American English • *the herb sage that promotes wisdom and is good for the liver*

Salomé, Shalom • Greek/Hebrew/Aramaic • *peace*

Salud • Roman Catholic • *Our Lady of Salvation*

Salwa • Arabic • *she who consoles others and gives a shoulder to cry on*

Samantha, Sam, Sammy, Sammi • Biblical/Hebrew/Jewish

Samsara • Sanskrit • *just passing through, referring to life being just part of a cycle*

Sandhya • Sanskrit • *twilight of the gods, devout, ritualistic*

Sarāb • Arabic • *a mirage; not as she seems from a distance*

Saroja • Sanskrit • *born in a lake, like a lotus*

Sarojini • Sanskrit • *lotus pond or lake; having lotuses*

Satin, Zaituni, Tsingtung • Chinese/Arabic/French/English/Latin • *soft, sleek, silky, shiny fabric*

Scarlett, Escarlate, Scarlata, Scarlet • Latin/Norman/English • *someone who dyes or sells fabrics of rich, radiant colours*

Siegrun, Sigrun, Sigi • *she who uses the runes or magic to gain power over her enemies*

Selima, Selim, Zelima • Arabic/ English • *peace*

Selma, Zelma, Selima • German/ Scandinavian • *unknown roots*

Serenissima • Italian • *serene*

Shafīqa • Arabic • *a compassionate, charitable woman*

Shakonda • African American • *unknown origin*

Shamīm • Arabic • *a woman who is fragrant and smells as sweet as perfume*

Shan • Chinese • *a woman who bears herself elegantly; like royalty or a model*

Shana, Shanae, Shania, Shanee, Siani, Siân • American English/ British Welsh

Shandy, Shandi, Shandigaff • American English • *from the drink Shandigaff*

Shanta • Sanskrit • *she who finds inner peace through yoga or meditation*

Shanti • Sanskrit • *she who finds tranquillity and serenity through yoga*

Sharmila • Sanskrit/Hindi • *she who is selfless, modest and protective*

Shashi • Sanskrit • *having a hare, referring to the moon*

Shatha • Arabic • *sweet-smelling, fragrant*

Shula, Shulamit • Hebrew/Jewish • *peacefulness*

Simran • English • *no roots*

Sinéad, Janet, Jeanette, Seònaid, Shona, Seona • English/Scots Gaelic • *God is gracious or gift of God*

Siobhán, Joan, Jehanne, Shevaun, Chevonne, Chevaun, Chevaunne, Shevaunne, Jehanne, Joan • English/ Norman French • *Biblical/Irish Gaelic • God is gracious or gift of God*

Sioned, Janet • English/British Welsh • *God is gracious or gift of God*

Sissy, Sisi, Sissey, Sissie, Elisabeth • Jewish/Hebrew/Bavarian • *God is my oath*

Sissel, Cecily • Scandinavian/ English • *old Roman family name Caecilius, from the Latin, meaning blind*

Siwan, Joan • British/Welsh • *sea trout*

Sky, Skye • Gaelic • *take your pick, the sky as in heaven or Skye as in the island in Scotland*

Sneh • Sanskrit • *aromatic oils good for affection and tenderness*

Socorro • Roman Catholic • *Our Lady of Perpetual Succour*

Sofia, Sophia, Sofya, Sofie, Sophie, Sofie, Sophy, • Greek • *wisdom*

Sonia, Sonya, Sonje • Greek • *wisdom*

Soledad, Sol • Roman Catholic • *Our Lady of Solitude*

Sroel, Israel • Jewish/Yiddish • *one who strives with God*

Stacey, Stacy, Stace, Eustacia, Stacie, Staci • English/Greek • *confused roots; could mean juicy, tasty grapes!*

Stella, Stella Maris • Latin • *a star and Star of the Seas (often used to describe the Virgin Mary)*

Su'ād • Arabic • *origin not known*

Suhād, Suhair • Arabic • *insomnia*

Sumati • Sanskrit • *good thoughts, devout in prayer*

Summer, Haf, Sumor • Anglo-Saxon • *someone born in the summer months (southern hemisphere)*

Sybil, Sybille, Sybilla, Sybilla, Sibilia, Sibella, Sibéal, Cybille, Sibilla, Sibella, Cybil, Cybill • Greek mythology • *a woman with the power to predict; a devotee of Apollo, the sun god*

Tabitha, Dorcas, Tabby, Tabea • Biblical/Aramaic • *fawn, doe, gazelle, antelope*

Talia, Talya, Natalya, Thalia • Latin/Russian • *the birth of Jesus Christ or reborn with faith*

Tamara, Tamar, Tammy, Tammie • Hebrew/Jewish/Russian/Biblical • *date palm*

Tara • Sanskrit • *a shining star who carries the troubles of the world on her shoulders*

Tārub • Arabic • *a woman who enraptures and bewitches*

Tasha, Natasha • Latin • *the birth of Jesus Christ or reborn with faith*

Tempe, Temnein • Greek • *a valley in Greece; the legendary home of the Muses, the nine goddesses of the arts and sciences*

Teresa, Theresa, Terri, Tessa, Tes, Teresia, Theresia, Treeza, Thérèse, Resi • Italian/Spanish/Portuguese • *unknown root*

Tessa, Tess, Theresa, Tessie, Tessy • Italian/Spanish/Portuguese • *unknown root; pet name for Teresa*

Tetty, Tettie, Elizabeth • English • *pet name for Elizabeth*

Texas, Tex, Teyas • Native American • *friends, and of course someone from Texas; especially 3rd March*

Thecia, Theokleia • Greek • *glory of God*

Theodora, Dora, Teodora, Feodora • Greek • *God-given or giving to God or God's gift*

Theodosia, Dosy, Theodosis • Greek • *God-given*

Theokleia, Thecia, Tekla • Greek • *glory of God*

Thera, Theresa • Greek • *vague origins; could be short for Theresa or Greek isle of Thera*

Thessaly, Thessalie • Greek/Illyrian • *an area and city of northern Greece; unknown root*

Thurayya, Surayya • Arabic • *coping with sorrow and sadness*

Thursday • Anglo-Saxon/Norse • *Thor's day; Thor is equivalent to Jupiter*

Tia, Laetitia, Lucretia, Tiana, Tiara • Spanish/Portuguese • *aunty or short form of any name ending in -tia*

Tikvah, Tikva • Biblical/Jewish/Hebrew • *hope*

Ting • Chinese • *graceful*

Tirion • British/Welsh • *kind and gentle*

Tita • Latin • *old Roman name, unknown origin*

Tonette, Tonette, Antoinette • African American • *modern name based on Toni*

Toltse, Dolce, Dulcie • Jewish/Yiddish/Italian • *sweet*

Toni, Tonia, Tonia, Tonya, Antonia, Antoinette • Estruscan/Roman • *Roman family name but with confused origins*

Topaz • Biblical/Hebrew/Greek • *God is good*

Tova, Tofa, Turid, Tove, Tufa • Norse • *the god Thor made me beautiful*

Trinity, Trinidad • Roman Catholic •

the Holy Trinity
Trixie, Trix, Trix, Beatrix, Beatrice •
blessed through life
Tulip, Tiwlip • English • *flower of enchantment: tulip*

'Umniya • Arabic • *your wish is my desire*
Úna, Unity, Oona, Oonagh, Euna •
Irish Gaelic • *uncertain root; hungry or lamb*

Veronica, Verona, Bérénice, Ronnie, Ronni, Roni, Veraicon, Véronique, Veronika, Vroni • Latin • *true image: vera icon*
Vimala • Sanskrit • *a peerless person, pure as crystal*
Virginia, Verginius, Ginny, Ginnie, Virginie • Latin • *Roman family name Vergilius but confusion reigned when the spelling was changed to Virgilius, which means the maiden or virga as in stick*
Virtudes • Roman Catholic/Spanish • *seven Christian virtues*

Wen • Chinese • *refinement*
Wenling • Chinese • *refined jade wind chime*
Whitney, Whitley, Witney, Hwitleah, Whiteney • Anglo-Saxon • *the white island*
Wynne, Wynn, Wine • British Welsh/Anglo-Saxon • *a friend and/ or one who is blessed and sacred*

Xiang • Chinese • *fragrant*
Xialian • Chinese • *little lotus*
Xingjuan • Chinese • *getting more graceful every day*
Xiuying • Chinese • *graceful flower*

Ya • Chinese • *grace*
Yana, Jana • Biblical/English/Latin • *God is gracious or gift of God*
Yasmīn, Jasmina, Yasmina • Swahili • *sweetness*
Yelisaveta, Elisabeth • Hebrew/ Jewish • *God is my oath*
Yola, Yolanda, Yolande, Jolenta • Germanic/Frankish/Norman • *uncertain origin*
Ysuelt, Isolde • French/British Welsh • *a beautiful Irish Princess*
Yuan • Chinese • *shining peace*
Yunru • Chinese • *charming*

Zelma, Selma • German/ Scandinavian • *unknown roots*
Zena, Zina, Alexina • Russian/ Greek • *descended from Zeus*
Zenobia, Zenobios, Zenbios, Zenovial • Greek • *Zeus, Jupiter, life*
Zhane • American English • *unknown roots of British surname*
Zhenzhen • Chinese • *my precious*
Zina, Zinaida • Greek • *descended from Zeus*
Zinovia, Zina, Zenais, Zenovia, Zenobia • Greek • *life of Zeus*
Zuleika, Zulēkha • Arabic/Jewish • *unknown origin*

ARIES

21st March to 20th April

Planet: Mars

Day: Tuesday

Stones: diamond and bloodstone

Metals: iron and steel

Colours: scarlet, red, vermilion, primal red, crimson, madder red

Design: straight lines, strong lines as in stripes, nothing soft, gentle or wavy

Trees: all thorn-bearing trees and those whose leaves are red

Flora: geranium and all thorn-bearing trees and those whose leaves are red, mustard thistles, hollyhocks, red-hot poker, snapdragons

Celebrity Arians: Herb Alpert • Hans Christian Andersen • Warren Beatty • Wallace Beery • Otto Bismarck • Marlon Brando • Matthew Broderick • Jerry Brown • Claudia Cardinale • Mariah Carey • David Cassidy • Jackie Chan • Richard Chamberlain • Lon Chaney • Charlie Chaplin • Eric Clapton • Francis Ford Coppola • Joan Crawford • Russell Crowe • Leonardo da Vinci • Timothy Dalton • Bette Davis • Doris Day • Celine Dion • Betty Ford • Aretha Franklin • Sir David Frost • Robert Frost • James Garner • Sir Alec Guinness • Arthur Hailey • Emmylou Harris • Hugh Hefner • William Holden • Harry Houdini • A E Houseman • Olivia Hussey • Eric Idle • Henry James • Thomas Jefferson • Elton John • Shirley Jones • David Letterman • Henry Mancini • Jayne Mansfield • Marcel Marceau • Ali McGraw • Hayley Mills • Elizabeth Montgomery • Dudley Moore • William Morris • Eddie Murphy • Leonard Nimoy • Gregory Peck • Mary Pickford • Colin Powell • Andre Previn • Dennis Quaid • Debby Reynolds • Diana Ross • Ricky Schroder • Steven Seagal • Omar Sharif • Tiny Tim • Spencer Tracy • Sir Peter Ustinov • Vincent van Gogh • Sarah Vaughan • Christopher Walken • Michael York.

Planetary Influences: see Mars at the back of this book (page 444)

Boys

Ace, Acer, As • Latin/American English • *number one!*

Achilles, Achilleus, Achille, Achilleo, Aquiles, Akhilleus • Greek/Greek mythology • *from the River Akehloos, a classic Greek hero*

Achim, Akim, Joachim, Akim, Yakim • Hebrew/Jewish • *made and created by God*

Adelard, Adelhard • Germanic • *what a strong-looking and noble boy*

Aiden, Aidan, Áedán, Aodhán, Aoghan, Aodhagán, Edan, Eden, Aeddan • Irish Gaelic • *fire god*

Aitor • Basque • *founder of the Basques, local hero*

Ajit • Sanskrit • *he who cannot be beaten*

'Alā • Arabic • *excellent and supreme*

Alaric, Aliric • Germanic • *a foreign power or powerful, ruling stranger, perhaps invader*

Alastair, Alistair, Allaster, Alec, Alaois, Alexander, Alasdair, Sandy • Scots Gaelic/Greek • *the man/warrior/leader who protects or defends his people*

Albert, Albrecht, Adalbert, Adalbrecht, Adelbrecht, Alberto, Albeart, Adalberht, Al, Bert, Albie, Alby, Bertie, Athelbert • French/Germanic/Anglo-Saxon • *bright and noble*

Alexander, Alexandre, Alexis, Alastair, Alasdair, Sandy, Alessandro, Alessio, Aleksandr, Aleksei, Alejandro, Alejo, Alec, Alick, Alex, Sandaidh, Lexy, Lexie, Alastar, Alasdair, Alistair, Alexandre, Aleixandre, Aleksandr,

Aleksandar, Aleksanteri, Sandor, Alick, Ailig, Alec • Greek • *the man/warrior/leader who protects or defends his people*

Alfonso, Alphonse, Alonso, Alonzo • Spanish/Visigothic • *royal at the ready*

Alfonso, Alphonse, Adalfuns, Alphonsus, Anluan, Fonzie, Fonsie, Fonso • Spanish/Visigothic • *ready for battle, noble fighter, proactive!*

Alistair, Alasdair, Alisdair, Alastair, Alister, Alaster, Allaster, Alistair • Scots Gaelic/Greek • *the man/warrior/leader who protects or defends his people*

Amiaz • Jewish/Hebrew • *my people/tribe are strong*

Amittai • Jewish/Hebrew • *being true, honest, candid*

Amīn • Arabic • *honest as the day is long*

Amjad, Amgad • Arabic • *glorious*

Andrew, André, Andreas, Andries, Aindréas, Aindriu, Andrea, Andrei, Anders, Aindrea, Anndra, Andras, Drew, Andy, Aindrias, Aindriu, Aindrea, Anndra, Andries, Andrés, Andrei, Andrzej, Jedrzej, Andrej, Ondrej, Andrija, Antero, Endre, Andrius, Andrejs • Biblical/Greek • *a real sexy, macho man*

Angus, Aonghas, Aengus, Angie, Angaidh, Gus • Scots Gaelic • *Celtic god, there is only one choice*

Annibale, Hannibal, Hannbaal • winning the favour of the chief or the lord

Antiochos, Antiekhein, Antioco • to hold out against all the odds

Aodh, Áed • Irish Gaelic • *fire, Celtic sun god*

Arailt, Harold • Scots Gaelic • *ruler of the army, chief of the tribe*

Archibald, Archibold, Archie, Ercanbold, Gilleasbaig, Gillespie, Baldie, Archy • Norman French/ German Frankish • *the real deal; genuine, bold and brave*

Ardal • Irish Gaelic • *top man for valour, he fights like a bear*

Aries • Greek • *the first zodiac sign*

Aristide, Aristides, Aristos • *the best*

Armand, Hermann, Armin, Arminius, Armando • Germanic/ Latin • *soldier*

Arseni, Arsenios, Arsene, Arsenio • Greek • *a very sexy boy*

Art • Irish Gaelic • *champion*

Asdrubale, Asrubaal • Phoenician/ Italian • *give aid to the lord or receive it*

Ashraf • Arabic • *honourable and distinguished*

'Asim • Arabic • *protector*

Augustus, Auguste, Gus, Augustín, Augustine, Agostino, Augusto, Avgust, Agustin, Aghaistin, Aibhistin, Augustijn, Agustin, Agusti, Agostinho, Agostino, Avgustin, Tauno, Agoston, Augustinas, Augere, Austin • Latin • *great, the max, magnificent, expansive, nobody does it better*

Austin, Awstin, Awstyn, Austen, Austyn, Augustinius, Augustine • English/Latin • *the tops! The very best, el supremo*

'Azīz • Arabic • *unconquerable, adored*

Bala, Balu • Sanskrit • *young*

Balder • Norse • *ruler or chief prince, said to be pure and beautiful*

Baldev • Sanskrit • *God of Strength and playboy!*

Baldomero • Germanic/Frankish • *a man famous for being brave*

Baldwin, Maldwyn, Baudouin • English • *a bold and brave friend*

Baldur, Baldr • Norse • *son of Odin*

Barry, Baz, Bazza, Barra, Bairre, Barrie, Barri • Irish Gaelic • *fair-headed boy*

Bayard, Bay • French/English • *a man with hint of tint of red hair*

Bearach, Biorach • Irish Celtic • *sharp, pointed*

Beathan • Scots Gaelic • *life*

Bechor • Jewish/Hebrew/Sephardic • *first-born*

Berthold, Barthold, Bertil • German • *splendid, powerful ruler*

Bertram, Bertie, Bert, Bertrand, Beltrán, Burt, Albert • German • *bright*

Berwyn, Barrwyn • British/Welsh • *white or fair-headed*

Bharat • Sanskrit • *taken care of, God of Fire*

Blake • English • *my lovely mousey coloured hair*

Bleddyn, Blaiddyn • British/Welsh • *wolf or hero*

Boaz • Jewish/Hebrew • *strength*

Booth • Anglo-Saxon • *a gamekeeper's hut or wee house*

Boyd • Irish • *blond*

Brant, Brand • Anglo-Saxon • *firebrand, spitfire*

Brendan, Brendon, Breandán, Brendanus • Latin • *prince, heir*

Bodie, Brody • Scots Gaelic • *a castle or fortress*

Burton • Anglo-Saxon • *a town with a castle or fort*

Cadell • British/Welsh • *battle-scarred man*

Cadfael • British/Welsh • *prince of*

warriors, battle prince

Cadfan • British/Welsh • *summit of the battle*

Cadoc, Cadog • British/Welsh • *battle*

Cadwgan, Cadwgawn, Cadogan • British/Welsh • *a man who has won honour and glory in battle*

Cadwaladr, Cadwalader • British/Welsh • *battle leader, warrior chief*

Cainneach, Kenny • Irish Celtic • *handsome, beautiful founder of Kilkenny*

Caleb, Kaleb • Hebrew/Jewish • *he who rages like a dog, needs anger management!*

Cameron, Camron, Kamerson, Kamran, Camsron • Scots Gaelic • *crooked nose*

Campbell, Cambell, Cambeul • Scots Gaelic • *crooked mouth*

Caolite • Irish Gaelic • *origins vague; linked to legendary sprinter Mac Ronain*

Caungula • Angolian • *leader or chief of the people*

Carroll, Cearbhall • Irish Gaelic • *hacking or cutting with a sharp weapon*

Cathal, Cal • Irish Gaelic • *battle ruler, commander*

Cathán • Irish Gaelic • *battle, war, fight*

Cathair, Cathaoir • Irish Gaelic • *battle man, soldier*

Cearbhall • Irish Gaelic • *hacking, slashing*

Chad, Tchad • English • *a man from the warlike place*

Chaim, Hyam • Jewish/Hebrew • *life*

Chandler • English • *a candle maker*

Changming • Chinese • *forever bright*

Chase, Chace • English • *hunter*

Chester, Caer, Castra • English/Roman • *a fortress or encampment*

Christhard • German • *as brave and strong as Christ*

Cillian, Killian, Kilian • Irish Gaelic • *fight or church*

Cinnéidigh, Kennedy • Irish Gaelic • *ugly head*

Claiborne, Clayborne, Claiborn, Clayborn • Anglo-Saxon/American English • *honouring a founder Virginian colonist, surname of an influential American family who came from Westmorland in Great Britain*

Clay, Clayton • American/English • *I am a mere mortal*

Cledwyn • British/Welsh • *a man who might be rough and ready on the outside but on the inside he is holy, spiritual and soft*

Clovis • Germanic/Frankish • *a famed warrior or fighter*

Coinneach, Kenneth • Scots Gaelic • *handsome, beautiful, sexy*

Colbert • French/Germanic/Frankish • *he has a such a bright helmet, he is famous for it*

Conall, Conell, Connell • Irish Celtic • *strong as a wolf*

Conán • Irish Gaelic • *Irish wolfhound*

Conn • Irish Celtic • *chief, leader*

Connor, Conor, Conner, Conchobhar • Irish Celtic • *dog lover*

Conrad, Konrad, Corrado • Germanic • *one who gives forthright and candid advice*

Conroy, Conraoi • Irish Gaelic • *keeper of the dogs*

Conway, Conwy, Connmhaigh,

**Connmhach, Conbhuide,
Cubhuide, Connmhach** • Gaelic/
British/Welsh • *golden hound or dog
or head-smasher!*
**Crispin, Crispian, Crispinus,
Crispus** • Latin • *the curly-headed
chap*
Cuán • Irish Celtic • *dog or hound*
**Cyril, Kyrillos, Cyrille, Kiri, Kyrios,
Kiril, Searle** • Greek • *lord or chief*
Cyrus, Cy, Kyros, Kyrios • Greek •
lord or chief

Da • Chinese • *attain, accomplish,
achieve*
Dag • Norse • *day*
Dai, Dei • British/Welsh • *this chap
shines forth*
Daithi • Irish Gaelic • *swift*
Dallas, Dalfhas • Scots Gaelic/
American/English • *the village of
Dallas in Moray, north Britain; a
place where cowpokes or drovers
would rest their weary bones
overnight*
**Damián, Damianos, Damien,
Demyan** • Greek • *vague roots but
could be 'to kill'*
Dante, Durante • Latin • *strong and
steadfast, personal name originally*
Davu • Kenyan • *beginning*
Delroy, Del • Caribbean/French •
son or servant of the king or leader
Devlin • Irish Gaelic • *fierce, brave,
hardy warrior*
**Diarmuid, Dermot, Diarmuit,
Diarmit** • *unsure but perhaps
without envy*
**Dickon, Richard, Dick, Dicky,
Dickie** • Germanic/Norman • *strong,
brave and powerful*
Dieter • Germanic • *the army of the
people*

Dietwald • Germanic • *powerful
people, ruling tribe*
**Dominic, Dominick, Dom,
Dominique, Domingo, Dominicus,
Dominus** • Latin/Roman Catholic
• *Lord, as in St Dominic, founder of
the Dominican order*
**Donagh, Donnchadh, Donough,
Donncha, Duncan, Donn, Don** •
Irish Gaelic • *brown noble chieftain*
**Donovon, Donovan, Donndubhan,
Donndubhain** • *brown, dark, black-
haired chief or leader*
Duncan, Donnchadh • Celtic •
brown chief or noble leader
Duyi • Chinese • *independent and
at one*

Eairdsidh, Archie, Eairrsidh • Scots
Gaelic • *the real deal; genuine, bold
and brave*
Earnán, Ernan • Irish Gaelic • *iron*
**Eckhard, Eckehard, Eggert,
Eckhardt, Eckehardt** • *all-powerful;
the point of a sword*
Eden, Edan • Hebrew/Jewish •
*Garden of Eden, a place of sheer
pleasure*
Edgar, Edgard, Eadgar • Anglo-
Saxon • *he who wins riches and titles
through battle*
Edom • Biblical/Hebrew/Jewish •
red
Egan, Aogán • Irish Gaelic • *fire,
Celtic sun god Aodh*
Egbert, Bert • Anglo-Saxon • *by the
edge of his sword he famously rules*
Egil, Egill • Norse • *edge, rim, point*
Egmont, Egmunt • Germanic •
*protected by the edge or point of a
sword*
Egon • Germanic • *point or sharp
edge of a sword*

Ehrenfried, Arnfried • Germanic • *peace with honour or person who, like the eagle, has power, but uses it as a deterrent*

Éimhín • Irish Gaelic • *speedy, fast, swift, prompt, quick*

Einar • Norse • *single warrior fighter*

Einion, Einwys • British/Welsh • *anvil*

Eirik, Erik • Norse • *total ruler, singular chief*

Eladio, Helladio • Greek • *a man from Greece*

Elmer, Elmar • Germanic • *famous swordsman*

Elof • Scandinavian • *the single descendant/heir*

Emery, Amauri, Emauri, Amalric • Germanic/Frankish • *he gains power over others by his vitality and courage*

Emile, Aemilius, Émilien, Aemilus, Emil, Emilio • Latin • *rival, competitor*

Emlyn, Aemilianus, Aemilius, Aemulus • British/Welsh/Latin • *vague roots, possibly means a rival*

Emyr • British/Welsh • *ruler, king, lord, chief*

Emmerich, Heimerich • Germanic • *strength in home or family*

Enos • Biblical/Hebrew/Jewish • *mankind*

Erdmut, Erdmuth, Hartmut • Germanic • *indomitable spirit*

Erhard, Erhardt • Germanic • *honoured because of his strength and fortitude*

Eric, Erik, Erick, Erich, Einnrik, Eirik • Norse • *one ruler or king alone, no other*

Esmond • Anglo-Saxon • *a handsome man filled with grace who protects his family or home*

Eunan, Ádhamhnán, Adomnae, Ádhamh • Irish Gaelic • *he's a right little horror! Strikes fear in my heart, tearaway*

Everard, Everett, Evrard, Eoforhard • Anglo-Saxon • *as brave as a boar or pig*

Ezekiel, Zeke • Biblical/Jewish/Hebrew • *God gives me strength*

Fa • Chinese • *starting out*

Fabio, Fabius • Latin • *Roman family name who were powerful during the republic*

Fabrizio, Fabrice, Fabricius, Fabricio • Italian/Etruscan • *Roman family name, one noted for his incorruptibility*

Fachtna, Festus • Irish Gaelic • *contentious, belligerent, hostile*

Faivish, Phoibos, Shimshon, Shraga, Fayvel, Feivel • Jewish/Yiddish/Aramaic • *God of the Sun, Apollo or linked to Samson*

Fakhri • Arabic • *diligent, high achiever, gets where he wants on merit*

Fanus • Ethiopian • *a bright light*

Fang • Chinese • *upright, honest, fair*

Fathi • Arabic • *conqueror or freedom giver*

Fawzi • Arabic • *victorious and triumphant, reaching the pinnacle*

Fāyiz • Arabic • *the winner, numero uno*

Fearadhach, Farry, Ferdie • Irish Gaelic • *butch, macho man*

Fergal, Fearghal • Irish Gaelic • *man of valour, man of courage*

Fergus, Fearghas, Ferrer • Irish/Scots Gaelic • *vital, dynamic man*

Ferrer, Ferris, Phiarais, Piaras

• Roman Catholic/Catalan • *blacksmith*

Ferruccio, Ferro • Latin • *man of iron*

Fergus, Fearghas • Scots Gaelic • *a dynamic man*

Fife, Fyfe • Gaelic • *someone from the kingdom of Fife; Fif was a Pictish hero*

Finlay, Findlay, Fionnlagh, Finley, Finnleik, Fionnlaogh • Scots Gaelic/ Norse • *fair, blond warrior or hero or war hero*

Firoz • Arabic • *champion and successful*

Fitzroy, Fitz • Norman/English • *often the bastard son of the king*

Flaithrí, Florry, Flurry • *prince, king*

Flann, Flannán • Irish Gaelic • *red*

Flynn, Floinn, Flann • Irish Gaelic • *red, ruddy, flushed*

Folker, Volker, Folke, Folkvar, Falkor • Norse • *protecting the people, the tribe*

Foma, Thomas • Russian/Biblical • *twin*

Fox, Sionnach, Fiksl • Anglo-Saxon • *a person who has features or colouring like a fox*

Frank, Franklin, Frankie • Germanic • *a loyal and free man or from the Frankish tribe*

Frédéric, Frederick, Frederik, Fritz, Fred, Phredd, Freddie, Fredick, Fredric, Friedrich, Frerik, Freek, Fredrik, Federico, Frederico, Fryderyk, Bedrich, Rieti, Frigyes • Germanic/Frankish • *peaceful but powerful ruler*

Friedemann • German • *man of peace*

Friedhelm • German • *well protected man in a helmet who comes in peace*

Galadima • Hausa African • *prince*

Gang • Chinese • *strong*

Gary, Garry, Gaz, Gazza • Germanic/French • *spear bearer or carrier*

Gauthier, Walter • Germanic • *commander of the army*

Gebhard, Gebbert, Geert, Gerd • German • *gifted with strength*

Geming • Chinese • *radical revolution*

Germaine, Jermaine, Germanus, Germain • French/Latin • *brother*

Germain, Germanus • Latin • *brother*

Gervaise, Gervase, Jervaise, Jervais, Gervais, Gervas, Gervasio • Germanic/Frankish • *unknown origin; possibly a man with a spear or something pointed*

Gérald, Jed, Ged, Jerrold, Gerry, Jerry, Geraud, Geraldo, Gerallt, Garret, Garrett, Gearóid, Jarrett, Gerolt, Gennaro • Germanic/ Frankish • *he who rules with a spear*

Gérard, Gerrard, Gerardo, Gerry, Jerry • Germanic/Frankish • *brave and bold with a spear*

Gerhard, Gerhardt, Geert, Gert • Germanic • *strong, dedicated swordsman*

Gerlach • Germanic • *playful and sporting swordsman*

Ghālib • Arabic • *conqueror and victorious*

Ghassān • Arabic • *youth*

Gideon • Hebrew/Jewish • *he who cuts someone down to size*

Gilroy, Giollaruadh • Scots Gaelic • *the red-haired boy*

Ginger • American/English • *someone with red or carrot-coloured hair*

Gjord, Gyrd, Jul • Norse • *God of Peace*

Gladstone, Glaedstan • Anglo-Saxon • *the stone where the red kite lands*

Gobbán • Irish Gaelic • *blacksmith*

Goddard, Godeheard • Anglo-Saxon • *hardy, strong and brave*

Godfrey, Godefroy, Gofraidh, Godfrid, Godfred • Germanic/Frankish • *God of Peace*

Gonzalo • Germanic/Visigothic • *personal name connected to battle, war*

Gottfried, Götz • Germanic • *God of Peace, God bring me peace*

Gotthard • Germanic • *God give me strength*

Gérard, Jed, Ged, Jerrold, Gerry, Jerry, Gerrard, Geraud, Gerardo, Geraud, Gearóid, Gérald, Geraldo, Gerallt • Germanic/Frankish • *a brave, strong man with a spear as his weapon*

Gruffudd, Griff, Griffith, Griffinus, Griffin, Grippiud, Gripiud, Gutun, Gutyn, Guto • *prince of lords*

Gunther, Gunter, Gunnar, Gunder, Gunne, Gunni • Germanic • *the army brings strife and lays the land waste*

Gustav, Gustave, Gus, Gustaf, Gösta, Gustavus, Gustavo • Scandinavian • *staff or supporter of the Goths*

Gwatcyn, Watkin • British/Welsh • *commander of the army*

Gwynedd • British/Welsh • *happiness or named after the British Welsh princedom of Gwynedd based on Snowdonia area where the ancient Brits (Welsh) fought the Anglo-Saxons in guerrilla warfare*

Gwythyr, Gwydyr, Victor • Latin • *victorious!*

Harding, Hearding • American/English • *I belong to Heard's tribe; strong and brave*

Hardy, Hardi • Germanic/Frankish • *a brave and stoic chap*

Harold, Harald • Anglo-Saxon • *ruler of the army, chief of the tribe*

Hartmann, • Germanic • *hard man!*

Hartmut • Germanic • *indomitable spirit*

Hartwig • Germanic • *strong, loyal and devoted in battle*

Harvard, Hereward, Hervard • American/English • *the vigilant soldier, the army guard*

Harvey, Harve, Harv, Hervé, Haervy • Breton Celtic • *a man who shows himself worthwhile in battle –*

Hāsim • Arabic • *decisive, incisive and quick*

Hātim • Arabic • *decisive and focussed*

Haydn, Heiden, Heidano, Hayden, Haydon • Germanic • *heathen or pagan*

Heilwig • German • *war is a deterrent*

Herbert, Bert, Herebeorht, Herb, Herbie, Heribert • German • *a famous army that carries all before it; a shining light*

Herleif, Härlief, Herlof, Herluf, Herliev • Norse • *personal* • *warlike descendant*

Herman, Hermann • German • *soldier*

Hildebrand • Germanic • *flaming sword, battle success*

Hildebrecht • Germanic • *bright light in the battle*

Holger, Hogge • Norse • *an warlike island-dweller with a sharp weapon*

Hongqi • Chinese • *red glag or banner*

Hopcyn, Hopkin, Hob, Robert • British/Welsh • *famous and bright*

Howard, Howerd, Haward • Scandinavian • *high or noble guardian or defender*

Hudson, Hudde, Richard • Anglo-Saxon • *strong and powerful* • *confused origin pet name of Richard*

Hugh, Huw, Hugues, Hugo, Aodh, Hughie, Hewie, Huey, Hewie, Hughie, Huwie • Germanic/Frankish • *heart, mind and spirit*

Hugo, Hugh • Germanic/Frankish/Latin • *heart, mind and spirit*

Humbert, Humberto • Germanic • *he who fights like a bear cub*

Humphrey, Humfrey, Humphry, Humfry, Hunfrid, Humff, Wmffre • Germanic/Frankish • *someone when aroused will fight like a bear cub but until then is a peaceful soul*

Hunter • American/English • *a person involved in all aspects of hunting*

Huojin • Chinese • *fire metal*

Husām • Arabic • *wword, sabre, rapier*

Hyacinth, Hyakinthos • Greek/English • *love and passion*

Iarlaithe, Jarlath • Irish Gaelic • *vague origins but maybe chief, leader*

Idris • British/Welsh • *an passionate loving lord or lord of passion and desire*

Inderjit • Sanskrit • *victor of Indra*

Ingram, Engelram • Norman/Norse • *Norman family name after the Viking fertility god, Ing, and his pet raven*

Ingvar, Yngvar • Norse • *Warrior God who brings fertility and male potency*

Iorwerth, Iolo, Iolyn, Yorath • British/Welsh • *a handsome, beautiful Lord or Chief*

Jacinto, Hyakinthos, Hyacinthe • Greek/Spanish • *love and passion*

Jalāl, Galāl • Arabic • *great and glorious*

Jagdish • Sanskrit • *ruler of the world, Brahma, Vishnu and Shiva*

Jai, Jay, Jaye • Sanskrit • *victory!*

Jamāl • Arabic • *physically, drop dead gorgeous*

Janmuhammad • Persian • *breath of Muhammed*

Jarod, Jarrod, Gerald • English • *he who rules with a spear*

Jarrett, Garrett • Irish/English • *he who rules with a spear*

Jarvis, Jervis • Germanic/Frankish/English • *unknown origin; possibly a man with a spear or something pointed*

Jayakrishna • Sanskrit • *victorious Krishna*

Jayant • Sanskrit • *victorious son of Indra*

Jayashanka • Sanskrit • *victorious Shiva*

Jaywant • Sanskrit • *he has the power to be victorious*

Jerker, Jerk, Erik • Scandinavian • *one ruler or king alone, no other*

Jerold, Jerrold, Gerald, Jerry, Gerry • English • *he who rules with a spear*

Jerrard, Gerrard, Gerard • American/English • *he who rules with a spear*

Jevon, Jeavon, Jeevan, Jovene • English/Norman • *young*

Jianjun • Chinese • *building the army*

Jian • Chinese • *healthy*

Jitendra, Jitender, Jitinder • Sanskrit • *all-powerful, all-mighty, in control*

Jocelyn, Jocelyne, Joscelyne, Joselyn, Josceline, Joslyn, Joss, Gautzelin, Joscelin • Norman • *someone from the Germanic tribe of the Gauts*

Julián, Jules, Julianus, Julius, Julyan, Jolyon, Julien, Julio, Jools • Latin • *a Roman name; the most famous bearer being Gaius Julius Caesar*

Junior, Junia • Biblical • *youth*

Just, Juste, Justus • Latin • *just, fair and honest*

Justin, Justyn, Justinus, Justus, Iestyn • Latin • *a Roman name; just, fair and honest*

Kaie, Cathal, Caile, Cayle, Cale, Kail, Kaile, Kayle • Irish Gaelic • *battle ruler, commander*

Kang • Chinese • *well being*

Karan • Sanskrit • *ear of the warrior king*

Karl, Charles, Karlmann • Germanic • *freeman*

Keegan, Aodhagain, Aodhagán, Aogán, Aodh • Irish/English • *fire, Celtic sun god*

Kelsey, Ceolsige • Anglo-Saxon • *ship of victory*

Kemp, Kemper, Kempa, Kempe • Anglo-Saxon/English • *a warrior champion at sports*

Kenneth, Ken, Cinaed, Cainnech, Coinneach, Kennith, Kenny, Cenydd, Canice, Canicius, Cainneach • Latin/ English/Gaelic • *handsome, gorgeous, pleasing to the eye and rather adorable!*

Kenelm, Cenehelm • Anglo-Saxon • *he who is a bold and assertive warrior protected by his magic helmet*

Kennedy, Cinnéidigh • Irish Gaelic • *ugly head*

Khālid • Arabic • *indestructible*

Khalipha, Caliph • Arabic • *successor, heir*

Khwaja • Persian • *the master*

Kilroy, Gilroy • English • *the red-haired boy*

Klaus, Claus, Nikolaus • Germanic/ Dutch • *victory over or with the people*

Kolya, Nikolai • Russian • *victory over or with the people*

Kumar • Sanskrit • *beautiful Prince Skanda*

Kynaston, Cynefripestun • Anglo-Saxon • *the homestead or village of a peaceful royal or noble personage*

Ladislas, Ladislaw, Ladislaus, Wadislaw, Vladislav, Laszlo; Volodslav • Latin/Slavic • *glorious ruler, rules with glory*

Lal • Sanskrit/Prakrit • *dear, sweet, darling one; king*

Lancelot, Lance • British Welsh/ Celtic mythology • *unknown origin but name given to a famous knight of King Arthur's Round Table*

Leif, Leaf, Leiv • Norse • *heir of the realm*

Léopold, Luitpold, Leopoldo • Germanic/Bavarian • *bold man*

Lewis, Lewie, Lou, Louis, Lew • Anglo-Saxon/Germanic Frankish • *someone who gains fame through waging war and conflict; a hero, he*

who vanquishes and is revered
Lex, Alex, Alexander, Lexie, Lexis,
Lexy • Greek • *the man/warrior/*
leader who protects or defends his
people
Lomán • Irish Gaelic/Irish English •
bare, as in I survive with nothing
Longwei • Chinese • *dragon*
greatness
Lorcán • Irish Gaelic • *fierce and*
fiery
Louie, Louis, Lewie, Lewi, Lou,
Luthais, Ludwig, Lodewijk, Ludvig,
Lovis, Luis, Lluis, Luigi, Lodovico,
Lutz, Ludwig, Ludvig, Ludwik,
Luthais • Germanic/Frankish •
a person who gains fame through
waging war; a hero who vanquishes
the enemy and is revered by his
people
Ludovic, Ludovik, Ludovicus,
Hludwig, Maoldomhnaich, Ludo,
Ludwig, Lutz • Germanic • *famous*
in war
Luitgard • Germanic • *protector of*
the people
Luther, Liutheri, Luither •
Germanic • *army of the people*

Mackenzie, Maccoinnich,
Coinneach, Makenzie, Makensie,
Mckenzie, Mack • English/Scots
Gaelic • *handsome, gorgeous,*
pleasing to the eye and rather
adorable!
Madog, Madoc, Aodh • British/
Welsh • *fiery and fortunate*
Magnus, Maghnus, Mànus, Måns,
Mogens, Mànas • Latin • *a great*
man
Maitland, Maltalent, Mautalent,
Mautalant • Anglo-Saxon/Norman
• *bad-tempered or from Mautalant,*

a barren place in France
Mani, Subrahmanya • Sanskrit •
jewel with potent qualities; the penis
Manlio, Manlius • Latin • *Roman*
family name famous for republican
leanings
Mansūr • Arabic • *victor, conqueror*
Marat • Russian/French • *named*
after a Swiss-born French revolu-
tionary, Jean-Paul Marat
Marcel, Marcellus, Marcus,
Marcellin, Marcello, Marcelino,
Marcelo • Latin • *named after Mars,*
God of Sex and War
March, Marche, Mensis • Norman
• *a person who lives on the borders,*
the Marches or born in the month of
March, named after the God of War
and Sex, Mars
Mark, Marcus, Marc, Marco,
Marcas, Marcus, Markus, Marcos,
Marek, Marko, Markku • Latin •
named after Mars, God of Sex and War
Marlon, Marclon • Latin/Norman
• *named after Mars, God of Sex and*
War
Marmaduke, Maelmaedoc,
Maedoc, Maolmaodhog, Duke •
Irish Gaelic/English • *follower of*
fiery Madog
Marquis, Marcuis • Norman • *Lord*
of the Marches, borders between
England and Wales
Martin, Martyn, Martinus, Martis,
Marty, Mairtin, Maratan, Martainn,
Merten, Maarten, Martijn, Morten,
Mårten, Martinho, Martino,Marcin,
Martti, Marton, Marty, Marti •
Latin/English • *named after Mars,*
God of Sex and War
Maxwell, Max • Anglo-Saxon • *the*
well of Magnus or Mack, a great man
Maynard, Maginhard • Germanic/

Frankish • *strong and brave*

Medardo • Germanic • *personal name plus a strong, hard chap*

Meilyr, Maglorix • British/Welsh • *chief or ruler*

Miles, Michael, Milo, Myles, Maoilios • Latin • *soldier of God*

Milo • Slavic/Latin • *grace and favour or soldier*

Mohammed, Muhammed, Mohammad, Mohamed, Muhammad, Muhammed, Mo • praiseworthy and possessing the finest perfect qualities

Mohan • Sanskrit • *enchantment; one of the five arrows of love*

Montgomery, Montgomeric, Monty • Germanic/Norman • *the powerful man from the hill country*

Mukesh • Sanskrit • *Shiva the conqueror of the wild boar/pig, demon god*

Munīr • Arabic • *shining, dazzling, glorious*

Murchadh, Murrough • Irish Gaelic • *sea battle or war*

Nagendra • Sanskrit • *good god amongst the snakes and elephants*

Nā'il • Arabic • *he who cannot lose, always comes up smelling of roses*

Naldo • Spanish/Visigothic • *wise, powerful and strong*

Nanne, Nannulf, Anders • Scandinavian/Norse • *daring, audacious wolf*

Naphtali • Biblical/Hebrew/Jewish • *wrestling or wrestler*

Narayan, Narain • Sanskrit • *destiny of man; son of creation*

Narottam • Sanskrit • *best of men*

Nasr, Nasser • Arabic • *winner takes all*

Neal, Neil, Neale, Nigel, Niall • Irish Gaelic/English • *passionate, champion, winner, dead sexy, really desirable; some say it means a man who cannot commit*

Nelson, Nell, Neil • English • *passionate, champion, winner, dead sexy, really desirable; some say it means a man who cannot commit*

Niall, Neal, Neale, Nile, Niles, Neil • Gaelic • *passionate, champion, winner, dead sexy, really desirable; some say it means a cloudy man*

Niallghus, Niallgus • Irish Gaelic • *a man who is a strong and powerful champion*

Nicasio, Nikasios • victorious

Nicanor, Nikaner • Greek • *victorious man*

Nicholas, Nikolaos, Nicolás, Nickolas, Nick, Nik, Nico, Nicky, Nioclás, Neacal, Nikolaus, Niklaus, Nicolaas, Nikolaas, Niklaas, Niels, Nils, Nicolao, Nicolau, Nicola, Niccolo, Nicolo, Nikolai, Mikolaj, Mikolas, Mikulas, Nikola, Nikolaj, Niilo, Miktos, Mykolas, Nik, Niklas, Nels, Neacal, Nikelaos • Greek/English • *victory for or over the people*

Nicol, Nicholl, Nicola, Nichola, Nichol, Nicole • English • *victory for or over the people*

Nicodemus, Nikodemos, Nicodème, Nico, Nicodim, Nicodemo • Greek/Latin • *victory for or over the people*

Nicophoros, Nikephoros, Nikifor • Greek • *brings victory*

Nicostrato, Nico, Nike • Greek • *victorious army*

Nikita, Aniketos • Greek/Russian • *unconquered; name of Orthodox saint*

Nolan, Nuallain, Nuallan, Nuall • Irish Gaelic • *champion charioteer*
Nolasco • Latin • *personal name honouring the man who rescued the Christians from the Moslems during the Crusade*

Odd, Oddbjörn • Norse • *the sharp point of a weapon*
Osborne, Osbourne, Osbourn, Osborn • Anglo-Saxon/ Scandinavian • *a warrior with the strength of a bear as given by God*

Pancras, Pankratios, Pancrazio, Pancraz, Pankrati • Greek • *all-powerful*
Parker • American/English • *a person who is a warden or game-keeper in hunting park or chase*
Pascal, Paschalis, Pascha, Pasquale, Pascual • Latin/French • *pascal lamb; Easter time*
Penn • American/English • *a hill or pen for domestic animals*
Pesah, Pesach, Pascal • Hebrew/ Jewish • *Passover*
Pimen, Poimen • Greek • *shepherd*
Prabhakar • Sanskrit • *bringer or maker of light, candles*
Prabhu • Sanskrit • *sun god, God of Fire*
Pradbodh • Sanskrit • *springtime; awakening of nature, flowers*
Prakash • Sanskrit • *a famous, radiant person*
Pran • Sanskrit • *vitality, life breath and force*
Pratap • Sanskrit • *warrior king*
Preben, Pridbjörn, Pritbor • Scandinavian • *he's like a bear, in battle he comes to the fore*
Primitivo, Primitivus • Latin • *the first, earliest saints or martyrs*
Primo, Primus • Latin • *numero uno, number one!*

Qiu • Chinese • *autumn or fall (southern hemisphere)*
Quan • Chinese • *hot springs*

Radwan • Arabic • *pleasure and enjoyment*
Raghīd • Arabic • *freedom loving and devil-may-care*
Raghu • Sanskrit • *swift, fast*
Raghnall, Raonull, Rannal, Ronald • Norse • *wise, decisive chief or an oracle of the gods or kings*
Rainier, Rayner • Germanic/ Frankish • *adviser to the army; army commander*
Rajkumar • Sanskrit • *prince, heir*
Ramón, Raimundo, Raymond • Catalan/Germanic • *adviser, protector*
Randall, Randell, Randal, Randel, Randle, Randy • Germanic/Norman • *rim of a shield, wolf*
Randolf, Randolph, Randy, Randulf • Germanic • *rim of a shield, wolf*
Raymond, Ray, Raimund, Raginmund, Raimondo, Raimundo • Germanic/Frankish • *adviser to the army; army commander*
Rayner, Rainer, Raginheri, Raginhari, Reiner, Raniero, Ragnar, Regner, Rainerio • Germanic/ Frankish • *adviser to the army; army commander*
Read, Reed, Red, Reod • Anglo-Saxon • *a person with red hair or a ruddy complexion*
Reagan, Regan, Riagain • Irish Gaelic/English • *descendant of*

Riagain, the impulsive or impatient one

Reginald, Reg, Reggie, Reginaldus, Reynold, Reginwald • Germanic/ Norman • *advice rule*

Reid, Read, Red • English • *Scots/ English border name for red-headed person*

Renshu • Chinese • *good and strong*

Reuben, Reuven, Rube, Rubén • Biblical/Hebrew/Jewish • *behold, a son!*

Rhodri, Rhodrhi • British/Welsh • *ruler of the wheel; king who rules by his chariot*

Rhydderch, Roderick • British/ Welsh • *a man who is reddish brown in complexion*

Rhys, Reece, Rees • British/Welsh • *ardent, dead sexy or enthusiasm*

Richard, Rich, Rick, Dick, Ricky, Rickie, Dicky, Dickie, Richie, Ristéard, Ruiseart, Rhisiart, Rikhart, Rikhard, Ricardo, Riccardo, Ryszard, Rihard, Rikard, Rihards, Ritchie, Rhisiart, Hudson, Hudde • Germanic/Norman • *strong, brave and powerful*

Roald, Hrod • Norse • *famous ruler, famous chief*

Robert, Rob, Robbie, Rodberht, Reodbeorht, Bob, Rob, Bobby, Robin, Roibéard, Raibeart, Rupprecht, Robrecht, Rupert, Robbert, Roberto, Roopertti, Roberts, Rabbie, Rab, Rigoberto • Germanic • *famous and bright*

Robin, Robben, Robert • Germanic • *famous and bright*

Roderick, Rod, Roddy, Rodric, Rory, Ruaridh • Germanic/ Visigothic • *famous and powerful*

Rodrigo, Hrodric, Ruy • Spanish/

Visigothic • *a man with fame and power such as El Cid*

Roger, Rodge, Roge, Rodger, Rogier, Rodgar, Ruggiero, Ruggero, Roar, Rogerio, Hrothgar • Germanic/Norman • *famous spear, someone who used the spear and became famous for it*

Roland, Rodland, Rowland, Roly, Rowley, Rolie, Rolland, Roldan, Rolant • Germanic • *famed throughout land*

Ronald, Ron, Ronnie, Ronny, Roni, Ranald, Randal, Rognvald • Norse • *adviser to the gods or king*

Rong • Chinese • *martial and aggressive*

Rory, Ruaidhrí, Ruairidh, Roderick, Roy, Ruadh • Gaelic • *fiery temper or red-headed*

Rosendo • Visigothic • *a man on the path to fame*

Roshan • Persian/Urdu • *splendid, glorious/famous*

Rostislav • Slavic • *to seize or grab victory*

Rötger, Rüdiger • Germanic • *fame with a knife or spear*

Rowan, Ruadhan • Gaelic/English • *descendant of Ruadhan, little red one*

Roy, Ruadh • Gaelic • *red*

Ruiadhri, Rory, Ruarí • Irish • *the red king*

Rufus, Rufino, Ruffino, Rufinus • Latin • *red-haired*

Rupert, Ruprecht, Robert • Germanic/Dutch • *famous and bright*

Russell, Russ, Rous, Rousel, Russel, Rusty • Norman • *little red one*

Sasha, Sacha, Shura • French/ Greek/Russian • *the man/warrior/*

leader who protects or defends his people

Sachdev • Sanskrit • *truth of God, totally honest*

Safdar • Arabic • *a man who breaks ranks; loose cannon*

Sander, Alexander • Norwegian/ Greek • *the man/warrior/leader who protects or defends his people*

Sandro, Sonny • Italian

Sandy, Alex, Sandaidh, Sawney • Scots Gaelic/Greek • *the man/ warrior/leader who protects or defends his people*

Sanjay • Sanskrit • *victorious, triumphant*

Sanjeev • Sanskrit • *reviving, resuscitating*

Sardar • Muslim/Persian/Sikh • *top man*

Sarfraz • Muslim/Persian • *hold your head up high with dignity*

Sekar • Sanskrit • *summit, the best at what you do*

Sender, Zender • Jewish/Greek • Greek • *the man/warrior/leader who protects or defends his people*

Shahnawaz • Muslim/Persian • *cherisher of kings*

Shahzad • Muslim/Persian • *prince*

Shakil • Arabic • *handsome*

Shan • Chinese • *mountain, symbolic of success, eternal and ambition*

Shanyuan • Chinese • *foot of the mountain*

Sharīf • Arabic • *eminent in his field*

Shi • Chinese • *symbolic of strength and support*

Shraga • Jewish/Hebrew • *God of the Sun, Apollo or linked to Samson*

Siegbert • Germanic • *quick, famous victory*

Siegfried • Germanic • *victory, peace*

Sieghard • Germanic • *strong, solid victory*

Sigmund, Siegmund, Sigismund • Germanic • *a personal name meaning victorious and protector*

Siegwald, Sigiswald, Sigurd, Sjur, Sjurd • Germanic/Norse • *protector, victory*

Sloan, Sluaghhadain • Irish Gaelic • *a descendant of Sluaghadh, the tribe who go on raids and quick attacks*

Solomon, Shlomo, Sol, Solly, Saloman • Biblical/Hebrew/Jewish • *peace*

Stanilas, Stanislaus, Stanislaw, Aneislis, Stanislav • Slavic • *glory to the court, glorious courtier or politician*

Steel, Style, Styal, Steele • Anglo-Saxon • *a person who works with hard metal*

Sture, Stura • Scandinavian/ Swedish • *wilful, contrary, independent spirit*

Sultan • Arabic • *ruler, leader*

Sumanjit • Sanskrit • *he who conquerors the demon Sumana*

Surjit • Sanskrit • *he who has conquered the Gods*

Swaran • Sanskrit • *beautiful colour, golden*

Talbot, Talbod, Tal • Germanic/ Frankish/Norman • *a personal name meaning to destroy despatches (messages)*

Taylor, Tayler, Tayla, Taillier, Taleare • Anglo-Saxon/Norman • *a person who cuts, a tailor*

Teàrlach, Toirdhealbhach • Irish

Gaelic • *a man who takes the initiative, starts things*

Tempest, Tempeste, Tempestas • Latin • *nickname for a person with a tempestuous temperament*

Terence, Terentius, Terry, Toirdhealbhach, Tel, Terrance, Terrence • Latin/Irish Gaelic • *from the Roman family name Terentius and Irish for someone who takes the initiative*

Theobald, Peudbald, Theo, Thibault, Tiobold • Germanic

Tiernan, Tighearnan, Tighearnach, Tierney • Irish Gaelic • *lord or chief*

Tikhon • Greek • *bullseye! Hitting the mark or target*

Tiordhealbhach, Tárlach, Traolach, Turlough • Irish Gaelic • *instigator, initiator*

Trahaearn, Traherne • British/Welsh • *iron*

Traynor, Threinfhir, Threinfear, Treanfear • Irish Gaelic • *son of Threinfar meaning a strong man, winner*

Tristan, Trystan, Tristram, Tristam, Trystram, Tristram, Dristan, Drystan • British/Welsh • *rowdy, rebellious, blue, melancholic, chaotic*

Tuathal, Toal • Irish Gaelic • *chief of the clan or tribe*

Tudur, Tudor, Tudyr, Teutorix • British/Welsh • *king or chief of the tribe*

Tybalt, Theobald • Germanic • *a tribe of people known for their boldness in the face of adversity*

Tycho, Tychon • Greek • *hitting the mark, honest and true*

Uarraig, Kennedy • Irish Gaelic • *a fierce, temperamental man who is burdened with pride*

Ugo, Hugo, Hugh • Germanic • *heart, mind and spirit*

'Umar, Omar • Arabic • *to flourish and to make the complex simple*

Usain • Caribbean English • *modern invention: the fastest man in the world is Usain Bolt!*

Uwe • Germanic/Norse • *sharp blade, in awe*

Uzi • Jewish/Hebrew • *power and might*

Vasant • Sanskrit • *springtime*

Vasu • Sanskrit • *simply the best!*

Victor, Vic, Viktor, Vittore, Vittorio • Latin • *conqueror, winner*

Vidal, Vitale, Hayyim • Latin/Jewish • *to life!*

Viggo, Vigge • Norse • *a personal name meaning warlike*

Vijay • Sanskrit • *prizes or booty from victory*

Vikram, Vik • Sanskrit • *hero*

Vincent, Vince, Vincens, Vincentis, Vinnie, Uinseann, Vinzenz, Vicente, Vicenc, Vincenzo, Wincenty, Vincenc, Vinko, Vincentas, Vinzenz, Vincente • Latin • *to conquer*

Vinod • Sanskrit • *recreation, leisure, pleasure and sport*

Vitale, Vitalis • Latin • *full of life*

Vitus • Latin • *life*

Vivien, Vyvyan, Viv, Vi, Béibhinn • Latin/Norman • *Roman name Vivianus meaning life*

Vladimir, Volodya, Valdemar, Waldemar • Slavic • *great, famous leader or ruler*

Vladislav • Slavic • *glorious leader or ruler*

Volk, Wolf, Volkhard • Germanic • *strong people*

Vumilia • Swahili • *have courage, bear patiently*

Vyacheslav, Wenceslas • Slavic/Latin • *greater and even greater glory*

Wajīh • Arabic • *a man people want to emulate, their role model*

Waldemar, Waldo, Wald, Walker, Wealcere, Wealcan, Woldemar • Germanic • *famous ruler*

Walīd • Arabic • *newly born or reborn*

Walter, Waldhari, Wealdhere, Wat, Walt, Walther, Wolter, Valter, Gualtiero, Gwallter • Germanic • *commander of the army*

Watkin, Wat, Walter • Germanic • *commander of the army*

Wei • Chinese • *impressive strength and energy leading to greatness*

Weimin • Chinese • *honour the people with greatness*

Wenceslas, Ventieslav, Wenzel • Slavic • *greater and even greater glory*

Werner, Verner, Wernher • Germanic • *a Werin soldier, belonging to the Werin army*

Werther, Werter, Wetzel • Germanic • *a worthy soldier, a noble army*

Wieland • Germanic • *war land*

Wilbur, Willburh • Anglo-Saxon • *he who has the will to build a fort or protected village*

William, Wilhelm, Will, Bill, Willy, Willie, Billy, Willis, Wilmot, Ulliam, Uilleam, Gwilym, Willem, Willi,

Vilhelm, Vilhjalm, Guillaume, Guillermo, Guillem, Guilherme, Guglielmo, Vilem, Viljem, Vilmos, Vilhelmas, Vilhelms, Wim • Germanic/Norman • *his helmet gives him magical protection and the will to win*

Willibald • Germanic • *terrific will, bold and brave*

Wilmot, Willmott, William • Germanic/Norman • *pet name for William*

Wyatt, Wigheard • Anglo-Saxon/Norman • *a person who is brave and strong in war*

Wystan, Wigstan • Anglo-Saxon • *memorial stone where the battle was fought*

Xander, Alexander • Greek • *the man/warrior/leader who protects or defends his people*

Xiabo • Chinese • *little fighter*

Xing • Chinese • *arising, ascending*

Yaroslav • Slavic • *glorious spring*

Yingjie • Chinese • *hero, courageous, brave*

Yong • Chinese • *brave and courageous*

Yorath, Iorwerth • British/Welsh • *a handsome, beautiful lord or chief*

Zeke, Ezekiel • Biblical/Jewish/Hebrew • *God gives me strength*

Zihao • Chinese • *heroic son*

Zixin • Chinese • *self-confident*

Zoab • Nigerian • *strong, brave*

Girls

Aegle, Aglaia • Greek • *splendid radiance*

'Āisha, Aishah, Ayesha • Arabic • *alive; Mohammed's third and favourite wife*

Alastriona • Scots Gaelic/Greek • *the warrior/leader who protects or defends her people*

Alethea, Althea, Aletheia • Greek • *truth*

Alexandra, Alexa, Alexis, Sandra, Sandy, Lexy, Alix, Alexandria, Alexandrina, Alexia, Aleksandra, Alexina • Greek • *the warrior/leader who protects or defends her people*

Alexia • Greek • *one who defends*

Alickina, Kina, Keena • Greek/Gaelic • *the warrior/leader who protects or defends her people*

Alix • Greek • *one who defends*

Alpha, Alfa • Greek/Jewish • *first letter of Greek alphabet*

Alphonsine, Alphonsia • Spanish/Visigothic • *ready for battle, noble fighter, proactive!*

Amanda, Miranda, Manda, Mandy • Latin • *she is fit to be adored and armoured ready for attack!*

Amāni • Arabic • *desire, passion*

Amelia, Emelia, Emilia, Amélie • Latin • *rival, competitor*

Andra, André, Andrea, Andriana, Andrine, Andy, Andree, Anndra • Biblical/Greek • *a real sexy person*

Anniella • Roman Catholic • *little lamb*

Antigone • Greek • *contrary, the antithesis, born against the odds or contrary to conditions*

April, Avril, Averil, Aprilis • Latin • *to open as in springtime flowers*

Armelle, Artmael • Breton Celtic • *a female chief who is a steady as a rock*

Artemis, Diana • Greek/Latin • *Goddess of the Moon and the Hunt*

Asenath • Biblical/Egyptian • *she is Daddy's little princess*

Asia, Aysha, Ayeesha • Greek/Assyrian • *the east*

Aston • Anglo-Saxon • *the village to the east*

Audra, Audrey, Audrie, Audry, Audrina • Anglo-Saxon • *strength and noble of character*

Autumn, Autumnus • Latin • *a season of the year (southern hemisphere)*

'Azza • Arabic • *pride and power*

Bala • Sanskrit • *young*

Baozhai • Arabic • *precious hairpin*

Belaynesh • Ethiopian • *you are above all*

Bérénice, Bernice, Binnie, Bearnas, Berenike, Pherenike • Greek/Macedonian • *personal name; bringer of victory*

Bertha, Berthe, Berta • Germanic • *bright and famous*

Billie • Germanic/Norman • *her helmet gives her magical protection and the will to win*

Bionda • Italian • *blondie!*

Blanche, Bianca, Blanca • pure white, blonde

Bobbie, Roberta • Germanic • *famous and bright*

Bodil, Bothild, Botilda • Norse • *compensation for the battle*

Borghild • Norwegian • *fortified for the battle*

Brenda • Norse • *sword*

Brünhild, Brünhilde • Germanic • *battle armour*

Bunty, Buntie, Lamb • English • *pet name for a lamb: to bunt was to nuzzle*

Cameron • Gaelic • *crooked nose*

Cassia, Kezia • Latin • *thy name is vanity!*

Cheyenne, Sahiyena • French Canadian • *a Native American tribe from Dakota*

Chiara, Clare, Claire, Clara, Ciara, Kiarah, Kiara, Kiera, Clair, Clarette, Clarinda, Clarrie, Clarus • Latin/Italian • *bright, famous, crystal-clear*

Chunhua • Chinese • *spring flower*

Chuntao • Chinese • *spring peach*

Cindy, Cynthia, Lucinda, Cendrillon, Sindy, Cinderella • French • *cinders from the fire*

Clare, Claire, Clara, Chiara, Klara, Kiara, Clara, Kiarah • Latin/English • *bright, famous, crystal-clear*

Clarice, Claritia • Latin/French/English • *bright, famous, crystal-clear*

Clarissa, Clarisa, Clarice, Clarrisse, Clarisse, Claris, Clarissa, Cáitir • Latin • *bright, famous, crystal-clear*

Clelia, Cloelia • Latin • *a heroine, part true, part fantasy, she was a hostage who escaped back to Rome by swimming the River Tiber*

Clothilde • Germanic • *famed through war and battles*

Colette, Nichola, Nicola, Collette, Col, Colle, Colla, Nicolette • Greek/French • *victory for or over the people*

Cyra • Greek • *lord or chief*

Cynthia, Kynthia, Kynthos, Cyndy, Cindy, Sindy, Cinzia, Chintzia • Greek • *Mount Kynthos on the island of Delos is the birthplace*

of Artemis, Goddess the Moon and the Hunt

Dallas, Dallas, Dalfhas • Scots Gaelic/American/English • *the village of Dallas in Moray, north Britain; a place where cowpokes or drovers would rest their weary bones overnight*

Dana, Ana • Irish Gaelic • *name of an ancient Celtic fertility goddess, especially in Ireland*

Danae • Greek mythology • *her great-grandfather founded the Greek tribe of Danai or Argives; she was raped by Zeus/Jupiter when he appeared to her as a shower of gold, and she gave birth to the hero Perseus*

Dandan • Chinese • *my (red) cinnabar*

Dawn, Aurora, Dawne, Duha, Dagung • Anglo-Saxon • *daybreak!*

Deanna, Diana, Deana, Artemis, Deanne, Diane • Roman mythology • *Goddess of the Moon and Hunting*

Diana, Diane, Diahann, Dianna, Dian, Dianne, Deanne, Dyan, Di, Diandrea • Roman mythology • *Goddess of the Moon and Hunting*

Dionne, Deonne, Diahann • American English • *Goddess of the Moon and Hunting*

Dominica, Dominique, Dominga • Latin/Roman Catholic • *Lord, as in St Dominic, founder of the Dominican order*

Drew • Biblical/Greek/Scots English • *a real sexy person*

Dwynwyn • British Welsh • *Goddess of Love and Relationships*

Eiddwen, Eiddunwen • British/ Welsh • *fond, passionate, desire, holy, white, fair*

Eimear, Émer, Eimh • Irish Gaelic • *vague origins but comes from the word for swift, the bird, describing a person who is fast and quick*

Elfriede, Adalfrid, Elfreda • Germanic • *peace is noble*

Elma • Germanic • *famous swordsperson*

Emelia, Amelia, Emilia • Latin/ Italian • *old Roman family name meaning rival, competitor*

Emily, Aemilia, Aemilius, Émilie • Latin • *old Roman family name meaning rival, competitor*

Erdemute, Erdmuthe • Germanic • *indomitable spirit*

Erica, Ericka, Erika • Norse • *one ruler alone, no other*

Ermenhilde, Ermenhild, Irmhild, Irmhilde • Germanic • *a whole load of muscle!*

Ermine, Hermine • German • *soldier*

Esther, Esta, Hester, Haddasah, Eistir, Ester • Hebrew/Persian/Jewish • *Myrtle, Star and Persian Goddess of Fertility, Love and War, Ishtar*

Estrild, Easter, Eastre • Anglo-Saxon • *Goddess of Spring at war!*

Eunice, Nike • Greek • *well-deserved victory, nice one!*

Eve, Eva, Aoife, Éabha, Evita, Havva, Evie, Hayya, Eve, Evelyn, Evelina, Eubh, Evalina, Evelina, Aibhilin • Biblical/Hebrew/Jewish • *mother of all living, life itself*

Evelyn, Éibhleann, Aibhilin • Irish Gaelic/English • *desired by others*

Fauziya • Swahili • *victorious*

Fayza • Arabic • *champion, a winning woman*

Fiedhelm, Fedelma, Fidelma • Irish Gaelic • *unknown origins but given to a beautiful Irish Bouddicca*

Feivel, Faivish • Jewish/Yiddish/ Aramaic • *God of the Sun, Apollo or linked to Samson*

Fiamma, Fiammetta • Italian • *fiery*

Fina, Seraphina • Jewish/Hebrew • *the burning ones*

Flair, Flairer • American English/ French • *showing an individual talent*

Flavia, Favius, Flavie • Latin • *old Roman family name meaning yellow-haired*

Gabrielle, Gabriella, Gabi, Gaby, Gabby, Gabriel, Gabriele, Gabriela • Biblical/Hebrew/Jewish • *person of God*

Geneva, Geneve, Ginevra • French • *after the Swiss city or can be variant of Jennifer or short form of Geneviève*

Geneviève, Jennifer, Genoveffa, Ginevra • Celtic • *a female chief or leader of the tribe of people*

Geraldine, Gerry • Germanic/ Frankish • *she who rules with a spear*

Geraldine, Gerry • Germanic/ Frankish • *brave and bold with a spear*

Gerd, Gerda, Gärd, Garo • Norse • *Goddess of Fertility, protection as in a fort or castle*

Gerlinde, Gerlind • Germanic • *sport spear*

Gertrude, Gert, Gertie, Gerde, Gertrud, Gerda, Gertraud, Gertraut, Gertrudis • Germanic • *she is a dear woman with strength,* *superlative with a spear*

Gertrun • Germanic • *magic spear*

Ginger • English • *someone with red hair!*

Gloria, Gloriana, Glory • Latin • *glorious!*

Goldie, Blondie, Guinevere • American English • *a girl with blond hair*

Gormlaith, Gormflaith • Irish Gaelic • *a splendid, illustrious woman or princess*

Griselda, Grizelda, Grizel, Grishild • Germanic • *grey battle*

Guinevere, Gwenhwyfar, Goldie • English/British/Welsh • *blondie!*

Gumersinda • Spanish/Visigothic • *the path of man or woman*

Gunilla, Gunnhild, Gunhild, Gunn • Norse • *ready for battle and prepared to attack*

Gunnborg • Norse • *a fort or castle ready for attack*

Gunna • Norse • *strife*

Gunnvor, Gunvor, Gunver • Norse • *cautious and prepared for battle*

Gwenfrewi • British/Welsh • *time for reconciliation*

Gwyneth, Gwynedd, Gwynneth, Gwenith, Gwynaeth • British/Welsh • *happiness or named after the British Welsh princedom of Gwynedd, based on Snowdonia area where the ancient Brits (Welsh) fought the Anglo-Saxons in guerrilla warfare*

Gytha, Gyth, Gudrid • Anglo-Saxon/Norse • *discord or beautiful god*

Harmony, Harmonie • English • *concord, unity, friendship*

Harriet, Henriette, Henrietta, Hattie, Hennie, Hettie • German/French/English • *a famous army that carries all before it; a shining light*

Hebe, Hebos • Greek • *the Goddess of Youth*

Hedda, Hedwig • Germanic • *contentious and warlike*

Hedwig, Edwige, Hedda, Haduwig, Edvige, Hedvig • Germanic • *contentious and warlike*

Heike • Germanic • *a famous army that carries all before it; a shining light*

Helga, Heilag, Hella • Norse • *successful, prosperity, wealth*

Helme, Friedhelm, Helma • Germanic • *well-protected woman who comes in peace*

Helmina, Wilhelmina, Helmine • Germanic • *her helmet gives her magical protection and the will to win*

Henrietta, Henriette, Enriqueta • German/French/Spanish • *a famous army that carries all before it; a shining light*

Hephzibah, Hepzibah, Hepsie, Effie • Biblical • *my delight is in her (my newborn daughter)*

Herlinda • Germanic • *a compassionate army*

Hermine • Germanic • *a female soldier*

Hertha • Norse • *Norse Goddess of Fertility*

Hester, Esther, Hettie, Hetty • English • *Myrtle, Star and Persian Goddess of Fertility, Love and War, Ishtar*

Hilda, Hylda, Hilde, Elda • Germanic • *battleaxe*

Hildebrande • Germanic • *flaming sword into battle*

Hildegard, Hildegarde • Germanic
• *battlefield*
Hildegund, Hildegunde •
Germanic • *battle and strife*
Hillevi • Danish • *safe and protected in war*
Hiltraud, Hiltrud • Germanic •
strength in battle
Hjördis, Hjorrdis • Norse • *warrior goddess, great with the sword!*
Honesty, Honesta, Honestas, Honor, Honour • Norman/Latin •
truthful, fair and frank
Hong • Chinese • *red*
Huguette, Huette • Germanic/
Frankish/French • *heart, mind and spirit*

Ilene, Eileen • Norman French/
modern English • *desired by others*
Imelda • Germanic/Visigothic • *the whole complete battle*
Inderjit • Sanskrit • *victory over Indra*
Inge, Inga, Ingeborg, Ingrid, Ingfrid, Ingetraud, Ingegerd, Ingegärd, Inger • Norse • *protected by Ing, the God of Fertility*
Ingrid • Norse • *a beautiful woman blessed by the God of Fertility*
Irma, Erma, Ermen, Irmgard, Irmtraud, Irmen, Irmengard, Ermengard, Irmgard, Irmingard, Irmentrud, Ermentrud, Irmentraud • all and nothing less
Isadora, Isidoro, Izzy • Greek/
Egyptian • *a gift from the goddess Isis, deity of magic and life*
Isolde, Isolda, Iseult, Esyllt •
Arthurian mythology/British Welsh
• *a beautiful Irish princess*
Ismene • Greek mythology • *Greek tragedy!*

Jaya • Sanskrit • *victory!*
Jayanti • Sanskrit • *all-conquering*
Jayashree • Sanskrit • *Goddess of Victory*
Jemima • Biblical/Hebrew/Jewish •
dove; as bright as day
Jinghua • Chinese • *what a splendid situation!*
Jocelyn, Joselyn, Jocelyne, Joscelyn, Josceline, Joslyn, Joss, Céline, Gautzeline, Joscel, Joscein, Joscelyn • Norman • *someone from the Germanic tribe of the Gauts*
Juno, Úna • Irish Gaelic/Roman/
English • *uncertain roots; starvation or lamb*
Jyoti • Sanskrit • *light of mind, light of freedom, light of paradise*

Karama • Arabic • *a generous spirit*
Keelin, Kylin, Cianian, Cilan •
British/Welsh/Gaelic • *companion or friend*
Kelly, Kelley, Kellie, Ceallach
• Irish Gaelic • *bright-headed, quick-tempered*
Kennedy, Cinnéidigh • Irish Gaelic
• *ugly head*
Keren, Kerenhappuch, Keran, Kerin, Kerrin, Keron, Kerena, Kerina • Biblical/Hebrew/Jewish
• *ray of light or rye painted in the shape of a horn*
Khadīja, Khadīga • Arabic • *a premature baby or birth*
Kia, Kiaora • New Zealand/English/
Maori • *be well*
Kinga, Kinegunde, Kinge •
Germanic • *in the face of strife she is brave and courageous*
Klara, Clara • German/Latin •
bright, famous, crystal-clear
Kriemhild, Kriemhilde • Germanic

• *the mask of battle*
Kumari • Sanskrit • *daughter or princess*
Kyra, Cyra • Greek • *lord or chief*

Lacey, Lassy, Lassie, Lacy • Norman/Irish • *Norman baronial name Lassy who became powerful in Ireland in the medieval period*
La Keisha • African American • *THE favourite daughter*
Lalita • Sanskrit • *this girl is as playful as a kitten; affectionate and amorous*
Lark, Lawerce • North American/Australian/English/Anglo-Saxon • *dawn song*
Latasha, Latisha, Natasha, Tasha • African American • *combo of Laetisha and Natasha*
Laura, Laurel, Laureen, Laurene, Laurelle, Laurie, Laure, Laurette, Lora, Lowri • Latin • *laurel tree, sacred to those who are victorious and honoured*
Lauretta, Loretta, Lorette • Latin/Italian • *laurel tree, sacred to those who are victorious and honoured*
Leela, Lila • Sanskrit • *very sexy*
Lena, Yelena, Helen • Greek/Russian • *ray of sunshine, sunbeam, sunny*
Lexie, Alexandra, Alexis, Alex, Lexy, Lexis, Leagsaidh, Lexine • Greek • *the warrior/leader who protects or defends her people*
Liqiu • Chinese • *beautiful autumn (southern hemisphere)*
Liv, Lif • Norse • *life*
Loredana • literary Italian • *heroine in a novel!*
Loreen, Lorene • Latin/Gaelic • *laurel tree, sacred to those who are*

victorious and honoured
Lorelle, Laura • Latin/French • *laurel tree, sacred to those who are victorious and honoured*
Loretta, Lauretta, Loreto • Roman Catholic/Italian • *laurel tree, sacred to those who are victorious and honoured*
Lorraine, Lotharingia, Lorrain, Lorrayne, Lori, Lorri • Germanic/Lotharigian • *land of the people of Lothar and his famous army*
Louise, Lou, Lulu, Lodwig, Louisa, Lovisa, Lovise, Liùsaidh • Frankish • *famous in war or battle*
Louella, Luella, Lou • Latin/Italian • *famous in war or battle*
Lowri, Laura • British/Welsh/Latin • *laurel tree, sacred to those who are victorious and honoured*
Ludovica • Germanic • *she finds her fame in war*
Luisa, Louisa, Luise, Lulu, Lou • Spanish/Frankish • *famous in war or battle*
Lulu, Luisa, Luise, Louise • German/Frankish • *famous in war or battle*
Lyudmila, Lyuda, Ludmil • Slavic • *a tribe of kind people, a family of gracious folks*

Mackenzie, Mackenzee, Makenzie, Makensie, Makensey, Mckenzie, Coinneach, MacCoinnich, Mickenzie • English/Gaelic • *handsome, gorgeous, pleasing to the eye and rather adorable!*
Madhu • Sanskrit • *she is as sweet as honey and younger than springtime*
Madīha • Arabic • *praiseworthy, commendable*
Madison, Maddison, Mady,

Maddie • American/English • *child of Maud or Matilda, the battleaxe*

Maha • Arabic • *oryx, an antelope with large, beautiful eyes*

Maia, Maya, Mya • Latin • *Roman Goddess of Youth, Life, Rebirth, Love and Sexuality*

Maitland, Maltalent, Mautalent • Anglo-Saxon/Norman • *bad-tempered or from Mautalant, a barren place in France*

Malvina, Malamhin, Maggi, Maggie, Malamhin • cosmetic Scots • *name created by poet James McPherson, meaning smooth brow in Gaelic*

Manara • Arabic • *she sends out a radiant light like a pharo (lighthouse)*

Marcella, Marcelle, Marcelline, Marceline, Marcelina, Marcela, Marcellina, Marcellus, Marsaili • Latin • *named after Mars, God of Sex and War*

Marcia, Marsha, Marcie, Marcy, Marci • Latin • *named after Mars, God of Sex and War*

Meirionwen • British/Welsh • *a British prince who gave his name to the County of Meirionydd or Merioneth*

Martine, Martina, Mari, Martie, Marty, Martinus • Latin/English • *named after Mars, God of Sex and War*

Matilda, Mahthild, Mehthild, Mathilda, Tilda, Mattie, Matty, Tilly, Tillie, Mechtild, Mechthilde, Mechtilde, Machteld, Matilde, Mathilde, Mathilda, Matilde, Matylda, Martta, Matild, Mafalda, Matilde • Germanic • *mighty in battle*

Maud, Matilda, Mahauld, Maauld,

Maude, Mallt • Dutch/Flemish • *mighty in battle*

Maxine, Max, Maxie • Latin • *the greatest!*

Meredith, Meredydd • British/Welsh • *unknown prefix plus lord*

Minnie, Wilhelmina • Germanic/Norman • *her helmet gives her magical protection and the will to win*

Mireille, Mireio, Miriam, Mary, Miranda, Mireio, Mirella • Provençal • *to admire*

Missy, Missie • American English • *mistress!*

Muna • Arabic • *sexy, desirable and gives out hope and optimism*

Munira • Arabic • *radiant, bright, sends out a light*

Nāhid • Arabic • *a girl who is becoming a woman*

Naila • Arabic • *she is an all-round winner*

Najāh, Nagāh • Arabic • *a woman who is progressive and successful*

Nanna • Norse • *daring one!*

Netta, Nettie • Gaelic/English • *confused origins; passionate in all she does, a champion*

Nia, Niamh, Neve • British/Welsh/Irish • *beautiful and bright*

Nia, Nyah • Swahili • *with a purpose*

Niamh, Neve, Nia • Irish Gaelic • *beautiful and bright*

Nibāl • Arabic • *a quiver of arrows*

Nichola, Nicola, Nicki, Nicky, Nicolasa • Greek/English • *victory for or over the people*

Nichole, Nicole, Nicki, Nicky, Nikki, Nicholette, Nicolette • Greek/English • *victory for or over the people*

Nigella • black as pitch or passionate, dead sexy, really desirable; maybe a commitment phobe
Nikita, Anitketos Greek/Russian • invincible
Nilsine, Nicola • Norwegian/ Swedish/Greek • *victory for or over the people*
Ninghong • Chinese • *serene red or I would rather be red*
Nola, Fionnuala • Irish Gaelic • *descended from Nolan or champion chariot fighter*
Nolene, Noleen, Nolan • English Australian/Irish Gaelic • *champion charioteer*
Nura, Nūr • Arabic • *this woman will light up your life and she has unique features*

Órla, Ona, Anona, Fíona, Honor, Orfhlaith, Orflaith, Orlaith • Irish Gaelic • *golden lady or princess*

Paraskeue, Praskovya • Greek • *Good Friday, the Friday before Easter Sunday*
Pascale, Pascuala • Latin/French • *pascal lamb; Easter time*
Patribha • Sanskrit • *clever, radiant, imaginative and precocious*
Primrose, Primarosa • Latin • *the first rose*

Queenie, Victoria, Cwene, Cwen • Anglo-Saxon/English • *popular name for Victoria*
Qiu • Chinese • *autumn (southern hemisphere)*
Qiuyue • Chinese • *autumn moon (southern hemisphere)*
Quan • Chinese • *thermal spring*

Rachel, Rachael, Rachelle, Rae, Rella, Ráichéal, Rachele, Rakel • Biblical/Hebrew/Jewish • *ewe (female sheep)*
Radha • Sanskrit • *success!*
Raelene, Rae • Germanic/Frankish/ English Australian • *adviser to the army; army commander*
Raghda • Arabic • *a carefree woman who enjoys life*
Ragnhild, Raghnallt, Regina, Raghnaid • Norse • *seek counsel from the gods in war*
Raimunde, Raimund, Raimonda • Germanic/Frankish • *adviser to the army; army commander*
Ramona • Catalan/Visigothic • *adviser, protector*
Raquel, Raquelle, Rachel • Biblical/ Hebrew/Jewish • *ewe (female sheep)*
Rati • Sanskrit • *she desires; gives sexual pleasure and carnal knowledge*
Reagan, Regan, Riagain • Irish Gaelic/English • *descendant of Riagain, the impulsive or impatient one*
Rhonda, Ronda • British Welsh • *good with the lance or spear*
Rhonwen, Rowena, Rhawnwen • British/Welsh • *fair lance or holy spear*
Ricarda • Germanic • *strong, brave and powerful*
Richelle • Germanic/French • *strong, brave and powerful*
Rigborg • Danish/Germanic • *fortified and powerful*
Robbin, Robbie, Roberta • Germanic • *famous and bright*
Roberta, Robbie • Germanic • *famous and bright*
Robyn, Robin • Germanic • *famous*

and bright

Romilda • Germanic • *famous in battle*

Rong • Chinese • *macho woman; tomboy*

Roswithe, Roswitha • Germanic • *famous and strong*

Rowen, Ruadhan • Gaelic/English • *descendant of Ruadhan, little red one*

Roxy • American English • *flashy, glitzy but just a little nouvelle riche!*

Rusty, Rusti, Russus • Latin/Norman • *little red one*

Ryanne, Ryan, Riain • Irish Gaelic/English • *little king, descendant of Riain*

Sabāh • Arabic • *morning*

Sabina, Sabine • Latin • *from the Sabine women who were kidnapped by the Romans*

Sahar • Arabic • *morning has broken, dawn*

Salma • Arabic • *a person who looks after those she loves; a protector*

Sandra, Sandy, Alessandra, Alexandra, Sandi, Saundra, Sander • *the warrior/leader who protects or defends her people*

Sappho • literary Greek • *poetess Sappho, noted for her verse honouring lesbian passion*

Sarai • Biblical/Jewish/Hebrew • *contentious*

Sarah, Sara, Zara, Sally, Sadie, Sari • Biblical/Jewish/Hebrew • *princess*

Sarita, Sarah • Biblical/Spanish • *princess*

Sarala • Sanskrit • *as straight as the pine and honest as the day is long*

Sasha, Alexandra, Sashura, Shura • Greek • *the warrior/leader who protects or defends her people*

Saskia, Sachs • Dutch/Germanic • *Saxon, the tribe*

Sayidana • Swahili • *our princess*

Scarlett, Escarlate, Scarlata, Scarlet • Latin/Norman/English • *someone who dyes or sells fabrics of rich, radiant colours*

Sieghilde, Siedlind, Siedlinde, Sigi • Germanic • *conqueror in battle; winner takes all*

Seraphina, Seraphim, Serafina, Fina, Serafima • Jewish/Hebrew • *the burning ones*

Sharada • Sanskrit • *autumn (southern hemisphere)*

Sharman, Charmaine, Sherman • Anglo-Saxon • *shearer, someone who trimmed woven cloth*

Sindy, Cindy, Sinda • French • *cinders from the fire*

Sixten • Swedish • *victory stone*

Slava • Slavic • *glorious*

Sondra, Sandra • American English • *modern name for Sandra*

Sorcha, Sarah, Sally • Irish Gaelic • *brightness*

Suyin • Chinese • *straight-talking*

Suranne • English • *combo of Sarah and Anne*

Svetlana, Sveta, Photine • Slavic/Greek • *light*

Swanhild, Swanhilda, Swanhilde, Svanhild • Saxon • *she glides through conflict (battle) like a swan*

Talitha • Biblical/Aramaic • *little girl*

Tate, Tata • Anglo-Saxon • *personal name of an Anglo-Saxon*

Tawny, Tauny, Tawney, Taune, Tane • Anglo-Saxon/Norman • *someone with light brown hair*

Taylor, Tayler, Tayla, Taillier, Taleare • Anglo-Saxon/Norman • *a person* *who cuts, a tailor*

Teàrlag • Irish Gaelic • *a woman who takes the initiative, starts things*

Tempest, Tempeste, Tempestas • Latin/Norman/English • *nickname for a person with a wild temperament*

Terri, Terry, Theresa, Terryl • Latin/Irish Gaelic • *from the Roman family name Terentius and Irish for someone who takes the initiative*

Theda, Teud, Theodosia • Latin • *people, tribe or race*

Thelma, Thelema • Greek • *to wish or have the will*

Tiara, Tia • Greek/Latin • *half a crown! The Persians used to wear hats like the Coneheads!*

Tierney, Tighearnach, Tighearnaigh • Irish Gaelic • *lord or chief*

Tilda, Matilda, Tilde, Mathilde • Germanic • *mighty in battle*

Tilly, Tillie, Tilli, Tili • Germanic • *mighty in battle*

Tori, Tory, Toria • English • *short form of Victoria*

Trista, Trysta • American English/British Welsh • *rowdy, rebellious, blue, melancholic, chaotic*

Trixie, Trix, Trix, Beatrix, Beatrice • *blessed through life*

Tuesday • Anglo-Saxon/Norse • *Tiw's day, equivalent to Mars*

Ujana • Kiswahili • *youth*

'Umniya • Arabic • *your wish is my desire*

Úna, Unity, Oona, Oonagh, Euna • Irish Gaelic • *uncertain roots; starvation or lamb*

Usha • Sanskrit • *Goddess of the Dawn*

Valda • American English • *combo of Valerie and Linda or Glenda*

Valene • African American • *combo of Valerie and 'ene'*

Valérie, Valeria, Valère, Val • French/Latin • *old Roman name Valerius, meaning healthy, robust and strong*

Valetta, Etta, Valletta • Italian • *combo of Val and -etta: capital of Malta*

Valmai, Val, Falmai • British Welsh/Australian English • *mayflower or combo of Valerie and May*

Verity, Veritas, Verus • Latin/Norman • *truth and honesty*

Victoria, Vicky, Vickie, Vicki, Vikki, Tory, Toria, Vita, Victoire, Viktoria, Vittoria, Bhictoria • Latin/English • *conqueror, winner*

Vigdis • Norse/Norwegian • *Goddess of War*

Vijayalakshhmi, Vijayashree • Sanskrit • *Goddess of Victory*

Vita, Victoria • Latin • *life; also short name for Victoria*

Vivienne, Vivien, Viv, Vi, Vivi, Vivienne, Vivianne, Béibhinn • Latin/Norman • *Roman name Vivianus meaning life*

Walburg, Walburga • Germanic • *she rules over a stronghold or fort*

Waltraud, Waltrud, Waltrude • Germanic • *rules with great strength*

Wanda, Wenda, Wendelin • Germanic/Polish/Slavic • *a member of the Slav tribe living between the Elbe and Oder*

Wenqian • Chinese • *madder red*

Wilhelmina, Mina, Minnie, Billie, Wilma • Germanic/Norman • *her helmet gives her magical protection*

and the will to win
Winona • Native American • *Sioux tribe, name reserved for the first daughter*
Winta • Ethiopian • *desire*

Xiaodan • Chinese • *little dawn*
Xiaofan • Chinese • *rather ordinary or ordinary dawn*
Xiaojian • Chinese • *little healthy*
Xiaojing • Chinese • *morning luxury*
Xiaoli • Chinese • *morning jasmine*
Xiaotong • Chinese • *dawn red*

Ysuelt, Isolde • French/British Welsh • *a beautiful Irish princess*
Yuan • Chinese • *shining peace*

Zelda, Griselda, Grizelda • Germanic • *grey battle*
Zhenzhen • Chinese • *my precious*
Zita, Zeta, Zetein, Zitta • Tuscan • *wee girl*
Zoe • Greek • *life*
Zongying • Chinese • *heroine the others look up to; a role model*
Zula • South African/Zulu • *someone from the Zulu tribe*

TAURUS

21st April to 21st May

Planet: Venus

Day: Friday

Stone: emerald

Metal: copper

Colours: nature colours: grass green, sky blue, earth brown. Rich, strong colours associated with Mother Nature.

Design: wavy shapes and voluptuous contours

Trees: apple, pear, fig and all fruit trees, oak, orchard trees, rose trees, ash

Flora: rose, foxglove, cowslip, primulas, columbines, mallows, meadow and field plants

Famous Taureans: Andre Agassi • Eddie Albert • Madeleine Albright • Dante Alighieri • Fred Astaire • David Beckham • Annette Benning • Candice Bergen • Irving Berlin • Tony Blair • Lucrezia Borgia • Johannes Brahms • Charlotte Bronte • Pierce Brosnan • Robert Browning • Carol Burnett • Glen Campbell • Catherine the Great • Cher • Rita Coolidge • Gary Cooper • Oliver Cromwell • Bing Crosby • Bobby Darin • Moshe Dayan • Honoré de Balzac • Catherine de Medici • Queen Elizabeth II • Ella Fitzgerald • Henry Fonda • Sigmund Freud • Stewart Granger • Ulysses S Grant • William Randolph Hearst • Katharine Hepburn • Rudolph Hess • Emperor Hirohito • Adolf Hitler • Jack Klugman • Vladimir Lenin • Joe Lewis • Wladziu Valentino Liberace • George Lucas • Niccolo Machiavelli • Shirley MacLaine • Lee Majors • Guglielmo Marconi • Karl Marx • Yehudi Menuhin • Hosni Mubarak • Ed Murrow • Jack Nicholson • Florence Nightingale • Ryan O'Neal • Eva Perone • Sergei Prokofiev • Maximilien Robespierre • Sugar Ray Robinson • Odette Sansom • Pete Seeger • David O Selznick • William Shakespeare • Dr Benjamin Spock • James Stewart • Barbra Streisand • Shirley Temple Black • Uma Thurman • Anthony Trollope • Harry S Truman • Rudolph Valentino • Joachim von Ribbentrop • Rick Wakeman • Duke of Wellington • Orson Wells • Stevie Wonder.

Planetary Influences: see Venus at the back of this book (page 448)

Boys

Abbondio, Abundius, Abundans • Latin • *abundant*

'Abd-al-Fattāh • Arabic • *servant of the opener of the gates of prosperity*

'Abd-al-Rāziq, 'Abd-al-Razzāq, 'Abd-er-Razzā • Arabic • *servant of the provider, Allah*

'Abd-al-Salām, Abdes Salām • Arabic • *servant of the peaceable, Allah*

'Abd-al-Wahhāb • Arabic • *servant of the giver, Allah*

Adam, Addam, Ádhamh, Adamo, Adán, Adama • Biblical/Hebrew/Jewish • *earth*

Adelard, Adelhard • Germanic • *what a strong-looking and noble boy*

Adie, Adaidh, Adam • Scots Gaelic • *earth*

Aegidus, Agid, Giles • Latin/Greek • *kid, a young goat*

Aeneas, Aineas, Ainein, Angus • Greek • *singing praises*

Aiguo • Chinese • *patriotic, I love the land of my birth*

Alan, Alain, Ailin, Ailean, Alyn, Alun, Allan, Allen • Celtic • *vague origins but likely to be a rock*

Albion • Latin/Celtic • *possibly meaning white or rocky cliff, white cliffs of Dover*

Aleph • Jewish/Hebrew • *ox*

Algernon, Algy, Algie • Norman • *a man with a moustache/hairy-faced*

Alton • English • *place name meaning village by a river*

Ambjørn, Arnbjörn • Norse • *eagle and bear*

Amīr • Arabic • *ruler, prince, caliph or prosperous, wealthy*

Amnon • Biblical/Jewish/Hebrew • *faithful, loyal*

Amrit • Sanskrit • *immortal, divine foods*

Antiochos, Antiekhein, Antioco • *to hold out against all the odds*

Antrim, Aontraim • Irish Gaelic • *county in Ulster, Great Britain meaning one wee house!*

Ardal • Irish Gaelic • *top man for valour, he fights like a bear*

Arkadi, Arkadios • Greek • *a man from Arcadia*

Arrigo, Enrico • Germanic/Spanish/Italian • *power comes from the home or family (meaning nation too)*

Arthur, Arturo, Artair, Arthur, Artorius, Art • British/Welsh • *unknown origins possibly bear man*

Armstrong • English • *surname perhaps meaning as chap with strong arms*

Ashley • English • *ash wood or forest*

Athan, Athanase, Athanasius, Afanasi, Athanasios, Athanatos • Latin/Greek • *eternal life*

Atholl, Athfodla • Gaelic • *New Ireland, area of Perthshire*

Auberon, Oberon, Bron, Adalber, Adalbern • Norman/Germanic/Frankish

Audley • Anglo-Saxon • *surname meaning Aldgyth's (feminine) clearing*

Ayman • Arabic • *blessed be, wealthy*

Bailey, Bailie, Baily, Bailee, Baileigh, Baylie, Baylee, Bayley, Bayleigh • English • *the bailiff!*

Baldev • Sanskrit • *God of Strength and playboy!*

Barclay, Berkeley, Berkley •

Anglo-Saxon • *birch tree or wood*

Barrett, Barratt • English • *a trader, merchant*

Baxter, Baker • English • *a man who bakes bread* • *a baker!*

Bem • Nigerian • *peace*

Benigno, Benignus • Latin • *a very kind man*

Bentley • Anglo-Saxon • *the meadow of crooked grass*

Benton • Anglo-Saxon • *the crooked farm*

Bernard, Bernie, Bearnard, Bernhardt, Berndt, Bernhard, Bernt, Bernardo, Bernat, Benno, Ber • Germanic • *strong and hardy like a bear*

Björn, Bjarne • Swedish/Norse • *bear*

Blair, Blaire, Blar • Scots Gaelic • *plain or field or meadow*

Blume, Blumke • Jewish/Yiddish • *flower*

Bo, Bosse • Scandinavian • *I have my own home*

Boaz • Jewish/Hebrew • *strength*

Boleslav • Russian • *distinctly large and rather glorious*

Bond • English • *a man into husbandry and a farmer at heart*

Booth • Anglo-Saxon • *a gamekeeper's hut or wee house*

Brad, Bradford, Bradley, Bradleigh, Braeden, Braden, Brayden • Anglo-Saxon • *a man from the broad meadow, ford, farm or clearing*

Bramwell • Anglo-Saxon • *the well or water by the broom shrub*

Brandon, Brandan, Branden, Brandyn, Don, Branton • Anglo-Saxon • *the hill filled with a shrub called broom*

Braxton • Anglo-Saxon • *the village*

of the badger (brock)

Brewster • English • *a man who brews, a brewer*

Brigham • English • *a hamlet or village round a bridge*

Brighton • English • *the fair farm*

Brinley, Brynley • Anglo-Saxon • *burnt field or meadow*

Brock • Anglo-Saxon • *little pig or badger*

Bodie, Brody • Scots Gaelic • *a castle or fortress*

Bruno • Germanic • *brown*

Bryn • British/Welsh • *hill*

Buck • American/English • *cowboy, stag or doe*

Burkhard • Germanic • *safe harbour, strong protection*

Burnett, Burnet • Norman • *brown complexion or hair, toasted colouring*

Burton • Anglo-Saxon • *a town with a castle or fort*

Byron • Anglo-Saxon • *the place with a byre or cattle shed; a person who looked after oxen*

Cade, Kade, Caden, Kaden • English • *a man made of stout and sturdy stuff*

Cai, Kay • British/Welsh • *rejoice!*

Cain, Kane, Cane • Jewish/Hebrew • *a craftsman*

Caius • Latin • *a man of the earth*

Calvin, Cal, Cathal, Calbhach, Calvagh • Latin/ Irish Gaelic • *bald*

Callisto, Kallistos • Greek • *most fair, simply the best*

Carlyle, Carlisle, Carlile • British Welsh • *the place or castle belonging to Lugavalos, a personal name honouring the Celtic God of the Sun and Creativity*

Carmine • Latin • *song*

Carter • English • *a man who drives a wagon or cart!*

Caspar, Casper • Germanic • *treasurer, banker*

Cavan, Cafan, Chabháin • Irish Gaelic • *hollow*

Caxton, Kakktun, Kokkton • Anglo-Saxon/Norse • *a lump of land for an enclosure or straggled-out settlement; disordered*

Chadwick, Ceadelwic • English • *a man from the industrious farm*

Chanden • Sanskrit • *sandalwood*

Chase, Chace • English • *hunter*

Chauncey, Chauncy • English • *the chancellor*

Chester, Caer, Castra • English/Latin • *a fortress or encampment*

Chuanli • Chinese • *propagating prosperity*

Cleveland • English • *a tribe from the hills (Cleveland Hills, North Riding of Yorkshire)*

Cliff, Clifford, Clifton, Clive • English • *the ford over the river by the slope or cliff*

Clint, Clinton • Anglo-Saxon • *the settlement by or on the hill*

Clive • English • *the man who lives in a cave or cliff*

Comfort • American/English • *secure, safe*

Constantine, Constanz, Costin, Constantin, Cystenian, Constant • Latin • *constant, steadfast, loyal, devoted*

Cornelius, Cornell, Corneille • Latin • *Roman family name, connected to Cornucopia and the horn of plenty*

Cyprian, Cyprianus • Latin • *the man who comes from Cyprus, the isle of Venus or Aphrodite*

Dáire • Irish Gaelic • *fertile*

Dale • English • *a valley dweller*

Dallas, Dalfhas • Scots Gaelic/American/English • *the village of Dallas in Moray, north Britain; a place where cowpokes or drovers would rest their weary bones overnight*

Dalton, Daleton • Anglo-Saxon • *the village in the valley*

Damodar • Indian • *a rope round his belly, to prevent mischief!*

Dana • Irish Gaelic/American/English • *Celtic fertility goddess*

Dante, Durante • Latin • *strong and steadfast, personal name originally*

Darragh, Dair, Dáire, Darach, Daragh, Darach, Dara • Irish Gaelic • *son of oak*

Darby, Derby, Diurby • Norse • *deer park or enclosure*

Darius, Dareios, Darayavahush, Darayamiy • Greek/Persian • *he who possesses, looks after the good and wellness of all*

Dennis, Denis, Denys, Den, Dionysios, Denny, Dioniso, Dionizy, Denes, Dionysius • Greek/French • *named after the god Dionysius*

Denton, Den • Anglo-Saxon • *the place in the valley*

Dermot, Diarmaid, Dermid, Diarmad, Diairmit • Irish Gaelic • *not a bad bone in his body*

Desmond, Deasún, Des, Deasmhumhnach • Irish Gaelic • *a man from south Munster (around Cork)*

Devlin • Irish Gaelic • *fierce, brave, hardy warrior*

Devin, Damhain • Irish Gaelic/American English • *descendant of* *the Damhan; fawn, deer*

Dickon, Richard, Dick, Dicky, Dickie • Germanic/Norman • *strong, brave and powerful*

Dietfried • Germanic • *people of peace or peaceful people*

Digby • Norse • *the place in or by the ditch, Dikiby or Digby in Lincolnshire*

Dionysus, Bacchus • Greek • *Dionysus, God of Wine, Orgies and Partying*

Donagh, Donnchadh, Donough, Donncha, Duncan, Donn, Don • Irish Gaelic • *brown noble chieftain*

Donovon, Donovan, Donndubhan, Donndubhain • brown, dark black-haired chief or leader

Drake, Draca, Drago • English/Dutch • *a male duck but more in honour of great English seaman Sir Francis Drake*

Dubhdara • Irish Gaelic • *black oak*

Dudley, Dud • Anglo-Saxon • *the Worcestershire town of Dudley, Dudda's clearing in the wood*

Duncan, Donnchadh • Celtic • *brown chief or noble leader*

Dwight, Diot, Dionysa • English • *a woman (that's right: female!) who worships the God of Orgies*

Dwyer, Duibhuidhir • Irish Gaelic • *personal name meaning brown, black, tawny, dark yellow, maybe sensible and wise*

Eairdsidh, Archie, Eairrsidh • Scots Gaelic • *the real deal; genuine, bold and brave*

Earnest, Ernest, Eornost • Germanic • *a very serious, tenacious person who never gives up*

Ebbo • Germanic • *boar or pig*

Eberhard, Evert, Ebbo • powerful boar or pig

Ebun • Nigerian • *gift*

Eden, Edan • Hebrew/Jewish • *Garden of Eden, a place of sheer pleasure*

Edward, Ed, Eddie, Eideard, Eudard, Edvard, Édouard, Eduardo, Duarte, Edoardo, Edvard, Eduard, Eetu, Ned, Ted, Neddy, Teddy, Ewart, Eadbhárd, Eadweard • Anglo-Saxon • *a person who guards his riches, blessed with wealth*

Edwin, Edwyn, Eardwine • Anglo-Saxon • *a wealthy, prosperous friend*

Ehrenfried, Arnfried • Germanic • *peace with honour or person who, like the eagle, has power, but uses it as a deterrent*

Ehrenreich • Germanic • *honour-able and rich*

Éibhear • *origin unknown but name of the Son of Mil, leader of Gaels that conquered Ireland*

Eldon, Elsdon, Elladun • Anglo-Saxon • *Ella's hill in County Durham*

Ellair, Ceallair, Cellarius, Cella, Ellar • Scots Gaelic • *a person who works in pub or monastery as a steward*

Elton • Anglo-Saxon • *Ella's hamlet or village*

Emrys, Ambrose • British/Welsh • *immortal, eternal*

Enrique, Heinrich, Henry • Visigothic/Germanic • *power comes from the home or family (meaning nation too)*

Éoghan, Ewan • Irish Gaelic • *born of yew wood*

Ephraim, Evron, Effie, Yefrem, Efraín • Hebrew/Jewish • *fruitful*

Erdmann, Hartmann • earth man, man of earth

Erin, Éirinn • Irish • *romantic name poets give to Ireland*

Erwin, Irwin • Germanic • *a good, loyal and honoured friend*

Esbjörn, Esben • Scandinavian • *God is as strong as a bear or where the bear is worshipped as a deity*

Ethan • Biblical/Hebrew/Jewish • *longevity, strong and firm*

Étienne, Stephen • French/Greek • *crown or garland*

Euan, Éoghan, Ewan, Ewen, Evan • Gaelic • *yew tree*

Eustace, Eustakhios, Euistathios, Eustache, Eustaquio • Greek/French • *confused roots; could mean juicy, tasty grapes!*

Everard, Everett, Evrard, Eoforhard • Anglo-Saxon • *as brave as a boar or pig*

Everton, Eofortun • Anglo-Saxon • *the place where the wild boar or pigs live*

Ewan, Éoghan • Irish Gaelic • *born of yew*

Fabián, Fabianus, Fabius, Fabien • Latin • *old Roman family name meaning a bean*

Festus, Fachtna, Feichín, Fester, Vester • Latin • *sturdy and steadfast*

Farquhar, Fearchar • Scots Gaelic • *what a dear, loving man*

Fidel, Fidelis • Latin • *faithful to the end*

Firmin, Firminus, Firmino, Fermin • Latin • *he who cannot be moved, firm*

Flint, Fflint • English • *hard rock*

Florenz, Florentius, Florenzo • Latin • *he flourishes and blossoms*

Florian, Florentius, Florenti, Florencio • Latin • *flowery and*

romantic

Forbes, Forba • Scots Gaelic • *a Scots surname based on Forbes in Aberdeenshire, meaning fields*

Frédéric, Frederick, Frederik, Fritz, Fred, Phredd, Freddie, Fredick, Fredric, Friedrich, Frerik, Freek, Fredrik, Federico, Frederico, Fryderyk, Bedrich, Rieti, Frigyes • Germanic/Frankish • *peaceful but powerful ruler*

Friedemann • German • *man of peace*

Fuhua • *fortunes flourishing and growing*

Galen, Galenus, Galene • Latin/Greek • *calmness*

Gang • Chinese • *strong*

Gardner • English/Germanic/Frankish • *the main gardener for a big house or religious building*

Garfield • Anglo-Saxon • *a person who lives near a field shaped like a pyramid or triangle*

Garner, Gernier • Norman • *a person who worked in a granary*

Garth, Gärd • Norse • *a man who lives near a farm or paddock*

Gen • Chinese • *root*

George, Georgie, Geordie, Seoirse, Seòras, Deòrsa, Siors, Siorus, Siorys, Georg, Jörg, Jurgen, Joris, Joren, Jurg, Jørgen, Jorn, Göran, Jöran, Örjan, Georges, Jordi, Jorge, Giorgio, Georgi, Yuri, Yegor, Yura, Jerzy, Jiri, Juraj, Jure, Yrjo, Gyorgy, Jurgis, Juris, Georgos, Geergain, Georgios • Greek/Latin/Norman • *farmer or someone who works on the land*

Giles, Gyles, Aegidius, Aigidios, Gilles, Aegidus, Gide, Gil • Latin/

Greek/English • *kid, a young goat*

Glen, Glenn, Gleann • Scots Gaelic • *valley*

Glyn, Glynn • British/Welsh • *valley*

Glyndwr, Glendower • British/ Welsh • *valley of water*

Goddard, Godeheard • Anglo-Saxon • *hardy, strong and brave*

Gopal • Sanskrit • *cowherd, the king of the earth*

Göran, Örjan, Jöran, Jörn • Scandinavian/Serbo-Croat • *man from the mountains*

Gotam • Sanskrit • *ox, symbol of wealth*

Govind • Sanskrit • *cow finder linked to gods Indra and Krishna*

Grafton, Graftun • Anglo-Saxon • *a grove within a village*

Graham, Graeme, Grahame, Grandham, Granham • Anglo-Saxon • *I live in a gravelly place; Grantham, Lincolnshire*

Grant, Grand, Grande • Anglo-Saxon/Norman • *a large, portly person*

Granville, Grenville • Norman • *large village or town*

Grayson, Greifi, Greyve • Norse/ English • *son of a steward, a publican*

Grover • American/English • *a man who lives in or near a grove of trees*

Grwn • British/Welsh • *ridge, embankment*

Gulzar • Persian • *rose garden*

Guowei • Chinese • *status quo*

Guy, Gy, Guido, Wido • Germanic/ Frankish • *wide or wooden*

Haakon, Håkon, Hagen, Håkan • Norse/Germanic • *high-born son, relative, like a horse/fort, stockade*

Habacuc, Habakkuk • Biblical/ Jewish/Hebrew • *embrace, a kiss*

Hadley, Hadleigh, Haedleah • Anglo-Saxon • *a clearing where the heather grows*

Hale, Halh • Anglo-Saxon • *a person who lives off the beaten track; perhaps a hermit*

Hall, Heall, Halle, Halldor, Hallstein, Halstein, Halsten, Hallsten • *rock*

Halvard, Halvor, Hallvard, Hallvor, Halvar • Scandinavian • *defender like a rock*

Hamilton • Anglo-Saxon • *a flat-topped hill or mound, like Cape Town's mountain*

Hamza, Hamzah • Arabic • *strong, unmoved*

Hardy, Hardi • Germanic/Frankish • *a brave and stoic chap*

Hari • Sanskrit • *pet name for Vishnu or Krishna, preservation of the universe*

Hārith • Arabic • *provider, lion*

Harlan, Harland, Harley • English/ American • *grey rock or fields where the hares run*

Hartley, Hartleigh • Anglo-Saxon • *the clearing where the deer feed and gather*

Hartmann, • Germanic • *hard man!*

Hartwig • Germanic • *strong, loyal and devoted in battle*

Hartwin • Germanic • *a faithful friend*

Hārūn, Aaron • Arabic • *mountain of strength*

Hāshim • Arabic • *crusher, breaks bread*

Hassan, Hasan • Arabic • *a beautiful and beneficent man*

Haydn, Heiden, Heidano, Hayden,

Haydon • Germanic • *heathen or pagan*

Heath • English • *scrubland*

Hedley, Hedleigh, Headley • Anglo-Saxon • *the clearing where the heather grows*

Helge, Heilag, Helje • Scandinavian • *Middle Ages personal name meaning wealthy*

Heng • Chinese • *eternal, forever*

Henry, Henri, Harry, Anraí, Einrí, Eanraig, Heinrich, Henrik, Henrike, Hinrich, Hendrik, Enrique, Enric, Henrique, Enrico, Henryk, Hal, Jindrich, Heikki, Henrikas, Henning, Harris, Harry, Henry, Harry, Hank, Hawkin • Germanic • *power comes from the home or family (meaning nation too)*

Hershel, Herschel, Hirsch, Heshel, Heshi • Jewish/Yiddish • *a hart, deer or stag*

Hilary, Hillary, Hilare, Hilario, Ilar • Latin • *as in hilarious!*

Hilton, Hill, Hyll • Anglo-Saxon • *a village on a hill or hump*

Hillel • Jewish/Hebrew • *praise him!*

Hirsh, Hirsch • Jewish/Yiddish • *a hart, deer or stag*

Hudson, Hudde, Richard • Anglo-Saxon • *strong and powerful; confused origin; pet name of Richard*

Humbert, Humberto • Germanic • *he who fights like a bear cub*

Humphrey, Humfrey, Humphry, Humfry, Hunfrid, Humff, Wmffre • Germanic/Frankish • *someone when aroused will fight like a bear cub but until then is a peaceful soul*

Hunter • American/English • *a person involved in all aspects of hunting*

Hussein, Husayn • Arabic • *exqui-site, precious, beautiful*

Huxley • Anglo-Saxon • *Hucca's wood or clearing*

Ibrāhīm, Abraham • Arabic • *father of the tribes or nations*

Idwal, Iudwal • British/Welsh • *master of the ramparts and turrets*

Igor, Ivor, Ifor, Yherr • Russian/Scandinavian • *the army with archers who shoot with bows of yew*

Ihāb • Arabic • *gift, promise*

Ilario, Hilarius, Hilaris, Illari, Illarion • Latin • *cheerful, merry, hilarious!*

Ingram, Engelram • Norman/Norse • *Norman family name after the Viking fertility god, Ing, and his pet raven*

Ingvar, Yngvar • Norse • *warrior God who brings fertility and male potency*

Innes, Aonghas, Inis • Scots Gaelic • *an island or man from Innes in Moray*

Irène, Irenaeus, Eirenaios, Irina • Greek • *peaceable man*

Irwin, Erwyn, Irwyn, Everwyn • *a good, loyal and honoured friend*

Isaac, Zak, Zac, Zack, Ike, Izaak, Isak • Biblical • *unsure roots; probably the hireling or the laugh of a baby*

Isidore, Izzy, Izzie, Isidoros, Isidor, Isidro, Isidoro • Greek/Egyptian

Islwyn, Isllwyn • British/Welsh • *below the grove of trees*

Issachar • Biblical/Jewish/Hebrew • *a hireling*

Ithel, Iudhael • British/Welsh • *a generous but common man who behaves like a goodly prince or lord; philanthropist*

Ivar, Iver • Scandinavian • *archer warrior whose bow is made of yew*

Ivo, Yves, Ivon • Germanic • *yew tree*
Ivor, Ifor, Yherr, Iobhar, Íomhar • Scandinavian/Norse • *the army with archers who shoot with bows of yew*
Ivory • African American • *tusks and teeth of certain animals like the elephant*

Jabez • Biblical/Jewish/Hebrew • *I bear him with sorrow, sorrowful*
Jābir, Gābir, Jabr, Gabr • Arabic • *compassionate, comforter*
Jalāl, Galāl • Arabic • *great and glorious*
Jahangir • Persian • *he's got the whole world in his hands*
Jamāl • Arabic • *physically, drop-dead gorgeous*
Japheth, Yapheth • Biblical/Jewish/Hebrew • *growth, development, expansion*
Jasper, Jaspar, Casper, Caspar • English/Persian • *treasurer, gift of gold*
Javan, Jevon, Jeavon, Jeevon • Biblical/Hebrew/Jewish • *wine*
Javed • Persian • *eternal*
Jawdat, Gawdat • Arabic • *kindness personified and supreme*
Jianguo • Chinese • *patriotic*
Jianyu • Chinese • *building the universe*
Jinān • Arabic • *beautiful gardens, paradise*
Jingguo • Chinese • *building the nation*
Jitendra, Jitender, Jitinder • Sanskrit • *all-powerful, all-mighty, in control*
Jody, Jude • American/English • *uncertain root, possibly from Jude meaning praise*

Jörg, George, Jurgen, Jørgen, Georgianus, Jörn • Scandinavian • *farmer or someone who works on the land*
Jūda, Gūda • Arabic • *goodness and kindness transcend all*
Judah, Judas • Biblical/Hebrew/Jewish • *praise*
Jude, Judas • Biblical/Greek • *praise*

Kai, Gerhard, Klaus, Gaius, Caius, Caietanus, Kajetan, CAyo, Kaj, Kad • Norse/Scandinavian • *hen*
Kailash • Sanskrit • *paradise of Shiva and Kubera's home, the God of Wealth*
Kamāl, Kāmil • Arabic/Sanskrit • *perfection, beyond compare, pink*
Karam, Karīm • Arabic • *generous, magnimous, philanthropic*
Karp, Karpos • Greek • *fruity*
Kay, Caius, Gaius • Latin • *a man of the earth*
Kedar • African American • *mighty, dark*
Keir, Kerr, Kjarr • Norse • *a person who lives in marshes covered in shrubs and brushwood*
Keith • British/Welsh • *wood, copse or thicket or a man from East Lothian*
Kelvin, Kelvyn • Scots/English • *if you come from Kelvinside, Glasgow or by the river, this is the root of the name*
Kendall, Kendal, Kendale, Kendel, Kendell, Kendle, Kendyl, Cynddelw • Anglo-Saxon/British/Welsh • *someone who worships Celtic deities or a place in Westmorland, Kendal, named after River Kent*
Kendrick, Kenrick, Cenric, Ceneric, Cynwrig, Maceanrig, Cyneric •

British/Welsh/Scots Gaelic • *a sacred place high on a hill, or son of Henry or royal power*
Kenzie, Keziah, Kenzee, MacKenzie • English/Scots Gaelic • *the cassia tree or shortened MacKenzie*
Kermit, Dhiarmuid, Dermot • English • *not a bad bone in his body*
Kevin, Caioimhin, Keven, Kevan, Kevyn, Caoimhean • English/ Irish Gaelic • *beloved, beautiful, enchanting*
Khālid • Arabic • *indestructible*
Khayrat • Arabic • *good deed, kind actions*
Kingsley, King, Kingsly, Kingslie, Cyningesleah • Anglo-Saxon/ English • *the clearing or woods that belong to the king*
Knut, Cnut, Knud • Norse • *a knot or man who is short, squat and stocky*
Kondrati, Quadratus • *a person with a figure like a square*
Konstantin, Constantinus • Latin • *constant, steadfast, loyal, devoted*
Kyle, Caol • Gaelic • *narrow in geographical terms; a region in Ayrshire*
Kynaston, Cynefripestun • Anglo-Saxon • *the homestead or village of a peaceful royal or noble personage*

Lachlan, Lachlann, Lochlann, Lochlan, Lachie, Lockie, Loughlin, Lochlainn Lochlainn, Lachlan, Laughlin, Loughlin • Scots Gaelic • *a man from the land of the lochs or Norway; especially 17th May*
Lachtna • Irish Gaelic • *milk or creamy coloured*
Lambert, Landbeorht, Lamprecht, Lammert • Germanic • *famous,*
wonderful land, very patriotic
Lamin • African/Sierra Leonese • *honest, trustworthy*
Landon, Langdon, Langdun • Anglo-Saxon • *the long hill*
Lane, Layne • Anglo-Saxon • *a narrow pathway or roadway*
Laoghaire, Leary • Irish • *herd of calves; name of Dun Laoghaire, was Kingstown*
Lasairióna, Lassarina, Lasrina • Irish Gaelic • *flame, red-coloured wine*
Layton, Leighton, Leyton • Anglo-Saxon • *farm or field where leeks are grown*
Lee, Leigh • Anglo-Saxon • *a clearing in the wood*
Leland, Layland, Leyland • Anglo-Saxon • *land that is used for growing crops over years and left fallow for one*
Lennox, Levenach, Lenox • Scots Gaelic • *the place of the elm trees*
Léopold, Luitpold, Leopoldo • Germanic/Bavarian • *bold man*
Leslie, Les, Leascuilinn, Lesslyn • Scots Gaelic • *the place where holly grows*
Li • Chinese • *profit, business acumen and respectable*
Linden, Linde, Lyndon, Lynden • Anglo-Saxon • *lime tree*
Linford, Lindford, Lynford • Anglo-Saxon • *the lime trees or flax plant that grow by the ford in the river*
Linton, Lynton • Anglo-Saxon • *the village by or with a lime tree*
Linton, Lynton • Anglo-Saxon • *the place where the lime tree or flax plants grow*
Liwei • Chinese • *profit and greatness*

Macharia • Kenyan • *lasting friend*

Madhukar • Sanskrit • *the bee, sweet as honey*

Mahmūd • Arabic • *respected and laudable*

Makram • Arabic • *giving, generous and magnificent*

Mam'ūn • Arabic • *reliable and trusted*

Manāl • Arabic • *materially prosperous*

Manfred, Manffred, Mainfred, Manfried, Manfredo • Germanic • *man of peace*

Mani, Subrahmanya • Sanskrit • *jewel with potent qualities; the penis*

Manley, Manly • Anglo-Saxon • *common land, for all men*

March, Marche, Mensis • Norman • *a person who lives on the borders, the Marches*

Marley, Maeremyrig • Anglo-Saxon • *the pleasant field or boundary enclosure of the pine martens*

Marquis, Marcuis • Norman • *Lord of the Marches, borders between England and Wales*

Mason, Macon, Macian • Germanic/Frankish/Anglo-Saxon • *a person who makes things with stone*

Mathúin, Mathghamhain, Mahon • Irish • *bear*

Maynard, Maginhard • Germanic/Frankish • *strong and brave*

Medardo • Germanic • *personal name plus a strong, hard chap*

Meinhard • Germanic • *strong as a rock*

Mercer, Mercy, Mercier, Mercarius, Merx • Norman/Latin • *a merchant*

Merdardo • Germanic • *unknown beginning but ends with strong and hardy*

Myrddin, Merlyn, Merlin • British/Welsh • *sea fort or sea hill*

Miller, Mille, Milne, Mylen • English • *a person who works in a mill*

Milton, Mylentun, Milt • Anglo-Saxon • *the homestead or village by or with a mill*

Montgomery, Montgomeric, Monty • Germanic/Norman • *the powerful man from the hill country*

Morton, Morten, Moses, Mort, Mortun • Anglo-Saxon • *village by or on moorland*

Muir, More • Scots/English • *moorland*

Murgatroyd, Royd • English • *clearing belonging to Margaret*

Nadīm • Arabic • *best friend, companion you share your social life with*

Nādir • Arabic • *rare, priceless, precious*

Nagendra • Sanskrit • *good god amongst the snakes and elephants*

Nā'il • Arabic • *he who cannot lose, always comes up smelling of roses*

Na'īm • Arabic • *he who enjoys his own company; happy is his lot*

Nanda • Sanskrit • *joy, happiness, child (especially son), many riches*

Naphtali • Biblical/Hebrew/Jewish • *wrestling or wrestler*

Nāsir, Nazir • Arabic • *a good ally and friend; helping and supportive*

Naveed • Persian • *glad tidings, invite to the wedding or something just as jolly*

Ned, Edward • Anglo-Saxon • *a careful, prudent ruler who looks after his riches and possessions*

Neo • African • *gift*

Niaz • Persian • *prayer, gift, sacrifice*

Njord, Nerthus • Norse • *Norse God of Sea and Fertility*

Noam • Jewish/Hebrew • *joy, pleasure and happiness*

Norman, Nordman, Tormod • Germanic • *a man from the north; Norseman or Viking*

Norris, Norreis • Germanic/Frankish • *a person who has migrated from the north to Normandy; Norseman or Viking*

Norton, Nordtun • Anglo-Saxon • *the northern village, homestead or enclosure*

Nyabera • Kenyan • *the good one*

Oakley, Oakleigh • American/English • *an oak wood or clearing in the forest*

Oberon, Auberon • Norman/Germanic/Frankish • *as noble as a bear*

Oisín, Ossian, Osheen • Irish Gaelic • *stag*

Oleg, Helgi • Norse • *prosperous, the chap who created Kiev, Ukraine*

Oliver, Olivier, Olivarius, Ollie, Oleifr, Noll • Germanic/Frankish/Norse • *olive tree*

Onisim, Anisim • Greek • *useful, worthwhile*

Omri • Jewish/Hebrew • *sheaf of wheat*

Örjan, Jurian, George • Scandinavian • *farmer or someone who works on the land*

Orpheus, Orfeo • Greek • *beautiful voice; in legend a Thracian musician who married Eurydice, stolen by Pluto*

Orazio, Horatius, Horatio • Estruscan • *personal family name*

Oren, Oran, Orin, Orren, Orrin • Biblical/Hebrew/Jewish • *a pine tree*

Orlando, Roland • Italian • *a person who is famous for the real estate they own; land, territory*

Orson, Orsursus • Norman • *bear cub*

Osborne, Osbourne, Osbourn, Osborn • Anglo-Saxon/Scandinavian • *a warrior with the strength of a bear as given by God*

Oscar, Oskar • Irish • *friend of wildlife, especially deer and stags*

Osian, Oisín, Ossian, Oisein • Gaelic • *stag*

Otis, Ote, Ode • Germanic/Frankish • *wealthy, prosperous*

Otmar, Ottmar, Ottomar • Germanic • *famed riches*

Otto • Germanic • *riches, a royal and imperial name*

Parker • American/English • *a person who is a warden or gamekeeper in hunting park or chase*

Patrice, Patrick • Latin/French/Irish Gaelic • *patrician*

Patrick, Pàdraig, Pat, Paddy, Patsy, Páraic, Patrice, Patricio, Patrizio, Porick, Podge, Pàra, Pàdair, Pàidean, Padrig, Paddy, Patrick, Pat, Patrice • Latin/Irish Gaelic • *patrician*

Pàrlan, Parthalán • Gaelic • *uncertain origin may be linked to Irish for Bartholomew*

Pearce, Pierce, Perais • Norman • *the rock or stone*

Peleg • Biblical/Hebrew/Jewish • *division, border or boundary*

Pelham, Peotlaham, Peolham • Anglo-Saxon • *Peola's homestead or farm*

Penn • American/English • *a hill*

or pen for domestic animals
**Percival, Parsifal, Parzifal,
Perceval, Peredur, Percy, Perce,
Perce, Pearce, Pierce, Percy, Piers,
Perceval, Perce** • Celtic/Norman
• *Celtic name of Peredur; Peredur's
valley*
**Percy, Piers, Percival, Perci,
Persiacum, Persius, Perse,
Percehaie, Percerhaie** • Latin/
Gaulish • *Pierce's hedge*
Perry, Pirige, Peregrine • Anglo-
Saxon • *a person who owns or lives
near a pear tree*
Pesah, Pesach, Pascal • Hebrew/
Jewish • *Passover*
**Peter, Pete, Petros, Peadar, Pedr,
Piet, Pieter, Per, Petter, Par, Pierre,
Pedro, Perico, Pere, Pietro, Piero,
Pyotr, Piotr, Petr, Petar, Pekka,
Peitari, Peteris, Petras, Petrus,
Petya, Pette, Pedr, Pier** • Greek •
the rock or stone
Piaras, Piers, Pierce, Pearce • Irish
Gaelic/English • *Pierce's hedge*
**Philbert, Filaberht, Philibert,
Filbert** • Greek/Germanic/Frankish
• *dear, beloved*
Philo, Philon • Greek • *love*
**Phineas, Fineas, Panhsj, Phinehas,
Pinchas** • Hebrew/Jewish/Biblical •
*a person from Nubia, now southern
Egypt or northern Sudan, or from
the snake's mouth*
Ping • Chinese • *stable and secure*
Pitambar • Sanskrit • *saffron*
Pitt • Anglo-Saxon • *a man who
lives in a pit*
Placido, Placidus • Latin/Italian •
calm, quiet, placid
Potter • American English •
someone who sells pots
Pradbodh • Sanskrit • *springtime;*

awakening of nature, flowers
Preben, Pridbjörn, Pritbor •
Scandinavian • *he's like a bear in
battle, he comes to the fore*
Precious • American English •
someone who is precious, invaluable
Prokhoros, Prokhor • Greek • *very
artistic, chief of a troupe of singers,
dancers, actors*
**Prokopios, Prokopi, Prokofi,
Prokope** • Greek • *successful*
Prosper, Prosperus, Prospero •
Latin • *a person who prospers*
**Prudenzio, Prudentius, Prudens,
Prudencio** • Latin • *prudent*

Qāsim • Arabic • *giver*
Quartus • Latin • *four*
Qiu • Chinese • *autumn or fall
(southern hemisphere)*
**Quentin, Quintinus, Quintus,
Quintin, Quinton, Cwentun** • Latin
• *Roman family name meaning
number five*
Quincy, Quincey, Cuinchy, Quintus
• Latin • *the number five*
Quinn, Cuinn • English/Irish Gaelic
• *descendant of Cuinn*
Quirinius • Latin • *governor*

Radwan • Arabic • *pleasure and
enjoyment*
Ra'fat • Arabic • *mercy, compassion,
forgiveness*
Rajiv • Sanskrit • *striped and/or the
blue lotus*
Ratan • Prakrit • *jewel*
Ratilal • Prakrit • *Lord of Love and
Pleasure*
Reid • Anglo-Saxon • *someone who
lives in a clearing in the woods*
Renshu • Chinese • *good and strong*
Riaz • Arabic • *green fields, often*

with an equine connection

Richard, Rich, Rick, Dick, Ricky, Rickie, Dicky, Dickie, Richie, Ristéard, Ruiseart, Rhisiart, Rikhart, Rikhard, Ricardo, Riccardo, Ryszard, Rihard, Rikard, Rihards, Ritchie, Rhisiart, Hudson, Hudde • Germanic/Norman • *strong, brave and powerful*

Ridley, Reodleah • Anglo-Saxon • *clearing of reeds*

Riley, Rygeleah, Reilly, Raghallach, Ryley • Anglo-Saxon/Irish Gaelic • *a field where the rye crop has been cleared*

Riscu • African • *prosperity*

Robhartach, Rob • Irish • *bringer or broker of prosperity and wealth*

Roscoe, Raskog • Norse • *the wood where the doe and deer gather*

Ross, Rós • Gaelic • *family name from geographical term for a headland or promontory*

Royce, Royston, Royse • English • *the town or place of the rose or roses*

Royle, Rygehyll, Royal • Anglo-Saxon • *the hill where rye is grown*

Sābir, Sabri • Arabic • *patience is a virtue, persevere*

Sachdev • Sanskrit • *truth of God, totally honest*

Sakhr • Arabic • *solid as a rock*

Salāma • Arabic • *keeping safe, self-protection*

Sālih • Arabic • *devout, devoted*

Sālim, Salīm • Arabic • *safe, unharmed*

Samīh • Arabic • *tolerant, generous*

Sanford, Stanford, Stamford • Anglo-Saxon • *the ford in the river is where the sandy soil is*

Satish • Sanskrit • *the fact of a matter, the true reality*

Scott • Gaelic • *a man from Ireland who settles in Scotland*

Seth • Sanskrit • *vague root but white or bridge*

Shādi • Arabic • *singer*

Shākir • Arabic • *thankful and grateful*

Shalom • Jewish/Hebrew • *peace*

Shamshad • Persian • *tall as a box tree*

Shan • Chinese • *mountain symbolic of success, eternal and ambition*

Shanyuan • Chinese • *foot of the mountain*

Sharma • Sanskrit • *protect, comfort, joy*

Shaw, Sceaga, Skog • Anglo-Saxon • *a wood or copse of trees*

Shelby • Norse • *willow farm*

Sheldon • Anglo-Saxon • *steep-sided valley; embankment*

Shi • Chinese • *symbolic of strength and support*

Shining • Chinese • *let the world be at peace*

Sioltach, Sholto • Scots Gaelic • *the sower of the seed*

Shukri • Arabic • *giving thanks*

Siddhartha • Sanskrit • *Buddha; attainment*

Siegbjorn • Norse/Swedish • *bear victory*

Silas, Silouanus, Silvanus, Silva • Latin

Silvester, Silver, Sylvester, Silvano, Silvestro, Silvestre, Sly, Slie • Latin • *a person from the woods or forest*

Silvio, Silvius • Latin/Italian/Spanish/Portuguese • *someone who loves or inhabits the woods or forest*

Sinclair • Norman • *baronial name from Saint-Clair who received earl-*

doms in Caithness and Orkney
Siyu • Chinese • *thinking of the
planet Earth*
**Solomon, Shlomo, Sol, Solly,
Saloman** • Biblical/Hebrew/Jewish
• *peace*
Spencer • Anglo-Saxon • *similar
to a quartermaster, someone who
dispenses provisions or goods*
Sridhar • Sanskrit • *bearing,
possessing the Goddess of Light,
Beauty and Wealth, Sri*
Srikant • Sanskrit • *Shiva's beautiful
throat*
Srikant • Sanskrit • *beloved of Sri,
Goddess of Light, Beauty and Wealth*
Sroel • Jewish/Yiddish • *Israel*
Stacey, Eustace • English/Greek
• *confused roots, could mean juicy,
tasty grapes!*
Stafford • Anglo-Saxon • *the river
ford good for landing*
Standish, Stanedisc, Stan • Anglo-
Saxon • *the field or meadow filled
with stones*
Stanley, Stan, Stanleah • Anglo-
Saxon • *the clearing filled with stones*
**Stefan, Stephan, Stephanos,
Steven, Steve, Steff, Stevie,
Stiofán, Stiana, Steaphan,
Steffan, Steffen, Stefan, Staffan,
Étienne, Stéphane, Estéban,
Esteve, Estevao, Stefano, Stepan,
Szczepan, Stjepan, Stevan, Istvan,
Steponas** • Greek • *a crown or
garland*
Stein, Steyne, Sten, Steen, Steinn •
Norse • *stone*
Stone, Stan • Anglo-Saxon • *stone*
Suleimān, Sulaymān • Biblical/
Arabic • *peace*
Sundar, Sunder • Sanskrit •
beautiful

Sunil • Sanskrit • *very dark blue*
Sushil • Sanskrit • *a hail and hearty
chap*
Sylvain, Silvano • Italian • *a person
from the woods or forest*

Tage, Taki, Taka • Scandinavian •
to take or grab, receive, guarantor
Tāmir • Arabic • *rich in dates and
figs and all good things*
Tanner • American English • *a
person who cleans and tans hides*
Tarun, Taroon • Sanskrit • *dawn, the
early sun, young, tender growth of
love and romance*
Tegan, Teg • British/Welsh • *a
rather lovely or beautiful person*
Terrell, Tyrell • Norman • *a person
who is hard to pull this way or that,
very fixed!*
Thornton, Thorn, Tornton • Anglo-
Saxon • *the village where the thorn
bush grows*
Tingguang • Chinese • *bright
garden or courtyard*
Tirso, Thyrsos • Oriental • *follower
of Dionysus (Bacchus)*
**Torbjørn, Thorbjørn, Torben,
Torbern** • Old Norse • *the god Thor
with the strength of a bear*
Torolf, Torulf, Torolv • Norse • *the
god Thor with the strength of a wolf*
**Torsten, Torstein, Thorstein,
Thorsteinn** • Norse • *the god Thor
with the strength of a stone*
Travis, Traverser • Norman •
*someone who worked collecting tolls
on the roads or highways, crossing
roads*
**Traynor, Threinfhir, Threinfear,
Treanfear** • Irish Gaelic • *son of
Threinfar, meaning a strong man,
winner*

Trefor, Trevor, Trev, Tref • British/ Welsh • *a large settlement or village*

Tremaine, Tremayne, Tremen • British/Welsh/Kernow • *Cornish for homestead and stone*

Trenton, Trent • American English • *means the settlement by the Trent, or after William Trent, the British Quaker founder of the New Jersey city*

Trevelyan, Treelian, Trevelien • British/Welsh/Kernow • *Cornish for the homestead or village of Elian (local personage)*

Trond, Tron • Norse • *a man from Trondelag in Norway*

Trofim, Trophimos • Greek • *fruitful, goodness, sustaining*

Truman, Treowemann, Trueman • Anglo-Saxon/American/English • *a trusted man*

Tryggve, Tryggr, Trygve • Norse • *trusty and true*

Turner • English • *a person who makes objects by turning them on a lathe or wheel*

Tyrone, Ty, Tir Eoghain • Irish Gaelic • *a man from County Tyrone, Ulster; the land of Owen*

Tyrell, Tyrrell, Tirel, Terrell • a person who is hard to pull this way or that, very fixed!

Tyson, Ty, Tison • Greek/Norman • *female name for Dionysius, God of Wine, or meaning a hot-tempered person*

Udo • Germanic • *riches*

Ùisdean, Eysteinn, Hugh, Hùisdean • Irish Gaelic • *a man who is forever unchanging, like a stone*

Ulric, Wulfric, Ulrick, Ulrich, Utz • Germanic/Anglo-Saxon • *power and riches; wolf power*

Ultach, Ultán • Irish • *a man from Ulster; especially 3rd May*

Umberto, Humbert • Italian/ Germanic • *he who fights like a bear cub*

Urs, Ursus • Latin • *bear*

Uwamahoro • Rwandan • *peacemaker*

Vasant • Sanskrit • *springtime*

Veit, Wido, Guy • Germanic • *wood or wide*

Vere, Ver, Vern, Vernon • Celtic/ Gaulish • *alder tree*

Vergil, Virgil • Latin • *family name with confused origins; could refer to Virgo the maiden or virga as in stick*

Vernon, Vere, Vern • Gaulish • *alder tree*

Vester, Silvester • Latin • *a person from the woods or forest*

Virgil, Vergilius, Virgilius, Vergil, Virgilio, Vigil • Latin • *Roman family name Vergilius but confusion reigned when the spelling was changed to Virgilius, which means the maiden or virga as in stick*

Vlas, Blasius, Blaesus, Blaise, Vlasi • Latin • *area of the throat; St Blaise rules the throat*

Vumilia • Swahili • *have courage, bear patiently*

Wayne, Waegen • Anglo-Saxon • *a carter or cartwright; wagon driver*

Wei • Chinese • *impressive strength and energy leading to greatness*

Weiyuan • Chinese • *strong roots*

Wentworth, Winterwort • Anglo-Saxon • *winter enclosure or paddock*

Wesley, Westley, Wes, Wez • Anglo-Saxon • *the meadow, wood or*

clearing to the west
Weston, Westun • Anglo-Saxon • *village or farm to the west*
Wilberforce, Wilberfoss, Wilburgfoss, Wilbur • Anglo-Saxon/ Latin • *Wilburg's ditch*
Wilbur, Willburh • Anglo-Saxon • *he who has the will to build a fort or protected village*
Wilfrid, Wilfrit, Walfrid, Wilfrey, Wilf, Wilfried, Vilfred • Germanic • *the will for peace*
Willard, Will Wilheard • Anglo-Saxon • *a person with tremendous willpower, powerful in every way*
Willibald • Germanic • *will, bold and brave*
Willibrand • Germanic • *will and flaming sword*
Willoughby, Weligbyr • Anglo-Saxon/Norse • *the village by the willow tree*
Wilmer, Wilmaer • Anglo-Saxon • *he is famous for his will-power and strength of character*
Winston, Wynnstan • Anglo-Saxon • *stone of joy*
Winthrop, Winthorpe • Anglo-Saxon • *Wynna's village*
Winton, Winntun, Withigtun, Winatun • Anglo-Saxon • *village with a pasture*
Witold • Germanic • *ruler of the wood or wide country*
Woodrow, Woody • English • *a hamlet with a row of houses*
Woody, Carpenter • English • *nickname for a carpenter or worker with wood*
Worth, Worth, Weorth • Anglo-Saxon • *hamlet of a main village*

Xolani • Xhosa South Africa • *please forgive*

Yaoting • Chinese • *honouring the garden or family*
Yaroslav • Slavic • *glorious spring*
Yāsir, Yusri • Arabic • *wealthy, prosperous*
Yefrem, Ephraim • Russian/ Hebrew/Jewish • *fruitful*
Yehudi • Biblical/Hebrew/Jewish • *jew*
Yi • Chinese • *sure and resolute*
Yilma • Ethiopian • *may he prosper*
Yitzhak, Isaac • Jewish/Hebrew • *unsure roots probably the hireling or the laugh of a baby*
Yorick, Jorck, George • Danish/ Greek • *farmer or someone who works on the land*
York, Yorke, Jorvik • Anglo-Saxon/ Norse • *boar or pig farm*
Yuri, Yura, Georgi • Russian/Greek • *farmer or someone who works on the land*
Yusra • Arabic • *rich, well endowed*
Yusheng • Chinese • *jade birth*
Yves, Ive, Ivo, Ivon • French/ Germanic • *yew tee*

Zayd • Arabic • *growth, increase*
Zedong • Chinese • *east of the marshes*
Zhengsheng • Chinese • *powerful country*
Zhengzhong • Chinese • *loyal and trustworthy*
Zhiqiang • Chinese • *strength of will*
Zhong • Chinese • *steadfast and devoted*
Ziyād • Arabic • *to grow and build*
Zoab • Nigerian • *strong, brave*
Zuhayr • Arabic • *little flowers*

Girls

Abilene, Abbie, Abby, Abbey, Abi, Lena • Biblical/Jewish/Hebrew • *an area of Palestine or the Holy Land, meaning grass or grasses*

Abīr • Arabic • *fragrant*

Abla • Arabic • *voluptuous*

Acacia, Akakia, Wattle • Greek/Latin • *acacia wood, holy wood that had special powers as a hex against evil*

Ada, Adah • Biblical/Jewish/Hebrew • *adornment to make one beautiful*

Adamina • Biblical/Hebrew/Jewish • *earth*

Adélaide • Germanic • *noble, kind and caring*

Aeron, Agrona • British/Welsh • *Celtic Goddess of Battle or Agriculture*

Afanen • British/Welsh • *raspberry*

Agapia, Agafya • Greek • *love*

Agatha, Agathe, Aggie, Agata, Ågot, Águeda, Agathos • Greek • *good and honourable*

Ai • Chinese • *loving*

Aileen, Eileen, Ailie • Irish Gaelic • *desired by others*

Aimee, Aimi • French • *beloved one*

Alaina, Alana, Alayna, Alanna, Alannah, Alanah, Allana, Alanda, Alanis, Ailin • Gaelic • *vague origins but likely to be a rock*

Alice, Alicia, Alesha, Alisia, Alys, Alisha, Alissa, Alesha, Alisa, Alissa, Ailish, Alis, Alys • Norman • *noble, kind and caring*

Alina, Allina • Arabic • *noble and lovely*

Alison, Allie, Ally, Aly, Alysoun, Aliyah, Aaliyah, Allison, Allyson •

Norman • *noble, kind and caring*

Allana, Alana • Gaelic • *vague origins but likely to be a rock*

Alma, Almus • Latin • *nourishing, nurturing, kind like a mother*

Amabel, Annabel, Mabel, Amabilis • Latin/Norman • *loveable*

Amāni • Arabic • *desire, passion*

Amber, Ambar • Latin/Arabic • *beautiful golden-coloured fossilised resin*

Amīna • Arabic • *peaceful, secure*

Amrit • Sanskrit • *divine, immortal, good enough to eat*

Amy, Amie, Aimie, Aimee • Norman • *beloved*

Angharad • British/Welsh • *love*

Anise, Annis, Annice, Anis • Latin/Greek/French • *aniseed plant*

Anniella • Roman Catholic • *little lamb*

Anona, Annona • Latin • *unsure root but possibly corn supply*

Anthea, Antheia • Greek • *flowery*

Anthousa, Anfisa • Greek • *flower*

Anwen, Annwen • British/Welsh • *blessed and beautiful*

Anwyl, Annwyl • British/Welsh • *beloved, darling, dear*

April, Avril, Averil, Aprilis • Latin • *to open as in springtime flowers*

Aranrhod • British/Welsh • *huge, big, round, plump and humped!*

Arantxa, Arancha, Aranzazu • Basque • *place name meaning thorn bush*

Armana • African • *faithful*

Armelle, Artmael • Breton Celtic • *a female chief who is a steady as a rock*

Ashley, Ashleigh, Ashlee, Ashlie, Ashly, Lee, Leigh • Anglo-Saxon • *ash wood or forest*

Ashlyn, Ashlynne, Ashlynn,

Ashlynne, Ash, Lyn • Anglo-Saxon/ British Welsh • *ash tree by the lake*
Ashton • Anglo-Saxon • *the village with an ash tree*
Asia, Aysha, Ayeesha • Greek/ Assyrian • *the east*
Aspen, Aespe • Anglo-Saxon • *the aspen tree*
Aston • Anglo-Saxon • *the village to the east*
Astrid, Åsta, Sassa • Norse • *love*
Atholl, Athol, Athole • Gaelic • *'New Ireland' area of Perthshire*
Audra, Audrey, Audrie, Audry, Audrina • Anglo-Saxon • *strength and noble of character*
Augusta, Augustina, Augustine, Agustina, August • Latin • *great, the max, magnificent, expansive, nobody does it better*
Autumn, Autumnus • Latin • *a season of the year (southern hemisphere)*
Avdotya, Eudokia, Eudokein • Greek • *she seems a nice, good girl*
Aveline, Éibhlin, Ailbhilin, Ellin, Eileen • French/Irish Gaelic • *desired by others*
Azucena, Susannah • Arabic/ Spanish • *madonna lily*

Bahīja, Bahīga • Arabic • *joyful, beautiful woman*
Bahiyya • Arabic • *a beautiful, radiant, dazzling woman*
Bailey • English • *the bailiff!*
Bano • Persian • *lady, princess, bride*
Baozhai • Arabic • *precious hairpin*
Bathsheba, Sheba, Bathsheeva • Biblical/Jewish/Hebrew • *daughter of the oath*
Bay, Baie, Baca, Bacca • Latin/ Norman • *bay tree*

Beatrice, Beatrix, Bea, Bee, Beattie, Beatriz, Beitiris, Betrys, Viatrix, Viator, Beatus • *blessed through life*
Beau • French • *beautiful and bonny girl*
Becca, Beck, Becky, Bekki, Rébecca • Biblical/Jewish/Aramaic • *unknown origins; many suggestions, from cattle stall to snare*
Bella, Isabella • Italian • *beautiful*
Belinda, Bella, Belle • literary • *from bella meaning beautiful*
Bernadette, Bernine, Berneen, Bernadetta, Benedetta, Bettina • Germanic • *strong and hardy like a bear*
Bernardine, Bernadine, Bernarda • Roman Catholic • *strong and hardy like a bear*
Bernita • Germanic • *strong and hardy like a bear*
Berry, Berie • Anglo-Saxon • *as in fruit and veg*
Bethany, Beth • Biblical/Jewish/ Hebrew • *village outside Jerusalem where Jesus stayed in Holy Week before travelling to Jerusalem for Palm Sunday; it means house of figs or dates*
Bevin, Béibhinn • Irish Gaelic • *fair lady*
Bibi • Persian • *lady of the house*
Bina, Albina, Devorah, Deborah, Binah, Bine, Binke • Jewish/Hebrew/Yiddish • *bee or understanding*
Blair • Scots Gaelic • *plain or field or meadow*
Bláithín, Bláthnat, Blanid, Bianaid • Irish Gaelic • *flower*
Blodyn, Blodeyn, Blod • British/ Welsh • *flower*
Blodwedd, Blodeuwedd, Blod •

British/Welsh • *flower face or face like a flower*

Blodwen, Blodwyn, Blod • British/Welsh • *sacred, holy flowers*

Blossom, Blostm • Anglo-Saxon • *blossom flowers*

Bona, Bonus • Latin • *good*

Bonita, Bonnie, Bonny, Bonitus, Bonito • Latin/Spanish • *pretty and good*

Brandy, Brandyewijn • Dutch/Anglo-Saxon • *distilled wine or the hill filled with a shrub called broom*

Brayne, Broyn, Brayndel • Jewish/Yiddish • *brown*

Briar, Briony, Bryony, Bryonia • Anglo-Saxon/Greek • *a thorny plant or shrub*

Brunella • Germanic • *brown*

Bunty, Buntie, Lamb • English • *pet name for a lamb; to bunt was to nuzzle*

Buthayna, Busayna, Bathua • Arabic • *flat, fertile land*

Calista, Kallista • Greek • *the fairest and most beautiful in the land*

Canna • Latin/Australian English • *reed; bright flowers that grow in warm climes like Oz*

Caprice, Capriccio, Capra • Italian • *hedgehog hair and as intransigent as a goat*

Cara, Kara • Italian/Irish Gaelic • *beloved friend*

Caris, Charis, Karis, Carissa • Greek • *brace*

Carmen • Spanish • *song*

Caron • British Welsh • *to love*

Carys, Gladys, Gwladys, Cerys • British/Welsh • *loving*

Celandine, Dina • English/Greek • *a swallow and a flower*

Celyn • British/Welsh • *holly*

Ceri, Kerry • British/Welsh • *romantic, holy and beautiful*

Cerise, Cherise • French • *cherry as in fruit*

Chanel, Chanelle, Shanelle • French/modern • *in honour of Gabrielle CoCo Chanel, founder of the perfume house*

Changchang • Chinese • *my flourishing*

Changying • Chinese • *flourishing and lustrous*

Chardonnay • modern French/English • *a variety of grape that makes the wine Chardonnay*

Charis, Karis, Caris, Clarissa, Charisse • Greek • *grace*

Chelsea, Kelsey, Chelsey, Chelsie • Anglo-Saxon • *the chalk landing place in Chelsea, Middlesex*

Cherish, Cherir • Norman • *to treasure something priceless or invaluable*

Cherry, Cherie, Cherrie • French • *darling fruit!*

Chloe, Chloris, Cloris, Khloris, Khloe • Greek • *another name for the Goddess of Fertility, Demeter or Ceres*

Chorine, Choreen, Corinne, Corinna • French • *chorus or dancing girl*

Chunhua • Chinese • *spring flower*

Chuntao • Chinese • *spring peach*

Cinnamon, Kinnamon • Greek/Jewish • *brown-coloured spice*

Clematis, Klematis, Clem, Clemmie • Greek • *climbing plant or vine, meaning twig or branch*

Clova, Clove, Clover, Clavus, Clafre • Latin/French • *the spice that when dried looks like a nail*

Colleen, Coleen, Coline, Colina, Collinna, Colinette, Colinetta, Coletta, Cailin • Irish Gaelic/ American English/Australian • *ordinary girl or maiden*

Condoleezza • Italian • *con dolcezza, a musical term meaning 'play sweetly or with sweetness'*

Constance, Connie, Konnie, Constantia, Konstanze, Contanze • Latin • *constancy; steadfast and faithful*

Cora, Kore, Coretta, Corinne, Corinna, Korina, Coreen, Corrinne • Latin/Greek • *maiden*

Cordelia, Cordellia, Cordula, Cordis • literary invention • *possibly from Latin for heart; by William Shakespeare for the virtuous daughter in* King Lear

Corinne, Corinna, Korinna • French/Greek • *maiden*

Cornelia • Latin • *Roman family name, connected to Cornucopia and the horn of plenty*

Cuifen • Chinese • *emerald fragrance*

Dagmar • Slavic/Danish • *a combo of peace, day, dear, maiden*

Dagny, Dagna, Dagne • Norse • *a new day, the dawn*

Daffodil, Deaffodil, Asphodel, Daffy, Daphne • Dutch • *a flower*

Dáirine, Darina • Irish Gaelic • *fertile woman*

Daisy, Daegesage, Margaret, Marguerite • Anglo-Saxon • *day's eye because it closes its petals at night*

Daiyu • Chinese • *black jade*

Dale • English • *a valley dweller*

Dallas, Dallas, Dalfhas • Scots Gaelic/American/English • *the*

village of Dallas in Moray, north Britain; a place where cowpokes or drovers would rest their weary bones overnight

Damaris, Damalis, Damascena • Biblical/Greek • *calf*

Damask • Arabic • *the city of Damascus, Syria and the damask rose*

Damhnait, Davnat, Damh • *fawn, stag or deer*

Dana, Ana • Irish Gaelic • *name of an ancient Celtic fertility goddess, especially in Ireland*

Danika, Danica • Slavic • *morning star*

Daphne, Laurel, Lorel, Lorer • Greek • *the laurel tree*

Daria • Greek/Persian • *he who possesses, looks after the good and wellness of all*

Dassa, Dassah, Hadassah, Esther • Hebrew/Persian/Jewish • *Myrtle, Star and Persian Goddess of Fertility, Love and War, Ishtar*

Dawn, Aurora, Dawne, Duha, Dagung • Anglo-Saxon • *daybreak!*

Deborah, Debra, Debbie, Debora, Debrah, Deb, Debbi, Debby, Debi, Debs, Devorah, Dvoire • Biblical/ Hebrew/Jewish • *bee*

Deirdre, Deidre • Irish Gaelic • *woman*

Delice, Delyse, Delicia, Delysia, Delicae, Delicius, Delite, Delicia • Latin • *angel delight!*

Delwyn • British/Welsh • *pretty, love, pure, sacred*

Delyth, Gwenyth • British/Welsh • *pretty, love, neat*

Demelza • Cornish/Kernow • *a place name in Cornwall*

Denise, Denese, Denice, Deneze,

Deniece, Dionysia • Greek •
*Dionysus, God of Wine, Orgies and
Partying*

Devin, Damhan, Damhain • Irish
Gaelic • *descendant of Damhan,
connected to the fawn or deer*

Dharma, Karma, Nirvana, Samsara
• Sanskrit • *custom, tradition or
decree from on high*

Digna • Latin • *worthy*

Dietlind • Germanic • *tender, soft
and kind; people love her*

Dilys, Dylis, Dyllis • British/Welsh •
loyal, true and genuine

Diva, Divine • Italian • *goddess!*

Dobre, Dobe, Dobro • Jewish/
Yiddish • *good and kind person*

Donla, Dunnflaith • brown lady

Donna • Italian • *lady*

Dorcas, Tabitha, Deòiridh • Greek
• *fawn, doe, gazelle, antelope*

Dulcie, Dowse, Dulcia, Dulcis •
Latin • *sweet*

Dvoire, Devorah • Jewish/Yiddish
• *bee*

Dwynwyn • British/Welsh • *Goddess
of Love and Relationships*

Dymphna, Damhnait, Dympna •
Irish/Flemish • *uncertain origins;
fawn or deer*

Eber, Ebba • Germanic • *boar or pig*

**Ernestine, Ernestina, Earnestine,
Earnestina** • *serious in all things and
will fight to the death; means business to the point of obsession*

Ebba, Eadburga • Anglo-Saxon •
prosperity, fortress

**Edith, Eden, Edun, Edon, Edie,
Edyth, Edythe, Eadgyth** • Anglo-
Saxon • *prosperity, riches and strife
or war, possibly she who gains her
wealth through the booty of war*

Edna, Eden, Ednah, Eithne •
Jewish/Hebrew • *pleasure and
delight*

Edwina, Edwardina • Anglo-Saxon
• *a person who guards her riches,
blessed with wealth*

Eglantine, Aiglent • English •
sweetbriar

Eileen, Aileen, Eibhlín, Eilín •
Norman French • *desired by others*

Elreen, Eirene, Irène • Greek • *peace*

Elaine, Helen, Elain, Elayne, Eliana
• British/Welsh • *hind, fawn, doe*

Elfriede, Adalfrid, Elfreda •
Germanic • *peace is noble*

Elle • American English/French •
French for 'she'

Élodie, Elodia • Germanic/
Visigothic • *foreign wealth*

Elvira • Germanic/Visigothic • *true
wealth, foreign*

Emerald, Emmarald, Esmeralda
• American/English/Spanish • *the
green precious stone*

Erin, Errin, Éirinn • Irish • *Eire, old
name for Ireland*

**Ermengard, Ermgard, Irmgard,
Irmengard, Irmingard** • Germanic •
this entire enclosure is mine

Ermintrude, Trude, Trudy •
Germanic/Frankish • *you are my
entire world, my beloved*

Ernesta, Ernestina, Erna, Ernestina
German • *serious in all things and
will fight to the death; means business to the point of obsession*

**Esmé, Esmee, Esmie, Aestimare,
Aestimatus, Edme** • Latin • *priceless, highly prized and valued*

**Esther, Esta, Hester, Haddasah,
Eistir, Ester** • Hebrew/Persian/Jewish
• *Myrtle, Star and Persian Goddess
of Fertility, Love and War, Ishtar*

Estrild, Easter, Eastre • Anglo-Saxon • *Goddess of Spring at war!*

Etta, Rosetta, Henrietta • Italian • *female*

Eudocia, Eudoxia, Eudokia • Biblical/Greek/Latin • *of fine appearance and comfortable, easy to be with*

Eve, Eva, Aoife, Éabha, Evita, Havva, Evie, Hayya, Eve, Evelyn, Evelina, Eubh, Evalina, Evelina, Aibhilin • Biblical/Hebrew/Jewish • *mother of all living, life itself*

Evelyn, Éibhleann, Aibhilin • Irish Gaelic/English • *desired by others*

Evette, Yvette • English/French • *yew tree*

Evonne, Yvonne • English/French • *yew tree*

Fabia, Fabienne, Fabiola • Latin • *old Roman family name meaning a bean*

Fang • Chinese • *fragrant*

Farida • Arabic • *a gem, a precious stone*

Fania, Stefania • Italian/Greek • *a crown or garland*

Fawziyya • Arabic • *accomplished and successful woman*

Felicity, Flick, Felcitas, Felicita, Felicidad • Latin • *good fortune*

Fenfang • Chinese • *perfumed, aromatic*

Fennel, Faeniculum, Faenum • Latin • *hay turned into a spice*

Fíona, Fionn, Ffion, Ffion, Fina • Irish Gaelic • *vine*

Fiorella, Fiore • Italian • *flower*

Fleur • Norman • *flower*

Flora, Floris, Flo, Florence, Floella, Florrie, Ffloraidh • Latin • *old Roman family name meaning flower*

Florence, Florentius, Florentia, Flo, Florance, Floss, Florrie, Flossie • *like a flower, blooming and blossoming*

Florentina, Florentinus, Florenz, Florens • Latin • *she flourishes and blossoms*

Florida, Floridus • Spanish • *flowery*

Flower, Fleur, Fiorella • Norman • *flower*

Freda, Frederica, Freddie, Frieda, Elfreda, Winifred, Frederika, Friede, Friederike • *peace*

Freya, Froja, Frouwa, Friday, Frøya, Freia, Freyja • Norse • *lady referring to the Goddess of Love, Freya*

Friday • Norse/English • *Freya's day, the Goddess of Love and Beauty*

Gaenor, Gaynor, Geinor, Cainwryr • British/Welsh • *beautiful maiden*

Gaia, Ge • Greek • *Goddess of the Earth, mum of Saturn and Uranus*

Galina, Gala, Galene • Greek • *calm*

Garnet, Grenate, Granatum • Norman/Latin • *either a dealer in pomegranates or the precious stone*

Gemma, Jemma • Italian • *precious jewel*

Geneva, Geneve, Ginevra • French • *after the Swiss city, or can be variant of Jennifer or short form of Geneviève*

Geneviève, Jennifer, Genoveffa, Ginevra • Celtic • *a female chief or leader of the tribe of people*

Genista, Genesta • Latin • *the shrub plant called broom, a bright yellow colour*

Georgina, Georgena, Georgette, Georgene, Georgia, Jorja, Georgiana, Georgie, Georgina, Georgine, Georene • Greek/Latin/

Norman • *farmer or someone who works on the land*

Gerd, Gerda, Gärd, Garo • Norse • *Goddess of Fertility, protection as in a fort or castle*

Gillian, Gill, Jill, Gillyflower, Gillaine, Jillian, Jilly, Gilly • Latin • *from Julius, a Roman name*

Gita • Sanskrit • *everyone sings her praises*

Gitte, Gittel, Birgitte • Jewish/Yiddish • *good girl*

Glenn, Glen, Glenna, Glennette, Glenette • Scots Gaelic • *valley*

Gráinne, Grania, Granya • Irish Gaelic • *unknown roots but possibly Goddess of the Harvest*

Guinevere, Gaynor, Gayner, Gayna, Gaenor • British/Welsh • *beautiful maiden*

Gull, Gudgull • Norse/Swedish • *God of Gold, Mammon*

Gunnborg • Norse • *a fort or castle ready for attack*

Gwenyth, Gwenith • British/Welsh • *wheat, romantic word for the pick of the crop!*

Habība • Arabic • *beloved one*
Habibunah • Swahili • *our beloved*
Hadassah, Dassah, Esther • Hebrew/Persian/Jewish • *Myrtle, Star and Persian Goddess of Fertility, Love and War, Ishtar*
Hadīl • Arabic • *a woman with a voice like the cooing of doves, soft, lovely voice*
Hadya • Arabic • *a woman with inner peace*
Hailey, Hayley, Hallie, Haylee, Hailee, Haley, Haleigh, Hegleah • Anglo-Saxon • *meaning a clearing for hay*

Hannah, Hanna, Hanā • Arabic • *blissful, happy woman filled with wellbeing*

Hannelore • Germanic • *combo of Hannah and Eleanor*

Happy, Merry, Happie, Merrie • Norse/English • *prosperity, abundance, good fortune*

Hazel, Haesel • Anglo-Saxon • *the hazel tree, for the Celts a magic tree*

Heather, Hather • English • *moorland plant in rich purple hues*

Helga, Heilag, Hella • Norse • *successful, prosperity, wealth*

Hephzibah, Hepzibah, Hepsie, Effie • Biblical • *my delight is in her (my newborn daughter)*

Hertha • Norse • *Norse Goddess of Fertility*

Hester, Esther, Hettie, Hetty • English • *Myrtle, Star and Persian Goddess of Fertility, Love and War, Ishtar*

Hilary, Hillary, Hilarie, Hilly, Hilario • Latin • *hilarious!*

Holly, Hollie, Holi, Holeg, Holin • Anglo-Saxon

Honey, Honeg, Honig • Anglo-Saxon • *sweet nectar, someone who is sweet*

Honeysuckle • English • *a climbing vine with fragrant flowers*

Hortense, Hortensia, Hortensius, Hortus • French/Latin • *old Roman family name meaning garden*

Hualing • Chinese • *flourishing fu-ling (herb used in oriental medicine)*

Huian • Chinese • *kind peace*

Huifang • Chinese • *kind and fragrant*

Huiliang • Chinese • *kind and good*

Huiling • Chinese • *wise jade wind chime*

Huda • Arabic • *a woman who is wise and judicious counsellor or adviser; agony aunt*

Hyacinth, Jacinth, Jacinthe, Jacintha, Hyakinthos • Greek/English • *love and passion*

Ianthe, Violet, Flower, Ionanthos, Iolanthe • Greek • *a beautiful deep purple flower*

Ihsān • Arabic • *charity, generosity*

Ilene, Eileen • Norman French/modern English • *desired by others*

Imogen, Innogen, Inghean, Imogene • Celtic • *girl, maiden*

Inge, Inga, Ingeborg, Ingrid, Ingfrid, Ingetraud, Ingegerd, Ingegärd, Inger • Norse • *protected by Ing, the God of Fertility*

Ingrid • Norse • *a beautiful woman blessed by the God of Fertility, Ing*

Iola, Iole • Greek • *violet, the flower*

Irène, Eirene, Irina, Ira, Arina • Greek • *peace*

Isabis • South African • *beautiful to see*

Isolde, Isolda, Iseult, Esyllt • Arthurian mythology/British Welsh • *a beautiful Irish princess*

I'tidāl • Arabic • *everything in moderation*

Ivy, Ifig • Anglo-Saxon • *ivy: the climbing plant known as the survivor*

Jacinta, Hyacinth, Jacinthe • Greek/Spanish/French • *love and passion*

Jamala, Gamala • Arabic • *beautiful woman*

Jamila, Gamila • Arabic • *graceful as well as beautiful*

Janina • Tunisian • *garden*

Jasmine, Jasmyn, Jazmin, Jazmine, Yasmīn, Yasmine, Jasmina, Yasmina, Jaslyn, Jaslynne • Persian/Norman • *evergreen shrub or vine with glorious fragrance*

Jawāhir, Gawāhir • Arabic • *a dazzling jewel*

Jennifer, Jen, Jenefer, Jenny, Jeni, Jenifer, Jenine, Jennifer, Jenni, Jennefer, Jannifer, Jenine, Jennine, Jeannine • Arthurian mythology/British Cornish • *beautiful maiden*

Jenessa, Jen • African American • *combo of Jennifer and Vanessa*

Jenna, Genna, Jena • Arthurian mythology/British Cornish • *beautiful maiden*

Jessica, Jesca, Jessika, Jess, Jessie, Jesse, Jessye, Teasag,

Iscah • Biblical/literary • *William Shakespeare's invention from the Biblical name Jesca or Iscah*

Jia • Chinese • *beautiful*

Jiayi • Chinese • *a woman's place is in the home*

Jiayang • Chinese • *a woman flourishes and blossoms in the home*

Jinana • Arabic • *a woman as beautiful and mystical as the Garden of Eden*

Jing • Chinese • *stillness, contemplation or luxurious, comfort*

Jingfei • Chinese • *forever fragrant*

Jody, Jodene, Jodie, Jodi, Jude, Judith • Biblical/Hebrew/Jewish • *praise*

Jonquil, Jonquille, Junco, Juncus • French/English/Spanish • *plant: reed*

Ju • Chinese • *chrysanthemum*

Judith, Judi, Judy, Judie, Jutte, Jutta, Julitta • Biblical/Hebrew/Jewish • *praise*

Julitta, Julitt, Julip, Judith •

Biblical/Latin • *praise*
Juniper, Jennifer, Rothem, Juniperus • Biblical/Hebrew/Jewish/Latin • *desert shrub that was used to build the Temple of Solomon*
Juno, Úna • Irish Gaelic/Roman/English • *uncertain roots; hungry or lamb*
Jutte, Jutta, Jude, Judith • Biblical/Germanic • *praise*

Kailash • Sanskrit • *mountain home of Kubera, the God of Wealth*
Kamala • Sanskrit • *beautiful pink*
Kanta • Sanskrit • *you are desirable because you are so lovely*
Karama • Arabic • *a generous spirit*
Karenza, Carenza • British/Welsh/Kernow • *love, loving to be loved*
Kay, Kaye • Latin • *a man of the earth*
Keeva, Caoimhe, Caomhe • Gaelic • *beautiful*
Kiera, Keira • Norse • *a person who lives in marshes covered in shrubs and brushwood*
Kenda, Kendala, Kendall • Anglo-Saxon/British/Welsh • *someone who worships Celtic deities, or a place in Westmorland, Kendal, named after River Kent*
Kendra, Kendrick • British/Welsh • *British/Welsh/Scots Gaelic • a sacred place high on a hill, or son of Henry or royal power*
Kenzie • English/Scots Gaelic/Biblical • *the cassia tree or shortened MacKenzie*
Keturah • Biblical/Hebrew/Jewish • *incense, the strong perfume from frankincense used to purify in sacred places*
Kezia, Cassia, Kizzie, Kizzy, Keziah,

Kenzie • Biblical/Hebrew/Jewish • *the cassia tree, known as the bark of cinnamon in the USA and Canada*
Khayriyya • *a woman with a charitable heart*
Kyla • Gaelic • *narrow in geographical terms; a region in Ayrshire*
Kyra, Kyria, Kira • Greek • *lady*

Lakshmi • Sanskrit • *lucky girl in matters of luck, money and beauty*
Lamyā • Arabic • *a woman with fulsome brown lips*
Lan • Chinese • *orchid*
Lana, Alana, Alanah, Lanna, Svetlana • American English • *vague origins but likely to mean a rock*
Lanfen • Chinese • *perfumed orchid*
Larch, Larche, Larix • American English/German/Latin • *sacred tree to the shaman*
Lark, Lawerce • North American/Australian/English/Anglo-Saxon • *dawn song*
Laura, Laurel, Laureen, Laurene, Laurelle, Laurie, Laure, Laurette, Lora, Lowri, Lauryn • Latin • *laurel tree, sacred to those who are victorious and honoured*
Lauretta, Loretta, Lorette • Latin/Italian • *laurel tree, sacred to those who are victorious and honoured*
Laverne, Lavern • American English/Gaulish • *alder tree*
Leela, Lila • Sanskrit • *very sexy*
Leigh, Lee • Anglo-Saxon • *a clearing in the wood*
Lesley, Lesslyn • Scots Gaelic • *the place where holly grows*
Lia, Rosalia, Rosalie, Leah • Latin/Italian • *rose*
Libe, Liebe • Jewish/Yiddish/German • *love or darling*

Lifen • Chinese • *beautiful fragrance*
Lilian, Lilly, Lily, Lili, Lillian, Lilium, Lily, Lillie, Lilly, Lili, Lilli • Latin/
Norman • *flower that is associated with purity and resurrection*
Liling • Chinese • *beautiful jade wind chime*
Lin • Chinese • *beautiful jade*
Līna • Arabic • *a woman with the figure of a palm tree*
Linda, Belinda, Lynda, Lindie, Lindy, Lyn, Lynn, Lynne, Linden, Lin, Lyn, Lynne, Linnet, Lindsey, Lenda • Spanish/Visigothic/ Germanic • *pretty, passive, tender and soft*
Lindall, Lindale, Linda, Lindell, Lindal • Anglo-Saxon • *valley where the flax grows*
Linden, Linda, Lindie • Anglo-Saxon • *lime tree*
Liqiu • Chinese • *beautiful autumn (southern hemisphere)*
Loreen, Lorene • Latin/Gaelic • *laurel tree, sacred to those who are victorious and honoured*
Lorelle, Laura • Latin/French • *laurel tree, sacred to those who are victorious and honoured*
Loretta, Lauretta, Loreto • Roman Catholic/Italian • *laurel tree, sacred to those who are victorious and honoured*
Lorinda • American English • *combo of Laura and Linda*
Lorna, Lorne, Latharna • English/ Scots Gaelic • *Scottish place name, Lorne, Argyll*
Lowri, Laura • British/Welsh/Latin • *laurel tree, sacred to those who are victorious and honoured*
Lubna • Arabic • *storax tree that has sweet, honey-like sap, used to make*

perfume and incense; a fragrant, perfumed, honey-tasting woman as intoxicating as incense
Luli • Chinese • *dewy jasmine*
Lynette, Lynette, Linnet, Linotte, Linnette, Linette • Spanish/French • *pretty, passive, tender and soft*

Mabel, Mab, Amabel, Amabilia, Mabilia, Mabelle, Amiabel, Maybelle, Maybella • Norman/ English • *lovely*
Madhu • Sanskrit • *she is as sweet as honey and younger than springtime*
Madhur • Sanskrit • *sweetie!*
Madonna, Madge • American Italian • *my lady*
Madrona, Matrona • Jewish • *from the name Matron, a wish for the baby girl to become a mother herself*
Maha • Arabic • *oryx, an antelope with large, beautiful eyes*
Mahāsin • Arabic • *charming and admirable qualities*
Maia, Maya, Mya • Latin • *Roman Goddess of Youth, Life, Rebirth, Love and Sexuality*
Maidie, Maid, Maegden • Old English • *maiden*
Marja • Finnish/Estonian • *berry as in fruit*
Manala • Arabic • *to acquire, to attain, to own*
Marjolaine • French • *marjoram, the herb*
Martha, Marthe, Marthja, Martja, Märta, Martta • Biblical/Aramaic • *lady*
Marwa • Arabic • *a fragrant plant and shiny pebble*
Matrona • Latin • *lady*
May, Mae, Maybelle, Maybella • Anglo-Saxon • *the magical*

hawthorn tree which is also known as may; the month of May

Medea, Medesthai • Greek mythology • *a Colchian princess in 'Jason and the Golden Fleece'; means to contemplate and reflect*

Meifen, Meixiang • Chinese • *plum fragrance*

Meili • Chinese • *beautiful*

Meilin • Chinese • *plum jade*

Meirong • Chinese • *beautiful soul and personality*

Meixiu • Chinese • *beautiful grace*

Melissa, Melita, Melitta Lissa, Melissa, Lyssa Lita, Melita, Melitta • Greek • *honey bee*

Melody, Melodie, Melodia, Melosaeidein • Greek • *the singing of songs*

Merry, Merrily, Merilee, Marylee, Marilee • American English • *to be merry*

Mignon, Mignonette, Minette • French • *little darling, cutie, sweetie*

Mildred, Mildpryd, Mildburh, Mildgyd • Anglo-Saxon • *a gentle strength*

Millena, Milenna • Czech • *grace and favour*

Mimosa, Mimus • Latin • *yellow plant that means mime or mimic*

Mingxia • Chinese • *bright rosy glow*

Mingyu • Chinese • *bright jade*

Miranda, Randa, Randy, Randie, Amanda • literary invention/Latin • *William Shakespeare invented this name for his heroine in* The Tempest: *admire, wonder at or in awe of her loveliness*

Morag, Mór, Móirín, Moreen • Irish/Scots Gaelic • *great, large, huge*

Morna, Muirne • Scots Gaelic • *beloved*

Morven, Morvern, Mhorbhairne, Morbheinn • Scots • *area of north Argyll or big peak*

Morwenna, Morwen, Morwyn • British/Welsh • *maiden*

Muhayya • Arabic • *she has such a lovely, beautiful face*

Myfanwy, Myf • British/Welsh • *your lady, your woman*

Myrna, Muirne, Morna • Irish Gaelic • *beloved*

Myrtle, Myrtille, Myrtilla, Myrta • Latin/Norman/Greek • *a tree with fragrant leaves; in Greek it means perfumed*

Nada • Arabic • *she is like the morning dew and generous with it*

Nadira, Nadra • Arabic • *a woman who is rare and precious*

Nadiyya • Arabic • *a woman who is as fresh and moist as morning dew*

Naʿīma • Arabic • *a woman who is contented and happy*

Najiba, Nagiba • Arabic • *cultured, cultivated and a cut above the rest*

Naomi, Noémie, Noemi • Biblical/Hebrew/Jewish • *pleasant and good*

Nápla, Annabel, Anabl, Anable, Anaple, Amable • Norman/English/Irish • *lovely*

Nasrīn • Persian/Arabic • *wild rose, a star set in the constellation of the Eagle and the Lyre*

Nawāl • Arabic • *a gift bestowed or given*

Nerissa, Nereis • literary invention/Greek • *sea sprite or nymph, Nerissa was invented by William Shakespeare for Portia's lady-in-waiting in* The Merchant of Venice

Neroli • Italian • *an aromatic oil based on bitter orange; founded by*

Princess Anne Marie de la Tremoille of Neroli

Nerys • British/Welsh • *lady*

Nia, Nyah • Swahili • *with a purpose*

Nihād • Arabic • *ground that resembles a female's breasts and contours*

Ni'mat • Arabic • *a woman who is good to have around*

Niu • Chinese • *I am a girl*

Norma • artistic Italian • *Felice Romani invented the name for Bellini's opera*

Normina • *a man from the north; Norseman or Viking*

Nuying • Chinese • *girl flower*

Odette, Odet, Oda • Germanic/Frankish • *prosperity and good fortune*

Odile, Odila, Ottilie, Ottoline • Germanic • *prosperous and wealthy*

Oksana, Oxana • Russian • *praise God*

Olga, Helgi • Norse • *prosperous*

Olive, Olivia, Oliff, Oliffe, Oliva • Latin • *olive tree, a symbol of peace and abundance*

Olivia, Olive, Oliva • literary invention/Latin • *William Shakespeare named Olivia as the rich heiress in* The Tempest

Órla, Ona, Anona, Fíona, Honor, Orfhlaith, Orflaith, Orlaith • Irish Gaelic • *golden lady or princess*

Ornella, Ornelia, Ornetta, Ornello • Tuscan • *the flowering ash tree*

Ottilie, Odile, Odila • Germanic • *prosperous and wealthy*

Ottoline • Germanic • *prosperous and wealthy*

Padma • Sanskrit • *lotus flower, energy centres of the chakra*

Padmavati • Sanskrit • *full of lotus flowers*

Paleley, Sudan • sweet

Pansy, Pensee • Norman • *flower whose name means 'thought'*

Parthenope, Parthenosops • Greek mythology • *maiden as in the goddess Athene in her form and face; one of the Sirens, who lured men to her with their enchanting, bewitching voices, was named Parthenope*

Parvin • Sanskrit • *the Pleiades, a cluster in the constellation of Taurus, called the weeping sisters*

Patrice, Patricia • Latin/French/Irish Gaelic • *patrician*

Patricia, Patrice, Pat, Tricia, Trisha, Trish, Patty, Pattie, Patti, Patsy, Patrizia • Latin/Irish Gaelic • *patrician*

Patty, Pattie, Patricia, Martha, Patti • English • *pet name for Patricia and Martha*

Paudeen, Páidín • Irish Gaelic/English • *pet name for Patricia*

Payton, Peyton • Anglo-Saxon • *Paega's village or hamlet*

Paz • Roman Catholic • *Our Lady of Peace*

Peijing • Chinese • *admiring luxuriance*

Peizhi • Chinese • *admiring iris*

Penelope, Pen, Penelops, Penny, Penni • Greek • *uncertain origin but 'duck' is one suggestion*

Perdita, Perdie, Purdee, Purdy, Perditus • Latin/literary invention • *William Shakespeare invented the name from the Latin 'lost' as one of his characters in* The Winter's Tale

Pernilla, Pella, Pernille, Petronel, Petronilla • Latin/Greek/Swedish •

a stone or someone who lives in the country
Petronel, Petronella, Petronilla, Petronius • Latin • *a Roman family name, Petronius, that could be connected to St Peter*
Petula • Latin • *Tagetis Petula aka French marigold*
Petal • English • *one of the often brightly coloured parts of a flower immediately surrounding the reproductive organs; a division of the corolla; a term of endearment*
Petra, Peta, Piera, Peta, Petra • Greek • *the rock or stone*
Philomena, Philomenus, Philomenes, Phileinmenos, Philoumena, Filumena, Filomena • Greek/Germanic • *loyal, strong friend, platonic friendship*
Phyllis, Phillida, Phyllis, Phyllidos, Phyllidis, Phyllida, Phyllicia, Phylicia • Greek mythology • *a Thracian queen, Phyllis died for love and transformed herself into an almond tree; her name means leaves or leaf and she is a symbol of undying love and friendship*
Pierce, Pearce, Perse, Pierette, Peta • Greek • *the rock or stone*
Poppy, Popaeg, Papaver • Latin/Anglo-Saxon • *the flower*
Portia, Porcia, Porcius, Porcus, Porsha • Latin • *Roman family name of Porcus, meaning pig*
Premiata • Sanskrit • *symbolic of the plant or flower of love*
Primrose, Primarosa • Latin • *the first rose*
Priya • Sanskrit • *beloved one*
Prunella, Ella, Pru, Prue • Latin • *pruna: plum*

Qiang • Chinese • *rose*
Qing • Chinese • *navy blue*

Rachel, Rachael, Rachelle, Rae, Rella, Ráichéal, Rachele, Rakel • Biblical/Hebrew/Jewish • *ewe (female sheep)*
Rhamantus, Rhamanta • British/Welsh • *romantic*
Rakaya • Tunisian • *sweet*
Rana • Arabic • *a beautiful object or being*
Randa • Arabic • *a desert-bound sweet perfumed tree*
Raquel, Raquelle, Rachel • Biblical/Hebrew/Jewish • *ewe (female sheep)*
Rathnait, Ronit • Irish Gaelic • *a woman of grace and prosperity*
Rati • Sanskrit • *she desires; gives sexual pleasure and carnal knowledge*
Rébecca, Rebekah, Beathag, Becca, Becks, Bex, Becky, Becki, Rella, Rebekka, Reba • Biblical/Jewish/Hebrew/Aramaic • *shadowy or vague origins, possibly connected to 'cattle stall' but doubtful*
Reisel, Reise, Rose, Reisl, Rella, Rele • Jewish/Yiddish • *rose*
Renxiang • Chinese • *lucky fragrance*
Rhea Silvia • Latin/Roman mythology • *mother of Romulus and Remus, founders of Rome*
Rhian, Rian, Rhianu • British/Welsh • *maiden*
Rhoda, Rhodon, Rose, Roda, Rodos • Greek • *rose or someone from the island of roses, Rhodes*
Ricarda • Germanic • *strong, brave and powerful*
Richelle • Germanic/French • *strong, brave and powerful*

Rigborg • Danish/Germanic • *fortified and powerful*

Riley, Rileigh, Ryley, Reilly, Rygelegh, Roghallach • Anglo-Saxon/Irish Gaelic • *a field where the rye crop has been cleared*

Rīm • Arabic • *white antelope*

Róisín, Rosheen, Rós, Rose, Rhosyn • Irish Gaelic • *rose*

Rosa, Rose, Roschen, Rosetta, Rosita • Latin • *the flower rose*

Rosalba • Italian • *rose white*

Rosalie, Rosalia • Latin/French • *the flower rose*

Rosalinda • Latin • *lovely or pretty rose*

Rosangela • Italian • *combo of Rosa and Angela*

Roseanne, Rosanne, Rosanna, Rosannagh, Rozanne • English • *combo of Rose and Anne*

Rose, Rosa, Rosie • English/Latin • *the flower rose*

Roselle, Rozelle • English/French • *the flower rose*

Rosetta, Rosa • Italian • *pet form of Rosa*

Roshanara • Persian • *her beauty is like honey to the bee, she is a magnet of loveliness*

Rosita, Rosa • Spanish • *pet form of Rosa*

Roxanne, Roxane, Roxana, Roxanna, Roxy, Rozanne • Latin/Greek/Persian • *dawn*

Ruiling • Chinese • *lucky jade wind chime*

Ruolan • Chinese • *like an orchid*

Ruomei • Chinese • *like a plum*

Sabāh • Arabic • *morning*

Sabriyya • Arabic • *a woman who is patient, persevering and dedicated*

Sadhbh, Syve, Sive, Sabia • Irish Gaelic • *sweet as honey*

Saffron, Safran • Arabic/Norman • *the saffron or Spanish crocus; the most expensive spice in the world*

Safiyya • Arabic • *the best friend anyone could have*

Sage, Sauge, Sapius • English/Norman/American English • *the herb sage that promotes wisdom and is good for the liver*

Sahar • Arabic • *morning has broken, dawn*

Salha • Arabic • *devoted and dedicated*

Salma • Arabic • *a person who looks after those she loves; a protector*

Salomé, Shalom • Greek/Hebrew/Aramaic • *peace*

Salwa • Arabic • *she who consoles others and gives a shoulder to cry on*

Satin, Zaituni, Tsingtung • Chinese/Arabic/French/English/Latin • *soft, sleek, silky, shiny fabric*

Savannah, Savanna • American English/Spanish • *treeless plain*

Sawsan • Arabic • *lily of the valley*

Selima, Selim, Zelima • Arabic/English • *peace*

Serenissima • Italian • *serene*

Shādya • Arabic • *singer, the voice*

Shakira • Arabic • *thankful and grateful*

Shamīm • Arabic • *a woman who is fragrant and smells as sweet as perfume*

Shamshad • Persian • *like a box tree, she is lean, tall and elegant*

Shoshanna, Shoshana, Shannah, Susanna • Biblical/Jewish/Hebrew • *the flower lily, which means rose in modern Hebrew*

Sharada • Sanskrit • *autumn*

(southern hemisphere)

Sharon, Sharron, Sharona, Sharonda • Biblical • *a place called Sharon on the coastal plain of the Holy Land; and for the shrub the Rose of Sharon*

Shatha • Arabic • *sweet-smelling, fragrant*

Shula, Shulamit • Hebrew/Jewish • *peacefulness*

Silvestra • Latin • *a person from the woods or forest*

Silvius • Latin • *someone who loves or inhabits the woods or forest*

Sita • Sanskrit • *she ploughs a straight furrow; symbolic of all wifely virtures and Goddess of Nature*

Sneh • Sanskrit • *aromatic oils good for affection and tenderness*

Sorrel, Sorrell, Sorell, Sorel, Sur • Norman/German/Frankish • *the herb sorrel with its sour leaves*

Solveig, Solvig, Solvej • Norse • *strength through the family or home*

Song • Chinese • *pine tree*

Sri • Sanskrit • *a royal personage who radiates the light of goodness, beauty and wealth*

Stacey, Stacy, Stace, Eustacia, Stacie, Staci • English/Greek • *confused roots; could mean juicy, tasty grapes!*

Steffanie, Stéphanie, Steph, Steffi, Stefanie, Steff • Greek • *a crown or garland*

Stéphanie, Steff, Steph, Steffie, Steffy, Stevie, Stefanie, Steffany, Stephania, Stephana, Stefania, Estefania, Stevie • Greek • *a crown or garland*

Sukie, Sukey, Susan • English • *pet form of Susan*

Susan, Susanna, Suzan, Sue, Su, Soo, Susie, Suzie, Susy, Suzy, Sukie, Sukey, Siùsan, Sue, Susan, Susanna, Susannah, Suzanne, Su, Soo • English/Biblical • *the flower lily, which means rose in modern Hebrew*

Susanna, Shoshana, Shoshan, Susana, Suzanna, Suzannah, Susannah, Slùsan, Siusaidh, Susanne, Suzanne, Zuzanna, Zuzana, Suzana, Zsuzsanna, Susann, Susi, Sanna, Zanna • Biblical/English • *lily*

Shushila • Sanskrit • *she has a lovely nature and is so placid too*

Susie, Suzie, Susi • English • *short form of Susan or Susannah*

Suzanne, Susanna, Suzette, Suzie • Biblical/French • *the flower lily, which means rose in modern Hebrew*

Swanhild, Swanhilda, Swanhilde, Svanhild • Saxon • *she glides through conflict (battle) like a swan*

Sylvestra, Silvestra • Latin • *a person from the woods or forest*

Sylvia, Silvia, Sylvie, Silvia, Sylvia, Sylve • Latin/English/French/Italian • *Rhea Silvia, mother of the founders of Rome*

Tabitha, Dorcas, Tabby, Tabea • Biblical/Aramaic • *fawn, doe, gazelle, antelope*

Tallulah, Talulla, Tuilelaith • Irish Gaelic/English • *abundance, lady and princess*

Tamara, Tamar, Tammy, Tammie • Russian/Biblical/Hebrew/Jewish • *date palm*

Tansy, Tanesie, Athanasia • Greek/Norman • *herb: tansy, giving immortality*

Tara, Teamhair, Tarra, Taree • Irish Gaelic • *a hill that was the seat of*

the high kings of Ireland
Tegan, Teagan, Teigan, Tiegan, Teg
• British/Welsh • *lovely*
Tempe, Temnein • Greek • *a valley
in Greece; the legendary home of the
Muses, the nine goddesses of the arts
and sciences*
Thalia, Talia, Thallein • Greek •
*one of the nine Muses; the Goddess
of Comedy, whose name means to
prosper comedically*
Thanā • Arabic • *a woman ready to
praise and be praised; everything she
does deserves praise*
Thelma, Thelema • Greek • *to wish
or have the will*
Themba • Zulu • *trusted*
Tia, Laetitia, Lucretia, Tiana, Tiara •
Spanish/Portuguese • *aunty or short
form of any name ending in -tia*
Tierra • American Spanish • *land,
earth, terra firma*
Tirzah, Tirza, Thirzah, Thirza
• Biblical/Hebrew/Jewish • *a
delightful woman*
Toltse, Dolce, Dulcie • Jewish/
Yiddish/Italian • *sweet*
Torborg, Thorbjorg • Norse • *forti-
fied place belonging to the god Thor*
Tova, Tofa, Turid, Tove, Tufa • Norse
• *the god Thor made me beautiful*
Treasa, Trean • Irish Gaelic • *a
woman of intense, immense strength*
Tuilelaith, Talulla, Talullah • Irish
Gaelic • *a lady of abundance*
Tulip, Tiwlip • English • *flower of
enchantment: tulip*

Ulla • Norse • *willpower and
determination*
Ulrike, Ulrika, Ulla • Germanic/
Anglo-Saxon • *from riches comes
power; wolf power*

'Um-Kalthūm • Arabic • *mother
of a little cherub!*
Úna, Unity, Oona, Oonagh, Euna
• Irish Gaelic • *uncertain roots;
hungry or lamb*
Ursula, Ursa, Urchi • Latin •
she-bear
Usha • Sanskrit • *Goddess of the
Dawn*
Ute, Uda • Germanic • *heritage,
roots, belonging*

Valentina, Valentine, Val, Tina
• Latin • *flourishing, blooming,
blossoming*
Valérie, Valeria, Valère, Val •
French/Latin • *old Roman name
Valerius meaning healthy, robust and
strong*
Valmai, Val, Falmai • British Welsh/
Australian English • *mayflower or
combo of Valerie and May*
Vashti • Biblical/Hebrew/Persian •
thread or beautiful woman
Velinda • American English • *an
extension of Linda*
Velma • modern English/Greek •
to wish or have the will
Venus, Venustas, Aphrodite •
Latin/Greek • *Goddess of Beauty
and Love*
Verna, Verona, Verena • American
English/Gaulish • *alder tree*
Viola, Violet, Vi • Latin • *the flower:
violet*
Violet, Violette, Violetta, Violeta, Vi
• Latin/Norman • *the flower: violet*
**Virginia, Verginius, Ginny, Ginnie,
Virginie** • Latin • *Roman family
name Vergilius but confusion reigned
when the spelling was changed to
Virgilius, which means the maiden
or virga as in stick*

Wafā • Arabic • *a faithful, loyal, devoted woman*

Walburg, Walburga • Germanic • *she rules over a stronghold or fort*

Waltraud, Waltrud, Waltrude • Germanic • *rules with great strength*

Wahiba • Arabic • *a generous woman who gives her all*

Wenling • Chinese • *refined jade wind chime*

Widād • Arabic • *an affectionate, friendly girl*

Willa • Anglo-Saxon • *a person with tremendous willpower, powerful in every way*

Willow, Welig • Anglo-Saxon

Wilma, Wilhelmina, Billie, Wilmette, Wilmetta • Anglo-Saxon • *she is famous for her willpower and strength of character*

Winifred, Winfred, Win, Winnie, Wynnfrith, Gwenfrewi, Winfriede, Winfried • Germanic • *a kind, peace-loving friend*

Wudasse • Ethiopian • *praise*

Xia • Chinese • *rosy clouds*

Xianavane • Mozambiquan • *to propagate*

Xiaojing • Chinese • *morning luxury*

Xiaozhi • Chinese • *little iris; long life and prosperity*

Xiuying • Chinese • *graceful flower*

Yael, Jael • Biblical/Hebrew/Jewish • *a wild goat*

Yanlin • Chinese • *forest of swallows; also Beijing, Chinese capital*

Yarrow, Yarrowe, Gearwe • Anglo-Saxon/English • *the herb yarrow*

Yasmīn, Jasmina, Yasmina • Swahili • *sweetness*

Yehudit • Jewish/Hebrew • *praise*

Yetta, Etta, Yehudit, Judith, Esther • Jewish/Yiddish/Slavic • *many associations with the names of Judith and Esther, and also Slavic names connected with Etta*

Yingtai • Chinese • *terrace of flowers*

Yuan • Chinese • *shining peace*

Yubi • Chinese • *jade emerald*

Yuming • Chinese • *jade brightness*

Yusheng • Chinese • *jade birth*

Yusra • *a woman who attracts wealth, prosperity and good things*

Yves, Eve • French/Germanic • *yew tree*

Yvette, Yves • French/Germanic • *yew tree*

Yvonne, Yvon, Yves • French/Germanic • *yew tree*

Zahra • Arabic • *she shines like a fully blossomed flower*

Zaibunissa • Persian • *a woman of sheer beauty*

Zara, Zahr • Arabic • *flower*

Zeinab, Zaynab • Arabic • *a glorious, admired sweet-smelling plant*

Zhu • Chinese • *bamboo: a lucky plant; symbol of happiness, wealth and health*

Zindzi • South African • *stability*

Zinnia • German • *a flower from Mexico named after botanist JG Zinn*

Zubaida • Arabic • *marigold*

GEMINI

22nd May to 21st June

Planet: Mercury

Day: Wednesday

Stones: agate and garnet

Metal: mercury

Colours: daffodil, yellow, light bright shades of blue, hints of tints, billows of colour that start strong and fade into almost nothing

Design: shapes and patterns that tell a story, lines and contours that join and connect

Trees: hazel, walnut and all nut-bearing trees, bonsai, myrtle

Flora: daffodil, lily of the valley, lavender, lilacs

Celebrity Geminis: Paula Abdul • James Arness • Josephine Baker • Harriet Beecher Stowe • Jim Belushi • Sandra Bernhard • Pat Boone • Helena Bonham Carter • Boy George • Barbara Bush • George Bush • Rosemary Clooney • Joan Collins • Sir Arthur Conan Doyle • Jacques Cousteau • Tony Curtis • Johnny Depp • Bruce Dern • Isadora Duncan • Bob Dylan • Clint Eastwood • Anthony Eden • Ralph Waldo Emerson • Douglas Fairbanks Snr • Sir Ian Fleming • Errol Flynn • Anne Frank • Judy Garland • Paul Gauguin • King George V • Steffi Graf • Thomas Hardy • Bob Hope • Hedda Hopper • Ben Johnson • Angelina Jolie • Tom Jones • Tom Jones • Sally Kellerman • John F Kennedy • Nicole Kidman • Gladys Knight • Anna Kournikova • Patti Labelle • Christopher Lee • Peggie Lee • Barry Manilow • Dean Martin • Queen Mary of Teck • Paul McCartney • Sir Ian McKellen • Marilyn Monroe • Claudio Monteverdi • Robert Montgomery • Audie Murphy • Liam Neeson • Sir Lawrence Olivier • Cole Porter • Vincent Price • Prince • Aleksandr Pushkin • Prince Rainier III • Basil Rathbone • Lionel Ritchie • Joan Rivers • Isabella Rossellini • Salman Rushdie • Rosalind Russell • Dorothy L Sayers • Robert Shumann • Wallis Simpson • Nancy Sinatra • Igor Stravinsky • Jessica Tandy • Donald Trump • Kathleen Turner • Queen Victoria • Richard Wagner (composer) • John Wayne • Dennis Weaver • Johnny Weissmuller • Gene Wilder • William Butler Yeats • Brigham Young.

Planetary Influences: see Mercury at the back of this book (page 450)

Boys

'Abd-al-Hādi • Arabic • *servant of the guide, Allah*

Achilles, Achilleus, Achille, Achilleo, Aquiles, Akhilleus • Greek • *from the River Akehloos*

Adina, Adin • Jewish/Hebrew • *so slender!*

Adnān • Arabic • *uncertain root; may mean settler*

Adrian, Adrien, Adriano, Hadrianus • Latin • *a man from Hadria which the Adriatic Sea is named*

Ainsley, Ainslie, Ainslee, Ainslie • English • *a person from the village of Annesley or Ansley*

Åke, Achatius, Åge • Germanic/ Norse • *either ancestor or the semi-precious stone garnet*

Alaric, Aliric • Germanic • *a foreign power or powerful, ruling stranger, perhaps invader*

Albert, Albrecht, Adalbert, Adalbrecht, Adelbrecht, Alberto, Albeart, Adalberht, Al, Bert, Albie, Alby, Bertie, Athelbert • French/ Germanic/Anglo-Saxon • *bright and noble*

Aled • modern British/Welsh • *child*

Algot • Norse • *elf and gothic*

Alger, Algie, Aelfgaer • Anglo-Saxon • *an old enchanted, noble spear with magical powers, possibly from a sacred location*

Alpha • Greek/Jewish • *first letter of Greek alphabet*

Amias • French/Biblical/Hebrew • *someone from Amiens in Picardie, or love God*

Amos • Biblical/Jewish/Hebrew •

to carry the Lord like St Christopher

Angelo, Ángel, Angelos • Greek/ Latin • *messenger of God*

Antip, Antipas, Antipater • just like your father!

Anwar • Arabic • *crystal-clear and bright*

Antshel, Anshel, Amshel • Jewish/Yiddish

Archer, Archier, Arcarius, Archarius • Norman/Latin • *surname meaning a bowman or archer*

Arkadi, Arkadios • Greek • *a man from Arcadia*

Arfon • British/Welsh • *area of Caernarfon and Gwynedd*

Arran • cosmetic Scots • *an island in the Firth of Clyde, part of Buteshire*

Armani, Armanno, Hariman • Lombardic/Italian/Germanic • *freeman*

Arseni, Arsenios, Arsene, Arsenio • Greek • *a very sexy boy*

Aulay, Amhladh, Amlaidh, Olaf • Scots Gaelic/Norse • *ancestor, heir, descendant*

Auliffe, Amhlaoibh • Irish Gaelic/ Norse • *ancestor, heir, descendant*

Bakr • young camel

Bala, Balu • Sanskrit • *young*

Balder • Norse • *ruler or chief prince, said to be pure and beautiful*

Baldev • Sanskrit • *God of Strength and playboy!*

Baldur, Baldr • Norse • *son of Odin*

Barnabas, Barnaby, Barney, Barny, Barnabé, Bernebe, Barnaba, Barna, Bernabé • Biblical/Greek • *son of consolation*

Barrett, Barratt • English • *a trader, merchant*

Barry, Baz, Bazza, Barra, Bairre,

Barrie, Barri • Irish Gaelic • *fair-headed boy*

Barrington, Bearain • Norman/Anglo-Saxon • *a person from Barentin, France or the village of Barrington*

Bartholomew, Barton, Bart, Barthélemy, Bartholomaus, Bartolomé • Biblical/Jewish/Hebrew • *son of Tolmai from Galilee*

Beau • French • *beautiful and bonny boy*

Bearach, Biorach • Irish Gaelic • *sharp, pointed*

Beathan • Scots Gaelic • *life*

Benjamin, Ben, Benny, Bennie, Benjamim, Benjie, Benji, Benjy, Venyamin, Binyamin, Benno, Bendik • Hebrew/Jewish • *son of my right hand, my right-hand man*

Benson, Bensington • English • *son of Benedict*

Benvenuto • Latin • *welcome*

Bertram, Bertie, Bert, Bertrand, Beltrán, Burt, Albert • German • *bright*

Bevan, Evan, Bev • British/Welsh • *son of Evan*

Bingwen • Chinese • *clever, cultivated*

Blaine, Blane • Scots Gaelic • *mellow yellow*

Blakeney • English • *he from the black island*

Bob, Bobbie, Bobby, Robbie, Robert • American/English/Germanic • *bright, famous and clever*

Boone • Norman/English • *a man from Bohon, France*

Boris, Borislav, Borya, Boba, Baurice • Russian • *small, little*

Börries, Liborius • German/Celtic • *to be free!*

Brad, Bradford, Bradley, Bradleigh, Braeden, Braden, Brayden • Anglo-Saxon • *a man from the broad meadow, ford, farm or clearing*

Brendan, Brendon, Breandán, Brendanus • Latin • *prince, heir*

Brett, Bret • Celtic • *a man from Brittany*

Broder, Bror • Scandinavian • *brother, especially for youngest son*

Broderick • British/Welsh • *son of Rhydderch*

Brooklyn • Dutch • *name of a New York borough*

Bruce • Norman/English • *someone from Bruis*

Bryson • American/English • *son of Brice*

Cadfael • British/Welsh • *prince of warriors, battle prince*

Cain, Kane, Cane • Jewish/Hebrew • *a craftsman*

Cairbre, Carbrey, Carbry • Irish Gaelic • *charioteer, horse driver*

Caolán, Kelan, Keelan • Irish Gaelic • *slender, slim, trim*

Caolite • Irish Gaelic • *origins vague; linked to legendary sprinter Mac Ronain*

Carlos, Carolus, Charles • Spanish/Latin • *freeman*

Carlton • English • *the place of the free men*

Carter • English • *a man who drives a wagon or cart!*

Celso, Celsus • Latin • *tall, lofty, beanpole*

Cedric • literary name • *invented by Sir Walter Scott*

Chaim, Hyam • Jewish/Hebrew • *life*

Chandler • English • *a candle maker*

Changming • Chinese • *forever bright*

Chapman, Ceappman • Anglo-Saxon • *pedlar, door-to-door salesman, merchant*

Chao • Chinese • *superior, improved*

Charles, Carl, Karl, Carlo, Carlos, Séarlas, Teàrlach, Slarl, Karel, Carel, Charel, Carles, Karol, Carol, Kaarle, Karoly, Karolis, Charlie, Charley • Germanic • *a freeman*

Chas, Chaz, Chuck, Chuckie, Chukkie • American/English • *little Charles*

Charlton, Chas, Chaz, Chuck, Chuckie, Chukkie • English • *the place where the free men live*

Chonglin • Chinese • *second brother unicorn*

Christopher, Chris, Christian, Crìsdean, Karsten, Christiaan, Carsten, Christer, Chretien, Cristiano, Krysztian, Krisztian, Christie, Christy, Kristy, Kristopher, Christopha, Kristopha, Críostóir, Christoph, Christofoor, Kristafoor, Kristoffer, Christophe, Cristobál, Cristofol, Cristovao, Cristoforo, Krzysztof, Krystof, Hristo, Risto, Kristof, Kristaps, Kit, Kester • Greek • *the man who bears Jesus Christ*

Claiborne, Clayborne, Claiborn, Clayborn • Anglo-Saxon/American English • *honouring a founder Virginian colonist, surname of an influential American family who came from Westmorland in Great Britain*

Cleon • African American • *invented name*

Clyde • American/English • *a famous Scottish river*

Colwyn, Dafydd • British/Welsh • *place name*

Comhghall, Comgall, Cowall • Irish Gaelic • *together, jointly, ransom*

Comhghán • Irish Gaelic • *twins!*

Conrad, Konrad, Corrado • Germanic • *one who gives forthright and candid advice*

Corin, Quirinus, Quirino • Latin • *an ancient Roman deity connected to Romulus*

Courtney, Curt, Kurt, Curtis, Courtenay • Norman • *the barony of Courtenay*

Creighton, Crichton, Criochiune • Scots Gaelic/English • *someone from Crichton in Midlothian*

Cuthbert, Bert, Cuddy, Cuddie, Cuithbeart • Anglo-Saxon • *a man well known for what he does, his personality or wit*

Cyprian, Cyprianus • Latin • *the man who comes from Cyprus, the isle of Venus or Aphrodite*

Daithi • Irish Celtic • *swift*

Daley, Dalaigh, Dalach, Daly • Irish Gaelic • *altogether now! A gathering or a moot*

Dalmazio, Dalmatius, Dalmacio • Latin • *a person from Dalmatia in the Adriatic*

D'Arcy, Darcy • Norman • *a man from the barony of D'Arcy*

Darell, Darrell, Darrel, Darryll, Daryl, Darryl • Norman/American/English • *a chap from D'airelle, a barony in Normandy*

David, Dave, Davy, Dewi, Dafydd, Dai, Davie, Davey, Dàibhidh, Davide, Taavi, Daw, Dawson, Dawūd, Dewi, Dewydd, David, Dai • Biblical/Hebrew • *vague origins but possibly from a baby word meaning darling one*

Delroy, Del • Caribbean/French •
son or servant of the king or leader
Denver • Anglo-Saxon/American/
English • *named after Denver
(Denafaer) in Norfolk, east Britain,
meaning where the Danes or Vikings
crossed the river*
Denzel, Densil, Denzil, Denzell •
Cornish/British • *local name from
Kernow or west Britain, which
became known as Cornwall*
**Desmond, Deasún, Des,
Deasmhumhnach** • Irish Gaelic •
*a man from south Munster (around
Cork)*
Devereux • Norman • *someone from
the barony of Evreux in Eure*
Dewey, Dewy • British/Welsh/
American/English • *possibly the
English spelling of Dewi, which
means David, darling one*
**Diarmuid, Dermot, Diarmuit,
Diarmit** • *unsure roots but perhaps
without envy*
Dilip • Sanskrit • *patron of Delhi
the city*
Diyā • Arabic • *brightness*
Doran, Deoradhain, Deoradh •
traveller, such as pilgrim or stranger
**Dorian, Dorien, Dorieus, Dorianus,
Doron** • literary name • *Oscar
Wilde's invention for* The Portrait of
Dorian Gray; *a Greek connection for
the people who settled in southern
Greece*
**Doyle, Dubhghaill, Dubhghall,
Dùghall, Dougal, Dugal, Dugald** •
Scots Gaelic • *black, dark, stranger*
Duyi • Chinese • *independent and
at one*

**Eckhard, Eckehard, Eggert,
Eckhardt, Eckehardt** • *all-powerful;*
the point of a sword
Efisio, Ephesius, Ephesus •
Sardinian • *a person from Ephesus in
Asia Minor*
Egbert, Bert • Anglo-Saxon • *by the
edge of his sword he famously rules*
Egil, Egill • Norse • *edge, rim, point*
Egmont, Egmunt • Germanic •
*protected by the edge or point of a
sword*
Egon • Germanic • *point or sharp
edge of a sword*
Éimhín • Irish • *speedy, fast, swift,
prompt, quick*
Eladio, Helladio • Greek • *a man
from Greece*
Eli • Hebrew/Jewish • *God's height,
probably tall*
Eligio, Eligius, Eligere, Eloy • Latin/
Italian/Spanish • *to choose, given a
choice*
Elmer, Elmar • Germanic • *famous
swordsman*
Emerson • English • *son of Emery*
Englebert, Engelbrecht • Germanic
• *bright angel*
Enda,Éanna • Irish Gaelic • *like a
bird*
Erland, Orland • Norse • *a stranger
or traveller from another land*
Ermete, Hermes • Greek •
messenger of the gods
Errol, Erol, Erroll, Eryl • Scottish •
*Scots surname from a place name
in Perthshire*
Erskine • Scottish • *a place name
in Renfrewshire*
**Eunan, Ádhamhán, Adomnae,
Ádhamh** • Irish Gaelic • *he's a right
little horror! Strikes fear in my heart*
**Eutrope, Eutropios, Eutropos,
Eutropio** • Greek • *what a nice polite
boy and so clever and versatile*

Fa • Chinese • *starting out*

Fahīm • Arabic • *a man of deep understanding and wisdom*

Fanus • Ethiopian • *a bright light*

Farīd • Arabic • *unique, beyond compare*

Farūq, Farouk • Arabic • *clever, intuitive and wise*

Fergus, Fearghas, Ferrer • Irish/ Scots Gaelic • *vital, dynamic man*

Fife, Fyfe • Gaelic • *someone from the kingdom of Fife; Fif was a Pictish hero*

Fikri • Arabic • *intellectual and contemplative*

Filiberto • Germanic • *very bright, royal house of Savoy name*

Fingal, Fionnghall, Fingall • Gaelic • *blond, fair stranger or traveller or Viking settler*

Finn • Scandinavian • *a man from Finland/Suomi*

Fitzgerald, Fitz • Norman/English • *son of Gerald*

Fitzroy, Fitz • Norman/English • *often the bastard son of the king*

Flaithrí, Florry, Flurry • prince, king

Flinders, Flanders • English • *a Flemish person from Flanders*

Foka, Phocas • Greek • *someone from Phocaea in Asia Minor*

Foma, Thomas • Russian/Biblical • *twin*

Forbes, Forba- Scots Gaelic • a Scots surname based on Forbes in Aberdeenshire, meaning fields

Francis, Francisco, Fran, Franciscus, Frank, France, François, Francesco, Franz • Latin • *to be French, someone from France*

Frank, Franklin, Frankie • Germanic • *a loyal and free man or from the Frankish tribe*

Franz • German/Italian • *to be French, someone from France*

Fridtjof • Norse • *quiet, like a thief in the night*

Frode, Frodi, Frod • Scandinavian • *a knowledgable man, well-informed*

Fry, Frig, Freo, Frio • Anglo-Saxon/ Norse • *either free man or a small man*

Fulgenzio, Fulgentius, Fulgens, Fulgencio • Latin • *shining*

Fulton • Scots • *Scottish surname based on a place in Ayrshire now extinct*

Gaétan, Gaetano, Caietanus • Latin • *a man from Caieta in Latium*

Galadima • Hausa African • *prince*

Gallagher Gallchobhar • Irish Gaelic • *foreign ally, helpful stranger*

Garnet, Grenate, Granatum • Norman/Latin • *either a dealer in pomegranates or the precious stone*

Garrison, Gary, Garry • American/ English • *someone from Garriston in North Riding of Yorkshire*

Gary, Garry, Gaz, Gazza • Germanic/French • *spear bearer or carrier*

Gaston • geographic • *a man from Gascony*

Gavino, Gabinus, Gabino • Sardinian/Latin • *a man from Gabium*

Geoffrey, Jeffrey, Jeff, Geoffroi, Geoff, Godofredo, Sieffre • Germanic/Frankish/Lombardic • *a stranger in your own land or foreigner who pledges allegiance*

Germaine, Jermaine, Germanus, Germain • French/Latin • *brother*

Gershom, Gershorn, Gersham • Biblical/Jewish/Hebrew • *a stranger there*

Germain, Germanus • Latin •
brother
**Gervaise, Gervase, Jervaise,
Jervais, Gervais, Gervas, Gervasio**
• Germanic/Frankish • *unknown
origin; possibly a man with a spear
or something pointed*
**Gerald, Jed, Ged, Jerrold, Gerry,
Jerry, Geraud, Geraldo, Gerallt,
Garret, Garrett, Gearóid, Jarrett,
Gerolt, Gennaro** • Germanic/
Frankish • *he who rules with a spear*
**Gérard, Gerrard, Gerardo, Gerry,
Jerry** • Germanic/Frankish • *brave
and bold with a spear*
Gerhard, Gerhardt, Geert, Gert
• Germanic • *strong, dedicated
swordsman*
Gerlach • Germanic • *playful and
sporting swordsman*
German, Germanus • Latin •
brother in God
Gernot • Germanic • *he needs a
spear*
Ghassān • Arabic • *youth*
**Giles, Gyles, Aegidius, Aigidios,
Gilles, Aegidus, Gide, Gil** • Latin/
Greek/English • *kid, a young goat*
Gino, Giorgino, Luigino • Latin •
clipped name
Gladwin • Anglo-Saxon • *an opti-
mistic, positive friend*
Gonzogue • *patron of young people*
Göran, Örjan, Jöran, Jörn •
Scandinavian/Serbo-Croat • *man
from the mountains*
Gordon • Scottish • *unknown
origins; could spring from place
name in Aberdeenshire or similar
in Normandy*
**Graham, Graeme, Grahame,
Grandham, Granham** • Anglo-
Saxon • *I live in a gravelly place;*

Grantham, Lincolnshire
**Gérard, Jed, Ged, Jerrold, Gerry,
Jerry, Gerrard, Geraud, Gerardo,
Geraud, Gearóid, Gerald, Geraldo,
Gerallt** • Germanic/Frankish • *a
brave, strong man with a spear as his
weapon*
Gerhard, Gerhardt, Geert, Gert
• Germanic • *strong, dedicated
swordsman*
Gerlach • Germanic • *playful and
sporting swordsman*
**Gregory, Gregorios, Gregor, Greg,
Gregg, Greig, Greagoir, Griogair,
Grigor, Joris, Greger, Gregers,
Grégoire, Gregorio, Grigori,
Grzegorz, Rehor, Grgur, Reijo,
Gergely, Grigor** • Greek • *watchful*
Grover • American/English • *a man
who lives in or near a grove of trees*
**Gruffudd, Griff, Griffith, Griffinus,
Griffin, Grippiud, Gripiud, Gutun,
Gutyn, Guto** • British/Welsh •
prince of lords

Haakon, Håkon, Hagen, Håkan •
Norse/Germanic • *high-born son,
relative, like a horse/fort, stockade*
Hāfiz • Arabic • *devoted scholar,
guardian, foster*
Halfdan, Halvdan • Norse • *a man
who is half Danish; especially 5th
June*
Harper • English/American • *a
person who plays a harp!*
Harvard, Hereward, Hervard •
American/English • *the vigilant
soldier, the army guard*
Hāsim • Arabic • *decisive, incisive
and quick*
Hātim • Arabic • *decisive and
focused*
Hector, Hektor, Ekhain, Eachann,

Eachdonn • Greek/Scots Gaelic • *brown horse*

Hermes, Hermolaos, Yermolai • Greek • *the god Hermes, messenger of the gods or the people*

Hernán, Fernando, Hernando • Spanish • *a man at peace wherever he is; always ready and prepared to travel*

Hesketh, Hesskeid • Norse • *where the horses race, a Viking hippodrome*

Hildebrand • Germanic • *flaming sword, battle success*

Hildebrecht • Germanic • *bright light in the battle*

Hilary, Hillary, Hilare, Hilario, Ilar • Latin • *as in hilarious!*

Hilton, Hill, Hyll • Anglo-Saxon • *a village on a hill or hump*

Hippolyte, Hippolytos, Hipolito • Greek • *a free spirit (horse!)*

Hiram, Ahiram • Phoenician/ Jewish/Hebrew • *brother of the exalted one*

Hopcyn, Hopkin, Hob, Robert • British/Welsh • *famous and bright*

Hubert, Hugbert, Huppert, Hupprecht, Hobart • Germanic • *brilliant heart and famed mind*

Hugh, Huw, Hugues, Hugo, Aodh, Hughie, Hewie, Huey, Hewie, Hughie, Huwie • Germanic/ Frankish • *heart, mind and spirit*

Hugo, Hugh • Germanic/Frankish/ Latin • *heart, mind and spirit*

Husām • Arabic • *sword, sabre, rapier*

Innes, Aonghas, Inis • Scots Gaelic • *an island, or man from Innes in Moray*

Innocenzo, Innocentius, Innocens, Innokenti, Inocencio • innocent, childlike; many saints and popes

named this

Ira • Hebrew/Jewish • *vigilant, observant, watchful*

Italo, Italus • Latin • *father of Romulus and Remus, founders of Rome*

Ithel, Iudhael • British/Welsh • *a generous but common man who behaves like a goodly prince or lord; philanthropist*

Jada • Biblical/Hebrew/Jewish • *he knows*

Jahangir • Persian • *he's got the whole world in his hands*

Jakada • Hausa West African • *the messenger*

Jarod, Jarrod, Gerald • English • *he who rules with a spear*

Jarrett, Garrett • Irish/English • *he who rules with a spear*

Jarvis, Jervis • Germanic/Frankish/ English • *unknown origin; possibly a man with a spear or something pointed*

Jeffrey, Geoffrey, Jeff, Geoff, Jefferson, Jeffery, Jeffry, Jep • *a stranger in your own land or foreigner who pledges allegiance*

Jenson, John, Jan • English • *son of Jan or John*

Jérôme, Hieronymos, Jerry, Jerrie, Jeri, Jerónimo, Geronimo, Hierosonoma • Greek • *I bear a holy name*

Jerold, Jerrold, Gerald, Jerry, Gerry • English • *he who rules with a spear*

Jerrard, Gerrard, Gerard • American/English • *he who rules with a spear*

Jevon, Jeavon, Jeevan, Jovene • English/Norman • *young*

Jing • Chinese • *a boy born in the*

capital city Beijing or regional capital
Jordan, Judd, Hayarden • Hebrew/
Jewish • *flowing down*
Junior, Junia • Biblical • *youth*

Kajetan, Caitanus, Gaetano,
Kayetan • Latin • *man from Caieta*
Karanja • Kenyan • *he who guides*
Karl, Charles, Karlmann • Germanic
• *freeman*
Kasi • Sanskrit • *radiant; Varanasi or
Benares, sacred city on the Ganges*
Keanu • Hawaiian • *cool breeze from
the mountains*
Keiller, Keilor, Keiller • Canadian/
English • *Scots surname from a place
in Perthshire*
Keith • British/Welsh • *wood, copse
or thicket, or a man from East
Lothian*
Kellen, Kelan, Cailein, Ailein,
McKellern, Macailein, Maccailein •
Gaelic • *slender, slim, trim, or son of
Alan or son of Colin*
Kelvin, Kelvyn • Scots/English • *if
you come from Kelvinside, Glasgow
or by the river, this is the root of the
name*
Kent, Kenton, Kenntun, Cenatun,
Cynetun • British/Welsh • *someone
from the British kingdom (now
county) and tribe of the Cantii*
Kenya • English • *someone from the
African land of Kenya*
Kerry, Ceri • English/British/Welsh •
after the Celtic Goddess of Poetry
Khalipha, Caliph • Arabic •
successor, heir
Kilroy, Gilroy • English • *the red-
haired boy*
Kimberley, Kimberly, Kim, Kym •
Anglo-Saxon/American English
• *after the South African town of*

*Kimberley where the British took on
the Boers*
Kishore • Sanskrit • *colt, a young
horse*
Kumar • Sanskrit • *beautiful Prince
Skanda*
Kyle, Caol • Gaelic • *narrow in
geographical terms; a region in
Ayrshire*

Lachlan, Lachlann, Lochlann,
Lochlan, Lachie, Lockie, Loughlin,
Lochlainn Lochlainn, Lachlan,
Laughlin, Loughlin • Scots Gaelic •
*a man from the land of the lochs or
Norway*
Lamont, Lagman, Logmad • Norse
• *a man of the law; legal person*
Laoiseach, Laois, Louis, Lewis, Leix
• Irish • *a man from County Leix*
Lark, Lawerce • Anglo-Saxon/
Australian/North American • *the
lark, the bird*
Laurence, Lawrence, Larry,
Laurentius, Laurentum, Laurie,
Lawrie, Labhrás, Labhrainn,
Lorenz, Laurens, Lars, Laurent,
Lorencio, Llorenc, Laurenco,
Lorenzo, Lawson, Lavrentios,
Lavrenti, Laurencjusz,
Wawrzyniec, Vavrinec, Lovrenc,
Lauri, Lasse, Lassi, Lorinc, Laz,
Lenz, Lavrenti • Latin • *man from
Laurentum, the capital of the Latins*
Leif, Leaf, Leiv • Norse • *heir of the
realm*
Lester, Ligoracaester, Ligoracastra
• Anglo-Saxon • *the place of the
Roman fort on the River Soar*
Levi, Levy • Hebrew/Jewish •
making a connection
Liang • Chinese • *bright, luminous,
radiant*

Licio, Lycius • Latin • *man from Lycia in Asia Minor*

Lincoln, Lindum • British/Welsh • *Roman fort by the lake*

Liu • Chinese • *flowing*

Llywarch, Lugumarcos • British/Welsh • *the horse god or God of the Horses*

Logan • Scots Gaelic • *a family name or someone from Logan in Ayrshire*

Lonán, Lonain • Irish Gaelic • *blackbird*

Lorin, Loren, Lorrin, Laurence • Latin • *man from Laurentum, the capital of the Latins*

Lorne, Latharna, Lorn • Canadian/English • *Scottish place name Lorne, Argyll*

Lucas, Luka, Luke, Luca, Loukas • East European/Greek • *man from Loucania, a Greek colony in southern Italy*

Lucian, Lucianus, Lucius, Lucien, Luciano, Lucio, Lux • Latin • *light*

Ludger, Luitger • Friesian • *place name derived from famous monk*

Lughaidh, Lewis, Lewie, Louis, Louie • *bright and shiny*

Luke, Lucas, Loukas, Lukas, Luc, Lluc, Lluch, Lukasz, Luukas, Lukacs, Luka • Greek • *man from Loucania, a Greek colony in southern Italy*

Lyle, De L'isle • Norman Gaelic • *someone from the isles or marshy land*

Mabon • British/Welsh • *son or son of*

Macey, Macciscum, Maccius • Norman/Latin • *someone from Massey, Normandy*

Madison, Madde, Madeleine, Maud • American English • *son of Maud or Matilda, the battleaxe*

Māhir • Arabic • *clever, dexterous, skilful*

Malachi, Malachy, Maoileachlainn • Biblical/Irish Gaelic • *my messenger or follower of St Seachnall or St Secundinus*

Maurice, Moris, Morris, Mo, Maurus, Moritz, Maurizio, Mauricius, Mavriki, Mauricio, Maurits • Latin • *a dark swarthy person as in a Moor from Arabia*

Mauro • Latin • *a Moor as in Arab; early followers of St Benedictine*

Meinrad • Germanic • *unswayed, determined counsellor*

Meir, Meier, Meyer, Myer, Maier, Mayr • Jewish/Hebrew • *giving light*

Melvin, Melvyn, Mel, Melvin, Melville, Melvyn, Malleville • *a man from a bad place*

Mengyao • Chinese • *a parent's wish for a wise child*

Mercer, Mercy, Mercier, Mercarius, Merx • Norman/Latin • *a merchant*

Merl, Meriel, Merle, Merula • Norman/Latin • *a blackbird*

Methodius, Mefodi • Greek • *following the path or road, spiritual as much as a traveller*

Meurig, Mauricius, Mouric, Meuric, Maurice • British/Welsh • *a dark swarthy person as in a Moor from Arabia*

Michelangelo • Bibilical • *angel*

Midhat • Arabic • *tribute*

Mihangel, Michael • British/Welsh • *Michael the Archangel*

Milan, Milano • Czech/Italian • *grace and favour or someone who comes from Milan, Italy*

Mirza • Persian • *subserviant prince*
Montague, Montaigu, Monty •
Norman/Latin • *a person from the
pointed hill particularly Montaigu,
La Manche, Normandy*
**Montgomery, Montgomeric,
Monty** • Germanic/Norman • *the
powerful man from the hill country*
**Montmorency, Montmaurentius,
Monty** • Roman/Gaulish/Norman • *the dark hill, possibly linked to Moors
or Arabs*
Morris, Maurice, Mo, Miuris •
English/Latin • *a dark swarthy
person as in a Moor from Arabia*
Munīr • Arabic • *shining, dazzling,
glorious*
Murray, Moray, Muireach • Scots
Gaelic • *a person from Moray*

Nadīm • Arabic • *best friend, companion
you share your social life with*
Nājib, Nāgib • Arabic • *cultured,
cultivated, in a class of his own*
Napoleon, Napoleone • Italian •
*unsure origin; may mean sons of the
mist or the Naples Lion*
**Narcissus, Narkissos, Narcisse,
Narciso** • Greek/Latin • *linked with
the daffodil but unsure origins*
Nataraj • Sanskrit • *Lord of the
Dance*
Neal, Neil, Neale, Nigel, Niall •
Irish Gaelic/English • *passionate,
champion, winner, dead sexy, really
desirable, some say it means a man
who cannot commit*
Nelson, Nell, Neil • English •
*passionate, champion, winner, dead
sexy, really desirable, some say it
means a man who cannot commit*
Neopmuk • Czech • *someone
from the town of Pomuk; St John of*

Pomuk, patron saint of Bohemia
Nigel, Nigellus, Nihel, Neil •
Latin/English • *black as pitch or
passionate, dead sexy, really desir-
able, maybe a commitment phobe*
Nino, Giannino • Latin/Spanish •
the boy, referring to the Christ child
Nizār • Arabic • *confused origin;
might mean small or little one*
Nolan, Nuallain, Nuallan, Nuall •
Irish Gaelic • *champion charioteer*
Norbert, Nordberht • Germanic • *a
bright light from the north, northern
lights, Aurora Borealis*
Norman, Nordman, Tormod •
Germanic • *a man from the north;
Norseman or Viking*
Norris, Norreis • Germanic/
Frankish • *a person who has
migrated from the north to
Normandy; Norseman or Viking*

Odd, Oddbjörn • Norse • *the sharp
point of a weapon*
Oded • Jewish/Hebrew • *he who
encourages or persuades, compelling*
**Olaf, Olav, Anuleif, Olof, Ottwolf,
Ola, Ole, Oluf, Olov, Olaus, Olai** •
Norse • *ancestor, heir, descendant*
Omar, 'Umar • Biblical/Hebrew/
Arabic • *talkative*
Orville • literary invention • *Lord
Orville was created by Fanny Burney
in her novel* Evelina
Ottokar, Odovacar • Germanic •
*being watchful and observant brings
riches*

Pacey, Pacciacum, Passy, Paccius •
Latin/Gaulish • *a man called Paccius
or from the town of Passy*
Pajonga • Sierra Leonese • *walk tall,
tall man*

Palmer • English • *a pilgrim who had been to the Holy Land and returned with a palm branch*

Palmiro, Palmiere • Latin/Spanish • *a pilgrim who brought back a palm from the Holy Land*

Parry, Parri • British/Welsh • *son of Harry or Harri*

Parthalán, Párthlán, Pártlán, Partnán, Bartholomew, Berkely, Barclay • Latin/Irish • *first ever citizen of Ireland after the Biblical flood; Biblical, meaning son of Tolmai from Galilee*

Párlan, Parthalán • Gaelic • *uncertain origin; may be linked to Irish for Bartholomew*

Paul, Paulus, Pol, Pål, Poul, Pall, Pauwel, Påvel, Pablo, Pau, Paulo, Paolo, Pavlos, Pavao, Pavle, Paavo, Paulius, Pablo • Latin • *Roman family name meaning little or small*

Paulino, Pablo, Paulus • Spanish/Italian • *Roman family name meaning little or small*

Paco, Francis, Francisco • Spanish • *to be French, someone from France*

Peregrine, Peregrinus, Perry, Pellegrino • Latin • *stranger, wanderer, foreigner*

Persis • Biblical/Greek • *a Persian woman*

Philip, Phil, Phillipos, Phileinhippos, Pip, Pilib, Filib, Philipp, Filip, Philippe, Phillip, Felipe, Felip, Filipe, Filippo, Filip, Vilppu, Fulop, Filipes, Philipp, Pino • Greek • *friend or lover of horses*

Phineas, Fineas, Panhsj, Phinehas, Pinchas • Hebrew/Jewish/Biblical • *a person from Nubia, now southern Egypt or northern Sudan, or from the snake's mouth*

Porter, Porteour, Portare, Portier • Norman • *a person who carries*

Potter • American English • *someone who sells pots*

Prabhakar • Sanskrit • *bringer or maker of light, candles*

Pran • Sanskrit • *vitality, life breath and force*

Pravin • Sanskrit • *dexterous, clever and skilful*

Price, Pryce, Rhys • British/Welsh • *son of Rhys*

Proinséas, Francis • Irish/Latin • *to be French, someone from France*

Prokhoros, Prokhor • Greek • *very artistic, chief of a troupe of singers, dancers, actors*

Qi • Chinese • *enlightened, wonderment and intellectual*

Qusay • Arabic • *vague origin but could mean someone who comes from a long way away*

Raghīd • Arabic • *freedom loving and devil-may-care*

Raghu • Sanskrit • *swift, fast*

Rajkumar • Sanskrit • *prince, heir*

Ramiro • Spanish/Visigothic • *a man famous for his advice and counselling*

Ramón, Raimundo, Raymond • Catalan/Germanic • *adviser, protector*

Rearden, Ríordan, Rordan, Ríoghbhardán • English/Irish Gaelic • *wee poet king*

Reginald, Reg, Reggie, Reginaldus, Reynold, Reginwald • Germanic/Norman • *advice*

Reineke, Reine • Germanic • *counsellor*

Reinhard, Reinhardt, Reine •

Germanic • *strong, firm advice*
Reinhold, Reinwald, Reine •
Germanic • *splendid, wonderful
adviser*
Reinmar, Reine • Germanic •
famous adviser, speaker
Remus, Remo • Latin • *with
Romulus, founder of Rome*
Reuben, Reuven, Rube, Rubén •
Biblical/Hebrew/Jewish • *behold,
a son!*
**Reynold, Reginald, Reynaud,
Raginwald, Reginald, Ray,
Reynard, Ragin, Renard, Ray,
Rinaldo, Reinaldo, Rheinallt** •
Germanic/Norman • *advice rule*
Rhett, Rhet, Raedt, Raet • Dutch •
advice, counsel
Rhodri, Rhodrhi • British/Welsh •
*ruler of the wheel; king who rules by
his chariot*
Riaz • Arabic • *green fields, often
with an equine connection*
Ríordan, Rearden, Ríoghbhardán •
Irish • *poet king or king of the poets*
**Robert, Rob, Robbie, Rodberht,
Reodbeorht, Bob, Rob, Bobby,
Robin, Roibéard, Raibeart,
Rupprecht, Robrecht, Rupert,
Robbert, Roberto, Roopertti,
Roberts, Rabbie, Rab, Rigoberto** •
Germanic • *famous and bright*
Robin, Robben, Robert • Germanic
• *famous and bright*
Rogelio, Rogelius, Rogellus • Latin
• *unknown origin, maybe request*
**Roger, Rodge, Roge, Rodger,
Rogier, Rodgar, Ruggiero,
Ruggero, Roar, Rogerio, Hrothgar**
• Germanic/Norman • *famous spear,
someone who used the spear and
became famous for it*
Rodney, Rod, Roddy • Anglo-Saxon

• *famous island; a person from there*
**Roman, Romanus, Romain,
Romano** • Latin/Czech/Polish/
Romanian • *to be Roman*
Romeo, Romaeus • Latin • *a pilgrim
who has visited Rome*
Romulus, Romolo • Latin • *someone
from Rome; one of the founders of
Rome*
**Ronald, Ron, Ronnie, Ronny, Roni,
Ranald, Randal, Rognvald** • Norse •
adviser to the gods or king
Ross, Rós • Gaelic • *family name
from geographical term for a head-
land or promontory*
Rötger, Rüdiger • Germanic • *fame
with a knife or spear*
Royce, Royston, Royse • English •
the town or place of the rose or roses
Ru • Chinese • *Confucian scholar*
Rune, Runi, Runolf, Run • Norse
• *named after the Norse magical
alphabet*
Rupert, Ruprecht, Robert •
Germanic/Dutch • *famous and
bright*
Rurik, Hrodrik, Roderick • Norse •
*famous ruler, the name of the man
who founded Russia's Novogorod, the
Big New City*
Rushdi • Arabic • *old head on young
shoulders; ahead of his years*
Ruslan • literary invention/Russian
• *meaning unknown; name was used
by Aleksandr Pushkin in his poem
'Ruslan and Ludmila'*
**Russell, Russ, Rous, Rousel, Russel,
Rusty** • Norman • *little red one*
Ryan, Rian, Riain • Irish Gaelic •
little king, descendant of Riain

**Sacheverell, Sautechevreuil,
Sachie** • Norman • *surname*

from place name Saute Chevreuil, meaning roebuck leap

Safdar • Arabic • *a man who breaks ranks; loose cannon*

Sa'īd • Arabic • *happy-go-lucky*

Samuel, Shemuel, Shaulmeel, Sam, Sammy, Sawyl • Biblical/Hebrew/Jewish • *name of God, God has heard, listen to God*

Saul • Biblical/Hebrew/Latin • *asked for, prayed for, yearned for*

Scott • Gaelic • *a man from Ireland who settles in Scotland*

Seth • Biblical/Hebrew • *appointed to a certain place*

Shahzad • Muslim/Persian • *prince*

Shamshad • Persian • *tall as a box tree*

Sheridan, Sirideain • Irish Gaelic • *descendant of Sirideain, the searcher*

Shirong • Chinese • *reward as a result of learning*

Shukri • Arabic • *giving thanks*

Simeon • English/Biblical/Hebrew • *he has heard*

Simón, Siomon, Sim, Simidh, Sieman, Simao, Simone, Semyon, Szymon, Simo, Sim, Simmie • Biblical/Hebrew/Jewish • *hearkening, hearing*

Sinclair • Norman • *baronial name from Saint-Clair, who received earldoms in Caithness and Orkney*

Skylar, Schuyler • Dutch/American English • *scholar, schoolteacher*

Sly • American English • *a person who is full of guile and basically sly as a fox!*

Somerled, Sumarlid, Summerlad, Somhairle, Sorley • Scots Gaelic/Norse • *summer traveller*

Somhairle • Irish Gaelic/Norse • *summer traveller*

Stian, Stigand, Kris, Stig • *wanderer*

Sture, Stura • Scandinavian/Swedish • *wilful, contrary, independent spirit*

Sumantra • Sanskrit • *a person who is well versed in the classics*

Sven, Sveinn, Svein, Svend • Norse/Swedish • *young boy*

Sverre, Sverri, Sverra • Norse/Norwegian • *spinning, swirling about*

Swift • Anglo-Saxon • *the bird, but describing a person who is fast and quick*

Tad, Tadhg, Thaddeus, Tig, Tim, Taddeo, Teague, Teigue, Tadeo • Irish Gaelic • *poet, wise man, philosopher*

Taffy, Taf, Dafydd • British/Welsh • *the universal nickname for someone from Wales/Cymru (or called David), after the River Taff that flows through Cardiff/Caerdydd*

Tage, Taki, Taka • Scandinavian • *to take or grab, receive, guarantor*

Talāl • Arabic • *morning dew or fine rain*

Talbot, Talbod, Tal • Germanic/Frankish/Norman • *a personal name meaning to destroy despatches (messages)*

Tam, Tammy, Thomas, Tommy, Tom • Greek/Aramaic • *twin*

Tammaro • Germanic • *clever; famous mind*

Tara • Sanskrit • *shining light for the saviour; carrying the Lord*

Taras, Tarasio • Greek • *man from Tarentum in northern Italy*

Tavish, Tamhas, Thomas • Scots Gaelic/English • *twin*

Tengfei • Chinese • *soaring high*

Thomas, Thos, Tom, Tommy, Tomás, Tamhas, Tomos, Tommaso, Foma, Tomasz, Toma, Tomaz, Tuomo, Toms, Didymos • Biblical/Aramaic/Greek • *twin*

Tingzhe • Chinese • *judgement or wisdom is required*

Tiordhealbhach, Tárlach, Traolach, Turlough • Irish Gaelic • *instigator, initiator*

Tracy, Thraciusacum, Tracey • Latin/Gaulic • *a person from a place in Normandy called Tracy!*

Trent, Trenton • British/Welsh • *after the River Trent in the English Midlands; its root meaning is to travel or journey*

Trenton, Trent • American English • *means the settlement by the Trent, or after William Trent, the British Quaker founder of the New Jersey city*

Trond, Tron • Norse • *a man from Trondelag in Norway*

Troy, Trey, Troyes • someone from the French city of Troyes, or, more powerful, in memory of the Troy (in modern-day Turkey) of Greek mythology

Tucker, Tucian • Anglo-Saxon/American English • *surname originally meaning to tease and torment*

Ty, Tyler, Tyrone, Tye, Tyrese • American English• *clipped name*

Tyrese, Tyreece, Ty • American English • *invented name*

Tyrone, Ty, Tir Eoghain • Irish Gaelic • *a man from County Tyrone, Ulster; the land of Owen*

Ugo, Hugo, Hugh • Germanic • *heart, mind and spirit*

Ultach, Ultán • Irish • *a man from Ulster*

'Umar, Omar • Arabic • *to flourish and to make the complex simple*

Urban, Urbanus • Latin • *a person who lives in the city*

Urowo • Kenyan • *tall*

Usain • Caribbean English • *a modern invention but first name of fastest man in the world, Usain Bolt!*

Uwe • Germanic/Norse • *sharp blade, in awe*

Valéry, Val • Germanic • *foreign power*

Varfolomel, Bartholomew • Biblical • *son of Tolmai from Galilee*

Vasant • Sanskrit • *springtime*

Vaughan, Vaughn, Fychan, Bychan • British/Welsh • *small, little*

Vinay • Sanskrit • *education, intelligence, learning*

Vinod • Sanskrit • *recreation, leisure, pleasure and sport*

Vitale, Vitalis • Latin • *full of life*

Vitus • Latin • *life*

Vivien, Vyvyan, Viv, Vi, Béibhinn • Latin/Norman • *Roman name Vivianus, meaning life*

Vlas, Blasius, Blaesus, Blaise, Vlasi • Latin • *area of the throat, perhaps person with a lisp*

Voshon • African American • *invented name*

Wallace, Wallis, Waleis, Wally • Anglo-Saxon • *foreigner*

Warren, Warin, Varenne • Germanic/Norman • *a person from La Varenne, Normandy*

Waseme • Swahili • *let them talk*

Wayne, Waegen • Anglo-Saxon • *a carter or cartwright; wagon driver*

Wendice • African American • *invented name*

Willibrand • Germanic • *will and flaming sword*

Wilson, Will • English • *son of William*

Worede • Ethiopian • *came from above*

Xayvion • African American • *invented name*

Xiang • Chinese • *circling in the air*

Xue • Chinese • *studious, knowledge*

Yaro • Hausa South African • *son*

Yaroslav • Slavic • *glorious spring*

Yefim, Euphemios • Russian/Greek • *eloquent, articulate speaker*

Yingpei • Chinese • *to be admired*

Zāhir • Arabic • *radiant, bright, luminous*

Zamir • Arabic • *ideas, mental thoughts*

Zengguang • Chinese • *growing brightness*

Zhen • Chinese • *astonishment surprises*

Zihao • Chinese • *heroic son*

Girls

Abilene, Abbie, Abby, Abbey, Abi, Lena • Biblical/Jewish/Hebrew • *an area of Palestine or the Holy Land, meaning grass or grasses*

Abishag, Avishag • Biblical/Jewish/Hebrew • *wise and educated*

Adria, Adrianne, Adrienne, Adrianna, Adriana • Latin • *a person from Hadria which the Adriatic Sea is named*

Adrienne, Adriana • Latin • *a person from Hadria which the Adriatic Sea is named*

Africa • Latin • *the dark continent*

Áine • Irish • *as bright, as radiant as the Queen of the Faeries*

Aingeal • Irish • *angel*

Alba • Latin/Germanic • *white or elfin*

Alberta, Albertina • French/Germanic/Anglo-Saxon • *bright and noble*

Aledwen • British/Welsh • *child*

Alfreda, Freddie, Fred • Anglo-Saxon • *supernatural, faerie counsel, help*

Allegra • Italian • *happy, jolly, frisky*

Alpha, Alfa • Greek/Jewish • *first letter of Greek alphabet*

Amaryllis, Amaryssein • Greek • *to sparkle*

Angel, Ángela, Angelina, Angeline, Angie, Ange, Angelos • Greek • *messenger of God*

Angela, Angelita • Latin/Greek • *messenger of God*

Ángeles • Spanish/Roman Catholic • *Our Lady of the Angels*

Angelica, Angélique, Angelika • Latin • *a girl of the angels*

Angosto • Spanish/Galician/Roman Catholic • *Our Lady of Angosto, a place where the Virgin appeared*

Anise, Annis, Annice, Anis • Latin/Greek/French • *aniseed plant*

Anitra • literary invention • *created by Henrik Ibsen as the name of an Arabic princess in* Peer Gynt

Annunziata, Nunzia, Anunciación, Anunciata • Roman Catholic • *announcing the birth of Jesus to Mary*

Aphra, Afra • Latin • *a woman from Africa, the dark continent*

Arianrhod • British/Welsh • *silver wheel*

Armani • Lombardic/Italian/Germanic • *freeman*

Asenath • Biblical/Egyptian • *she is Daddy's little princess*

Atalanta, Atlanta • mythological/American English • *capital of the US state of Georgia*

Athene, Athena, Athina, Athenai • Greek • *Greek Goddess of Wisdom and protector of the city of Athens*

Atholl, Athol, Athole • Gaelic • *'New Ireland' area of Perthshire*

Attracta, Athracht • Latin • *she is like a magnet, she draws people to her*

Autumn, Autumnus • Latin • *a season of the year (southern hemisphere)*

Auxilio • Spanish/Roman Catholic • *Mary the helper; especially 24th May*

Avdotya, Eudokia, Eudokein • Greek • *she seems a nice, good girl*

Bala • Sanskrit • *young*

Bano • Persian • *lady, princess, bride*

Barbara, Babette, Babs, Barbra, Barb, Barbie, Baibín, Báirbre,

Varvara, Varya, Barbro • Greek •
a foreign woman
Bathsheba, Sheba, Bathsheeva •
Biblical/Jewish/Hebrew • *daughter*
of the oath
Beathag • Irish Gaelic • *life*
Beau • French • *beautiful and bonny*
girl
Bertha, Berthe, Berta • Germanic •
bright and famous
Bina, Albina, Devorah,
Deborah, Binah, Bine, Binke •
Jewish/Hebrew/Yiddish • *bee or*
understanding
Blythe, Blithe • Anglo-Saxon •
a sanguine spirit
Bobbie, Roberta • Germanic •
famous and bright
Brenda • Norse • *sword*
Brittany, Britney • Latin • *the Celtic-*
speaking province of north-west
France, so-called due to the influx
of Celts from Cornwall when the
Romans invaded, and who trans-
ferred Britannia, their name for the
island, across to this part of France
Brooklyn, Lyn, Breukelen • Dutch
• *a district of New York City when it*
was New Amsterdam under Dutch
control, meaning broken land
Bushra • Arabic • *happy news, glad*
tidings and fine omen

Caileigh, Kayley, Kayleigh, Caleigh,
Caollaidhe • Irish Gaelic • *a*
descendant of Caollaidhe, the prefix
meaning a slender man
Calico • Indian • *a light cotton fabric*
from Calicut a port in Kerala state
Caoilfhionn, Caoilainn, Keelin,
Caolffionn • Irish • *slender and*
white maiden
Careen • literary invention • *one of*

Scarlett O'Hara's sisters in Gone with
the Wind
Carla, Carlene, Charlene, Charlotte,
Carlotta, Charlotta, Carleen,
Carlin, Carlina, Carlyn, Carlynne,
Carline, Carolina, Caroline, Carly,
Karly, Carley, Carola, Carlie, Carli,
Carolyn, Caro, Carrie, Carol, Carole,
Caryl, Caryll, Sharlene, Charlie,
Charley, Lotte, Lottie, Tottie •
Italian/English/Germanic
Casey, Casy, KC, Kacey, Kaci, Kacie
• Irish Gaelic • *a watchman; keeps*
guard in war
Celandine, Dina • English/Greek •
a swallow and a flower
Ceridwen, Ceridwynn, Ceri •
British/Welsh • *Goddess of Poetry*
Charline, Charlene, Sharlene,
Shalene • French/American English/
Australian/Germanic • *a freeman*
Charlotte, Carlotta, Karlotte,
Karlotta, Séarlait • French/
Germanic • *a freeman*
Chenguang • Chinese • *morning*
light
Cheyenne, Sahiyena • French
Canadian • *an Indian tribe from*
Dakota
Chiara, Clare, Claire, Clara, Ciara,
Kiarah, Kiara, Kiera, Clair, Clarette,
Clarinda, Clarrie, Clarus • Latin/
Italian • *bright, famous, crystal-clear*
Chorine, Choreen, Corinne,
Corinna • French • *chorus or*
dancing girl
Clare, Claire, Clara, Chiara, Klara,
Kiara, Clara, Kiarah • Latin/English
• *bright, famous, crystal-clear*
Clarice, Claritia • Latin/French/
English • *bright, famous,*
crystal-clear
Clarissa, Clarisa, Clarice, Clarrisse,

Clarisse, Claris, Clarissa, Cáitir • Latin • *bright, famous, crystal-clear*
Clíodhna, Clíona • Irish Gaelic • *vague origin; one of the three daughters of the poet Libra*
Consilia, Conseja • Roman Catholic • *Mary of Good Counsel and Advice*
Cordelia, Cordellia, Cordula, Cordis • literary invention • *possibly from Latin for heart, by William Shakespeare for the virtuous daughter in* King Lear
Courtney • Norman • *the barony of Courtenay*

Dahlia, Dale, Dalia, Dalya, Dahl, Dale • Swedish • *named after botanist Anders Dahl from Sweden*
Damask • Arabic • *the city of Damascus, Syria, and the damask rose*
Darcy • Norman • *a person from the barony of D'Arcy*
Daryl, Daryll • Norman/American/English • *a person from D'Airelle, a barony in Normandy*
Davina, Davida, Davena, Davinia • Biblical/Hebrew • *vague origins but possibly from a baby word meaning darling one*
Deborah, Debra, Debbie, Debora, Debrah, Deb, Debbi, Debby, Debi, Debs, Devorah, Dvoire • Biblical/Hebrew/Jewish • *bee*
Demelza • Cornish/Kernow • *a place name in Cornwall*
Deryn • British/Welsh • *blackbird*
Disgleirio • British/Welsh • *bright, glittering, dazzling*
Diketi • Swahili/Kenyan • *small*
Dimity, Dimitos • Irish/Greek • *a light cotton fabric from Italy meaning two double warp thread!*

Ditanny, Diktamnon • Greek/Cretan • *the name of a medicinal plant on Mount Dikte in Crete*
Diyā • Arabic • *bright and breezy*
Doris, Dorris • Greek • *a tribe of Greece, the Dorian women from Doros, southern mainland Greece, from the name son of or gift to the Hellenes*
Dvoire, Devorah • Jewish/Yiddish • *bee*

Echo, Ekho • Greek • *a word that has come to mean a nymph who pined after the beautiful boy Narcissus, who was only interested in himself; as a result she was left with nothing but her voice*
Eimear, Émer, Eimh • Irish Gaelic • *vague origins but comes from the word for swift, the bird, describing a person who is fast and quick*
Eirian • British/Welsh • *silvery bright, beautiful*
Eithne, Edna, Ena, Etna, Ethna, Ethenia • Irish/Gaelic • *kernel*
Elaine, Helen • Greek/French • *sunbeam, ray of sun, coming from the name for the Greeks, the Hellen(es)*
Eleanor, Alienor, Ellenor, Elinor, Elenor, Nell, Ellen, Nellie, Nelly, Eleanora, Eléonore • Germanic/Frankish/Provençal • *prefix means foreign or stranger; the suffix is unknown*
Ellen, Helen, Elin, Elen, Ella, Elena, Nell, Nelly, Nellie, Ellena, Ellenor • modern English • *shortened form of Helen and Eleanor*
Ella, Ellen • Germanic • *foreigner, stranger*
Ellie, Elly, Eilidh, Ailie • Germanic/

Frankish/Provençal • *short for Eleanor*

Elma • Germanic • *famous swordsperson*

Élodie, Elodia • Germanic/ Visigothic • *foreign wealth*

Eloi, Eligere, Eligius • Latin • *to choose*

Elvina, Alvina • Anglo-Saxon • *elfin, noble or faerie friend*

Elvira • Germanic/Visigothic • *true wealth, foreign*

Ena, Ina, Eithne • English/Irish/ Gaelic • *kernel*

Esther, Esta, Hester, Haddasah, Eistir, Ester • Hebrew/Persian/ Jewish • *Myrtle, Star and Persian Goddess of Fertility, Love and War, Ishtar*

Eulalia, Eulalie, Lalien, Eulalee, Eula, Olalla • Greek • *good to talk*

Euphemia, Eppie, Hephzibah, Eufemia, Euphémie, Effie, Eppie, Effemy, Hephzibah • Greek/Latin • *good to talk*

Evangeline, Evangelina • Greek/ Latin/French • *good tidings from the gospel*

Evelyn, Eveline, Avaline, Ava, Evelyne, Eveleen, Éibhleann, Aibhilin • English/Norman • *from a French girl's name that became an English surname*

Fancy, Fantasy • American English • *whim, vagary*

Fanny, Frances • English/Latin • *to be French, someone from France*

Feige, Fayge, Feygl, Vogel, Zipporah • Jewish/Yiddish • *bird*

Felicia, Felice, Felis, Feliz, Fenicia, Phoenicia, Felicie • Latin • *happy-go -lucky*

Fikriyya • Arabic • *pensive, contemplative, intelligent, intellectual*

Flair, Flairer • American English/ French • *showing an individual talent*

Franca • French • *a girl from France*

Frances, Proinséas • English/Latin • *to be French, someone from France*

Francesca, France, Francene, Fran, Frances, Fanny, Françoise, Franceen, Franziska, Frankie, Francine, Francisca • Italian/Latin • *to be French, someone from France*

Frauke • German • *a lady from northern Germany*

Gae, Gay, Gaye • English • *bright, jolly, cherry, sanguine*

Garnet, Grenate, Granatum • Norman/Latin • *either a dealer in pomegranates or the precious stone*

Geneva, Geneve, Ginevra • French • *after the Swiss city, or can be variant of Jennifer or short form of Geneviève*

Genista, Genesta • Latin • *the shrub plant called broom, a bright yellow colour*

Geraldine, Gerry • Germanic/ Frankish • *he who rules with a spear*

Gerardine, Gerry • Germanic/ Frankish • *brave and bold with a spear*

Gerlinde, Gerlind • Germanic • *sport spear*

Germaine, Jermaine • Latin • *brother*

Gertrude, Gert, Gertie, Gerde, Gertrud, Gerda, Gertraud, Gertraut, Gertrudis • Germanic • *she is a dear woman with strength, superlative with a spear*

Gertrun • Germanic • *magic spear*

Ghislain, Ghislaine, Giselle, Gisil
• Germanic/Frankish • *to pledge or
promise something or someone to
confirm an alliance*

Gigi • French • *pet name for Giselle,
to pledge or promise something or
someone to confirm an alliance*

Gioconda, Jucunda • Latin • *happy,
jovial, jocund*

Giselle, Gisil, Gisella, Gisela, Gigi •
Germanic/Frankish • *pledge*

Goretti • Roman Catholic • *named
after Maria Goretti, patron saint of
youth*

Gormlaith, Gormflaith • Irish
Gaelic • *a splendid, illustrious
woman or princess*

Greer, Grier • Greek/Scots English
• *from a Scottish surname, Gregor,
meaning watchful*

Guadalupe, Guadeloupe • Roman
Catholic • *site of a convent with the
famous image of the Virgin Mary*

Gypsy • Roman/Egyptian • *meaning
an Egyptian, thought to be travellers
from Asia*

Hadassah, Dassah, Esther •
Hebrew/Persian/Jewish • *Myrtle,
Star and Persian Goddess of Fertility,
Love and War, Ishtar*

Hadīl • Arabic • *a woman with a
voice like the cooing of doves, soft,
lovely voice*

Haidee, Aidoios • Greek/literary •
Lord Byron character in Don Juan,
meaning modest

Harmony, Harmonie • English •
concord, unity, friendship

Harper • English/American • *a
person who plays a harp!*

Hayfā • Arabic • *slender, delicate
flower*

Hazel, Haesel • Anglo-Saxon • *the
hazel tree, for the Celts a magic tree*

Hebe, Hebos • Greek • *the Goddess
of Youth*

Heledd, Hyledd • British Welsh/
Celtic mythology • *not entirely sure
of its root but it is the name of a
princess whose name is at the heart
of a lament for her brother's death*

Hermione, Hermia • Greek • *the god
Hermes, messenger of the gods or the
people*

Hester, Esther, Hettie, Hetty •
English • *Myrtle, Star and Persian
Goddess of Fertility, Love and War,
Ishtar*

Hikmat • Arabic • *wisdom*

Hilary, Hillary, Hilarie, Hilly, Hilario
• Latin • *hilarious!*

Hjördis, Hjorrdis • Norse • *warrior
goddess great with the sword!*

Huguette, Huette • Germanic/
Frankish/French • *heart, mind and
spirit*

Huifen • Chinese • *wise and fragrant*

Ibtisām • Arabic • *a woman
wreathed in smiles and laughter*

Idony, Idone, Idunn, Idonea •
Norse • *Goddess of the Apples of
Eternal Youth*

Ilona, Helen • Hungarian •
*sunbeam, ray of sun, coming
from the name for the Greeks, the
Hellen(es)*

**Imogen, Innogen, Inghean,
Imogene** • Celtic • *girl, maiden*

Ina, Ena, Ines, Agnes • English/
Irish/Gaelic • *kernel*

India • English • *as in India, the
country*

Iona, Nonie • Latin/Gaelic • *sacred
island in Hebrides in north Britain*

Ione, Nonie • English • *Ionian islands*

Isaura • Latin • *a woman from Isauria in Asia Minor (Turkey)*

Isla • Scots • *name of Hebridean island in north Britain*

Ismene • Greek mythology • *Greek tragedy!*

Jada, Yada • Biblical/Hebrew/Jewish • *he knows*

Jancis, Jancie • English literary • *combo of Frances and Jan, from the novel* Precious Bane *by Mary Webb*

Jay, Jaye, Jai • English • *named after the letter 'J', short and snappy*

Jessica, Jesca, Jessika, Jess, Jessie, Jesse, Jessye, Teasag, Iscah • Biblical/literary • *William Shakespeare's invention from the Biblical name Jesca or Iscah*

Jocasta • literary Greek • *mother of Oedipus, tragic figure in classical mythology*

Jocelyn, Joselyn, Jocelyne, Joscelyn, Josceline, Joslyn, Joss, Céline, Gautzeline, Joscel, Joscein, Joscelyn • Norman • *someone from the Germanic tribe of the Gauts*

Joely, Jolene, Jolie, Jollie, Joleen, Jolie, Joli, Jol • Norse/French • *pretty one, also gay and festive; yuletide*

June • English • *born in the month of June*

Jyoti • Sanskrit • *light of mind, light of freedom, light of paradise*

Kaneesha • African American • *modern invention that means nothing*

Karla, Carla • Scandinavian/English/Germanic • *a freeman*

Karlene, Karleen, Carlene, Carleen • American English • *a freeman*

Karlotte, Karlotta, Carlottam, Charlotte • German/Scandinavian • *a freeman*

Karola, Carolyn, Karoline, Karolina, Carolina, Carola, Karoline • Scandinavian/English/Germanic • *a freeman*

Kayla, Kayley, Kaylah • American English • *a descendent of Caollaidhe, the prefix meaning a slender person*

Kayley, Kayleigh, Kayly, Kaylie, Kayli, Kaylee, Kaileley, Kailey, Kaily, Kalie, Kalee, Kaleigh, Cayleigh, Caileigh, Caleigh, Kayley, Kayleigh, Caollaidhe, Kailey, Kayley, Kaley • Irish Gaelic • *a descendant of Caollaidhe, the prefix meaning a slender person*

Keelin, Kylin, Cianian, Cilan • British/Welsh/Gaelic • *companion or friend*

Keely, Keeley, Kayley, Keighley • Irish Gaelic • *a descendant of Caollaidhe, the prefix meaning a slender person*

Keisha, Nkisa • West African • *favourite daughter*

Kelly, Kelley, Kellie, Ceallach • Irish Gaelic • *bright-headed, quick-tempered*

Kerry, Keri, Ceri • English/British/ Welsh/Irish Gaelic • *after the Celtic Goddess of Poetry*

Klara, Clara • German/Latin • *bright, famous, crystal-clear*

Kumari • Sanskrit • *daughter or princess*

Kylie, Kyley, Kylee, Kyleigh, Kyla, Kelly • Australian/Aborigine • *boomerang is said to be the ethnic meaning but it seems more likely* *to be an invention of Kyle and Kelly!*

Lacey, Lassy, Lassie, Lacy • Norman/Irish • *Norman baronial name Lassy, who became powerful in Ireland in the medieval period*

La Keisha • African American • *THE favourite daughter*

Lalage, Lalagein, Lally, Lailie, Lalla, La-La • Greek • *to chatter on endlessly, loquacious*

Lalita • Sanskrit • *this girl is as playful as a kitten; affectionate and amorous*

Larissa, Lara, Larry, Larrisah • Russian/Greek • *unsure meaning; perhaps someone from a town near Thessaloniki, in northern Greece*

Lark, Lawerce • North American/ Australian/English/Anglo-Saxon • *dawn song*

Lata • Sanskrit • *she is as supple as a tendril*

Lauren, Lauryn, Loren, Lorenna, Laurenna, Laurie, Lori • Latin • *man from Laurentum, the capital of the Latins*

Lavender, Lavanda, Levandulova, Lavendelbla, Lavendel, Kahvatulilla, Laventelinsininen, Lavande, Blasseslila, Levendulaszinu, Ljosfjolublarlitur, Ungukebiruan, Melakrasa, Lawendowy, Cor de Alfazema, Lillalavendelfarget • Norman/ English • *a beautiful bluey/lilac-coloured shrub*

Lavinia, Lavinium, Luvinia • Etruscan/Roman mythology • *wife of King Aeneus and mother of the Roman people*

Lena, Leena, Leesa, Leni, Lene,

Magdalena, Helena, Selena • English • *the end of a longer name*

Leocardia, Leukados • Latin • *clear and bright as crystal*

Leonora, Eleonora, Léonore, Elenonore, Eleanore, Lenora, Lennora, Lennorah, Lenorah, Lena • Germanic/Frankish/ Provençal

Liberty, Liberta, Libertas • English/ Norman/Latin • *freedom*

Linnéa, Linnaea • Swedish • *name honouring botanist Carl von Linne*

Liqin • Chinese • *beautiful zither (musical instrument)*

Lisha • American English • *the suffix of any name ending with -cia, e.g. Patricia!*

Liv, Lif • Norse • *life*

Loredana • cosmetic Italian • *heroine in a novel!*

Lorna, Lorne, Latharna • English/ Scots Gaelic • *Scottish place name Lorne, Argyll*

Lottie, Lotte, Charlotte • French/ Germanic • *a freeman*

Luana, Luanna, Luanne, Luan • cinematic Italian • *made up for 1932 movie* End of the Trail; *Luana, the sacred virgin*

Lydia, Lydie • Greek • *woman from Lydia*

Lyra • Latin • *lyre, a stringed musical instrument*

Macey, Masey, Macie, Macy, Maci, Macciacum • Norman/Latin • *someone from Massey, Normandy*

Madhu • Sanskrit • *she is as sweet as honey and younger than springtime*

Madison, Maddison, Mady, Maddie • American/English • *son of Maud or Matilda, the battleaxe*

Maia, Maya, Mya • Latin • *Roman*

Goddess of Youth, Life, Rebirth, Love and Sexuality
Maitland, Maltalent, Mautalent
• Anglo-Saxon/Norman • *bad-tempered or from Mautalant, a barren place in France*
Malak • Arabic • *angel*
Malvina, Malamhin, Maggi, Maggie, Malamhin • cosmetic Scots
Mame, Mamie Margaret, Mary
• American English • *short for Margaret or Mary*
María de los Ángeles, Mary-Ange • Spanish • *Mary of the Angels*
Meirionwen • British/Welsh • *a British prince who gave his name to the County of Meirionydd or Merioneth*
Maura, Mavra • Latin • *Moor, as in Arab*
Mavis, Mave, Maeve • Breton Celtic/Norman • *song thrush*
May, Mae, Maybelle, Maybella
• Anglo-Saxon • *the magical hawthorn tree which is also known as may; the month of May*
Medea, Medesthai • Greek mythology • *a Colchian princess in 'Jason and the Golden Fleece'; means to contemplate and reflect*
Meifeng • Chinese • *beautiful wind*
Meihui • Chinese • *beautiful wisdom*
Meinir • British/Welsh • *thin, long and slender*
Meinwen • British/Welsh • *thin, slender, pale and white*
Melissa, Melita, Melitta Lissa, Melissa, Lyssa Lita, Melita, Melitta
• Greek • *honey bee*
Merle, Meriel, Merula • Norman/Latin • *a blackbird*
Mertice • African American • *modern invention*
Mimosa, Mimus • Latin • *yellow*

plant that means mime or mimic
Mina, Wilhelmina, Calumina, Normina • Scots Gaelic • *short name for any name ending in -mina!*
Miranda, Randa, Randy, Randie, Amanda • literary invention/Latin • *William Shakespeare invented this name for his heroine in* The Tempest: *admire, wonder at or in awe of her loveliness*
Montserrat • Catalan • *the Lady of Montserrat, a Benedictine monastery near Barcelona*
Morven, Morvern, Mhorbhairne, Morbheinn • Scots • *area of north Argyll or big peak*
Munira • Arabic • *radiant, bright, send out a light*
Myrtle, Myrtille, Myrtilla, Myrta • Latin/Norman/Greek • *a tree with fragrant leaves; in Greek it means perfumed*

Nadiyya • Arabic • *a woman who is as fresh and moist as morning dew*
Nāhid • Arabic • *a girl who is becoming a woman*
Najāh, Nagāh • Arabic • *a woman who is progressive and successful*
Narelle, Narellan • Australian Aborigine • *an ethnic name with no known roots although there is a town called Narellan in New South Wales*
Nastasia, Anastasia • Greek/Russian • *short form of Anastasia; resurrection*
Nell, Nella, Nellie, Nelly, Eleanor, Ellen, Helen • *English short name for Eleanor, Ellen or Helen*
Nerissa, Nereis • literary invention/Greek • *sea sprite or nymph Nerissa was invented by William Shakespeare for Portia's lady-in-*

waiting in The Merchant of Venice
Nessa, Agnessa, Agnes, Vanessa
• English • *short form of any name ending in -nessa!*
Nettie, Annette, Jeannette •
English • *short form of all names ending in -nette*
Nia, Niamh, Neve • British/Welsh/ Irish • *beautiful and bright*
Niamh, Neve, Nia • Irish Gaelic • *beautiful and bright*
Nina, Nena, Ninette, Ninon, Antonina • Russian • *short form of names that end in -nina*
Nita, Neats, Anita, Juanita • Spanish • *short form of names ending in -nita!*
Normina • *a person from the north; Norseman or Viking*
Nuha • Arabic • *a woman who is clever, intellectual and cerebrally bright*

Olympe, Olympia • Greek • *a woman from Olympus, the mountain of the Gods*
Olivia, Olive, Oliva • literary invention/Latin • *William Shakespeare named Olivia as the rich heiress in* The Tempest
Ona, Anona, Fiona, Honor • English • *shortened name for any that end in -ona*
Onora, Nora, Honora • English • *shortened name for any ending in -nora*
Órla, Ona, Anona, Fíona, Honor, Orfhlaith, Orflaith, Orlaith • Irish Gaelic • *golden lady or princess*

Paige, Page • American English • *a page boy to a great lord or lady*
Pamela, Pam, Pammy, Pamella •

poetic invention • *Sir Philip Sidney, Elizabethan (First) poet, created the name*
Pansy, Pensee • Norman • *flower whose name means 'thought'*
Paula, Paola • Latin/Italian/English • *Roman family name meaning little or small*
Paulette, Paula, Paulina, Paola • Latin • *Roman family name meaning little or small*
Pauline, Paulina • Latin/French • *Roman family name meaning little or small*
Penelope, Pen, Penelops, Penny, Penni • Greek • *uncertain origin but 'duck' is one suggestion*
Perdita, Perdie, Purdee, Purdy, Perditus • Latin/literary invention • *William Shakespeare invented the name from the Latin 'lost' as one of his characters in* The Winter's Tale
Pernilla, Pella, Pernille, Petronel, Petronilla • Latin/Greek/Swedish • *a stone or someone who lives in the country*
Persis • Biblical/Greek • *a Persian woman*
Philippa, Phil, Philippina • Greek • *friend or lover of horses*
Philomena, Philomenus, Philomenes, Phileinmenos, Philoumena, Filumena, Filomena • Greek/Germanic • *loyal, strong friend, platonic friendship*
Pilar • Roman Catholic • *Our Lady of the Pillar; appearance of the Virgin on a pillar at Zaragossa*
Pippa, Philippa • Greek • *friend or lover of horses*
Pixie • English • *playful sprite, mischievous, naughty*
Patribha • Sanskrit • *clever, radiant,*

imaginative and precocious

Precious • American English • *dear; beloved: a precious child*

Presentación • Roman Catholic/Spanish • *presentation of the Virgin at the Temple in Jerusalem*

Psyche, Psykhe • Greek • *butterfly, spirit and soul*

Qiao • Chinese • *dexterous girl*

Qiaohui • Chinese • *dexterous and sagacious*

Qiaolian • Chinese • *eternally dexterous*

Qingling • Chinese • *celebrating understanding*

Qingzhao • Chinese • *clear understanding, crystal illumination*

Rabāb • Arabic • *a musical instrument like a violin*

Radegund, Radegunde • Germanic • *a counsellor, adviser in times of trouble*

Raelene, Rae • Germanic/Frankish/English Australian • *adviser to the army; army commander*

Raffaella, Rafaela • Biblical • *archangel*

Raimunde, Raimund, Raimonda • Germanic/Frankish • *adviser to the army; army commander*

Randa, Miranda, Randy • American English • *shortened Miranda*

Ravenna • Italian • *an Italian city; someone from Ravenna, the capital of Roman mosaic*

Rāwiya • Arabic • *a narrator of classical Arabic poetry and prose and beautiful speaker*

Reagan, Regan, Riagain • Irish Gaelic/English • *descendant of Riagain, the impulsive or impatient one*

Rene, Renata, Irene, Renee, Doreen, Maureen • English • *short for any name ending in -reen or -rene*

Rhetta • Dutch • *advice, counsel*

Rhona, Rona • Scots • *name of Hebridean island off northern Britain*

Ricki, Ricky, Rikki, Riki • English • *short form of any name ending in -rick*

Rita, Magarita • Spanish • *short form of Margarita*

Robbin, Robbie, Roberta • Germanic • *famous and bright*

Roberta, Robbie • Germanic • *famous and bright*

Robyn, Robin • Germanic • *famous and bright*

Rochelle, Rachelle • Germanic/French/American English • *rest a while*

Ros, Roz, Rosalind, Rosamund • English • *shortened for any name beginning with Ros*

Rosalind, Rosaleen, Rosalyn, Roslind, Rosaline, Rosalin, Rosalynne, Rosalynn • Germanic/Frankish • *horse, tender and soft, passive and weak*

Rosamund, Rosmund, Rosamunda, Rosamond, Roschen • Germanic • *horse protector*

Rowen, Ruadhan • Gaelic/English • *descendant of Ruadhan, little red one*

Roxanne, Roxane, Roxana, Roxanna, Roxy, Rozanne • Latin/Greek/Persian • *dawn*

Ruda • Slavic • *ingenious*

Rusty, Rusti, Russus • Latin/Norman • *little red one*

Ryanne, Ryan, Riain • Irish Gaelic/

English • *little king, descendant of Riain*

Sabāh • Arabic • *morning*
Sadie, Sarah, Sara, Sarai • English • *pet form of Sarah*
Sahar • Arabic • *morning has broken, dawn*
Sally, Sal, Sarah • English • *another name for Sarah, meaning princess*
Samantha, Sam, Sammy, Sammi • Biblical/Hebrew/Jewish • *the name of God, God has heard, listen to God*
Saoirse, Seersha • Irish Gaelic • *freedom, liberation*
Sappho • literary Greek • *poetess Sappho, noted for her verse honouring lesbian passion*
Sarah, Sara, Zara, Sally, Sadie, Sari • Biblical/Jewish/Hebrew • *princess*
Sarita, Sarah • Biblical/Spanish • *princess*
Saraswati • Sanskrit • *filled with waters of knowledge of the arts, learning and academia*
Sayidana • Swahili • *our princess*
Scarlett, Escarlate, Scarlata, Scarlet • Latin/Norman/English • *someone who dyes or sells fabrics of rich, radiant colours*
Sebastienne • Latin/French • *someone from Sebaste in Asia Minor (now Turkey)*
Senga • Gaelic • *slender*
Shakuntala • Sanskrit • *a rare bird*
Shamshad • Persian • *like a box tree she is lean, tall and elegant*
Sharon, Sharron, Sharona, Sharonda • Biblical • *a place called Sharon on the coastal plain of the Holy Land; and for the shrub, the Rose of Sharon*
Sky, Skye • Gaelic • *take your pick, the sky as in heaven or Skye as in the island in Scotland*
Skylar, Schuyler • Dutch/American English • *scholar, school teacher*
Sloane, Sloan • English • *after Sloane Square in London, name given to a Sloane Ranger*
Sofia, Sophia, Sofya, Sofie, Sophie, Sofie, Sophy, • Greek • *wisdom*
Sonia, Sonya, Sonje • Greek • *wisdom*
Sprite, Spiritus, Esprit • American English • *a mischievous spirit*
Sunita • Sanskrit • *she's a good girl who gives wise advice*
Sunny, Sunnie • English • *cheery, cheerful, full of joy; a sunny disposition*
Svea, Svearike, Sverige • Swedish • *patriotic name for Sweden; especially 6th June*
Svetlana, Sveta, Photine • Slavic/Greek • *light*
Sylphide, Sylva, Silva, Sylpha • Latin/French • *airborne, invisible spirits; sylph-like*

Taghrīd • Arabic • *bird song*
Tahiyya • Arabic • *hello!*
Talitha • Biblical/Aramaic • *little girl*
Tallulah, Talulla, Tuilelaith • Irish Gaelic/English • *abundance, lady and princess*
Tamsin, Thomasina, Tammy, Tammie, Tamzin • Biblical/Aramaic/Greek • *twin*
Teal, Teale, Teling • German/Dutch/English • *a bird!*
Tempe, Temnein • Greek • *a valley in Greece; the legendary home of the Muses, the nine goddesses of the arts and sciences*
Thalia, Talia, Thallein • Greek •

one of the nine Muses; the Goddess of Comedy whose name means to prosper comedically

Thera, Theresa • Greek • *vague origins; could be short for Theresa or Greek isle of Thera*

Thessaly, Thessalie • Greek/Illyrian • *an area and city of northern Greece; unknown root*

Tia, Laetitia, Lucretia, Tiana, Tiara • Spanish/Portuguese • *aunty or short form of any name ending in -tia*

Tiffany, Theophania, Theosphainein • English/Greek • *Epiphany: God will appear*

Tori, Tory, Toria • English • *short form of Victoria*

Tottie, Charlotte, Lottie, Totty, Lotte, Carlotta • English • *short form of Charlotte*

Tracey, Trace, Tracie, Tracy • Latin/Gaulic • *a person from a place in Normandy called Tracy!*

Trude, Gertraud, Gertrude, Traute, Trudy, Traude • German • *short form of any name ending in -raud or -raude*

Trina, Treena, Catrina, Treena • English • *short form of any name ending in -tina*

Trinity, Trinidad • Roman Catholic • *the Holy Trinity*

Trudy, Trudi, Trudie, Gertrude, Ermintrude, Ermentrud, Trude • English/German • *short form of any name ending in -rude*

Uhuti • Swahili • *my sister*

Ujana • Kiswahili • *youth*

Uma • Sanskrit • *turmeric or flax; messenger of the gods*

Usha • Sanskrit • *Goddess of the Dawn*

Vanessa, Nessa, Venessa • literary invention/Dutch • *created by Jonathan Swift from his lover's Dutch surname Vanhomrigh*

Venetia, Venice, Venezia • Italian • *someone from Venice, celebrating the city of Venezia*

Verona, Veronica • Italian/English • *someone from the city of Verona*

Visitacion • Roman Catholic/Spanish • *the Virgin Mary visits her sister Elisabeth*

Vita, Victoria • Latin • *life, also short name for Victoria*

Vivienne, Vivien, Viv, Vi, Vivi, Vivienne, Vivianne, Béibhinn • Latin/Norman • *Roman name Vivianus, meaning life*

Wallis, Wally • Anglo-Saxon • *foreigner*

Wednesday • Anglo-Saxon/Norse • *Woden's day, Wodnesdaeg*

Wendy, Wenda, Wendi, Gwendolen • literary invention • *JM Barrie created it for his book* Peter Pan *from his own nursery name Fwendy-Wendy meaning friend*

Widād • Arabic • *an affectionate, friendly girl*

Xanthe, Xanthos • Greek • *bright yellow*

Xena • Greek • *stranger, foreigner*

Xenia • Greek • *hospitality and a welcome to or from a stranger or foreigner*

Xiaohui • Chinese • *little wisdom*

Xiaosheng • Chinese • *small at birth*

Yan • Chinese • *like a swallow or drop-dead gorgeous*

Ying • Chinese • *a clever girl*

Zena, Zina, Xena • Russian/Greek • *stranger, foreigner*

Zéphyrine, Zephyrus, Zephyros • Latin/Greek/French • *the west wind or breeze*

Zipporah, Zip, Zippor • *little bird*

Ziska, Zissi, Franziska • German • *to be French, someone from France*

Zita, Zeta, Zetein, Zitta • Tuscan • *wee girl*

CANCER

22nd June to 23rd July

Planet: Moon

Day: Monday

Stones: pearl and moonstone

Metal: silver

Colours: silver, misty blues, dove greys, white, cream and ivory lemon

Design: ripple effects like on water, soft indistinct lines, gentle wispy waves

Trees: lemon, lime, and all trees rich in sap

Flora: white and cream roses and all flowers and plants that respond to the moon and come alive at night, morning glory, verbena, lotus, any plants that grow near river banks, lilies and all white flowers, hydrangea

Cancer celebrities: Georgio Armani • Arthur Ashe • Dan Aykroyd • Kevin Bacon • Mary Baker Eddy • Theda Bara • Ingmar Bergman • Gary Busey • Julius Caesar • Pierre Cardin • Lesley Caron • John Cusack • Olivia de Havilland • Dihann Carroll • Bill Cosby • Tom Cruise • His Holiness the Dalai Lama XIV • Jack Dempsey • Diana (Princess of Wales) • Phyllis Diller • Nelson Eddy • Edward VIII (Duke of Windsor) • Gerald Ford • Harrison Ford • Bob Fosse • John Glen • Merv Griffin • Tom Hanks • Ernest Hemingway • King Henry VIII • Tab Hunter • Angelica Huston • Helen Keller • Kris Kristofferson • Cheryl Ladd • Gina Lollobrigida • Nelson Mandela • Imelda Marcos • Brigit Nielsen • George Orwell • Camilla Parker Bowles (Duchess of Cornwall) • Dame Diana Rigg • Ginger Rogers • Linda Ronstadt • Jane Russell • Neil Simon • OJ Simpson • Sylvester Stallone • Barbara Stanwick • Cat Stevens • Meryl Streep • Donald Sutherland • Mike Tyson • Prince William • Robin Williams.

Planetary Influences: see Moon at the back of this book (pages 453)

Boys

'**Abd-al-Latīf** • Arabic • *servant of the kind, Allah*

'**Abd-al-Rahīm, Abder Rahīm** • Arabic • *servant of the compassionate, Allah*

Abdalrahman, Abderrahman • Arabic • *servant of the merciful, Allah*

'**Abd-al-Rāziq, 'Abd-al-Rāzzaq, 'Abd-er-Razzā** • Arabic • *servant of the provider, Allah*

Abraham, Abe, Avraham, Avrom, Abe, Avhamon • Hebrew/Aramaic • *father of the tribes or nations*

Achilles, Achilleus, Achille, Achilleo, Aquiles, Akhilleus • Greek • *from the River Akehloos*

Achim, Akim, Joachim, Akim, Yakim • Hebrew/Jewish • *made and created by God*

Addison, Addie, Adie • modern English • *originally surname*

Adnān • Arabic • *uncertain root; may mean settler*

Adrian, Adrien, Adriano, Hadrianus • Latin • *a man from Hadria which the Adriatic Sea is named*

Afon, Avon • British/Welsh • *river*

Aiguo • Chinese • *patriotic, I love the land of my birth*

Ailpein, Alpine, Alpin • Pictish/Scots Gaelic • *white*

Ainsley, Ainslie, Ainslee, Ainslie • English • *a person from the village of Annesley or Ansley*

Aitor • Basque • *founder of the Basques, local hero*

Åke, Achatius, Åge • Germanic/Norse • *either ancestor or the semi-precious stone garnet*

Alastair, Alistair, Allaster, Alec, Alaois, Alexander, Alasdair, Sandy • Scots Gaelic/Greek • *the man/warrior/leader who protects or defends his people*

Alban, Albanus, Albie, Alby • Latin • *confused origins; perhaps Alba meaning white or Albion meaning Britain*

Albion • Latin/Celtic • *possibly meaning white or rocky cliff, white cliffs of Dover*

Aled • modern British/Welsh • *child*

Alexander, Alexandre, Alexis, Alastair, Alasdair, Sandy, Alessandro, Alessio, Aleksandr, Aleksei, Alejandro, Alejo, Alec, Alick, Alex, Sandaidh, Lexy, Lexie, Alastar, Alasdair, Alistair, Aleixandre, Aleksandar, Aleksanteri, Sandor, Alick, Ailig, Alec • Greek • *the man/warrior/ leader who protects or defends his people*

Alexis, Alexein • Greek • *he who defends*

Alby, Ailbhe • Irish Gaelic • *white*

Alistair, Alasdair, Alisdair, Alastair, Alister, Alaster, Allaster, Alistair • Scots Gaelic/Greek • *the man/ warrior/leader who protects or defends his people*

Alton • English • *place name meaning village by a river*

Álvaro, Alwar • Visigothic/Spanish • *guarding, defending*

Amadeus, Amédée, Gottlieb, Amedeo • Latin/Germanic • *love God or God of Love!*

Amias • French/Biblical/Hebrew • *someone from Amiens in Picardie or love God*

Amiaz • Jewish/Hebrew • *my people/ tribe are strong*

Amos • Biblical/Jewish/Hebrew • *to carry the Lord like St Christopher*

Amrit • Sanskrit • *immortal, divine foods*

Åmund, Agmund • Norse • *living on the edge, seeks protection*

Anand • Sanskrit • *blissfully happy*

Anatole, Anatoly, Anatoli • Greek • *sunrise*

Aneurin, Aneirin, Nye, Neirin • *modest and noble*

Antip, Antipas, Antipater • *just like your father!*

Anthony, Antony, Tony, Antain, Antaine, Anton, Antoine, Antonio, Antoni, Antonin, Antoninus, Ante, Antun, Antal, Antanas, Anthos, Antwan, Antonino, Nino, Ninny, Anthony, Antoine, Anton, Antonio, Antonius • Etruscan/Roman • *Roman family name but with confused origins*

Antrim, Aontraim • Irish Gaelic • *county in Ulster, Great Britain meaning one wee house!*

Arailt, Harold • Scots Gaelic • *ruler of the army, chief of the tribe*

Archer, Archier, Arcarius, Archarius • Norman/Latin • *surname meaning a bowman or archer*

Arfon • British/Welsh • *area in the princedom of Gwynedd around Caernarfon*

Arjun • Sanskrit • *white*

Arkadi, Arkadios • Greek • *a man from Arcadia*

Arran • cosmetic Scots • *an island in the Firth of Clyde, part of Buteshire*

Arrigo, Enrico • Germanic/Spanish/ Italian • *power comes from the home or family (meaning nation too)*

Arjun • Sanskrit • *white and silver*

Arran • English • *island making up county of Buteshire*

Artemas, Artyom, Artemios, Artemidoros, Artemisthenes, Artemus • Biblical/Greek • *he who worships, has the strength or bears the gift of the goddess Artemis/Diana or is a gift from the divine huntress*

Arwel • British/Welsh • *I wept over you*

Asaph • Biblical/Hebrew/Jewish • *collector*

Asdrubale, Asrubaal • Phoenician/ Italian • *give aid to the lord or receive it*

'Asim • Arabic • *protector*

Åsmund, Assmund • *protected by the gods*

Aston • Anglo-Saxon • *the village to the east*

Atholl, Athfodla • Gaelic • *'New Ireland' area of Perthshire*

'Ātif • Arabic • *compassionate and sympathetic*

Atilla, Attlius, Attilio • Latin/ Etruscan • *family name from Rome*

Audley • Anglo-Saxon • *surname meaning Aldgyth's (feminine) clearing*

Aulay, Amhladh, Amlaidh, Olaf • Scots Gaelic/Norse • *ancestor, heir, descendant*

Auliffe, Amhlaoibh • Irish Gaelic/ Norse • *ancestor, heir, descendant*

Aurelius, Aurèle, Aurel, Aureus, Aurelio • Latin • *Roman family name meaning golden*

Axel, Absalom • Biblical/Hebrew/ Danish • *father is peace*

Ayman • Arabic • *blessed be, wealthy*

Azriel • Jewish/Hebrew • *God helps*

Badr, Budūr • Arabic • *full moon*

Bai • Chinese • *white*

Baptiste, Baptist, Bautista • Biblical • *John the Baptist*

Barnabas, Barnaby, Barney, Barny, Barnabé, Bernebe, Barnaba, Barna, Bernabé • Biblical/Greek • *son of consolation*

Barrington, Bearain • Norman/Anglo-Saxon • *a person from Barentin, France or the village of Barrington*

Bartholomew, Barton, Bart, Barthélemy, Bartholomaus, Bartolomé • Biblical/Jewish/Hebrew • *son of Tolmai from Galilee*

Baruch • Biblical/Jewish/Hebrew • *blessed*

Bāsim • Arabic • *smiling!*

Beatus, Beat • Swiss • *blessed*

Beau • French • *beautiful and bonny boy*

Bechor • Jewish/Hebrew/Sephardic • *first born*

Benjamin, Ben, Benny, Bennie, Benjamim, Benjie, Benji, Benjy, Venyamin, Binyamin, Benno, Bendik • Hebrew/Jewish • *son of my right hand, my right-hand man or son of the south, re-named by his father Jacob from his original name, son of my sorrow*

Benedict, Bennett, Benneit, Benedikt, Bendt, Bent, Benoît, Benito, Benet, Bento, Benedetto, Venedikt, Benedykt, Pentii, Benedek, Bendikts, Beynish, Benes, Benedictus, Benneit • Latin • *blessed*

Benigno, Benignus • Latin • *a very kind man*

Benson, Bensington • English • *son of Benedict*

Beresford, Beverley • Anglo-Saxon • *the ford in the river where the beaver lives*

Berwyn, Barrwyn • British/Welsh • *white or fair-headed*

Bilal, Bilil • Arabic • *moist*

Blakeney • English • *he from the black island*

Blythe, Blithe, Bly • English • *I'm HAPPY!*

Bo, Bosse • Scandinavian • *I have my own home*

Boleslav • Russian • *distinctly large and rather glorious*

Bojing • Chinese • *to win admiration and respect*

Boone • Norman/English • *a man from Bohon, France*

Brad, Bradford, Bradley, Bradleigh, Braeden, Braden, Brayden • Anglo-Saxon • *a man from the broad meadow, ford, farm or clearing*

Brady, Braidy, Bragha • Irish Gaelic • *descendant of Bradach, one of Bradach's bunch*

Braxton • Anglo-Saxon • *the village of the badger (brock)*

Brent, Brenton • British/Welsh • *holy river or hill*

Brett, Bret • Celtic • *a man from Brittany*

Brigham • English • *a hamlet or village round a bridge*

Brook, Brooke • English • *a small river*

Bruce • Norman/English • *someone from Bruis*

Burgess • Anglo-Saxon • *a man who is on a town council*

Burkhard • Germanic • *safe harbour, strong protection*

Burton • Anglo-Saxon • *a town with a castle or fort*

Cainneach, Kenny • Irish Celtic
• *handsome, beautiful founder of Kilkenny*

Callum, Colm, Calum, Columba, Cole, Colmán, Colum • Latin/Scots Gaelic • *dove*

Camille, Camillo, Camillus, Camilo • Latin/French • *Roman family name, perfection*

Caungula • Angolan • *leader or chief of the people*

Carlyle, Carlisle, Carlile • British Welsh • *the place or castle belonging to Lugavalos, a personal name honouring the Celtic God of the Sun and Creativity*

Cecil, Cesil • Latin/English • *old Roman family name Caecilius, from the Latin, meaning blind*

Chad, Tchad • English • *a man from the warlike place*

Chadwick, Ceadelwic • English • *a man from the industrious farm*

Chandra • Sanskrit • *the moon*

Chandrakant • Sanskrit • *moonstone*

Charlton, Chas, Chaz, Chuck, Chuckie, Chukkie • English • *the place where the free men live*

Chester, Caer, Castra • English/ Roman • *a fortress or encampment*

Christopher, Chris, Christian, Crísdean, Karsten, Christiaan, Carsten, Christer, Chretien, Cristiano, Krysztian, Krisztian, Christie, Christy, Kristy, Kristopher, Christopha, Kristopha, Críostóir, Christoph, Christofoor, Kristafoor, Kristoffer, Christophe, Cristobál, Cristofol, Cristovao, Cristoforo, Krzysztof, Krystof, Hristo, Risto, Kristof, Kristaps, Kit, Kester • Greek • *the man who bears Jesus Christ*

Christhard • German • *as brave and strong as Christ*

Christian, Carsten, Christer, Kristian, Criosd, Crìsdean • Latin • *follower of Christ*

Claiborne, Clayborne, Claiborn, Clayborn • Anglo-Saxon/American English • *honouring a founder Virginian colonist, surname of an influential American family who came from Westmorland in Great Britain*

Claus, Klaus, Niklaus • German • *the people are victorious*

Cledwyn • British/Welsh • *a man who might be rough and ready on the outside but on the inside he is holy, spiritual and soft*

Clem, Clément, Clemmie, Cliamain, Clemente • Latin • *merciful, gentle, compassionate*

Cleveland • English • *a tribe from the hills (Cleveland Hills, North Riding of Yorkshire)*

Cliff, Clifford, Clifton, Clive • English • *the ford over the river by the slope or cliff*

Clint, Clinton • Anglo-Saxon • *the settlement by or on the hill*

Clive • English • *the man who lives in a cave or cliff*

Clyde • American/English • *a famous Scottish river*

Coby • Hebrew/Jewish • *he who supplants someone else*

Cody, Cuidightheact, Macoda • Irish Gaelic • *descendant of Oda, a helpful soul*

Coinneach, Kenneth • Scots Gaelic • *handsome, beautiful, sexy*

Colombe, Columba, Callum, Colmán, Colm, Colum, Columbano • Latin • *dove*

Colin, Collin, Coll, Nicholas, Cailean • English/Scots Gaelic • *dove*

Colwyn, Dafydd • British/Welsh • *place name*

Comfort • American/English • *secure, safe*

Constantine, Constanz, Costin, Constantin, Cystenian, Constant • Latin • *constant, steadfast, loyal, devoted*

Cornelius, Cornell, Corneille • Latin • *Roman family name, connected to Cornucopia and the horn of plenty*

Coty, Cote • American/English/French • *a river bank*

Courtney, Curt, Kurt, Curtis, Courtenay • Norman • *the barony of Courtenay*

Crawford • Anglo-Saxon • *ford where the crows gather at the river*

Creighton, Crichton, Criochiune • Scots Gaelic/English • *someone from Crichton in Midlothian*

Cyprian, Cyprianus • Latin • *the man who comes from Cyprus, the isle of Venus or Aphrodite*

Dáire • Irish Gaelic • *fertile*

Dale • English • *a valley dweller*

Daley, Dalaigh, Dalach, Daly • Irish Gaelic • *altogether now! A gathering or a moot*

Dallas, Dalfhas • Scots Gaelic/American/English • *the village of Dallas in Moray, north Britain; a place where cowpokes or drovers would rest their weary bones overnight*

Dalton, Daleton • Anglo-Saxon • *the village in the valley*

Dalmazio, Dalmatius, Dalmacio • Latin • *a person from Dalmatia in the Adriatic*

Daniel, Dan, Danny, Danyal, Deiniol, Daniele, Daniil, Taneli,

Dannie • Biblical/Hebrew/Jewish • *God is my judge*

Dana • Irish Gaelic/American/English • *Celtic fertility goddess*

D'Arcy, Darcy • Norman • *a man from the barony of D'Arcy*

Darell, Darrell, Darryll, Darryl, Darell, Darrell, Darrel, Darryll, Daryl, Darryl • Norman/American/English • *a chap from D'airelle, a barony in Normandy*

David, Dave, Davy, Dewi, Dafydd, Dai, Davie, Davey, Dàibhidh, Davide, Taavi, Daw, Dawson, Dawūd, Dewi, Dewydd, David, Dai • Biblical/Hebrew • *vague origins but possibly from a baby word meaning darling one*

Davis, Davies • American/English • *in honour of Jefferson Davis, leader of the Dixie states*

Demetrius, Demetrio, Dmitri, Dimitar, Dmitriy • Greek/Russian • *follower of the goddess Demeter*

Denton, Den • Anglo-Saxon • *the place in the valley*

Denver • Anglo-Saxon/American/English • *named after Denver (Denafaer) in Norfolk, east Britain, meaning where the Danes or Vikings crossed the river*

Denzel, Densil, Denzil, Denzell • Cornish/British • *local name from Kernow or west Britain, which became known as Cornwall*

Derek, Dereck, Derrick, Deryck, Del, Dirk, Theodoric • German/Dutch • *God's gift*

Dermot, Diarmaid, Dermid, Diarmad, Diairmit • Irish Gaelic • *not a bad bone in his body*

Desmond, Deasún, Des, Deasmhumhnach • Irish Gaelic •

a man from south Munster (around Cork)

Detlev, Dietlieb, Detlef • Germanic • *an inheritance by or from the people*

Devereux • Norman • *someone from the barony of Evreux in Eure*

Devdan • Sanskrit • *gift of the gods*

Devin, Damhain • Irish Gaelic/ American English • *descendant of the Damhan; fawn, deer*

Devon • British/Welsh • *the tribe of the Dumnonos, who worshipped the Celtic god of the same name*

Dewey, Dewy • British/Welsh/ American/English • *possibly the English spelling of Dewi, which means David, darling one*

Diarmuid, Dermot, Diarmuit, Diarmit • *unsure but perhaps without envy*

Diego, Didacus, Santiago • Spanish • *supplanter, a cuckoo in the nest! Edging out someone to take their place against their will*

Dieter • Germanic • *the army of the people*

Dietfried • Germanic • *people of peace or peaceful people*

Dietmar, Theodemar, Theodemaris • Germanic • *famous people or person*

Dietrich, Diederick, Terry • Germanic • *people power or powerful person*

Dietwald • Germanic • *powerful people, ruling tribe*

Dieudonné • French • *God-given*

Digby • Norse • *the place in or by the ditch, Dikiby or Digby in Lincolnshire*

Dilip • Sanskrit • *patron of Delhi the city*

Dilwyn • British/Welsh • *fair, blonde, white, blessed, sacred, holy*

Donat, Donato, Donatus, Donatien, Donatianus • given by God

Dorian, Dorien, Dorieus, Dorianus, Doron • literary name • *Oscar Wilde's invention for* The Portrait of Dorian Gray; *a Greek connection for the people who settled in southern Greece*

Dorotheos, Dorofei • Greek • *gift of God*

Dositheos, Dosifei • Greek • *God-given*

Douglas, Doug, Dougie, Duggie, Dubhglas • *black stream or pool*

Dudley, Dud • Anglo-Saxon • *the Worcestershire town of Dudley, Dudda's clearing in the wood*

Éamonn, Éamon, Edmund, Éaman, Éamann • Irish Gaelic/English • *a rich man who protects others*

Ernest, Earnest, Eornost • Germanic • *a very serious, tenacious person who never gives up*

Edmund, Edmond, Eumann, Edmundo, Eadmund • Anglo-Saxon • *protector, defender*

Efisio, Ephesius, Ephesus • Sardinian • *a person from Ephesus in Asia Minor*

Ehud • Jewish/Hebrew • *compassionate and pleasant*

Éibhear • *origin unknown but name of the Son of Mil, leader of Gaels that conquered Ireland*

Eladio, Helladio • Greek • *a man from Greece*

Elias, Eli • Biblical/Greek • *Yahweh is God*

Eliezer, Eleazar, Eli • Jewish/Hebrew • *God's help*

Elijah, Eliezer, Elisha, Eli, Eliyahu, Eli • Jewish/Hebrew • *Yahweh is God*

Elisud, Elus, Ellis • British/Welsh • *a kind, benevolent man*

Elliott, Eliott, Elliot, Elias, Elijah • English • *Yahweh is God*

Elof • Scandinavian • *the single descendant/heir*

Elton • Anglo-Saxon • *Ella's hamlet or village*

Elwyn, Alyn • British/Welsh • *white, fair, blessed, sacred and holy*

Emmanuel, Emanuel, Manny, Immanuel • Hebrew/Jewish • *God is with us or amongst us*

Emmerich, Heimerich • Germanic • *strength in home or family*

Enos • Biblical/Hebrew/Jewish • *mankind*

Enrique, Heinrich, Henry • Visigothic/Germanic • *power comes from the home or family (meaning nation too)*

Ernest, Ern, Ernie, Ernst, Ernesto • German • *serious in all things and will fight to the death; means business to the point of obsession*

Errol, Erol, Erroll, Eryl • Scottish • *Scots surname from a place name in Perthshire*

Erskine • Scottish • *a place name in Renfrewshire*

Esmond • Anglo-Saxon • *a handsome man filled with grace who protects his family or home*

Eusebio, Eusebios, Eusebes • Greek • *revered, pious*

Evan, Iefan, Ieuan, Ifan • British/Welsh • *from John, Johannes; God is gracious or gift of God*

Euandros, Evander, Íomhar • Greek/Latin • *a fine good man*

Evelyn • English/French • *a French girl's name that became an English surname*

Ezekiel, Zeke • Biblical/Jewish/Hebrew • *God gives me strength*

Ezio, Aetius, Aetios • Latin • *Roman family name meaning eagle*

Ezra, Esdras • Biblical/Jewish/Hebrew • *help!*

Fabián, Fabianus, Fabius, Fabien • Latin • *old Roman family name meaning a bean*

Fabio, Fabius • Latin • *Roman family name; who were powerful during the republic*

Fabrizio, Fabrice, Fabricius, Fabricio • Italian/Etruscan • *Roman family name; one noted for his incorruptibility*

Fādi • Arabic • *redeemer, saviour, God*

Faraj • Arabic • *solves worries and grief*

Faysal, Feisal • *a man or judge who knows the difference between good and bad, right and wrong*

Fearchar • Irish Gaelic • *dear, nice man*

Feliciano, Felcius, Felix • Latin • *what a happy chappie!*

Feidhlimidh, Felim, Phelim, Fidelminus • Irish Gaelic • *always chaste and virtuous*

Feliciano, Felicianus, Felix • Latin • *happy-go-lucky*

Felix • Latin • *happy-go-lucky*

Fenn, Fenton • Anglo-Saxon • *marshy, wetlands*

Ferapont, Therapon • Greek • *he who worships*

Farquhar, Fearchar • Scots Gaelic • *what a dear, loving man*

Filat, Feofilakt, Theophylaktos •

Greek • *protected by God*

Fingal, Fionnghall, Fingall • Gaelic • *blond, fair stranger or traveller or Viking settler*

Finn, Fionn • Irish Gaelic • *white, fair*

Finn • Scandinavian • *a man from Finland/Suomi*

Fínnen, Finnan, Fionnán, Finnian, Finian • Irish Gaelic • *white, fair*

Finlay, Findlay, Fionnlagh, Finley, Finnleik, Fionnlaogh • Scots Gaelic/Norse • *fair, blond warrior or hero or war hero*

Fionnbarr, Fionnbharr, Finbar • Irish Gaelic • *his head is white, fair and blond*

Flavio, Flavien, Flavianus, Flavius • Latin • *old Roman family name meaning yellow-haired*

Flinders, Flanders • English • *a Flemish person from Flanders*

Floyd, Lloyd, Llwyd • English/British Welsh • *grey*

Foka, Phocas • Greek • *someone from Phocaea in Asia Minor*

Folker, Volker, Folke, Folkvar, Falkor • Norse • *protecting the people, the tribe*

Forbes, Forba • Scots Gaelic • *a Scots surname based on Forbes in Aberdeenshire, meaning fields*

Ford • Anglo-Saxon • *the shallow part of a river you can walk across*

Francis, Francisco, Fran, Franciscus, Frank, France, François, Francesco, Franz • Latin • *to be French, someone from France*

Frank, Franklin, Frankie • Germanic • *a loyal and free man or from the Frankish tribe*

Franz • German/Italian • *to be French, someone from France*

Fraser, Frazer, Frazier, Frisselle, Fresel, Freseliere, Frasier • Norman French/Scots English • *Scots family name with no known origins*

Frédéric, Frederick, Frederik, Fritz, Fred, Phredd, Freddie, Fredick, Fredric, Friedrich, Frerik, Freek, Fredrik, Federico, Frederico, Fryderyk, Bedrich, Rieti, Frigyes • Germanic/Frankish • *peaceful but powerful ruler*

Friedemann • German • *man of peace*

Friedhelm • German • *well-protected man in a helmet who comes in peace*

Fulk, Volk, Folk, Fulke • Germanic/Frankish • *the people*

Fulton • Scottish • *Scottish surname based on a place in Ayrshire now extinct*

Gabriel, Gabby, Gaby, Gabriele • Biblical/Hebrew/Jewish • *man of God*

Gaétan, Gaetano, Caietanus • Latin • *a man from Caieta in Latium*

Gamaliel • Jewish/Hebrew • *benefit of God*

Garfield • Anglo-Saxon • *a person who lives near a field shaped like a pyramid or triangle*

Garrison, Gary, Garry • American/English • *someone from Garriston in North Riding of Yorkshire* •

Garth, Gärd • Norse • *a man who lives near a farm or paddock*

Gaston • geographic • *a man from Gascony*

Gautam • Sanskrit • *descendant of Gotam*

Gavino, Gabinus, Gabino • Sardinian/Latin • *a man from Gabium*

Gen • Chinese • *root*

Giulio • Latin • *old Roman family name*

Glanville, Claenfeld • Norman • *surname derived from place in Normandy which is a cleared field*

Glen, Glenn, Gleann • Scots Gaelic • *valley*

Glyn, Glynn • British/Welsh • *valley*

Glyndwr, Glendower • British/Welsh • *valley of water*

Godfrey, Godefroy, Gofraidh, Godfrid, Godfred • Germanic/Frankish • *God of Peace*

Gordon • Scottish • *unknown origins; could spring from place name in Aberdeenshire or similar in Normandy*

Gottfried, Götz • Germanic • *God of Peace, God bring me peace*

Gotthelf • Germanic • *God help me*

Gottlieb, Theophilus • Germanic • *love God*

Gottlob • Germanic • *praise God*

Grafton, Graftun • Anglo-Saxon • *a grove within a village*

Graham, Graeme, Grahame, Grandham, Granham • Anglo-Saxon • *I live in a gravelly place; Grantham, Lincolnshire*

Grant, Grand, Grande • Anglo-Saxon/Norman • *a large, portly person*

Granville, Grenville • Norman • *large village or town*

Grover • American/English • *a man who lives in or near a grove of trees*

Guoliang • Chinese • *where you are there is kindness*

Gwilym, Gwilim, Gwillym, William • British Welsh • *his helmet gives him magical protection and the will to win*

Gwyn, Gwynn, Wyn • British/Welsh • *white, holy, sacred and blond*

Gwynfor • British/Welsh • *a large, grand man who is sacred, holy, blessed and fair*

Hāfiz • Arabic • *devoted scholar, guardian, foster*

Hale, Halh • Anglo-Saxon • *a person who lives off the beaten track; perhaps a hermit*

Halvard, Halvor, Hallvard, Hallvor, Halvar • Scandinavian • *defender like a rock*

Hamdi • Arabic • *praise be, grateful*

Hamish, James, Sheumais, Seumas • Scots Gaelic • *supplanter, a cuckoo in the nest! Edging out someone to take their place against their will*

Handel, Hans, Hans, Hansel, Johannes • Germanic • *God is gracious or gift of God*

Hāni • Arabic • *happy, gay*

Hannibal, Haanbaal • Phoenician • *I give the Lord grace and favour or he gives it to me*

Harding, Hearding • American/English • *I belong to Heard's tribe; strong and brave*

Hārith • Arabic • *provider, lion*

Harold, Harald • Anglo-Saxon • *ruler of the army, chief of the tribe*

Hāshim • Arabic • *crusher, breaks bread*

Håvard • Norse • *high protector*

Heber, Éibhear • Irish Gaelic/Biblical/Jewish/Hebrew • *an enclave, a ghetto*

Heddwyn • British/Welsh • *tranquil and peaceful; white, fair and sacred*

He • Chinese • *yellow river*

Hefin • British/Welsh • *summer*

Heimo • German • *east, west, home's best*

Henry, Henri, Harry, Anraí, Einrí, Eanraig, Heinrich, Henrik, Henrike, Hinrich, Hendrik, Enrique, Enric, Henrique, Enrico, Henryk, Hal, Jindrich, Heikki, Henrikas, Henning, Harris, Harry, Henry, Harry, Hank, Hawkin • Germanic • *power comes from the home or family (meaning nation too)*

Hercules, Herakles, Athairne, Hercule, Ercwlff • Latin • *the glory of Hera or Juno, Queen of the Gods*

Herleif, Härlief, Herlof, Herluf, Herliev • Norse • *warlike descendant*

Hilary, Hillary, Hilare, Hilario, Ilar • Latin • *as in hilarious!*

Hilton, Hill, Hyll • Anglo-Saxon • *a village on a hill or hump*

Hillel • Jewish/Hebrew • *praise him!*

Hishām • Arabic • *crusher (as in sacred bread) and giver*

Hjalmar • Norse • *magic helmet that protects the wearer*

Horace, Horatius, Horatio • Etruscan • *Roman family name with no certain root*

Horatio, Horatius, Horace • Etruscan • *Roman family name with no certain root*

Howard, Howerd, Haward • Scandinavian • *high or noble guardian or defender*

Huan • Chinese • *happy*

Hyam • Jewish/Hebrew • *a person who prays for the ill or dying for their recovery*

Iago, Jacob, James • Biblical • *supplanter, a cuckoo in the nest! Edging out someone to take their place against their will*

Ian, Iain, John • Scots Gaelic • Biblical • *God is gracious or gift of God*

Ianto, Ifan, Ieuan, Iohannes, John, Iefan, Ioan • British/Welsh • *God is gracious or gift of God*

Ib, Jepp, Jacob • Scandinavian • *supplanter, a cuckoo in the nest! Edging out someone to take their place against their will*

Ibrāhīm, Abraham • Arabic • *father of the tribes or nations*

Ignazio, Ignatius, Ignus, Ignace, Ignaz, Egnatius, Ignati, Ignacio • Latin/Estruscan • *Roman family name*

Ihsān • Arabic • *charitable, giver*

Ilario, Hilarius, Hilaris, Illari, Illarion • Latin • *cheerful, merry, hilarious!*

Illtud, Iltyd • British/Welsh • *a multitude or congregation of people/ the public*

Ingemar, Ingmar • Norse • *famous, well known to God*

Ingram, Engelram • Norman/Norse • *Norman family name after the Viking fertility god, Ing, and his pet Raven*

Ingvar, Yngvar • Norse • *warrior god who brings fertility and male potency*

Inigo • Spanish • *Roman family name*

Innes, Aonghas, Inis • Scots Gaelic • *an island, or man from Innes in Moray, north Britain*

Innocenzo, Innocentius, Innocens, Innokenti, Inocencio • *innocent, childlike; many saints and popes named this*

Iosif, Osip, Joseph • Biblical/Jewish/ Hebrew • *God will add another son*

Irène, Irenaeus, Eirenaios, Irina • Greek • *peaceable man*

Irvine, Irvin, Erwin, Irving, Israel • British/Welsh • *fresh, clear water*
Isaac, Zak, Zac, Zack, Ike, Izaak, Isak • Biblical • *unsure roots; probably the hireling or the laugh of a baby*
Isaiah, Izzy, Isaïe • Biblical/Jewish/Hebrew • *God is salvation*
'Isām • Arabic • *protection, keeper of the faith*
Iser, Iserl, Issur • Jewish/Yiddish • *he who strives with God*
'Ismat • Arabic • *innocent and without sin*
Israel, Jacob • Biblical/Jewish/Hebrew • *he who strives with God*
Italo, Italus • Latin • *father of Romulus and Remus, founders of Rome*
Ivan, John, Ewan • Russian • *God is gracious or gift of God*

Jabez • Biblical/Jewish/Hebrew • *I bear him with sorrow, sorrowful*
Jābir, Gābir, Jabr, Gabr • Arabic • *compassionate, comforter*
Jack John, Jankin, Jan, Jehan, James, Jacques, Jock, Jake, Jak, Jac, Jackie, Jackson, Jacky, Jackin • English • *God is gracious or gift of God*
Jada • Biblical/Hebrew/Jewish • *he knows*
Ja'far, Ga'far • Arabic • *stream, brook*
James, Iacomus, Jago, Jaime, Jamie, Jim, Jamey, Jimmy, Jimmie, Séamas, Séamus, Seumas, Seumus, Hamish, Jaume, Jacques, Jaume, Jaimes, Giacomo, Jameson, Jamieson, Jamey, Jamee, Jami, Jaimie, Jem, Jacobus • Biblical/Latin • *supplanter, a cuckoo in the*

nest! Edging out someone to take their place against their will
Jake, Jack • English • *God is gracious or gift of God*
Jamshed • Muslim/Parsis • *king and founder of Persopolis*
Jan, John, Johannes • Germanic/Slavic • *God is gracious or gift of God*
Jared, Jarred, Jarod, Jarrod • Biblical • *descent*
Jason, Jayson, Iason • Greek • *healer or he who heals*
Javier, Xavier • Roman Catholic/Basque • *the new house*
Jawdat, Gawdat • Arabic • *kindness personified and supreme*
Jean, Jehan, Gene • French • *God is gracious or gift of God*
Jed, Jedidiah, Ged • Biblical/Hebrew/Jewish • *beloved of God*
Jenkin, Jankin, Siencyn • British/Welsh • *God is gracious or gift of God*
Jens, Jons, Johann • Scandinavian • *God is gracious or gift of God*
Jeremiah, Jeremy, Jerry, Jem, Gerry, Jeremias • Biblical/Hebrew/Jewish • *appointed by God*
Jeremy, Jem, Jeremiah • Biblical/English • *appointed by God*
Jérôme, Hieronymos, Jerry, Jerrie, Jeri, Jerónimo, Geronimo, Hierosonoma • Greek
Jesse, Jess, Jessie, Jessi, Jessye • Biblical/Hebrew/Jewish • *gift*
Jianguo • Chinese • *patriotic*
Jiang • Chinese • *Yangtze River*
Jim, Jimmy, James • English • *supplanter, a cuckoo in the nest! Edging out someone to take their place against their will*
Jing • Chinese • *a boy born in the capital city Beijing or regional capital*

Jingguo • Chinese • *building the nation*

Joe, Jo, Joey • English • *God will add another*

Joachim, Jo, Johoiachin, Joaquin, Jochim, Jochem, Jochen, Joakim, Jokum • Biblical • *created by God*

Job, Joby, Jobey • Biblical/Jewish/ Hebrew • *persecuted*

Jocelyn, Jocelyne, Joscelyne, Joselyn, Josceline, Joslyn, Joss, Gautzelin, Joscelin • Norman • *someone from the Germanic tribe of the Gauts*

Jock, Jocky, Jack • Scots • *nickname for a man from Scotland*

John, Iohannes, Johannes, Ioannes, Johannan, Johanan, Eóin, Seán, Ian, Iain, Seathan, Ieuan, Siôn, Johann, Johannes, Jan, Jens, Johan, Jons, Jon, Jan, Johan, Jean, Juan, Joan, Joao, Giovanni, Gianni, Ioannis, Iannis, Ivan, Juhani, Jussi, Hannu, Janos, Janis, Johnnie, Johnny, Jack, Hank, Jonathan, Johnathan, Jonny, Jon, Johnson, Juwan, Johnston, Johnstone, Jones • Biblical/English/Latin • *God is gracious or gift of God*

Jonathan, Jon, Jonn, Johnny, Johnnie, Jonathen, Jonathon • Biblical • *God has given*

Jonah, Jon, Jonas • Biblical/ Hebrew/Jewish • *dove*

Jordan, Judd, Hayarden • Hebrew/ Jewish • *flowing down*

Joseph, Jo, Joey, Jose, Josef, Yosef, Joe, Jo, Seosamh, Ioseph, Josef, Jozef, Josep, Giuseppe, Iosif, Josip, Jooseppi • Biblical/Hebrew/Jewish

Joshua, Josh • Biblical/Hebrew/ Jewish • *God is my salvation*

Josiah, Josh • Biblical/Hebrew/ Jewish • *God heals*

Jozsef, Osip, Jazeps, Juozapas • Biblical/Jewish/Hebrew • *God will add another son*

Juan, John • Biblical/Greek/Spanish • *God is gracious or gift of God*

Jūda, Gūda • Arabic • *goodness and kindness transcend all*

Julián, Jules, Julianus, Julius, Julyan, Jolyon, Julien, Julio, Jools • Latin • *a Roman family name that gives its name to month of July*

Justin, Justyn, Justinus, Justus, Iestyn • Latin • *a Roman family name*

Kai, Gerhard, Klaus, Gaius, Caius, Caietanus, Kajetan, Cayo, Kaj, Kad • Norse/Scandinavian • *hen*

Kailash • Sanskrit • *paradise of Shiva and Kubera's home, the God of Wealth*

Kajetan, Caitanus, Gaetano, Kayetan • Latin • *man from Caieta*

Kamil, Camillus • Latin • *order of Monks who nursed the sick*

Kasi • Sanskrit • *radiant; Varanasi or Benares, sacred city on the Ganges*

Keaton • Anglo-Saxon • *the homestead of Kea*

Keelan, Keelahan, Ceileachain • British/Welsh/ Irish Gaelic • *companion or friend; descendant of Keelahan*

Keenan, Cianain, Cian, Cianin • Irish Gaelic • *descendant of Cianan, old and ancient*

Keiller, Keilor, Keiller • Canadian/ English • *Scots surname from a place in Perthshire*

Keir, Kerr, Kjarr • Norse • *a person who lives in marshes covered in shrubs and brushwood*

Keith • British/Welsh • *wood, copse or thicket, or a man from East Lothian*

Kelvin, Kelvyn • Scots/English • *if you come from Kelvinside, Glasgow or by the river, this is the root of the name*

Kendall, Kendal, Kendale, Kendel, Kendell, Kendle, Kendyl, Cynddelw • Anglo-Saxon/British/Welsh • *someone who worships Celtic deities or a place in Westmorland, Kendal, named after River Kent*

Kent, Kenton, Kenntun, Cenatun, Cynetun • British/Welsh • *someone from the British kingdom (now county) and tribe of the Cantii*

Kenya • English • *someone from the African country of Kenya*

Kjell, Keld, Kjetil, Kjeld, Ketill, Ketil • *sacred kettle or cauldron*

Kimberley, Kimberly, Kim, Kym • Anglo-Saxon/American English • *after the South African town of Kimberley where the British took on the Boers*

Kirk, Kirkja • Norse • *a church or someone who lives near one*

Klaus, Claus, Nikolaus • Germanic/Dutch • *victory over or with the people*

Kilment, Clément, Clemens • Latin • *merciful*

Kolya, Nikolai • Russian • *victory over or with the people*

Konstantin, Constantinus • Latin • *constant, steadfast, loyal, devoted*

Kyle, Caol • Gaelic • *narrow in geographical terms; a region in Ayrshire*

Kynaston, Cynefripestun • Anglo-Saxon • *the homestead or village of a peaceful royal or noble personage*

Lachlan, Lachlann, Lochlann, Lochlan, Lachie, Lockie, Loughlin, Lochlainn, Lachlan, Laughlin, Loughlin • Scots Gaelic • *a man from the land of the lochs or Norway*

Lachtna • Irish Gaelic • *milk or creamy coloured*

Lakshman, Laxman • Sanskrit • *the mark of God; most auspicious*

Lal • Sanskrit/Prakrit • *dear, sweet, darling one; king*

Lambert, Landbeorht, Lamprecht, Lammert • Germanic • *famous, wonderful land, very patriotic*

Lamin • African/Sierra Leonese • *honest, trustworthy*

Laoiseach, Laois, Louis, Lewis, Leix • Irish • *a man from County Leix*

Laurence, Lawrence, Larry, Laurentius, Laurentum, Laurie, Lawrie, Labhrás, Labhrainn, Lorenz, Laurens, Lars, Laurent, Lorencio, Llorenc, Laurenco, Lorenzo, Lawson, Lavrentios, Lavrenti, Laurencjusz, Wawrzyniec, Vavrinec, Lovrenc, Lauri, Lasse, Lassi, Lorinc, Laz, Lenz, Lavrenti • Latin • *man from Laurentum, the capital of the Latins*

Lazarus, Laz, Lazare, Eleazar, Lazaros, Lazar • Biblical/Greek/Aramaic/Hebrew • *God is my helper*

Leberecht • Protestant German • *live your life properly, give it to God*

Léger, Luitger, Leodegar, Leo • Germanic • *a tribe of people with spears*

Lemuel • Hebrew/Jewish • *devoted to God*

Lester, Ligoracaester, Ligoracastra • Anglo-Saxon • *the place of the Roman fort on the River Soar*

Li • Chinese • *profit, business*

acumen and respectable

Liam, Ulliam, William • Irish
Gaelic/Norman • *willpower, with a
helmet, possibly magic, to give divine
protection*

Licio, Lycius • Latin • *man from
Lycia in Asia Minor*

Lincoln, Lindum • British/Welsh •
Roman fort by the lake

Linden, Linde, Lyndon, Lynden •
Anglo-Saxon • *lime tree*

Lindsay, Lindissi • Anglo-Saxon
• *old Saxon kingdom whose root
means Lelli's island*

Linford, Lindford, Lynford •
Anglo-Saxon • *the lime trees or flax
plant that grow by the ford in the
river*

Linton, Lynton • Anglo-Saxon • *the
village by or with a lime tree*

Ling • Chinese • *compassionate and
understanding*

Linton, Lynton • Anglo-Saxon •
*the place where the lime tree or flax
plants grow*

Logan • Scots Gaelic • *a family
name or someone from Logan in
Ayrshire*

Lonnie, Lonso, Lenny • Spanish/
Visigothic • *royal at the ready*

Lorin, Loren, Lorrin, Laurence •
Latin • *man from Laurentum, the
capital of the Latins*

Lorne, Latharna, Lorn • Canadian/
English • *Scottish place name Lorne,
Argyll*

**Lutz, Ludwig, Ludvig, Ludwik,
Luthais** • Germanic/Frankish •
*a person who gains fame through
waging war; a hero who vanquishes
the enemy and is revered by his people*

Lucas, Luka, Luke, Luca, Loukas •
East European/Greek • *man from
Loucania, a Greek colony in southern
Italy*

Ludger, Luitger • Friesian • *place
name derived from famous monk*

Luitgard • Germanic • *protector of
the people*

**Luke, Lucas, Loukas, Lukas, Luc,
Lluc, Lluch, Lukasz, Luukas,
Lukacs, Luka** • Greek • *man from
Loucania, a Greek colony in southern
Italy*

Luther, Liutheri, Luither •
Germanic • *army of the people*

Lyle, De L'isle • Norman/Gaelic •
*someone from the isles or marshy
land*

Macey, Macciscum, Maccius •
Norman/Latin • *someone from
Massey, Normandy*

Madhav • Sanskrit • *descendant
of Madhu (Krishna)*

**Madison, Madde, Madeleine,
Maud** • American English • *son
of Maud or Matilda, the battleaxe*

**Maitland, Maltalent, Mautalent,
Mautalant** • Anglo-Saxon/Norman
• *bad-tempered or from Mautalant,
a barren place in France*

**Makarios, Macaire, Macario,
Makari** • Greek • *blessed one*

Malcolm, Maelcoluim, Maelcoluim
• Scots Gaelic • *follower of St
Columba, the dove*

**Mallory, Mallery, Malheure,
Malerie** • Norman • *unhappy or
unfortunate one*

Ma'mūn • Arabic • *reliable and
trusted*

Manār • Arabic • *light of goodness*

**Manfred, Manffred, Mainfred,
Manfried, Manfredo** • Germanic •
man of peace

Manley, Manly • Anglo-Saxon • *common land, for all men*

Manlio, Manlius • Latin • *Roman family name famous for republican leanings*

Manuel, Emmanuel • Biblical/Spanish • *God is with us or amongst us*

Mario, Marius • Latin • *from Roman family name and male version of Mary*

Marius • Latin • *Roman family name; clouded meaning but associated with someone of or from the sea*

Marsh, Marshall, Marshal, Mersc • Anglo-Saxon • *a person who lives on marshy ground or fen land*

Mathias, Matthias, Matthaeus, Matthäus, Mattathia • Biblical/ Greek/Jewish/Aramaic/Latin • *gift of God*

Matthew, Matt, Mathew, Mattathia, Maitiu, Matthias, Maitias, Mata, Matha, Matthäus, Matthijs, Mads, Mathies, Mats, Mathieu, Mateo, Mateu, Mateus, Matteo, Mattia, Matvei, Mateusz, Maciej, Matej, Matyas, Matija, Matti, Matyas, Mate, Mattanah, Mattaniah, Mattathah, Mattatha, Mattathiah, Mattathias • Biblical/ Hebrew/Jewish/English • *gift of God*

Melchior, Melkquart, Melchiorre • Jewish/Christian • *city of the King*

Melvin, Melvyn, Mel, Melvin, Melville, Melvyn, Malleville • *a man from a bad place*

Mengyao • Chinese • *a parent's wish for a wise child*

Merton • Anglo-Saxon • *lakeside village*

Michael, Micah, Micheal, Meical, Mihangel, Machiel, Mikael, Mikkel, Michel, Miguel, Miquel, Michele,

Mikhail, Michal, Mihovil, Mihajlo, Mihael, Mikko, Mihaly, Mike, Mick, Micky, Mikey, Mickey, Meical • Biblical/Hebrew/Jewish/English • *who is like God?*

Milan, Milano • Czech/Italian • *grace and favour, or someone who comes from Milan, Italy*

Milo • Slavic/Latin • *grace and favour or soldier*

Milton, Mylentun, Milt • Anglo-Saxon • *the homestead or village by or with a mill*

Mingli • Chinese • *lighting up propriety*

Minzhe • Chinese • *sensitive, wise*

Misha, Micha, Mikhail • Russian • *he who is like God*

Mitchell, Michael, Michel, Mitch • Norman/English • *he who is like God*

Modesto, Modest • Latin • *modest*

Mohammed, Muhammed, Mohammad, Mohamed, Muhammad, Muhammed, Mo • *praiseworthy and possessing the finest perfect qualities*

Monday • Anglo-Saxon • *mona's daeg, the moon's day*

Monroe, Munro, Munrow, Monro, Munroe, Bunrotha • Gaelic • *mouth of the River Roe, near Derry, Ulster*

Montague, Montaigu, Monty • Norman/Latin • *a person from the pointed hill, particularly Montaigu, La Manche, Normandy*

Montgomery, Montgomeric, Monty • Germanic/Norman • *the powerful man from the hill*

Mordecai, Motke, Motl, Marduk • Biblical/Persian • *he who worships the God of Magic and Water*

Mortimer, Mortemer, Muiriartach •

Norman • *dead sea or stagnant lake place or new village*

Morton, Morten, Moses, Mort, Mortun • Anglo-Saxon • *village by or on moorland*

Moses, Moshe, Moïse, Moss, Moses, Mostyn, Monty • Biblical/Hebrew/Egyptian • *born of God*

Mostyn, Mostun • English • *mossy settlement or enclosure; place name in Flintshire*

Motke, Mordecai, Motl • Biblical/Jewish/Yiddish • *he who worships the God of Magic and Water,*

Muhammed • Arabic • *sacred qualities, scrupulous*

Muhsin • Arabic • *good to others, compassionate*

Mun'im • Arabic • *charitable, donor*

Murray, Moray, Muireach • Scots Gaelic • *a person from Moray*

Mustafa, Mustapha • pure, the chosen one

Mu'tasim • Arabic • *trust in God or the Lord*

Nabīl • Arabic • *royal born or noble birth*

Nahman, Nahum, Naum • Jewish • *comforter*

Nāji, Nāgi • Arabic • *rescued and saved*

Nāsir, Nazir • Arabic • *a good ally and friend; helping and supportive*

Nathan, Nat, Jonathan, Nathen • Biblical/Hebrew/Jewish • *God has given*

Nathaniel, Nat, Nathanael, Natanaele • Biblical/Greek/English • *God has given*

Neopmuk • Czech • *someone from the town of Pomuk; St John of Pomuk, patron saint of Bohemia*

Neville, Neuville • Norman • *a new*

place or new village

Newton, Newt, Neowe • Anglo-Saxon • *a new village or new homestead*

Nianzu • Chinese • *ancestors revered*

Niaz • Persian • *prayer, gift, sacrifice*

Nicholas, Nikolaos, Nicolás, Nickolas, Nick, Nik, Nico, Nicky, Nioclás, Neacal, Nikolaus, Niklaus, Nicolaas, Nikolaas, Niklaas, Niels, Nils, Nicolao, Nicolau, Nicola, Niccolo, Nicolo, Nikolai, Mikolaj, Mikolas, Mikulas, Nikola, Nikolaj, Niilo, Miktos, Mykolas, Nik, Niklas, Nels, Neacal, Nikelaos • Greek/English • *victory for or over the people*

Nicol, Nicholl, Nicola, Nichola, Nichol, Nicole • English • *victory for or over the people*

Nicodemus, Nikodemos, Nicodème, Nico, Nicodim, Nicodemo • Greek/Latin • *victory for or over the people*

Norris, Norreis • Germanic/Frankish • *a person who has migrated from the north to Normandy; Norseman or Viking*

Norton, Nordtun • Anglo-Saxon • *the northern village, homestead or enclosure*

Nyabera • Kenyan • *the good one*

Olaf, Olav, Anuleif, Olof, Ottwolf, Ola, Ole, Oluf, Olov, Olaus, Olai • Norse • *ancestor, heir, descendant*

Oleg, Helgi • Norse • *prosperous, the chap who created Kiev, Ukraine*

Olijimi • Nigerian • *God gave me this*

Onofre • Egyptian • *a man who opens up to God*

Ophelos, Ofelos • Greek • *help!*

Orazio, Horatius, Horatio •

Estruscan • *personal family name*
Osbert, Osbeorht • Anglo-Saxon • *illuminated by God, famous for his devotion*
Osmond, Osmund, Oz • Anglo-Saxon • *God is my protector*
Ove, Aghi • Norse • *frightened or in awe of a weapon of terror*
Owen, Owain, Éoghan, Eóin, Eugenius • Latin/British/Welsh • *born of Esos or Aesos, a Celtic god that was big in Gaul (now France)*

Pacey, Pacciacum, Passy, Paccius • Latin/Gaulish • *a man called Paccius or from the town of Passy*
Paris, Parisii • Latin/Celtic • *member of the Parisii tribe, origins unknown*
Parnell, Parnel • Irish/English • *named after Irish republican Charles Parnell*
Parthalán, Párthlán, Pártlán, Partnán, Bartholomew, Berkely, Barclay • Latin/Irish • *first ever citizen of Ireland after the Biblical flood; Biblical meaning: son of Tolmai from Galilee*
Patrice, Patrick • Latin/French • *patrician*
Patrick, Pádraig, Pat, Paddy, Patsy, Páraic, Patrice, Patricio, Patrizio, Porick, Podge, Pàra, Pàdair, Pàidean, Padrig, Paddy, Patrick, Pat, Patrice • Latin/Irish Gaelic • *patrician*
Pàrlan, Parthalán • Gaelic • *uncertain origin; may be linked to Irish for Bartholomew*
Paul, Paulus, Pol, Pål, Poul, Pall, Pauwel, Påvel, Pablo, Pau, Paulo, Paolo, Pavlos, Pavao, Pavle, Paavo, Paulius, Pablo • Latin • *Roman family name meaning little or small*
Paulino, Pablo, Paulus • Spanish/

Italian • *Roman family name meaning little or small*
Payton, Peyton • Anglo-Saxon • *Paega's place*
Paco, Francis, Francisco • Spanish • *to be French, someone from France; especially 14th July*
Pelham, Peotlaham, Peolham • Anglo-Saxon • *Peola's homestead or farm*
Penn • American/English • *a hill or pen for domestic animals*
Pepe, Pepito, Joseph, José • Spanish • *God is my salvation*
Philbert, Filaberht, Philibert, Filbert • Greek/Germanic/Frankish • *dear, beloved*
Phoenix, Phoinix • Latin/Greek • *mythical bird that represents rebirth or reincarnation*
Pimen, Poimen • Greek • *shepherd*
Ping • Chinese • *stable and secure*
Pompeo, Pompeius • Latin • *Roman family name*
Pontius, Ponzio, Poncio • Latin • *family name; origin unknown*
Prasad • Sanskrit • *by the grace of God, gifts from the deity to the worshippers*
Preston, Preosttun • Anglo-Saxon • *priest's town*
Proinséas, Francis • Irish/Latin • *to be French, someone from France; especially 14th July*
Pryderi • British/Welsh • *a carer, someone who is anxious*

Quartus • Latin • *four*
Quentin, Quintinus, Quintus, Quintin, Quinton, Cwentun • Latin • *Roman family name*
Qi • Chinese • *enlightened, wonderment and intellectual*

Qingsheng • Chinese • *celebrating birth*

Quinn, Cuinn • English/Irish Gaelic • *descendant of Cuinn*

Quirce, Quiricus • Latin • *name of a three-year-old child martyred with his mother in Tarsus in AD 304*

Ra'fat • Arabic • *mercy, compassion, forgiveness*

Rafferty, Rabhartaigh, Robhartaigh, Raff • Irish Gaelic • *descendant of Robhartaigh*

Raghav • Sanskrit • *from name for Rama, descendant of Raghu*

Rajab, Ragab • Arabic • *seventh month of the Muslim calendar*

Rajkumar • Sanskrit • *prince, heir*

Rajnish • Sanskrit • *ruler of the night*

Rakesh • Sanskrit • *ruler of the full moon*

Ramesh • Sanskrit • *night-time tranquillity and serenity; sleep*

Ramón, Raimundo, Raymond • Catalan/Germanic • *adviser, protector*

Raphael, Rafael, Rafa, Rapha, Raffaele • Biblical/Jewish/Hebrew • *God has healed*

Ra'ūf • Arabic • *caring and compassionate*

Reagan, Regan, Riagain • Irish Gaelic/English • *descendant of Riagain, the impulsive or impatient one*

Rémy, Remigius, Remi, Remigio, Remix • Latin • *oarsman or man at the tiller*

Renato, Renatus • Latin • *reborn*

René, Renatus, Renato • Latin • *reborn; resurrected*

Reuben, Reuven, Rube, Rubén • Biblical/Hebrew/Jewish • *behold, a son!*

Rida • Arabic • *affirmation, validation by God (Allah); contented*

Riley, Rygeleah, Reilly, Raghallach, Ryley • Anglo-Saxon/Irish Gaelic • *a field where the rye crop has been cleared*

Rio • Portuguese/Spanish • *river*

River, Rivere, Rivieres • English/French • *river*

Rodion, Herodion • Greek • *follower of Hera, wife of Zeus*

Rodney, Rod, Roddy • Anglo-Saxon • *famous island; a person from there*

Roland, Rodland, Rowland, Roly, Rowley, Rolie, Rolland, Roldan, Rolant • Germanic • *famed throughout land*

Roman, Romanus, Romain, Romano • Latin/Czech/Polish/Romanian • *to be Roman*

Ross, Rós • Gaelic • *family name from geographical term for a headland or promontory*

Rowan, Ruadhan • Gaelic/English • *descendant of Ruadhan, little red one*

Royce, Royston, Royse • English • *the town or place of the rose or roses*

Royle, Rygehyll, Royal • Anglo-Saxon • *the hill where rye is grown*

Rupchand • Sanskrit • *as beautiful as the moon*

Rurik, Hrodrik, Roderick • Norse • *famous ruler, the name of the man who founded Russia's Novogorod, the Big New City*

Ryan, Riain • Irish Gaelic • *little king, descendant of Riain*

Sasha, Sacha, Shura • French/Greek/Russian • *the man/warrior/leader who protects or defends his people*

Sachdev • Sanskrit • *truth of God, totally honest*

Safā • Arabic • *pure and sincere*

Salāma • Arabic • *keeping safe, self protection*

Sālih • Arabic • *devout, devoted*

Sālim, Salīm • Arabic • *safe, unharmed*

Samuel, Shemuel, Shaulmeel, Sam, Sammy, Sawyl • Biblical/ Hebrew/Jewish • *name of God, God has heard, listen to God*

Sander, Alexander • Norwegian/ Greek • *the man/warrior/leader who protects or defends his people*

Sandro, Sonny • Italian

Sandy, Alex, Sandaidh, Sawney • Scots Gaelic/Greek • *the man/ warrior/leader who protects or defends his people*

Santiago, Iago, Jacobus, James • Spanish • *supplanter, a cuckoo in the nest! Edging out someone to take their place against their will*

Sava, Sabas, Sabbas, Saba • Greek/Jewish

Scott • Gaelic • *a man from Ireland who settles in Scotland*

Séamus, Shamus, Séamas, James, Seumas • Gaelic • *supplanter, a cuckoo in the nest! Edging out someone to take their place against their will*

Seán, Shane, Shaughan, Shaughn, Shaun, Shawn • Irish Gaelic/ English • *supplanter, a cuckoo in the nest! Edging out someone to take their place against their will*

Seathan, Jean, Jehan • Scots Gaelic/French/Biblical/English/ Latin • *God is gracious or gift of God*

Sender, Zender • Jewish/Greek • *the man/warrior/leader who protects or defends his people*

Serge, Sergio, Sergius • Latin/ Etruscan • *old Roman family name*

Sergei, Serzha • Russian/Etruscan • *old Roman name of vague roots*

Seth • Sanskrit • *vague root but white or bridge*

Severiano, Severus, Severo, Severinus, Sören, Severinus, Severino, Seve • Latin • *Roman family name meaning stern, austere*

Sextus, Sesto, Seissylt • Latin • *sixth or number six*

Shafiq • Arabic • *compassionate*

Shākir • Arabic • *thankful and grateful*

Shankar, Sankar • Sanskrit • *confers welfare, to look after*

Shabbetai, Shabbath, Shabath, Shabtai • Jewish/Hebrew • *the Sabbath*

Sharma • Sanskrit • *protect, comfort, joy*

Shashi • Sanskrit • *having a hare, referring to the moon*

Shea, Shae, Shay • Irish Gaelic • *descendant of Séaghdha*

Shelby • Norse • *willow farm*

Sheridan, Sirideain • Irish Gaelic • *descendant of Sirideain, the searcher*

Shi • Chinese • *symbolic of strength and support*

Shiva • Sanskrit • *beautiful, timely, death and regeneration*

Shneur, Senior • Jewish/Yiddish • *senior*

Shukri • Arabic • *giving thanks*

Shunyuan • Chinese • *following back to the roots or source*

Sidney, Sydney • Anglo-Saxon • *an ait, a small island in a river or a wide river meadow*

Sigmund, Siegmund, Sigismund • Germanic • *a personal name meaning victorious and protector*

Siegwald, Sigiswald, Sigurd, Sjur, Sjurd • Germanic/Norse • *protector, victory*

Silver, Siolfor, Seolfor • Anglo-Saxon • *the metal silver*

Simeon • English/Biblical/Hebrew • *he has heard*

Simón, Siomon, Sim, Simidh, Sieman, Simao, Simone, Semyon, Szymon, Simo, Sim, Simmie • Biblical/Hebrew/Jewish • *hearkening, hearing*

Sirideán • Irish Gaelic • *unsure roots; likely to be someone who seeks*

Skipper, Schipper • Dutch/Scandinavian • *boss, ship's captain or someone who skips across ships*

Slane, Slaney, Sluaghhadain • Irish Gaelic • *descendant of Sluaghadhan*

Slater • Anglo-Saxon • *a surname for someone who fixes slates on a roof*

Sloan, Sluaghhadain • Irish Gaelic • *a descendant of Sluaghadh, the tribe who go on raids and quick attacks*

Spencer • Anglo-Saxon • *similar to a quartermaster, someone who dispenses provisions or goods*

Srinivas • Sanskrit • *house of Sri*

Sroel • Jewish/Yiddish • *Israel*

Stafford • Anglo-Saxon • *the river ford good for landing*

Stamford, Stanford, Stan • Anglo-Saxon • *where the stones are, you can ford the river*

Standish, Stanedisc, Stan • Anglo-Saxon • *the field or meadow filled with stones*

Stirling, Ystrefelyn • British/Welsh/Anglo-Saxon • *Melyn's tribe or people*

Suhayl • Arabic • *the bright star of Canopus constellation*

Taffy, Taf, Dafydd • British/Welsh • *the universal nickname for someone from Wales/Cymru (or called David), after the River Taff that flows through Cardiff/Caerdydd*

Tage, Taki, Taka • Scandinavian • *to take or grab, receive, guarantor*

Tāha • Arabic • *opening letters of the 20th sura in the Koran*

Tāhir • Arabic • *oh so pure, chaste and virtuous*

Tāmir • Arabic • *rich in dates and figs and all good things*

Tasgall, Taskill, Asketill • Norse • *the sacred pot or cauldron*

Teodosio • Greek • *God-given*

Terence, Terentius, Terry, Toirdhealbhach, Tel, Terrance, Terrence • Latin/Irish Gaelic • *from the Roman family name Terentius and Irish for someone who takes the initiative*

Thaddeus, Labbaeus, Theodoras, Theodotos, Thad, Tad • Biblical/Aramaic/Greek • *given by God or God's gift*

Thelonius, Till, Tillo • Germanic/Dutch • *the people*

Theobald, Peudbald, Theo, Thibault, Tiobold • Germanic • *a tribe of people known for their boldness in the face of adversity*

Théodore, Theo, Ted, Teddy, Theodor, Theodoor, Teodor, Teodoro, Feodor, Fyodr, Teuvo, Tivador, Todor, Teodors, Theodoric, Tiobad, Ted, Teddy, Edward, Theodos, Theodosios, Teodosio, Todos, Theodoros • Greek • *God-given or giving to God or God's gift*

Thierry, Theodoric • French/Greek • *ruler of the people*

Thornton, Thorn, Tornton •

Anglo-Saxon • *the village where the thorn bush grows*

Till, Dietrich • Germanic • *the people*

Timothy, Tim, Tadhg, Timmy, Timotheus, Timotheos, Timetheo, Timmy, Tiger, Timothee, Timo, Timoteo, Timofei • Biblical/Latin/Greek • *honour God*

Tingguang • Chinese • *bright garden or courtyard*

Tobias, Tobiah, Tobijah, Toby • Biblical/Hebrew/Greek • *God is good*

Tony, Anthony, Tone, Tönjes, Antonius, Tonio • Estruscan/Roman • *Roman family name but with confused origins*

Torcall, Torquil • Norse • *the sacrificial or sacred cauldron of Thor, the God of Thunder*

Torquil, Torkel, Thorkel, Torkild, Torkjell, Torkil • Norse • *sacred kettle or cauldron*

Tracy, Thraciusacum, Tracey • Latin/Gaulic • *a person from a place in Normandy called Tracy!*

Traugott • Germanic • *trust in God*

Travis, Traverser • Norman • *someone who worked collecting tolls on the roads or highways, crossing roads*

Trefor, Trevor, Trev, Tref • British/Welsh • *a large settlement or village*

Tremaine, Tremayne, Tremen • British/Welsh/Kernow • *Cornish for homestead and stone*

Trent, Trenton • British/Welsh • *after the River Trent in the English Midlands; its root meaning is to travel or journey*

Trenton, Trent • American English • *means the settlement by the Trent, or after William Trent, the British*

Quaker founder of the New Jersey city

Trevelyan, Treelian, Trevelien • British/Welsh/Kernow • *Cornish for the homestead or village of Elian (local personage)*

Trofim, Trophimos • Greek • *fruitful, goodness, sustaining*

Tuathal, Toal • Irish Gaelic • *chief of the clan or tribe*

Tudur, Tudor, Tudyr, Teutorix • British/Welsh • *king or chief of the tribe*

Tullio, Tullius • Latin • *a Roman family name*

Tulsi • Sanskrit • *the herb, basil; so holy is also a goddess*

Tybalt, Theobald • Germanic • *a tribe of people known for their boldness in the face of adversity*

Ulysses, Odysseus, Odyssesthai, Ulick, Ulisse, Ulises • Greek/Latin • *a person who hates*

Urban, Urbanus • Latin • *a person who lives in the city*

Vance, Van • Anglo-Saxon • *meaning fenland or marshland*

Vanya, Ivan • Russian • *God is gracious or gift of God*

Varfolomel, Bartholomew • Biblical • *son of Tolmai from Galilee*

Volk, Wolf, Volkhard • Germanic • *strong people*

Volkmar • Germanic • *famous people*

Wade, Wadan, Wada, Gewaed • Anglo-Saxon • *a ford, as in river, to wade across*

Walid • Arabic • *newly born or reborn*

Warwick, Waerwic, Werwic •

Anglo-Saxon • *industrial area by a dam or weir*

Washington, Wassingtun • Anglo-Saxon • *the village or tribe of Wassa*

Weimin • Chinese • *honour the people with greatness*

Weiyuan • Chinese • *strong roots*

Wendell, Wendel • Germanic • *a member of the Slav tribe living between the Elbe and Oder*

Wenyan • Chinese • *refined, chic, chaste and gifted*

Whitney, Whiteney • Anglo-Saxon • *the white island*

Wilbur, Willburh • Anglo-Saxon • *he who has the will to build a fort or protected village*

Willoughby, Weligbyr • Anglo-Saxon/Norse • *the village by the willow tree*

Windsor, Windelsora • Anglo-Saxon • *the place on the river with a windlass (special crane to move heavy weights)*

Winton, Winntun, Withigtun, Winatun • Anglo-Saxon • *village with a pasture*

Woodrow, Woody • English • *a hamlet with a row of houses*

Worth, Worth, Weorth • Anglo-Saxon • *hamlet of a main village*

Wyndham, Windham, Wymondham • Anglo-Saxon • *the village of Wigmund*

Wynfor, Wyn • British/Welsh • *white, blonde, holy, blessed*

Xander, Alexander • Greek • *the man/warrior/leader who protects or defends his people*

Xavier, Javier, Etcheberria, Xaver • Roman Catholic/Basque • *the new house*

Xiaodan • Chinese • *little dawn*

Xiaosi • Chinese • *thoughts of offspring*

Xolani • Xhosa South Africa • *please forgive*

Yadav • Sanskrit • *descendant of Yadu or Krishna*

Yahya, John • Arabic/Biblical • *God is gracious or gift of God*

Yaochuan • Chinese • *honouring the river*

Yaoting • Chinese • *honouring the garden or family*

Yaozu • Chinese • *honouring the ancestors and the past*

Yigael • Jewish/Hebrew • *he shall be redeemed*

Yitzhak, Isaac • Jewish/Hebrew • *unsure roots; probably the hireling or the laugh of a baby*

Yosef, Joseph, Yūsuf • Jewish/Hebrew/Arabic • *God is my salvation*

Yuan, Juan, John • Manx Gaelic • *God is gracious or gift of God*

Yuanjun • Chinese • *master or child of the Yuan river*

Yuri, Yura, Georgi • Russian/Greek • *farmer or someone who works on the land*

Yūsuf, Joseph • Arabic/Biblical • *God is my salvation*

Yusheng • Chinese • *jade birth*

Zachary, Zach, Zak • Greek/English/Biblical • *God has remembered*

Zacharias, Zak, Zechariah, Zachariah, Zakaria, Zach • Biblical/Jewish/Hebrew • *God has remembered*

Zaki • Arabic • *chaste, virginal*

Zakariyya, Zakariya • Biblical/
Arabic • *God has remembered*
Zebadiah, Zabdi, Zabadiah,
Zebedee • Biblical/Hebrew/Jewish
• *living with, to dwell; Yahweh has
given*
Zechariah • Biblical/Jewish/Hebrew
• *God has remembered*

Zelig, Selig • Jewish/Yiddish •
happy and counting my blessings
Zemin • Chinese • *favoured people*
Zhengsheng • Chinese • *powerful
country*
Zhong • Chinese • *steadfast and
devoted*

Girls

Abigail, Abbie, Abby, Abbey, Abbigail, Abbiegail, Abbygail, Abigayle, Abi • Biblical/Jewish/ Hebrew • *my father is joy, father is exaltation*

Abital, Avital • Biblical/Jewish/ Hebrew • *dewy and moist*

Abla • Arabic • *voluptuous*

Adélaide • Germanic • *noble, kind and caring*

Adria, Adrianne, Adrienne, Adrianna, Adriana • Latin • *a person from Hadria after which the Adriatic Sea is named*

Adrienne, Adriana • Latin • *a person from Hadria after which the Adriatic Sea is named*

Aeronwen • British/Welsh • *white, sacred and fair*

Afāf • Arabic • *chastity, refinement, elegance*

Afon • British/Welsh • *river*

Agatha, Agathe, Aggie, Agata, Ågot, Águeda, Agathos • Greek • *good and honourable*

Agnès, Aggie, Aigneis, Inés, Agnese, Agnessa, Agnieszka, Anezka, Aune, Agnese, Agne, Annis, Annys, Annice, Aigneis, Agnethe, Agnetis, Agnete, Ågot • Greek • *pure and holy*

Agrippina, Agrafena • Latin/ Estruscan • *family name of old Roman family*

Ailbhe • Irish Gaelic • *white*

Áine • Irish • *as bright, as radiant as the Queen of the Faeries*

'Āisha, Aishah, Ayesha • Arabic • *alive; Mohammed's third and favourite wife*

Alastriona • Scots Gaelic/Greek • *the warrior/leader who protects or defends her people*

Alba • Latin/Germanic • *white or elfin*

Albina, Bina, Albus, Albius • Latin • *Roman family name meaning white*

Alexandra, Alexa, Alexis, Sandra, Sandy, Lexy, Alix, Alexandria, Alexandrina, Alexia, Aleksandra, Alexina • Greek • *the warrior/leader who protects or defends her people*

Alexia • Greek • *Greek* • *she who defends*

Alice, Alicia, Alesha, Alisia, Alys, Alisha, Alissa, Alesha, Alisa, Alissa, Ailish, Alis, Alys • Norman • *noble, kind and caring*

Alickina, Kina, Keena • Greek/ Gaelic • *the warrior/leader who protects or defends her people*

Alison, Allie, Ally, Aly, Alysoun, Aliyah, Aaliyah, Allison, Allyson • Norman • *noble, kind and caring*

Alix • Greek • *one who defends*

Aliza, Freyde • Jewish/Hebrew • *joyful and gay*

Alma, Almus • Latin • *nourishing, nurturing, kind like a mother*

Alva, Alvah, Ailbhe, Alvina • Scots Gaelic • *white*

Amīna • Arabic • *peaceful, secure*

Amparo • Roman Catholic/Spanish • *may the Virgin Mary protect me and all Christians*

Anais, Ana, Anya • Biblical/Catalan/ Provençal • *God has favoured me*

Angosto • Spanish/Galician/Roman Catholic • *Our lady of Angosto, a place where the Virgin appeared*

Anita, Ana • Spanish/ Biblical • *God has favoured me*

Ann, Anne, Anna, Annabel,

Annette, Annetta, Anouk, Anni, Annelie, Anneli, Annella, Annabell, Annabella, Annabelle, Belle, Annie, Anna, Anneke, Anke, Anoushka, Anouska, Arabella, Arabel Anna, Ana • Biblical/Jewish/ Hebrew • *God has favoured me*

Annalisa, Annaliesa, Annalise, Annelise, Annelies, Anneli • German • *combo of Anne and Elisabeth; God has favoured me, plus God is my oath*

Anneka, Anika, Annika, Anna, Anniken • German/Dutch • *God has favoured me*

Anniella • Roman Catholic • *little lamb*

Anona, Annona • Latin • *unsure root but possibly corn supply*

Antonia, Anthonia • Estruscan/ Roman • *Roman family name but with confused origins*

Antigone • Greek • *contrary, the antithesis, born against the odds or contrary to conditions*

Antoinette, Toinette, Tonette, Antonella, Antonia, Toni, Antonina • Estruscan/Roman • *Roman family name but with confused origins*

Anwen, Annwen • British/Welsh • *blessed and beautiful*

Aranrhod • British/Welsh • *huge, big, round, plump and humped!*

Armana • African • *faithful*

Armelle, Artmael • Breton Celtic • *a female chief who is as steady as a rock*

Artemis, Diana • Greek/Latin • *Goddess of the Moon and the Hunt*

Asenath • Biblical/Egyptian • *she is Daddy's little princess*

Ashanti • Ghanian • *tribe from Ghana*

Aslög, Asslaug, Åslaug • Swedish • *God-consecrated*

Ashton • Anglo-Saxon • *the village with an ash tree*

Aston • Anglo-Saxon • *the village to the east*

Atalanta, Atlanta • mythological/ American English • *capital of US state of Georgia*

Athene, Athena, Athina, Athenai • Greek • *Greek Goddess of Wisdom and protector of the city of Athens*

Aurelia, Auriol • Latin • *Roman family name meaning golden*

'Awātif • Arabic • *affectionate and tender*

Azucena, Susannah • Arabic/ Spanish • *madonna lily*

Beata, Beate • Swiss • *blessed*

Beatrice, Beatrix, Bea, Bee, Beattie, Beatriz, Beitiris, Betrys, Viatrix, Viator, Beatus • blessed through life

Beau • French • *beautiful and bonny girl*

Béibhin, Béibhinn, Bébhionn, Bébinn • Irish Gaelic • *white lady, fair lady*

Beile, Beyle, Beylke • Jewish/ Yiddish/Slavic • *white, pale, beautiful*

Benedicta, Benedicte, Benita • Latin • *blessed*

Bess, Bessie, Bet, Beth, Elizabeth, Elisabeth, Bethan, Betsy, Betty, Bette, Bettina, Buffy, Beitidh, Elisheba • Hebrew/Greek • *God is my oath or God is my abundance*

Bethany, Beth • Biblical/Jewish/ Hebrew • *village outside Jerusalem where Jesus stayed in Holy Week before travelling to Jerusalem for Palm Sunday; it means house of figs or dates*

Bethlehem, Belem • Biblical/ Jewish/Hebrew • *where Jesus was born*

Beulah • Biblical/Hebrew • *married*

Beverley, Beverly, Bev • Anglo-Saxon • *the stream of the beavers*

Bevin, Béibhinn • Irish Gaelic • *fair lady*

Berwen • British Welsh • *fair or white-headed*

Bethan, Beth • British/Welsh • *God is my oath or God is my abundance*

Bianca, Blanca • Italian/Spanish • *white*

Bibi • Persian • *lady of the house*

Billie • Germanic/Norman • *her helmet gives her magical protection and the will to win*

Blanche, Bianca, Blanca • pure white, blonde

Blodwen, Blodwyn, Blod • British/ Welsh • *sacred, holy flowers*

Bona, Bonus • Latin • *good*

Bonita, Bonnie, Bonny, Bonitus, Bonito • Latin/Spanish • *pretty and good*

Borghild • Norwegian • *fortified for the battle*

Brady, Braidy • Irish Gaelic • *descendant of Bradach, one of Bradach's bunch*

Branwen, Bronwen, Brangwen • British/Welsh • *raven or beast that is holy, sacred and white*

Brenna, Braonan • American English/Irish Gaelic • *descendant of Braonan; meaning moist, droplet of water*

Brittany, Britney, Britannia • Latin • *the Celtic-speaking province of north-west France, so-called due to the influx of Celts from Cornwall when the Romans invaded and who* transferred Britannia, their name for the island, across to this part of France

Brónach, Bronagh • Irish Gaelic • *sad and sorrowful*

Brooke, Brook, Broc • Anglo-Saxon • *a person who lives near a brook or stream*

Brooklyn, Lyn, Breukelen • Dutch • *a district of New York City when it was New Amsterdam under Dutch control, meaning broken land*

Brünhild, Brünhilde • Germanic • *battle armour*

Budūr, Badr • Arabic • *full moon*

Bunty, Buntie, Lamb • English • *pet name for a lamb; to bunt was to nuzzle*

Caileigh, Kayley, Kayleigh, Caleigh, Caollaidhe • Irish Gaelic • *a descendant of Caollaidhe, the prefix meaning a slender person*

Caitlín, Katherine, Aikaterine, Caitlyn, Kaitlyn, Catriona, Caitríona, Catrina, Katrina, Cáit, Caitrín, Catraoine, Kathleen, Katelyn, Cate, Ceit, Katharos • Greek/Irish Gaelic • *pure or purity*

Calaminag, Calumina, Columbine, Columba • Scots Gaelic • *dove*

Calista, Callie, Callie, Calixta, Calixtus • Latin • *cup as in a Christian chalice or holy grail*

Cameo, Cammeo • Italian/Oriental • *carving of a silhouette on a mineral such as ivory*

Camilla, Milla, Millie, Milly, Camille, Camila • Latin/French • *Roman family name*

Candice, Candace, Canditia, Candy, Candi • Latin/Ethiopian • *pure and sincere; whiter than white*

Caoilfhionn, Caoilainn, Keelin, Caolffionn • Irish Gaelic • *slender and white maiden*

Caoimhe, Keeva • Irish Gaelic • *full of grace, very lovely and so tender*

Caren, Karen, Carin, Karin, Carina, Karina • Danish/Greek • *pure or purity*

Carey, Ciardha, Carrie • English/ Irish Gaelic • *pure and descendant of Ciardha*

Caris, Charis, Karis, Carissa • Greek • *grace*

Carmel, Carmella, Carmelina, Camelita, Carmen, Carmine, Carmela • Roman Catholic • *Our Lady of Carmel, the mountain where early Christians lived as hermits and later became the Carmelite order of monks*

Casilda • Spanish • *unsure origins; an 11th-century Moorish saint, she lived in Toledo*

Catherine, Katherine, Catharine, Katharine, Cathryn, Caterina, Kathryn, Cathrine, Kathrine, Catríona, Caitríona, Catalina, Catrin • Greek • *pure or purity*

Cecilia, Cécile, Cecily, Cecelia, Cissie, Cissey, Sessy, Sissi, Sissy, Cecille, Cecilie, Cacille, Cacilia, Caecilia, Cicely • Latin/English • *old Roman family name Caecilius, from the Latin, meaning blind*

Ceinwen • British/Welsh • *lovely, beautiful, sacred and white*

Celia, Célie, Caelia, Caelum, Celina • Latin • *Roman family name meaning heaven*

Céleste, Celestine, Celestina, Celia, Celine, Marcelline, Caelius, Caelia, Caelestis • Latin • *Roman family name meaning heaven*

Céline, Caelina, Marceline, Marcelline, Caelius, Celina • Latin/French • *Roman family name meaning heaven*

Chalice • Latin • *cup as in a Christian chalice or holy grail*

Chandra • Sanskrit • *the moon*

Chandrakanta • Sanskrit • *night, time of the moon*

Chantal, Chantelle, Shantell • French • *in honour of St Jeanne-Françoise, a woman of great charity and virtue who married the Baron de Chantal; when he died she adopted a severe religious life following St Francis of Sales*

Charis, Karis, Caris, Clarissa, Charisse • Greek • *grace*

Charisma, Karrisma, Kharisma • Greek • *spiritual blessings*

Chausika • Swahili • *of the night*

Chelsea, Kelsey, Chelsey, Chelsie • Anglo-Saxon • *the chalk landing place in Chelsea, Middlesex*

Cherith, Cheryth • Biblical • *a dry riverbed at a place called Cherith*

Chevonne, Siobhán, Shivaun • English/American/Irish Gaelic • *God is gracious or gift of God*

Cheyenne, Sahiyena • French Canadian • *an Indian tribe from Dakota*

Chiara, Clare, Claire, Clara, Ciara, Kiarah, Kiara, Kiera, Clair, Clarette, Clarinda, Clarrie, Clarus • Latin/ Italian • *bright, famous, crystal-clear*

Chloe, Chloris, Cloris, Khloris, Khloe • Greek • *another name for the Goddess of Fertility, Demeter or Ceres*

Christine, Christiana, Chris, Chrissy, Christianne, Christina, Cristina, Kristina, Chriselda,

Chrissie, Christa, Christabel, Christabella, Christabelle, Cristobel, Christobel, Christelle, Christella, Christel, Christene, Christeen, Cristina, Cairistine, Cairistiòna, Crystin • Scots Gaelic/ Latin • *follower of Christ*

Christian, Christiane, Christiana, Anna, Christie, Christy, Kristy, Christina, Chris, Tina, Cristiona, Cairistiòna, Stineag, Cairistine, Crystin, Kristin, Kristina, Kerstin, Kirsten, Krzystyna, Kirsti, Kirsty, Krisztiana, Krisztina • Scots Gaelic/ Latin • *follower of Christ*

Cilla, Priscilla, Pricus, Prissy • Biblical/Latin • *Roman family name meaning ancient, old*

Ciorstaidh, Ciostag, Kirsty, Kirstie, Chirsty, Curstaidh, Curstag • Scots Gaelic/Scandinavian/Latin • *follower of Christ*

Clare, Claire, Clara, Chiara, Klara, Kiara, Clara, Kiarah • Latin/English • *bright, famous, crystal-clear*

Clarice, Claritia • Latin/French/ English • *bright, famous, crystal-clear*

Clarissa, Clarisa, Clarice, Clarrisse, Clarisse, Claris, Clarissa, Cáitir • Latin • *bright, famous, crystal-clear*

Claudia, Claudine, Claude, Claudinia, Claudette, Klavdia • Latin

Clémentine, Clem, Clemmie • Latin/French • *merciful, gentle, compassionate*

Clemency, Clemencie, Clementis • Latin • *leniency and mercy*

Clodagh • Irish Gaelic • *a river in County Tipperary*

Cody, Codi, Codie, Codee, Codey, Cuidightheach • Irish Gaelic/

American English • *descendant of Cuidightheach, a helpful and caring person*

Colleen, Coleen, Coline, Colina, Collinna, Colinette, Colinetta, Coletta, Cailin • Irish Gaelic/ American English/Australian • *ordinary girl or maiden*

Colette, Nichola, Nicola, Collette, Col, Colle, Colla, Nicolette • Greek/French • *victory for or over the people*

Columbina, Columbine, Bina, Binnie, Colimbina, Colombe • Latin • *dove*

Constance, Connie, Konnie, Constantia, Konstanze, Contanze • Latin • *constancy; steadfast and faithful*

Cornelia • Latin • *Roman family name, connected to Cornucopia and the horn of plenty*

Courtney • Norman • *the barony of Courtenay*

Crescentia, Kreszenz • Latin/ Bavarian • *growing, flourishing as in the waxing crescent moon; a positive omen*

Cyd, Syd, Sidney • Anglo-Saxon • *an ait, a small island in a river or a wide river meadow*

Cynthia, Kynthia, Kynthos, Cyndy, Cindy, Sindy, Cinzia, Chintzia • Greek • *Mount Kynthos on the island of Delos is the birthplace of Artemis, the Goddess of the Moon and the Hunt*

Dáirine, Darina • Irish Gaelic • *fertile woman*

Dale • English • *a valley dweller*

Dallas, Dallas, Dalfhas • Scots Gaelic/American/English • *the*

village of Dallas in Moray, north Britain; a place where cowpokes or drovers would rest their weary bones overnight

Dana, Ana • Irish Gaelic • *name of an ancient Celtic fertility goddess especially in Ireland*

Danae • Greek mythology • *her great-grandfather founded the Greek tribe of Danai or Argives; she was raped by Zeus/Jupiter when he appeared to her as a shower of gold, and she gave birth to the hero Perseus*

Daniella, Danielle, Danya, Daniele, Daniela • Biblical/Hebrew/Jewish • *God is my judge*

Danya, Donya • American English/ Biblical/Hebrew/Jewish • *God is my judge*

Darcy • Norman • *someone from the barony of D'Arcy*

Daria • Greek/Persian • *she who possesses, looks after the good and wellness of all*

Darya • Persian • *a good, royal ruler*

Daryl, Daryll • Norman/American/ English • *someone from D'airelle, a barony in Normandy*

Dassa, Dassah, Hadassah, Esther • Hebrew/Persian/Jewish • *Myrtle, Star and Persian Goddess of Fertility, Love and War, Ishtar*

Davina, Davida, Davena, Davinia • Biblical/Hebrew • *vague origins but possibly from a baby word meaning darling one*

Dawn, Aurora, Dawne, Duha, Dagung • Anglo-Saxon • *daybreak!*

Deanna, Diana, Deana, Artemis, Deanne, Diane • Roman mythology • *Goddess of the Moon and Hunting*

Deirdre, Deidre • Irish Gaelic • *woman*

Delphine, Delfina, Delphina • Latin • *a woman from Delphi, the place of the oracle of the Gods*

Delia, Delos • Greek • *birthplace of the goddess Artemis*

Delwyn • British/Welsh • *pretty, love, pure, sacred*

Demelza • Cornish/Kernow • *a place name in Cornwall*

Demi, Demetria • Greek • *follower of the goddess Demeter*

Desiree, Desire • Latin • *longed for!*

Devi • Sanskrit • *Her Majesty the Queen*

Devin, Damhan, Damhain • Irish Gaelic • *descendant of Damhan, connected to the fawn or deer*

Devon, Devonne • British/Welsh • *the tribe of the Dumnonos, who worshipped the Celtic god of the same name*

Dharma, Karma, Nirvana, Samsara • Sanskrit • *custom, tradition or decree from on high*

Diana, Diane, Diahann, Dianna, Dian, Dianne, Deanne, Dyan, Di, Diandrea • Roman mythology • *Goddess of the Moon and Hunting*

Dietlind • Germanic • *tender, soft and kind; people love her*

Dilwen • British/Welsh • *white, fair, true, genuine and sacred*

Dilys, Dylis, Dyllis • British/Welsh • *loyal, true and genuine*

Dionne, Deonne, Diahann • American English • *Goddess of the Moon and Hunting*

Diorbhail, Devorgilla • Scots Gaelic • *true testimony*

Disa, Hjördis, Tordis • Norse • *goddess*

Diva, Divine • Italian • *goddess!*

Dixie • American English/Cajun •

someone from the American South/
Confederate states

Dobre, Dobe, Dobro • Jewish/
Yiddish • *good and kind person*

Dolly, Dorothy, Dolores, Dora •
English/Greek • *gift from God*

Dominica, Dominique, Dominga
• Latin/Roman Catholic • *Lord,
as in St Dominic, founder of the
Dominican order*

Domitilla, Domitius • Latin • *a
Roman imperial family name*

Donatella, Donatus • Latin • *given
by God*

Donna • Italian • *lady*

**Dora, Isedore, Isadora, Theodora,
Doria, Dorinda, Dory** • Greek • *gift*

Doreen, Dorean, Dorene, Dorine •
Greek/Irish • *gift*

Dorian, Dorienne, Dorean • literary
• *dor is Greek for gift; Oscar Wilde's
invention for* The Portrait of Dorian
Gray; *most likely from the Dorian
women of southern mainland Greece*

Doris, Dorris • Greek • *a tribe of
Greece, the Dorian women from
Doros, southern mainland Greece,
from the name son of or gift to the
Hellenes*

**Dorothea, Dorothy, Dorothee,
Dorothie, Dot, Dottie, Dotty,
Dodie, Dolly, Dorofei, Dorotheos,
Dorete, Dee** • Greek • *gift from God*

Drusilla, Drausus, Drasus • Latin •
from the old Roman family name

Du'ā • Arabic • *prayer and worship*

**Ernestine, Ernestina, Earnestine,
Earnestina** • *serious and tenacious
in all things and will fight to the
death; means business to the point
of obsession*

Ebba, Eadburga • Anglo-Saxon •

prosperity, fortress

Eiddwen, Eiddunwen • British/
Welsh • *fond, passionate, desire,
holy, white, fair*

Eilwen, Aelwen • British/Welsh •
white, sacred, fair brow

Eira • British/Welsh • *snow*

Eirian • British/Welsh • *silvery
bright, beautiful*

Eirwen • British/Welsh • *pure as
snow*

Eleri • British/Welsh • *unknown
root, might be a river name*

Elaine, Helen • Greek/French
• *sunbeam, ray of sun, coming
from the name for the Greeks, the
Hellen(es)*

**Ellen, Helen, Elin, Elen, Ella, Elena,
Nell, Nelly, Nellie, Ellena, Ellenor** •
modern English • *shortened form
of Helen and Eleanor*

**Elizabeth, Elisabeth, Elisheba,
Elise, Eliza, Elisa, Elsa, Liza, Lisa,
Liz, Beth, Bet, Bess, Lisbet, Lisbeth,
Lysbeth, Elsie, Bessie, Bessy, Betty,
Betsy, Tetty, Libby, Lizzie, Lizzy,
Buffy, Eilis, Ealasaid, Elisabet,
Elisabete, Elisabetta, Elisavet,
Yelizaveta, Elzbieta, Alzbeta,
Elizabeta, Erzsebet, Elspeth, Eliza**
• Biblical/Hebrew/Jewish • *God is
my oath*

Elisha, Eleesha • Jewish/Hebrew •
Yahweh is God

Ellis • Biblical/Greek • *Yahweh is
God*

Elma • American English • *combo
of Elizabeth and Mary*

**Elspeth, Elsbeth, Elspie, Elsie,
Elspet, Elizabeth** • Scots English/
Biblical • *God is my oath*

Elva, Alva • Scots Gaelic • *white*

Élise, Elyse, Elysia, Alicia, Elisabeth

• Biblical/French • *God is my oath*
Emelia, Amelia, Emilia • Latin/
Italian • *old Roman family name
meaning rival, competitor*
Émer, Eimear, Eimer, Eimhir • Irish
• *vague origins, perhaps chastity and
purity, beauty and wisdom*
Emily, Aemilia, Aemilius, Émilie
• Latin • *old Roman family name
meaning rival, competitor*
Encarnación, Incarnatio • Roman
Catholic • *incarnation of Jesus Christ*
**Engracia, Enkrates, Encratis,
Encratia, Gratia** • Latin • *grace*
Ernesta, Ernestina, Erna, Ernestina
• German • *serious and tenacious
in all things and will fight to the
death; means business to the point of
obsession*
**Esmé, Esmee, Esmie, Aestimare,
Aestimatus, Edme** • Latin • *price-
less, highly prized and valued*
Esperanza, Sperantia • Latin • *hope
for resurrection of Jesus Christ and
life everlasting*
**Esther, Esta, Hester, Haddasah,
Eistir, Ester** • Hebrew/Persian/
Jewish • *Myrtle, Star and Persian
Goddess of Fertility, Love and War,
Ishtar*
Etta, Rosetta, Henrietta • Italian •
female
Eudocia, Eudoxia, Eudokia •
Biblical/Greek/Latin • *of fine
appearance and comfortable, easy
to be with*
Eudora, Dora, Doron • Greek •
a good gift; gift
**Eve, Eva, Aoife, Éabha, Evita,
Havva, Evie, Hayya, Eve, Evelyn,
Evelina, Eubh, Evalina, Evelina,
Aibhilin** • Biblical/Hebrew/Jewish •
mother of all life, life itself

**Evelyn, Eveline, Avaline, Ava,
Evelyne, Eveleen, Éibhleann,
Aibhilin** • English/Norman • *from
a French girl's name that became an
English surname*

Fabia, Fabienne, Fabiola • Latin •
*old Roman family name meaning a
bean*
Fadīla • Arabic • *a moral, ethical,
virtuous woman*
Faith • English • *she who trusts in
God, faithful follower*
Fakhriyya • Arabic • *this woman
is glorious and expects nothing for
nothing; everything is unconditional*
Fanny, Frances • English/Latin • *to
be French, someone from France*
Fātima • Arabic/Muslim/Roman
Catholic • *abstainer from all bad or
wicked things; mother*
Fenella, Fionnuala, Finella, Finola •
Scots Gaelic • *white, fair, shoulders*
Fern, Fearn • Anglo-Saxon • *the
plant that repels evil spirits*
Fidda, Fizza • Arabic • *silver*
Fiedhelm, Fedelma, Fidelma • Irish
• *unknown origins but given to a
beautiful Irish Bouddicca*
Fiesta, Festa • Latin/Spanish •
*celebration, particularly over a baby's
birth*
Fifi, Joséphine • French/Biblical/
Hebrew/Jewish • *short name for
Joséphine, meaning God is my
salvation*
Fiona, Fionn, Ffion • Scots Gaelic/
British Welsh • *white, fair*
**Finola, Fionnuala, Fionola, Nuala,
Finuala, Fionnguala, Fenella,
Finella, Finola** • Scots Gaelic •
white, fair, shoulders
Flavia, Favius, Flavie • Latin •

old Roman family name meaning yellow-haired

Flora, Floris, Flo, Florence, Floella, Florrie, Ffloraidh • Latin • old Roman family name meaning flower

Franca • French • a girl from France

Frances, Proinséas • English/Latin • to be French, someone from France

Francesca, France, Francene, Fran, Frances, Fanny, Françoise, Franceen, Franziska, Frankie, Francine, Francisca • Italian/Latin • to be French, someone from France

Frauke • German • a lady from northern Germany

Friedelinde • Germanic • soft, tender, gentle and peaceful

Frume, Fromm • Jewish/Yiddish • pious, devout and virtuous

Fulvia, Fulvius • Latin • an old Roman family name meaning dark, dusky, exotic

Gabrielle, Gabriella, Gabi, Gaby, Gabby, Gabriel, Gabriele, Gabriela • Biblical/Hebrew/Jewish • woman of God

Gae, Gay, Gaye • English • bright, jolly, cheery, sanguine

Gail, Gael, Abigail, Gaelle, Gaile, Gale, Gayle • Biblical/Jewish/ Hebrew • shortened Abigail: my father is joy, father is exaltation

Gauri, Gowri • Sanskrit • white

Genette, Jeanette • Biblical/ English/Latin • God is gracious or gift of God

Geneva, Geneve, Ginevra • French • after the Swiss city, or can be variant of Jennifer or short form of Geneviève

Genevieve, Jennifer, Genoveffa, Ginevra • Celtic • a female chief or leader of the tribe of people

Gerd, Gerda, Gärd, Garo • Norse • Goddess of Fertility, protection as in a fort or castle

Ghadīr • Arabic • stream, brook, watercourse

Ghufrān • Arabic • forgiveness

Giachetta • Biblical • LADY James! Supplanter, a cuckoo in the nest! Edging out someone to take their place against their will

Gillian, Gill, Jill, Gillyflower, Gillaine, Jillian, Jilly, Gilly • Latin • from Julius, a Roman name

Ginikanwa, Gini • Nigerian • what is more precious than a child?

Ginny, Virginia, Jane, Jaine, Ginnie, Jinny • Biblical/English/Latin • pet name for Virginia or Jane, meaning God is gracious or gift of God

Gioconda, Jucunda • Latin • happy, jovial, jocund

Giovanna • Biblical/English/Latin • LADY John! God is gracious or gift of God

Gita • Sanskrit • everyone sings her praises

Giuletta, Giulia • Latin/Italian • from Julius, an old Roman name

Giuseppina • Biblical/Italian • LADY Joseph! God is my salvation

Gladys, Gwladys, Gwladus • British/Welsh • uncertain origins but said to be a local form of Claudia from the old Roman family name Claudius

Glenn, Glen, Glenna, Glennette, Glenette • Scots Gaelic • valley

Glenda, Gwenda • British/Welsh • good, clean, pure and holy

Glenys, Glynis, Glennis, Glenis, Glenice, Glenise, Glennys, Glynnis • British/Welsh • pure and holy

Godiva • Anglo-Saxon/Latin •
God's gift

**Godelieve, Godliva, Godleva,
Godliob** • Germanic • *good or dear
one*

**Grace, Gracie, Gratia, Grazia,
Graziella, Gracia , Graciela** • Latin
• *grace*

**Greta, Gretta, Greet, Gretchen,
Margaretta, Margareta, Grete,
Margarette, Margarethe** • Greek/
Norman/English • *pearl*

Griet, Margriet • North Germanic
• *pearl*

**Gwen, Gwendolen, Gwendoline,
Gwenllian, Gwendolin,
Gwendolyne, Gwendolyn,
Gwenfrewi** • British/Welsh • *white*

Gwenda • British/Welsh • *a good,
holy, pure woman*

Gwendolen, Gwendoline • British/
Welsh • *white or silver sacred ring*

Gwenfrewi • British/Welsh • *time
for reconciliation*

Gwenllian • British/Welsh • *fair,
white complexion*

Gwyneira • British/Welsh • *pure as
snow*

Hadassah, Dassah, Esther •
Hebrew/Persian/Jewish • *Myrtle,
Star and Persian Goddess of Fertility,
Love and War, Ishtar*

Haidee, Aidoios • Greek/literary
• *Lord Byron named a character
Haidee in Don Juan, meaning
modest*

Hāla • Arabic • *ring or halo around
the moon*

Hannah, Hanna, Hanā • Arabic •
*blissful, happy woman filled with
wellbeing*

Hannah, Hanne, Johanna, Hanna

• Biblical/Jewish/Hebrew • *God has
favoured me*

Hanān • Arabic • *as tender as a
woman's heart*

Hansine • Germanic • *God is
gracious or gift of God*

Hefina • British/Welsh • *summer girl*

**Helen, Helena, Hélène, Elena,
Elen, Elin** • Greek/English • *ray of
sunshine, sunbeam, sunny; another
analogy is it means torch of the
moon*

Helme, Friedhelm, Helma •
Germanic • *well-protected woman
who comes in peace*

Helmina, Wilhelmina, Helmine
• Germanic • *her helmet gives her
magical protection and the will to
win*

**Hephzibah, Hepzibah, Hepsie,
Effie** • Biblical • *my delight is in her
(my newborn daughter)*

Herlinda • Germanic • *a compassionate army*

Hertha • Norse • *Norse Goddess
of Fertility*

Hester, Esther, Hettie, Hetty •
English • *Myrtle, Star and Persian
Goddess of Fertility, Love and War,
Ishtar*

Hiba • Arabic • *a gift or prize from
God*

**Hilary, Hillary, Hilarie, Hilly, Hilario,
Illaria** • Latin • *hilarious!*

Hilda, Hylda, Hilde, Elda •
Germanic • *battleaxe*

Hillevi • Danish • *safe and protected
in war*

Hope, Hopa • Anglo-Saxon •
*Christians' belief in the resurrection
and life everlasting*

Horatia • Etruscan • *Roman family
name with no certain root*

Hortense, Hortensia, Hortensius, Hortus • French/Latin • *old Roman family name meaning garden*
Huan • Chinese • *happiness*
Huiliang • Chinese • *kind and good*
Huiqing • Chinese • *kind and affectionate*
Huizhong • Chinese • *wise devotion*
Huda • Arabic • *a woman who is wise and judicious counsellor or adviser; agony aunt*

Ibtisām • Arabic • *a woman wreathed in smiles and laughter*
Ihāb • Arabic • *a gift from God*
Ihsān • Arabic • *charity, generosity*
Ilona, Helen • Hungarian • *sunbeam, ray of sun, coming from the name for the Greeks, the Hellen(es)*
Ilse, Ilsa, Elisabeth • Germanic/Biblical • *God is my oath*
Imān • Arabic • *faith, belief*
In'ām • Arabic • *a gift given or bestowed by God*
Inanna, Anna • Sumerian • *Queen of Heaven*
Inés, Inez, Agnès • Spanish/Greek • *pure and holy*
Inge, Inga, Ingeborg, Ingrid, Ingfrid, Ingetraud, Ingegerd, Ingegärd, Inger • Norse • *protected by Ing, the God of Fertility*
Ingrid • Norse • *a beautiful woman blessed by the God of Fertility, Ing*
Iona, Nonie • Latin/Gaelic • *sacred island in Hebrides in north Britain*
Ione, Nonie • English • *Ionian islands*
Isabel, Isobel, Isa, Isabella, Isabelle, Isobelle, Isobella, Izzy, Izzie, Sibéal, Iseabail, Ishbel, Isbel, Elizabeth • Spanish/Biblical/

Hebrew/Jewish • *God is my oath*
Isaura • Latin • *a woman from Isauria in Asia Minor (Turkey)*
Isla • Scots • *name of Hebridean island in north Britain*

Jacalyn, Jacqueline, Jackalyn, Jaclyn • Biblical/Latin/English • *supplanter, a cuckoo in the nest! Edging out someone to take their place against their will*
Jacqueline, Jackalyn, Jacalyn, Jacqualine, Jacqueline, Jacquelyn, Jacquelyne, Jacquiline, Jacaline, Jacuelline, Jacqueline, Jacklyn, Jaclyn, Jacki, Jackie, Jacky, Jacqui, Jacquie, Jaqui, Jaki, Jakki, Jacquelyn, Jacquelynn • Biblical/Latin/French • *supplanter, a cuckoo in the nest! Edging out someone to take their place against their will*
Jacquetta, Giachetta • Biblical/Latin/Italian • *supplanter, a cuckoo in the nest! Edging out someone to take their place against their will*
Jada, Yada • Biblical/Hebrew/Jewish • *he knows*
Jaime, Jame, Jamesina, Jamie, Jamey, Jamee, Jami, Jaimie, Jaimee • Biblical/Latin/Spanish • *supplanter, a cuckoo in the nest! Edging out someone to take their place against their will*
Jana, Yana, Jan • Biblical/English/Latin • *God is gracious or gift of God*
Jane, Jeanne, Jehanne, Jaine, Jayne, Jain, Jean, Joan, Janie, Janey, Joanna, Jaynie, Síne, Siân, Johanna, Hanne, Hansine, Johanne, Janja, Jannja, Sheena Jensine, Jonna, Jeanne, Juanna, Juana, Giovanna, Gianna, Hana, Jana, Janeen, Janelle, Jaynia •

Biblical/French/Latin • *God is gracious or gift of God*

Janet, Jannet, Janett, Janette, Jan, Janetta, Janeta, Seònaid, Shona, Seona • Biblical/English/Latin • *God is gracious or gift of God*

Janice, Janis, Janise, Jannice, Jan • Biblical/French/Latin • *God is gracious or gift of God*

Jan, Janna • Biblical/English • *God is gracious or gift of God*

Jean, Joan, Jane, Jeanne, Jehanne, Jehanna, Jeane, Jeana, Gina, Jeanna, Jeane, Jeanetta, Jeanette, Jeanie, Jeanine, Jeannette, Jeanne, Jeanett, Jenette, Jennet, Jenet, Ginett, Ginnette, Ginetta, Ginnetta, Jeannie, Jeannine, Jeannique, Jannike • Biblical/French • *God is gracious or gift of God*

Jemima • Biblical/Hebrew/Jewish • *dove; as bright as day*

Jerrie, Jerry, Geri, Gerry • Biblical/English • *appointed by God*

Jiayi • Chinese • *a woman's place is in the home*

Jiayang • Chinese • *a woman flourishes and blossoms in the home*

Jill, Jillian, Gillian, Gill, Jilly, Gilly, Jillie • Latin • *from Julius, a Roman name*

Jinghua • Chinese • *what a splendid situation!*

Jo, Joe, Joanna, Joanne, Jody, Josephine, Josie, Josey • Biblical/Greek • *God is gracious or gift of God*

Joan, Ionna, Iohanna, Joanna, Johanna, Joanne, Johanne, Joanie, Joni, Siobhán, Chevanne, Siubhan, Jane, Shevaune, Chevaune, Shona, Shevanne, Joann, Seonag

• Biblical/Norman • *God is gracious or gift of God*

Jocasta • literary Greek • *mother of Oedipus, tragic figure in classical mythology*

Jocelyn, Joselyn, Jocelyne, Joscelyn, Josceline, Joslyn, Joss, Céline, Gautzeline, Joscel, Joscein, Joscelyn • Norman • *someone from the Germanic tribe of the Gauts*

Joelle, Joël • Biblical/Hebrew/Jewish/French • *God*

Joely, Jolene, Jolie, Jollie, Joleen, Jolie, Joli, Jol • Norse/French • *pretty one; also gay and festive; yuletide*

Johanna, Johna, Johannah, Johanne, Joanna, Joanne, Jo, Jannike • Biblical/Latin • *God is gracious or gift of God*

Jonina • modern English/Biblical/English • *God is gracious or gift of God*

Jordan, Hayarden, Jordana • Hebrew/Jewish • *flowing down*

Josefa, Yosefa • Bibilical/Hebrew/Jewish • *God will provide me with another son*

Joséphine, Josefine, Josephina, Josefina, Jo, Josie, Jozie, Josette, Fifi, Posy, Josefa, Jozefa, Josée, Josiane, Seosaimhín, Josianne, Josiane • Biblical/French • *God will provide me with another son*

Joy, Joie, Gaudia • Latin/French • *joyful in the Lord*

Juan • Chinese • *gracious*

Juanita, Janita, Janita • Spanish • *God is gracious or gift of God*

Julia, Juli, Julie, Giulia, Julietta, Guilietta, Juliet, Juliette, Guiliette, Juliana, Julianus, Julianna, Julianne, Julián, Juliane, Julieann,

**Julien, Julieanne, Julienne Jools,
Julia, Jules, Juleen, Julianne** • Latin
• *a Roman family name*
June • English • *born in the month
of June*
Juno, Hera • Greek/Roman • *Queen
of the Gods, Greek and Roman
pantheon*
Juno, Úna • Irish Gaelic/Roman/
English • *uncertain roots; starvation
or lamb*
Justina, Justine • Latin • *a Roman
name*

Kailash • Sanskrit • *mountain home
of Kubera, the God of Wealth*
Kanti • Sanskrit • *you are as beau-
tiful as the moon*
Karen, Katherine, Kaz • Danish/
Greek/English • *pure or purity*
Karina, Carina • Scandinavian/
Polish/Russian/Greek/English •
pure or purity
**Katerina, Catarina, Katarina,
Katherine, Katya** • Russian/Greek •
Greek • pure or purity
Katelyn, Caitlín • Greek/Irish Gaelic
• *pure or purity*
**Katharine, Katharos, Katherine,
Aikaterine, Hecate, Kathryn,
Katharyn, Kathrin, Katherine,
Catherine, Catharine, Cathryn,
Kate, Kath, Cath, Cate, Kathy,
Cathy, Kathie, Katty, Cat, Katie,
Kitty, Caitrín, Katrine, Catraoine,
Caitlín, Catriona, Caitríona,
Catrin, Katrien, Katrijn, Katharina,
Catalina, Caterina, Ekaterini,
Yekaterina, Katerina, Katarzyna,
Katarina, Ekaterina, Kaarin,
Kaarina, Karen, Katlin, Caron,
Carin, Katha, Katheryn, Katlyn, Kit,
Katherine, Kitty, Kittie** • Greek •**

pure or purity
**Kathleen, Caitlín, Kathlene,
Cathleen, Kath, Kathy, Kathlyn,
Käthe** • Greek/Irish Gaelic • *pure
or purity*
**Katia, Katya, Yekaterina, Katja,
Katharina** • Russian/Greek • *pure
or purity*
**Katrine, Karina, Carina, Catrina,
Katrina** • Danish/German/Greek •
pure or purity
Kausalya • Sanskrit • *a member
of the Kosala family of people*
Kayla, Kayley, Kaylah • American
English • *a descendant of
Caollaidhe, the prefix meaning a
slender person*
**Kayley, Kayleigh, Kayly, Kaylie,
Kayli, Kaylee, Kaileley, Kailey,
Kaily, Kalie, Kalee, Kaleigh,
Cayleigh, Caileigh, Caleigh
Caileigh, Kayley, Kayleigh, Caleigh,
Caollaidhe, Kailey, Kayley, Kaley**
• Irish Gaelic • *a descendant of
Caollaidhe, the prefix meaning a
slender person*
Keely, Keeley, Kayley, Keighley
• Irish Gaelic • *a descendent of
Caollaidhe, the prefix meaning a
slender person*
Keila • African American • *refuge*
Kiera, Keira • Norse • *a person who
lives in marshes covered in shrubs
and brushwood*
Kenda, Kendala, Kendall • Anglo-
Saxon/British/Welsh • *someone who
worships Celtic deities, or a place in
Westmorland, Kendal, named after
River Kent*
Khadīja, Khadīga • Arabic • *a
premature baby or birth*
Khayriyya • *a woman with a chari-
table heart*

Kia, Kiaora • English/New Zealand/ Maori • *be well*

Kimberley, Kim, Kimberly, Kimberlie, Kimberlee, Kimberleigh, Kimberli, Kymberley, Kym • Anglo-Saxon/American English • *etymology is a personal name such as Kimma's wood or clearing. But gained popularity after the South African town of Kimberley where the British took on the Boers*

Kirsten, Christine, Kristine, Kerstin • Danish/Norwegian/English/ Latin • *follower of Christ*

Kirstie, Kirstin, Kirsty, Kirstie, Christine, Chirsty, Ciorstaidh, Ciorstag, Curstaidh, Curstag • Scots English • *Latin* • *follower of Christ*

Kiva • Jewish/Hebrew/Romanian • *protected one*

Klara, Clara • German/Latin • *bright, famous, crystal-clear*

Kreszenz, Crescentia • Latin/ Bavarian • *growing like the moon*

Kris, Kristina, Kristina, Kristen • Swedish/Czech/Latin • *follower of Christ*

Krista, Christa • German/Latin • *follower of Christ*

Kristie, Christie, Kirstie, Kristina, Kristy • American English • *Latin* • *follower of Christ*

Kristina, Kristine, Christine, Christina, Kristeen, Kristene, Kerstin, Kirsten, Tina • Swedish/ Czech/Latin • *follower of Christ*

Kumari • Sanskrit • *daughter or princess*

Kyla • Gaelic • *narrow in geographical terms; a region in Ayrshire*

Kyra, Kyria, Kira • Greek • *lady*

Lacey, Lassy, Lassie, Lacy • Norman/Irish • *Norman baronial*

name Lassy, who became powerful in Ireland in the medieval period

Leila, Laila, Layla, Leyla • Arabic • *a beautiful dark woman, as enchanting as the night, intoxicating*

Lara, Larissa, Larrisah • Russian/ Greek • *unsure meaning; perhaps someone from a town near Thessaloniki, in northern Greece*

Laraine, Larraine, Lareina, Lareine • African American • *the queen*

Larissa, Lara, Larry • Russian/Greek • *unsure meaning; perhaps someone from a town near Thessaloniki, in northern Greece*

Lauren, Lauryn, Loren, Lorenna, Laurenna, Laurie, Lori • Latin • *someone from Laurentum, the capital of the Latins*

Lavinia, Lavinium, Luvinia • Etruscan/Roman mythology

Layla • Arabic • *a beautiful dark woman, as enchanting as the night, intoxicating to the senses*

Leah, Léa, Lia, Azalea, Lee, Leia • Biblical/Hebrew/Jewish • *weary*

Leda • Greek mythology • *Queen of Sparta who was raped by Zeus/ Jupiter in the shape of a swan*

Leila, Laila, Layla, Leyla, Lela, Lila • Arabic • *a beautiful dark woman, as enchanting as the night, intoxicating to the senses*

Leocardia, Leukados • Latin • *clear and bright as crystal*

Leontina, Léontine • Italian/French • *family name of Leontius, meaning lion*

Lettice, Leticia, Laetitia, Letitia, Letizia, Letty, Lettie • Latin/English • *overcome with joy and happiness*

Lexie, Alexandra, Alexis, Alex, Lexy, Lexis, Leagsaidh, Lexine

• Greek • *the warrior/leader who protects or defends her people*

Líadan • Irish Gaelic • *grey*

Libby, Elizabeth • English • *God is my oath*

Lidwina, Liduina, Luzdivina • Germanic • *friendly people*

Liese, Elisabeth • German • *God is my oath*

Life, Liffey • Irish legend • *she who gave her name to a river*

Lili, Lilli, Elisabeth • German • *God is my oath*

Lilian, Lilly, Lily, Lili, Lillian, Lilium, Lily, Lillie, Lilly, Lili, Lilli • Latin/Norman • *flower that is associated with purity and resurrection*

Lina • Arabic • *a woman with the figure of a palm tree*

Linda, Belinda, Lynda, Lindie, Lindy, Lyn, Lynn, Lynne, Linden, Lin, Lyn, Lynne, Linnet, Lindsey, Lenda • Spanish/Visigothic/Germanic • *pretty, passive, tender and soft*

Linden, Linda, Lindie • Anglo-Saxon • *lime tree*

Lisa, Liza, Elyse, Lise, Liese, Élise, Elisabeth • French/German • *God is my oath*

Lisette, Lise, Elisabeth, Lysette, Lise, Lys, Liz, Lis, Elisbet, Liza, Eliza, Lisa, Lizzie, Lizzy, Lizi, Elizabeth • English/French • *God is my oath*

Livia, Livius • Latin • *Roman family name Livius, uncertain origin but maybe means a hue of the colour blue*

Logan • Scots • *Scottish surname based on place in Ayrshire*

Lone, Abelone, Magdelone • Danish • *Mary Magdelene aka Mary of Magdala, woman healed of evil spirits*

Lorinda • American English • *combo of Laura and Linda*

Lorna, Lorne, Latharna • English/Scots Gaelic • *Scottish place name Lorne, Argyll*

Lorraine, Lotharingia, Lorrain, Lorrayne, Lori, Lorri • Germanic/Lotharigian • *land of the people of Lothar and his famous army*

Lourdes, Lurdes • Roman Catholic • *a French place of pilgrimage where a young girl had visions of the Virgin*

Lucretia, Lucrece, Lucrezia, Lucretius • Latin • *Roman family name*

Lujayn • Arabic • *silver*

Luli • Chinese • *dewy jasmine*

Lydia, Lydie • Greek • *woman from Lydia*

Lynette, Lynette, Linnet, Linotte, Linnette, Linette • Spanish/French

Lyudmila, Lyuda, Ludmil • Slavic • *a tribe of kind people, a family of gracious folks*

Mabel, Mab, Amabel, Amabilia, Mabilia, Mabelle, Amiabel, Maybelle, Maybella • Norman/English • *lovely*

Macey, Masey, Macie, Macy, Maci, Macciacum • Norman/Latin • *someone from Massey, Normandy*

Madeleine, Madelaine, Magdalene, Magdala, Madelene, Madlyn, Madelyn, Madalene, Madaline, Madoline, Magdalen, Maddie, Maddy, Maddalena • Biblical/French • *Mary Magdelene aka Mary of Magdala, woman healed of evil spirits*

Madonna, Madge • American Italian • *my lady*

Madrona, Matrona • Jewish • *from the name Matron, a wish for the baby girl to become a mother herself*
Mairwen • British/Welsh • *white and pure virgin*
Magali, Magalie • Provençal • *pearl*
Magda, Magdalene, Magadelena, Lena • Biblical/Slavic/German • *Mary Magdelene aka Mary of Magdala, woman healed of evil spirits*
Maggie, Margaret, Magaidh • Scots Gaelic/Greek/Latin/Norman • *pearl*
Mahalia, Mahalah, Mahali • Biblical/Jewish/Hebrew/Aramaic • *unsure; either tender or marrow – perhaps tender down to her marrow!*
Mahāsin • Arabic • *charming and admirable qualities*
Mai, Maria, Margit • Scandinavian • *combo of Maria/Mary and Margaret*
Maisie, Margaret, Mairéad, Maisy • Greek/Scots Gaelic/English • *pearl*
Maitland, Maltalent, Mautalent • Anglo-Saxon/Norman • *bad-tempered or from Mautalant, a barren place in France*
Malati • Sanskrit • *she is like the jasmine, she is even more beautiful at night*
Malikiya • Swahili • *my queen*
Malkah, Malka • Jewish/Hebrew • *queen*
Mallory, Malerie, Mallery • Norman
Mame, Mamie Margaret, Mary • American English • *short for Margaret or Mary*
Manon, Marie • Biblical/French • *pet name for Marie*
Manuela • Biblical/Spanish • *God is with us or amongst us*
Maoilosa • Irish Gaelic • *follower of Jesus Christ*
Mara, Naomi • Biblical/Jewish/

Hebrew • *bitter*
Margaret, Margeurite, Margarita, Margarites, Margaron, Pearl, Marina, Margery, Marjory, Marjorie, Magarette, Margaretta, Meg, Peg, Madge, Marge, Maggie, Meg, Meggie, Peggy, Peggie, Peggi, Margie, May, Daisy, Mairéad, Mairghead, Mared, Marged, Marget, Mererid, Margaretha, Margareta, Margarethe, Margrit, Margret, Meta, Margriet, Margrethe, Marit, Merete, Mereta, Mette, Margeurite, Margarita, Margarida, Margherita, Margareta, Malgorzata, Marketa, Marketta, Margrieta, Margarita, Margaretha, Margherita, Margrethe, Margit, Maighread, Maretta, Mared, Marged • Greek • *pearl*
Margot, Margaux, Marguerite, Margarete, Margit • French/Greek/Latin/Norman • *pearl*
Margery, Marjorie, Marjorie, Marjory, Marjie, Margaret, Margery, Margie, Marjy, Marji, Marga, Marge, Marsaili • Greek/English
María José • Roman Catholic • *combo of Mary the Virgin and Joseph the father*
Marie • French • *Virgin Mary, special patroness of France*
Marietta, Mariella, María, Mairéad, Margaret, Mariette, Maretta • Biblical/Italian • *Mary Magdelene aka Mary of Magdala, woman healed of evil spirits*
Marina, Marinus, Marius, Marna • Latin • *Roman family name; clouded meaning but associated with someone of or from the sea*

Marla, Marlene, Magdalene •
modern • *Mary Magdelene aka
Mary of Magdala, woman healed
of evil spirits*

Marlene, Maria, Magdalena •
German • *Mary Magdelene aka
Mary of Magdala, woman healed
of evil spirits*

Marna, Marnie • Swedish/Latin
• *Roman family name; clouded
meaning but associated with
someone of or from the sea*

Marsha • Anglo-Saxon • *a person
who lives on marshy ground or fen
land*

**Martha, Marthe, Marthja, Martja,
Märta, Martta** • Biblical/Aramaic
• *lady*

Matrona • Latin • *lady*

**Meg, Margaret, Mag, Magg,
Maggie, Megan, Meggie** • Greek/
Latin/English • *pearl*

**Megan, Meg, Meghan, Meaghan,
Meagan, Marged, Margaret** •
Greek/Gaelic • *pearl*

Mehetabel, Mehitabel • Biblical/
Jewish/Hebrew • *God makes happy*

Mehjibin • Persian • *she has a face
that is as beautiful as the temples of
the moon*

Meinwen • British/Welsh • *thin,
slender, pale and white*

Meirong • Chinese • *beautiful soul
and personality*

Meixiu • Chinese • *beautiful grace*

Mercedes • Roman Catholic • *Our
Lady of Mercies, alluding to the
Virgin Mary*

Mercedes, Merche, Mercy, Mary •
Spanish • *Mary of Mercies*

Mercia, Mercy, Mecedes, Merces
• Latin • *showing compassion for
others' plight*

**Merete, Margareta, Mereta, Mette,
Meta** • Greek/Latin/Danish • *pearl*

Michaela, Mikayla, Mica, Micah •
Biblical/Hebrew/Jewish/English •
who is like God?

Michal • Biblical/Jewish/Hebrew •
brook

**Michele, Michelle, Michel, Chelle,
Shell, Micheline** • Biblical/Hebrew/
Jewish/English • *who is like God?*

Mignon, Mignonette, Minette •
French • *little darling, cutie, sweetie*

**Mildred, Mildpryd, Mildburh,
Mildgyd** • Anglo-Saxon • *a gentle
strength*

Milla, Camilla, Camille • Latin/
French • *Roman family name;
perfection*

Millena, Milenna • Czech • *grace
and favour*

Mingzhu • Chinese • *bright pearl*

Minnie, Wilhelmina • Germanic/
Norman • *her helmet gives her
magical protection and the will to
win*

**Mireille, Mireio, Miriam, Mary,
Miranda, Mireio, Mirella** •
Provençal • *to admire*

Missy, Missie • American English •
mistress!

**Monica, Monere, Monique,
Monika** • Latin/Phoenician •
cautious counsel, to advise or warn

Morag, Mór, Móirín, Moreen • Irish
Scots Gaelic • *great, large, huge*

Muhayya • Arabic • *she has such a
lovely, beautiful face*

Muhsina • Arabic • *a charitable,
kind and compassionate woman*

Myfanwy, Myf • British/Welsh •
your lady, your woman

Nadira, Nadra • Arabic • *a woman who is rare and precious*

Nāhid • Arabic • *a girl who is becoming a woman*

Naʿīma • Arabic • *a woman who is contented and happy*

Najāt, Nagāt • Arabic • *a woman who has been saved, rescued or redeemed, or helps others to confess*

Najwa, Nagwa • Arabic • *secrets abound, a woman who is discreet and confidential, keeper of secrets*

Nan, Nancy, Nanette, Ann • Biblical/Jewish/Hebrew • *pet form of Ann, of uncertain origins: God has favoured me*

Nancy, Nan, Ann, Annis, Agnès, Nancie, Nanci, Nance • Biblical/Jewish/Hebrew • *pet form of Ann, of uncertain origins: God has favoured me*

Nanette, Nan • Biblical/Jewish/Hebrew/French • *pet form of Ann, of uncertain origins: God has favoured me*

Naomi, Noémie, Noemi • Biblical/Hebrew/Jewish • *pleasant and good*

Nápla, Annabel, Anabl, Anable, Anaple, Amable • Norman/English/Irish • *lovely*

Natalia, Natalya, Natalie, Natasha • Latin/Russian • *the birth of Jesus Christ or reborn with faith*

Natalie, Nathalie, Natalia • Latin/French • *the birth of Jesus Christ or reborn with faith*

Natasha, Natalia, Noel • Latin/Russian • *the birth of Jesus Christ or reborn with faith*

Nazaret, Nazareth • Roman Catholic • *Jesus Christ's native village*

Nerina, Nerine, Nereus • Greek/Latin • *sea god/family name Nero or Nerio*

Nerys • British/Welsh • *lady*

Nesta, Nester, Nostos, Agnès • British Welsh/Greek • *pure and holy*

Ngaio • New Zealand Maori • *a clever tribe or people*

Nichola, Nicola, Nicki, Nicky, Nicolasa • Greek/English • *victory for or over the people*

Nihād • Arabic • *ground that resembles a female's breasts and contours*

Nilsine, Nicola • Norwegian/Swedish/Greek • *victory for or over the people*

Niʿmat • Arabic • *a woman who is good to have around*

Niu • Chinese • *I am a girl*

Noelle • Latin/Norman • *nativity of Christ: Christmas*

Nóra, Honora, Norah, Nonie • Irish Gaelic/Latin • *an honoured woman*

Noreen, Nóirín, Norene, Norine, Honoria • Irish Gaelic/Latin • *an honoured woman*

Normina • *a man from the north; Norseman or Viking*

Nyamekye • Ghanaian • *given by God*

Oksana, Oxana • Russian • *praise God*

Olive, Olivia, Oliff, Oliffe, Oliva • Latin • *olive tree, a symbol of peace and abundance*

Olwen, Olwin, Olwyn • footprint, path, white, sacred

Olufemi • Nigerian • *God loves me*

Ophelia, Ophelos • Italian/Greek • *help!*

Oralie, Aurelie, Aurelia, Oralee • Latin/French • *Roman family name meaning golden*

Órla, Ona, Anona, Fíona, Honor, Orfhlaith, Orflaith, Orlaith • Irish Gaelic

Owena • British/Welsh • *born of Esos or Aesos, Celtic deity*

Paleley • Sudanese • *sweet*

Paloma, Palumba • Latin • *dove*

Payton, Peyton • Anglo-Saxon • *Paega's village or hamlet*

Pearl, Perle, Peninnah, Perla • Jewish/Hebrew • *pearl*

Peg, Peggy, Peggi, Margaret, Meg, Pegeen, Peigín, Peig, Peigi • Greek/Latin/Norman • *pearl*

Peninnah, Pen, Pearl, Perle, Peninna, Penina • Biblical/Hebrew/Jewish • *coral or pearl, beautiful pink underwater mineral found in warm water*

Pernilla, Pella, Pernille, Petronel, Petronilla • Latin/Greek/Swedish

Petronilla, Petronel, Petronella, Petronius • Latin • *a Roman family name, Petronius, that could be connected to St Peter*

Persis • Biblical/Greek • *a Persian woman*

Petula, Pet, Petulare • Latin/Christian • *to ask or plead humbly for mercy or forgiveness*

Phoebe, Phoibos, Phoebus • Latin/Greek • *bright, Goddess of the Moon*

Phyllis, Phillida, Phyllis, Phyllidos, Phyllidis, Phyllida, Phyllicia, Phylicia • Greek mythology • *a Thracian queen, Phyllis died for love and transformed herself into an almond tree; her name means leaves or leaf and she is a symbol of undying love and friendship*

Pia, Pius • Italian • *pious*

Piedad • Roman Catholic • *Our Lady of Piety*

Portia, Porcia, Porcius, Porcus, Porsha • Latin • *Roman family name of Porcus, meaning pig*

Posy, Posey, Josephine, Poesy • Biblical/English • *God will provide me with another son*

Precious • American English • *dear, beloved, a precious child*

Prisca, Priscilla, Priscus • Biblical/Latin • *Roman family name meaning ancient or old*

Priscilla, Cilla, Prissy, Priscus • Biblical/Latin • *Roman family name meaning ancient or old*

Purificación • Roman Catholic/Spanish • *Feast of the Purification when Virgin purges of the uncleanliness associated with childbirth*

Purnima • Sanskrit • *full moon*

Queenie, Victoria, Cwene, Cwen • Anglo-Saxon/English • *popular name for Victoria*

Qingge • Chinese • *crystal house*

Qingzhao • Chinese • *clear understanding, crystal illumination*

Qiuyue • Chinese • *autumn moon*

Rachel, Rachael, Rachelle, Rae, Rella, Ráichéal, Rachele, Rakel • Biblical/Hebrew/Jewish • *ewe (female sheep)*

Radwa • Arabic • *an area in the holy city of Mecca*

Rafferty, Rabhartaigh, Robhartach • Irish Gaelic • *descendant of Robhartaigh*

Ragnborg, Ramborg • Norse • *decisions and protection from the gods*

Raine, Reine, Rayne, Regina • French/Germanic • *queen*

Rajani, Rajni • Sanskrit • *something*

of the night... as dark as night
Rajni • Sanskrit • *queen of the night*
Ramona • Catalan/Visigothic •
adviser, protector
Raquel, Raquelle, Rachel • Biblical/
Hebrew/Jewish • *ewe (female sheep)*
Ravenna • Italian • *an Italian city;*
someone from Ravenna, the capital
of Roman mosaic
Renée, Reenie, Rena, Renatus,
Renata, Serena, Rina • Latin •
reborn; resurrected
Refugio • Roman Catholic • *Our*
Lady of the Refuge
Regina, Queenie, Raine, Régine,
Raghnailt, Ragnhild • Latin/Roman
Catholic • *queen (of heaven)*
Renata, Renée, René, Renate •
Latin • *reborn*
Rhea, Silvia • Latin/Roman
mythology • *mother of Romulus and*
Remus, founders of Rome
Rhianna, Rhiannon, Reanna,
Rianna, Rhianon, Riannon,
Rheanna, Rigantona, Rhianna,
Reanne, Rhiannon, Rigantona •
British Welsh/Celtic mythology •
great queen
Rhona, Rona • Scots • *name of*
Hebridean island off northern
Britain
Rida • Arabic • *one who has God's*
(Allah's) approval
Rigborg • Danish/Germanic • *forti-*
fied and powerful
Riley, Rileigh, Ryley, Reilly,
Rygelegh, Roghallach • Anglo-
Saxon/Irish Gaelic • *a field where*
the rye crop has been cleared
Rīm • Arabic • *white antelope*
Ríonach, Rina, Caterina, Katerina,
Carina, Sabrina, Regina, Ríona,
Rio, Rioghnach, Rinach • Irish

Gaelic • *royalty; like a queen*
Rio • Portuguese/Spanish • *river*
Rochelle, Rachelle • Germanic/
French/American English • *rest a*
while
Rocio • Roman Catholic • *Our Lady*
of the Dews, or tears shed for the
wickedness of the world
Rosalba • Italian • *rose white*
Rosalind, Rosaleen, Rosalyn,
Roslind, Rosaline, Rosalin,
Rosalynne, Rosalynn • Germanic/
Frankish • *horse, tender and soft,*
passive and weak
Rou • Chinese • *mild and gentle*
Rowen, Ruadhan • Gaelic/English •
descendant of Ruadhan, little red one
Roxanne, Roxane, Roxana,
Roxanna, Roxy, Rozanne • Latin/
Greek/Persian • *dawn*
Ryanne, Ryan, Riain • Irish Gaelic/
English • *little king, descendant of*
Riain

Sabāh • Arabic • *morning*
Sabrina • Celtic mythology • *from*
the river goddess who lived in the
River Severn
Sadie, Sarah, Sara, Sarai • English •
pet form of Sarah
Safā • Arabic • *a pure, chaste woman*
who is sincere and goodly
Sahar • Arabic • *morning has*
broken, dawn
Salha • Arabic • *devoted and*
dedicated
Sally, Sal, Sarah • English • *another*
name for Sarah, princess
Salma • Arabic • *a person who looks*
after those she loves; a protector
Salwa • Arabic • *she who consoles*
others and gives a shoulder to cry on
Samantha, Sam, Sammy, Sammi •

Biblical/Hebrew/Jewish • *the name of God, God has heard, listen to God*
Sandra, Sandy, Alessandra, Alexandra, Sandi, Saundra, Sander • the warrior/leader who protects or defends her people
Sandhya • Sanskrit • *twilight of the gods, devout, ritualistic*
Sarabeth • American English • *combo of Sara and (Eliza)beth*
Sarah, Sara, Zara, Sally, Sadie, Sari • Biblical/Jewish/Hebrew • *princess*
Sarita, Sarah • Biblical/Spanish • *princess*
Sasha, Alexandra, Sashura, Shura • Greek • *the warrior/leader who protects or defends her people*
Saskia, Sachs • Dutch/Germanic • *Saxon, the tribe*
Sayidana • Swahili • *our princess*
Sebastienne • Latin/French • *a man from Sebaste in Asia Minor (now Turkey)*
Selina, Selena, Selene, Slie, Sly • Greek • *Goddess of the Moon*
Séverine, Severina, Severa • Latin • *Roman family name, austere, severe*
Shae, Shea, Séaghdha • Irish Gaelic • *descendant of Séaghdha*
Shafiqa • Arabic • *a compassionate, charitable woman*
Shakira • Arabic • *thankful and grateful*
Shana, Shanae, Shania, Shanee, Siani, Siân • American English/British Welsh • *God is gracious or gift of God*
Shane • Irish Gaelic/English • *supplanter, a cuckoo in the nest! Edging out someone to take their place against their will*
Shannagh, Shannah, Seanaigh, Seanach • Irish Gaelic • *surname;*

descendant of Seanach
Shoshanna, Shoshana, Shannah, Susanna • Biblical/Jewish/Hebrew • *the flower lily, which means rose in modern Hebrew*
Sharmila • Sanskrit/Hindi • *she who is selfless, modest and protective*
Shaughan, Shaun, Shaughn, Shawn • Irish Gaelic/English • *supplanter, a cuckoo in the nest!*
Silver, Silvette, Argentia • Anglo-Saxon • *silver, the metal*
Silvius • Latin • *someone who loves or inhabits the woods or forest*
Simone • Biblical/Hebrew/Jewish • *hearkening, hearing*
Sinéad, Janet, Jeanette, Seònaid, Shona, Seona • English/Scots Gaelic • *God is gracious or gift of God*
Siobhán, Joan, Jehanne, Shevaun, Chevonne, Chevaun, Chevaunne, Shevaunne, Jehanne, Joan • English/Norman French/Biblical/Irish Gaelic • *God is gracious or gift of God*
Sioned, Janet • English/British Welsh • *God is gracious or gift of God*
Sissy, Sisi, Sissey, Sissie, Elisabeth • Jewish/Hebrew/Bavarian • *God is my oath*
Sissel, Cecily • Scandinavian/English • *old Roman family name Caecilius, from the Latin, meaning blind*
Siv • Norse • *bride or wife, name of Thor's golden-haired missus*
Siwan, Joan • British/Welsh • *sea trout*
Sky, Skye • Gaelic • *take your pick, the sky as in heaven or Skye as in the island in Scotland*

Slane, Slaney Irish Gaelic •
descendant of Sluaghadhan
Socorro • Roman Catholic • *Our
Lady of Perpetual Succour*
Sondra, Sandra • American English
• *modern name for Sandra*
Solange, Sollemnia, Sollemna •
Latin • *solemn*
Solveig, Solvig, Solvej • Norse •
strength through the family or home
Sroel, Israel • Jewish/Yiddish • *one
who strives with God*
Sultana • Arabic • *empress, queen*
Sukie, Sukey, Susan • English • *pet
form of Susan*
Sumati • Sanskrit • *good thoughts,
devout in prayer*
Summer, Haf, Sumor • Anglo-
Saxon • *someone born in the
summer months*
Sunny, Sunnie • English • *cheery,
cheerful, full of joy; a sunny
disposition*
**Susan, Susanna, Suzan, Sue, Su,
Soo, Susie, Suzie, Susy, Suzy,
Sukie, Sukey, Siùsan, Sue, Susan,
Susanna, Susannah, Suzanne, Su,
Soo** • English/Biblical • *the flower
lily, which means rose in modern
Hebrew*
**Susanna, Shoshana, Shoshan,
Susana, Suzanna, Suzannah,
Susannah, Siùsan, Siusaidh,
Susanne, Suzanne, Zuzanna,
Zuzana, Suzana, Zsuzsanna,
Susann, Susi, Sanna, Zanna** •
Biblical/English • *lily*
Susie, Suzie, Susi • English • *short
form of Susan or Susannah*
Suzanne, Susanna, Suzette, Suzie
• Biblical/French • *the flower lily,
which means rose in modern Hebrew*
Svea • Swedish • *patriotic name for*
Sweden
**Sybil, Sybille, Sybilla, Sibylla,
Sibilia, Sibella, Sibéal, Cybille,
Sibilla, Sibella, Cybil, Cybill** • Greek
mythology • *a woman with the
power to predict; a devotee of Apollo,
the sun god*
Sydney, Sid, Sidney • Anglo-Saxon
• *an ait, a small island in a river or a
wide river meadow*
**Sylvia, Silvia, Sylvie, Silvia, Sylvia,
Sylve** • Latin/English/French/Italian
• *Rhea Silvia: mother of the founders
of Rome*

Talia, Talya, Natalya, Thalia • Latin/
Russian • *the birth of Jesus Christ or
reborn with faith*
Talitha • Biblical/Aramaic • *little girl*
Tallulah, Talulla, Tuilelaith • Irish
Gaelic/English • *abundance, lady
and princess*
Tanya, Tania, Tanja • Latin • *Sabine
Roman family name*
Tara • Sanskrit • *a shining star who
carries the troubles of the world on
her shoulders*
Tasha, Natasha • Latin • *the birth of
Jesus Christ or reborn with faith*
Tate, Tata • Anglo-Saxon • *personal
name of an Anglo-Saxon*
**Tatiana, Tanya, Tatyana, Tatianus,
Tatius** • Latin/Russian • *Sabine
Roman family name, Tatius, of vague
origins*
Teleri • British/Welsh • *your river*
Tempe, Temnein • Greek • *a valley
in Greece; the legendary home of the
Muses, the nine goddesses of the arts
and sciences*
Terri, Terry, Theresa, Terryl •
Latin/Irish Gaelic • *from the Roman
family name Terentius and Irish for*

someone who takes the initiative
Thanā • Arabic • *a woman ready to praise and be praised; everything she does deserves praise*
Thea, Dorothea • Greek • *short name for Dorothea*
Thecia, Theokleia • Greek • *glory of God*
Theda, Teud, Theodosia • Latin • *people, tribe or race*
Themba • Zulu • *trusted*
Theodora, Dora, Teodora, Feodora • Greek • *God-given or giving to God or God's gift*
Theodosia, Dosy, Theodosis • Greek • *God-given*
Theokleia, Thecia, Tekla • Greek • *glory of God*
Thurayya, Surayya • Arabic • *coping with sorrow and sadness*
Tirion • British/Welsh • *kind and gentle*
Tirzah, Tirza, Thirzah, Thirza • Biblical/Hebrew/Jewish • *a delightful woman*
Tita • Latin • *old Roman name, unknown*
Toni, Tonia, Tonia, Tonya, Antonia, Antoinette • Estruscan/Roman • *Roman family name but with confused origins*
Topaz • Biblical/Hebrew/Greek • *God is good*
Tordis • Norse • *goddess connected to Thor*
Tracey, Trace, Tracie, Tracy • Latin/ Gaulic • *a person from a place in Normandy called Tracy!*
Trixie, Trix, Trix, Beatrix, Beatrice • *blessed through life*
Tuilelaith, Talulla, Talullah • Irish Gaelic • *a lady of abundance*

'Umayma • Arabic • *little mother*
'Um-Kalthūm • Arabic • *mother of a little cherub!*
Ummi • Swahili • *my mother*
Úna, Unity, Oona, Oonagh, Euna • Irish Gaelic • *uncertain roots; hungry or lamb*
Usha • Sanskrit • *Goddess of the Dawn*
Ute, Uda • Germanic • *heritage, roots, belonging*

Valérie, Valeria, Valère, Val • French/Latin • *old Roman name Valerius meaning healthy, robust and strong*
Venetia, Venice, Venezia • Italian • *someone from Venice, celebrating the city of Venezia*
Vera, Verus • Slavic • *a woman with faith*
Verona, Veronica • Italian/English • *someone from the city of Verona*
Vesta, Hestia • Latin • *Roman Goddess of the Hearth; Hestia is the same in the Greek pantheon*
Vienna, Wien, Vindo, Vianna • Celtic • *white*
Vimala • Sanskrit • *a peerless person, pure as crystal*
Virginia, Verginius, Ginny, Ginnie, Virginie • Latin • *Roman family name Vergilius but confusion reigned when the spelling was changed to Virgilius which means the maiden or virga as in stick*
Virtudes • Roman Catholic/Spanish • *seven Christian virtues*
Visitacion • Roman Catholic/ Spanish • *the Virgin Mary visits her sister Elisabeth*
Vivienne, Vivien, Viv, Vi, Vivi, Vivienne, Vivianne, Béibhinn • Latin/Norman

Vivien, Vivian, Vivienne, Béibhinn • Celtic/Irish Gaelic/Arthurian Legend • *white or fair lady*

Wafā • Arabic • *a faithful, loyal, devoted woman*

Wanda, Wenda, Wendelin • Germanic/Polish/Slavic • *a member of the Slav tribe living between the Elbe and Oder*

Weici • Chinese • *a mother's love*

Whitney, Whitley, Witney, Hwitleah, Whiteney • Anglo-Saxon • *the white island*

Widād • Arabic • *an affectionate, friendly girl*

Wilhelmina, Mina, Minnie, Billie, Wilma • Germanic/Norman

Willow, Welig • Anglo-Saxon • *the tree that loves water and ruled by the moon*

Wanda, Wenda, Wendelin • Germanic/Polish/Slavic • *a member of the Slav tribe living between the Elbe and Oder*

Xaveria • Roman Catholic/Basque • *the new house*

Xenia • Greek • *hospitality and a welcome to or from a stranger or foreigner*

Xiaodan • Chinese • *little dawn*

Xiaofan • Chinese • *rather ordinary or ordinary dawn*

Xiaosheng • Chinese • *small at birth*

Xiaowen • Chinese • *morning clouds*

Xue • Chinese • *snow meaning white, pure as the driven stuff*

Xueman • Chinese • *snowy composure and grace*

Ya • Chinese • *grace*

Yana, Jana • Biblical/English/Latin • *God is gracious or gift of God*

Yejide • Nigerian • *the image of her mother*

Yekaterina, Aikaterine, Katherine • Greek/Russian • *pure or purity*

Yelena, Helen, Helena • Russian/Greek • *ray of sunshine, sunbeam, sunny; another analogy is it means torch of the moon*

Yelisaveta, Elisabeth • Hebrew/Jewish • *God is my oath*

Yentl, Gentille • French/Jewish/Yiddish • *kind, goodly*

Ysuelt, Isolde • French/British Welsh • *a beautiful Irish princess*

Yue • Chinese • *moon*

Yun • Chinese • *cloud*

Yusheng • Chinese • *jade birth*

Zakiyya • Arabic • *a woman who is innocent and pure*

Zélie, Célie, Celia, Zaylie, Zaylee, • French/Latin • *Roman family name meaning heaven*

Zelah • Biblical/Hebrew/Jewish • *literal meaning is 'side'; one of the 14 cities of the tribe of Benjamin*

Zena, Zina, Alexina • Russian/Greek • *descended from Zeus*

Zina, Zinaida • Greek • *descended from Zeus*

Ziska, Zissi, Franziska • German • *to be French, someone from France; especially 14th July*

Zita, Zeta, Zetein, Zitta • Tuscan • *wee girl*

Zula • South African/Zulu • *someone from the Zulu tribe*

LEO

24th July to 23rd August

Planet: Sun

Day: Sunday

Stone: ruby

Metal: gold

Colours: gold, golden yellow, amber, yellow, flame red and orange

Design: all bold shapes, designs and contours coming out from a strong motif/motifs

Trees: all trees that flourish in hot climates, citrus trees (apart from lime and lemon), bay, laurel, palm

Flora: daisy, dandelion, sunflower, marigold, bougainvillea, hibiscus, sundew, celandine, larkspur, goldenrod, heliotropes, passion flower, narcissus, heartsease

Celebrity Leos: Princess Anne • Neil Armstrong • Lucille Ball • Ethel Barrymore • William 'Count' Basie • Menachem Begin • George Bernard Shaw • Madame Helena Blavatski • Ann Blyth • Napoleon Bonaparte • Clara Bow • Emily Brontë • Keith Carradine • Fidel Castro • Coco Chanel • Bill Clinton • Davy Crockett • Cecil B DeMille • Robert De Niro • Dolores del Rio • Madame du Barry • Alexandre Dumas • Amelia Earhart • Queen Elizabeth (the Queen Mother) • Eddie Fisher • Sir Ian Fleming • Henry Ford • Kathie Lee Gifford • Robert Graves • Alex Haley • George Hamilton • Mata Hari • Alfred Hitchcock • Timothy Hutton • Dustin Hoffman • Herbert Hoover • Whitney Houston • John Huston • Aldous Huxley • Mick Jagger • Magic Johnson • Carl Jung • Jacqueline Kennedy Onassis • T E Lawrence • Jennifer Lopez • Myrna Loy • Madonna • Princess Margaret • Benito Mussolini • Ogden Nash • Annie Oakley • Peter O'Toole • Roman Polanski • Beatrix Potter • Robert Redford • Sir Joshua Reynolds • Kenny Rogers • Susan Saint James • Jill Saint John • Arnold Schwarzenegger • Norma Shearer • Martin Sheen • Percy Bysshe Shelly • Christian Slater • Wesley Snipes • Yves St Laurent • Patrick Swayze • Claus von Bülow • Alfred Lord Tennyson • Andy Warhol • Shelley Winters • Orville Wright

Planetary Influences: see Sun at the back of this book (pages 456)

Boys

Abner, Avner • Biblical/Hebrew • *father of light*

Abram • Biblical/Hebrew • *high father*

Achim, Akim, Joachim, Akim, Yakim • Hebrew/Jewish • *made and created by God*

Adelard, Adelhard • Germanic • *what a strong looking and noble boy*

Aeneas, Aineas, Ainein, Angus • Greek • *singing praises*

Aiden, Áidàn, Aedan, Aodhán, Aoghan, Aodhagán, Edan, Eden, Aeddan • Irish Gaelic • *fire god*

'Alā • Arabic • *excellent and supreme*

Alastair, Alistair, Allaster, Alec, Alaois, Alexander, Alasdair, Sandy • Scots Gaelic/Greek • *the man/warrior/leader who protects or defends his people*

Albert, Albrecht, Adalbert, Adalbrecht, Adelbrecht, Alberto, Albeart, Adalberht, Al, Bert, Albie, Alby, Bertie, Athelbert • French/Germanic/Anglo-Saxon • *bright and noble*

Aldo, Adal • Germanic • *noblesse oblige*

Alexander, Alexandre, Alexis, Alastair, Alasdair, Sandy, Alessandro, Alessio, Aleksandr, Aleksei, Alejandro, Alejo, Alec, Alick, Alex, Sandaidh, Lexy, Lexie, Alastar, Alasdair, Alistair, Aleixandre, Aleksandar, Aleksanteri, Sandor, Alick, Ailig, Alec • Greek • *the man/warrior/leader who protects or defends his people*

Alfonso, Alphonse, Alonso, Alonzo • Spanish/Visigothic • *royal at the ready*

Alfonso, Alphonse, Adalfuns, Alphonsus, Anluan, Fonzie, Fonsie, Fonso • Spanish/Visigothic • *ready for battle, noble fighter, proactive!*

Algernon, Algy, Algie • Norman • *a man with a moustache/hairy faced*

'Ali • Arabic • *the most sublime*

Alistair, Alasdair, Alisdair, Alastair, Alister, Alaster, Allaster, Alistair • Scots Gaelic/Greek • *the man/warrior/leader who protects or defends his people*

Amadeus, Amédée, Gottlieb, Amedeo • Latin/Germanic • *Love God or God of Love!*

Amador, Amator • Spanish • *lover*

Amancio • Latin • *loving*

Amato, Amatus, Amado • Latin • *beloved*

Amias • French/Biblical/Hebrew • *someone from Amiens in Picardie or Love God*

Amīr • Arabic • *ruler, prince, caliph or prosperous, wealthy*

Armitabh • Sanskrit • *eternal splendour*

Amjad, Amgad • Arabic • *glorious*

Amnon • Biblical/Jewish/Hebrew • *faithful, loyal*

Amos • Biblical/Jewish/Hebrew • *to carry the Lord like St Christopher*

Amrit • Sanskrit • *immortal, divine foods*

Anatole, Anatoly, Anatoli • Greek • *sunrise*

Andrew, André, Andreas, Andries, Aindréas, Aindriu, Andrea, Andrei, Anders, Aindrea, Anndra, Andrés, Andras, Andre, Drew, Andy, Aindrias, Aindriu, Aindrea, Anndra, Andras, Andries, Andrei,

Andrzej, Jedrzej, Andrej, Ondrej, Andrija, Antero, Endre, Andrius, Andrejs • Biblical/Greek • *a real sexy, macho man*

Angus, Aonghas, Aengus, Angie, Angaidh, Gus • Scots Gaelic • *Celtic god, there is only one choice*

Annibale, Hannibal, Hannbaal • *winning the favour of the chief or the lord*

Antip, Antipas, Antipater • *just like your father!*

Aodh, Áed • Irish Gaelic • *fire, Celtic sun god*

Apollinaire, Apollo, Apollinaris • Italian/Greek • *Apollo, sun god*

Apollo, Apollinaris, Apollone • Latin/Greek • *God of the Sun*

Arduino, Hartwinn • Germanic • *best friend*

Ariel • Biblical/Hebrew/Jewish • *lion of God*

Aristide, Aristides, Aristos • *the best*

Arseni, Arsenios, Arsene, Arsenio • Greek • *a very sexy boy*

Arye, Yehuda, Judah • Jewish/Hebrew • *lion*

Åsa, Ase, Ass • Norse • *God, deity*

Asdrubale, Asrubaal • Phoenician/Italian • *give aid to the lord or receive it*

Ashraf • Arabic • *honourable and distinguished*

Åsmund, Assmund • *protected by the gods*

Augustine, Augustus, Austin • *great, the max, magnificent, nobody does it better*

Augustus, Auguste, Gus, Augustín, Augustine, Agostino, Augusto, Avgust, Agustin, Aghaistin, Aibhistin, Augustijn, Agustin, Agusti, Agostinho, Agostino,

Avgustin, Tauno, Agoston, Augustinas, Augere • Latin • *great, the max, magnificent, expansive, nobody does it better*

Aulay, Amhladh, Amlaidh, Olaf • Scots Gaelic/Norse • *ancestor, heir, descendant*

Auliffe, Amhlaoibh • Irish Gaelic/Norse • *ancestor, heir, descendant*

Aurelius, Aurèle, Aurel, Aureus, Aurelio • Latin • *Roman family name meaning golden*

Austin, Awstin, Awstyn, Austen, Austyn, Augustinius, Augustine • English/Latin • *the tops! The very best, el supremo*

Azriel • Jewish/Hebrew • *God helps*

Babar • Turkish • *lion*

Bahā • Arabic • *splendour*

Balder • Norse • *ruler or chief prince, said to be pure and beautiful*

Baldev • Sanskrit • *God of Strength and playboy!*

Balthasar, Balthazar, Balzer, Baltasar • *sun king, protect the king*

Baron • English/Norman • *noble man*

Barry, Baz, Bazza, Barra, Bairre, Barrie, Barri • Irish Gaelic • *fair-headed boy*

Basil, Bazil, Baz, Basiel, Basilio, Basilios, Basileu, Bazyli, Vasilios, Vasili, Pasi • Greek • *king*

Bayard, Bay • French/English • *a man with a hint of red hair*

Beau • French • *beautiful and bonny boy*

Beathan • Scots Gaelic • *life*

Bechor • Jewish/Hebrew/Sephardic • *first born*

Benjamin, Ben, Benny, Bennie, Benjamim, Benjie, Benji, Benjy,

Venyamin, Binyamin, Benno, Bendik • Hebrew/Jewish • *son of my right hand, my right hand man or son of the south, re-named by his father Jacob from his original name, son of my sorrow*

Benson, Bensington • English • *son of Benedict*

Berthold, Barthold, Bertil • German • *splendid, powerful ruler*

Bertram, Bertie, Bert, Bertrand, Beltrán, Burt, Albert • German • *bright*

Berwyn, Barrwyn • British/Welsh • *white or fair-headed*

Bevan, Evan, Bev • British/Welsh • *son of Evan*

Bharat • Sanskrit • *taken care of, God of Fire*

Bharvesh • Sanskrit • *Lord or King of the World, linked to Shiva*

Bhaskar • Sanskrit • *bright light, the sun*

Blaine, Blane • Scots Gaelic • *mellow yellow*

Blake • English • *my lovely mousey coloured hair*

Bob, Bobbie, Bobby, Robbie, Robert • American/English/Germanic • *bright, famous and clever*

Boleslav • Russian • *distinctly large and rather glorious*

Boqin • Chinese • *win respect*

Boyd • Irish • *blond*

Brant, Brand • Anglo-Saxon • *fire-brand, spitfire*

Brendan, Brendon, Breandán, Brendanus • Latin • *prince, heir*

Brian, Bryan, Bryant, Bryon • Irish Gaelic • *high or royal born, noble*

Caesar, César, Kaiser, Tsar • Latin • *leader*

Caerwyn, Carwyn, Caradog, Caradoc • British/Welsh • *sacred love*

Caungula • angola • *leader or chief of the people*

Carlyle, Carlisle, Carlile • British Welsh • *the place or castle belonging to Lugavalos, a personal name honouring the Celtic god of the Sun and Creativity*

Cassian, Cassianus, Cassius • Latin • *thy name is vanity!*

Cassidy • Irish Gaelic • *curly- or wavy-haired*

Cassius • Latin • *thy name is vanity!*

Césaire, Caesarius • French/Latin • *hairy, hursuit*

Chaim, Hyam • Jewish/Hebrew • *life*

Christopher, Chris, Christian, Crìsdean, Karsten, Christiaan, Carsten, Christer, Chretien, Cristiano, Krysztian, Krisztian, Christie, Christy, Kristy, Kristopher, Christopha, Kristopha, Críostóir, Christoph, Christofoor, Kristafoor, Kristoffer, Christophe, Cristobál, Cristofol, Cristovao, Cristoforo, Krzysztof, Krystof, Hristo, Risto, Kristof, Kristaps, Kit, Kester • Greek • *the man who bears Jesus Christ*

Christhard • German • *as brave and strong as Christ*

Christmas, Noël • English/French • *the nativity of Jesus Christ*

Ciriaco, Cyriacus, Kyriakos • Latin/Greek • *lord*

Clarence • English/Latin • *Dux Clarentiae, a royal title*

Clitus, Kleio, Clio, Kleitos • Latin/Greek • *famous, splendid*

Conley, Conlaodh • *a person who is pure and chaste as Aodh*

Conn • Irish Celtic • *chief, leader*

Constantine, Constanz, Costin, Constantin, Cystenian, Constant • Latin • *constant, steadfast, loyal, devoted*

Corin, Quirinus, Quirino • Latin • *an ancient Roman deity connected to Romulus*

Coy, McKay, McCoy • American/English • *the real McCoy; son of Aodh, Celtic sun god*

Crispin, Crispian, Crispinus, Crispus • Latin • *the curly-headed chap*

Cyril, Kyrillos, Cyrille, Kiri, Kyrios, Kiril, Searle • Greek • *lord or chief*

Cyrus, Cy, Kyros, Kyrios • Greek • *lord or chief*

Dai, Dei • British/Welsh • *this chap shines forth*

Daniel, Dan, Danny, Danyal, Deiniol, Daniele, Daniil, Taneli, Dannie • Biblical/Hebrew/Jewish • *God is my judge*

Dana • Irish Gaelic/American/English • *Celtic fertility goddess*

Darwin, Deorwine • Anglo-Saxon • *dear, good, bosom buddy*

David, Dave, Davy, Dewi, Dafydd, Dai, Davie, Davey, Dàibhidh, Davide, Taavi, Daw, Dawson, Dawŭd, Dewi, Dewydd, David, Dai • Biblical/Hebrew • *vague origins but possibly from a baby word meaning darling one*

Dayaram • Sanskrit • *as kind and tender as Rama, the perfect man/divinity*

Demetrius, Demetrio, Dmitri, Dimitar • Greek • *follower of the goddess Demeter*

Derek, Dereck, Derrick, Deryck, Del, Dirk, Theodoric • German/Dutch • *God's gift*

Dev, Deb, Deo • Sanskrit • *royal title, your majesty, God*

Devdan • Sanskrit • *gift of the gods*

Dewey, Dewy • British/Welsh/American/English • *possibly the English spelling of Dewi, which means David, darling one*

Dieudonné • French • *God-given*

Dinesh • Sanskrit • *Lord of the Day, the sun*

Dipak • Sanskrit • *God of Love, glows like a little lamp*

Disgleirio • modern Welsh • *bright and dazzling*

Diyā • Arabic • *brightness*

Dominic, Dominick, Dom, Dominique, Domingo, Dominicus, Dominus • Latin/Roman Catholic • *Lord, as in St Dominic, founder of the Dominican order*

Dónal, Domhnall, Donall • Irish Gaelic • *ruler of the world*

Donald, Don, Donny, Donnie, Donnell, Dolly, Dhomhnuill, Domhnall • Scots Gaelic • *world ruler*

Donat, Donato, Donatus, Donatien, Donatianus • given by God

Donovon, Donovan, Donndubhan, Donndubhain • brown, dark black-haired chief or leader

Dorotheos, Dorofei • Greek • *gift of God*

Dositheos, Dosifei • Greek • *God-given*

Duncan, Donnchadh • Celtic • *brown chief or noble leader*

Earl, Earle, Erle • American/English • *a noble man*

Eden, Edan • Hebrew/Jewish •

Garden of Eden, a place of sheer pleasure

Edgar, Edgard, Eadgar • Anglo-Saxon • *he who wins riches and titles through battle*

Edric • Anglo-Saxon • *a powerful, rich ruler*

Edsel, Etzel • Germanic • *nobleman or father*

Egan, Aogán • Irish • *fire, Celtic sun god, Aodh*

Ehrenreich • Germanic • *honourable and rich*

Eirik, Erik • Norse • *total ruler, singular chief*

Eli • Hebrew/Jewish • *God's height, probably tall*

Elias, Eli • Biblical/Greek • *Yahweh is God*

Eliezer, Eleazar, Eli • Jewish/Hebrew • *God's help*

Elijah, Eliezer, Elisha, Eli, Eliyahu, Eli • Jewish/Hebrew • *Yahweh is God*

Elisud, Elus, Ellis • British/Welsh • *a kind, benevolent man*

Elliott, Eliott, Elliot, Elias, Elijah • English • *Yahweh is God*

Elof • Scandinavian • *the single descendant/heir*

Elroy, Leroy, Rex, Roy, Roi • Spanish/French • *king*

Emmanuel, Emanuel, Manny, Immanuel • Hebrew/Jewish • *God is with us or amongst us*

Emyr • British/Welsh • *ruler, king, lord, chief*

Erasmus, Erazmus, Eran • Greek/Latin • *to love*

Erastus, Rastus • Biblical/Greek • *beloved*

Eric, Erik, Erick, Erich, Einnrik, Eirik • Norse • *one ruler or king alone, no other*

Ethan • Biblical/Hebrew/Jewish • *longevity, strong and firm*

Étienne, Stephen • French/Greek • *crown*

Eugene, Gene, Eugenios, Eugen, Eugenio • Greek • *well bred and high born*

Evan, Iefan, Ieuan, Ifan • British/Welsh • *from John, Johannes; God is gracious or gift of God*

Ewald, Ewawalt • Germanic • *a wise and just ruler; powerful leader, lawful ruler, judge*

Ezekiel, Zeke • Biblical/Jewish/Hebrew • *God gives me strength*

Fādi • Arabic • *redeemer, saviour, God*

Fairfax, Faegarfeax • English • *lovely long hair*

Fahd • Arabic • *leopard, panther, puma*

Faivish, Phoibos, Shimshon, Shraga, Fayvel, Feivel • Jewish/Yiddish/Aramaic • *God of the Sun, Apollo or linked to Samson*

Ferapont, Therapon • Greek • *he who worships*

Fergus, Fearghas, Ferrer • Irish/Scots Gaelic • *vital, dynamic man*

Farquhar, Fearchar • Scots Gaelic • *what a dear, loving man*

Fergus, Fearghas • Scots Gaelic • *a dynamic man*

Fidel, Fidelis • Latin • *faithful to the end*

Fife, Fyfe • Gaelic • *someone from the kingdom of Fife; Fif was a Pictish hero*

Filat, Feofilakt, Theophylaktos • Greek • *protected by God*

Filiberto • Germanic • *very bright, royal house of Savoy name*

Fingal, Fionnghall, Fingall • Gaelic • *blond, fair stranger or traveller or Viking settler*

Finlay, Findlay, Fionnlagh, Finley, Finnleik, Fionnlaogh • Scots Gaelic/ Norse • *fair, blond warrior or hero or war hero*

Fionnbarr, Fionnbharr, Finbar • Irish • *his head is white, fair and blond*

Fiontan, Fintan • Irish • *fiery and fair*

Firmin, Firminus, Firmino, Fermin • Latin • *he who cannot be moved; firm*

Fitzroy, Fitz • Norman/English • *often the bastard son of the king*

Flaithrí, Florry, Flurry • *prince, king*

Flavio, Flavien, Flavianus, Flavius • Latin • *old Roman family name meaning yellow-haired*

Fox, Sionnach, Fiksl • Anglo-Saxon • *a person who has features or colouring like a fox*

Fu'ād • Arabic • *the heart*

Fürchtegott • German • *fear God*

Gamaliel • Jewish/Hebrew • *benefit of God*

Ganesh • Sanskrit • *Lord of the Hosts*

Gaylord, Gaillard, Gay, Gaye • Norman • *a dandy or popinjay*

Gesualdo • Germanic • *I pledge to rule*

Gerlach • Germanic • *playful and sporting swordsman*

Gilbert, Gib, Gibb, Gilberto • Germanic/Frankish/Roman Catholic

Gideon • Hebrew/Jewish • *he who cuts someone down to size*

Gilroy, Giollaruadh • Scots Gaelic • *the red-haired boy*

Ginger • American/English • *someone with red or carrot-coloured hair*

Gjord, Gyrd, Jul • Norse • *God of Peace*

Gleb, Gudeif • Norse/Russian • *he who lives his life like a god or saint; heir of God*

Godfrey, Godefroy, Gofraidh, Godfrid, Godfred • Germanic/ Frankish • *God of Peace*

Godwin, Godwine, Win • Anglo-Saxon • *God is my friend*

Goodwin, Godwine • Anglo-Saxon • *not to be confused with Godwin; it means a good friend*

Gopal • Sanskrit • *cowherd, the King of the Earth*

Goronwy, Gronw • British/Welsh • *uncertain origin but by legend an adulterer who went too far!*

Gottfried, Götz • Germanic • *God of Peace, God bring me peace*

Gotthard • Germanic • *God give me strength*

Gotthelf • Germanic • *God help me*

Gotthold, Gottwald • Germanic • *wonderful (lovely) God*

Gottlieb, Theophilus • Germanic • *love God*

Gottlob • Germanic • *praise God*

Gerlach • Germanic • *playful and sporting swordsman*

German, Germanus • Latin • *brother in God*

Gruffudd, Griff, Griffith, Griffinus, Griffin, Grippiud, Gripiud, Gutun, Gutyn, Guto • *prince of lords*

Guaire • Irish Gaelic • *proud and noble, upstanding*

Gui • Chinese • *honourable, noble*

Guowei • Chinese • *status quo*

Haakon, Håkon, Hagen, Håkan •
Norse/Germanic • *high-born son,
relative*

Habīb • Arabic • *beloved, adored*

Habimana • Rwandan • *there is God*

Haidar • Arabic • *lion*

**Handel, Hans, Hans, Hansel,
Johannes** • Germanic • *God is
gracious or gift of God*

Hank, Hankin • Norman/English
• *mixed roots; short form of Jehan,
John or Henry*

Hannibal, Haanbaal • Phoenician
• *I give the Lord grace and favour or
he gives it to me*

Harinder • Sikh • *Hari (Vishnu) and
Indra, the supreme god*

Harish • Sanskrit • *Lord of the
Monkeys, Vishnu*

Hārith • Arabic • *provider, lion*

Harold, Harald • Anglo-Saxon •
ruler of the army, chief of the tribe

Hartwin • Germanic • *a faithful
friend*

Hefin • British/Welsh • *summer*

Henning • Scandinavian • *short
form of Henrik and Johannes*

Heng • Chinese • *eternal, forever*

**Herbert, Bert, Herebeorht, Herb,
Herbie, Heribert** • German • *a
famous army that carries all before
it; a shining light*

Hildebrecht • Germanic • *bright
light in the battle*

**Honore, Honoratus, Honorius,
Ynyr** • Latin • *an honoured man*

Hopcyn, Hopkin, Hob, Robert •
British/Welsh • *famous and bright*

Heul, Haul • British/Welsh • *sun*

**Hugh, Huw, Hugues, Hugo, Aodh,
Hughie, Hewie, Huey, Hewie,
Hughie, Huwie** • Germanic/
Frankish • *heart, mind and spirit*

Hugo, Hugh • Germanic/Frankish/
Latin • *heart, mind and spirit*

Hui • Chinese • *magnificent*

Husni • Arabic • *a person of
excellence*

Hyacinth, Hyakinthos • Greek/
English • *love and passion*

Hywel, Hywell, Howell • British/
Welsh • *conspicuous by his eminence*

Iagan, Aodh, Aodhagán • Irish
Gaelic • *the Celtic sun god*

Ian, Iain, John • Scots Gaelic •
Biblical • *God is gracious or gift of
God*

**Ianto, Ifan, Ieuan, Iohannes, John,
Iefan, Ioan** • British/Welsh • *God is
gracious or gift of God*

Iarlaithe, Jarlath • Irish • *vague
origins but maybe chief, leader*

Ibrāhīm, Abraham • Arabic • *father
of the tribes or nations*

Idris • British/Welsh • *a passionate
loving lord or lord of passion and
desire*

Igal • Biblical/Hebrew/Jewish •
redeemer

Ingemar, Ingmar • Norse • *famous,
well known to God*

Iorwerth, Iolo, Iolyn, Yorath •
British/Welsh • *a handsome, beautiful lord or chief*

Iosif, Osip, Joseph • Biblical/Jewish/
Hebrew • *God will add another*

Ipati, Hypatios, Hypatos • Greek •
most high, el supremo!

Irwin, Erwyn, Irwyn, Everwyn •
a good, loyal and honoured friend

Isaiah, Izzy, Isaïe • Biblical/Jewish/
Hebrew • *God is salvation*

Iser, Iserl, Issur • Jewish/Yiddish •
he who strives with God

Ishmael, Ismā'īl • Arabic • *receiver*

of the divine spirit; listen to God
Israel, Jacob • Biblical/Jewish/
Hebrew • *he who strives with God*
Italo, Italus • Latin • *father of
Romulus and Remus, founders of
Rome*
Ithel, Iudhael • British/Welsh • *a
generous but common man who
behaves like a goodly prince or lord;
philanthropist*
Ivan, John, Ewan • Russian • *God
is gracious or gift of God*

Jacinto, Hyakinthos, Hyacinthe •
Greek/Spanish • *love and passion*
**Jack John, Jankin, Jan, Jehan,
James, Jacques, Jock, Jake, Jak,
Jac, Jackie, Jackson, Jacky, Jackin** •
English • *God is gracious or gift of God*
Jalāl, Galāl • Arabic • *great and
glorious*
Jagannath • Sanskrit • *Lord of the
World, Vishnu, as in sacred Puri*
Jagdish • Sanskrit • *ruler of the
world, Brahma, Vishnu and Shiva*
Jahangir • Persian • *he's got the
whole world in his hands*
Jake, Jack • English • *God is
gracious or gift of God*
Jamshed • Muslim/Parsis • *king and
founder of Persopolis*
Jan, John, Johannes • Germanic/
Slavic • *God is gracious or gift of God*
Jasper, Jaspar, Casper, Caspar •
English/Persian • *treasurer, gift of
gold*
Jean, Jehan, Gene • French • *God is
gracious or gift of God*
Jed, Jedidiah, Ged • Biblical/
Hebrew/Jewish • *beloved of God*
Jenkin, Jankin, Siencyn • British/
Welsh • *God is gracious or gift of
God*

Jens, Jons, Johann • Scandinavian •
God is gracious or gift of God
**Jeffrey, Geoffrey, Jeff, Geoff,
Jefferson, Jeffery, Jeffry, Jep** •
Anglo-Saxon • *a stranger in your
own land or foreigner who pledges
allegiance*
**Jeremiah, Jeremy, Jerry, Jem,
Gerry, Jeremias** • Biblical/Hebrew/
Jewish • *appointed by God*
Jeremy, Jem, Jeremiah • Biblical/
English • *appointed by God*
Jerker, Jerk, Erik • Scandinavian •
one ruler or king alone, no other
Jinhai • Chinese • *golden sea*
Jinjing • Chinese • *golden mirror*
Joe, Jo, Joey • English • *God will
add another*
**Joachim, Jo, Johoiachin, Joaquin,
Jochim, Jochem, Jochen, Joakim,
Jokum** • Biblical • *created by God*
Jobst, Jodocus, Iodoc • Latin/
Breton Celtic • *lord*
Joël, Yahel • Biblical/Hebrew/Jewish
• *God*
**John, Iohannes, Johannes,
Ioannes, Johannan, Johanan, Eóin,
Seán, Ian, Iain, Seathan, Ieuan,
Siôn, Johann, Johannes, Jan, Jens,
Johan, Jons, Jon, Jan, Johan, Jean,
Juan, Joan, Joao, Giovanni, Gianni,
Ioannis, Iannis, Ivan, Juhani, Jussi,
Hannu, Janos, Janis, Johnnie,
Johnny, Jack, Hank, Jonathan,
Johnathan, Jonny, Jon, Johnson,
Juwan, Johnston, Johnstone,
Jones** • Biblical/English/Latin • *God
is gracious or gift of God*
**Jonathan, Jon, Jonn, Johnny,
Johnnie, Jonathen, Jonathon** •
Biblical • *God has given*
**Joseph, Jo, Joey, Jose, Josef, Yosef,
Joe, Jo, Seosamh, Ioseph, Josef,**

Jozef, Josep, Giuseppe, Iosif, Josip, Jooseppi • Biblical/Hebrew/Jewish
Joshua, Josh • Biblical/Hebrew/Jewish • *God is my salvation*
Joyce, Josce, Josse, Joducus, Ioduc, Joss • Breton Celtic • *lord*
Jozsef, Osip, Jazeps, Juozapas • Biblical/Jewish/Hebrew • *God will add another son*
Juan, John • Biblical/Greek/Spanish • *God is gracious or gift of God*
Julián, Jules, Julianus, Julius, Julyan, Jolyon, Julien, Julio, Jools • Latin • *a Roman family name that gives its name to the month of July*
Junjie • Chinese • *beautiful, brilliant*
Justin, Justyn, Justinus, Justus, Iestyn • Latin • *a Roman name*

Kapil • Sanskrit • *the colour of a monkey!*
Kapiton, Capito • Latin • *big-headed*
Karan • Sanskrit • *ear of the warrior king*
Kåre, Kari • Scandinavian • *curly-haired*
Kasi • Sanskrit • *radiant; Varanasi or Benares, sacred city on the Ganges*
Keegan, Aodhagain, Aodhagán, Aogán, Aodh • Irish/English • *fire, Celtic sun god*
Kemp, Kemper, Kempa, Kempe • Anglo-Saxon/English • *a warrior champion at sports*
Kendrick, Kenrick, Cenric, Ceneric, Cynwrig, Maceanrig, Cyneric • British/Welsh/Scots Gaelic • *a sacred place high on a hill, or son of Henry or royal power*
Kennard, Ceneweard, Cyneheard • Anglo-Saxon • *he who is keen or even royal, and a fierce defender of others*

Kevin, Caioimhin, Keven, Kevan, Kevyn, Caoimhean • English/Irish Gaelic • *beloved, beautiful, enchanting*
Khalīl • Arabic • *best friend*
Khalipha, Caliph • Arabic • *successor, heir*
Khurshid • Persian • *the sun*
Khwaja • Persian • *the master*
Kingsley, King, Kingsly, Kingslie, Cyningesleah • Anglo-Saxon/English • *the clearing or woods that belong to the king*
Kiran • Sanskrit • *a ray of light*
Kirill, Kyrillos, Cyril • Greek • *belongs to the Lord*
Knut, Cnut, Knud • Norse • *a knot or man who is short, squat and stocky*
Kondrati, Quadratus • *a person with a figure like a square*
Konstantin, Constantinus • Latin • *constant, steadfast, loyal, devoted*
Kumar • Sanskrit • *beautiful Prince Skanda*
Kynaston, Cynefripestun • Anglo-Saxon • *the homestead or village of a peaceful royal or noble personage*

Ladislas, Ladislaw, Ladislaus, Wadislaw, Vladislav, Laszlo; Volodslav • Latin/Slavic • *glorious ruler, rules with glory*
Lakshman, Laxman • Sanskrit • *the mark of God; most auspicious*
Lal • Sanskrit/Prakrit • *dear, sweet, darling one; king*
Laoghaire, Leary • Irish • *herd of calves, name of Dun Laoghaire, was Kingstown*
Lazarus, Laz, Lazare, Eleazar, Lazaros, Lazar • Biblical/Greek/Aramaic/Hebrew • *God is my helper*

Leander, Leandro, Leandros, Leander, Leandros, Leonaner, Lee, Léandre • Greek • *lion man, man with the strength of a lion*

Leif, Leaf, Leiv • Norse • *heir of the realm*

Leib, Lowe, Arye • Jewish/Hebrew • *lion*

Lemuel • Hebrew/Jewish • *devoted to God*

Leo, Léon, Leodegar, Luitger • Latin • *lion*

Léon, Levon, Leonzio, Leontius, Leontis, Leonti • Latin • *leo the lion! Or like a lion*

Leonidas, Leonid • Greek • *lion*

Léonard, Lennard, Len, Lenny, Lennie, Leonardo, Leonhard, Lienhard, Lennart • Latin/ Germanic • *strong as a lion*

Léonce, Leonzio, Leoncio, Leontius • Italian/Latin • *lion*

Leroy, Elroy, Lee-Roy • Spanish/ French • *king*

Lev • Russian • *lion*

Lex, Alex, Alexander, Lexie, Lexis, Lexy • Greek • *the man/warrior/ leader who protects or defends his people*

Liang • Chinese • *bright, luminous, radiant*

Linus, Linos • Greek • *the song of Linus, a Greek musician who taught Hercules*

Lionel, Leo, Lion, Léon • Norman/Anglo-Saxon

Llewelyn, Llew, Lugobelinos, Llewellyn, Llywelyn, Llywellyn, Lyn • British/Welsh • *lion*

Lonnie, Lonso, Lenny • Spanish/ Visigothic • *royal at the ready*

Lothar • Germanic/Frankish • *famous, royal army*

Madog, Madoc, Aodh • British/ Welsh • *fiery and fortunate*

Mahesh • Sanskrit • *great ruler*

Mājid • Arabic • *brighter than a star*

Mani, Subrahmanya • Sanskrit • *jewel with potent qualities; the penis*

Manuel, Emmanuel • Biblical/ Spanish • *God is with us or amongst us*

Marquis, Marcuis • Norman • *Lord of the Marches, borders between England and Wales*

Marvin, Mervyn • British Welsh/ English • *he's a lord or eminent being down to his marrow*

Mathias, Matthias, Matthaeus, Matthäus, Mattathia • Biblical/Greek/ Jewish/Aramaic/Latin • *gift of God*

Matthew, Matt, Mathew, Mattathia, Maitiu, Matthias, Maitias, Mata, Matha, Matthäus, Matthijs, Mads, Mathies, Mats, Mathieu, Mateo, Mateu, Mateus, Matteo, Mattia, Matvei, Mateusz, Maciej, Matej, Matyas, Matija, Matti, Matyas, Mate, Mattanah, Mattaniah, Mattathah, Mattatha, Mattathiah, Mattathias • Biblical/Hebrew/Jewish/English

Maxim, Max, Maximus, Maxime, Massimo, Maksim, Maximo, Macsen • Latin • *the greatest!*

Maxwell, Max • Anglo-Saxon • *the well of Magnus or Mack, a great man*

Meilyr, Maglorix • British/Welsh • *chief or ruler*

Melchior, Melkquart, Melchiorre • Jewish/Christian • *city of the king*

Melek, Elimelek • Biblical/Jewish/ Hebrew • *king*

Meredith, Meredydd, Maredudd, Meredudd • uncertain beginning but ends with Lord

Merfyn, Mervin, Mervyn, Marvin, Mervyn • British/Welsh • *he's a lord or eminent being down to his marrow*

Michael, Micah, Micheal, Meical, Mihangel, Machiel, Mikael, Mikkel, Michel, Miguel, Miquel, Michele, Mikhail, Michal, Mihovil, Mihajlo, Mihael, Mikko, Mihaly, Mike, Mick, Micky, Mikey, Mickey, Meical • Biblical/Hebrew/Jewish/English • *who is like God?*

Miles, Michael, Milo, Myles, Maoilios • Latin • *soldier of God*

Misha, Micha, Mikhail • Russian • *he who is like God*

Mitchell, Michael, Michel, Mitch • Norman/English • *he who is like God*

Mohammed, Muhammed, Mohammad, Mohamed, Muhammad, Muhammed, Mo • *praiseworthy and possessing the finest perfect qualities*

Mohan • Sanskrit • *enchantment; one of the five arrows of love*

Moses, Moshe, Moïse, Moss, Moses, Mostyn, Monty • Biblical/Hebrew/Egyptian • *born of God*

Mujtaba • Arabic • *the chosen one*

Mukhtār • Arabic • *preferred to all others*

Mungo, Munghu, Munga, Fychi, • British/Welsh • *carissimus amicus, meaning dearest friend; pet name of St Kentigern*

Munīr • Arabic • *shining, dazzling, glorious*

Mustafa, Mustapha • pure, the chosen one

Mu'tasim • Arabic • *trust in God or the Lord*

Mu'tazz • Arabic • *proud and powerful*

Nabīl • Arabic • *royal born or noble birth*

Nadīm • Arabic • *best friend, companion you share your social life with*

Nagendra • Sanskrit • *good god amongst the snakes and elephants*

Napoleon, Napoleone • Italian • *unsure origin; may mean sons of the mist or the Naples Lion*

Narcissus, Narkissos, Narcisse, Narciso • Greek/Latin • *linked with the daffodil but unsure origins*

Narendra • Sanskrit • *shaman, witchdoctor, doctor king*

Naresh • Sanskrit • *ruler of men*

Naveed • Persian • *glad tidings, invite to the wedding or something just as jolly*

Ned, Edward • Anglo-Saxon • *a careful, prudent ruler who looks after his riches and possessions*

Nestor, Nestore • Greek • *personal name King of Pylos, in legend one of the Greeks (bearing gifts!) at Troy*

Nino, Giannino • Latin/Spanish • *the boy, referring to the Christ Child*

Noam • Jewish/Hebrew • *joy, pleasure and happiness*

Noble, Nobilis • American English/Norman Latin • *someone who has noble qualities even if not born aristocratic*

Nolasco • Latin • *personal name honouring the man who rescued the Christians from the Moslems during the Crusade*

Nūr • Arabic • *luminous*

Obadiah, Abdullah • Biblical/Hebrew/Jewish • *servant of God*

Obed • Hebrew/Jewish • *God's servant*

Onofre • Egyptian • *a man who opens up to God*

Orpheus, Orfeo • Greek • *beautiful voice; in legend a Thracian musician who married Eurydice, stolen by Pluto*

Orlando, Roland • Italian • *a person who is famous for the real estate they own; land, territory*

Osama, Usama • Arabic • *predator, as in a killer cat such as lion or lioness*

Osbert, Osbeorht • Anglo-Saxon • *illuminated by God, famous for his devotion*

Osborne, Osbourne, Osbourn, Osborn • Anglo-Saxon/Scandinavian

Osmond, Osmund, Oz • Anglo-Saxon • *God is my protector*

Oswald, Osweald, Oz, Ozzy, Osvaldo • Anglo-Saxon • *my ruler is God or God rules*

Oswin, Oswine, Oz • Anglo-Saxon • *God is my friend*

Otto • Germanic • *riches, a royal and imperial name*

Owen, Owain, Éoghan, Eóin, Eugenius • Latin/British/Welsh • *born of Esos or Aesos, a Celtic god that was big in Gaul (now France)*

Ozzy, Oz, Ozzie • Anglo-Saxon • *shortened version of any name beginning with Os, meaning God*

Pancras, Pankratios, Pancrazio, Pancraz, Pankrati • Greek • *all-powerful*

Parry, Parri • British/Welsh • *son of Harry or Harri*

Parthalán, Párthlán, Pártlán, Partnán, Bartholomew, Berkely, Barclay • Latin/Irish • *first ever citizen of Ireland after the Biblical flood; Biblical meaning son of Tolmai from Galilee*

Patrice, Patrick • Latin/French/Irish Gaelic • *patrician*

Patrick, Pádraig, Pat, Paddy, Patsy, Páraic, Patrice, Patricio, Patrizio, Porick, Podge, Pàra, Pàdair, Pàidean, Padrig, Paddy, Patrick, Pat, Patrice • Latin/Irish Gaelic • *patrician*

Pàrlan, Parthalán • Gaelic • *uncertain origin; may be linked to Irish for Bartholomew*

Pepe, Pepito, Joseph, José • Spanish • *God is my salvation*

Philbert, Filaberht, Philibert, Filbert • Greek/Germanic/Frankish • *dear, beloved*

Philo, Philon • Greek • *love*

Pitambar • Sanskrit • *saffron*

Prabhu • Sanskrit • *sun god, God of Fire*

Pradeep • Sanskrit • *glorious light, natural or artificial*

Prakash • Sanskrit • *a famous, radiant person*

Pramod • Sanskrit • *joy, happiness, pleasure*

Pran • Sanskrit • *vitality, life breath and force*

Prasad • Sanskrit • *by the grace of God, gifts from the deity to the worshippers*

Pratap • Sanskrit • *warrior king*

Price, Pryce, Rhys • British/Welsh • *son of Rhys*

Prince, Princeps • Latin/English • *royal title*

Prokhoros, Prokhor • Greek • *very artistic, chief of a troupe of singers, dancers, actors*

Purushottam • Sanskrit • *divine being*

Quentin, Quintinus, Quintus, Quintin, Quinton, Cwentun • Latin • *Roman family name meaning number five*

Quincy, Quincey, Cuinchy, Quintus • Latin • *the number five*

Radwan • Arabic • *pleasure and enjoyment*

Raghnall, Raonull, Rannal, Ronald • Norse • *wise, decisive chief or an oracle of the gods or kings*

Ragnvald • Norse • *an oracle of the gods or kings*

Raj, Raju • Sanskrit • *king, royal*

Rajab, Ragab • Arabic • *seventh month of the Muslim calendar*

Rajendra • Sanskrit • *mighty king, mighty ruler*

Rajesh, Raj • Sanskrit • *above the law, above the king, divine*

Rajkumar • Sanskrit • *prince, heir*

Ramadān • Arabic • *ninth month of the Muslim calendar: the hot month*

Rameshwar, Ramnath • Sanskrit • *Lord Rama*

Ramsay, Ramsa, Ramsey • Anglo-Saxon • *island of wild garlic (good for the heart)*

Rastus, Erastus • Biblical/Greek • *beloved*

Ratilal • Prakrit • *Lord of Love and Pleasure*

Ravi • Sanskrit • *the sun god*

Ravindra • Sanskrit • *mightiest of suns*

Read, Reed, Red, Reod • Anglo-Saxon • *a person with red hair or a ruddy complexion*

Rearden, Ríordan, Rordan, Ríoghbhardán • English/Irish Gaelic • *wee poet king*

Régis • French/Provençal • *the ruler*

Reid, Read, Red • English • *Scots/English border name for red-headed person*

Remus, Remo • Latin • *with Romulus, founder of Rome*

Reuben, Reuven, Rube, Rubén • Biblical/Hebrew/Jewish • *behold, a son!*

Reuel • Biblical/Jewish/Hebrew • *friend of God*

Rex • Latin • *king*

Rhodri, Rhodrhi • British/Welsh • *ruler of the wheel; king who rules by his chariot*

Rida • Arabic • *affirmation, validation by God (Allah); contented*

Rian, Ryan, Riain • Irish Gaelic/English • *little king, descendant of Riain*

Ríordan, Rearden, Ríoghbhardán • Irish • *poet king or king of the poets*

Roald, Hrod • Norse • *famous ruler, famous chief*

Robert, Rob, Robbie, Rodberht, Reodbeorht, Bob, Rob, Bobby, Robin, Roibéard, Raibeart, Rupprecht, Robrecht, Rupert, Robbert, Roberto, Roopertti, Roberts, Rabbie, Rab, Rigoberto • Germanic • *famous and bright*

Robin, Robben, Robert • Germanic • *famous and bright*

Roman, Romanus, Romain, Romano • Latin/Czech/Polish/Romanian • *to be Roman*

Romulus, Romolo • Latin • *someone from Rome; one of the founders of Rome*

Ronald, Ron, Ronnie, Ronny, Roni, Ranald, Randal, Rognvald • Norse • *adviser to the gods or king*

Rory, Ruaidhrí, Ruairidh, Roderick, Roy, Ruadh • Gaelic • *fiery temper or red-headed*

Roshan • Persian/Urdu • *splendid, glorious/famous*

Roy, Roi • French • *king*

Ruiadhrí, Rory, Ruarí • Irish • *the red king*

Rufus, Rufino, Ruffino, Rufinus • Latin • *red-haired*

Rupert, Ruprecht, Robert • Germanic/Dutch • *famous and bright*

Ryan, Riain • Irish Gaelic • *little king, descendant of Riain*

Sasha, Sacha, Shura • French/Greek/Russian • *Greek • the man/warrior/leader who protects or defends his people*

Sachdev • Sanskrit • *truth of God, totally honest*

Safwat • Arabic • *choice and best*

Salvatore, Salvator, Salvador, Sal • Latin • *saviour*

Sāmi • Arabic • *elevated, sublime*

Samson, Shimshon, Shemesh, Sampson, Sansone, Sammy, Sammie, Sansone • Biblical/Hebrew/Jewish • *the sun*

Samuel, Shemuel, Shaulmeel, Sam, Sammy, Sawyl • Biblical/Hebrew/Jewish • *name of God, God has heard, listen to God*

Sander, Alexander • Norwegian/Greek • *the man/warrior/leader who protects or defends his people*

Sandro, Sonny • Italian/Greek • *the man/warrior/leader who protects or defends his people*

Sandy, Alex, Sandaidh, Sawney • Scots Gaelic/Greek • *the man/warrior/leader who protects or defends his people*

Sardar • Muslim/Persian/Sikh

Sarfraz • Muslim/Persian • *hold*

your head up high with dignity

Sayyid • Arabic • *lord and master*

Seathan, Jean, Jehan • Scots Gaelic/French/Biblical/English/Latin • *God is gracious or gift of God*

Sekar • Sanskrit • *summit, the best at what you do*

Selwyn, Selewyn, Selewine, Silvanus, Silas, Selwin • Anglo-Saxon • *prosperous, high-flying friend*

Sender, Zender • Jewish/Greek • *the man/warrior/leader who protects or defends his people*

Shah • Muslim/Persian/Sufi • *king, God, lord, emperor, divine mystic*

Shahjahan • Muslim/Persian • *king of the World*

Shahnawaz • Muslim/Persian • *cherisher of kings*

Shahzad • Muslim/Persian • *prince*

Shabbetai, Shabbath, Shabath, Shabtai • Jewish/Hebrew • *the Sabbath*

Sher • Muslim/Persian • *lion*

Shraga • Jewish/Hebrew • *God of the Sun, Apollo or linked to Samson*

Simeon • English/Biblical/Hebrew • *he has heard*

Simón, Siomon, Sim, Simidh, Sieman, Simao, Simone, Semyon, Szymon, Simo, Sim, Simmie • Biblical/Hebrew/Jewish • *hearkening, hearing*

Somerled, Sumarlid, Summerlad, Somhairle, Sorley • Scots Gaelic/Norse • *summer traveller*

Somhairle • Irish Gaelic/Norse • *summer traveller*

Spike • English • *a nickname for a person whose hair sticks up like a permanent bad-hair day*

Stanilas, Stanislaus, Stanislaw,

Aneislis, Stanislav • Slavic • *glory to the court, glorious courtier or politician*
Stefan, Stephan, Stephanos, Steven, Steve, Steff, Stevie, Stiofán, Stiana, Steaphan, Steffan, Steffen, Stefan, Staffan, Étienne, Stéphane, Estéban, Esteve, Estevao, Stefano, Stepan, Szczepan, Stjepan, Stevan, Istvan, Steponas • Greek • *a crown or garland*
Sultan • Arabic • *ruler, leader*
Surendra, Surinder • Sanskrit • *the most powerful of the gods*
Suresh • Sanskrit • *ruler of the gods*
Surya • Sanskrit • *sun*
Swaran • Sanskrit • *beautiful colour, golden*
Svyatoslav, Syvantoslav • Slavic • *sacred glory*

Taqi • Arabic • *God-fearing*
Tara • Sanskrit • *shining light for the saviour; carrying the Lord*
Tarun, Taroon • Sanskrit • *dawn, the early sun, young, tender growth of love and romance*
Teodosio • Greek • *God-given*
Terrell, Tyrell • Norman • *a person who is hard to pull this way or that, very fixed!*
Thaddeus, Labbaeus, Theodoras, Theodotos, Thad, Tad • Biblical/Aramaic/Greek • *given by God or God's gift*
Theo, Théodore, Theobald, Theodor, Teodoro • Greek • *God*
Theodore, Theo, Ted, Teddy, Theodor, Theodoor, Teodor, Teodoro, Feodor, Fyodr, Teuvo, Tivador, Todor, Teodors, Theodoric, Tiobad, Ted, Teddy, Edward,

Theodos, Theodosios, Teodosio, Todos, Theodoros • Greek • *God-given or giving to God or God's gift*
Theophilus, Theosphilos, Theo, Théophile, Teofilo • Biblical/Greek • *God's friend or friend of God*
Thierry, Theodoric • French/Greek • *ruler of the people*
Tiernan, Tighearnan, Tighearnach, Tierney • Irish Gaelic • *lord or chief*
Timothy, Tim, Tadhg, Timmy, Timotheus, Timotheos, Timetheo, Timmy, Tiger, Timothee, Timo, Timoteo Timofei • Biblical/Latin/Greek • *honour God*
Tobias, Tobiah, Tobijah, Toby • Biblical/Hebrew/Greek • *God is good*
Tochukwa • Nigerian • *praise God*
Traugott • Germanic • *trust in God*
Troy, Trey, Troyes • *someone from the French city of Troyes, or, more powerful, in memory of the Troy (in modern-day Turkey) of Greek mythology*
Tudur, Tudor, Tudyr, Teutorix • British/Welsh • *king or chief of the tribe*
Tulsi • Sanskrit • *the herb basil; so holy is also a goddess*
Tyrell, Tyrrell, Tirel, Terrell • a person who is hard to pull this way or that, very fixed!

Uarraig, Kennedy • Irish Gaelic • *a fierce, temperamental man who is burdened with pride*
Ughtred, Uhtraed • Anglo-Saxon • *dawn counsel; a person who is good and wise in the mornings*
Ugo, Hugo, Hugh • Germanic • *heart, mind and spirit*
Ùisdean, Eysteinn, Hugh,

Hùisdean • Irish Gaelic • *a man who is forever unchanging like a stone*
Umashankar • Sanskrit • *union of two people*
Uriah, Urias, Uriel • Biblical/Jewish/ Hebrew • *God is light*
Urien, Orbogen • British/Welsh • *born with a silver spoon in his mouth; privileged*
Uttam • Sanskrit • *the ultimate*
Uwamahoro • Rwandan • *peacemaker*
Uzziah, Uziah • Biblical/Jewish/ Hebrew • *power of Yahweh*
Uzziel, Uziel • Biblical/Jewish/ Hebrew • *power of God*

Vanya, Ivan • Russian • *God is gracious or gift of God*
Varfolomel, Bartholomew • Biblical • *son of Tolmai from Galilee*
Vasili, Basilios • Greek • *royal*
Vasu • Sanskrit • *simply the best!*
Venkat • Sanskrit • *sacred mountain near Madras*
Vidal, Vitale, Hayyim • Latin/Jewish • *to life!*
Vinod • Sanskrit • *recreation, leisure, pleasure and sport*
Vishwanath • Sanskrit • *lord of all*
Vitale, Vitalis • Latin • *full of life*
Vitus • Latin • *life*
Vivien, Vyvyan, Viv, Vi, Béibhinn • Latin/Norman • *Roman name Vivianus, meaning life*
Vladimir, Volodya, Valdemar, Waldemar • Slavic • *great, famous leader or ruler*
Vladislav • Slavic • *glorious leader or ruler*
Vyacheslav, Wenceslas • Slavic/ Latin • *greater and even greater glory*

Waldemar, Waldo, Wald, Walker, Wealcere, Wealcan, Woldemar • Germanic • *famous ruler*
Wasīm, Wazim • Arabic • *what a stunner! Beautiful to look at, delightful to know*
Wei • Chinese • *impressive strength and energy leading to greatness*
Weimin • Chinese • *honour the people with greatness*
Weishing • Chinese • *born great*
Wenceslas, Ventieslav, Wenzel • Slavic • *greater and even greater glory*
Willard, Will, Wilheard • Anglo-Saxon • *a person with tremendous willpower, powerful in every way*
Wilmer, Wilmaer • Anglo-Saxon • *he is famous for his willpower and strength of character*
Witold • Germanic • *ruler of the wood or wide country*
Wynfor, Wyn • British/Welsh • *white, blonde, holy, blessed*

Xander, Alexander • Greek • *the man/warrior/leader who protects or defends his people*
Xerxes • Persian • *king*
Xianliang • Chinese • *worthy of brightness*
Xiaodan • Chinese • *little dawn*

Yahya, John • Arabic/Biblical • *God is gracious or gift of God*
Yakim, Akim • *created by God*
Yaro • Hausa of South Africa • *son*
Yashpal • Sanskrit • *cherishes splendour*
Yehiel, Jehiel • Biblical/Hebrew/ Jewish • *God lives*
Yeremiah • Uganda • *exalted*
Yevgeni, Eugenios, Eugene •

Russian • *well bred and high born*
Yingpei • Chinese • *to be admired*
Yongliang • Chinese • *forever light and bright*
Yoram • Biblical/Jewish/Hebrew • *Yahweh is high*
Yorath, Iorwerth • British/Welsh • *a handsome, beautiful lord or chief*
Yosef, Joseph, Yūsuf • Jewish/Hebrew/Arabic • *God is my salvation*
Yuan, Juan, John • Manx Gaelic • *God is gracious or gift of God*
Yūsuf, Joseph • Arabic/Biblical • *God is my salvation*

Zachary, Zach, Zak • Greek/English/Biblical • *God has remembered*
Zacharias, Zak, Zechariah,

Zachariah, Zakaria, Zach • Biblical/Jewish/Hebrew
Zāhir • Arabic • *radiant, bright, luminous*
Zakariyya, Zakariya • Biblical/Arabic • *God has remembered*
Zeb, Zebedee, Zebulun • Biblical/Hebrew/Greek • *gift of Jehovah*
Zabulun, Zabulon, Zebulon, Zabal • Biblical/Hebrew/Jewish • *exaltation*
Zechariah • Biblical/Jewish/Hebrew • *God has remembered*
Zeke, Ezekiel • Biblical/Jewish/Hebrew • *God gives me strength*
Zengguang • Chinese • *growing brightness*
Zhiqiang • strength of will
Zihao • Chinese • *heroic son*

Girls

Abigail, Abbie, Abby, Abbey, Abbigail, Abbiegail, Abbygail, Abigayle, Abi • Biblical/Jewish/ Hebrew • *my father is joy, father is exaltation*

Ada, Adah • Biblical/Jewish/Hebrew • *adornment to make one beautiful*

Adelheid, Adalheid, Aleida, Aleit, Alke, Elke • Germanic • *noble woman, carries herself well*

Adeltraud • Germanic • *strong and noble*

Adélaide • Germanic • *noble, kind and caring*

Adèle, Adelle, Addie, Addi, Addy, Adeline, Adelina, Aline Adela, Adella, Alette • French • *noble*

Aegle, Aglaia • Greek • *splendid radiance*

Afāf • Arabic • *chasity, refinement, elegance*

Agapia, Agafya • Greek • *love*

Ai • Chinese • *loving*

Aimee, Aimi • French • *beloved one*

Alastriona • Scots Gaelic/Greek • *the warrior/leader who protects or defends her people*

Alberta, Albertina • French/ Germanic/Anglo-Saxon • *bright and noble*

Alexandra, Alexa, Alexis, Sandra, Sandy, Lexy, Alix, Alexandria, Alexandrina, Alexia, Aleksandra, Alexina • Greek • *the warrior/leader who protects or defends her people*

Alice, Alicia, Alesha, Alisia, Alys, Alisha, Alissa, Alesha, Alisa, Alissa, Ailish, Alis, Alys • Norman • *noble, kind and caring*

Alickina, Kina, Keena • Greek/ Gaelic • *the warrior/leader who protects or defends her people*

Aline, Adeline, Alainn • French/ Gaelic • *noble*

Alison, Allie, Ally, Aly, Alysoun, Aliyah, Aaliyah, Allison, Allyson • Norman • *noble, kind and caring*

Allina, Alina • French • *noble*

Aloha • Polynesian/Hawaiian • *love*

Amabel, Annabel, Mabel, Amabilis • Latin/Norman • *loveable*

Amaryllis, Amaryssein • Greek • *to sparkle*

Amber, Ambar • Latin/Arabic • *beautiful golden-coloured fossilised resin*

Amy, Amie, Aimie, Aimee • Norman • *beloved*

Anais, Ana, Anya • Biblical/Catalan/ Provençal • *God has favoured me*

Andrea, André, Andra, Andriana, Andrine, Andy, Andree, Anndra • Biblical/Greek • *a real sexy person*

Angharad • British/Welsh • *love*

Anita, Ana • Spanish/ Biblical • *God has favoured me*

Ann, Anne, Anna, Annabel, Annette, Annetta, Anouk, Anni, Annelie, Anneli, Annella, Annabell, Annabella, Annabelle, Belle, Annie, Anna, Anneke, Anke, Anoushka, Anouska, Arabella, Arabel Anna, Ana • Biblical/Jewish/ Hebrew • *God has favoured me*

Annalisa, Annaliesa, Annalise, Annelise, Annelies, Anneli • German • *combo of Anne and Elisabeth; God has favoured me plus God is my oath*

Anneka, Anika, Annika, Anna, Anniken • German/Dutch • *God has favoured me*

Annemarie, Annmarie, Annamarie,

Annamaria • modern • *combo of Anne and Maria; God has favoured me*

Anwyl, Annwyl • British/Welsh • *beloved, darling, dear*

Apollinaria, Apollonia, Apolline, Apolloneia, Abelone • Italian/Greek • *the god Apollo*

Ariel, Arielle, Ariella • Biblical/Hebrew/Jewish • *lion of God*

Armana • African • *faithful*

Åsa, Ase • Norse • *God*

Aslög, Asslaug, Åslaug • Swedish • *God-consecrated*

Asmā • Arabic • *prestigious*

Aster • Ethiopian • *star*

Astra, Estelle, Aster, Stella, Astrum • Greek/Latin • *star*

Astrid, Åsta, Sassa • Norse • *love*

Atarah, Atara, Kreine • Biblical/Jewish/Hebrew/Yiddish • *crown*

Audra, Audrey, Audrie, Audry, Audrina • Anglo-Saxon • *strength and noble of character*

Augusta, Augustina, Augustine, Agustina, August • Latin • *great, the max, magnificent, expansive, nobody does it better*

Aurelia, Auriol • Latin • *Latin • Roman family name meaning golden*

Aurelie • Latin/French • *Roman family name meaning golden*

Aurora, Dawn, Aurore • Latin • *the sun comes up*

'Azza • Arabic • *pride and power*

Bahiyya • Arabic • *a beautiful, radiant, dazzling woman*

Baozhai • Arabic • *precious hairpin*

Bay, Baie, Baca, Bacca • Latin/Norman • *bay tree*

Beathag • Irish Gaelic • *life*

Belaynesh • Ethiopian • *you are above all*

Bertha, Berthe, Berta • Germanic • *bright and famous*

Bess, Bessie, Bet, Beth, Elizabeth, Elisabeth, Bethan, Betsy, Betty, Bette, Bettina, Buffy, Beitidh, Elisheba • Hebrew/Greek • *God is my oath or God is my abundance*

Bethlehem, Belem • Biblical/Jewish/Hebrew • *where Jesus was born*

Bethan, Beth • British/Welsh • *God is my oath or God is my abundance*

Bionda • Italian • *blondie!*

Bobbie, Roberta • Germanic • *famous and bright*

Breanna, Brianna, Breanne • Irish Celtic • *high or royal born, noble*

Bridget, Briget, Bridgid, Brigid, Biddy, Bride, Bridy, Bridie, Bridey, Brigitte, Britt, Brighid, Birgit, Brigette, Birgitta, Brigitta, Bedelia, Bríd, Breda, Breeda, Bree, Bríghe, Brídín, Bri, Brighida, Berit, Britta, Birgitte, Birthe, Birte, Ffraid • Irish Gaelic • *the exalted one*

Cara, Kara • Italian/Irish Gaelic • *beloved friend*

Caron • British Welsh • *to love*

Carys, Gladys, Gwladys, Cerys • British/Welsh • *loving*

Cassia, Kezia • Latin • *thy name is vanity!*

Celia, Célie, Caelia, Caelum, Celina • Latin • *Roman family name meaning heaven*

Céleste, Celestine, Celestina, Celia, Celine, Marcelline, Caelius, Caelia, Caelestis • Latin • *Roman family name meaning heaven*

Céline, Caelina, Marceline, Marcelline, Caelius, Celina • Latin/French • *Roman family name meaning heaven*

Chanel, Chanelle, Shanelle • French/Modern • *in honour of Gabrielle CoCo Chanel, founder of the perfume house; especially 19th August*

Chaya, Eve, Arye • Jewish/Hebrew • *lion*

Chenguang • Chinese • *morning light*

Cherie, Cheri, Cherie, Cheree, Sheree, Querida • French • *darling*

Cherry, Cherie, Cherrie • French • *darling fruit!*

Chevonne, Siobhán, Shivaun • English/American/Irish Gaelic • *God is gracious or gift of God*

Chiara, Clare, Claire, Clara, Ciara, Kiarah, Kiara, Kiera, Clair, Clarette, Clarinda, Clarrie, Clarus • Latin/Italian • *bright, famous, crystal-clear*

Chloe, Chloris, Cloris, Khloris, Khloe • Greek • *another name for the Goddess of Fertility, Demeter or Ceres*

Chorine, Choreen, Corinne, Corinna • French • *chorus or dancing girl*

Chrystal, Crystal, Chrystalla, Chrystellina, Khyros, Khrysos • Greek • *gold*

Celandine, Dina • English/Greek • *a flower*

Cindy, Cynthia, Lucinda, Cendrillon, Sindy, Cinderella • French • *cinders from the fire*

Cleopatra, Cleo, Clio, Kleos, Kleio, Kleopatra • Greek/Ptolemaic • *glory to father*

Constance, Connie, Konnie, Constantia, Konstanze, Contanze • Latin • *constancy; steadfast and faithful*

Corazón • Roman Catholic • *sacred heart, the heart of Jesus Christ*

Corona • Latin • *crown*

Cressida, Cressa, Criseida, Criseyde, Khryseis • Greek • *gold*

Cushla • Irish Gaelic • *the beat of my heart*

Cyra • Greek • *lord or chief*

Dagny, Dagna, Dagne • Norse • *a new day, the dawn*

Daisy, Daegesage, Margaret, Marguerite • Anglo-Saxon • *day's eye because it closes its petals at night*

Damask • Arabic • *the city of Damascus, Syria and the damask rose*

Danae • Greek mythology • *her great-grandfather founded the Greek tribe of Danai or Argives; she was raped by Zeus/Jupitêr when he appeared to her as a shower of gold, and she gave birth to the hero Perseus*

Dandan • Chinese • *my (red) cinnabar*

Danika, Danica • Slavic • *morning star*

Daphne, Laurel, Lorel, Lorer • Greek • *the laurel tree*

Darlene, Darleen • American English/Australian • *darling*

Darya • Persian • *a good, royal ruler*

Dassa, Dassah, Hadassah, Esther • Hebrew/Persian/Jewish • *Myrtle, Star and Persian Goddess of Fertility, Love and War, Ishtar*

Davina, Davida, Davena, Davinia • Biblical/Hebrew • *vague origins but possibly from a baby word meaning darling one*

Dawn, Aurora, Dawne, Duha, Dagung • Anglo-Saxon • *daybreak!*

Delice, Delyse, Delicia, Delysia,

Delicae, Delicius, Delite, Delicia • Latin • *angel delight!*

Della, Adela • French • *noble*

Devi • Sanskrit • *Her Majesty the Queen*

Devon, Devonne • British/Welsh • *the tribe of the Dumnonos, who worshipped the Celtic god of the same name*

Disgleirio • British/Welsh • *bright, glittering, dazzling*

Disa, Hjördis, Tordis • Norse • *goddess*

Diva, Divine • Italian • *goddess!*

Dolina, Dolag, Donella • Scots Gaelic • *world ruler*

Dolly, Dorothy, Dolores, Dora • English/Greek • *gift from God*

Domitilla, Domitius • Latin • *a Roman imperial family name*

Donatella, Donatus • Latin • *given by God*

Donella, Donna • Scots Gaelic • *world ruler*

Dora, Isedore, Isadora, Theodora, Doria, Dorinda, Dory • Greek • *gift*

Doreen, Dorean, Dorene, Dorine • Greek/Irish • *gift*

Dorian, Dorienne, Dorean • literary name • *dor is Greek for gift. Oscar Wilde's invention for* The Portrait of Dorian Gray; *most likely from the Dorian women of southern mainland Greece*

Doris, Dorris • Greek • *a tribe of Greece, the Dorian women from Doros, southern mainland Greece, from the name son of or gift to the Hellenes*

Dorothea, Dorothy, Dorothee, Dorothie, Dot, Dottie, Dotty, Dodie, Dolly, Dorofei, Dorotheos, Dorete, Dee • Greek • *gift from God*

Drew • Biblical/Greek/Scots English • *a real sexy person*

Dwynwyn • British/Welsh • *Goddess of Love and Relationships*

Earla, Erla, Earlina, Erline, Earline, Earlene, Earleen • American/English • *a noble person*

Ehuang • Chinese • *august beauty*

Éibhleann, Eibhliu, Evlin • Irish Gaelic • *beautiful, radiant*

Eiddwen, Eiddunwen • British/Welsh • *fond, passionate, desire, holy, white, fair*

Electra, Ellettra • Greek • *brilliant*

Elaine, Helen • Greek/French • *sunbeam, ray of sun, coming from the name for the Greeks, the Hellen(es)*

Éliane, Liane, Aeliana, Eliana, Aelianus • Latin/Greek • *sun*

Ellen, Helen, Elin, Elen, Ella, Elena, Nell, Nelly, Nellie, Ellena, Ellenor • modern English • *shortened form of Helen and Eleanor*

Elizabeth, Elisabeth, Elisheba, Élise, Eliza, Elisa, Elsa, Liza, Lisa, Liz, Beth, Bet, Bess, Lisbet, Lisbeth, Lysbeth, Elsie, Bessie, Bessy, Betty, Betsy, Tetty, Libby, Lizzie, Lizzy, Buffy, Eilis, Ealasaid, Elisabet, Elisabete, Elisabetta, Elisavet, Yelizaveta, Elzbieta, Alzbeta, Elizabeta, Erzsebet, Elspeth, Eliza • Biblical/Hebrew/Jewish • *God is my oath*

Elisha, Eleesha • Jewish/Hebrew • *Yahweh is God*

Elita, Elire • American English • *elite person, upper class, VIP*

Elle • American English/French • *French for 'she'*

Ellis • Biblical/Greek • *Yahweh is God*

Elspeth, Elsbeth, Elspie, Elsie, Elspet, Elizabeth • Scots English/ Biblical • *God is my oath*

Élise, Elyse, Elysia, Alicia, Elisabeth • Biblical/French • *God is my oath*

Emily, Aemilia, Aemilius, Émilie • Latin • *old Roman family name meaning rival, competitor*

Erica, Ericka, Erika • Norse • *one ruler or king alone, no other*

Ermintrude, Trude, Trudy • Germanic/Frankish • *you are my entire world, my beloved*

Esther, Esta, Hester, Haddasah, Eistir, Ester • Hebrew/Persian/ Jewish • *Myrtle, Star and Persian Goddess of Fertility, Love and War, Ishtar*

Estelle, Stella • Latin/Norman • *star*

Étaín, Éadaoin, Eaden • Irish Gaelic • *the jealous Celtic sun goddess*

Ethel • Anglo-Saxon • *noble*

Eudora, Dora, Doron • Greek • *a good gift*

Eugenia, Eugenios, Eugenius, Eugenie • Greek • *well bred and high born*

Eydl, Edel • Jewish/Yiddish • *noble*

Faith • English • *she who trusts in God, faithful follower*

Fania, Stefania • Italian/Greek • *a crown or garland*

Fiedhelm, Fedelma, Fidelma • Irish Gaelic • *unknown origins but given to a beautiful Irish Bouddicca*

Feivel, Faivish • Jewish/Yiddish/ Aramaic • *God of the sun, Apollo or linked to Samson*

Fiamma, Fiammetta • Italian • *fiery*

Fiesta, Festa • Latin/Spanish • *celebration, particularly over a baby's birth*

Fifi, Joséphine • French/Biblical/ Hebrew/Jewish • *short name for Joséphine, meaning God is my salvation*

Filomena, Philomena, Philomenes, Phileinmenos, Philomenus • Greek • *love, strength*

Fina, Seraphina • Jewish/Hebrew • *the burning ones*

Flair, Flairer • American English/ French • *showing an individual talent*

Freya, Froja, Frouwa, Friday, Frøya, Freia, Freyja • Norse • *lady referring to the Goddess of Love*

Freyde, Freud, Freude • Jewish/ Yiddish • *joy unconfined*

Gabrielle, Gabriella, Gabi, Gaby, Gabby, Gabriel, Gabriele, Gabriela • Biblical/Hebrew/Jewish • *person of God*

Gail, Gael, Abigail, Gaelle, Gaile, Gale, Gayle • Biblical/Jewish/ Hebrew • *shortened Abigail; my father is joy, father is exaltation*

Genista, Genesta • Latin • *the shrub plant called broom, a bright yellow colour*

Gerlinde, Gerlind • Germanic • *soft and tender; spear*

Gillian, Gill, Jill, Gillyflower, Gillaine, Jillian, Jilly, Gilly • Latin • *from Julius, a Roman family name that gives its name to the month of July*

Ginger • English • *someone with red hair!*

Ginikanwa, Gini • Nigerian • *what is more precious than a child?*

Ginny, Virginia, Jane, Jaine, Jane, Ginnie, Jinny • Biblical/English/ Latin • *pet name for Virginia or Jane;*

God is gracious or gift of God
Giovanna • Biblical/English/Latin • *LADY John! God is gracious or gift of God*
Giuletta, Giulia • Latin/Italian • *from Julius, an old Roman name*
Giuseppina • Biblical/Italian • *LADY Joseph! God shall add another son; God is my salvation*
Gloria, Gloriana, Glory • Latin • *glorious!*
Godiva • Anglo-Saxon/Latin • *God's gift*
Golda, Golde • Jewish/Yiddish • *gold*
Goldie, Blondie, Guinevere • American English • *a girl with blond hair*
Guinevere, Gwenhwyfar, Goldie • English/British/Welsh • *blondie!*
Gull, Gudgull • Norse/Swedish • *God of Gold, Mammon*
Gwenyth, Gwenith • British/Welsh • *wheat, romantic word for the pick of the crop!*
Gytha, Gyth, Gudrid • Anglo-Saxon/Norse • *discord or beautiful god*

Habība • Arabic • *beloved one*
Habibunah • Swahili • *our beloved*
Hadassah, Dassah, Esther • Hebrew/Persian/Jewish • *Myrtle, Star and Persian Goddess of Fertility, Love and War, Ishtar*
Hannah, Hanne, Johanna, Hanna • Biblical/Jewish/Hebrew • *God has favoured me*
Hansine • Germanic • *God is gracious or gift of God*
Harmony, Harmonie • English • *concord, unity, friendship*
Heaven, Heofon • American

English/Anglo-Saxon • *where God lives and good people go after this life*
Hefina • British/Welsh • *summer girl*
Heidi, Adelheid, Adélaide, Heide • Germanic • *noble woman, carries herself well*
Heike • Germanic • *a famous army that carries all before it; a shining light*
Helen, Helena, Hélène, Elena, Elen, Elin • Greek/English • *ray of sunshine, sunbeam, sunny*
Henrietta, Henriette, Enriqueta • German/French/Spanish • *a famous army that carries all before it; a shining light*
Hephzibah, Hepzibah, Hepsie, Effie • Biblical • *my delight is in her (my newborn daughter)*
Hester, Esther, Hettie, Hetty • English • *Myrtle, Star and Persian Goddess of Fertility, Love and War, Ishtar*
Heulog • British/Welsh • *sunny*
Heulwen • British/Welsh • *sunshine*
Hiba • Arabic • *a gift or prize from God*
Hildebrande • Germanic • *flaming sword into battle*
Hong • Chinese • *red*
Honor, Honour, Honora, Honorah, Honoria, Honoré, Honorine, Honorina, Norine, Noreen • Norman/Latin • *an honoured woman*
Hulda, Huldah • sweet, lovable, adorable
Hyacinth, Jacinth, Jacinthe, Jacintha, Hyakinthos • Greek/English • *love and passion*

Ihāb • Arabic • *a gift from God*
Ilayne, Elaine • Greek/modern

English • *sunbeam, ray of sun, coming from the name for the Greeks, the Hellen(es)*

Ilona, Helen • Hungarian • *sunbeam, ray of sun, coming from the name for the Greeks, the Hellen(es)*

Ilse, Ilsa, Elisabeth • Germanic/ Biblical • *God is my oath*

In'ām • Arabic • *a gift given or bestowed by God*

Inanna, Anna • Sumerian • *Queen of Heaven*

India • English • *as in India, the country*

Isabel, Isobel, Isa, Isabella, Isabelle, Isobelle, Isobella, Izzy, Izzie, Sibéal, Iseabail, Ishbel, Isbel, Elizabeth • Spanish/Biblical/ Hebrew/Jewish • *God is my oath*

Isadora, Isidoro, Izzy • Greek/ Egyptian • *a gift from the goddess Isis, deity of magic and life*

Isolde, Isolda, Iseult, Esyllt • Arthurian mythology/British Welsh • *a beautiful Irish princess*

Jalīla, Galīla • Arabic • *exalted on high*

Jana, Yana, Jan • Biblical/English/ Latin • *God is gracious or gift of God*

Jane, Jeanne, Jehanne, Jaine, Jayne, Jain, Jean, Joan, Janie, Janey, Joanna, Jaynie, Síne, Siân, Johanna, Hanne, Hansine, Johanne, Janja, Jannja, Sheena Jensine, Jonna, Jeanne, Juanna, Juana, Giovanna, Gianna, Hana, Jana, Janeen, Janelle, Jaynia • Biblical/French/Latin

Janet, Jannet, Janett, Janette, Jan, Janetta, Janeta, Seònaid, Shona, Seona • Biblical/English/Latin •

God is gracious or gift of God

Janice, Janis, Janise, Jannice, Jan, Janeth • Biblical/French/Latin • *God is gracious or gift of God*

Jan, Janna • Biblical/English • *God is gracious or gift of God*

Jawāhir, Gawāhir • Arabic • *a dazzling jewel*

Jean, Joan, Jane, Jeanne, Jehanne, Jehanna, Jeane, Jeana, Gina, Jeanna, Jeane, Jeanetta, Jeanette, Jeanie, Jeanine, Jeannette, Jeanne, Jeanett, Jenette, Jennet, Jenet, Ginett, Ginnette, Ginetta, Ginnetta, Jeannie, Jeannine, Jeannique, Jannike • Biblical/ French • *God is gracious or gift of God*

Jemima • Biblical/Hebrew/Jewish • *dove; as bright as day*

Jerrie, Jerry, Geri, Gerry • Biblical/ English • *appointed by God*

Jill, Jillian, Gillian, Gill, Jilly, Gilly, Jillie • from Julius, a Roman family names that gives its name to the month of July

Jo, Joe, Joanna, Joanne, Jody, Josephine, Josie, Josey • Biblical/ Greek • *God is gracious or gift of God*

Joan, Ionna, Iohanna, Joanna, Johanna, Joanne, Johanne, Joanie, Joni, Siobhán, Chevanne, Siubhan, Jane, Shevaune, Chevaune, Shona, Shevanne, Joann, Seonag • Biblical/Norman • *God is gracious or gift of God*

Joelle, Joël • Biblical/Hebrew/ Jewish/French • *God*

Johanna, Johna, Johannah, Johanne, Joanna, Joanne, Jo, Jannike • Biblical/Latin • *God is gracious or gift of God*

Jonina • Biblical/English • *God is gracious or gift of God*

Josefa, Yosefa • Bibilical/Hebrew/ Jewish • *God will provide me with another son*

Joséphine, Josefine, Josephina, Josefina, Jo, Josie, Jozie, Josette, Fifi, Posy, Josefa, Jozefa, Josée, Josiane, Seosaimhín, Josianne, Josiane • Biblical/French • *God will provide me with another son*

Joy, Joie, Gaudia • Latin/French • *joyful in the Lord*

Juanita, Janita, Janita • Spanish • *God is gracious or gift of God*

Julia, Juli, Julie, Giulia, Julietta, Guilietta, Juliet, Juliette, Guiliette, Juliana, Julianus, Julianna, Julianne, Julián, Juliane, Julieann, Julien, Julieanne, Julienne Jools, Julia, Jules, Juleen, Julianne • Latin • *a Roman name which becomes month of July*

Juno, Hera • Greek/Roman • *Queen of the Gods, Greek and Roman pantheon*

Jyoti • Sanskrit • *light of mind, light of freedom, light of paradise*

Karenza, Carenza • British/Welsh/ Kernow • *love, loving to be loved*

Karīma • Arabic • *a woman with a noble personality and generous too boot!*

Kelly, Kelley, Kellie, Ceallach • Irish Gaelic • *bright-headed, quick-tempered*

Keren, Kerenhappuch, Keran, Kerin, Kerrin, Keron, Kerena, Kerina • Biblical/Hebrew/Jewish • *ray of light or eye painted in the shape of a horn*

Kreine, Kroine, Crean, Kreen,

Krone, Corona • Jewish/Yiddish • *crown*

Kristel, Krystal, Chrystal • German/ Greek • *gold*

Krone, Corona • German/Latin • *crown*

Lacey, Lassy, Lassie, Lacy • Norman/Irish • *Norman baronial name Lassy, who became powerful in Ireland in the medieval period*

Lalita • Sanskrit • *this girl is as playful as a kitten; affectionate and amorous*

Lani, Leilani • Polynesian/Hawaiian • *sky, heaven*

Laoise, Leesha, Luigseach • Irish Gaelic • *unsure origins but most possibly Lug, Goddess of Light/ someone from County Laoise*

Laraine, Larraine, Lareina, Lareine • African American • *the queen*

Laura, Laurel, Laureen, Laurene, Laurelle, Laurie, Laure, Laurette, Lora, Lowri • Latin • *laurel tree, sacred to those who are victorious and honoured*

Lauretta, Loretta, Lorette • Latin/ Italian • *laurel tree, sacred to those who are victorious and honoured*

Lavinia, Lavinium, Luvinia • Etruscan/Roman mythology • *wife of King Aeneus and mother of the Roman people*

Liane, Leeanne, Éliane, Leann, Leanna, Lean • French/Latin/Greek • *sun*

Leda • Greek mythology • *Queen of Sparta who was raped by Zeus/ Jupiter in the shape of a swan*

Lena, Yelena, Helen • Greek/ Russian • *ray of sunshine, sunbeam, sunny*

Leona, Léonie, Léon, Leoni, Leonia, Leonne, Liona • Latin • *lion*
Leontina, Léontine • Italian/French • *family name of Leontius, meaning lion*
Lexie, Alexandra, Alexis, Alex, Lexy, Lexis, Leagsaidh, Lexine • Greek • *the warrior/leader who protects or defends her people*
Liane, Lianne, Elianus, Helianus, Lian, Liana, Liann, Lianne, Lianna, Éliane • French/Latin/Greek • *sun*
Libby, Elizabeth • English • *God is my oath*
Libe, Liebe • Jewish/Yiddish/German • *love or darling*
Liese, Elisabeth • German • *God is my oath*
Lili, Lilli, Elisabeth • German • *God is my oath*
Lisa, Liza, Elyse, Lise, Liese, Élise, Elisabeth • French/German • *God is my oath*
Lisette, Lise, Elisabeth, Lysette, Lise, Lys, Liz, Lis, Elisbet, Liza, Eliza, Lisa, Lizzie, Lizzy, Lizi, Elizabeth • English/French • *God is my oath*
Liv, Lif • Norse • *life*
Lleucu, Leucu, Lughaidh, Lugh, Lucy, Lucía, Lugh, Lugus • British Welsh/Latin • *light*
Llewella, Lugobelinos • British/Welsh • *lion!*
Lolonyo • Ghanaian • *love is beautiful*
Loreen, Lorene • Latin/Gaelic • *laurel tree, sacred to those who are victorious and honoured*
Lorelle, Laura • Latin/French • *laurel tree, sacred to those who are victorious and honoured*
Loretta, Lauretta, Loreto • Roman Catholic/Italian • *laurel tree, sacred to those who are victorious and honoured*
Lowri, Laura • British/Welsh/Latin • *laurel tree, sacred to those who are victorious and honoured*
Luana, Luanna, Luanne, Luan • cosmetic Italian • *made up for a 1932 movie; Luana, the sacred virgin*
Lucía, Lucilla, Lucy, Lucie, Luce, Lucetta, Luciana • Latin • *light*
Lucien, Lucienne • Latin • *light*
Lucilla, Lucille, Lucy, Lucille, Lucy, Luci • Latin • *light*
Lucinda, Lucía, Sinda, Cindy, Sindy, Lucy, Lucinde • Latin • *light*
Lucie, Lucy, Lucinda, Luíseach, Lucía, Lucinde, Liùsaidh • Norman/Latin • *light*
Lyra • Latin • *a stringed musical instrument*

Mabel, Mab, Amabel, Amabilia, Mabilia, Mabelle, Amiabel, Maybelle, Maybella • Norman/English • *lovely*
Maia, Maya, Mya • Latin • *Roman Goddess of Youth, Life, Rebirth, Love and Sexuality*
Malikiya • Swahili • *my queen*
Malkah, Malka • Jewish/Hebrew • *queen*
Manara • Arabic • *she sends out a radiant light like a pharo (lighthouse)*
Manuela • Biblical/Spanish • *God is with us or amongst us*
Marisol • Spanish • *combination of María and Sol (sun)*
Marva, Marvalee • American English • *he's a lord or eminent being down to his marrow*
Maxine, Max, Maxie • Latin • *the greatest!*
Mehetabel, Mehitabel • Biblical/

Jewish/Hebrew • *God makes for happiness*

Meredith, Meredydd • British/Welsh • *unknown prefix plus lord*

Michaela, Mikayla, Mica, Micah • Biblical/Hebrew/Jewish/English • *who is like God?*

Michele, Michelle, Michel Chelle, Shell, Micheline • Biblical/Hebrew/Jewish/English • *who is like God?*

Mignon, Mignonette, Minette • French • *little darling, cutie, sweetie*

Mirabelle, Mirabella, Mirabellis, Mirari, Mirabilis • Latin/French • *wonderful, glorious*

Mireille, Mireio, Miriam, Mary, Miranda, Mireio, Mirella • Provençal • *to admire*

Mona, Muadhnait, Monos, Muadh • Irish Gaelic • *noble*

Munira • Arabic • *radiant, bright, send out a light*

Myrna, Muirne, Morna • Irish Gaelic • *beloved*

Nan, Nancy, Nanette, Ann • Biblical/Jewish/Hebrew • *pet form of Ann, of uncertain origins: God has favoured me*

Nancy, Nan, Ann, Annis, Agnès, Nancle, Nanci, Nance • Biblical/Jewish/Hebrew • *pet form of Ann, of uncertain origins: God has favoured me*

Nanette, Nan • Biblical/Jewish/Hebrew/French • *pet form of Ann, of uncertain origins: God has favoured me*

Natalia, Natalya, Natalie, Natasha • Latin/Russian • *the birth of Jesus Christ or reborn with faith*

Natalie, Nathalie, Natalia • Latin/French • *the birth of Jesus Christ*

or reborn with faith

Natasha, Natalia, Noel • Latin/Russian • *the birth of Jesus Christ or reborn with faith*

Nazaret, Nazareth • Roman Catholic • *Jesus Christ's native village*

Nawāl • Arabic • *a gift bestowed or given*

Nell, Nella, Nellie, Nelly, Eleanor, Ellen, Helen • *English short name for Eleanor, Ellen or Helen*

Neroli • Italian • *an aromatic oil based on bitter orange, founded by Princess Anne Marie de la Tremoille of Neroli*

Nia, Niamh, Neve • British/Welsh/Irish • *beautiful and bright*

Niamh, Neve, Nia • Irish Gaelic • *beautiful and bright*

Ninghong • Chinese • *serene red or I would rather be red*

Nyamekye • Ghanian • *given by God*

Olympe, Olympia • Greek • *a woman from Olympus, the mountain of the gods*

Oksana, Oxana • Russian • *praise God*

Olufemi • Nigerian • *God loves me*

Oralle, Aurelle, Aurella, Oralee • Latin/French • *Roman family name meaning golden*

Oriana, Aurum, Oriane • Spanish/Norman • *uncertain roots but may mean gold*

Órla, Ona, Anona, Fíona, Honor, Orfhlaith, Orflaith, Orlaith • Irish Gaelic • *golden lady or princess*

Patrice, Patricia • Latin/French • *Latin/Irish Gaelic • patrician*

Patricia, Patrice, Pat, Tricia, Trisha,

Trish, Patty, Pattie, Patti, Patsy, Patrizia, Pat, Patsy • Latin/Irish Gaelic • *patrician*

Paudeen, Páidín • Irish Gaelic/ English • *pet name for Patricia*

Peijing • Chinese • *admiring luxuriance*

Petula • Latin • *tagetis petula aka French marigold*

Philomena, Philomenus, Philomenes, Phileinmenos, Philoumena, Filumena, Filomena • Greek/Germanic

Phyllis, Phillida, Phyllis, Phyllidos, Phyllidis, Phyllida, Phyllicia, Phylicia • Greek mythology • *a Thracian queen, Phyllis died for love and transformed herself into an almond tree; her name means leaves or leaf and she is a symbol of undying love and friendship*

Posy, Posey, Josephine, Poesy • Biblical/English • *God will provide me with another son*

Precious • American English • *dear; beloved: a precious child*

Premiata • Sanskrit • *symbolic of the plant or flower of love*

Priya • Sanskrit • *beloved one*

Queenie, Victoria, Cwene, Cwen • Anglo-Saxon/English • *popular name for Victoria*

Raine, Reine, Rayne, Regina • French/Germanic • *queen*

Raisa • Slavic • *paradise, heaven*

Rajni • Sanskrit • *queen of the night*

Regina, Queenie, Raine, Régine, Raghnailt, Ragnhild • Latin/Roman Catholic • *queen (of heaven)*

Rexanne, Roxanne, Roxane • Latin • *queen*

Rhianna, Rhiannon, Reanna, Rianna, Rhianon, Riannon, Rheanna, Rigantona, Rhianna, Reanne, Rhiannon, Rigantona • British Welsh/Celtic mythology • *great queen*

Ríonach, Rina, Caterina, Katerina, Carina, Sabrina, Regina, Ríona, Rio, Rioghnach, Rinach • Irish Gaelic • *royalty; like a queen*

Ritz, Ritzy • American English • *posh hotel name*

Robbin, Robbie, Roberta • Germanic • *famous and bright*

Roberta, Robbie • Germanic • *famous and bright*

Robyn, Robin, Robina • Germanic • *famous and bright*

Roxanne, Roxane, Roxana, Roxanna, Roxy, Rozanne • Latin/ Greek/Persian • *dawn*

Roxy • American English • *flashy, glitzy but just a little nouvelle riche!*

Ruby, Rube, Rubinus, Rubeus • Latin • *the gemstone, ruby*

Rukmini • Sanskrit • *dripping with gold*

Ryanne, Ryan, Riain • Irish Gaelic/ English • *little king, descendant of Riain*

Sabāh • Arabic • *morning*

Saffron, Safran • Arabic/Norman • *the saffron or Spanish crocus; the most expensive spice in the world*

Safiyya • Arabic • *the best friend anyone could have*

Sahar • Arabic • *morning has broken*

Samantha, Sam, Sammy, Sammi • Biblical/Hebrew/Jewish • *the name of God, God has heard, listen to God*

Sanā • Arabic • *a brilliant, radiant woman*

Sandra, Sandy, Alessandra, Alexandra, Sandi, Saundra, Sander • the warrior/leader who protects or defends her people

Sandhya • Sanskrit • *twilight of the gods, devout, ritualistic*

Saniyya • Arabic • *wonderful, dazzling woman*

Sasha, Alexandra, Sashura, Shura • Greek • *the warrior/leader who protects or defends her people*

Satin, Zaituni, Tsingtung • Chinese/Arabic/French/English/Latin • *soft, sleek, silky, shiny fabric*

Savitri • Sanskrit • *I belong to the sun god!*

Seraphina, Seraphim, Serafina, Fina, Serafima • Jewish/Hebrew • *the burning ones*

Seren, Serena, Serenus • British/Welsh • *star*

Shahīra • Arabic • *destiny for fame and fortune*

Shahnaz • Persian • *the glory of kings*

Shan • Chinese • *a woman who bears herself elegantly; like royalty or a model*

Shana, Shanae, Shania, Shanee, Siani, Siân • American English/British Welsh • *God is gracious or gift of God*

Sindy, Cindy, Sinda • French • *cinders from the fire*

Sinéad, Janet, Jeanette, Seònaid, Shona, Seona • English/Scots Gaelic • *God is gracious or gift of God*

Siobhán, Joan, Jehanne, Shevaun, Chevonne, Chevaun, Chevaunne, Shevaunne, Jehanne, Joan • English/Norman French/Biblical/Irish Gaelic • *God is gracious or gift of God*

Sioned, Janet • English/British Welsh • *God is gracious or gift of God*

Sissy, Sisi, Sissey, Sissie, Elisabeth • Jewish/Hebrew/Bavarian • *God is my oath*

Siv • Norse • *bride or wife; name of Thor's golden-haired missus*

Slava • Slavic • *glorious*

Sloane, Sloan • English • *after Sloane Square in London; name given to a Sloane Ranger*

Sondra, Sandra • American English • *modern name for Sandra*

Sorcha, Sarah, Sally • Irish Gaelic • *brightness*

Sri • Sanskrit • *a royal personage who radiates the light of goodness, beauty and wealth*

Sroel, Israel • Jewish/Yiddish • *one who strives with God*

Star, Starr, Stella • English • *a star (heavenly rather than celebrity)*

Steffanie, Stéphanie, Steph, Steffi, Stefanie, Steff • Greek • *a crown or garland*

Stella, Stella Maris • Latin • *a star and Star of the Seas (often used to describe the Virgin Mary)*

Stéphanie, Steff, Steph, Steffie, Steffy, Stevie, Stefanie, Steffany, Stephania, Stephana, Stefania, Estefania, Stevie • Greek • *a crown or garland*

Suha • Arabic • *star*

Sultana • Arabic • *empress, queen*

Sujata • Sanskrit • *excellent character or born of nobility*

Summer, Haf, Sumor • Anglo-Saxon • *someone born in the summer*

Sunday, Sunnandaeg, Sunnedaeg • Anglo-Saxon • *the sun's day*

Sunniva, Sunnegifu, Synnøve, Synneva, Synnøv, Synne • English • *gift from the sun*

Sunny, Sunnie • English • *cheery, cheerful, full of joy; a sunny disposition*

Svetlana, Sveta, Photine • Slavic/Greek • *light*

Sybil, Sybille, Sybilla, Sibylla, Sibilia, Sibella, Sibéal, Cybille, Sibilla, Sibella, Cybil, Cybill • Greek mythology • *a woman with the power to predict; a devotee of Apollo, the sun god*

Talia, Talya, Natalya, Thalia • Latin/Russian • *the birth of Jesus Christ or reborn with faith*

Tara, Teamhair, Tarra, Taree • Irish Gaelic • *a hill that was the seat of the high kings of Ireland*

Tara • Sanskrit • *a shining star who carries the troubles of the world on her shoulders*

Tasha, Natasha • Latin • *the birth of Jesus Christ or reborn with faith*

Tawny, Tauny, Tawney, Taune, Tane • Anglo-Saxon/Norman • *someone with light brown hair*

Tempe, Temnein • Greek • *a valley in Greece; the legendary home of the Muses, the nine goddesses of the arts and sciences*

Tetty, Tettie, Elizabeth • English • *pet name for Elizabeth*

Thanā • Arabic • *a woman ready to praise and be praised; everything she does deserves praise*

Thea, Dorothea • Greek • *short name for Dorothea*

Thecia, Theokleia • Greek • *glory of God*

Theodora, Dora, Teodora, Feodora • Greek • *God-given or giving to God or God's gift*

Theodosia, Dosy, Theodosis • Greek • *God-given*

Theokleia, Thecia, Tekla • Greek • *glory of God*

Thheiba • Arabic • *gold bar*

Topaz • Biblical/Hebrew/Greek • *God is good*

Tordis • Norse • *goddess connected to Thor*

Tori, Tory, Toria • English • *short form of Victoria*

Usha • Sanskrit • *Goddess of the Dawn*

Victoria, Vicky, Vickie, Vicki, Vikki, Tory, Toria, Vita, Victoire, Viktoria, Vittoria, Bhictoria • Latin/English • *conqueror, winner*

Vita, Victoria • Latin • *life; also short name for Victoria*

Vivienne, Vivien, Viv, Vi, Vivi, Vivienne, Vivianne, Béibhinn • Latin/Norman • *Roman name Vivianus, meaning life*

Wenqian • Chinese • *madder red*

Wynne, Wynn, Wine • British Welsh/Anglo-Saxon • *a friend and/or one who is blessed and sacred*

Xanthe, Xanthos • Greek • *bright yellow*

Xiaodan • Chinese • *little dawn*

Xiaojing • Chinese • *morning luxury*

Xiaotong • Chinese • *dawn red*

Yana, Jana • Biblical/English/Latin • *God is gracious or gift of God*

Yelena, Helen, Helena • Russian/

Greek • *ray of sunshine, sunbeam, sunny*
Yelisaveta, Elisabeth • Hebrew/Jewish • *God is my oath*

Zarina • Persian • *she is golden*
Zenith, Samtarras • Arabic • *overhead (celestial) path*

Zhenzhen • Chinese • *my precious*
Zoe • Greek • *life*
Zongying • Chinese • *heroine the others look up to; a role model*
Zubaida • Arabic • *marigold*

VIRGO

24th August to 23rd September

Planet: Mercury

Day: Wednesday

Stones: peridot and garnet

Metal: mercury

Colours: autumn and harvest shades, beige, fawn, camel, wheat, russet red, apple green

Design: shapes and patterns that tell a story, lines and contours that join and connect

Trees: horse chestnut, hazel, walnut and all nut-bearing trees, bonsai, olive

Flora: tulip, small colourful dainty flowers, especially border plants to make neat rows

Celebrity Virgos: Prince Albert • Sir Richard Attenborough • Lauren Bacall • Johann Sebastian Bach • Anne Bancroft • Ingrid Bergman • Leonard Bernstein • Jacqueline Bissett • Rossano Brazzi • Anton Bruckner • William Rice Burroughs • Maurice Chevalier • Agatha Christie • King Chulalongkorn • James Coburn • Claudette Colbert • Jimmy Connors • Sean Connery • Jackie Cooper • Elvis Costello • Brian De Palma • Antonin Dvorak • Queen Elizabeth I • Mama Cass Elliot • Gloria Estefan • Jose Feliciano • Greta Garbo • Richard Gere • Barry Gibb • Elliot Gould • Linda Gray • Buddy Hackett • Prince Harry • Pee-wee Herman • Buddy Holly • Gustav Holst • Amy Irving • Jeremy Irons • Christopher Isherwood • Ivan the Terrible • Michael Jackson • Lyndon Johnson • Tommy Lee Jones • Michael Keaton • Stephen King • DH Lawrence • Sophia Loren • Louis XIV ('the Sun King') • Mickey Mouse • Rocky Marciano • Bill Murray • Bob Newhart • Aristotle Onassis • Arnold Palmer • Regis Philbin • River Phoenix • Otis Redding • Keanu Reeves • Cliff Robertson • Peter Sellers • Charlie Sheen • Mary Shelley • Dame Edith Sitwell • Oliver Stone • William H Taft • Mother Teresa • Count Leo Tolstoy • Lilly Tomlin • Twiggy (model) • Johann Wolfgang von Goethe • Raquel Welch • Tuesday Weld • HG Wells • Queen Wilhelmina • Yasser Arafat • Darryl F Zanuck.

Planetary Influences: see Mercury at the back of this book (page 450)

Boys

Abbán, Abbot • Irish Gaelic • *abbot: the head or superior of a monastery*

'Abd-al-Āti • Arabic • *servant of giver, Allah*

'Abd-al-Āziz • Arabic • *servant of the mighty Allah*

'Abd-al-Fattāh • Arabic • *servant of the opener of the gates of prosperity*

'Abd-al-Hādi • Arabic • *servant of the guide, Allah*

'Abd-al-Hakīm • Arabic • *servant of the wise, Allah*

'Abd-al-Halīm • Arabic • *servant of the patient, Allah*

'Abd-al-Hamīd • Arabic • *servant of the praiseworthy, Allah*

'Abd-al-Jawād • Arabic • *servant of the magnimous, Allah*

'Abd-al-Karīm • Arabic • *servant of the generous, Allah*

'Abd-al-Latīf • Arabic • *servant of the kind, Allah*

'Abd-al-Mu'ti • Arabic • *servant of the giver, Allah*

'Abd-al-Qādir • Arabic • *servant of the capable, Allah*

'Abd-al-Rahīm, Abder Rahīm • Arabic • *servant of the compassionate, Allah*

Abdalrahman, Abderrahman • Arabic • *servant of the merciful, Allah*

'Abd-al-Rāziq, 'Abd-al-Razzāq, 'Abd-er-Razzā • Arabic • *servant of the provider, Allah*

'Abd-al-Salām, Abdes Salām • Arabic • *servant of the peaceable, Allah*

'Abd-al-Wahhāb • Arabic • *servant of the giver, Allah*

Abdullah, 'Abd-Allāh • Arabic • *servant of Allah*

Abel, Hevel • Biblical • *breath, saint for the dying*

Adam, Addam, Ádhamh, Adamo, Adán, Adama • Biblical/Hebrew/Jewish • *earth*

Adie, Adaidh, Adam • Scots Gaelic • *earth*

Adina, Adin • Jewish/Hebrew • *so slender!*

Adrian, Adrien, Adriano, Hadrianus • Latin • *a man from Hadria after which the Adriatic Sea is named*

'Ahmad, Ahmed • Arabic • *highly commendable*

Ailpein, Alpine, Alpin • Pictish/Scots Gaelic • *white*

'Ali • Arabic • *sublime*

Amerigo, Emmerich • Spanish/Visigothic • *a person who works hard to gain power*

Amias • French/Biblical/Hebrew • *someone from Amiens in Picardie or love God*

Aneislis • Irish Gaelic • *careful, pensive, thoughtful*

Amīn • Arabic • *honest as the day is long*

Amos • Biblical/Jewish/Hebrew • *to carry the Lord like St Christopher*

Amrit • Sanskrit • *immortal, divine foods*

Aneurin, Aneirin, Nye, Neirin • *modest and noble*

Angelo, Ángel, Angelos • Greek/Latin • *messenger of God*

Anisim, Onisim, Onesimos • Greek • *useful, worthwhile*

Anacleto, Anacletus, Anakletos, Aniceto • Latin/Greek • *invocation*

Aram • Biblical/Hebrew • *tall*

Arkadi, Arkadios • Greek • *a man from Arcadia*

Artemis, Artyom, Artemios, Artemas, Artemus Artemisthenes • Greek • *he who worships or follows Artemis/Diana or is a gift from the divine virgin huntress*

Artemidoros • Greek • *gift of Artemis*

Artemisthenes • Greek • *strength of Artemis*

Asa • Biblical/Hebrew/Jewish • *doctor, one who heals*

Ashish • Sanskrit • *prayer, wish or blessing*

Augustine, Augustus, Austin • *great, the max, magnificent, nobody does it better*

Augustus, Auguste, Gus, Augustín, Augustine, Agostino, Augusto, Avgust, Agustin, Aghaistin, Aibhistin, Augustijn, Agustin, Agusti, Agostinho, Agostino, Avgustin, Tauno, Agoston, Augustinas, Augere • Latin • *great, the max, magnificent, expansive, nobody does it better*

Azriel • Jewish/Hebrew • *God helps*

Bai • Chinese • *white*

Bala, Balu • Sanskrit • *young*

Balder • Norse • *ruler or chief prince, said to be pure and beautiful*

Baptiste, Baptist, Bautista • Biblical • *John the Baptist*

Barak • Arabic • *blessing*

Barclay, Berkeley, Berkley • Anglo-Saxon • *birch tree or wood*

Barrett, Barratt • English • *a trader, merchant*

Barrington, Bearain • Norman/Anglo-Saxon • *a person from Barentin, France or the village of Barrington*

Bastien, Sébastien, Sebastián • Greek • *venerable, wise*

Bellarmino • Roman Catholic/Jesuit • *named after Italian saint, Roberto Bellarmino; especially 17th September*

Bingwen • Chinese • *clever/cultivated*

Birger, Birghir, Byrghir, Børje, Birre, • Norse • *helper*

Blaise, Blaize, Blas • Latin/French • *to limp, limping*

Blume, Blumke • Jewish/Yiddish • *flower*

Bob, Bobbie, Bobby, Robbie, Robert • American/English/Germanic • *bright, famous and clever*

Bodo • Gemanic • *messenger, glad tidings*

Bojing • Chinese • *to win admiration and respect*

Bond • English • *a man into husbandry and a farmer at heart*

Booker • English • *a man who bleaches the laundry*

Boone • Norman/English • *a man from Bohon, France*

Booth • Anglo-Saxon • *a gamekeeper's hut or wee house*

Boqin • Chinese • *win respect*

Boris, Borislav, Borya, Boba, Baurice • Russian • *small, little*

Börries, Liborius • German/Celtic • *to be free!*

Brett, Bret • Celtic • *a man from Brittany*

Bruce • Norman/English • *someone from Bruis*

Burgess • Anglo-Saxon • *a man who is on a town council*

Cain, Kane, Cane • Jewish/Hebrew • *a craftsman*

Caius • Latin • *a man of the earth*

Callum, Colm, Calum, Columba, Cole, Colmán, Colum • Latin/Scots Gaelic • *dove*

Camille, Camillo, Camillus, Camilo • Latin/French • *Roman family name, perfection*

Caolán, Kelan, Keelan • Irish Gaelic • *slender, slim, trim*

Carey, Cary, Karey, Kary • English • *pure*

Carter • English • *a man who drives a wagon or cart!*

Casey, KC, Casy, Kacy, Kacey, Kasey • Irish Gaelic • *a watchman; keeps guard in war*

Caspar, Casper • Germanic • *treasurer, banker*

Ceallach, Kelly • Irish Gaelic • *fairhaired or monk church monastery*

Cecil, Cesil • Latin/English • *old Roman family name Caecilius, from the Latin, meaning blind*

Celso, Celsus • Latin • *tall, lofty, beanpole*

Cedric • literary name • *invented by Sir Walter Scott*

Chadwick, Ceadelwic • English • *a man from the industrious farm*

Chapman, Ceappman • Anglo-Saxon • *pedlar, door-to-door salesman, merchant*

Chao • Chinese • *superior, improved*

Chauncey, Chauncy • English • *the chancellor*

Cheng • Chinese • *accomplished*

Christopher, Chris, Christian, Crìsdean, Karsten, Christiaan, Carsten, Christer, Chretien, Cristiano, Krysztian, Krisztian, Christie, Christy, Kristy, Kristopher,

Christopha, Kristopha, Críostóir, Christoph, Christofoor, Kristafoor, Kristoffer, Christophe, Cristobál, Cristofol, Cristovao, Cristoforo, Krzysztof, Krystof, Hristo, Risto, Kristof, Kristaps, Kit, Kester • Greek • *the man who bears Jesus Christ*

Clark, Clarke, Clarkson • English • *a clerk, as in penpusher*

Claude, Claud, Claudius, Claudio • Late • *a lame man*

Clem, Clément, Clemmie, Cliamain, Clemente • Latin • *merciful, gentle, compassionate*

Cody, Cuidightheact, Macoda • Irish Gaelic • *descendant of Oda, a helpful soul*

Colombe, Columba, Callum, Colmán, Colm, Colum, Columbano • Latin • *dove*

Colin, Collin, Coll, Nicholas, Cailean • English/Scots Gaelic • *dove*

Comhghán • Irish Celtic • *twins!*

Conley, Conlaodh • *a person who is pure and chaste as Aodh*

Corin, Quirinus, Quirino • Latin • *an ancient Roman deity connected to Romulus*

Cosmo, Kosmas, Cosimo, Kosmos • Greek • *there is beauty in order*

Creighton, Crichton, Criochiune • Scots Gaelic/English • *someone from Crichton in Midlothian*

Cuthbert, Bert, Cuddy, Cuddie, Cuithbeart • Anglo-Saxon • *a man well known for what he does, his personality or wit*

Cynddelw • British/Welsh • *he who worships holy and sacred images, pagan or Christian*

Cyprian, Cyprianus • Latin • *the man who comes from Cyprus, the isle of Venus or Aphrodite*

Dalmazio, Dalmatius, Dalmacio •
Latin • *a person from Dalmatia in
the Adriatic*

Damon, Daman, Damaso • Greek
• *a man full of self-control or a man
who tames*

D'Arcy, Darcy • Norman • *a man
from the barony of D'Arcy*

**Darell, Darrell, Darryll, Darryl,
Darell, Darrell, Darrel, Darryll,
Daryl, Darryl** • Norman/American/
English • *a chap from D'airelle, a
barony in Normandy*

**Darius, Dareios, Darayavahush,
Darayamiy** • Greek/Persian • *he
who possesses, looks after the good
and wellness of all*

Darnell, Darnel • Norman • *not
entirely known origins but possibly a
type of grass or shrub*

**Dean, Dino, Deane, Dene Denu,
Decanus, Dane** • Anglo-Saxon
• *a man who served as dean in a
Christian church or cathedral*

Delun • Chinese • *virtuous,
respected*

Deming • Chinese • *virtuous, bright*

Delroy, Del • Caribbean/French •
son or servant of the king or leader

**Demetrius, Demetrio, Dmitri,
Dimitar** • Greek • *follower of the
goddess Demeter*

**Dermot, Diarmaid, Dermid,
Diarmad, Diairmit** • Irish Gaelic •
not a bad bone in his body

**Desmond, Deasún, Des,
Deasmhumhnach** • Irish Gaelic •
*a man from south Munster (around
Cork)*

Devereux • Norman • *someone from
the barony of Evreux in Eure*

Devdas • Sanskrit • *servant of the
gods*

Dexter, Dex, Dexy • Anglo-Saxon/
Latin • *a female dyer/laundress or
right-handed*

Dilwyn • British/Welsh • *fair,
blonde, white, blessed, sacred, holy*

**Dominic, Dominick, Dom,
Dominique, Domingo, Dominicus,
Dominus** • Latin/Roman Catholic
• *Lord, as in St Dominic, founder of
the Dominican order*

Doran, Deoradhain, Deoradh
• Irish Gaelic • *traveller, such as
pilgrim or stranger*

Dwyer, Duibhuidhir • Irish Gaelic
• *personal name meaning brown,
black, tawny, dark yellow; maybe
sensible and wise*

Efisio, Ephesius, Ephesus •
Sardinian • *a person from Ephesus
in Asia Minor (Turkey)*

Éimhín • Irish • *speedy, fast, swift,
prompt, quick*

Eladio, Helladio • Greek • *a man
from Greece*

Eli • Hebrew/Jewish • *God's height,
probably tall*

Eliezer, Eleazar, Eli • Jewish/Hebrew
• *God's help*

Ellair, Ceallair, Cellarius, Cella, Ellar
• Scots Gaelic • *a person who works
in pub or monastery as a steward*

Elwyn, Alyn • British/Welsh • *white,
fair, blessed, sacred and holy*

**Emmanuel, Emanuel, Manny,
Immanuel** • Hebrew/Jewish • *God is
with us or amongst us*

**Ephraim, Evron, Effie, Yefrem,
Efraín** • Hebrew/Jewish • *fruitful*

Erdmann, Hartmann • *earth man,
man of earth*

Erland, Orland • Norse • *a stranger
or traveller from another land*

Ermete, Hermes • Greek • *messenger of the gods*

Eusebio, Eusebios, Eusebes • Greek • *revered, pious*

Eutrope, Eutropios, Eutropos, Eutropio • Greek • *what a nice polite boy and so clever and versatile*

Fabrizio, Fabrice, Fabricius, Fabricio • Italian/Etruscan • *Roman family name; one noted for his incorruptibility*

Fādil • Arabic • *generous, respected and conscientious*

Fahīm • Arabic • *a man of deep understanding and wisdom*

Fakhri • Arabic • *diligent, high achiever, gets where he wants on merit*

Fang • Chinese • *upright, honest, fair*

Faraj • Arabic • *solves worries and grief*

Farūq, Farouk • Arabic • *clever, intuitive and wise*

Faysal, Feisal • *a man or judge who knows the difference between good and bad, right and wrong*

Feidhlimidh, Felim, Phelim, Fidelminus • Irish Gaelic • *always chaste and virtuous*

Ferdinand, Ferdinando, Hernan, Ferdi, Ferdie, Fernand • Spanish Visigothic • *a man at peace wherever he is; always ready and prepared to travel*

Fernando, Ferdinando, Hernando, Fernán, Hernán • Spanish Visigothic • *a man at peace wherever he is; always ready and prepared to travel*

Fikri • Arabic • *intellectual and contemplative*

Fingal, Fionnghall, Fingall • Gaelic • *blond, fair stranger or traveller or Viking settler*

Finn • Scandinavian • *a man from Finland/Suomi*

Fínnen, Fínnan, Fionnán, Finnian, Finian • Irish Gaelic • *white, fair*

Fletcher, Fletch, Flechier, Fleche • Norman/Germanic • *maker of arrows*

Flinders, Flanders • English • *a Flemish person from Flanders*

Foka, Phocas • Greek • *someone from Phocaea in Asia Minor*

Foma, Thomas • Russian/Biblical • *twin*

Francis, Francisco, Fran, Franciscus, Frank, France, François, Francesco, Franz • Latin • *to be French, someone from France*

Franz • German/Italian • *to be French, someone from France*

Frode, Frodi, Frod • Scandinavian • *a knowledgable man, well-informed*

Gaétan, Gaetano, Caietanus • Latin • *a man from Caieta in Latium*

Galen, Galenus, Galene • Latin/Greek • *calmness*

Gallagher Gallchobhar • Irish Gaelic • *foreign ally, helpful stranger*

Gennadi • Russian • *roots unknown; name of orthodox saint*

Gardner • English/Germanic/Frankish • *the main gardener for a big house or religious building*

Garner, Gernier • Norman • *a person who worked in a granary*

Garnet, Grenate, Granatum • Norman/Latin • *either a dealer in pomegranates or the precious stone*

Gaston • Geographic • *a man from Gascony*

Gavino, Gabinus, Gabino •
Sardinian/Latin • *a man from
Gabium*

**Geoffrey, Jeffrey, Jeff, Geoffroi,
Geoff, Godofredo, Sieffre** •
Germanic/Frankish/Lombardic
• *a stranger in your own land or
foreigner who pledges allegiance*

**George, Georgie, Geordie, Seoirse,
Seòras, Deòrsa, Siors, Siorus,
Siorys, Georg, Jörg, Jurgen, Joris,
Joren, Jurg, Jorgen, Jorn, Goran,
Joran, Orjan, Georges, Jorge, Jordi,
Giorgio, Georgi, Yuri, Yegor, Yura,
Jerzy, Jiri, Juraj, Jure, Yrjo, Gyorgy,
Jurgis, Juris, Georgos, Geergain,
Georgios** • Greek/Latin/Norman
• *farmer or someone who works on
the land*

Gershom, Gershorn, Gersham •
Biblical/Jewish/Hebrew • *a stranger
there*

Ghassān • Arabic • *youth*

Gilbert, Gib, Gibb, Gilberto
• Germanic/Frankish/Roman
Catholic • *he who pledges or sacri-
fices his life for greater things*

**Gillanders, Gilleainndreis,
Gillandrais** • Gaelic • *servant of St
Andrew*

Gilleonan, Gilleádhamhnain •
Gaelic • *servant of St Adomnan*

Gillespie, Gilleeasbaig • Gaelic •
bishop's servant

Gino, Giorgino, Luigino • Latin •
short name

Goito, Goyo, Goya, Gregorio •
Spanish • *watchful*

Gomer • Biblical/Jewish/Hebrew •
complete and wholesome

Gonzogue • *patron of young people*

Gottschalk • Germanic • *God or the
Lord's servant*

Grayson, Greifi, Greyve • Norse/
English • *son of a steward, a
publican*

**Gregory, Gregorios, Gregor, Greg,
Gregg, Greig, Greagoir, Griogair,
Grigor, Joris, Greger, Gregers,
Grégoire, Gregorio, Grigori,
Grzegorz, Rehor, Grgur, Reijo,
Gergely, Grigor** • Greek • *watchful*

Guangli • Chinese • *lighting up
virtue and propriety*

Gulzar • Persian • *rose garden*

Guoliang • Chinese • *where you are
there is kindness*

Guozhi • Chinese • *orderly and
organised*

**Gustav, Gustave, Gus, Gustaf,
Gösta, Gustavus, Gustavo** •
Scandinavian • *staff or supporter of
the Goths*

Gwyn, Gwynn, Wyn • British/Welsh
• *white, holy, sacred and blond*

Hādi • Arabic • *mentor, guru, reflective and spiritual*

Hadley, Hadleigh, Haedleah •
Anglo-Saxon • *a clearing where the
heather grows*

Harvard, Hereward, Hervard •
American/English • *the vigilant
soldier, the army guard*

Hāsim • Arabic • *decisive, incisive
and quick*

Hātim • Arabic • *decisive and
focused*

**Hector, Hektor, Ekhain, Eachann,
Eachdonn** • Greek/Scots Gaelic •
*restrained, holds himself back, brown
horse*

Heddwyn • British/Welsh • *tranquil
and peaceful white, fair and
sacred*

Hedley, Hedleigh, Headley •

Anglo-Saxon • *the clearing where the heather grows*

Hefin • British/Welsh • *summer*

Heilyn, Ynheilio • British/Welsh • *steward, keeper of the cellars*

Hemming, Heming • Norse • *chameleon-like, changes shape to camouflage*

Hermenigild, Hermengildo, Emengildo • Spanish/Visigothic • *a total sacrifice*

Hermes, Hermolaos, Yermolai • Greek • *the god Hermes, messenger of the gods or the people*

Hernán, Fernando, Hernando • Spanish • *a man at peace wherever he is; always ready and prepared to travel*

Hugh, Huw, Hugues, Hugo, Aodh, Hughie, Hewie, Huey, Hewie, Hughie, Huwie • Germanic/Frankish • *heart, mind and spirit*

Hugo, Hugh • Germanic/Frankish/Latin • *heart, mind and spirit*

Hyam • Jewish/Hebrew • *a person who prays for the ill or dying for their recovery*

Imām • Arabic • *leader and piety*

Innocenzo, Innocentius, Innocens, Innokenti, Inocencio • *innocent, childlike; many saints and popes named this*

Ira • Hebrew/Jewish • *vigilant, observant, watchful*

Isaac, Zak, Zac, Zack, Ike, Izaak, Isak • Biblical • *unsure roots; probably the hireling or the laugh of a baby*

'Ismat • Arabic • *innocent and without sin*

Issachar • Biblical/Jewish/Hebrew • *a hireling*

Italo, Italus • Latin • *father of*

Romulus and Remus, founders of Rome

Ivory • African American • *tusks and teeth of certain animals like the elephant*

Jagannath • Sanskrit • *Lord of the World, Vishnu, as in sacred Puri*

Jakada • Hausa West African • *the messenger*

Jason, Jayson, Iason • Greek • *healer or he who heals*

Jazz, Jos, Josh, Jed, Jay • American/English • *shortened name for almost any beginning with J!*

Jeffrey, Geoffrey, Jeff, Geoff, Jefferson, Jeffery, Jeffry, Jep • Anglo-Saxon • *a stranger in your own land or foreigner who pledges allegiance*

Jevon, Jeavon, Jeevan, Jovene • English/Norman • *young*

Jian • Chinese • *healthy*

Jonah, Jon, Jonas • Biblical/Hebrew/Jewish • *dove*

Jörg, George, Jurgen, Jørgen, Georgianus, Jörn • Scandinavian • *farmer or someone who works on the land*

Joshua, Josh • Biblical/Hebrew/Jewish • *God is my salvation*

Josiah, Josh • Biblical/Hebrew/Jewish • *God heals*

Junior, Junia • Biblical • *youth*

Kajetan, Caitanus, Gaetano, Kayetan • Latin • *man from Caieta*

Kalidas • Sanskrit • *servant of Kali*

Kamāl, Kāmil • Arabic/Sanskrit • *perfection, beyond compare, pink*

Kamil, Camillus • Latin • *order of monks who nursed the sick*

Kang • Chinese • *wellbeing*

Karp, Karpos • Greek • *fruity*

Kasi • Sanskrit • *radiant; Varanasi or Benares, sacred city on the Ganges*

Kay, Caius, Gaius • Latin • *a man of the earth*

Keith • British/Welsh • *wood, copse or thicket or a man from East Lothian*

Kellen, Kelan, Cailein, Ailein, McKellern, Macailein, Maccailein • Gaelic • *slender, slim, trim or son of Alan or son of Colin*

Kelly, Ceallach, Ceallaigh • Irish/English • *fair-haired or monk, church, monastery*

Kendrick, Kenrick, Cenric, Ceneric, Cynwrig, Maceanrig, Cyneric • British/Welsh/Scots Gaelic • *a sacred place high on a hill, or son of Henry or royal power*

Kent, Kenton, Kenntun, Cenatun, Cynetun • British/Welsh • *someone from the British kingdom (now county) and tribe of the Cantii*

Kenya • English • *someone from the African land of Kenya*

Kerry, Ceri • English/British/Welsh • *after the Celtic Goddess of Poetry*

Khayri • Arabic • *charitable, merciful, good*

Kilment, Clément, Clemens • Latin • *merciful*

Lane, Layne • Anglo-Saxon • *a narrow pathway or roadway*

Laurence, Lawrence, Larry, Laurentius, Laurentum, Laurie, Lawrie, Labhrás, Labhrainn, Lorenz, Laurens, Lars, Laurent, Lorencio, Llorenc, Laurenco, Lorenzo, Lawson, Lavrentios, Lavrenti, Laurencjusz, Wawrzyniec, Vavrinec, Lovrenc, Lauri, Lasse, Lassi, Lorinc, Laz, Lenz, Lavrenti • Latin • *man from Laurentum, the capital of the Latins*

Layton, Leighton, Leyton • Anglo-Saxon • *farm or field where leeks are grown*

Lazarus, Laz, Lazare, Eleazar, Lazaros, Lazar • Biblical/Greek/Aramaic/Hebrew • *God is my helper*

Leland, Layland, Leyland • Anglo-Saxon • *land that is used for growing crops over years and left fallow for one*

Levi, Levy • Hebrew/Jewish • *making a connexion*

Li • Chinese • *profit, business acumen and respectable*

Liaqat • Persian • *dignified, noble wise and clever*

Licio, Lycius • Latin • *man from Lycia in Asia Minor*

Ling • Chinese • *compassionate and understanding*

Linus, Linos • Greek • *the song of Linus, a Greek musician who taught Hercules*

Lorin, Loren, Lorrin, Laurence • Latin • *man from Laurentum, the capital of the Latins*

Ludger, Luitger • Friesian • *place name derived from famous monk*

Luke, Lucas, Loukas, Lukas, Luc, Lluc, Lluch, Lukasz, Luukas, Lukacs, Luka • Greek • *man from Loucania, a Greek colony in southern Italy*

Mabon • British/Welsh • *son or son of*

Mahendra, Mahinder, Mohinder • Sanskrit • *Great Indra, first great Buddhist missionary*

Māhir • Arabic • *clever, dexterous, skilful*

Mahmūd • Arabic • *respected and laudable*

Mainchín, Mannix • Irish • *monk*

Majdi, Magdi • Arabic • *conscientious and worthy of praise*

Makarios, Macaire, Macario, Makari • Greek • *blessed one*

Malachi, Malachy, Maoileachlainn • Biblical/Irish Gaelic • *my messenger or follower of St Seachnall or St Secundinus*

Malcolm, Maelcoluim, Maelcoluim • Scots Gaelic • *follower of St Columba, the Dove*

Ma'mūn • Arabic • *reliable and trusted*

Manār • Arabic • *light of goodness*

Maolra, Myles, Miles • Irish Gaelic/English • *follower of the Blessed Virgin Mary*

Mario, Marius • Latin • *from Roman family name and male version of Mary*

Marion, Marianus, Marius, Mariano • Latin • *follower of the Virgin Mary*

Masterman • Anglo-Saxon • *a butler*

Maurice, Moris, Morris, Mo, Maurus, Moritz, Maurizio, Mauricius, Mavriki, Mauricio, Maurits, • Latin • *a dark swarthy person as in a Moor from Arabia*

Mauro • Latin • *a Moor as in Arab; early followers of St Benedictine*

Maximilian, Maximilianus, Maximus, Max, Maximillian, Maximilien, Aemilianus • Latin/Germanic/Bavarian/Austrian • *a great person through industry and hard work*

Meir, Meier, Meyer, Myer, Maier, Mayr • Jewish/Hebrew • *giving light*

Meirion, Merrion, Marianus,

Marius • Latin • *follower of the Virgin Mary*

Mercer, Mercy, Mercier, Mercarius, Merx • Norman/Latin • *a merchant*

Methodius, Mefodi • Greek • *following the path or road, spiritual as much as a traveller*

Meurig, Mauricius, Mouric, Meuric, Maurice • British/Welsh • *a dark swarthy person as in a Moor from Arabia*

Michelangelo • Bibilical • *angel*

Midhat • Arabic • *tribute*

Miller, Mille, Milne, Mylen • English • *a person who works in a mill*

Milo • Slavic/Latin • *grace and favour or soldier*

Mingli • Chinese • *lighting up propriety*

Mirza • Persian • *subserviant prince*

Mitrofan, Metrophanes • Greek • *vision of the Mother Mary*

Mitya, Dmitri • Russian • *follower of the goddess Demeter*

Modesto, Modest • Latin • *modest*

Mohammed, Muhammed, Mohammad, Mohamed, Muhammad, Muhammed, Mo • *praiseworthy and possessing the finest perfect qualities*

Morris, Maurice, Mo, Miuris • English/Latin • *a dark swarthy person as in a Moor from Arabia*

Muhammed • Arabic • *sacred qualities, scrupulous*

Mustafa, Mustapha • *pure, the chosen one*

Narendra • Sanskrit • *shaman, witchdoctor, doctor king*

Naughton, Neachdan • Scots Gaelic • *pure*

Niaz • Persian • *prayer, gift, sacrifice*

Nikita, Aniketos • Greek/Russian

• *unconquered; name of Orthodox saint*

Niven, Naoimhean, Gillniven, Gillenaomh • Irish Gaelic/English • *servant of the saint*

Nyabera • Kenyan • *the good one*

Odhrán, Oran, Oren • Irish Gaelic • *ashen, pale*

Oleg, Helgi • Norse • *prosperous, the chap who created Kiev, Ukraine; especially 24th August*

Oliver, Olivier, Olivarius, Ollie, Oleifr, Noll • Germanic/Frankish/Norse • *olive tree*

Onisim, Anisim • Greek • *useful, worthwhile*

Omar, 'Umar • Biblical/Hebrew/Arabic • *talkative*

Omri • Jewish/Hebrew • *sheaf of wheat*

Örjan, Jurian, George • Scandinavian • *farmer or someone who works on the land*

Orlando, Roland • Italian • *a person who is famous for the real estate they own; land, territory*

Oscar, Oskar • Irish • *friend of wildlife, especially deer and stags*

Ottokar, Odovacar • Germanic • *being watchful and observant brings riches*

Paderau • modern Welsh • *a rosary*

Padma • Sanskrit • *lotus position, the chakra*

Pajonga • Sierra Leonese • *walk tall, tall man*

Palmer • English • *a pilgrim who had been to the Holy Land and returned with a palm branch*

Palmiro, Palmiere • Latin/Spanish • *a pilgrim who brought back a palm from the Holy Land*

Paul, Paulus, Pol, Pål, Poul, Pall, Pauwel, Påvel, Pablo, Pau, Paulo, Paolo, Pavlos, Pavao, Pavle, Paavo, Paulius, Pablo • Latin • *Roman family name meaning little or small*

Paulino, Pablo, Paulus • Spanish/Italian • *Roman family name meaning little or small*

Peleg • Biblical/Hebrew/Jewish • *division, border or boundary*

Percy, Piers, Percival, Perci, Persiacum, Persius, Perse, Percehaie, Percerhaie • Latin/Gaulish • *Pierce's hedge*

Peregrine, Peregrinus, Perry, Pellegrino • Latin • *stranger, wanderer, foreigner*

Piaras, Piers, Pierce, Pearce • Irish Gaelic/English • *Pierce's hedge*

Pius, Pio • Latin • *a man who is pious and respects*

Placido, Placidus • Latin/Italian • *calm, quiet, placid*

Porter, Porteour, Portare, Portier • Norman • *a person who carries*

Potter • American English • *someone who sells pots*

Pravin • Sanskrit • *dexterous, clever and skilful*

Preston, Preosttun • Anglo-Saxon • *priest's town*

Proinséas, Francis • Irish Gaelic/Latin • *to be French, someone from France*

Prudenzio, Prudentius, Prudens, Prudencio • Latin • *prudent*

Pryderi • British/Welsh • *a carer, someone who is anxious*

Qiu • Chinese • *autumn or fall*

Ra'fat • Arabic • *mercy, compassion, forgiveness*

Raghu • Sanskrit • *swift, fast*

Ram, Rama, Ramu, Ramakrishna, Ramgopal, Ramnarayan • Sanskrit • *nice, lovely, kind*

Ramadān • Arabic • *ninth month of the Muslim calendar: the hot month*

Ramiro • Spanish/Visigothic • *a man famous for his advice and counselling*

Ramón, Raimundo, Raymond • Catalan/Germanic • *adviser, protector*

Raphael, Rafael, Rafa, Rapha, Raffaele • Biblical/Jewish/Hebrew • *God has healed*

Ra'ūf • Arabic • *caring and compassionate*

Reineke, Reine • Germanic • *counsellor*

Reinhard, Reinhardt, Reine • Germanic • *strong, firm advice*

Reinhold, Reinwald, Reine • Germanic • *splendid, wonderful adviser*

Reinmar, Reine • Germanic • *famous adviser, speaker*

Remus, Remo • Latin • *with Romulus, founder of Rome*

Reynold, Reginald, Reynaud, Raginwald, Reginald, Ray, Reynard, Ragin, Renard, Ray, Rinaldo, Reinaldo, Rheinallt • Germanic/Norman • *advice rule*

Rhett, Rhet, Raedt, Raet • Dutch • *advice, counsel*

Riley, Rygeleah, Reilly, Raghallach, Ryley • Anglo-Saxon/Irish Gaelic • *a field where the rye crop has been cleared*

Rohan • Sanskrit • *ascension, healing, medicine*

Romulus, Romolo • Latin • *someone from Rome; one of the founders of Rome*

Ronald, Ron, Ronnie, Ronny, Roni, Ranald, Randal, Rognvald • Norse • *adviser to the gods or king*

Royle, Rygehyll, Royal • Anglo-Saxon • *the hill where rye is grown*

Ru • Chinese • *Confucian scholar*

Rune, Runi, Runolf, Run • Norse • *named after the Norse magical alphabet*

Rushdi • Arabic • *old head on young shoulders; ahead of his years*

Ruslan • literary invention/Russian • *meaning unknown; name was used by Aleksandr Pushkin in his poem 'Ruslan and Ludmila'*

Sābir, Sabri • Arabic • *patience is a virtue, persevere*

Sacheverell, Sautechevreuil, Sachie • Norman • *surname from place name Saute Chevreuil, meaning roebuck leap*

Safā • Arabic • *pure and sincere*

Sage, Sauge, Sapius • Anglo-Saxon

Salāh • Arabic • *righteous and devout religiously*

Sālih • Arabic • *devout, devoted*

Sāmi • Arabic • *elevated, sublime*

Samīr, Sameer • Arabic • *confidant at night, a night conversation*

Samuel, Shemuel, Shaulmeel, Sam, Sammy, Sawyl • Biblical/Hebrew/Jewish • *name of God, God has heard, listen to God*

Sancho, Sanctus • Latin/Spanish • *holy*

Sanjeev • Sanskrit • *reviving, resuscitating*

Shankar, Sankar • Sanskrit • *confers welfare*

Satish • Sanskrit • *the fact of a matter, the true reality*

Saul • Biblical/Hebrew/Latin • *asked for, prayed for, yearned for*

Scevola, Scaevola, Scaevus • *left-handed*

Scott • Gaelic • *a man from Ireland who settles in Scotland*

Seanán, Shannon , Senan • Irish Gaelic • *wise, mature and ancient*

Sebastián, Sebastianus, Sebastos, Sébastien, Sebastiano, Sevastyan • Latin/Greek • *a man from Sebaste in Asia Minor (now Turkey)*

Sekar • Sanskrit • *summit, the best at what you do*

Seth • Biblical/Hebrew • *appointed to a certain place*

Sextus, Sesto, Seissylt • Latin • *sixth or number six*

Shakīl • Arabic • *handsome*

Shākir • Arabic • *thankful and grateful*

Shalom • Jewish/Hebrew • *peace*

Shamshad • Persian • *tall as a box tree*

Shankar, Sankar • Sanskrit • *confers welfare, to look after*

Sharīf • Arabic • *eminent in his field*

Sherman, Sharman • Anglo-Saxon • *shears man, someone who trimmed woven cloth*

Sheridan, Sirideain • Irish Gaelic • *descendant of Sirideain, the searcher*

Shining • Chinese • *let the world be at peace*

Shirong • Chinese • *reward as a result of learning*

Shukri • Arabic • *giving thanks*

Sioltach, Sholto • Scots Gaelic • *the sower of the seed*

Siddhartha • Sanskrit • *Buddha*

Silas, Silouanus, Silvanus, Silva • Latin

Silvester, Silver, Sylvester, Silvano,

Silvestro, Silvestre, Sly, Slie • Latin • *a person from the woods or forest*

Silvio • Latin/Italian/Spanish /Portuguese

Silvius • *someone who loves or inhabits the woods or forest*

Simeon • English/Biblical/Hebrew • *he has heard*

Simón, Siomon, Sim, Simidh, Sieman, Simao, Simone, Semyon, Szymon, Simo, Sim, Simmie • Biblical/Hebrew/Jewish • *hearkening, hearing*

Simran • Sikh • *he who meditates, yogic*

Sirideán • Irish Gaelic • *unsure roots; likely to be someone who seeks*

Siyu • Chinese • *thinking of the planet Earth*

Skylar, Schuyler • Dutch/American English • *scholar, schoolteacher*

Slater • Anglo-Saxon • *a surname for someone who fixes slates on a roof*

Solomon, Shlomo, Sol, Solly, Saloman • Biblical/Hebrew/Jewish • *peace*

Somerled, Sumarlid, Summerlad, Somhairle, Sorley • Scots Gaelic/ Norse • *summer traveller*

Somhairle • Irish Gaelic/Norse • *summer traveller*

Sondre, Sindri • Norse/Norwegian • *no known origins but in Norse mythology a magical dwarf*

Spencer • Anglo-Saxon • *similar to a quartermaster, someone who dispenses provisions or goods*

Sriram • Sanskrit • *devotee or worshipper of the Lord Rama*

Stacey, Eustace • English/Greek • *confused roots; could mean juicy, tasty grapes!*

Stafford • Anglo-Saxon • *the river*

ford good for landing

Steel, Style, Styal, Steele • Anglo-Saxon • *a person who works with hard metal*

Stein, Steyne, Sten, Steen, Steinn • Norse • *stone*

Stian, Stigand, Kris, Stig • *wanderer*

Stuart, Stewart, Stu, Stew • French • *primarily a surname given to a person who served as a steward in a big house, manor or palace*

Stone, Stan • Anglo-Saxon • *stone*

Subhash • Sanskrit • *eloquent and articulate*

Suleimān, Sulaymān • Biblical/Arabic • *peace*

Sumantra • Sanskrit • *a person who is well versed in the classics*

Sven, Sveinn, Svein, Svend • Norse/Swedish • *young boy*

Swift • Anglo-Saxon • *the bird, describing a person who is fast and quick*

Sylvain, Silvano • Italian • *a person from the woods or forest*

Tad, Tadhg, Thaddeus, Tig, Tim, Taddeo, Teague, Teigue, Tadeo • Irish Gaelic • *poet, wise man, philosopher*

Tāhir • Arabic • *oh so pure, chaste and virtuous*

Tam, Tammy, Thomas, Tommy, Tom • Greek/Aramaic • *twin*

Tammaro • Germanic • *clever; famous mind*

Tancredo • Germanic • *thoughtful counsel*

Tanner • American English • *a person who cleans and tans hides*

Tara • Sanskrit • *shining light for the saviour; carrying the Lord*

Taras, Tarasio • Greek • *man from*

Tarentum in northern Italy

Tāriq • Arabic • *morning or evening star; night visitor*

Tavish, Tamhas, Thomas • Scots Gaelic/English • *twin*

Taylor, Tayler, Tayla, Taillier, Taleare • Anglo-Saxon/Norman • *a person who cuts, a tailor*

Thomas, Thos, Tom, Tommy, Tomás, Tamhas, Tomos, Tommaso, Foma, Tomasz, Toma, Tomaz, Tuomo, Toms, Didymos • Biblical/Aramaic/Greek • *twin*

Tingguang • Chinese • *bright garden or courtyard*

Tingzhe • Chinese • *judgement or wisdom is required*

Tracy, Thraciusacum, Tracey • Latin/Gaulish • *a person from a place in Normandy called Tracy!*

Travis, Traverser • Norman • *someone who worked collecting tolls on the roads or highways, crossing roads*

Trent, Trenton • British/Welsh • *after the River Trent in the English Midlands; its root meaning is to travel or journey*

Trond, Tron • Norse • *a man from Trondelag in Norway*

Troy, Trey, Troyes • *someone from the French city of Troyes, or, more powerful, in memory of the Troy (in modern-day Turkey) of Greek mythology*

Trofim, Trophimos • Greek • *fruitful, goodness, sustaining*

Truman, Treowemann, Trueman • Anglo-Saxon/American/English • *a trusted man*

Turner • English • *a person who makes objects by turning them on a lathe or wheel*

Ty, Tyler, Tyrone, Tye, Tyrese •
American English • *shortened name*
Tyler, Tylor, Ty, Tye, Tigele, Tegula
• Anglo-Saxon/Latin • *a man who
covers*
Tyrone, Ty, Tir Eoghain • Irish
Gaelic • *a man from County Tyrone,
Ulster; the land of Owen*

Ultach, Ultán • Irish Gaelic • *a man
from Ulster*
'Umar, Omar • Arabic • *to flourish
and to make the complex simple*
Usain • Caribbean English •
*unknown origins but the name of the
fastest man on earth, Usain Bolt (of
lightning!)*

Valère, Valerius, Valeri • Latin •
always to be healthy
Vaughan, Vaughn, Fychan, Bychan
• British/Welsh • *small, little*
Venkat • Sanskrit • *sacred mountain
near Madras*
Vergil, Virgil • Latin • *family name
with confused origins; could refer to
Virgo the maiden*
Vidal, Vitale, Hayyim • Latin/Jewish
• *to life!*
Vidkun, Vidkunn • Norse • *lateral
thinking, wise, experienced*
Vimal • Sanskrit • *peerless, perfection
and pure*
Vinay • Sanskrit • *education, intel-
ligence, learning*
**Virgil, Vergilius, Virgilius, Vergil,
Virgilio, Vigil** • Latin • *Roman
family name Vergilius but confu-
sion reigned when the spelling was
changed to Virgilius, which means
the maiden*
Vlas, Blasius, Blaesus, Blaise, Vlasi
• Latin • *area of the throat, perhaps*

*person with a lisp; St Blaise rules the
throat*
Vumilia • Swahili • *have courage,
bear patiently*

Warren, Warin, Varenne •
Germanic/Norman • *a person from
La Varenne, Normandy or a war
guard*
Warwick, Waerwic, Werwic •
Anglo-Saxon • *industrial area by a
dam or weir*
Wayne, Waegen • Anglo-Saxon •
a carter or cartwright; wagon driver
Webster, Webbestre • Anglo-Saxon
• *a weaver*
Wencheng • Chinese • *refined,
elegant and accomplished*
Wenyan • Chinese • *refined, chic,
chaste and gifted*
**Wilfrid, Wilfrit, Walfrid, Wilfrey,
Wilf, Wilfried, Vilfred** • Germanic •
the will for peace
Windsor, Windelsora • Anglo-
Saxon • *the place on the river with
a windlass (special crane to move
heavy weights)*
Woody, Carpenter • English • *nickname
for a carpenter or worker with wood*

Xue • Chinese • *studious, knowledge*

Yang • Chinese • *formed, perfection*
Yefim, Euphemios • Russian/Greek
• *eloquent, articulate speaker*
Yefrem, Ephraim • Russian/
Hebrew/Jewish • *fruitful*
Yigael • Jewish/Hebrew • *he shall be
redeemed*
Yi • Chinese • *sure and resolute*
Yitzhak, Isaac • Jewish/Hebrew •
*unsure roots; probably the hireling
or the laugh of a baby*

Yongzheng • Chinese • *eternally; forever scrupulous and conscientious*
Yorick, Jorck, George • Danish/Greek • *farmer or someone who works on the land*
Yūnis, Younis, Jonah • Arabic/Biblical • *dove*
Yuri, Yura, Georgi • Russian/Greek • *farmer or someone who works on the land*

Zaki • Arabic • *chaste, virginal*
Zamir • Arabic • *ideas, mental thoughts*
Zhengzhong • Chinese • *loyal and trustworthy*
Zhong • Chinese • *steadfast and devoted*
Zian • Chinese • *peaceful soul*
Zuhayr • Arabic • *little flowers*

Girls

Abilene, Abbie, Abby, Abbey, Abi, Lena • Biblical/Jewish/Hebrew • *an area of Palestine or the Holy Land, meaning grass or grasses*

Abishag, Avishag • Biblical/Jewish/ Hebrew • *wise and educated*

Acacia, Akakia, Wattle • Greek/ Latin • *acacia wood, holy wood that had special powers as a hex against evil*

Adamina • Biblical/Hebrew/Jewish • *earth*

Addolorata • Italian • *Our Lady (Virgin Mary) of Sorrows*

Adélaide • Germanic • *noble, kind and caring*

Adria, Adrianne, Adrienne, Adrianna, Adriana • Latin • *a person from Hadria after which the Adriatic Sea is named*

Adrienne, Adriana • Latin • *a person from Hadria after which the Adriatic Sea is named*

Aeron, Agrona • British/Welsh • *Celtic Goddess of Battle or Agriculture*

Aeronwen • British/Welsh • *white, sacred and fair*

Afāf • Arabic • *chastity, refinement, elegance*

Afanen • British/Welsh • *raspberry*

Agatha, Agathe, Aggie, Agata, Ågot, Águeda, Agathos • Greek • *good and honourable*

Agnès, Aggie, Aigneis, Inés, Agnese, Agnessa, Agnieszka, Anezka, Aune, Agnese, Agne, Annis, Annys, Annice, Aigneis, Agnethe, Agnetis, Agnete, Ågot • Greek • *pure and holy*

Ailbhe • Irish Gaelic • *white*

Albina, Bina, Albus, Albius • Latin • *Roman family name meaning white*

Alice, Alicia, Alesha, Alisia, Alys, Alisha, Alissa, Alesha, Alisa, Alissa, Ailish, Alis, Alys • Norman • *noble, kind and caring*

Alison, Allie, Ally, Aly, Alysoun, Aliyah, Aaliyah, Allison, Allyson • Norman • *noble, kind and caring*

Alva, Alvah, Ailbhe, Alvina • Scots Gaelic • *white*

Amalia • Latin/Germanic • *all work, no play*

Amparo • Roman Catholic/Spanish • *may the Virgin Mary protect me and all Christians*

Amrit • Sanskrit • *divine, immortal, good enough to eat*

Angel, Ángela, Angelina, Angeline, Angie, Ange, Angelos • Greek • *messenger of God*

Angela, Angelita • Greek/Latin • *messenger of God*

Ángeles • Spanish/Roman Catholic • *Our Lady of the Angels*

Angelica, Angélique, Angelika • Latin • *a girl of the angels*

Angosto • Spanish/Galician/Roman Catholic • *Our Lady of Angosto, a place where the Virgin appeared*

Angustias • Spanish/Roman Catholic • *Our Lady of Sufferings*

Anitra • literary invention • *created by Henrik Ibsen as the name of an Arabic princess in* Peer Gynt

Annunziata, Nunzia, Anunciación, Anunciata • Roman Catholic • *announcing the birth of Jesus to Mary*

Anona, Annona • Latin • *unsure root but possibly corn supply*

Anthea, Antheia • Greek • *flowery*

Anthousa, Anfisa • Greek • *flower*

Anwen, Annwen • British/Welsh • *blessed and beautiful*

Ariadne, Arianna, Ariana, Arianne • Greek/Cretean • *most holy*

Armelle, Artmael • Breton Celtic • *a female chief who is a steady as a rock*

Artemis, Diana • Greek/Latin • *virgin Goddess of the Moon and the Hunt*

Aslög, Asslaug, Åslaug • Swedish • *God-consecrated*

Asmā • Arabic • *prestigious*

Assumpta, Assunta, Asunción • Latin • *the assumption of the Virgin Mary into heaven*

Athene, Athena, Athina, Athenai • Greek • *Greek Goddess of Wisdom and protector of the city of Athens*

Avdotya, Eudokia, Eudokein • Greek • *she seems a nice, good girl*

Azalea, Azalia, Azeleos • Greek • *flower that flourishes in dry soil*

Azania, Azaria, Azelia • Greek • *flower that flourishes in dry soil*

Azucena, Susannah • Arabic/Spanish • *madonna lily*

Bala • Sanskrit • *young*

Bano • Persian • *lady, princess, bride*

Beata, Beate • Swiss • *blessed*

Beatrice, Beatrix, Bea, Bee, Beattie, Beatriz, Beitiris, Betrys, Viatrix, Viator, Beatus • *blessed through life*

Begoña • Spanish • *honouring the Virgin as patron of Bilbao*

Béibhin, Béibhinn, Bébhionn, Bébinn • Irish Gaelic • *white lady, fair lady*

Beige, Fawn • American English • *colour of undyed woollen cloth*

Beile, Beyle, Beylke • Jewish/Yiddish/Slavic • *white, pale, beautiful*

Benedicta, Benedicte, Benita • Latin • *blessed*

Berry, Berie • Anglo-Saxon • *as in fruit and veg*

Bevin, Béibhinn • Irish Gaelic • *fair lady*

Berwen • British Welsh • *fair or white-headed*

Bianca, Blanca • Italian/Spanish • *white*

Bina, Albina, Devorah, Deborah, Binah, Bine, Binke • Jewish/Hebrew/Yiddish • *bee or understanding*

Blaise, Blaize • Latin/French • *to limp, limping*

Bláithín, Bláthnat, Blanid, Bianaid • Irish Gaelic • *flower*

Blanche, Bianca, Blanca • *pure white, blonde*

Blodyn, Blodeyn, Blod • British/Welsh • *flower*

Blodwedd, Blodeuwedd, Blod • British/Welsh • *flower face*

Blodwen, Blodwyn, Blod • British/Welsh • *sacred, holy flowers*

Bona, Bonus • Latin • *good*

Bonita, Bonnie, Bonny, Bonitus, Bonito • Latin/Spanish • *pretty and good*

Branwen, Bronwen, Brangwen • British/Welsh • *raven or beast that is holy, sacred and white*

Caileigh, Kayley, Kayleigh, Caleigh, Caollaidhe • Irish Gaelic • *a descendant of Caollaidhe, the prefix meaning a slender man*

Caitlín, Katherine, Aikaterine, Caitlyn, Kaitlyn, Catriona, Caitríona, Catrina, Katrina, Cáit, Caitrín, Catraoine, Kathleen, Katelyn, Cate, Ceit, Katharos •

Greek/Irish Gaelic • *pure or purity*
**Calaminag, Calumina, Columbine,
Columba** • Scots Gaelic • *dove*
Calico • Indian • *a light cotton fabric
from Calicut, a port in Kerala state*
**Calista, Callie, Callie, Calixta,
Calixtus** • Latin • *cup as in a
Christian chalice or holy grail*
**Camilla, Milla, Millie, Milly,
Camille, Camila** • Latin/French •
Roman family name, perfection
Candelaria • Spanish/Roman
Catholic • *Candlemas, the purifica-
tion of the Virgin Mary*
**Candice, Candace, Canditia,
Candy, Candi** • Latin/Ethiopian •
pure and sincere; whiter than white
**Caoilfhionn, Caoilainn, Keelin,
Caolffionn** • Irish • *slender and
white maiden*
Caoimhe, Keeva • Irish Gaelic • *full
of grace, very lovely and so tender*
Careen • literary invention • *one of
Scarlett O'Hara's sisters in* Gone with
the Wind
**Caren, Karen, Carin, Karin, Carina,
Karina** • Danish/Greek • *pure or
purity*
Caris, Charis, Karis, Carissa • Greek
• *grace*
**Carmel, Carmella, Carmelina,
Camelita, Carmen, Carmine,
Carmela** • Roman Catholic • *Our
Lady of Carmel, the mountain where
early Christians lived as hermits and
later became the Carmelite order of
monks*
Casey, Casy, KC, Kacey, Kaci, Kacie
• Irish Gaelic • *a watchman; keeps
guard in war*
Casilda • Spanish • *unsure origins;
an 11th-century Moorish saint, she
lived in Toledo*

**Catherine, Katherine, Catharine,
Katharine, Cathryn, Caterina,
Kathryn, Cathrine, Kathrine,
Catriona, Caitríona, Catalina,
Catrin** • Greek • *pure or purity*
**Cecilia, Cécile, Cecily, Cecelia,
Cissie, Cissey, Sessy, Sissi, Sissy,
Cecille, Cecilie, Cacille, Cacilia,
Caecilia, Cicely** • Latin/English • *old
Roman family name Caecilius, from
the Latin, meaning blind*
Ceinwen • British/Welsh • *lovely,
beautiful, sacred and white*
Celandine, Dina • English/Greek •
a swallow and a flower
Ceri, Kerry • British/Welsh •
romantic, holy and beautiful
Ceridwen, Ceridwynn, Ceri •
British/Welsh • *Goddess of Poetry*
Cerise, Cherise • French • *cherry
as in fruit*
Chalice • Latin • *cup as in a
Christian chalice or holy grail*
Chantal, Chantelle, Shantell •
French • *in honour of St Jeanne-
Françoise, a woman of great
charity and virtue who married the
Baron de Chantal; when he died
she adopted a severe religious life
following St Francis of Sales*
Chardonnay • modern • *French/
English • a variety of grape that
makes the wine Chardonnay*
**Charis, Karis, Caris, Clarissa,
Charisse** • Greek • *grace*
Charisma, Karrisma, Kharisma •
Greek • *spiritual blessings*
Charity, Caridad, Caritas, Carus •
Latin • *dear charity; humanitarian*
Chastity, Chasity, Castitas, Castus •
Latin/English • *like a virgin!*
Cherry, Cherie, Cherrie • French •
darling fruit!

Chloe, Chloris, Cloris, Khloris, Khloe • Greek • *another name for the Goddess of Fertility, Demeter or Ceres*

Clémentine, Clem, Clemmie • Latin/French • *merciful, gentle, compassionate*

Clemency, Clemencie, Clementis • Latin • *leniency and mercy*

Cody, Codi, Codie, Codee, Codey, Cuidightheach • Irish Gaelic/American English • *descendant of Cuidightheach, a helpful and caring person*

Colleen, Coleen, Coline, Colina, Collinna, Colinette, Colinetta, Coletta, Cailin • Irish Gaelic/American English/Australian • *ordinary girl or maiden*

Columbina, Columbine, Bina, Binnie, Colimbina, Colombe • Latin • *dove*

Comfort • modern • *to soothe, pamper and look after*

Concepta • Irish • *the immaculate conception of the Virgin Mary*

Concetta • Roman Catholic • *Maria Concetta, the immaculate conception*

Concepción, Conchita, Concha • Spanish • *the immaculate conception of the Virgin Mary*

Consilia, Conseja • Roman Catholic • *Mary of Good Counsel and Advice*

Consolata, Consuelo • Roman Catholic • *Maria Consolata, Mary of Solace*

Cora, Kore, Coretta, Corinne, Corinna, Korina, Coreen, Corrinne • Latin/Greek • *maiden*

Cordelia, Cordellia, Cordula, Cordis • literary invention • *possibly from Latin for heart; by William Shakespeare for the virtuous*

daughter in King Lear

Corinne, Corinna, Korinna • French/Greek • *maiden*

Cornelia • Latin • *Roman family name, connected to Cornucopia and the horn of plenty*

Cruz • Roman Catholic • *cross, meaning Mary, Christ's mother, in agony at the foot of the cross; her son's crucifixion*

Cynthia, Kynthia, Kynthos, Cyndy, Cindy, Sindy, Cinzia, Chintzia • Greek • *Mount Kynthos on the island of Delos is the birthplace of Artemis, Goddess of the Moon and the Hunt*

Dagmar • Slavic/Danish • *a combo of peace, day, dear, maiden*

Daffodil, Deaffodil, Asphodel, Daffy, Daphne • Dutch • *a flower*

Dahlia, Dale, Dalia, Dalya, Dahl, Dale • Swedish

Darcy • Norman • *a man from the barony of D'Arcy*

Daria • Greek/Persian • *he who possesses, looks after the good and wellness of all*

Daryl, Daryll • Norman/American/English • *a chap from D'airelle, a barony in Normandy*

Deanna, Diana, Deana, Artemis, Deanne, Diane • Roman mythology • *virgin Goddess of the Moon and Hunting*

Deborah, Debra, Debbie, Debora, Debrah, Deb, Debbi, Debby, Debi, Debs, Devorah, Dvoire • Biblical/Hebrew/Jewish • *bee*

Deirdre, Deidre • Irish Gaelic • *woman*

Delphine, Delfina, Delphina • Latin • *a woman from Delphi, the place of the oracle of the gods*

Delia, Delos • Greek • *birthplace of*

the goddess Artemis

Demi, Demetria • Greek • *follower of the goddess Demeter*

Dena, Dina • Anglo-Saxon • *a man who served as dean in a Christian church or cathedral*

Deòiridh, Dorcas • Gaelic • *pilgrim*

Dextra • Anglo-Saxon/Latin • *a female dyer/laundress or right-handed*

Diana, Diane, Diahann, Dianna, Dian, Dianne, Deanne, Dyan, Di, Diandrea • Roman mythology • *virgin Goddess of the Moon and Hunting*

Digna • Latin • *worthy*

Dilwen • British/Welsh • *white, fair, true, genuine and sacred*

Dionne, Deonne, Diahann • American English • *virgin Goddess of the Moon and Hunting*

Dimity, Dimitos • Irish/Greek • *a light cotton fabric from Italy meaning two double warp thread!*

Ditanny, Diktamnon • Greek/Cretan • *the name of a medicinal plant on Mount Dikte in Crete*

Dolores, Deloris, Delores, Doloris, Lola, Lolita, Dolly • Roman Catholic • *Our Lady of the Seven Sorrows of the Virgin*

Dominica, Dominique, Dominga • Latin/Roman Catholic • *Lord, as in St Dominic, founder of the Dominican order*

Donna • Italian • *lady*

Du'ā • Arabic • *prayer and worship*

Dvoire, Devorah • Jewish/Yiddish • *bee*

Ehuang • Chinese • *august beauty*

Echo, Ekho • Greek • *a word that has come to mean a nymph*

who pined after the beautiful boy Narcissus, who was only interested in himself; as a result she was left with nothing but her voice

Eiddwen, Eiddunwen • British/Welsh • *fond, passionate, desire, holy, white, fair*

Eilwen, Aelwen • British/Welsh • *white, sacred, fair brow*

Eithne, Edna, Ena, Etna, Ethna, Ethenia • Irish/Gaelic • *kernel*

Eleanor, Alienor, Ellenor, Elinor, Elenor, Nell, Ellen, Nellie, Nelly, Eleanora, Eléonore • Germanic/Frankish/Provençal • *prefix means foreign or stranger; the suffix is unknown*

Elke, Adelheide • Germanic • *noble woman, carries herself well*

Ellen, Helen, Elin, Elen, Ella, Elena, Nell, Nelly, Nellie, Ellena, Ellenor • modern English • *shortened form of Helen and Eleanor*

Ellie, Elly, Eilidh, Ailie • Germanic/Frankish/Provençal • *short for Eleanor*

Elva, Alva • Scots Gaelic • *white*

Émer, Eimear, Eimer, Eimhir • Irish • *vague origins; perhaps chastity and purity, beauty and wisdom*

Ena, Ina, Eithne • English/Irish/Gaelic • *kernel*

Engracia, Enkrates, Encratis, Encratia, Gratia • Latin • *grace*

Esperanza, Sperantia • Latin • *hope*

Eulalia, Eulalie, Lalien, Eulalee, Eula, Olalla • Greek • *good to talk*

Euphemia, Eppie, Hephzibah, Eufemia, Euphémie, Euphemia, Effie, Eppie, Euphemia, Effemy, Hephzibah • Greek/Latin • *good to talk*

Fabia, Fabienne, Fabiola • Latin • *old Roman family name meaning a bean*

Fadīla • Arabic • *a moral, ethical, virtuous woman*

Fakhriyya • Arabic • *this woman is glorious and expects nothing for nothing; everything is unconditional*

Fanny, Frances • English/Latin • *to be French, someone from France*

Fātima • Arabic/Muslim/Roman Catholic • *abstainer from all bad or wicked things; mother*

Fawziyya • Arabic • *accomplished and successful woman*

Fenella, Fionnuala, Finella, Finola • Scots Gaelic • *white, fair, shoulders*

Fennel, Faeniculum, Faenum • Latin • *hay turned into a spice*

Fikriyya • Arabic • *pensive, contemplative, intelligent, intellectual*

Fiona, Fionn, Ffion • Scots Gaelic/British Welsh • *white, fair*

Fiorella, Fiore • Italian • *flower*

Finola, Fionnuala, Fionola, Nuala, Finuala, Fionnguala, Fenella, Finella, Finola • Scots Gaelic • *white, fair, shoulders*

Fleur • Norman • *flower*

Flora, Floris, Flo, Florence, Floella, Florrie, Ffloraidh • Latin • *old Roman family name meaning flower*

Florence, Florentius, Florentia, Flo, Florance, Floss, Florrie, Flossie • *like a flower, blooming and blossoming*

Florentina, Florentinus, Florenz, Florens • Latin • *she flourishes and blossoms*

Florida, Floridus • Spanish • *flowery*

Flower, Fleur, Fiorella • Norman • *flower*

Franca • French • *a girl from France*

Frances, Proinséas • English/Latin • *to be French, someone from France*

Francesca, France, Francene, Fran, Frances, Fanny, Françoise, Franceen, Franziska, Frankie, Francine, Francisca • Italian/Latin • *to be French, someone from France*

Frauke • German • *a lady from northern Germany*

Frume, Fromm • Jewish/Yiddish • *pious, devout and virtuous*

Gaenor, Gaynor, Geinor, Cainwryr • British/Welsh • *beautiful maiden*

Gaia, Ge • Greek • *Goddess of the Earth, mum of Saturn and Uranus*

Galina, Gala, Galene • Greek • *calm*

Garnet, Grenate, Granatum • Norman/Latin • *either a dealer in pomegranates or the precious stone*

Gauri, Gowri • Sanskrit • *white*

Georgina, Georgena, Georgette, Georgene, Georgia, Jorja, Georgiana, Georgie, Georgina, Georgine, Georene • Greek/Latin/Norman • *farmer or someone who works on the land*

Ghāda • Arabic • *young, graceful, refined woman*

Gilda • Germanic • *sacrifice*

Gina, Giorgina, Luigina, Ginette • Italian • *suffix for other name but on its own it is said to mean 'pure'*

Gislög, Gisillaug, Gislaug • Norse • *sacred hostage*

Gitte, Gittel, Birgitte • Jewish/Yiddish • *good girl*

Glenda, Gwenda • British/Welsh • *good, clean, pure and holy*

Glenys, Glynis, Glennis, Glenis, Glenice, Glenise, Glennys, Glynnis • British/Welsh • *pure and holy*

Goretti • Roman Catholic • *named*

after Maria Goretti, patron saint of youth

Grace, Gracie, Gratia, Grazia, Graziella, Gracia , Graciela • Latin • *grace*

Gráinne, Grania, Granya • Irish Gaelic • *unknown roots but possibly Goddess of the Harvest*

Greer, Grier • Greek/Scots English • *from a Scottish surname, Gregor, meaning watchful*

Gro, Groa, Gruach • Norse/Celtic • *evolving/old woman*

Guadalupe, Guadeloupe • Roman Catholic • *site of a convent with the famous image of the Virgin Mary*

Guinevere, Gaynor, Gayner, Gayna, Gaenor • British/Welsh • *beautiful maiden*

Gwen, Gwendolen, Gwendoline, Gwenllian, Gwendolin, Gwendolyne, Gwendolyn, Gwenfrewi • British/Welsh • *white*

Gwenda • British/Welsh • *a good, holy, pure woman*

Gwendolen, Gwendoline • British/ Welsh • *white or silver sacred ring*

Gwenllian • British/Welsh • *fair, white complexion*

Gwerful, Gwairmul • British/Welsh • *shy, modest compromising*

Gwenyth, Gwenith • British/Welsh • *wheat, romantic word for the pick of the crop!*

Hadīl • Arabic • *a woman with a voice like the cooing of doves, soft, lovely voice*

Hadya • Arabic • *a woman with inner peace*

Hafza • Arabic • *devoted to the Koran*

Haidee, Aidoios • Greek/literary •

Lord Byron called a character in Don Juan Haidee, meaning modest

Hailey, Hayley, Hallie, Haylee, Hailee, Haley, Haleigh, Hegleah • Anglo-Saxon • *meaning a clearing for hay*

Hayfā • Arabic • *slender, delicate flower*

Hebe, Hebos • Greek • *the Goddess of Youth*

Hefina • British/Welsh • *summer girl*

Heledd, Hyledd • British Welsh/ Celtic mythology • *not entirely sure of its root but it is the name of a princess whose name is at the heart of a lament for her brother's death*

Hermione, Hermia • Greek • *the god Hermes, messenger of the gods or the people*

Hortense, Hortensia, Hortensius, Hortus • French/Latin • *old Roman family name meaning garden*

Hualing • Chinese • *flourishing fu-ling (herb used in oriental medicine)*

Huguette, Huette • Germanic/ Frankish/French • *heart, mind and spirit*

Huizhong • Chinese • *wise devotion*

Huda • Arabic • *a woman who is wise and judicious counsellor or adviser; agony aunt*

Ida • Germanic/Frankish/Norman • *worker*

Idony, Idone, Idunn, Idonea • Norse • *Goddess of the Apples of Eternal Youth*

Ihsān • Arabic • *charity, generosity*

Immaculata, Immacolata, Immaculada • Roman Catholic • *stainless, peerless character, Mary of the Immaculate Conception*

Imogen, Innogen, Inghean,

Imogene • Celtic • *girl, maiden*
Ina, Ena, Ines, Agnès • English/
Irish/Gaelic • *kernel*
Inés, Inez, Agnès • Spanish/Greek •
pure and holy
Isaura • Latin • *a woman from
Isauria in Asia Minor (Turkey)*
'Ismat • Arabic • *she without sin,
perfection*
I'tidāl • Arabic • *everything in
moderation*

Jade, Ijada, Jada • Spanish • *stone
of the bowels*
Jancis, Jancie • English literary •
*combo of Frances and Jan, from the
novel* Precious Bane *by Mary Webb*
Janina • Tunisian • *garden*
Jay, Jaye, Jai • English • *named after
the letter 'J', short and snappy*
Jemima • Biblical/Hebrew/Jewish •
dove; as bright as day
**Jennifer, Jen, Jenefer, Jenny, Jeni,
Jenifer, Jenine, Jennifer, Jenni,
Jennefer, Jannifer, Jenine, Jennine,
Jeannine** • Arthurian mythology/
British Cornish • *beautiful maiden*
Jenna, Genna, Jena • Arthurian
mythology/British Cornish • *beau-
tiful maiden*
**Jessica, Jesca, Jessika, Jess,
Jessie, Jesse, Jessye, Teasag,
Iscah** • Biblical/literary • *William
Shakespeare's invention from the
Biblical name Jesca or Iscah*
Jiao • Chinese • *lovely, dainty*
Jie • Chinese • *hygiene and clean*
Jing • Chinese • *stillness, contempla-
tion or luxurious, comfort*
Jocasta • literary/Greek • *mother
of Oedipus, tragic figure in classical
mythology*
Juniper, Jennifer, Rothem,

Juniperus • Biblical/Hebrew/
Jewish/Latin • *desert shrub that
was used to build the Temple of
Solomon*
Jyoti • Sanskrit • *light of mind, light
of freedom, light of paradise*

Karen, Katherine, Kaz • Danish/
Greek/English • *pure or purity*
Karin, Karen, Katherine, Kari •
Swedish/Norwegian/Greek/English
• *pure or purity*
Karina, Carina • Scandinavian/
Polish/Russian/Greek/English •
pure or purity
Karita, Caritas, Caritas, Charity
• Swedish/Latin • *dear charity;
humanitarian*
Kasia • Polish/Slavic • *pure*
**Katerina, Catarina, Katarina,
Katherine, Katya** • Russian/Greek •
pure or purity
Katelyn, Caitlín • Greek/Irish Gaelic
• *pure or purity*
**Katharine, Katharos, Katherine,
Aikaterine, Hecate, Kathryn,
Katharyn, Kathrin, Catherine,
Catharine, Cathryn, Kate, Kath,
Cath, Cate, Kathy, Cathy, Kathie,
Katty, Cat, Katie, Kitty, Caitríona,
Caitrín, Katrine, Catraoine, Caitlín,
Catriona, Catrin, Katrien, Katrijn,
Katharina, Catalina, Caterina,
Ekaterini, Yekaterina, Katerina,
Katarzyna, Katarina, Ekaterina,
Kaarin, Kaarina, Karen, Katlin,
Caron, Carin, Katha, Katheryn,
Katlyn, Kit, Katherine, Kitty, Kittie** •
Greek • *pure or purity*
**Kathleen, Caitlín, Kathlene,
Cathleen, Kath, Kathy, Kathlyn,
Käthe** • Greek/Irish Gaelic • *pure
or purity*

Katia, Katya, Yekaterina, Katja, Katharina • Russian/Greek • *pure or purity*

Katrine, Karina, Carina, Catrina, Katrina • Danish/German/Greek • *pure or purity*

Kay, Kaye • Latin • *a woman of the earth*

Kayla, Kayley, Kaylah • American English • *a descendant of Caollaidhe, the prefix meaning a slender man*

Kayley, Kayleigh, Kayly, Kaylie, Kayli, Kaylee, Kaileley, Kailey, Kaily, Kalie, Kalee, Kaleigh, Cayleigh, Caileigh, Caleigh Caileigh, Kayley, Kayleigh, Caleigh, Caollaidhe, Kailey, Kayley, Kaley • Irish Gaelic • *a descendant of Caollaidhe, the prefix meaning a slender man*

Keely, Keeley, Kayley, Keighley • Irish Gaelic • *a descendant of Caollaidhe, the prefix meaning a slender man*

Kerry, Keri, Ceri • English/British/Welsh/Irish Gaelic • *after the Celtic Goddess of Poetry*

Keturah • Biblical/Hebrew/Jewish • *incense, the strong perfume from frankincense used to purify in sacred places*

Kia, Kiaora • English/New Zealand/Maori • *be well*

Kyra, Kyria, Kira • Greek • *lady*

Lalage, Lalagein, Lally, Lailie, Lalla, La-La • Greek • *to chatter on endlessly, loquacious*

Lara, Larissa, Larrisah • Russian/Greek • *unsure meaning; perhaps someone from a town near Thessaloniki, in northern Greece*

Larissa, Lara, Larry • Russian/Greek • *unsure meaning; perhaps someone from a town near Thessaloniki, in northern Greece*

Lata • Sanskrit • *she is as supple as a tendril*

Lawāhiz • Arabic • *shy glances, whispered secrets*

Li • Chinese • *upright*

Lilian, Lilly, Lily, Lili, Lillian, Lilium, Lily, Lillie, Lilly, Lili, Lilli • Latin/Norman • *flower that is associated with purity and resurrection*

Linda, Belinda, Lynda, Lindie, Lindy, Lyn, Lynn, Lynne, Linden, Lin, Lyn, Lynne, Linnet, Lindsey, Lenda • Spanish/Visigothic/Germanic • *pretty, passive, tender and soft*

Lisha • American English • *the suffix of any name ending with -cia e.g. Patricia!*

Lola, Dolores • Roman Catholic • *Our Lady of the Seven Sorrows of the Virgin*

Lolicia, Lola, Delicia • American English/Roman Catholic • *Our Lady of the Seven Sorrows of the Virgin*

Lolita, Lola, Lolita • Roman Catholic • *Our Lady of the Seven Sorrows of the Virgin*

Lone, Abelone, Magdelone • Danish • *Mary Magdelene aka Mary of Magdala, woman healed of evil spirits*

Loredana • literary Italian • *heroine in a novel!*

Lourdes, Lurdes • Roman Catholic • *a French place of pilgrimage where a young girl had visions of the Virgin*

Luana, Luanna, Luanne, Luan • cinematic Italian • *made up for a 1932 movie; Luana, the sacred virgin*

Luz, Lux, Luzdivina • Roman

Catholic • *Our Lady of Light; refer-*
ring to the Virgin
Lydia, Lydie • Greek • *woman from*
Lydia
Lynette, Lynette, Linnet, Linotte,
Linnette, Linette • Spanish/French

Mabel, Mab, Amabel, Amabilia,
Mabilia, Mabelle, Amiabel,
Maybelle, Maybella • Norman/
English • *lovely*
Macey, Masey, Macie, Macy, Maci,
Macciacum • Norman/Latin •
someone from Massey, Normandy
Madeleine, Madelaine,
Magdalene, Magdala, Madelene,
Madlyn, Madelyn, Madalene,
Madaline, Madoline, Magdalen,
Maddie, Maddy, Maddalena •
Biblical/French • *Mary Magdelene*
aka Mary of Magdala, woman
healed of evil spirits
Madīha • Arabic • *praiseworthy,*
commendable
Madonna, Madge • American
Italian • *my lady*
Mairwen • British/Welsh • *white*
and pure virgin
Magda, Magdalene, Magadelena,
Lena • Biblical/Slavic/German
• *Mary Magdelene aka Mary of*
Magdala, woman healed of evil spirits
Maia, Maya, Mya • Latin • *Roman*
Goddess of Youth, Life, Rebirth, Love
and Sexuality
Maidie, Maid, Maegden • old
English • *maiden*
Marja • Finnish/Estonian • *berry as*
in fruit
Malvina, Malamhin, Maggi,
Maggie, Malamhin • cosmetic
Scots • *name created by poet James*
McPherson meaning smooth brow

in Gaelic
Manon, Marie • Biblical/French •
pet name for Marie
María José • Roman Catholic •
combo of Mary the Virgin and Joseph
the father
Mariana, Marianus, Marianne,
Marius • Latin • *Latin* • *follower of*
the Virgin Mary
Marie • French • *Virgin Mary,*
special patroness of France
María de los Ángeles, Mary-Ange •
Spanish • *Mary of the Angels*
Mariel, Muriel, Meriel, Murielle,
Marielle • English • *combo of Mary*
and Muriel
Marietta, Mariella, María, Mairéad,
Margaret, Mariette, Maretta •
Biblical/Italian • *Mary Magdelene*
aka Mary of Magdala, woman
healed of evil spirits
Marigold, Golde • Anglo-Saxon •
Virgin Mary's flower
Marilee, Marylee, Marylou,
Marilene, Marilla, Marioa •
American English • *names all based*
on Mary or Maria: a drop of the sea
Marilyn, Mary, Maralyn, Marilynne,
Marylyn, Marylynn, Marilene,
Maralyn, Marilyn • modern English
• *combo of Mary and Lyn*
Marion, Marie, Margeret, Margery,
Marianus, Marion, Marian,
Marianne, Mariann, Marieanne,
Marianna, Meiriona • Latin/French
• *follower of the Virgin Mary*
Maris, Stella Maris • modern name
• *uncertain root but from Maria or*
Mary meaning Star of the Sea
Marisa, Maria, Marissa • *modern*
name based on Mary; a drop of the sea
Marisol • Spanish • *combination of*
Maria and Sol (sun)

Marla, Marlene, Magdalene •
modern • *Mary Magdelene aka
Mary of Magdala, woman healed
of evil spirits*

Marlene, Maria, Magdalena •
German • *Mary Magdelene aka
Mary of Magdala, woman healed
of evil spirits*

**Martha, Marthe, Marthja, Martja,
Märta, Martta** • Biblical/Aramaic
• *lady*

Martirio • Roman Catholic/Spanish
• *to be a martyr*

**Mary, Marie, Maria, Miriam, May,
Molly, Máire, Mair, Moira, Maura,
Mairia, Màiri, Màili, Mari, Marja,
Mariya, Marya, Marija, Marica,
Masha, Maryam, Moire** • Biblical/
French/English • *a drop of the sea*

Matrona • Latin • *lady*

Maura, Mary • Irish/Celtic/Latin •
a drop of the sea

**Maureen, Muirinn, Moreen,
Maírín, Maurene, Maurine, Máire,
Moirean, Moire, Mo** • Virgin Mary

May • English • *pet name for Mary
and Margaret*

Mercedes • Roman Catholic • *Our
Lady of Mercies, alluding to the
Virgin Mary*

Medea, Medesthai • Greek
mythology • *a Colchian princess in
'Jason and the Golden Fleece'; means
to contemplate and meditate*

Meinir • British/Welsh • *thin, long
and slender*

Meinwen • British/Welsh • *thin,
slender, pale and white*

Meirong • Chinese • *beautiful soul
and personality*

**Melissa, Melita, Melitta, Lissa,
Melissa, Lyssa, Lita, Melita, Melitta**
• Greek • *honey bee*

Mercedes, Merche, Mercy, Mary •
Spanish • *Mary of Mercies*

Mia, Maria • Swedish/Danish/
Biblical • *a drop of the sea*

Milagros • Roman Catholic • *Our
Lady of Miracles*

Milla, Camilla, Camille • Latin/
French • *Roman family name,
perfection*

Millena, Milenna • Czech • *grace
and favour*

Mimi, María, Mary • Italian • *pet
name for Maria or Mary*

Mimosa, Mimus • Latin • *yellow
plant that means mime or mimic*

**Mina, Wilhelmina, Calumina,
Normina** • Scots Gaelic • *short name
for any name ending in -mina!*

**Miranda, Randa, Randy, Randie,
Amanda** • literary invention/Latin
• *William Shakespeare invented
this name for his heroine in* The
Tempest: *admire, wonder at or in
awe of her loveliness*

Minerva • Latin • *Goddess of
Wisdom, Roman equivalent to
Athene*

**Miriam, Maryam, Mary, María,
Maiamne, Myriam, Mirjam** •
Biblical/Jewish/Hebrew • *uncertain
origins but is the root of Mary and
Maria*

Mitzi, Maria • Biblical/French/
Bavarian • *a drop of the sea*

**Moira, Moyra, Maura, Máire,
Mary, Moya** • Irish Gaelic/French •
Biblical/French/English • *a drop of
the sea*

Molly, Mollie, Mary, Mally •
Biblical/French/English • *a drop of
the sea*

**Monica, Monere, Monique,
Monika** • Latin/Phoenician •

cautious counsel, to advise or warn
Montserrat • Catalan • *Our Lady of Montserrat, a Benedictine monastery near Barcelona*
Morwenna, Morwen, Morwyn • British/Welsh • *maiden*
Muhayya • Arabic • *she has such a lovely, beautiful face*
Muhsina • Arabic • *a charitable, kind and compassionate woman*
Myra, Myrrha, Mary, Miranda, Mairéad • Latin • *anagram of Mary meaning myrrh, the embalming spice*
Myriam, Miriam • Biblical/French • *uncertain origins but is the root of Mary and Maria*

Najāh, Nagāh • Arabic • *a woman who is progressive and successful*
Najāt, Nagāt • Arabic • *a woman who has been saved, rescued or redeemed, or helps others to confess*
Najiba, Nagiba • Arabic • *cultured, cultivated and a cut above the rest*
Najwa, Nagwa • Arabic • *secrets abound, a woman who is discreet and confidential, keeper of secrets*
Nanda, Ferdinanda, Hernanda • Spanish/Italian • *short form of Ferdinanda or Hernanda; someone at peace wherever she is; always ready and prepared to travel*
Naomh • Irish Gaelic • *holy, saintly*
Naomi, Noémie, Noemi • Biblical/Hebrew/Jewish • *pleasant and good*
Nápla, Annabel, Anabl, Anable, Anaple, Amable • Norman/English/Irish • *lovely*
Natividad, Nativitas • Roman Catholic • *festival of the Nativity of the Virgin Mary, 5th September*
Nell, Nella, Nellie, Nelly, Eleanor, Ellen, Helen • *English short name for Eleanor, Ellen or Helen*
Nerissa, Nereis • literary invention/Greek • *sea sprite or nymph Nerissa, invented by William Shakespeare for Portia's lady-in-waiting in* The Merchant of Venice
Nessa, Neassa, Neasa, Ness • Irish Gaelic • *unknown meaning but the name of a character in Irish legend*
Nesta, Nester, Nostos, Agnès • British Welsh/Greek • *pure and holy*
Nettie, Annette, Jeannette • English • *short form of all names ending in -nette*
Nia, Nyah • Swahili • *with a purpose*
Nieves • Roman Catholic • *Our Lady of the Snows*
Ni'mat • Arabic • *a woman who is good to have around*
Nina, Nena, Ninette, Ninon, Antonina • Russian • *short form of names that end in -nina*
Ninette, Nina, Nadine • Russian/French/English • *Russian/French • from the name Nina*
Ning • Chinese • *tranquillity*
Nirvana • Sanskrit • *extinction, disappearance of the individual soul into the universal*
Nita, Neats, Anita, Juanita • Spanish • *short form of names ending in -nita!*
Norma • artistic Italian • *Felice Romani invented the name for Bellini's opera*
Normina • *a woman from the north; Norseman or Viking*
Nuha • Arabic • *a woman who is clever, intellectual and cerebrally bright*

Olive, Olivia, Oliff, Oliffe, Oliva • Latin • *olive tree, a symbol of peace and abundance*

Olivia, Olive, Oliva • literary invention/Latin • *William Shakespeare named Olivia as the rich heiress in* The Tempest

Olwen, Olwin, Olwyn • *footprint, path, white, sacred*

Olympia, Olympe • Greek • *woman from Olympus, home of the Greek gods*

Ona, Anona, Fiona, Honor • English • *shortened name for any that ends in -ona*

Onora, Nora, Honora • English • *shortened name for any ending in -nora*

Paderau • British/Welsh • *Lady of the Rosary, alludes to the Virgin Mary*

Padma • Sanskrit • *lotus flower, energy centres of the chakra*

Padmavati • Sanskrit • *full of lotus flowers*

Padmini • Sanskrit • *lotus pond or lake*

Paige, Page • American English • *a page boy to a great lord or lady*

Paloma, Palumba • Latin • *dove*

Pamela, Pam, Pammy, Pamella • poetic invention • *Sir Philip Sidney, Elizabethan (First) poet, created the name*

Pansy, Pensee • Norman • *flower whose name means 'thought'*

Parthenope, Parthenosops • Greek mythology • *maiden as in the goddess Athene in her form and face; one of the Sirens, who lured men to her with their enchanting, bewitching voices was named Parthenope*

Patience, Pati • Latin • *to suffer, a virtue*

Paula, Paola • Latin/Italian/English • *Roman family name meaning little or small*

Paulette, Paula, Paulina, Paola • Latin • *Roman family name meaning little or small*

Pauline, Paulina • Latin/French • *Roman family name meaning little or small*

Paz • Roman Catholic • *Our Lady of Peace*

Perdita, Perdie, Purdee, Purdy, Perditus • Latin/literary invention • *William Shakespeare invented the name from the Latin 'lost' as one of his characters in* The Winter's Tale

Peridot • Norman/English • *a green transparent variety of olivine, used as a gem; Virgo's birthstone*

Petula, Pet, Petulare • Latin/Christian • *to ask or plead humbly for mercy or forgiveness*

Pia, Pius • Italian • *pious*

Piedad • Roman Catholic • *Our Lady of Piety*

Pilar • Roman Catholic • *Our Lady of the Pillar; appearance of the Virgin on a pillar at Zaragossa*

Poppy, Popaeg, Papaver • Latin/Anglo-Saxon • *the flower*

Patribha • Sanskrit • *clever, radiant, imaginative and precocious*

Presentación • Roman Catholic/Spanish • *presentation of the Virgin at the Temple in Jerusalem*

Psyche, Psykhe • Greek • *butterfly, spirit and soul*

Purificación • Roman Catholic/Spanish • *Feast of the Purification, when Virgin purges of the uncleanliness associated with childbirth*

Qiao • Chinese • *dexterous girl*
Qiaohui • Chinese • *dexterous and sagacious*
Qiaolian • Chinese • *eternally dexterous*
Qingling • Chinese • *celebrating understanding*
Qingzhao • Chinese • *clear understanding, crystal illumination*

Radegund, Radegunde • Germanic • *a counsellor, adviser in times of trouble*
Radwa • Arabic • *an area in the holy city of Mecca*
Ragā, Rajā • Arabic • *perpetual anticipation is good for the soul*
Ramona • Catalan/Visigothic • *adviser*
Ravenna • Italian • *an Italian city; someone from Ravenna, the capital of Roman mosaic*
Rāwiya • Arabic • *a narrator of classical Arabic poetry and prose and beautiful speaker*
Refugio • Roman Catholic • *Our Lady of the Refuge*
Regina, Queenie, Raine, Régine, Raghnailt, Ragnhild • Latin/Roman Catholic • *queen (of heaven)*
Remedios • Roman Catholic • *Our Lady of the Remedies; through prayer the Virgin heals*
Rene, Renata, Irene, Renee, Doreen, Maureen • English • *short for any name ending in -reen or -rene*
Rhetta • Dutch • *advice, counsel*
Rhian, Rian, Rhianu • British/Welsh • *maiden*
Rida • Arabic • *one who has God's (Allah's) approval*
Riley, Rileigh, Ryley, Reilly,

Rygelegh, Roghallach • Anglo-Saxon/Irish Gaelic
Rita, Magarita • Spanish • *short form of Margarita*
Rocio • Roman Catholic • *Our Lady of the Dews, or tears shed for the wickedness of the world*
Rosaire, Rosario • Roman Catholic • *Our Lady of the Rosary*
Rosalind, Rosaleen, Rosalyn, Roslind, Rosaline, Rosalin, Rosalynne, Rosalynn • Germanic/Frankish • *horse, tender and soft, passive and weak*
Rou • Chinese • *mild and gentle*

Sabriyya • Arabic • *a woman who is patient, persevering and dedicated*
Safā • Arabic • *a pure, chaste woman who is sincere and goodly*
Sage, Sauge, Sapius • English/Norman/American English • *the herb sage that promotes wisdom and is good for the liver*
Salma • Arabic • *a person who looks after those she loves; a protector*
Salud • Roman Catholic • *Our Lady of Salvation*
Salwa • Arabic • *she who consoles others and gives a shoulder to cry on*
Samantha, Sam, Sammy, Sammi • Biblical/Hebrew/Jewish • *the name of God, God has heard, listen to God*
Sappho • literary Greek • *poetess Sappho, noted for her verse honouring lesbian passion*
Sarala • Sanskrit • *as straight as the pine and honest as the day is long*
Saraswati • Sanskrit • *filled with waters of knowledge of the arts, learning and academia*
Savannah, Savanna • American English/Spanish • *treeless plain*

Sawsan • Arabic • *lily of the valley*

Sebastienne • Latin/French • *someone from Sebaste in Asia Minor (now Turkey)*

Senga • Gaelic • *slender*

Serenissima • Italian • *serene*

Shafiqa • Arabic • *a compassionate, charitable woman*

Shamshad • Persian • *like a box tree, she is lean, tall and elegant*

Shoshanna, Shoshana, Shannah, Susanna • Biblical/Jewish/Hebrew • *the flower lily, which means rose in modern Hebrew*

Shanta • Sanskrit • *she who finds inner peace through yoga or meditation*

Shanti • Sanskrit • *she who finds tranquillity and serenity through yoga*

Sharifa • Arabic • *a woman who is eminent in her field and honourable to the nth degree*

Sharman, Charmaine, Sherman • Anglo-Saxon • *shearer, someone who trimmed woven cloth*

Sharmila • Sanskrit/Hindi • *she who is selfless, modest and protective*

Sharon, Sharron, Sharona, Sharonda • Biblical • *a place called Sharon on the coastal plain of the Holy Land; and for the shrub the Rose of Sharon*

Shula, Shulamit • Hebrew/Jewish • *peacefulness*

Silvestra • Latin • *a person from the woods or forest*

Simone • Biblical/Hebrew/Jewish • *hearkening, hearing*

Sissel, Cecily • Scandinavian/English • *old Roman family name Caecilius, from the Latin, meaning blind*

Sita • Sanskrit • *she ploughs a straight furrow; symbolic of all wifely virtures and Goddess of Nature*

Skylar, Schuyler • Dutch/American English • *scholar, school teacher*

Socorro • Roman Catholic • *Our Lady of Perpetual Succour*

Soledad, Sol • Roman Catholic • *Our Lady of Solitude*

Stella, Stella Maris • Latin • *a star and Star of the Seas (often used to describe the Virgin Mary)*

Sukie, Sukey, Susan • English • *pet form of Susan*

Sumati • Sanskrit • *good thoughts, devout in prayer*

Summer, Haf, Sumor • Anglo-Saxon • *someone born in the summer months*

Sunita • Sanskrit • *she's a good girl who gives wise advice*

Susan, Susanna, Suzan, Sue, Su, Soo, Susie, Suzie, Susy, Suzy, Sukie, Sukey, Siùsan, Sue, Susan, Susanna, Susannah, Suzanne, Su, Soo • English/Biblical • *the flower lily, which means rose in modern Hebrew*

Susanna, Shoshana, Shoshan, Susana, Suzanna, Suzannah, Susannah, Siùsan, Siusaidh, Susanne, Suzanne, Zuzanna, Zuzana, Suzana, Zsuzsanna, Susann, Susi, Susanna, Sanna, Zanna • Biblical/English • *lily*

Shushila • Sanskrit • *she has a lovely nature and is so placid too*

Silvius • Latin • *someone who loves or inhabits the woods or forest*

Susie, Susan, Suzie, Susi • English • *short form Susan or Susannah*

Suzanne, Susanna, Suzette, Suzie • Biblical/French • *the flower lily,*

which means rose in modern Hebrew
Sylvestra, Silvestra • Latin • *a person from the woods or forest*
Sylvia, Silvia, Sylvie, Silvia, Sylvia, Sylve • Latin/English/French/Italian • *Rhea Silvia, mother of the founders of Rome*

Talitha • Biblical/Aramaic • *little girl*
Tamsin, Thomasina, Tammy, Tammie, Tamzin • Biblical/Aramaic/Greek • *twin*
Taylor, Tayler, Tayla, Taillier, Taleare • Anglo-Saxon/Norman • *a person who cuts, a tailor*
Tegan, Teagan, Teigan, Tiegan, Teg • British/Welsh • *lovely*
Themba • Zulu • *trusted*
Tierra • American Spanish • *land, earth, terra firma*
Tirion • British/Welsh • *kind and gentle*
Tori, Tory, Toria • English • *short form of Victoria*
Tottie, Charlotte, Lottie, Totty, Lotte, Carlotta • English • *short form of Charlotte*
Tracey, Trace, Tracie, Tracy • Latin/Gaulic • *a person from a place in Normandy called Tracy!*
Trude, Gertraud, Gertrude, Traute, Trudy, Traude • German • *short form of any name ending in -raud or -raude*
Trina, Treena, Catrina,Treena • English • *short form of any name ending in -tina*
Trinity, Trinidad • Roman Catholic • *the Holy Trinity*
Trudy, Trudi, Trudie, Gertrude, Ermintrude, Ermentrud, Trude • English/German
Tyler, Tigele, Tegula, Tylor • Anglo-Saxon/Latin • *a man who covers structure with fabric*

Uhuti • Swahili • *my sister*
Ujana • Kiswahili • *youth*
Uma • Sanskrit • *turmeric or flax; messenger of the gods*

Valérie, Valeria, Valère, Val • French/Latin • *old Roman name Valerius, meaning healthy, robust and strong*
Vashti • Biblical/Hebrew/Persian • *thread or beautiful woman*
Velinda • American English • *an extension of Linda*
Venetia, Venice, Venezia • Italian • *someone from Venice, celebrating the city of Venezia*
Verity, Veritas, Verus • Latin/Norman • *truth and honesty*
Verona, Veronica • Italian/English • *someone from the city of Verona*
Vesta, Hestia • Latin • *Roman Goddess of the Hearth; Hestia is the same in the Greek pantheon*
Vienna, Wien, Vindo, Vianna • Celtic • *white*
Vimala • Sanskrit • *a peerless person, pure as crystal*
Virginia, Verginius, Ginny, Ginnie, Virginie • Latin • *Roman family name Vergilius but confusion reigned when the spelling was changed to Virgilius, which means the maiden*
Virtudes • Roman Catholic/Spanish • *seven Christian virtues*
Visitacion • Roman Catholic/Spanish • *the Virgin Mary visits her sister Elisabeth*
Vivien, Vivian, Vivienne, Béibhinn • Celtic/Irish Gaelic/Arthurian legend • *white or fair lady*

Wendy, Wenda, Wendi, Gwendolen • literary invention • *JM Barrie created it for his book* Peter Pan *from his own nursery name Fwendy-Wendy meaning friend*

Xiaojian • Chinese • *little healthy*
Xiaosheng • Chinese • *small at birth*
Xiuying • Chinese • *graceful flower*
Xueman • Chinese • *snowy composure and grace*

Yekaterina, Aikaterine, Katherine • Greek/Russian • *Greek* • *pure or purity*

Yentl, Gentille • French/Jewish/Yiddish • *kind, goodly*
Ying • Chinese • *a clever girl*
Yingtai • Chinese • *terrace of flowers*

Zakiyya • Arabic • *a woman who is innocent and pure*
Zara, Zahr • Arabic • *flower*
Zhu • Chinese • *bamboo: a lucky plant; symbol of happiness, wealth and health*
Zita, Zeta, Zetein, Zitta • Tuscan • *wee girl*

LIBRA

24th September to 23rd October

Planet: Venus

Day: Friday

Stone: sapphire

Metal: copper

Colours: all pastel shades, candy pink, baby blue, peach and apricot, lilacs and lavenders

Design: wavy shapes and voluptuous contours

Trees: ash, cherry, aspen, tulip tree, pocket handkerchief tree and all fragrant trees including some pines

Flora: fragrant roses, aster, pinks, delphinium, hyacinth, sweet william, friesa, fuschia, all blue and pink flowers, all sweet-smelling plants and shrubs

Celebrity Libras: June Allyson • Julie Andrews • Gene Autry • Bridget Bardot • David Ben-Gurion • Constance Bennett • Lenny Bruce • Truman Capote • Al Capp • James Earl 'Jimmy' Carter • Chubby Checker • James Clavell • Montgomery Clift • Michael Crichton • Aleister Crowley • Linda Darnell • Michael Douglas • Robert Duval • T S Elliot • Dwight Eisenhower • William Faulkner • Sarah Ferguson • Peter Finch • Carrie Fisher • F Scott Fitzgerald • Margot Fontaine • Mahatma Gandhi • Mohandas Gandhi • Greer Garson • George Gershwin • Lillian Gish • Bryant Gumball • Richard Harris • Helen Hayes • Rutherford Hayes • Susan Hayworth • Charlton Heston • Julio Iglesias • Jesse Jackson • Deborah Kerr • Evel Knievel • Lillie Langtry • Angela Lansbury • John Le Carré • John Lennon • Jenny Lind • Franz Liszt • John Lithgow • Carol Lombard • Bela Lugosi • Marcello Mastroianni • Penny Marshall • Groucho Marx • Walter Matthau • Linda McCartney • Arthur Miller • Yves Montand • Martina Navratilova • Olivia Newton-John • Oliver North • Eugene O'Neill • Luciano Pavarotti • Pope Paul VI • Pelé • George Peppard • John Profumo • Juliet Prowse • Randy Quaid • Christopher Reeve • Patti Regan • Mickey Rooney • Eleanor Roosevelt • Susan Sarandon • George C Scott • Dimitri Shostakovich • Suzanne Somers • Sting • Ed Sullivan • Margaret Thatcher • Archbishop Desmond Tutu • Jean-Claude Van Damme • Giuseppe Verdi • Gore Vidal • Lech Walesa • Barbara Walters • Sigourney Weaver • James Whitmore • Oscar Wilde • Catherine Zeta-Jones.

Planetary Influences: see Venus at the back of this book (page 448)

Boys

'Abd-al-Latīf • Arabic • *servant of the kind, Allah*

'Abd-al-Salām, Abdes Salām • Arabic • *servant of the peaceable, Allah*

Absalom, Absolon • Biblical/Hebrew • *father of peace*

Ādil • Arabic • *just and fair*

Aeneas, Aineas, Ainein, Angus • Greek • *singing praises*

'Ali • Arabic • *the most sublime*

Amadeus, Amédée, Gottlieb, Amedeo • Latin/Germanic • *love God or God of Love!*

Amador, Amator • Spanish • *lover*

Amal • Arabic • *hope, longing*

Amancio • Latin • *loving*

Amato, Amatus, Amado • Latin • *beloved*

Amias • French/Biblical/Hebrew • *someone from Amiens in Picardie or love God*

Amittai • Jewish/Hebrew • *being true, honest, candid*

Amīn • Arabic • *honest as the day is long*

Anil • Sanskrit • *air and wind*

Arduino, Hartwinn • Germanic • *best friend*

Arun • Sanskrit • *pinkish red*

Arwel • British/Welsh • *I wept over you*

'Ātif • Arabic • *compassionate and sympathetic*

Balder • Norse • *ruler or chief prince, said to be pure and beautiful*

Baldev • Sanskrit • *God of Strength and playboy!*

Barry, Baz, Bazza, Barra, Bairre,

Barrie, Barri • Irish Gaelic • *fair-haired boy*

Bāsim • Arabic • *smiling!*

Beau • French • *beautiful and bonny boy*

Bem • Nigerian • *peace*

Benvenuto • Latin • *welcome*

Bertram, Bertie, Bert, Bertrand, Beltrán, Burt, Albert • German • *bright*

Berwyn, Barrwyn • British/Welsh • *white or fair-haired*

Bingwen • Chinese • *clever/cultivated*

Birger, Birghir, Byrghir, Børje, Birre, • Norse • *helper*

Blume, Blumke • Jewish/Yiddish • *flower*

Bob, Bobbie, Bobby, Robbie, Robert • American/English/Germanic • *bright, famous and clever*

Bojing • Chinese • *to win admiration and respect*

Boyd • Irish • *blond*

Brad, Bradford, Bradley, Bradleigh, Braeden, Braden, Brayden • Anglo-Saxon • *a man from the broad meadow, ford, farm or clearing*

Brendan, Brendon, Breandán, Brendanus • Latin • *prince, heir*

Bunem • Jewish/Yiddish • *a good man*

Caerwyn, Carwyn, Caradog, Caradoc • British/Welsh • *sacred love*

Cai, Kay • British/Welsh • *rejoice!*

Cale, Caile, Cayle • English/American • *dog*

Cainneach, Kenny • Irish Celtic • *handsome, beautiful founder of Kilkenny*

Callisto, Kallistos • Greek • *most fair, simply the best*

Caleb, Kaleb • Hebrew/Jewish • *he who rages like a dog, needs anger management!*

Callum, Colm, Calum, Columba, Cole, Colmán, Colum • Latin/Scots Gaelic • *dove*

Caoimhín, Kevin • Irish Gaelic • *beloved, beautiful, enchanting*

Carmine • Latin • *song*

Cassian, Cassianus, Cassius • Latin • *thy name is vanity!*

Cassius • Latin • *thy name is vanity!*

Ceallach, Kelly • Irish Gaelic • *fair-haired or monk, church, monastery*

Cedric • literary name • *invented by Sir Walter Scott*

Chanden • Sanskrit • *sandalwood*

Changming • Chinese • *forever bright*

Chaoxiang • Chinese • *fortunate, hopeful*

Chongan • Chinese • *second brother of peace*

Chonglin • Chinese • *second brother unicorn*

Clem, Clément, Clemmie, Cliamain, Clemente • Latin • *merciful, gentle, compassionate*

Cody, Cuidightheact, Macoda • Irish Gaelic • *descendant of Oda, a helpful soul*

Coinneach, Kenneth • Scots Gaelic • *handsome, beautiful, sexy*

Colombe, Columba, Callum, Colmán, Colm, Colum, Columbano • Latin • *dove*

Colin, Collin, Coll, Nicholas, Cailean • English/Scots Gaelic • *dove*

Comhghall, Comgall, Cowall • Irish Celtic • *together, jointly, ransom*

Conán • Irish Gaelic • *Irish wolfhound*

Conley, Conlaodh • *a person who is pure and chaste as Aodh*

Connor, Conor, Conner, Conchobhar • Irish Gaelic • *dog lover*

Conroy, Conraoi • Irish Gaelic • *keeper of the dogs*

Constantine, Constanz, Costin, Constantin, Cystenian, Constant • Latin • *constant, steadfast, loyal, devoted*

Conway, Connmhaigh, Connmhach, Conbhuide, Cubhuide, Connmhach • Gaelic/British/Welsh • *golden hound or dog or head-smasher!*

Cuán • Irish Celtic • *dog or hound*

Curtis, Curt, Kurtis, Kurt • Norman • *a charming, courteous man*

Cuthbert, Bert, Cuddy, Cuddie, Cuithbeart • Anglo-Saxon • *a man well known for what he does, his personality or wit*

Cyprian, Cyprianus • Latin • *the man who comes from Cyprus, the isle of Venus or Aphrodite*

Dai, Dei • British/Welsh • *this chap shines forth*

Daley, Dalaigh, Dalach, Daly • Irish Gaelic • *altogether now! A gathering*

Damon, Daman, Damaso • Greek • *a man full of self-control or a man who tames*

Darius, Dareios, Darayavahush, Darayamiy • Greek/Persian • *he who possesses, looks after the good and wellness of all*

Darwin, Deorwine • Anglo-Saxon • *dear, good, bosom buddy*

David, Dave, Davy, Dewi, Dafydd,

Dai, Davie, Davey, Dàibhidh, Davide, Taavi, Daw, Dawson, Dawūd, Dewi, Dewydd, David, Dai • Biblical/Hebrew • *vague origins but possibly from a baby word meaning darling one*

Dayaram • Sanskrit • *as kind and tender as Rama, the perfect man/divinity*

Delun • Chinese • *virtuous, respected*

Deming • Chinese • *virtuous, bright*

Dennis, Denis, Denys, Den, Dionysios, Denny, Dioniso, Dionizy, Denes, Dionysius • Greek/French • *named after the god Dionysius*

Derek, Dereck, Derrick, Deryck, Del, Dirk, Theodoric • German/Dutch • *God's gift*

Desiderio, Desiderius, Desiderium • Latin • *longing*

Devdan • Sanskrit • *gift of the gods*

Dewey, Dewy • British/Welsh/American/English • *possibly the English spelling of Dewi, which means David, darling one*

Didier, Desiderius • Latin • *longing for*

Dietfried • Germanic • *people of peace or peaceful people*

Dieudonné • French • *God-given*

Dilwyn • British/Welsh • *fair, blonde, white, blessed, sacred, holy*

Dionysus, Bacchus • Greek • *Dionysus, God of Wine, Orgies and Partying*

Dipak • Sanskrit • *God of Love, glows like a little lamp*

Donat, Donato, Donatus, Donatien, Donatianus • *given by God*

Dorotheos, Dorofei • Greek • *gift of God*

Dositheos, Dosifei • Greek • *God-given*

Dwight, Diot, Dionysa • English • *a woman (that's right: female!) who worships the God of Orgies*

Ebun • Nigerian • *gift*

Eden, Edan • Hebrew/Jewish • *Garden of Eden, a place of sheer pleasure*

Ehrenfried, Arnfried • Germanic • *peace with honour or person who, like the eagle, has power, but uses it as a deterrent*

Ehrenreich • Germanic • *honourable and rich*

Ehud • Jewish/Hebrew • *compassionate and pleasant*

Eliezer, Eleazar, Eli • Jewish/Hebrew • *God's help*

Elisud, Elus, Ellis • British/Welsh • *a kind, benevolent man*

Eligio, Eligius, Eligere, Eloy • Latin/Italian/Spanish • *to choose, given a choice*

Elpidio, Elpidius, Elpidios • Latin/Greek • *hope*

Elwyn, Alyn • British/Welsh • *white, fair, blessed, sacred and holy*

Englebert, Engelbrecht • Germanic • *bright angel*

Enlai • Chinese • *favours foreseen*

Erasmus, Erazmus, Eran • Greek/Latin • *to love*

Erastus, Rastus • Biblical/Greek • *beloved*

Erin, Éirinn • Irish • *romantic name poets give to Ireland*

Erwin, Irwin • Germanic • *a good, loyal and honoured friend*

Esmé, Aestimare, Aestimatus • Latin • *truly esteemed and highly valued*

Ethan • Biblical/Hebrew/Jewish • *longevity, strong and firm*

Eutrope, Eutropios, Eutropos, Eutropio • Greek • *what a nice polite boy and so clever and versatile*

Evan, Iefan, Ieuan, Ifan, John, Johannes • British/Welsh • *God is gracious or gift of God*

Euandros, Evander, Íomhar • Greek/Latin • *a fine good man*

Evaristo, Euarestos • Greek • *a personal name; someone who wants to please everyone*

Ewald, Ewawalt • Germanic • *a wise and just ruler; powerful leader, lawful ruler, judge*

Fabrizio, Fabrice, Fabricius, Fabricio • Italian/Etruscan • *Roman family name; one noted for his incorruptibility*

Fādil • Arabic • *generous, respected and conscientious*

Fang • Chinese • *upright, honest, fair*

Faraj • Arabic • *solves worries and grief*

Faysal, Feisal • *a man or judge who knows the difference between good and bad, right and wrong*

Fearchar • Irish Gaelic • *dear, nice man*

Feliciano, Felcius, Felix • Latin • *what a happy chappie!*

Feidhlimidh, Felim, Phelim, Fidelminus • Irish Gaelic • *always chaste and virtuous*

Ferdinand, Ferdinando, Hernán, Ferdi, Ferdie, Fernand • Spanish Visigothic • *a man at peace wherever he is; always ready and prepared to travel*

Fernando, Ferdinando, Hernando,

Fernán, Hernán • Spanish Visigothic • *a man at peace wherever he is; always ready and prepared to travel*

Farquhar, Fearchar • Scots Gaelic • *what a dear, loving man*

Fikri • Arabic • *intellectual and contemplative*

Fingal, Fionnghall, Fingall • Gaelic • *blond, fair stranger or traveller or Viking settler*

Finn, Fionn • Irish Gaelic • *white, fair*

Fínnen, Fínnan, Fionnán, Finnian, Finian • Irish • *white, fair*

Finlay, Findlay, Fionnlagh, Finley, Finnleik, Fionnlaogh • Scots Gaelic/Norse • *fair, blond warrior or hero or war hero*

Fionnbarr, Fionnbharr, Finbar • Irish • *his head is white, fair and blond*

Fiontan, Fintan • Irish • *fiery and fair*

Florenz, Florentius, Florenzo • Latin • *he flourishes and blossoms*

Florian, Florentius, Florenti, Florencio • Latin • *flowery and romantic*

Frédéric, Frederick, Frederik, Fritz, Fred, Phredd, Freddie, Fredick, Fredric, Friedrich, Frerik, Freek, Fredrik, Federico, Frederico, Fryderyk, Bedrich, Rieti, Frigyes • Germanic/Frankish • *peaceful but powerful ruler*

Friedemann • German • *man of peace*

Fuhua • *fortunes flourishing and growing*

Gallagher, Gallchobhar • Irish Gaelic • *foreign ally, helpful stranger*

Garnet, Grenate, Granatum •
Norman/Latin • *a dealer in
pomegranates or garnets (semi-
precious stone)*
Gaylord, Gaillard, Gay, Gaye •
Norman • *a dandy or popinjay*
**Geoffrey, Jeffrey, Jeff, Geoffroi,
Geoff, Godofredo, Sieffre** •
Germanic/Frankish/Lombardic
• *a stranger in your own land or
foreigner who pledges allegiance*
**Germaine, Jermaine, Germanus,
Germain** • French/Latin • *brother*
Germain, Germanus • Latin •
brother
Gerlach • Germanic • *playful and
sporting swordsman*
Gjord, Gyrd, Jul • Norse • *God of
Peace*
Gladwin • Anglo-Saxon • *an opti-
mistic, positive friend*
**Godfrey, Godefroy, Gofraidh,
Godfrid, Godfred** • Germanic/
Frankish • *God of Peace*
Godwin, Godwine, Win • Anglo-
Saxon • *God is my friend*
Goodwin, Godwine • Anglo-Saxon
• *not to be confused with Godwin; it
means a good friend*
Gottfried, Götz • Germanic • *God of
Peace, God bring me peace*
Gottlieb, Theophilus • Germanic •
love God
Gottlob • Germanic • *God*
**Gratien, Gratianus, Gratus,
Graciano, Gratianus** • Latin • *most
pleasing*
Grazian, Gratianus, Gratus • Latin •
a very nice man
Guangli • Chinese • *lighting up
virtue and propriety*
Gui • Chinese • *honourable, noble*
Guiren • Chinese • *grateful*

Gulzar • Persian • *rose garden*
Guoliang • Chinese • *where you are
there is kindness*
Gwyn, Gwynn, Wyn • British/Welsh
• *white, holy, sacred and blond*
Gwynfor • British/Welsh • *a large,
grand man who is sacred, holy,
blessed and fair*

Habacuc, Habakkuk • Biblical/
Jewish/Hebrew • *embrace, a kiss*
Habīb • Arabic • *beloved, adored*
Hamdi • Arabic • *praise be, grateful*
**Handel, Hans, Hans, Hansel,
Johannes** • Germanic • *God is
gracious or gift of God*
Hāni • Arabic • *happy, gay*
Hannibal, Haanbaal • Phoenician
• *I give the Lord grace and favour or
he gives it to me*
Harper • English/American • *a
person who plays a harp!*
Hassan, Hasan • Arabic • *a beautiful
and beneficent man*
Heddwyn • British/Welsh • *tranquil
and peaceful white, fair and sacred*
**Hercules, Herakles, Athairne,
Hercule, Ercwlff** • Latin • *the glory
of Hera or Juno, Queen of the Gods*
Hernán, Fernando, Hernando •
Spanish • *a man at peace wherever
he is; always ready and prepared to
travel*
Hillel • Jewish/Hebrew • *praise him!*
Hong • Chinese • *great and wild
swan*
**Honore, Honoratus, Honorius,
Ynyr** • Latin • *an honoured man*
**Hubert, Hugbert, Huppert,
Hupprecht, Hobart** • Germanic •
brilliant heart and famed mind
**Hugh, Huw, Hugues, Hugo, Aodh,
Hughie, Hewie, Huey, Hewie,**

Hughie, Huwie • Germanic/
Frankish • *heart, mind and spirit*
Hugo, Hugh • Germanic/Frankish/
Latin • *heart, mind and spirit*
**Humphrey, Humfrey, Humphry,
Humfry, Hunfrid, Humff, Wmffre** •
Germanic/Frankish • *someone when
aroused will fight like a bear cub but
until then is a peaceful soul*
Hussein, Husayn • Arabic • *exqui-
site, precious, beautiful*
Hyacinth, Hyakinthos • Greek/
English • *love and passion*
Hyman, Hymen, Hymie, Hayyim
• Greek/Latin/Yiddish • *God of
Marriage*

Ian, Iain, John • Scots Gaelic/
Biblical • *God is gracious or gift of
God*
**Ianto, Ifan, Ieuan, Iohannes, John,
Iefan, Ioan** • British/Welsh • *God is
gracious or gift of God*
Idris • British/Welsh • *a passionate
loving lord or lord of passion and
desire*
Ihāb • Arabic • *gift, promise*
Ihsān • Arabic • *charitable, giver*
Iorwerth, Iolo, Iolyn, Yorath •
British/Welsh • *a handsome, beau-
tiful lord or chief*
Irène, Irenaeus, Eirenaios, Irina •
Greek • *peaceable man*
Irwin, Erwyn, Irwyn, Everwyn •
a good, loyal and honoured friend
Ishmael, Ismā'īl • Arabic • *receiver
of the divine spirit; listen to God*
**Isidore, Izzy, Izzie, Isidoros, Isidor,
Isidro, Isidoro** • Greek/Egyptian •
*a gift from the goddess Isis, deity of
magic and life*
'Ismat • Arabic • *innocent and
without sin*

Ithel, Iudhael • British/Welsh • *a
generous but common man who
behaves like a goodly prince or lord;
philanthropist*
Ivan, John, Ewan • Russian • *God is
gracious or gift of God*

Jacinto, Hyakinthos, Hyacinthe •
Greek/Spanish • *love and passion*
**Jack, John, Jankin, Jan, Jehan,
James, Jacques, Jock, Jake, Jak,
Jac, Jackie, Jackson, Jacky, Jackin**
• English • *God is gracious or gift of
God*
Jamāl, Gamāl • Arabic • *beautiful,
lovely, with poise*
Jake, Jack • English • *God is
gracious or gift of God*
Jan, John, Johannes • Germanic/
Slavic • *God is gracious or gift of God*
Jawdat, Gawdat • Arabic • *kindness
personified and supreme*
Jean, Jehan, Gene • French • *God is
gracious or gift of God*
Jenkin, Jankin, Siencyn • British/
Welsh • *God is gracious or gift of
God*
Jens, Jons, Johann • Scandinavian •
God is gracious or gift of God
**Jeffrey, Geoffrey, Jeff, Geoff,
Jefferson, Jeffery, Jeffry, Jep** •
Anglo-Saxon • *a stranger in your
own land or foreigner who pledges
allegiance*
Jesse, Jess, Jessie, Jessi, Jessye •
Biblical/Hebrew/Jewish • *gift*
Jinān • Arabic • *beautiful gardens,
paradise*
Jinjing • Chinese • *golden mirror*
**Joachim, Jo, Johoiachin, Joaquin,
Jochim, Jochem, Jochen, Joakim,
Jokum** • Biblical • *created by God*
Jody, Jude • American/English •

uncertain root; possibly from Jude,
meaning praise

John, Iohannes, Johannes,
Ioannes, Johannan, Johanan, Eóin,
Seán, Ian, Iain, Seathan, Ieuan,
Siôn, Johann, Johannes, Jan, Jens,
Johan, Jons, Jon, Jan, Johan, Jean,
Juan, Joan, Joao, Giovanni, Gianni,
Ioannis, Iannis, Ivan, Juhani, Jussi,
Hannu, Janos, Janis, Johnnie,
Johnny, Jack, Hank, Jonathan,
Johnathan, Jonny, Jon, Johnson,
Juwan, Johnston, Johnstone,
Jones • Biblical/English/Latin • *God*
is gracious or gift of God

Jonathan, Jon, Jonn, Johnny,
Johnnie, Jonathen, Jonathon •
Biblical • *God has given*

Jonah, Jon, Jonas • Biblical/
Hebrew/Jewish • *dove*

Juan, John • Biblical/Greek/Spanish
• *God is gracious or gift of God*

Jūda, Gūda • Arabic • *goodness and*
kindness transcend all

Judah, Judas • Biblical/Hebrew/
Jewish • *praise*

Jude, Judas • Biblical/Greek • *praise*

Judge, Dayan • Norman/Latin/
Hebrew/Jewish • *a rabbinic judge or*
legal judge

Junjie • Chinese • *beautiful, brilliant*

Just, Juste, Justus • Latin • *just, fair*
and honest

Justin, Justyn, Justinus, Justus,
Iestyn • Latin • *a Roman name which*
is rooted in just, fair and honest

Kalyan • Sanskrit • *most beautiful*
and fortunate

Kamāl, Kāmil • Arabic/Sanskrit •
perfection, beyond compare, pink

Keanu • Hawaiian • *cool breeze from*
the mountains

Keelan, Keelahan, Ceileachain
• British/Welsh/ Irish Gaelic •
companion or friend; descendant of
Keelahan

Kelly, Ceallach, Ceallaigh •
Irish/English • *fair-haired or monk,*
church, monastery

Kenneth, Ken, Cinaed, Cainnech,
Coinneach, Kennith, Kenny,
Cenydd, Canice, Canicius,
Cainneach • Latin/ English/Gaelic •
handsome, gorgeous, pleasing to the
eye and rather adorable!

Kennard, Ceneweard, Cyneheard
• Anglo-Saxon • *he who is keen or*
even royal, and a fierce defender of
others

Kermit, Dhiarmuid, Dermot •
English • *not a bad bone in his body*

Kerry, Ceri • English/British/Welsh •
after the Celtic Goddess of Poetry

Kevin, Caioimhin, Keven, Kevan,
Kevyn, Caoimhean • English/
Irish Gaelic • *beloved, beautiful,*
enchanting

Khayrat • Arabic • *good deed, kind*
actions

Khayri • Arabic • *charitable,*
merciful, good

Kimberley, Kimberly, Kim, Kym
• Anglo-Saxon/American English
• *after the South African town of*
Kimberley where the British took on
the Boers; especially 14th October

Kiran • Sanskrit • *a ray of light*

Kilment, Clément, Clemens • Latin
• *merciful*

Konstantin, Constantinus • Latin •
constant, steadfast, loyal, devoted

Kumar • Sanskrit • *beautiful Prince*
Skanda

Lal • Sanskrit/Prakrit • *dear, sweet, darling one; king*

Lamin • African/Sierra Leonese • *honest, trustworthy*

Lark, Lawerce • Anglo-Saxon/Australian/North American • *the lark, the bird*

Lazarus, Laz, Lazare, Eleazar, Lazaros, Lazar • Biblical/Greek/Aramaic/Hebrew • *God is my helper*

Leannán, Lennan, Lennon • Irish Gaelic • *fairy lover, fairy darling*

Lennon, Leannain • Irish Gaelic • *fairy lover, fairy darling*

Levi, Levy • Hebrew/Jewish • *making a connection*

Liang • Chinese • *bright, luminous, radiant*

Ling • Chinese • *compassionate and understanding*

Linus, Linos • Greek • *the song of Linus, a Greek musician who taught Hercules*

Lonán, Lonain • Irish Gaelic • *blackbird*

Lucian, Lucianus, Lucius, Lucien, Luciano, Lucio, Lux • Latin • *light*

Macharia • Kenyan • *lasting friend*

Mackenzie, Maccoinnich, Coinneach, Makenzie, Makensie, Mckenzie, Mack • English/Scots Gaelic • *handsome, gorgeous, pleasing to the eye and rather adorable!*

Madhukar • Sanskrit • *the bee, sweet as honey*

Majdi, Magdi • Arabic • *conscientious and worthy of praise*

Mājid • Arabic • *brighter than a star*

Malcolm, Maelcoluim, Maelcoluim • Scots Gaelic • *follower of St Columba , the dove*

Ma'mūn • Arabic • *reliable and trusted*

Manār • Arabic • *light of goodness*

Manfred, Manffred, Mainfred, Manfried, Manfredo • Germanic • *man of peace*

Marcel, Marcellus, Marcus, Marcellin, Marcello, Marcelino, Marcelo • Latin • *named after Mars, God of Sex and War*

March, Marche, Mensis • Norman • *a person who lives on the borders, the Marches or born in the month of March, named after God of War and Sex, Mars*

Marcus, Markus, Mark • Latin • *named after Mars, God of Sex and War*

Mark, Marcus, Marc, Marco, Marcas, Markus, Marcos, Marek, Marko, Markku • Latin • *named after Mars, God of Sex and War*

Marlon, Marclon • Latin/Norman • *named after Mars, God of Sex and War*

Martin, Martyn, Martinus, Martis, Marty, Mairtin, Maratan, Martainn, Merten, Maarten, Martijn, Morten, Mårten, Martinho, Martino,Marcin, Martti, Marton, Morten, Marty, Marti • Latin/English • *named after Mars, God of Sex and War*

Mathias, Matthias, Matthaeus, Matthäus, Mattathia • Biblical/Greek/Jewish/Aramaic/Latin • *gift of God*

Matthew, Matt, Mathew, Mattathia, Maitiu, Matthias, Maitias, Mata, Matha, Matthäus, Matthijs, Mads, Mathies, Mats, Mathieu, Mateo, Mateu, Mateus, Matteo, Mattia, Matvei, Mateusz, Maciej, Matej, Matyas, Matija,

Matti, Matyas, Mate, Mattanah, Mattaniah, Mattathah, Mattatha, Mattathiah, Mattathias • Biblical/Hebrew/Jewish/English • *gift of God*
Menahem, Mendel, Menachem • Jewish/Yiddish/Germanic • *comforter*
Mendel, Mandel, Menahem, Mandy • Jewish/Yiddish/Germanic • *comforter*
Merl, Meriel, Merle, Merula • Norman/Latin • *a blackbird*
Michael, Micah, Micheal, Meical, Mihangel, Machiel, Mikael, Mikkel, Michel, Miguel, Miquel, Michele, Mikhail, Michal, Mihovil, Mihajlo, Mihael, Mikko, Mihaly, Mike, Mick, Micky, Mikey, Mickey, Meical • Biblical/Hebrew/Jewish/English • *who is like God?*
Midhat • Arabic • *tribute*
Mingli • Chinese • *lighting up propriety*
Mirza • Persian • *subserviant prince*
Misha, Micha, Mikhail • Russian • *he who is like God*
Mitchell, Michael, Michel, Mitch • Norman/English • *he who is like God*
Mohammed, Muhammed, Mohammad, Mohamed, Muhammad, Muhammed, Mo
Mohan • Sanskrit • *enchantment; one of the five arrows of love*
Muhammed • Arabic • *sacred qualities, scrupulous*
Muhsin • Arabic • *good to others, compassionate*
Mukhtār • Arabic • *preferred to all others*
Mungo, Munghu, Munga, Fychi, • British/Welsh • *carissimus amicus, meaning dearest friend; pet name of St Kentigern*

Munīr • Arabic • *shining, dazzling, glorious*

Nadīm • Arabic • *best friend, companion you share your social life with*
Nahman, Nahum, Naum • Jewish • *comforter*
Nājib, Nāgib • Arabic • *cultured, cultivated, in a class of his own*
Nanne, Nannulf, Anders • Scandinavian/Norse • *daring, audacious wolf*
Naoise • Irish Gaelic • *vague; in legend the lover of Deirdre was Naoise*
Narayan, Narain • Sanskrit • *destiny of man; son of creation*
Narottam • Sanskrit • *best of men*
Nāsir, Nazir • Arabic • *a good ally and friend; helping and supportive*
Nataraj • Sanskrit • *Lord of the Dance*
Nathan, Nat, Jonathan, Nathen • Biblical/Hebrew/Jewish • *God has given*
Nathaniel, Nat, Nathanael, Natanaele • Biblical/Greek/English • *God has given*
Naveed • Persian • *glad tidings, invite to the wedding or something just as jolly*
Neo • African • *gift*
Nestor, Nestore • Greek • *personal name of King of Pylos, in legend one of the Greeks (bearing gifts!) at Troy*
Niaz • Persian • *prayer, gift, sacrifice*
Noah, Nahum, Noë • Biblical/English • *to rest*
Noam • Jewish/Hebrew • *joy, pleasure and happiness*
Noble, Nobilis • American English/Norman Latin • *someone who has*

noble qualities even if not born
aristocratic
Nyabera • Kenyan • *the good one*

**Octavian, Octavianus, Octavius,
Octavus, Octavio** • Latin • *a Roman
family name meaning the number
eight*
Oded • Jewish/Hebrew • *he who
encourages or persuades, compelling*
Olijimi • Nigerian • *God gave me this*
Omar, 'Umar • Biblical/Hebrew/
Arabic • *talkative*
Orpheus, Orfeo • Greek • *beautiful
voice; in legend a Thracian musi-
cian who married Eurydice, stolen
by Pluto*
Oswin, Oswine, Oz • Anglo-Saxon •
God is my friend

Patrice, Pat, Patrick • Latin/French/
Irish Gaelic • *patrician*
**Patrick, Pádraig, Pat, Paddy, Patsy,
Páraic, Patrice, Patricio, Patrizio,
Porick, Podge, Pàra, Pàdair,
Pàidean, Padrig, Paddy, Patrick,
Pat, Patrice** • Latin/Irish Gaelic •
patrician
Persis • Biblical/Greek • *a Persian
woman*
**Philbert, Filaberht, Philibert,
Filbert** • Greek/Germanic/Frankish
• *dear, beloved*
Philo, Philon • Greek • *love*
Pramod • Sanskrit • *joy, happiness,
pleasure*
Prem • Sanskrit • *love and affection*
Prokhoros, Prokhor • Greek • *very
artistic, chief of a troupe of singers,
dancers, actors*

Qingshan • Chinese • *celebrating
goodness*
Qiu • Chinese • *autumn or fall*

Radwan • Arabic • *pleasure and
enjoyment*
Ra'fat • Arabic • *mercy, compassion,
forgiveness*
Rafiq • Arabic • *friend, companion
who is gentle and kind*
Rainier, Rayner • Germanic/
Frankish • *adviser to the army; army
commander*
Rajab, Ragab • Arabic • *seventh
month of the Muslim calendar*
Rajiv • Sanskrit • *striped and/or the
blue lotus*
**Ram, Rama, Ramu, Ramakrishna,
Ramgopal, Ramnarayan** • Sanskrit
• *nice, lovely, kind*
Ramadān • Arabic • *ninth month of
the Muslim calendar: the hot month*
Ramiro • Spanish/Visigothic • *a
man famous for his advice and
counselling*
Ramón, Raimundo, Raymond
• Catalan/Germanic • *adviser,
protector*
Ranjit • Sanskrit • *charming,
coloured, rainbow*
Ranulf, Reginulf, Ran, Reginulf
• Norse • *adviser or counsellor to
wolves*
Rastus, Erastus • Biblical/Greek •
beloved
Ratilal • Prakrit • *Lord of Love and
Pleasure*
Ra'ūf • Arabic • *caring and
compassionate*
**Raymond, Ray, Raimund,
Raginmund, Raimondo, Raimundo**
• Germanic/Frankish • *adviser to the
army; army commander*

Rayner, Rainer, Raginheri, Raginhari, Reiner, Raniero, Ragnar, Regner, Rainerio • Germanic/ Frankish • *adviser to the army; army commander*

Reginald, Reg, Reggie, Reginaldus, Reynold, Reginwald • Germanic/Norman

Reineke, Reine • Germanic • *counsellor*

Reinhold, Reinwald, Reine • Germanic • *splendid, wonderful adviser*

Reinmar, Reine • Germanic • *famous adviser, speaker*

Reuel • Biblical/Jewish/Hebrew • *friend of God*

Reynold, Reginald, Reynaud, Raginwald, Reginald, Ray, Reynard, Ragin, Renard, Ray, Rinaldo, Reinaldo, Rheinallt • Germanic/Norman • *advice rule*

Rhett, Rhet, Raedt, Raet • Dutch • *advice, counsel*

Rhys, Reece, Rees • British/Welsh • *ardent, dead sexy*

Robert, Rob, Robbie, Rodberht, Reodbeorht, Bob, Rob, Bobby, Robin, Roibéard, Raibeart, Rupprecht, Robrecht, Rupert, Robbert, Roberto, Roopertti, Roberts, Rabbie, Rab, Rigoberto • Germanic • *famous and bright*

Robin, Robben, Robert • Germanic • *famous and bright*

Rocco, Rokko, Roc, Rokko, Rocky, Rok, Rocky, Roche, Roch, Roque • Germanic • *rest awhile*

Rodion, Herodion • Greek • *follower of Hera, wife of Zeus*

Ronald, Ron, Ronnie, Ronny, Roni, Ranald, Randal, Rognvald • Norse • *adviser to the gods or king*

Royce, Royston, Royse • English • *the town or place of the rose or roses*

Rupert, Ruprecht, Robert • Germanic/Dutch • *famous and bright*

Ruslan • literary invention/Russian • *meaning unknown; name was used by Aleksandr Pushkin in his poem 'Ruslan and Ludmila'*

Sachdev • Sanskrit • *truth of God, totally honest*

Safā • Arabic • *pure and sincere*

Samuel, Shemuel, Shaulmeel, Sam, Sammy, Sawyl • Biblical/ Hebrew/Jewish • *name of God, God has heard, listen to God*

Saul • Biblical/Hebrew/Latin • *asked for, prayed for, yearned for*

Seathan, Jean, Jehan • Scots Gaelic/French/Biblical/English/ Latin • *God is gracious or gift of God*

Septimus • Latin • *seventh or number seven*

Shādi • Arabic • *singer*

Shafīq • Arabic • *compassionate*

Shakīl • Arabic • *handsome*

Shākir • Arabic • *thankful and grateful*

Shalom • Jewish/Hebrew • *peace*

Shamīm • Arabic • *a very precious fragrant person*

Shankar, Sankar • Sanskrit • *confers welfare, to look after*

Sharma • Sanskrit • *protect, comfort, joy*

Shining • Chinese • *let the world be at peace*

Shukri • Arabic • *giving thanks*

Siegfried • Germanic • *victory peace*

Simeon • English/Biblical/Hebrew • *he has heard*

Simón, Siomon, Sim, Simidh,

Sieman, Simao, Simone, Semyon, Szymon, Simo, Sim, Simmie • Biblical/Hebrew/Jewish • *hearkening, hearing*

Sirideán • Irish Gaelic • *unsure roots, likely to be someone who seeks*

Sitaram • Sanskrit • *a union of bliss*

Solomon, Shlomo, Sol, Solly, Saloman • Biblical/Hebrew/Jewish • *peace*

Spencer • Anglo-Saxon • *similar to a quarter master, someone who dispenses provisions or goods*

Sridhar • Sanskrit • *bearing, possessing the Goddess of Light, Beauty and Wealth, Sri*

Srikant • Sanskrit • *beloved of Sri, Goddess of Light, Beauty and Wealth*

Stacey, Eustace • English/Greek • *confused roots; could mean juicy, tasty grapes!*

Stanilas, Stanislaus, Stanislaw, Aneislis, Stanislav • Slavic • *glory to the court, glorious courtier or politician*

Stefan, Stephan, Stephanos, Steven, Steve, Steff, Stevie, Stiofán, Stiana, Steaphan, Steffan, Steffen, Stefan, Staffan, Étienne, Stéphane, Estéban, Esteve, Estevao, Stefano, Stepan, Szczepan, Stjepan, Stevan, Istvan, Steponas • Greek • *a crown or garland*

Sterling, Sterrling • Anglo-Saxon • *little star*

Subhash • Sanskrit • *eloquent and articulate*

Suleimān, Sulaymān • Biblical/Arabic • *peace*

Sumantra • Sanskrit • *a person who is well versed in the classics*

Sundar, Sunder • Sanskrit • *beautiful*

Sushil • Sanskrit • *a hail and hearty chap*

Sverre, Sverri, Sverra • Norse/Norwegian • *spinning, swirling about, dancing under the influence*

Tāhir • Arabic • *oh so pure, chaste and virtuous*

Talāl • Arabic • *morning dew or fine rain*

Tāmir • Arabic • *rich in dates and figs and all good things*

Tancredo • Germanic • *thoughtful counsel*

Tāriq • Arabic • *morning or evening star; night visitor*

Tarun, Taroon • Sanskrit • *dawn, the early sun, young, tender growth of love and romance*

Tegan, Teg • British/Welsh • *a rather lovely or beautiful person*

Tengfei • Chinese • *soaring high*

Teodosio • Greek • *God-given*

Thaddeus, Labbaeus, Theodoras, Theodotos, Thad, Tad • Biblical/Aramaic/Greek • *given by God or God's gift*

Théodore, Theo, Ted, Teddy, Theodor, Theodoor, Teodor, Teodoro, Feodor, Fyodr, Teuvo, Tivador, Todor, Teodors, Theodoric, Tiobad, Ted, Teddy, Edward, Theodos, Theodosios, Teodosio, Todos, Theodoros • Greek • *God-given or giving to God or God's gift*

Theophilus, Theosphilos, Theo, Théophile, Teofilo • Biblical/Greek • *God's friend or friend of God*

Timothy, Tim, Tadhg, Timmy, Timotheus, Timotheos, Timetheo, Timmy, Tiger, Timothee, Timo, Timoteo Timofei • Biblical/Latin/Greek • *honour God*

Tingguang • Chinese • *bright garden or courtyard*

Tingzhe • Chinese • *judgement or wisdom is required*

Tirso, Thyrsos • Oriental • *follower of Dionysus (Bacchus)*

Tobias, Tobiah, Tobijah, Toby • Biblical/Hebrew/Greek • *God is good*

Tochukwa • Nigerian • *praise God*

Toribio, Turibius • Latin/Spanish • *unknown roots, very local Iberian name; especially 12th October*

Trofim, Trophimos • Greek • *fruitful, goodness, sustaining*

Truman, Treowemann, Trueman • Anglo-Saxon/American/English • *a trusted man*

Tryggve, Tryggr, Trygve • Norse • *trusty and true*

Tyson, Ty, Tison • Greek/Norman • *likely to stem from a girl's name for Dionysius, God of Wine*

Ughtred, Uhtraed • Anglo-Saxon • *dawn counsel; a person who is good and wise in the mornings*

Ugo, Hugo, Hugh • Germanic • *heart, mind and spirit*

Uilleac, Hugleik, Uilliam, Liam, Uilleag, Ulick • Norse • *a complete whole well-balanced man*

Umashankar • Sanskrit • *union of two people*

Uri, Yuri • Jewish/Hebrew • *light*

Uriah, Urias, Uriel • Biblical/Jewish/Hebrew • *God is light*

Uwamahoro • Rwandan • *peacemaker*

Vimal • Sanskrit • *peerless, perfection and pure*

Vinay • Sanskrit • *education, intelligence, learning*

Vinod • Sanskrit • *recreation, leisure, pleasure and sport*

Wasīm, Wazim • Arabic • *what a stunner! Beautiful to look at, delightful to know*

Wencheng • Chinese • *refined, elegant and accomplished*

Wenyan • Chinese • *refined, chic, chaste and gifted*

Wilfrid, Wilfrit, Walfrid, Wilfrey, Wilf, Wilfried, Vilfred • Germanic • *the will for peace*

Winfred, Wyn, Win, Wynnfrith, Winfried • Germanic • *a kind, peace-loving friend*

Wynfor, Wyn • British/Welsh • *white, blonde, holy, blessed*

Xiang • Chinese • *circling in the air*

Xianliang • Chinese • *worthy of brightness*

Xiu • Chinese • *graceful, cultivated*

Xolani • Xhosa South Africa • *please forgive*

Yahya, John • Arabic/Biblical • *God is gracious or gift of God*

Yakim, Akim • *created by God*

Yashpal • Sanskrit • *cherishes splendour*

Ye • Chinese • *bright*

Yefim, Euphemios • Russian/Greek • *eloquent, articulate speaker*

Yingpei • Chinese • *to be admired*

Yongliang • Chinese • *forever light and bright*

Yongzheng • Chinese • *eternally; forever scrupulous and conscientious*

Yorath, Iorwerth • British/Welsh • *a handsome, beautiful lord or chief*

You • Chinese • *friend*

Yuan, Juan, John • Manx Gaelic • *God is gracious or gift of God*
Yūnis, Younis, Jonah • Arabic/ Biblical • *dove*

Zadok • Biblical/Jewish/Hebrew • *just or righteous*
Zāhir • Arabic • *radiant, bright, luminous*
Zeb, Zebedee, Zebulun • Biblical/ Hebrew/Greek • *gift of Jehovah*
Zebadiah, Zabdi, Zabadiah, Zebedee • Biblical/Hebrew/Jewish • *living with, to dwell, Yahweh has given*

Zed, Zedekiah • Biblical/Jewish/ Hebrew • *justice of Yahweh*
Zeke, Ezekiel • Biblical/Jewish/ Hebrew • *God gives me strength*
Zelig, Selig • Jewish/Yiddish • *happy and counting my blessings*
Zhengzhong • Chinese • *loyal and trustworthy*
Zhong • Chinese • *steadfast and devoted*
Zian • Chinese • *peaceful soul*
Zuhayr • Arabic • *little flowers*

Girls

Abīr • Arabic • *fragrant*

Abishag, Avishag • Biblical/Jewish/Hebrew • *wise and educated*

Abla • Arabic • *voluptuous*

Ada, Adah • Biblical/Jewish/Hebrew • *adornment to make one beautiful*

Adélaide • Germanic • *noble, kind and caring*

Aegle, Aglaia • Greek • *splendid radiance*

Aeronwen • British/Welsh • *white, sacred and fair*

Afāf • Arabic • *chasity, refinement, elegance*

Agapia, Agafya • Greek • *love*

Agatha, Agathe, Aggie, Agata, Ågot, Águeda, Agathos • Greek • *good and honourable*

Ai • Chinese • *loving*

Ailbhe • Irish Gaelic • *white*

Aileen, Eileen, Ailie • Irish Gaelic • *desired by others*

Aimee, Aimi • French • *beloved one*

Áine • Irish • *as bright, as radiant as the Queen of the Faeries*

Aingeal • Irish • *angel*

Alba • Latin/Germanic • *white or elfin*

Alberta, Albertina • French/Germanic/Anglo-Saxon • *bright and noble*

Albina, Bina, Albus, Albius • Latin • *Roman family name meaning white*

Alethea, Althea, Aletheia • Greek • *truth*

Alice, Alicia, Alesha, Alisia, Alys, Alisha, Alissa, Alesha, Alisa, Alissa, Ailish, Alis, Alys • Norman • *noble, kind and caring*

Alina, Allina • Arabic • *noble and lovely*

Alison, Allie, Ally, Aly, Alysoun, Aliyah, Aaliyah, Allison, Allyson • Norman • *noble, kind and caring*

Alix • Greek • *he who defends*

Aliza, Freyde • Jewish/Hebrew • *joyful and gay*

Allegra • Italian • *happy, jolly, frisky*

Aloha • Polynesian/Hawaiian • *love*

Althena • modern • *a combo of Althea and Athene*

Alva, Alvah, Ailbhe, Alvina • Scots Gaelic • *white*

Amabel, Annabel, Mabel, Amabilis • Latin/Norman • *loveable*

Amaryllis, Amaryssein • Greek • *to sparkle*

Amice, Amity, Amita, Amicitia • Latin • *friendship*

Amy, Amie, Aimie, Aimee • Norman • *beloved*

Anais, Ana, Anya • Biblical/Catalan/Provençal • *God has favoured me*

Angel, Ángela, Angelina, Angeline, Angie, Ange, Angelos • Greek • *messenger of God*

Angela, Angelita • Latin • *Greek/Latin • messenger of God*

Angharad • British/Welsh • *love*

Anita, Ana • Spanish/ Biblical • *God has favoured me*

Anitra • literary invention • *created by Henrik Ibsen as the name of an Arabic princess in* Peer Gynt

Ann, Anne, Anna, Annabel, Annette, Annetta, Anouk, Anni, Annelie, Anneli, Annella, Annabell, Annabella, Annabelle, Belle, Annie, Anna, Anneke, Anke, Anoushka, Anouska, Arabella, Arabel Anna, Ana • Biblical/Jewish/Hebrew • *God has favoured me*

Annalisa, Annaliesa, Annalise, Annelise, Annelies, Anneli •

German • *combo of Anne and Elisabeth; God has favoured me plus God is my oath*

Anneka, Anika, Annika, Anna, Anniken • German/Dutch • *God has favoured me*

Annemarie, Annmarie, Annamarie, Annamaria • modern • *combo of Anne and Maria; God has favoured me*

Anthea, Antheia • Greek • *flowery*

Anthousa, Anfisa • Greek • *flower*

Anwen, Annwen • British/Welsh • *blessed and beautiful*

Anwyl, Annwyl • British/Welsh • *beloved, darling, dear*

Aoibheann, Aiobhinn • Irish • *beautiful*

Aoife, Aiobh, Esuvia • Gaelic/ Gaulish • *beauty*

Aphra, Afra • Latin • *a woman from Africa, the dark continent*

Asenath • Biblical/Egyptian • *she is Daddy's little princess*

Asha • Sanskrit • *hope*

Aster • Ethiopian • *star*

Astra, Estelle, Aster, Stella , Astrum • Greek/Latin • *star*

Astrid, Åsta, Sassa • Norse • *love*

Attracta, Athracht • Latin • *she is like a magnet, she draws people to her*

Auxilio • Spanish/Roman Catholic • *Mary the helper*

Avdotya, Eudokia, Eudokein • Greek • *she seems a nice, good girl*

'Awātif • Arabic • *affectionate and tender*

Azucena, Susannah • Arabic/ Spanish • *madonna lily*

Bahīja, Bahīga • Arabic • *joyful, beautiful woman*

Bahiyya • Arabic • *a beautiful, radiant, dazzling woman*

Bano • Persian • *lady, princess, bride*

Barbara, Babette, Babs, Barbra, Barb, Barbie, Baibín, Báirbre, Varvara, Varya, Barbro • Greek • *a foreign woman*

Basma • Arabic • *this woman melts your heart with her smile*

Bathsheba, Sheba, Bathsheeva • Biblical/Jewish/Hebrew • *daughter of the oath*

Beau • French • *beautiful and bonny girl*

Béibhin, Béibhinn, Bébhionn, Bébinn • Irish Gaelic • *white lady, fair lady*

Beile, Beyle, Beylke • Jewish/ Yiddish/Slavic • *white, pale, beautiful*

Bella, Isabella • Italian • *beautiful*

Belinda, Bella, Belle • literary • *from bella meaning beautiful*

Bess, Bessie, Bet, Beth, Elizabeth, Elisabeth, Bethan, Betsy, Betty, Bette, Bettina, Buffy, Beitidh, Elisheba • Hebrew/Greek • *God is my oath or God is my abundance*

Bethany, Beth • Biblical/Jewish/ Hebrew • *village outside Jerusalem where Jesus stayed in Holy Week before travelling to Jerusalem for Palm Sunday; it means house of figs or dates*

Beulah • Biblical/Hebrew • *married*

Bevin, Béibhinn • Irish Gaelic • *fair lady*

Berwen • British Welsh • *fair or white-headed*

Bethan, Beth • British/Welsh • *God is my oath or God is my abundance*

Bianca, Blanca • Italian/Spanish • *white*

Bibi • Persian • *lady of the house*
Bionda • Italian • *blondie!*
Bláithín, Bláthnat, Blanid, Bianaid •
Irish Gaelic • *flower*
Blanche, Bianca, Blanca • pure
white, blonde
Blodyn, Blodeyn, Blod • British/
Welsh • *flower*
Blodwedd, Blodeuwedd, Blod •
British/Welsh • *flower face*
Blossom, Blostm • Anglo-Saxon •
blossom flowers
Blythe, Blithe • Anglo-Saxon • *a
sanguine spirit*
Bobbie, Roberta • Germanic •
famous and bright
Bona, Bonus • Latin • *good*
**Bonita, Bonnie, Bonny, Bonitus,
Bonito** • Latin/Spanish • *pretty and
good*
Bushra • Arabic • *happy news, glad
tidings and fine omen*

**Calaminag, Calumina, Columbine,
Columba** • Scots Gaelic • *dove*
Calista, Kallista • Greek • *the fairest
and most beautiful in the land*
**Candice, Candace, Canditia,
Candy, Candi** • Latin/Ethiopian •
pure and sincere; whiter than white
Caoimhe, Keeva • Irish Gaelic • *full
of grace, very lovely and so tender*
Cara, Kara • Italian/Irish Gaelic •
beloved friend
Careen • literary invention • *one of
Scarlett O'Hara's sisters in* Gone with
the Wind
Caris, Charis, Karis, Carissa • Greek
• *grace*
**Carla, Carlene, Charlene,
Charlotte, Carlotta** • Italian/English
• *a freeman*
Carmen • Spanish • *song*

Caron • British Welsh • *to love*
Carys, Gladys, Gwladys, Cerys •
British/Welsh • *loving*
Cassia, Kezia • Latin • *thy name is
vanity!*
Ceinwen • British/Welsh • *lovely,
beautiful, sacred and white*
Celandine, Dina • English/Greek •
a swallow and a flower
Ceri, Kerry • British/Welsh •
romantic, holy and beautiful
Ceridwen, Ceridwynn, Ceri •
British/Welsh • *Goddess of Poetry*
Chanel, Chanelle, Shanelle •
French/Modern • *in honour of
Gabrielle CoCo Chanel, founder
of the iconic perfume house*
Changchang • Chinese • *my
flourishing*
Changying • Chinese • *flourishing
and lustrous*
**Charis, Karis, Caris, Clarissa,
Charisse** • Greek • *grace*
Charmaine, Charmian, Kharmion
• *created name, combo of charm and
lorraine*
**Cher, Cheryl, Cheree, Sheree,
Cherilyn, Sherilyn, Cherene,
Cherelle, Cherida, Phillida,
Querida** • modern invention •
combo of Cherry and Beryl
**Cherie, Cheri, Cherie, Cheree,
Sheree, Querida** • French • *darling*
Cherry, Cherie, Cherrie • French •
darling fruit!
**Cheryl, Cherry, Beryl, Cheryll,
Cherryl, Cherril, Cherrill, Sheryl**
• modern invention • *combo of
Cherry and Beryl*
Chevonne, Siobhán, Shivaun •
English/American/Irish Gaelic •
God is gracious or gift of God
Chiara, Clare, Claire, Clara, Ciara,

Kiarah, Kiara, Kiera, Clair, Clarette, Clarinda, Clarrie, Clarus • Latin/ Italian • *bright, famous, crystal-clear*

Chorine, Choreen, Corinne, Corinna • French • *chorus or dancing girl*

Chunhua • Chinese • *spring flower*

Chuntao • Chinese • *spring peach*

Clare, Claire, Clara, Chiara, Klara, Kiara, Clara, Kiarah • Latin/English • *bright, famous, crystal-clear*

Clarice, Claritia • Latin/French/ English • *bright, famous, crystal-clear*

Clarissa, Clarisa, Clarice, Clarrisse, Clarisse, Claris, Clarissa, Cáitir • Latin • *bright, famous, crystal-clear*

Clémentine, Clem, Clemmie • Latin/French • *merciful, gentle, compassionate*

Clemency, Clemencie, Clementis • Latin • *leniency and mercy*

Clíodhna, Clíona • Irish Gaelic • *vague origin; one of the three daughters of the poet Libra*

Cody, Codi, Codie, Codee, Codey, Cuidightheach • Irish Gaelic/ American English • *descendant of Cuidightheach, a helpful and caring person*

Colleen, Coleen, Coline, Colina, Collinna, Colinette, Colinetta, Coletta, Cailin • Irish Gaelic/ American English/Australian • *ordinary girl or maiden*

Columbina, Columbine, Bina, Binnie, Colimbina, Colombe • Latin • *dove*

Comfort • modern • *to soothe, pamper and look after*

Condoleezza • Italian • *con dolcezza, a musical term meaning 'play sweetly or with sweetness'*

Consilia, Conseja • Roman Catholic • *Mary of Good Counsel and Advice*

Constance, Connie, Konnie, Constantia, Konstanze, Contanze • Latin • *constancy; steadfast and faithful*

Cora, Kore, Coretta, Corinne, Corinna, Korina, Coreen, Corrinne • Latin/Greek • *maiden*

Coral, Corallia, Coralie, Corallium • Latin/Jewish • *beautiful pink underwater mineral found in reefs in warm waters*

Cordelia, Cordellia, Cordula, Cordis • literary invention • *possibly from Latin for heart; by William Shakespeare for the virtuous daughter in* King Lear

Corinne, Corinna, Korinna • French/Greek • *maiden*

Dagmar • Slavic/Danish • *a combo of peace, day, dear, maiden*

Daffodil, Deaffodil, Asphodel, Daffy, Daphne • Dutch • *a flower*

Dahlia, Dale, Dalia, Dalya, Dahl, Dale • Swedish • *named after botanist Anders Dahl from Sweden*

Daisy, Daegesage, Margaret, Marguerite • Anglo-Saxon • *day's eye because it closes its petals at night*

Damask • Arabic • *the city of Damascus, Syria and the damask rose*

Danika, Danica • Slavic • *morning star*

Daria • Greek/Persian • *he who possesses, looks after the good and wellness of all*

Darlene, Darleen • American English/Australian • *darling*

Dassa, Dassah, Hadassah, Esther • Hebrew/Persian/Jewish • *Myrtle,*

Star and Persian Goddess of Fertility, Love and War, Ishtar

Davina, Davida, Davena, Davinia • Biblical/Hebrew • *vague origins but possibly from a baby word meaning darling one*

Deirbhile, Dervilla, Derfile, Deirbhail • Irish • *daughter of Fal or the poet*

Deirdre, Deidre • Irish Gaelic • *woman*

Delphine, Delfina, Delphina • Latin • *a woman from Delphi, the place of the oracle of the Gods*

Delice, Delyse, Delicia, Delysia, Delicae, Delicius, Delite, Delicia • Latin • *angel delight!*

Delwyn • British/Welsh • *pretty, love, pure, sacred*

Delyth, Gwenyth • British/Welsh • *pretty, love, neat*

Denise, Denese, Denice, Deneze, Deniece, Dionysia • Greek • *Dionysus, God of Wine, Orgies and Partying*

Deryn • British/Welsh • *blackbird*

Dietlind • Germanic • *tender, soft and kind; people love her*

Dilwen • British/Welsh • *white, fair, true, genuine and sacred*

Disgleirio • British/Welsh • *bright, glittering, dazzling*

Diorbhail, DEvorgilla • Scots Gaelic • *true testimony*

Diva, Divine • Italian • *goddess!*

Diyā • Arabic • *bright and breezy*

Dobre, Dobe, Dobro • Jewish/Yiddish • *good and kind person*

Dolores, Deloris, Delores, Doloris, Lola, Lolita, Dolly • Roman Catholic

Dolly, Dorothy, Dolores, Dora • English/Greek • *gift from God*

Donatella, Donatus • Latin • *given*

by God

Donna • Italian • *lady*

Dora, Isedore, Isadora, Theodora, Doria, Dorinda, Dory • Greek • *gift*

Doreen, Dorean, Dorene, Dorine • Greek/Irish • *gift*

Dorian, Dorienne, Dorean • literary name • *dor is Greek for gift; Oscar Wilde's invention for* The Portrait of Dorian Gray; *most likely from the Dorian women of southern mainland Greece*

Doris, Dorris • Greek • *a tribe of Greece, the Dorian women from Doros, southern mainland Greece, from the name son of or gift to the Hellenes*

Dorothea, Dorothy, Dorothee, Dorothie, Dot, Dottie, Dotty, Dodie, Dolly, Dorofei, Dorotheos, Dorete, Dee • Greek • *gift from God*

Dulcie, Dowse, Dulcia, Dulcis • Latin • *sweet*

Dwynwyn • British/Welsh • *Goddess of Love and Relationships*

Echo, Ekho • Greek • *a word that has come to mean a nymph who pined after the beautiful boy Narcissus, who was only interested in himself; as a result she was left with nothing but her voice*

Edna, Eden, Ednah, Eithne • Jewish/Hebrew • *pleasure and delight*

Eglantine, Aiglent • English • *sweetbriar*

Éibhleann, Eibhliu, Evlin • Irish Gaelic • *beautiful, radiant*

Eiddwen, Eiddunwen • British/Welsh • *fond, passionate, desire, holy, white, fair*

Eilwen, Aelwen • British/Welsh •

white, sacred, fair brow
Eirian • British/Welsh • *silvery bright, beautiful*
Elreen, Eirene, Irène • Greek • *peace*
Elfriede, Adalfrid, Elfreda • Germanic • *peace is noble*
Elizabeth, Elisabeth, Elisheba, Elise, Eliza, Elisa, Elsa, Liza, Lisa, Liz, Beth, Bet, Bess, Lisbet, Lisbeth, Lysbeth, Elsie, Bessie, Bessy, Betty, Betsy, Tetty, Libby, Lizzie, Lizzy, Buffy, Eilis, Ealasaid, Elisabet, Elisabete, Elisabetta, Elisavet, Yelizaveta, Elzbieta, Alzbeta, Elizabeta, Erzsebet, Elspeth, Eliza • Biblical/Hebrew/Jewish • *God is my oath*
Elita, Elire • American English • *elite person, upper class, VIP*
Elle • American English/French • *French for 'she'*
Elma • American English • *combo of Elizabeth and Mary*
Eloi, Eligere, Eligius • Latin • *to choose*
Elspeth, Elsbeth, Elspie, Elsie, Elspet, Elizabeth • Scots English/Biblical • *God is my oath*
Eluned, Eiluned, Luned, Lunet, Lunete, Eilun • British/Welsh • *icon, image*
Elvina, Alvina • Anglo-Saxon • *elfin, noble or faerie friend*
Élise, Elyse, Elysia, Alicia, Elisabeth • Biblical/French • *God is my oath*
Émer, Eimear, Eimer, Eimhir • Irish • *vague origins, perhaps chastity and purity, beauty and wisdom*
Engracia, Enkrates, Encratis, Encratia, Gratia • Latin • *grace*
Ermintrude, Trude, Trudy • Germanic/Frankish • *you are my entire world, my beloved*

Esmé, Esmee, Esmie, Aestimare, Aestimatus, Edme • Latin • *priceless, highly prized and valued*
Esperanza, Sperantia • Latin • *hope*
Esther, Esta, Hester, Haddasah, Eistir, Ester • Hebrew/Persian/Jewish • *Myrtle, Star and Persian Goddess of Fertility, Love and War, Ishtar*
Estelle, Stella • Latin/Norman • *star*
Etta, Rosetta, Henrietta • Italian • *female*
Eudocia, Eudoxia, Eudokia • Biblical/Greek/Latin • *of fine appearance and comfortable, easy to be with*
Eudora, Dora, Doron • Greek • *a good gift*
Eulalia, Eulalie, Lalien, Eulalee, Eula, Olalla • Greek • *good to talk*
Euphemia, Eppie, Hephzibah, Eufemia, Euphémie, Euphemia, Effie, Eppie, Euphemia, Effemy, Hephzibah • Greek/Latin • *good to talk*
Evadne • Greek • *well, good, fine but the final suffix is confused in origin*
Evelyn, Eveline, Avaline, Ava, Evelyne, Eveleen, Éibhleann, Aibhilin • English/Norman • *from a French girl's name that became an English surname*

Fadīla • Arabic • *a moral, ethical, virtuous woman*
Fang • Chinese • *fragrant*
Faith • English • *she who trusts in God, faithful follower*
Fania, Stefania • Italian/Greek • *a crown or garland*
Fātima • Arabic/Muslim/Roman Catholic • *abstainer from all bad or wicked things; mother*

Fayza • Arabic • *champion, a winning woman*

Fiedhelm, Fedelma, Fidelma • Irish Gaelic • *unknown origins but given to a beautiful Irish Bouddicca*

Fenella, Fionnuala, Finella, Finola • Scots Gaelic • *white, fair, shoulders*

Fenfang • Chinese • *perfumed, aromatic*

Fikriyya • Arabic • *pensive, contemplative, intelligent, intellectual*

Filomena, Philomena, Philomenes, Phileinmenos, Philomenus • Greek • *love, strength*

Fiona, Fionn, Ffion • Scots Gaelic/British Welsh • *white, fair*

Fiorella, Fiore • Italian • *flower*

Finola, Fionnuala, Fionola, Nuala, Finuala, Fionnguala, Fenella, Finella, Finola • Scots Gaelic • *white, fair, shoulders*

Flair, Flairer • American English/French • *showing an individual talent*

Fleur • Norman • *flower*

Flora, Floris, Flo, Florence, Floella, Florrie, Ffloraidh • Latin • *old Roman family name meaning flower*

Florence, Florentius, Florentia, Flo, Florance, Floss, Florrie, Flossie • *like a flower, blooming and blossoming*

Florentina, Florentinus, Florenz, Florens • Latin • *she flourishes and blossoms*

Florida, Floridus • Spanish • *flowery*

Flower, Fleur, Fiorella • Norman • *flower*

Frauke • German • *a lady from northern Germany*

Freda, Frederica, Freddie, Frieda, Elfreda, Winifred, Frederika, Friede, Friederike • *peace*

Friedelinde • Germanic • *soft, tender, gentle and peaceful*

Freya, Froja, Frouwa, Friday, Frøya, Freia, Freyja • Norse • *lady referring to the Goddess of Love, Freya*

Friday • Norse/English • *Freya's day, the Goddess of Love and Beauty*

Frume, Fromm • Jewish/Yiddish • *pious, devout and virtuous*

Gae, Gay, Gaye • English • *bright, jolly, cherry, sanguine*

Gaenor, Gaynor, Geinor, Cainwryr • British/Welsh • *beautiful maiden*

Garnet, Grenate, Granatum • Norman/Latin • *either a dealer in pomegranates or the precious stone*

Gemma, Jemma • Italian • *precious jewel*

Genette, Jeanette • Biblical/English/Latin • *God is gracious or gift of God*

Geneva, Geneve, Ginevra • French • *after the Swiss city or can be variant of Jennifer or short form of Geneviève*

Genevieve, Jennifer, Genoveffa, Ginevra • Celtic • *a female chief or leader of the tribe of people*

Gertrude, Gert, Gertie, Gerde, Gertrud, Gerda, Gertraud, Gertraut, Gertrudis • Germanic • *she is a dear woman with strength, superlative with a spear*

Ghāda • Arabic • *young, graceful, refined woman*

Ghislain, Ghislaine, Giselle, Gisil • Germanic/Frankish • *to pledge or promise something or someone to confirm an alliance*

Ghufrān • Arabic • *forgiveness*

Gigi • French • *pet name for Giselle; to pledge or promise something or* *someone to confirm an alliance*

Ginny, Virginia, Jane, Jaine, Jane, Ginnie, Jinny • Biblical/English/ Latin • *pet name for Virginia or Jane; God is gracious or gift of God*

Giovanna • Latin • *LADY John!*

Giselle, Gisil, Gisella, Gisela, Gigi • Germanic/Frankish • *pledge to pledge or promise something or someone to confirm an alliance*

Gita • Sanskrit • *everyone sings her praises*

Gitte, Gittel, Birgitte • Jewish/ Yiddish • *good girl*

Glenda, Gwenda • British/Welsh • *good, clean, pure and holy*

Gloria, Gloriana, Glory • Latin • *glorious!*

Godiva • Anglo-Saxon/Latin • *God's gift*

Godelieve, Godliva, Godleva, Godliob • Germanic • *good or dear one*

Goldie, Blondie, Guinevere • American English • *a girl with blond hair*

Gormlaith, Gormflaith • Irish Gaelic • *a splendid, illustrious woman or princess*

Grace, Gracie, Gratia, Grazia, Graziella, Gracia , Graciela • Latin • *grace*

Gro, Groa, Gruach • Norse/Celtic • *evolving/old woman*

Guinevere, Gwenhwyfar, Goldie • English/British/Welsh • *blondie!*

Guinevere, Gaynor, Gayner, Gayna, Gaenor • British/Welsh • *beautiful maiden*

Gwenda • British/Welsh • *a good, holy, pure woman*

Gwenfrewi • British/Welsh • *time for reconciliation*

Gwerful, Gwairmul • British/Welsh • *shy, modest, compromising*

Gwyneth, Gwynedd, Gwynneth, Gwenith, Gwynaeth • British/ Welsh • *happiness or named after the British Welsh princedom of Gwynedd, based on Snowdonia area where the ancient Brits (Welsh) fought the Anglo-Saxons in guerrilla warfare*

Habība • Arabic • *beloved one*

Habibunah • Swahili • *our beloved*

Hadassah, Dassah, Esther • Hebrew/Persian/Jewish • *Myrtle, Star and Persian Goddess of Fertility, Love and War, Ishtar*

Hadīl • Arabic • *a woman with a voice like the cooing of doves, soft, lovely voice*

Hannah, Hanna, Hanā • Arabic • *blissful, happy woman filled with wellbeing*

Hannah, Hanne, Johanna, Hanna • Biblical/Jewish/Hebrew • *God has favoured me*

Hannelore • Germanic • *combo of Hannah and Eleanor*

Hanān • Arabic • *as tender as a woman's heart*

Hansine • Germanic • *God is gracious or gift of God*

Harmony, Harmonie • English • *concord, unity, friendship*

Harper • English/American • *a person who plays a harp!*

Helme, Friedhelm, Helma • Germanic • *well-protected man who comes in peace*

Herlinda • Germanic • *a compassionate army*

Hermine • Germanic • *a female soldier*

Hester, Esther, Hettie, Hetty •
English • *Myrtle, Star and Persian Goddess of Fertility, Love and War, Ishtar*

Heulog • British/Welsh • *sunny*

Hiba • Arabic • *a gift or prize from God*

Hjördis, Hjorrdis • Norse • *warrior goddess great with the sword!*

Honesty, Honesta, Honestas, Honor, Honour • Norman/Latin • *truthful, fair and frank*

Honey, Honeg, Honig • Anglo-Saxon • *sweet nectar, someone who is sweet*

Honeysuckle • English • *a climbing vine with fragrant flowers*

Honor, Honour, Honora, Honorah, Honoria, Honoré, Honorine, Honorina, Norine, Noreen •
Norman/Latin • *an honoured woman*

Hortense, Hortensia, Hortensius, Hortus • French/Latin • *old Roman family name meaning garden*

Huguette, Huette • Germanic/Frankish/French • *heart, mind and spirit*

Huian • Chinese • *kind, peace*

Huifang • Chinese • *kind and fragrant*

Huifen • Chinese • *wise and fragrant*

Huiliang • Chinese • *kind and good*

Huiling • Chinese • *wise, jade wind chime*

Huiqing • Chinese • *kind and affectionate*

Huda • Arabic • *a woman who is wise and judicious counsellor or adviser; agony aunt*

Hulda, Huldah • *sweet, lovable, adorable*

Hyacinth, Jacinth, Jacinthe,

Jacintha, Hyakinthos • Greek/English • *love and passion*

Idony, Idone, Idunn, Idonea •
Norse • *Goddess of the Apples of Eternal Youth*

Ihāb • Arabic • *a gift from God*

Ilse, Ilsa, Elisabeth • Germanic/Biblical • *God is my oath*

Imogen, Innogen, Inghean, Imogene • Celtic • *girl, maiden*

In'ām • Arabic • *a gift given or bestowed by God*

Inanna, Anna • Sumerian • *Queen of Heaven*

Indira • Sanskrit • *she is so beautiful, radiant, filled with splendour*

Ingrid • Norse • *a beautiful woman blessed by the god of fertility, Ing*

Irène, Eirene, Irina, Ira, Arina •
Greek • *peace*

Irma, Erma, Ermen, Irmgard, Irmtraud, Irmen, Irmengard, Ermengard, Irmgard, Irmingard, Irmentrud, Ermentrud, Irmentraud
• *all and nothing less*

Isabel, Isobel, Isa, Isabella, Isabelle, Isobelle, Isobella, Izzy, Izzie, Sibéal, Iseabail, Ishbel, Isbel, Elizabeth • Spanish • *Biblical/Hebrew/Jewish • God is my oath*

Isabis • South African • *beautiful to see*

Isadora, Isidoro, Izzy • Greek/Egyptian • *a gift from the goddess Isis, deity of magic and life*

Isaura • Latin • *a woman from Isauria in Asia Minor (Turkey)*

Isolde, Isolda, Iseult, Esyllt •
Arthurian mythology/British Welsh
• *a beautiful Irish princess*

Jamala, Gamala • Arabic • *beautiful woman*

Jamila, Gamila • Arabic • *graceful as well as beautiful*

Jana, Yana, Jan • Biblical/English/Latin • *God is gracious or gift of God*

Jancis, Jancie • English literary • *combo of Frances and Jan, from the novel* Precious Bane *by Mary Webb*

Jane, Jeanne, Jehanne, Jaine, Jayne, Jain, Jean, Joan, Janie, Janey, Joanna, Jaynie, Síne, Siân, Johanna, Hanne, Hansine, Johanne, Janja, Jannja, Sheena Jensine, Jonna, Jeanne, Juanna, Juana, Giovanna, Gianna, Hana, Jana, Janeen, Janelle, Jaynia • Biblical/French/Latin • *God is gracious or gift of God*

Janet, Jannet, Janett, Janette, Jan, Janetta, Janeta, Seònaid, Shona, Seona • Biblical/English/Latin • *God is gracious or gift of God*

Janice, Janis, Janise, Jannice, Jan • Biblical/French/Latin • *God is gracious or gift of God*

Janina • Tunisian • *garden*

Jan, Janna • Biblical/English • *God is gracious or gift of God*

Jasmine, Jasmyn, Jazmin, Jazmine, Yasmīn, Yasmine, Jasmina, Yasmina, Jaslyn, Jaslynne • Persian/Norman • *evergreen shrub or vine with glorious fragrance*

Jāthibiyya, Gāzbiyya • Arabic • *charm personified*

Jawāhir, Gawāhir • Arabic • *a dazzling jewel*

Jean, Joan, Jane, Jeanne, Jehanne, Jehanna, Jeane, Jeana, Gina, Jeanna, Jeane, Jeanetta, Jeanette, Jeanie, Jeanine, Jeannette, Jeanne, Jeanett, Jenette, Jennet,

Jenet, Ginett, Ginnette, Ginetta, Ginnetta, Jeannie, Jeannine, Jeannique, Jannike • Biblical/French • *God is gracious or gift of God*

Jemima • Biblical/Hebrew/Jewish • *dove; as bright as day*

Jennifer, Jen, Jenefer, Jenny, Jeni, Jenifer, Jenine, Jennifer, Jenni, Jennefer, Jannifer, Jenine, Jennine, Jeannine • Arthurian mythology/British Cornish • *beautiful maiden*

Jenessa, Jen • African American • *combo of Jennifer and Vanessa*

Jenna, Genna, Jena • Arthurian mythology/British Cornish • *beautiful maiden*

Jessica, Jesca, Jessika, Jess, Jessie, Jesse, Jessye, Teasag, Iscah • Biblical/literary • *William Shakespeare's invention from the Biblical name Jesca or Iscah*

Jewel, Jouel, Iocus • Latin/Norman • *rare stone that is a plaything, a delight to the eyes*

Jia • Chinese • *beautiful*

Jiao • Chinese • *lovely, dainty*

Jinana • Arabic • *a woman as beautiful and mystical as the Garden of Eden*

Jing • Chinese • *stillness, contemplation or luxurious, comfort*

Jingfei • Chinese • *forever fragrant*

Jinghua • Chinese • *what a splendid situation!*

Jo, Joe, Joanna, Joanne, Jody, Josephine, Josie, Josey • Biblical/Greek • *God is gracious or gift of God*

Joan, Ionna, Iohanna, Joanna, Johanna, Joanne, Johanne, Joanie, Joni, Siobhán, Chevanne, Siubhan, Jane, Shevaune, Chevaune,

Shona, Shevanne, Joann, Seonag •
Biblical/Norman
**Jody, Jodene, Jodie, Jodi, Jude,
Judith** • Biblical/Hebrew/Jewish •
praise
**Joely, Jolene, Jolie, Jollie, Joleen,
Jolie, Joli, Jol** • Norse/French •
*pretty one, also gay and festive;
yuletide*
**Johanna, Johna, Johannah,
Johanne, Joanna, Joanne, Jo,
Jannike** • Biblical/Latin • *God is
gracious or gift of God*
Jonina • Biblical/modern English •
God is gracious or gift of God
Joy, Joie, Gaudia • Latin/French •
joyful in the Lord
Juan • Chinese • *gracious*
Juanita, Janita, Janita • Spanish •
God is gracious or gift of God
**Judith, Judi, Judy, Judie, Jutte,
Jutta, Julitta** • Biblical/Hebrew/
Jewish • *praise*
Julitta, Julitt, Julip, Judith •
Biblical/Latin • *praise*
Juno, Hera • Greek/Roman • *Queen
of the Gods, Greek and Roman
pantheon*
Jutte, Jutta, Jude, Judith • Biblical/
Germanic • *praise*
Jyoti • Sanskrit • *light of mind, light
of freedom, light of paradise*

Kamala • Sanskrit • *beautiful pink*
Kanta • Sanskrit • *you are desirable
because you are so lovely*
Karenza, Carenza • British/Welsh/
Kernow • *love, loving to be loved*
Keelin, Kylin, Cianian, Cilan •
British/Welsh/Gaelic • *companion
or friend*
Keeva, Caoimhe, Caomhe • Gaelic
• *beautiful*

**Keren, Kerenhappuch, Keran,
Kerin, Kerrin, Keron, Kerena,
Kerina** • Biblical/Hebrew/Jewish
• *ray of light or eye painted in the
shape of a horn*
Kerry, Keri, Ceri • English/British/
Welsh/Irish Gaelic • *after the Celtic
Goddess of Poetry*
**Kimberley, Kim, Kimberly,
Kimberlie, Kimberlee,
Kimberleigh, Kimberli, Kymberley,
Kym** • Anglo-Saxon/American
English • *etymology is a personal
name such as Kimma's wood or
clearing. But gained popularity after
the South African town of Kimberley
where the British took on the Boers;
especially 14th October*
Kinga, Kinegunde, Kinge •
Germanic • *in the face of strife she is
brave and courageous*
Kyra, Kyria, Kira • Greek • *lady*

**Laetitia, Latisha, Leticia, Lettice,
Tish, Tisha** • Latin • *overcome with
joy and happiness*
Leila, Laila, Layla, Leyla • Arabic • *a
beautiful dark woman, as enchanting
as the night, intoxicating to the
senses*
Lakshmi • Sanskrit • *lucky girl in
matters of luck, money and beauty*
**Lalage, Lalagein, Lally, Lailie,
Lalla, La-La** • Greek • *to chatter on
endlessly, loquacious*
Lalita • Sanskrit • *this girl is as
playful as a kitten; affectionate and
amorous*
Lamyā • Arabic • *a woman with
fulsome brown lips*
Lanfen • Chinese • *perfumed orchid*
Laoise, Leesha, Luigseach • Irish
Gaelic • *unsure origins but most*

*possibly Lug, Goddess of Light;
someone from County Laoise*

Lark, Lawerce • North American/
Australian/English/Anglo-Saxon •
dawn song

Latasha, Latisha, Natasha, Tasha
• African American • *combo of
Laetisha and Natasha*

**Lavender, Lavanda, Levandulova,
Lavendelbla, Lavendel,
Kahvatulilla, Laventelinsininen,
Lavande, Blasseslila,
Levendulaszinu, Ljosfjolublarlitur,
Ungukebiruan, Melakrasa,
Lawendowy, Cor de Alfazema,
Lillalavendelfarget** • Norman/
English • *a beautiful bluey/lilac-
coloured shrub*

Layla • Arabic • *a beautiful dark
woman, as enchanting as the night,
intoxicating to the senses*

Leila, Laila, Layla, Leyla, Lela, Lila •
Arabic • *a beautiful dark woman, as
enchanting as the night, intoxicating
to the senses*

Lena, Yelena, Helen • Greek/
Russian • *ray of sunshine, sunbeam,
sunny*

**Lettice, Leticia, Laetitia, Letitia,
Letizia, Letty, Lettie** • Latin/English
• *overcome with joy and happiness*

Lia, Rosalia, Rosalie, Leah • Latin/
Italian • *rose*

Libby, Elizabeth • English • *God is
my oath*

Libe, Liebe • Jewish/Yiddish/
German • *love or darling*

Lidwina, Liduina, Luzdivina •
Germanic • *friendly people*

Liese, Elisabeth • German • *God is
my oath*

Lieselotte, Liselotte, Lilo • German
• *combo of Liese and Charlotte*

Lifen • Chinese • *beautiful fragrance*

Ligia, Eligia • Latin/Italian/Spanish
• *to choose, given a choice*

Lihua • Chinese • *beautiful China*

Lijuan • Chinese • *beautiful and
graceful*

Lilac, Lilak, Nilak • Persian/Arabic •
blue or hues of blue

Lili, Lilli, Elisabeth • German • *God
is my oath*

Liling • Chinese • *beautiful jade
wind chime*

Lïna • Arabic • *a woman with the
figure of a palm tree; voluptuous and
curved*

**Linda, Belinda, Lynda, Lindie,
Lindy, Lyn, Lynn, Lynne, Linden,
Lin, Lyn, Lynne, Linnet, Lindsey,
Lenda** • Spanish/Visigothic/
Germanic • *pretty, passive, tender
and soft*

Liqin • Chinese • *beautiful zither
(musical instrument)*

Liqiu • Chinese • *beautiful autumn*

**Lisa, Liza, Elyse, Lise, Liese, Élise,
Elisabeth** • French/German • *God
is my oath*

**Lisette, Lise, Elisabeth, Lysette,
Lise, Lys, Liz, Lis, Elisbet, Liza, Eliza,
Lisa, Lizzie, Lizzy, Lizi, Elizabeth** •
English/French • *God is my oath*

Livia, Livius • Latin • *Roman family
name Livius; uncertain origin but
maybe means a hue of the colour
blue*

**Lleucu, Leucu, Lughaidh, Lugh,
Lucy, Lucía, Lugh, Lugus** • British
Welsh • *Latin • light*

Lola, Dolores • Roman Catholic •
*Our Lady of the Seven Sorrows of the
Virgin*

Lolicia, Lola, Delicia • American
English/Roman Catholic

Lolonyo • Ghanaian • *love is beautiful*

Lolita, Lola, Lolita • Roman Catholic • *Our Lady of the Seven Sorrows of the Virgin*

Lorinda • American English • *combo of Laura and Linda*

Lottelore • modern • *combo of Lotte (Charlotte) and Lore (Eleanore)*

Lubna • Arabic • *storax tree that has sweet, honey-like sap, used to make perfume and incense. A fragrant, perfumed, honey-tasting woman as intoxicating as incense*

Lucía, Lucilla, Lucy, Lucie, Luce, Lucetta, Luciana • Latin • *light*

Lucien, Lucienne • Latin • *light*

Lucilla, Lucille, Lucy, Lucille, Lucy, Luci • Latin • *light*

Lucinda, Lucia, Sinda, Cindy, Sindy, Lucy, Lucinde • Latin • *light*

Lucie, Lucy, Lucinda, Luíseach, Lucía, Lucinde, Liùsaidh • Norman/ Latin • *light*

Luz, Lux, Luzdivina • Roman Catholic • *Our Lady of Light; referring to the Virgin*

Lydia, Lydie • Greek • *woman from Lydia*

Lynette, Lynette, Linnet, Linotte, Linnette, Linette • Spanish/French

Lyra • Latin • *a stringed musical instrument*

Lyudmila, Lyuda, Ludmil • Slavic • *a tribe of kind people, a family of gracious folks*

Mabel, Mab, Amabel, Amabilia, Mabilia, Mabelle, Amiabel, Maybelle, Maybella • Norman/ English • *lovely*

Mackenzie, Mackenzee, Makenzie, Makensie, Makensey, Mckenzie, Coinneach, MacCoinnich, Mickenzie • English/Gaelic • *handsome, gorgeous, pleasing to the eye and rather adorable!*

Madhu • Sanskrit • *she is as sweet as honey and younger than springtime*

Madhur • Sanskrit • *sweetie!*

Madīha • Arabic • *praiseworthy, commendable*

Maha • Arabic • *oryx: an antelope with large, beautiful eyes*

Mahalia, Mahalah, Mahali • Biblical/Jewish/Hebrew/Aramaic • *unsure; either tender or marrow – perhaps tender down to her marrow!*

Mahāsin • Arabic • *charming and admirable qualities*

Mai, Maria, Margit • Scandinavian • *combo of Maria/Mary and Margaret*

Maia, Maya, Mya • Latin • *Roman Goddess of Youth, Life, Rebirth, Love and Sexuality*

Maidie, Maid, Maegden • Old English • *maiden*

Malati • Sanskrit • *she is like the jasmine, she is even more beautiful at night*

Malak • Arabic • *angel*

Majella • Roman Catholic • *in honour of St Gérard Majella*

Manara • Arabic • *she sends out a radiant light like a pharo (lighthouse)*

Marcella, Marcelle, Marcelline, Marceline, Marcelina, Marcela, Marcellina, Marcellus, Marsaili • Latin • *named after Mars, God of Sex and War*

Marcia, Marsha, Marcie, Marcy, Marci • Latin • *named after Mars, God of Sex and War*

María José • Roman Catholic • *combo of Mary the Virgin and*

Joseph the father
Mariana, Marianus, Marianne, Marius • Latin • *Latin* • *follower of the Virgin Mary*

Maribella, Annabel, Christabel • Italian • *the suffix bella means beautiful*

Mariel, Muriel, Meriel, Murielle, Marielle • English • *combo of Mary and Muriel*

Marilyn, Mary, Maralyn, Marilynne, Marylyn, Marylynn, Marilene, Maralyn, Marilyn • modern English • *combo of Mary and Lyn*

Marion, Marie, Margeret, Margery, Marianus, Marion, Marian, Marianne, Mariann, Marieanne, Marianna, Meiriona • Latin/French • *follower of the Virgin Mary*

Marisol • Spanish • *combination of María and Sol (sun)*

Martha, Marthe, Marthja, Martja, Märta, Martta • Biblical/Aramaic • *lady*

Martine, Martina, Mari, Martie, Marty, Martinus • Latin/English • *named after Mars, God of Sex and War*

Matilda, Mahthild, Mehthild, Mathilda, Tilda, Mattie, Matty, Tilly, Tillie, Mechtild, Mechthilde, Mechtilde, Machteld, Matilde, Mathilde, Mathilda, Matilde, Matylda, Martta, Matild, Mafalda, Matilde • Germanic • *mighty in battle*

Matrona • Latin • *lady*

Maud, Matilda, Mahauld, Maauld, Maude, Mallt • Dutch/Flemish • *mighty in battle*

Mavis, Mave, Maeve • Breton Celtic/Norman • *song thrush*

Mercedes • Roman Catholic • *Our Lady of Mercies, alluding to the Virgin Mary*

Mehetabel, Mehitabel • Biblical/Jewish/Hebrew • *God makes happy*

Meifeng • Chinese • *beautiful wind*

Meili • Chinese • *beautiful*

Meirong • Chinese • *beautiful soul and personality*

Meixiu • Chinese • *beautiful grace*

Melinda, Mélanie, Lucinda • modern • *combo of Melanie and Lucinda*

Melody, Melodie, Melodia, Melosaeidein • Greek • *the singing of songs*

Mercedes, Merche, Mercy, Mary • Spanish • *Mary of Mercies*

Mercia, Mercy, Mecedes, Merces • Latin • *showing compassion for others' plight*

Merle, Meriel, Merula • Norman/Latin • *a blackbird*

Merry, Merrily, Merilee, Marylee, Marilee • American English • *to be merry*

Michaela, Mikayla, Mica, Micah • Biblical/Hebrew/Jewish/English • *who is like God?*

Michele, Michelle, Michel Chelle, Shell, Micheline • Biblical/Hebrew/Jewish/English • *who is like God?*

Mignon, Mignonette, Minette • French • *little darling, cutie, sweetie*

Millena, Milenna • Czech • *grace and favour*

Mingxia • Chinese • *bright rosy glow*

Mirabelle, Mirabella, Mirabellis, Mirari, Mirabilis • Latin/French • *wonderful, glorious*

Miranda, Randa, Randy, Randie, Amanda • literary invention/Latin • *William Shakespeare invented this name for his heroine in* The

Tempest: *admire, wonder at or in awe of her loveliness*
Mireille, Mireio, Miriam, Mary, Miranda, Mireio, Mirella • Provençal • *to admire*
Missy, Missie • American English • *mistress!*
Morna, Muirne • Scots Gaelic • *beloved*
Morwenna, Morwen, Morwyn • British/Welsh • *maiden*
Muhayya • Arabic • *she has such a lovely, beautiful face*
Muhsina • Arabic • *a charitable, kind and compassionate woman*
Munira • Arabic • *radiant, bright, send out a light*
Myfanwy, Myf • British/Welsh • *your lady, your woman*
Myrna, Muirne, Morna • Irish Gaelic • *beloved*
Myrtle, Myrtille, Myrtilla, Myrta • Latin/Norman/Greek • *a tree with fragrant leaves; in Greek it means perfumed*

Nadia, Nadya, Nadezhda, Nadine Nadezhda, Nadya • Russian • *hope*
Nadine, Nadia • Russian/French • *hope*
Nadira, Nadra • Arabic • *a woman who is rare and precious*
Nāhid • Arabic • *a girl who is becoming a woman*
Najiba, Nagiba • Arabic • *cultured, cultivated and a cut above the rest*
Nan, Nancy, Nanette, Ann • Biblical/Jewish/Hebrew • *pet form of Ann, of uncertain origins: God has favoured me*
Nancy, Nan, Ann, Annis, Agnès, Nancie, Nanci, Nance • Biblical/Jewish/Hebrew • *pet form of Ann,*

of uncertain origins: God has favoured me
Nanda, Ferdinanda, Hernanda • Spanish/Italian • *short form of Ferdinanda or Hernanda; someone who is at peace where they are but always ready to travel*
Nanette, Nan • Biblical/Jewish/Hebrew/French • *pet form of Ann, of uncertain origins: God has favoured me*
Naomi, Noémie, Noemi • Biblical/Hebrew/Jewish • *pleasant and good*
Nápla, Annabel, Anabl, Anable, Anaple, Amable • Norman/English/Irish • *lovely*
Nasrīn • Persian/Arabic • *wild rose, a star set in the constellation of the Eagle and the Lyre*
Nawāl • Arabic • *a gift bestowed or given*
Nerida, Nerys, Phillida, Phyllis, Nerissa, Nereis • British Welsh/Greek • *sea nymph or lady*
Nerissa, Nereis • literary invention/Greek • *sea sprite or nymph Nerissa, invented by William Shakespeare for Portia's lady-in-waiting in* The Merchant of Venice
Nerys • British/Welsh • *lady*
Niamh, Neve, Nia • Irish Gaelic • *beautiful and bright*
Nichelle, Nicole, Michelle • modern • *combo of Michelle and Nicole*
Ni'mat • Arabic • *a woman who is good to have around*
Niu • Chinese • *I am a girl*
Nóra, Honora, Norah, Nonie • Irish Gaelic/Latin • *an honoured woman*
Noreen, Nóirín, Norene, Norine, Honoria • Irish Gaelic/Latin • *an honoured woman*
Norma • artistic Italian • *Felice*

Romani invented the name for Bellini's opera

Nuala, Fionnuala, Nola • *fair hair down to her bonny shoulders*

Nuo • Chinese • *graceful*

Nura, Nūr • Arabic • *this woman will light up your life and she has unique features too*

Nuying • Chinese • *girl flower*

Nyamekye • Ghanaian • *given by God*

Octavia • Latin • *a Roman family name meaning the number eight*

Odette, Odet, Oda • Germanic/ Frankish • *prosperity and good fortune*

Olympe, Olympia • Greek • *a woman from Olympus, the mountain of the Gods*

Oksana, Oxana • Russian • *praise God*

Oktyabrina, October • Russian/ Latin/English • *commemorates the October revolution 1917*

Olive, Olivia, Oliff, Oliffe, Oliva • Latin • *olive tree, a symbol of peace and abundance*

Olivia, Olive, Oliva • literary invention/Latin • *William Shakespeare named Olivia as the rich heiress in* The Tempest

Ottavia • Latin/Italian • *personal name of Octavius, linked to number eight*

Paleley • Sudanese • *sweet*

Pamela, Pam, Pammy, Pamella • poetic invention • *Sir Philip Sidney and Elizabeth I created the name*

Pandora, Dora, Pandoran • Greek mythology • *all and every gift; alluding to Pandora's box that she*

was told never to open, when she did, she allowed everything evil and bad out, leaving the fairy Hope as the only thing left inside

Patrice, Patricia • Latin/French • Latin/Irish Gaelic • *patrician*

Patricia, Patrice, Pat, Tricia, Trisha, Trish, Patty, Pattie, Patti, Patsy, Patrizia • Latin/Irish Gaelic • *patrician*

Patty, Pattie, Patricia, Martha, Patti • English • *pet name for Patricia and Martha*

Paudeen, Páidín • Irish Gaelic/ English • *pet name for Patricia*

Paz • Roman Catholic • *our Lady of Peace*

Peijing • Chinese • *admiring luxuriance*

Peninnah, Pen, Pearl, Perle, Peninna, Penina • Biblical/Hebrew/ Jewish/Latin • *coral or pearl, a beautiful pink underwater mineral found in warm water*

Perdita, Perdie, Purdee, Purdy, Perditus • Latin/literary invention • *William Shakespeare invented the name from the Latin 'lost' as one of his characters in* The Winter's Tale

Persis • Biblical/Greek • *a Persian woman*

Petula, Pet, Petulare • Latin/ Christian • *to ask or plead humbly for mercy or forgiveness*

Petal • English • *one of the often brightly coloured parts of a flower immediately surrounding the reproductive organs; a division of the corolla; a term of endearment*

Philomena, Philomenus, Philomenes, Phileinmenos, Philoumena, Filumena, Filomena • Greek/Germanic • *loyal, strong*

friend, platonic friendship

Phyllis, Phillida, Phyllis, Phyllidos, Phyllidis, Phyllida, Phyllicia, Phylicia • Greek mythology • *a Thracian queen, Phyllis died for love and transformed herself into an almond tree; her name means leaves or leaf and she is a symbol of undying love and friendship*

Pilar • Roman Catholic • *Our Lady of the Pillar; appearance of the Virgin on a pillar at Zaragossa*

Piper, Pipere • English • *a pipe player*

Patribha • Sanskrit • *clever, radiant, imaginative and precocious*

Precious • American English • *dear; beloved: a precious child*

Premiata • Sanskrit • *symbolic of the plant or flower of love*

Primrose, Primarosa • Latin • *the first rose*

Priya • Sanskrit • *beloved one*

Qiang • Chinese • *rose*

Qiu • Chinese • *autumn*

Qiuyue • Chinese • *autumn Moon*

Rabāb • Arabic • *a musical instrument like a violin*

Radegund, Radegunde • Germanic • *a counsellor, adviser in times of trouble*

Raelene, Rae • Germanic/Frankish/English Australian • *adviser to the army; army commander*

Raghda • Arabic • *a carefree woman who enjoys life*

Rhamantus, Rhamanta • British/Welsh • *romantic*

Raimunde, Raimund, Raimonda • Germanic/Frankish • *adviser to the army; army commander*

Rajni • Sanskrit • *Queen of the Night*

Rakaya • Tunisian • *sweet*

Ramona • Catalan/Visigothic • *adviser, protector*

Randa • Arabic • *a desert-bound sweet perfumed tree*

Rathnait, Ronit • Irish Gaelic • *a woman of grace and prosperity*

Rāwiya • Arabic • *a narrator of classical Arabic poetry and prose and beautiful speaker*

Regina, Queenie, Raine, Régine, Raghnailt, Ragnhild • Latin/Roman Catholic • *queen (of heaven)*

Reisel, Reise, Rose, Reisl, Rella, Rele • Jewish/Yiddish • *rose*

Rhetta • Dutch • *advice counsel*

Rhian, Rian, Rhianu • British/Welsh • *maiden*

Rhianna, Rhiannon, Rianna, Rhianon, Riannon, Rheanna, Reanna, Reanne, Rigantona • British Welsh/Celtic mythology • *great queen*

Rhoda, Rhodon, Rose, Roda, Rodos • Greek • *rose or someone from the island of roses, Rhodes*

Ríonach, Rina, Caterina, Katerina, Carina, Sabrina, Regina, Ríona, Rio, Rioghnach, Rinach • Irish Gaelic • *royalty; like a queen*

Robbin, Robbie, Roberta • Germanic • *famous and bright*

Roberta, Robbie • Germanic • *famous and bright*

Robyn, Robin • Germanic • *famous and bright*

Rochelle, Rachelle • Germanic/French/American English • *rest a while*

Rocio • Roman Catholic • *Our Lady of the Dews, or tears shed for the wickedness of the world*

Róisín, Rosheen, Rós, Rose, Rhosyn • Irish Gaelic • *rose*

Roni, Veronica, Ronnie • Latin/ English • *shortened Veronica; true image*

Rosa, Rose, Roschen, Rosetta, Rosita • Latin • *the flower rose*

Rosalie, Rosalia • Latin/French • *the flower rose*

Rosalinda • Latin • *lovely rose*

Rosangela • Italian • *combo of Rosa and Angela*

Roseanne, Rosanne, Rosanna, Rosannagh, Rozanne • English • *combo of Rose and Anne*

Rose, Rosa, Rosie • English/Latin • *the flower rose*

Roselle, Rozelle • English/French • *the flower rose*

Rosetta • Italian • *pet form of Rosa*

Roshanara • Persian • *her beauty is like honey to the bee, she is a magnet of loveliness*

Rosita • Spanish • *pet form of Rosa*

Rowena, Rodwynn • Anglo-Saxon • *fame and joy*

Ruiling • Chinese • *lucky jade wind chime*

Rupinder • Sanskrit • *beauty beyond compare*

Ruth, Ruthi, Ruthie, Rut, Rutt, Roo • Biblical/Jewish/English • *unknown roots but in English: compassion*

Sabina, Sabine • Latin • *from the Sabine women who were kidnapped by the Romans*

Sadhbh, Syve, Sive, Sabia • Irish Gaelic • *sweet as honey*

Safā • Arabic • *a pure, chaste woman who is sincere and goodly*

Salma • Arabic • *a person who looks after those she loves; a protector*

Salomé, Shalom • Greek/Hebrew/ Aramaic • *peace*

Salwa • Arabic • *she who consoles others and gives a shoulder to cry on*

Samantha, Sam, Sammy, Sammi • Biblical/Hebrew/Jewish • *the name of God, God has heard, listen to God*

Sanā • Arabic • *a brilliant, radiant woman*

Saniyya • Arabic • *wonderful, dazzling woman*

Sapphire, Sappheiros • Greek/ Jewish • *the precious blue gemstone; birthstone of Libra*

Sarabeth • American English • *combo of Sara and (Eliza)beth*

Sarala • Sanskrit • *as straight as the pine and honest as the day is long*

Saraswati • Sanskrit • *filled with waters of knowledge of the arts, learning and academia*

Satin, Zaituni, Tsingtung • Chinese/ Arabic/French/English/Latin • *soft, sleek, silky, shiny fabric*

Scarlett, Escarlate, Scarlata, Scarlet • Latin/Norman/English • *someone who dyes or sells fabrics of rich, radiant colours*

Selima, Selim, Zelima • Arabic/ English • *peace*

Seren, Serena, Serenus • British/ Welsh • *star*

Serenissima • Italian • *serene*

Shādya • Arabic • *singer, the voice*

Shafīqa • Arabic • *a compassionate, charitable woman*

Shakira • Arabic • *thankful and grateful*

Shamīm • Arabic • *a woman who is fragrant and smells as sweet as perfume*

Shan • Chinese • *a woman who*

bears herself elegantly; like royalty or a model

Shana, Shanae, Shania, Shanee, Siani, Siân • American English/ British Welsh • *God is gracious or gift of God*

Shanice • American English • *combo of Shane and Janice*

Shoshanna, Shoshana, Shannah, Susanna • Biblical/Jewish/Hebrew • *the flower lily, which means rose in modern Hebrew*

Shaoqing • Chinese • *young blue*

Sharada • Sanskrit • *autumn*

Sharifa • Arabic • *a woman who is eminent in her field and honourable to the nth degree*

Sharissa • African American • *combo of Sharon and names that end in -rissa*

Sharon, Sharron, Sharona, Sharonda • Biblical • *a place called Sharon on the coastal plain of the Holy Land; and for the shrub, the rose of sharon*

Shatha • Arabic • *sweet-smelling, fragrant*

Shula, Shulamit • Hebrew/Jewish • *peacefulness*

Simone • Biblical/Hebrew/Jewish • *hearkening, hearing*

Sinéad, Janet, Jeanette, Seònaid, Shona, Seona • English/Scots Gaelic • *God is gracious or gift of God*

Siobhán, Joan, Jehanne, Shevaun, Chevonne, Chevaun, Chevaunne,Shevaunne, Jehanne, Joan • English/Norman/French/ Biblical/Irish Gaelic • *God is gracious or gift of God*

Sioned, Janet • English/British Welsh • *God is gracious or gift of God*

Sissy, Sisi, Sissey, Sissie, Elisabeth • Jewish/Hebrew/Bavarian • *God is my oath*

Siv • Norse • *bride or wife, name of Thor's golden-haired missus*

Sloane, Sloan • English • *after Sloane Square in London, name given to a Sloane Ranger (Fergie, Duchess of York!)*

Sneh • Sanskrit • *aromatic oils good for affection and tenderness*

Socorro • Roman Catholic • *Our Lady of Perpetual Succour*

Sorcha, Sarah, Sally • Irish Gaelic • *brightness*

Sri • Sanskrit • *a royal personage who radiates the light of goodness, beauty and wealth*

Stacey, Stacy, Stace, Eustacia, Stacie, Staci • English/Greek

Star, Starr, Stella • English • *a star (heavenly rather than celebrity)*

Steffanie, Stéphanie, Steph, Steffi, Stefanie, Steff • Greek • *a crown or garland*

Stella, Stella Maris • Latin • *a star and Star of the Seas (often used to describe the Virgin Mary)*

Stéphanie, Steff, Steph, Steffie, Steffy, Stevie, Stefanie, Steffany, Stephania, Stephana, Stefania, Estefania, Stevie • Greek • *a crown or garland*

Suha • Arabic • *star*

Sultana • Arabic • *empress, queen*

Sujata • Sanskrit • *excellent character or born of nobility*

Sukie, Sukey, Susan • English • *pet form of Susan*

Sunita • Sanskrit • *she's a good girl who gives wise advice*

Sunniva, Sunnegifu, Synnøve,

Synneva, Synnøv, Synne • English •
gift from the sun
Sunny, Sunnie • English • *cheery,
cheerful, full of joy; a sunny
disposition*
**Susan, Susanna, Suzan, Sue, Su,
Soo, Susie, Suzie, Susy, Suzy,
Sukie, Sukey, Siùsan, Sue, Susan,
Susanna, Susannah, Suzanne, Su,
Soo** • English/Biblical • *the flower
lily, which means rose in modern
Hebrew*
**Susanna, Shoshana, Shoshan,
Susana, Suzanna, Suzannah,
Susannah, Siùsan, Siusaidh,
Susanne, Suzanne, Zuzanna,
Zuzana, Suzana, Zsuzsanna,
Susann, Susi, Susanna, Sanna,
Zanna** • Biblical/English • *lily*
Shushila • Sanskrit • *she has a lovely
nature and is so placid too*
Susie, Susan, Suzie, Susi • English •
short form Susan or Susannah
Suzanne, Susanna, Suzette, Suzie
• Biblical/French • *the flower lily,
which means rose in modern Hebrew*
Suranne • English • *combo of Sarah
and Anne*
Svetlana, Sveta, Photine • Slavic/
Greek • *light*
**Swanhild, Swanhilda, Swanhilde,
Svanhild** • Saxon • *she glides
through conflict (battle) like a swan*
Sylphide, Sylva, Silva, Sylpha •
Latin/French • *airborne, invisible
spirits, sylph-like*

Taghrīd • Arabic • *bird song*
Tahiyya • Arabic • *hello!*
Tallulah, Talulla, Tuilelaith • Irish
Gaelic/English • *abundance, lady
and princess*
Tara • Sanskrit • *a shining star who*

*carries the troubles of the world on
her shoulders*
Tegan, Teagan, Teigan, Tiegan, Teg
• British/Welsh • *lovely*
Tempe, Temnein • Greek • *a valley
in Greece; the legendary home of the
Muses, the nine goddesses of the arts
and sciences*
Tetty, Tettie, Elizabeth • English •
pet name for Elizabeth
Thanā • Arabic • *a woman ready to
praise and be praised; everything she
does deserves praise*
Thea, Dorothea • Greek • *short
name for Dorothea; gift from God*
Theodora, Dora, Teodora, Feodora
• Greek • *God-given or giving to God
or God's gift*
Tikvah, Tikva • Biblical/Jewish/
Hebrew • *hope*
Ting • Chinese • *graceful*
Tirion • British/Welsh • *kind and
gentle*
Tirzah, Tirza, Thirzah, Thirza
• Biblical/Hebrew/Jewish • *a
delightful woman*
Toltse, Dolce, Dulcie • Jewish/
Yiddish/Italian • *sweet*
Tova, Tofa, Turid, Tove, Tufa • Norse
• *the god Thor made me beautiful*
Trudeliese • German • *combo of
Trude and Liese*
Tuilelaith, Talulla, Talullah • Irish
Gaelic • *a lady of abundance*

Unity, Unitas, Úna • Latin/English/
Irish • *to join together*

Valda • American English • *combo
of Valerie and Linda or Glenda*
Valene • African American • *combo
of Valerie and -ene*
Valentina, Valentine, Val, Tina

• Latin • *flourishing, blooming, blossoming*

Valetta, Etta, Valletta • Italian • *combo of Val and -etta; capital of Malta*

Valmai, Val, Falmai • British Welsh/ Australian English

Vanessa, Nessa, Venessa • literary invention/Dutch • *created by Jonathan Swift from his lover's Dutch surname, Vanhomrigh*

Vashti • Biblical/Hebrew/Persian • *thread or beautiful woman*

Velinda • American English • *an extension of Linda*

Venus, Venustas, Aphrodite • Latin/Greek • *Goddess of Beauty and Love*

Verity, Veritas, Verus • Latin/ Norman • *truth and honesty*

Veronica, Verona, Bérénice, Ronnie, Ronni, Roni, Veraicon, Véronique, Veronika, Vroni • Latin • *true image: vera icon*

Virtudes • Roman Catholic/Spanish • *seven Christian virtues*

Visitacion • Roman Catholic/ Spanish • *the Virgin Mary visits her sister Elisabeth*

Vivien, Vivian, Vivienne, Béibhinn • Celtic/Irish Gaelic/Arthurian Legend • *white or fair lady*

Wendy, Wenda, Wendi, Gwendolen • literary invention • *JM Barrie created it for his book* Peter Pan *from his own nursery name Fwendy-Wendy meaning friend*

Wahiba • Arabic • *a generous woman who gives her all*

Wen • Chinese • *refinement*

Wenling • Chinese • *refined jade wind chime*

Widād • Arabic • *an affectionate, friendly girl*

Winifred, Winfred, Win, Winnie, Wynnfrith, Gwenfrewi, Winfriede, Winfried • Germanic • *a kind, peace-loving friend*

Wudasse • Ethiopian • *praise*

Wynne, Wynn, Wine • British Welsh/Anglo-Saxon • *a friend and/ or one who is blessed and sacred*

Xenia • Greek • *hospitality and a welcome to or from a stranger or foreigner*

Xia • Chinese • *rosy clouds*

Xiang • Chinese • *fragrant*

Xiaojing • Chinese • *morning luxury*

Xiaoqing • Chinese • *little blue*

Xingjuan • Chinese • *getting more graceful every day*

Xiulan • Chinese • *graceful orchid*

Xiurong • Chinese • *charming personality*

Xiuying • Chinese • *graceful flower*

Xueman • Chinese • *snowy composure and grace*

Ya • Chinese • *grace*

Yan • Chinese • *like a swallow or drop-dead gorgeous*

Yasmīn, Jasmina, Yasmina • Swahili • *sweetness*

Yehudit • Jewish/Hebrew • *praise*

Yelena, Helen, Helena • Russian/ Greek • *ray of sunshine, sunbeam, sunny; another analogy is it means torch of the moon*

Yentl, Gentille • French/Jewish/ Yiddish • *kind, goodly*

Yetta, Etta, Yehudit, Judith, Esther • Jewish/Yiddish/Slavic • *many associations with the names of Judith and Esther and also Slavic names*

connected with Etta
Ysuelt, Isolde • French/British
Welsh • *a beautiful Irish princess*
Yuan • Chinese • *shining peace*
Yunru • Chinese • *charming*
Yusra • *a woman who attracts
wealth, prosperity and good things*

Zahra • Arabic • *she shines like a
fully blossomed flower*
Zaibunissa • Persian • *a woman
of sheer beauty*

Zeinab, Zaynab • Arabic • *a
glorious, admired sweet-smelling
plant*
Zéphyrine, Zephyrus, Zephyros •
Latin/Greek/French • *the west wind
or breeze*
Zita, Zeta, Zetein, Zitta • Tuscan •
wee girl
Zongying • Chinese • *heroine the
others look up to; a role model*

SCORPIO
24th October to 22nd November

Planets: Pluto and Mars

Day: Tuesday

Stones: opal, jet and bloodstone

Metals: iron and steel

Colours: black, wine, red, maroon, crimson

Design: strong straight lines as in stripes, nothing wavy; invisible marking or shapes that are seen after heat is applied

Trees: yew, bushy trees and all that have deep underground roots, blackthorn, black-eyed susan

Flora: rhododendron, chrysanthemum, gardenia, tulip, plants that trap insects like the Venus flytrap, all plants that demand much shade or even darkness and have tubers rather than roots, cactus

Celebrity Scorpios: Roseanne Arnold • Charles Atlas • Christian Barnard • Sarah Bernhardt • Alexander Borodin • Charles Bronson • Richard Burton • Truman Capote • Johnny Carson • Prince Charles • Petula Clark • John Cleese • Hillary Rodham Clinton • Jackie Coogan • Alistair Cooke • Walter Cronkite • Nicholas Culpepper • Marie Curie • Bo Derek • Danny DeVito • Leonardo DiCaprio • Fyodor Dostoevsky • Richard Dreyfuss • Sally Field • Jody Foster • Indira Gandhi • James Garfield • Art Garfunkel • Bill Gates • Joseph Goebbels • Whoopi Goldberg • Billy Graham • Harry Hamlin • Goldie Hawn • Katharine Hepburn • Rock Hudson • King Hussein of Jordan • Barbara Hutton • Lauren Hutton • John Keats • Grace Kelly • Bobby Kennedy • Kevin Kline • Hedy Lamarr • Burt Lancaster • Vivian Leigh • Martin Luther • Marie Antoinette • Joni Mitchell • Demi Moore • George Patton • William Penn • Pablo Picasso • James K Polk • Helen Reddy • Julia Roberts • Auguste Rodin • Roy Rogers • Erwin Rommel • Theodore Roosevelt • Winona Ryder • Carl Sagan • Martin Scorsese • Paul Simon • Jaclyn Smith • Elke Sommer • John Sousa • Robert Louis Stevenson • Bram Stoker • Joan Sutherland • Loretta Swit • Dylan Thomas • Mary Travers • Leo Trotsky • Ike Turner • Ted Turner • Voltaire • Henry Winkler

Planetary Influences: see Mars and Pluto at the back of this book (pages 444 and 459)

Boys

Aaron, Aron, Arron, Arun, Aharon, Arke, Arn, Arran • Biblical/Egyptian • *mountain of strength*

'Abbās • Arabic • *austere, severe*

Abel, Hevel • Biblical • *breath, saint for the dying*

Achilles, Achilleus, Achille, Achilleo, Aquiles, Akhilleus • Greek • *from the River Akehloos*

Ádhamhnán • Irish Gaelic • *great fear*

Adolph, Adolphe, Adelwolf, Adolfo • Germanic • *noble wolf*

Afon, Avon • British/Welsh • *river*

Ailill • Irish • *elf*

Ajit • Sanskrit • *he who cannot be beaten*

Alan, Alain, Ailin, Ailean, Alyn, Alun, Allan, Allen • Celtic • *vague origins but likely to be a rock*

Alaric, Aliric • Germanic • *a foreign power or powerful, ruling stranger, perhaps invader*

Alfio • Sicilian • *unknown root*

Algot • Norse • *elf and gothic*

Alfred, Alfie, Alf, Aelfraed, Alfredo • Anglo-Saxon • *supernatural, faerie counsel, help*

Alger, Algie, Aelfgaer • Anglo-Saxon • *an old enchanted, noble spear with magical powers, possibly from a sacred location*

Algernon, Algy, Algie • Norman • *a man with a moustache/hairy-faced*

Alirio • Spanish • *unknown origin*

Alvar, Alfhere, Álvaro • Anglo-Saxon/ Visigothic/Spanish • *army with faerie fighters, very Lord of the Rings!*

Alvin, Aelfwine, Athelwine • Anglo-Saxon • *elfin, noble or faerie friend*

Alwyn, Aylwin, Alvin • British/ Welsh/Anglo-Saxon • *he who has faerie friends*

Ambjørn, Arnbjörn • Norse • *eagle and bear*

Ambrose, Ambroise, Ambrosius, Ambrois, Ambroix, Ambrogio, Ambrosio, Ambrosios, Ambros, Emrys, Ambros, Ambrogio, Ambrozy, Ambroz • Latin • *immortal, eternal*

Amias, Amyas • English • *unknown root*

Amrit • Sanskrit • *immortal, divine foods*

Andrew, André, Andreas, Andries, Aindriu, Andrea, Andrei, Anders, Aindrea, Anndra, Andrés, Andras, Drew, Andy, Aindrias, Aindréas, Aindriu, Anndra, Andrei, Andrzej, Jedrzej, Andrej, Ondrej, Andrija, Antero, Endre, Andrius, Andrejs • Biblical/Greek • *a real sexy, macho man*

Aniketos, Aniceto • Greek/Russian • *invincible*

Anluan • Irish Gaelic • *unknown root; may mean war dog*

Anselm, Anselmo • Germanic • *divine face, divine protection (helmet)*

Antiochos, Antiekhein, Antioco • *to hold out against all the odds*

Anacleto, Anacletus, Anakletos, Aniceto • Latin/Greek • *invocation*

Anastasio, Anastasis • Greek • *resurrection*

Anthony, Antony, Tony, Antain, Antaine, Anton, Antoine, Antonio, Antoni, Antonin, Antoninus, Ante, Antun, Antal, Antanas, Anthos,

Antwan, Antonino, Nino, Ninny, Anthony, Antoine, Anton, Antonio, Antonius • Etruscan/Roman • *Roman family name but with confused origins*

Aquilina, Akilina • Latin • *like an eagle*

Are, Ari • Norse • *eagle*

Armand, Hermann, Armin, Arminius, Armando • Germanic/ Latin • *soldier*

Arnold, Arnaud, Arnd, Arndt, Arnaldo, Amwald • Germanic • *eagle power*

Arne • Norse • *eagle*

Arnulf • Germanic • *wolf eagle*

Arthur, Arturo, Artair, Arthur, Artorius, Art • British/Welsh • *unknown origins, possibly bear man*

Armstrong • English • *surname perhaps meaning a chap with strong arms*

Arnold, Arnald, Arnaud, Arnwald, Arn, Arnie • Germanic/Frankish • *he rules like an eagle*

Arseni, Arsenios, Arsene, Arsenio • Greek • *a very sexy boy*

Ashok • Sanskrit • *emotionally controlled*

Athan, Athanase, Athanasius, Afanasi, Athanasios, Athanatos • Latin/Greek • *eternal life*

Aubrey, Aubry, Alberic, Albric, Aelfric, Aubrey, Alberic, Albericus • Germanic/Anglo-Saxon/Latin • *he who has the power of the faeries*

Averill, Eoforhild, Alfred • Norman/ Anglo-Saxon • *supernatural, faerie favours*

Avery • Norman/Anglo-Saxon • *supernatural, faerie favours*

Averki, Aberkios • Greek • *unknown root*

'Azīz • Arabic • *unconquerable, adored*

Bailey, Bailie, Baily, Bailee, Baileigh, Baylie, Baylee, Bayley, Bayleigh • English • *the bailiff!*

Barnabas, Barnaby, Barney, Barny, Barnabé, Bernebe, Barnaba, Barna, Bernabé • Biblical/Greek • *son of consolation*

Barrymore • American English • *no known origins*

Benjamin, Ben, Benny, Bennie, Benjamim, Benjie, Benji, Benjy, Venyamin, Binyamin, Benno, Bendik • Hebrew/Jewish • *son of my right hand, my right-hand man or son of the south, re-named by his father Jacob from his original name, son of my sorrow*

Bharvesh • Sanskrit • *Lord or King of the World, linked to Shiva*

Bilal, Bilil • Arabic • *moist*

Blakeney • English • *he from the black island*

Bleddyn, Blaiddyn • British/Welsh • *wolf or hero*

Boniface, Bonifacio, Bonifacius, Bonifaz • Latin • *good fate*

Bran • British/Welsh • *raven*

Brock • Anglo-Saxon • *little pig or badger*

Brodie, Brody • Scots Gaelic • *a castle or fortress*

Brutus • Latin • *old Roman family name; originally meant dull or stupid but became synonymous with defeating tyranny*

Burton • Anglo-Saxon • *a town with a castle or fort*

Cadell • British/Welsh • *battle-scarred man*

Calvin, Cal, Cathal, Calbhach, Calvagh • Latin/ Irish Gaelic • *bald*

Cameron, Camron, Kamerson, Kamran, Camsron • Scots Gaelic • *crooked nose*

Campbell, Cambell, Cambeul • Scots Gaelic • *crooked mouth*

Carlyle, Carlisle, Carlile • British Welsh • *the place or castle belonging to Lugavalos, a personal name honouring the Celtic God of the Sun and Creativity*

Carroll, Cearbhall • Irish Gaelic • *hacking or cutting with a sharp weapon*

Cathair, Cathaoir • Irish Gaelic • *battle man, soldier*

Cearbhall • Irish Gaelic • *hacking, slashing*

Cecil, Cesil • Latin/English • *old Roman family name Caecilius, from the Latin, meaning blind*

Ceri, Kerry • British/Welsh/Irish Gaelic • *unknown origin; maybe the dark one*

Césaire, Caesarius • French/Latin • *hairy, hirsute*

Chad, Tchad • English • *a man from the warlike place*

Chase, Chace • English • *hunter*

Chester, Caer, Castra • English/ Roman • *a fortress or encampment*

Christhard • German • *as brave and strong as Christ*

Ciarán, Kieron, Cieran, Kieran, Kieren, Keiran • Irish Gaelic • *black*

Cinnéidigh, Kennedy • Irish Gaelic • *ugly head*

Coby • Hebrew/Jewish • *he who supplants someone else*

Coinneach, Kenneth • Scots Gaelic • *handsome, beautiful, sexy*

Colby, Colton • American/English/ Norse • *a man who makes charcoal or who has dark looks*

Conall, Conell, Connell • Irish Gaelic • *strong as a wolf*

Conán • Irish Gaelic • *Irish wolfhound*

Conway, Connmhaigh, Connmhach, Conbhuide, Cubhuide, Connmhach • Gaelic/ British/Welsh • *golden hound or dog or head-smasher!*

Corbin, Corbinian • Anglo-Saxon/ Norman • *crow*

Cormac, Cormag • Irish/Scots Gaelic • *origins vague*

Craig, Creag • Scots Gaelic • *rock*

Crawford • Anglo-Saxon • *ford where the crows gather at the river*

Crónán, Cronin • Irish Celtic • *dark, swarthy complexion*

Cuán • Irish Gaelic • *dog or hound*

Cugat, Cucuphas • Catalan • *unknown origin*

Cuimín, Comyn • Irish Gaelic • *bent, doubled-over, crooked*

Damián, Damianos, Damien, Demyan • Greek • *vague roots but could be 'to kill'*

Damon, Daman, Damaso • Greek • *a man full of self-control or a man who tames*

Daren, Darren, Darien, Darius, Darin, Darron, Daron • American/ English • *unknown origins*

Darnell, Darnel • Norman • *not entirely known origins but possibly a type of grass or shrub*

Declan, Deaglán • Irish Celtic • *unknown origins*

Dennis, Denis, Denys, Den, Dionysios, Denny, Dioniso, Dionizy, Denes, Dionysius •

Greek/French • *named after the god Dionysius*

Denver • Anglo-Saxon/American/ English • *named after Denver (Denafaer) in Norfolk, east Britain; meaning where the Danes or Vikings crossed the river*

Detlev, Dietlieb, Detlef • Germanic • *an inheritance by or from the people*

Devlin • Irish Gaelic • *fierce, brave, hardy warrior*

Diego, Didacus, Santiago • Spanish • *supplanter, a cuckoo in the nest! Edging out someone to take their place against their will*

Dionysus, Bacchus • Greek • *Dionysus, God of Wine, Orgies and Partying*

Donagh, Donnchadh, Donough, Donncha, Duncan, Donn, Don • Irish Gaelic • *brown noble chieftain*

Donovon, Donovan, Donndubhan, Donndubhain • *brown, dark black-haired chief or leader*

Douglas, Doug, Dougie, Duggie, Dubhglas • *black stream or pool*

Doyle, Dubhghaill, Dubhghall, Dùghall, Dougal, Dugal, Dugald • Scots Gaelic • *black, dark, stranger*

Drake, Draca, Drago • English/ Dutch • *a male duck but more in honour of great English seaman, Sir Francis Drake*

Drogo, Dorogo, Drog • Norman/ Slavic • *ghost or spirit: dear one*

Duald, Dubhaltach, Dubhfholtach • Irish Gaelic • *black-haired*

Duane, Dubhán, Dwane, Dwayne, Dwain, Dubhain • Irish Gaelic • *dark, black*

Dubhdara • Irish Gaelic • *black oak*

Duff, Dubh • Irish Gaelic • *dark or black-haired man*

Duncan, Donnchadh • Celtic • *brown chief or noble leader*

Dunstan • English/Roman Catholic • *dark stone*

Dwight, Diot, Dionysa • English • *a woman (that's right: female!) who worships the God of Orgies*

Dwyer, Duibhuidhir • Irish Gaelic • *personal name meaning brown, black, tawny, dark yellow; maybe sensible and wise*

Ernest, Earnest, Eornost • Germanic • *a very serious, tenacious person who never gives up*

Ebbo • Germanic • *boar or pig*

Eberhard, Evert, Ebbo • *powerful boar or pig*

Edgar, Edgard, Eadgar • Anglo-Saxon • *he who wins riches and titles through battle*

Edward, Ed, Eddie, Eideard, Eudard, Edvard, Édouard, Eduardo, Duarte, Edoardo, Edvard, Eduard, Eetu, Ned, Ted, Neddy, Teddy, Ewart, Eadbhárd, Eadweard • Anglo-Saxon • *a person who guards his riches, blessed with wealth*

Ehrenfried, Arnfried • Germanic • *peace with honour or person who, like the eagle, has power, but uses it as a deterrent*

Éibhear • Irish Gaelic • *unknown but name of the son of Mil, leader of Gaels that conquered Ireland*

Eilif • Scandinavian • *one alone, for always, evermore, eternal life*

Einion, Einwys • British/Welsh • *anvil*

Eirik, Erik • Norse • *total ruler, singular chief*

Ellair, Ceallair, Cellarius, Cella, Ellar

• Scots Gaelic • *a person who works in pub or monastery as a steward*
Elvis, Elwyn, Elwin, Elian, Allan • American/English • *unknown origins although there was a Hibernian St Elvis in the 6th century*
Emett, Emmett • Germanic/Frankish • *from the female name Emma; the real deal*
Emidio • Latin • *vague origin; patron saint of Ascoli Piceno*
Emile, Aemilius, Émilien, Aemilus, Emil, Emilio • Latin • *rival, competitor*
Emlyn, Aemilianus, Aemilius, Aemulus • British/Welsh/Latin • *vague roots, possibly means a rival*
Emrys, Ambrose • British/Welsh • *immortal, eternal*
Éoghan, Ewan • Irish Gaelic • *born of yew wood*
Eric, Erik, Erick, Erich, Einnrik, Eirik • Norse • *one ruler or king alone, no other*
Ermenegilde, Hermengildo • French/Visigothic • *a total sacrifice*
Ernest, Ern, Ernie, Ernst, Ernesto • German • *serious in all things and will fight to the death; means business to the point of obsession*
Esau, Esaw • Hebrew/Jewish • *hairy!*
Euan, Éoghan, Ewan, Ewen, Evan • Gaelic • *yew tree*
Eunan, Ádhamhnán, Adomnae, Ádhamh • Irish • *he's a right little horror! Strikes fear in my heart*
Eustace, Eustakhios, Euistathios, Eustache, Eustaquio • Greek/French • *confused roots; could mean juicy, tasty grapes!*
Everard, Everett, Evrard, Eoforhard • Anglo-Saxon • *as brave as a boar or pig*

Everton, Eofortun • Anglo-Saxon • *the place where the wild boar or pigs live*
Eyolf • Scandinavian • *lucky wolf, like a gift or talisman*
Ezio, Aetius, Aetios • Latin • *Roman family name meaning eagle*

Fachtna, Festus • Irish Gaelic • *contentious, belligerent, hostile*
Fardorgh, Feardocha • Irish Gaelic • *dark man*
Falk, Falke, Yehoshua • German/Yiddish • *hawk or falcon*
Faolán, Fillan, Foillan • Irish Gaelic • *wolf*
Fearadhach, Farry, Ferdie • Irish Gaelic • *butch, macho man*
Feichín, Fiach • Irish Gaelic • *raven*
Fengge • Chinese • *house of the phoenix*
Ferrer, Ferris, Phiarais, Piaras • Roman Catholic/Catalan • *blacksmith*
Ferruccio, Ferro • lain • *man of iron*
Fiachna, Fiach • Irish • *raven hunt, chase*
Fiachra, Fiach • Irish • *King of the Hunt, King of the Ravens*
Fihr • Arabic • *fusion*
Firmin, Firminus, Firmino, Fermin • Latin • *he who cannot be moved; firm*
Fitzroy, Fitz • Norman/English • *often the bastard son of the king*
Flint, Fflint • English • *hard rock*
Fraser, Frazer, Frazier, Frisselle, Fresel, Freseliere, Frasier • Norman French/Scots English • *Scots family name with no known origins*
Frédéric, Frederick, Frederik, Fritz, Fred, Phredd, Freddie, Fredick, Fredric, Friedrich, Frerik, Freek,

Fredrik, Federico, Frederico, Fryderyk, Bedrich, Rieti, Frigyes • Germanic/Frankish • *peaceful but powerful ruler*

Fridtjof • Norse • *quiet, like a thief in the night*

Frost, Freosan • Anglo-Saxon • *person who looks icy, cold, snowy white hair or beard*

Fulton • Scots • *Scottish surname based on a place in Ayrshire now extinct*

Gallagher, Gallchobhar • Irish Gaelic • *foreign ally, helpful stranger*

Gennadi • Russian • *roots unknown; name of orthodox saint*

Garbhán, Garvan • Irish Gaelic • *rough, cruel, wicked*

Gareth • Welsh/British • *unknown origins possibly, linked to Geraint*

Gavin, Gawain, Gauvain • Celtic • *unknown root*

Geming • Chinese • *radical revolution*

Gershom, Gershorn, Gersham • Biblical/Jewish/Hebrew • *a stranger there*

Gesualdo • Germanic • *I pledge to rule*

Gethin, Gethen, Cethin • British/Welsh • *dark, dusky, exotic*

Gilbert, Gib, Gibb, Gilberto • Germanic/Frankish/Roman Catholic • *he who pledges or sacrifices his life for greater things*

Gideon • Hebrew/Jewish • *he who cuts someone down to size*

Giulio • Latin • *old Roman family name with vague origins*

Gladstone, Glaedstan • Anglo-Saxon • *the stone where the red kite lands*

Gobbán • Irish Gaelic • *blacksmith*

Goronwy, Gronw • British/Welsh • *uncertain origin but by legend an adulterous murderer*

Grant, Grand, Grande • Anglo-Saxon/Norman • *a large, portly person*

Gregory, Gregorios, Gregor, Greg, Gregg, Greig, Greagoir, Griogair, Grigor, Joris, Greger, Gregers, Grégoire, Gregorio, Grigori, Grzegorz, Rehor, Grgur, Reijo, Gergely, Grigor • Greek • *watchful*

Gumersindo • Spanish/Visigothic • *path of man*

Gunther, Gunter, Gunnar, Gunder, Gunne, Gunni • Germanic • *the army brings strife and lays the land waste*

Guowei • Chinese • *status quo*

Gwalchmai • British/Welsh • *plain of the hawks or ospreys*

Gwynedd • British/Welsh • *happiness or named after the British Welsh princedom of Gwynedd, based on Snowdonia area where the ancient Brits (Welsh) fought the Anglo-Saxons in guerrilla warfare*

Haakon, Håkon, Hagen, Håkan • Norse/Germanic • *high-born son, relative, like a horse/fort, stockade*

Hādi • Arabic • *mentor, guru, reflective and spiritual*

Hall, Heall, Halle, Halldor, Hallstein, Halstein, Halsten, Hallsten • *rock*

Halldor • Norse • *rock, name of God of Thunder*

Halvard, Halvor, Hallvard, Hallvor, Halvar • Scandinavian • *defender like a rock*

Hamish, James, Sheumais, Seumas

• Scots Gaelic • *supplanter, a cuckoo in the nest! Edging out someone to take their place against their will*

Hamza, Hamzah • Arabic • *strong, unmoved*

Hank, Hankin • Norman/English • *mixed roots; short form of Jehan, John or Henry*

Hari • Sanskrit • *pet name for Vishnu or Krishna, preservation of the universe*

Harinder • Sikh • *Hari (Vishnu) and Indra, the supreme god*

Harlan, Harland, Harley • English/American • *grey rock or fields where the hares run*

Hartmann, • Germanic • *hard man!*

Hārūn, Aaron • Arabic • *mountain of strength*

Hāshim • Arabic • *crusher, breaks bread*

Hawk, Hauk, Hawke, Hafoc, Hawkeye • Anglo-Saxon/English • *bird of prey*

Haydn, Heiden, Heidano, Hayden, Haydon • Germanic • *heathen or pagan*

Haytham • Arabic • *young eagle*

Heber, Éibhear • Irish Gaelic/Biblical/Jewish/Hebrew • *an enclave, a ghetto*

Hector, Hektor, Ekhain, Eachann, Eachdonn • Greek/Scots Gaelic • *restrained, holds himself back, brown horse*

Heilyn, Ynheilio • British/Welsh • *steward, keeper of the cellars*

Heng • Chinese • *eternal, forever*

Hermenigild, Hermengildo, Emengildo • Spanish/Visigothic • *a total sacrifice*

Hishām • Arabic • *crusher (as in sacred bread) and giver*

Horace, Horatius, Horatio • Etruscan • *Roman family name with no certain root*

Horatio, Horatius, Horace • Etruscan • *Roman family name with no certain root*

Hosea • African American • *salvation*

Hudson, Hudde, Richard • Anglo-Saxon • *strong and powerful; confused origin; pet name of Richard*

Hunter • American/English • *a person involved in all aspects of hunting*

Hyacinth, Hyakinthos • Greek/English • *love and passion*

Hywel, Hywell, Howell • British/Welsh • *conspicuous by his eminence*

Iago, Jacob, James • Biblical • *supplanter, a cuckoo in the nest! Edging out someone to take their place against their will*

Iarlaithe, Jarlath • Irish • *vague origins but maybe chief, leader*

Ib, Jepp, Jacob • Scandinavian • *supplanter, a cuckoo in the nest! Edging out someone to take their place against their will*

Ibrāhīm, Abraham • Arabic • *father of the tribes or nations*

Idris • British/Welsh • *a passionate loving lord or lord of passion and desire*

Ifor, Ivor • British/Welsh • *no known origin but may be linked to the yew tree*

Igal • Biblical/Hebrew/Jewish • *redeemer*

Ignazio, Ignatius, Ignus, Ignace, Ignaz, Egnatius, Ignati, Ignacio • Latin/Estruscan • *Roman family name of uncertain roots*

Igor, Ivor, Ifor, Yherr • Russian/ Scandinavians • *the army with archers who shoot with bows of yew*

Indalecio, Indoletius • Latin • *unknown origin*

Inderjit • Sanskrit • *victor of Indra*

Ingram, Engelram • Norman/Norse • *Norman family name after the Viking fertility god, Ing and his pet raven*

Ingvar, Yngvar • Norse • *warrior god who brings fertility and male potency*

Inigo • Spanish • *Roman family name, no known roots*

Iorwerth, Iolo, Iolyn, Yorath • British/Welsh • *a handsome, beautiful lord or chief*

Ira • Hebrew/Jewish • *vigilant, observant, watchful*

Irvine, Irvin, Erwin, Irving, Israel • British/Welsh • *fresh, clear water*

Isaiah, Izzy, Isaïe • Biblical/Jewish/ Hebrew • *God is salvation*

Iser, Iserl, Issur • Jewish/Yiddish • *he who strives with God*

Isidore, Izzy, Izzie, Isidoros, Isidor, Isidro, Isidoro • Greek/Egyptian • *a gift from the goddess Isis, deity of magic and life*

Israel, Jacob • Biblical/Jewish/ Hebrew • *he who strives with God*

Ivar, Iver • Scandinavian • *archer warrior whose bow is made of yew*

Ivo, Yves, Ivon • Germanic • *yew tree*

Ivor, Ifor, Yherr, Iobhar, Iomhar • Scandinavian/Norse • *the army with archers who shoot with bows of yew*

Jabez • Biblical/Jewish/Hebrew • *I bear him with sorrow, sorrowful*

Jacinto, Hyakinthos, Hyacinthe •

Greek/Spanish • *love and passion*

James, Iacomus, Jago, Jaime, Jamie, Jim, Jamey, Jimmy, Jimmie, Séamas, Séamus, Seumas, Seumus, Hamish, Jaume, Jacques, Jaume, Jaimes, Giacomo, Jameson, Jamieson, Jamey, Jamee, Jami, Jaimie, Jem, Jacobus • Biblical/ Latin • *supplanter, a cuckoo in the nest! Edging out someone to take their place against their will*

Jagannath • Sanskrit • *Lord of the World, Vishnu, as in sacred Puri*

Jagdish • Sanskrit • *ruler of the world, Brahma, Vishnu and Shiva*

Jagjit • Sanskrit • *conqueror of the world*

Jamāl • Arabic • *physically, drop-dead gorgeous*

Javan, Jevon, Jeavon, Jeevon • Biblical/Hebrew/Jewish • *wine*

Javed • Persian • *eternal*

Jayakrishna • Sanskrit • *victorious Krishna*

Jayant • Sanskrit • *victorious son of Indra*

Jayashanka • Sanskrit • *victorious Shiva*

Jeffrey, Geoffrey, Jeff, Geoff, Jefferson, Jeffery, Jeffry, Jep • Anglo-Saxon • *a stranger in your own land or foreigner who pledges allegiance*

Jenson, John, Jan • English • *son of Jan or John*

Jim, Jimmy, James • English • *supplanter, a cuckoo in the nest! Edging out someone to take their place against their will*

Jitendra, Jitender, Jitinder • Sanskrit • *all-powerful, all-mighty, in control*

Job, Joby, Jobey • Biblical/Jewish/

Hebrew • *persecuted*

Jordan, Judd, Hayarden • Hebrew/ Jewish • *flowing down*

Joshua, Josh • Biblical/Hebrew/ Jewish • *God is my salvation*

Julián, Jules, Julianus, Julius, Julyan, Jolyon, Julien, Julio, Jools • Latin • *old Roman family name with vague origins*

Junaid • Muslim/Sufi • *in honour of a holy mystic*

Kedar • African American • *mighty, dark*

Keiran, Ciarán • Irish Gaelic • *black*

Kelsey, Ceolsige • Anglo-Saxon • *ship of victory*

Kelvin, Kelvyn • Scots/English • *if you come from Kelvinside, Glasgow or by the river, this is the root of the name*

Kenneth, Ken, Cinaed, Cainnech, Coinneach, Kennith, Kenny, Cenydd, Canice, Canicius, Cainneach • Latin/ English/Gaelic • *handsome, gorgeous, pleasing to the eye and rather adorable!*

Kenelm, Cenehelm • Anglo-Saxon • *he who is a bold and assertive warrior protected by his magic helmet*

Kennedy, Cinnéidigh • Irish Gaelic • *ugly head*

Kevin, Caioimhin, Keven, Kevan, Kevyn, Caoimhean • English/ Irish Gaelic • *beloved, beautiful, enchanting*

Khālid • Arabic • *indestructible*

Kieran, Ciarán • Irish Gaelic • *black*

Kjell, Keld, Kjetil, Kjeld, Ketill, Ketil • *sacred kettle or cauldron*

Knut, Cnut, Knud • Norse • *a knot or man who is short, squat and stocky*

Kondrati, Quadratus • *a person with a figure like a square*

Korbinian, Corvus, Hraban • Latin/ Frankish • *raven*

Krishna, Kishen, Kistna • Sanskrit • *black, dark, intense*

Kyran, Kieran, Ciarán • modern/ Irish Gaelic • *black*

Lancelot, Lance • British Welsh/ Celtic mythology • *unknown origin but name given to a famous knight of King Arthur's Round Table*

Lasairióna, Lassarina, Lasrina • Irish Gaelic • *flame red-coloured wine*

Leannán, Lennan, Lennon • Irish Gaelic • *fairy lover, fairy darling*

Lennon, Leannain • Irish Gaelic • *fairy lover, fairy darling*

Lester, Ligoracaester, Ligoracastra • Anglo-Saxon • *the place of the Roman fort on the River Soar*

Lewis, Lewie, Lou, Louis, Lew • Anglo-Saxon/Germanic Frankish • *someone who gains fame through waging war and conflict; a hero, he who vanquishes and is revered*

Liam, Ulliam, William • Irish Gaelic/Norman • *willpower, with a helmet, possibly magic, to give divine protection*

Lincoln, Lindum • British/Welsh • *Roman fort by the lake*

Liu • Chinese • *flowing*

Lleu, Lugg, Lughus, Lugh • British/ Welsh • *dark, bright and shining*

Lomán • Irish • *bare*

Lope, Lupus • Latin • *wolf*

Lorcán • Irish Gaelic • *fierce and fiery*

Louie, Louis, Lewie, Lewi, Lou, Luthais, Ludwig, Lodewijk, Ludvig,

Lovis, Luis, Lluis, Luigi, Lodovico, Lutz, Ludwig, Ludvig, Ludwik, Luthais • Germanic/Frankish • *a person who gains fame through waging war; a hero who vanquishes the enemy and is revered by his people*

Lovell, Louvel, Lou • Norman • *wolf cub*

Ludovic, Ludovik, Ludovicus, Hludwig, Maoldomhnaich, Ludo, Ludwig, Lutz • Germanic

Lyall, Lisle, Liulf • Norse • *vague origins and wolf*

Lycerius, Licerio • Latin • *possibly light or wolf*

Madison, Madde, Madeleine, Maud • American English • *son of Maud or Matilda, the battleaxe*

Maitland, Maltalent, Mautalent, Mautalant • Anglo-Saxon/Norman • *bad-tempered or from Mautalant, a barren place in France*

Mallory, Mallery, Malheure, Malerie • Norman • *unhappy or unfortunate one*

Mani, Subrahmanya • Sanskrit • *jewel with potent qualities; the penis*

Manlio, Manlius • Latin • *Roman family name; no known root but famous for republican leanings*

Marcel, Marcellus, Marcus, Marcellin, Marcello, Marcelino, Marcelo • Latin • *named after Mars, God of Sex and War*

March, Marche, Mensis • Norman • *a person who lives on the borders or the Marches, or named after the God of War and Sex, Mars*

Marcus, Markus, Mark • Latin • *named after Mars, God of Sex and War*

Mark, Marcus, Marc, Marco, **Marcas, Markus, Marcos, Marek, Marko, Markku** • Latin • *named after Mars, God of Sex and War*

Marlon, Marclon • Latin/Norman • *named after Mars, God of Sex and War*

Martin, Martyn, Martinus, Martis, Marty, Mairtin, Maratan, Martainn, Merten, Maarten, Martijn, Morten, Mårten, Martinho, Martino,Marcin, Martti, Marton, Marty, Marti • Latin/English • *named after Mars, God of Sex and War*

Maurice, Moris, Morris, Mo, Maurus, Moritz, Maurizio, Mauricius, Mavriki, Mauricio, Maurits, • Latin • *a dark swarthy person as in a Moor from Arabia*

Mauro • Latin • *a Moor as in Arab; early followers of St Benedictine*

Maxwell, Max • Anglo-Saxon • *the well of Magnus or Mack, a great man*

Medardo • Germanic • *personal name plus a strong, hard chap*

Meinhard • Germanic • *strong as a rock*

Melvin, Melvyn, Mel, Melvin, Melville, Melvyn, Malleville • *a man from a bad place*

Meredith, Meredydd, Maredudd, Meredudd • *uncertain beginning but ends with Lord*

Myrddin, Merlyn, Merlin • British/Welsh • *sea fort or sea hill*

Methodius, Mefodi • Greek • *following the path or road, spiritual as much as a traveller*

Meurig, Mauricius, Mouric, Meuric, Maurice • British/Welsh • *a dark swarthy person as in a Moor from Arabia*

Mordecai, Motke, Motl, Marduk • Biblical/Persian

Morgan, Morgannwg, Morcant •
British/Welsh • *vague beginning but
ends with ending, completion, full
circle*

Morley, Morleah • *a clearing or
wood by the marsh or in the swamp*

Morris, Maurice, Mo, Miuris •
English/Latin

Mortimer, Mortemer, Muiriartach •
Norman • *dead sea or stagnant lake*

Motke, Mordecai, Motl • Biblical/
Jewish/Yiddish • *he who worships
the God of Magic and Water,
Marduk*

Mstislav • Slavic • *vengeance brings
glory*

Muirgheas, Maurice, Muiris • Irish
Gaelic • *if I had a choice I'd choose
the sea*

Mukesh • Sanskrit • *Shiva, the
conqueror of the wild boar/pig
demon God*

Murchadh, Murrough • Irish Gaelic
• *sea battle or war*

Myron • Greek • *the embalming
spice, myrrh*

Nagendra • Sanskrit • *good god
amongst the snakes and elephants*

Nanne, Nannulf, Anders •
Scandinavian/Norse • *daring, audacious wolf*

Naoise • Irish • *vague; in legend the
lover of Deirdre was Naoise*

Naphtali • Biblical/Hebrew/Jewish •
wrestling or wrestler

Napoleon, Napoleone • Italian •
*unsure origin; may mean sons of the
mist or the Naples Lion*

Narayan, Narain • Sanskrit • *destiny
of man; son of creation*

**Narcissus, Narkissos, Narcisse,
Narciso** • Greek/Latin • *linked with*

the daffodil but unsure origins

Narendra • Sanskrit • *shaman,
witchdoctor, doctor king*

Nasr, Nasser • Arabic • *winner takes
all*

Neal, Neil, Neale, Nigel, Niall •
Irish Gaelic/English • *passionate,
champion, winner, dead sexy, really
desirable; some say it means a man
who cannot be monogamous*

Ned, Edward • Anglo-Saxon • *a
careful, prudent ruler who looks after
his riches and possessions*

Nelson, Nell, Neil • English •
*passionate, champion, winner,
dead sexy, really desirable; some
say it means a man who cannot be
monogamous*

Neopmuk • Czech • *someone
from the town of Pomuk; St John of
Pomuk, patron saint of Bohemia;
especially 28th October*

Nestor, Nestore • Greek • *personal
name of King of Pylos in legend, one
of the Greeks (bearing gifts!) at Troy*

Niall, Neal, Neale, Nile, Niles, Neil
• Gaelic • *passionate, champion,
winner, dead sexy, really desirable;
some say it means means a man who
cannot be monogamous or who is
vague or cloudy in life*

Niallghus, Niallgus • Irish Gaelic •
*a man who is a strong and powerful
champion*

Niaz • Persian • *prayer, gift, sacrifice*

Nigel, Nigellus, Nihel, Neil •
Latin/English • *black as pitch or
passionate, dead sexy, really desirable; but may mean a man who
cannot be monogamous*

Nikita, Aniketos • Greek/Russian
• *unconquered; name of Orthodox
saint*

Nizār • Arabic • *confused origin;
might mean small or little one*
Nolasco • Latin • *personal name
honouring the man who rescued the
Christians from the Moslems during
the Crusade*

Oded • Jewish/Hebrew • *he who
encourages or persuades, compelling*
Ottwolf, Otwolf • Germanic • *rich
wolf*
Ove, Aghi • Norse • *frightened or in
awe of a weapon of terror*

**Pancras, Pankratios, Pancrazio,
Pancraz, Pankrati** • Greek •
all-powerful
Pearce, Pierce, Perais • Norman •
the rock or stone
**Peter, Pete, Petros, Peadar, Pedr,
Piet, Pieter, Per, Petter, Par, Pierre,
Pedro, Perico, Pere, Pietro, Piero,
Pyotr, Piotr, Petr, Petar, Pekka,
Peitari, Peteris, Petras, Petrus,
Petya, Pette, Pedr, Pier** • Greek •
the rock or stone
**Phineas, Fineas, Panhsj, Phinehas,
Pinchas** • Hebrew/Jewish/Biblical •
*a person from Nubia, now southern
Egypt or northern Sudan, or from
the snake's mouth*
Phoenix, Phoinix • Latin/Greek •
*mythical bird that represents rebirth
or reincarnation*
Pompeo, Pompeius • Latin •
*Roman family name; with no known
origins*
Pontius, Ponzio, Poncio • Latin •
family name; origin unknown
Pran • Sanskrit • *vitality, life breath
and force*

Qiqiang • *enlightenment and
strength*
Qiu • Chinese • *autumn or fall*
Quan • Chinese • *hot springs*

Ralph, Rafe, Raulf, Ralf, Raoul, Raul
• Scandinavian/Germanic • *wolf
counsel*
Ramadān • Arabic • *ninth month of
the Muslim calendar: the hot month*
Ramesh • Sanskrit • *night time
tranquillity and serenity; sleep*
Rameshwar, Ramnath • Sanskrit •
Lord Rama
Ramsay, Ramsa, Ramsey • Anglo-
Saxon • *island of wild garlic*
**Randall, Randell, Randal, Randel,
Randle, Randy** • Germanic/Norman
• *rim of a shield, wolf*
**Randolf, Randolph, Randy,
Randulf** • Germanic • *rim of a
shield, wolf*
Ranulf, Reginulf, Ran, Reginulf
• Norse • *adviser or counsellor to
wolves*
Rául, Ralph • Spanish • *wolf counsel*
Raven, Rafn, Raefn • Anglo-Saxon/
Norse • *Odin's winged friend, the
Raven*
**Rémy, Remigius, Remi, Remigio,
Remix** • Latin • *oarsman or man at
the tiller*
Renato, Renatus • Latin • *reborn*
René, Renatus, Renato • Latin •
reborn; resurrected
Rhys, Reece, Rees • British/Welsh •
ardent, dead sexy
**Richard, Rich, Rick, Dick, Ricky,
Rickie, Dicky, Dickie, Richie,
Ristéard, Ruiseart, Rhisiart,
Rikhart, Rikhard, Ricardo,
Riccardo, Ryszard, Rihard, Rikard,
Rihards, Ritchie, Rhisiart, Hudson,**

Hudde • Germanic/Norman • *strong, brave and powerful*

Rolf, Rodwulf, Rudolf, Rollo, Rodolfo • Germanic • *famed wolf*

Rollo, Roul, Rolf • Norman • *famed wolf*

Rong • Chinese • *martial and aggressive*

Rudolf, Rudolphus, Rodwulf, Rolf, Rudolph, Rudy, Rudi, Rodolphe, Rudy, Rudolf, Rodolf, Hrodwolf, Rodolpho • Germanic • *famed wolf*

Samīr, Sameer • Arabic • *confidant at night, a night conversation*

Sandalio, Sandalius, Sandallius, Sandal • Spanish/Visigothic • *true wolf*

Sanjeev • Sanskrit • *reviving, resuscitating*

Santiago, Iago, Jacobus, James • Spanish • *supplanter, a cuckoo in the nest! Edging out someone to take their place against their will*

Séaghdha • Irish Gaelic • *like a hawk, fine and goodly*

Séamus, Shamus, Séamas, James, Seumas • Gaelic • *supplanter, a cuckoo in the nest! Edging out someone to take their place against their will*

Seán, Shane, Shaughan, Shaughn, Shaun, Shawn • Irish Gaelic/English • *supplanter, a cuckoo in the nest! Edging out someone to take their place against their will*

Serge, Sergio, Sergius • Latin/Etruscan • *old Roman family name with vague roots*

Sergei, Serzha • Russian/Etruscan • *old Roman name of vague roots*

Severiano, Severus, Severo, Severinus, Sören, Severinus,

Severino, Seve • Latin • *Roman family name meaning stern, austere*

Shah • Muslim/Persian/Sufi • *king, god, lord, emperor, divine mystic*

Shen • Chinese • *intense, deep and wary*

Shiva • Sanskrit • *beautiful, timely, death and regeneration*

Shyam • Sanskrit • *dark, black and handsome, sexy*

Simran • Sikh • *he who meditates, yogic*

Sly • American English • *a person who is full of guile and basically sly as a fox!*

Sondre, Sindri • Norse/Norwegian • *no known origins but in Norse mythology a magical dwarf*

Stacey, Eustace • English/Greek • *confused roots; could mean juicy, tasty grapes!*

Stein, Steyne, Sten, Steen, Steinn • Norse

Stuart, Stewart, Stu, Stew • French • *primarily a surname given to a person who served as a steward in a big house, manor or palace*

Stone, Stan • Anglo-Saxon • *stone*

Sture, Stura • Scandinavian/Swedish • *wilful, contrary, independent spirit*

Sumanjit • Sanskrit • *he who conquerors the demon Sumana*

Surendra, Surinder • Sanskrit • *the most powerful of the gods*

Suresh • Sanskrit • *ruler of the gods*

Surjit • Sanskrit • *he who has conquered the gods*

Talbot, Talbod, Tal • Germanic/Frankish/Norman • *a personal name meaning to destroy despatches (messages)*

Tanner • American English • *a person who cleans and tans hides*

Tasgall, Taskill, Asketill • Norse • *the sacred pot or cauldron*

Tate • English • *a personal name from medieval times, no known root*

Terrell, Tyrell • Norman • *a person who is hard to pull this way or that, very fixed!*

Tirso, Thyrsos • Oriental • *follower of Dionysus (Bacchus)*

Titus, Tito, Tiziano, Titianus, Titian • Latin • *old Roman name, unknown origins*

Tony, Anthony, Tone, Tönjes, Antonius, Tonio • Etruscan/Roman • *Roman family name but with confused origins*

Torcall, Torquil • Norse • *the sacrificial or sacred cauldron of Thor, the God of Thunder*

Tore, Ture • Norse • *a man like the god Thor*

Tormod, Torrmod • Norse • *a man with the courage of Thor, the God of Thunder*

Toribio, Turibius • Latin/Spanish • *unknown roots; very local Iberian name*

Torolf, Torulf, Torolv • Norse • *god Thor with the strength of a wolf*

Torquil, Torkel, Thorkel, Torkild, Torkjell, Torkil • Norse • *sacred kettle or cauldron*

Torsten, Torstein, Thorstein, Thorsteinn • Norse • *the god Thor with the strength of a stone*

Torvald, Thorwald • Norse • *ruler with the power of Thor*

Tory, Torir, Thor, Thori, Thorir • Norse/Danish • *Thor*

Toussaint • French • *tous les saints; a child who has the blessings of all the saints; particularly 31st October or 1st November*

Trahaearn, Traherne • British/Welsh • *iron*

Tristan, Trystan, Tristram, Tristam, Trystram, Tristram, Dristan, Drystan • British/Welsh • *rowdy, rebellious, blue, melancholic, chaotic*

Tullio, Tullius • Latin • *a Roman family name with hidden origins*

Tybalt, Theobald • Germanic • *a tribe of people known for their boldness in the face of adversity*

Tyrell, Tyrrell, Tirel, Terrell • *a person who is hard to pull this way or that, very fixed!*

Tyson, Ty, Tison • Greek/Norman • *girl's name for Dionysius, God of Wine or meaning a hot-tempered person*

Ùisdean, Eysteinn, Hugh, Hùisdean • Irish Gaelic • *a man who is forever unchanging like a stone*

Ulf, Uffe, Ulv • Norse • *wolf*

Ulric, Wulfric, Ulrick, Ulrich, Utz • Germanic/Anglo-Saxon • *power and riches; wolf power*

Ulysses, Odyseus, Odyssesthai, Ulick, Ulisse, Ulises • Greek/Latin • *a person who hates*

Uwe • Germanic/Norse • *sharp blade, in awe*

Uzi • Jewish/Hebrew • *power and might*

Vadim, Vladimir • Russian • *origin unknown*

Vance, Van • Anglo-Saxon • *meaning fenland or marshland*

Vasco, Velasco, Belasco, Velásquez • Spanish/Basque • *crow*

Viggo, Vigge • Norse • *a personal name meaning warlike*

Vijay • Sanskrit • *prizes or booty from victory*

Vikram, Vik • Sanskrit • *hero*

Vinayak • Sanskrit • *demonic*

Vincent, Vince, Vincens, Vincentis, Vinnie, Uinseann, Vinzenz, Vicente, Vicenc, Vincenzo, Wincenty, Vincenc, Vinko, Vincentas, Vinzenz, Vincente • Latin • *to conquer*

Vishnu • Sanskrit • *joint conqueror of demon Vrtra*

Vissarion, Bessarion • Greek • *origins vague*

Vladimir, Volodya, Valdemar, Waldemar • Slavic • *great, famous leader or ruler*

Vladislav • Slavic • *glorious leader or ruler*

Volk, Wolf, Volkhard • Germanic • *strong people*

Vsevolod, Pancras • Russian • *rules over all*

Walid • Arabic • *newly born or reborn*

Wei • Chinese • *impressive strength and energy leading to greatness*

Wieland • Germanic • *war land*

Wilbur, Willburh • Anglo-Saxon • *he who has the will to build a fort or protected village*

Willard, Will Wilheard • Anglo-Saxon • *a person with tremendous willpower, powerful in every way*

William, Wilhelm, Will, Bill, Willy, Willie, Billy, Willis, Wilmot, Ulliam, Uilleam, Gwilym, Willem, Willi, Vilhelm, Vilhjalm, Guillaume, Guillermo, Guillem, Guilherme, Guglielmo, Vilem, Viljem, Vilmos,

Vilhelmas, Vilhelms, Wim • Germanic/Norman • *his helmet gives him magical protection and the will to win*

Willibald • Germanic • *will, bold and brave*

Willibrand • Germanic • *will and flaming sword*

Wilmer, Wilmaer • Anglo-Saxon • *he is famous for his willpower and strength of character*

Wilmot, Willmott, William • Germanic/Norman • *pet name for William*

Wilson, Will • English • *son of William*

Wolf, Wulf, Wolfe • Germanic • *wolf*

Wolfgang, Wolf, Volf • Germanic • *where the wolf goes*

Wolfger, Wolf • Germanic • *wolf spear*

Wolfram, Wolf • Germanic • *wolf raven*

Wystan, Wigstan • Anglo-Saxon • *memorial stone where the battle was fought*

Xiabo • Chinese • *little fighter*

Yigael • Jewish/Hebrew • *he shall be redeemed*

Yi • Chinese • *sure and resolute*

Yingjie • Chinese • *hero, courageous, brave*

Yongnian • Chinese • *eternity, forever*

York, Yorke, Jorvik • Anglo-Saxon/Norse • *boar or pig farm*

Yves, Ive, Ivo, Ivon • French Germanic • *yew tree*

Zane • American English • *unknown roots of British surname*

Zedong • Chinese • *east of the marshes*

Zeev, Wolf, Binyamin, Benjamin • Jewish/Hebrew • *wolf: the symbol of the tribe of Binyamin or Benjamin as given by his father Jacob on his deathbed*

Zephaniah, Zep • Biblical/Jewish/Hebrew • *hidden by God*

Zhiqiang • Chinese • *strength of will*

Zhong • Chinese • *steadfast and devoted*

Zihao • Chinese • *heroic son*

Zoab • Nigerian • *strong, brave*

Girls

Acacia, Akakia, Wattle • Greek/ Latin • *acacia wood, holy wood that had special powers as a hex against evil*

Addolorata • Italian • *Our Lady (Virgin Mary) of Sorrows*

Agrippina, Agrafena • Latin/ Estruscan • *family name of old Roman family with no known roots*

Aileen, Eileen, Ailie • Irish Gaelic • *desired by others*

Ailsa, Ealasaid, Alfsigesey • Norse • *elfin victory, supernatural powers*

Aimee, Aimi • French • *beloved one*

Aisling, Aislin, Aislinn • *she who has visionary dreams*

Alaina, Alana, Alayna, Alanna, Alannah, Alanah, Allana, Alanda, Alanis, Ailin • Gaelic • *vague origins but likely to be a rock*

Alba • Latin/Germanic • *white or elfin*

Alfreda, Freddie, Fred • Anglo-Saxon • *supernatural, faerie counsel, help*

Allana, Alana Gaelic • vague origins but likely to be a rock

Althea, Althaia • Greek • *uncertain origin*

Althena • modern • *a combo of Althea and Athene*

Amanda, Miranda, Manda, Mandy • Latin • *she is fit to be adored and armoured ready for attack!*

Amāni • Arabic • *desire, passion*

Amber, Ambar • Latin/Arabic • *beautiful golden-coloured fossilised resin*

Amelia, Emelia, Emilia, Amélie • Latin • *rival, competitor*

Amrit • Sanskrit • *divine, immortal, good enough to eat*

Amy, Amie, Aimie, Aimee • Norman • *beloved*

Anastasis, Anastasia • Greek/ Russian • *resurrection*

Andra, André, Andrea, Andriana, Andrine, Andy, Andree, Anndra • Biblical/Greek • *a sexy person*

Angustias • Spanish/Roman Catholic • *Our Lady of Sufferings*

Anona, Annona • Latin • *unsure root but possibly corn supply*

Antonia, Anthonia • Estruscan/ Roman • *Roman family name but with confused origins*

Antigone • Greek • *contrary, the antithesis, born against the odds or contrary to conditions*

Antoinette, Toinette, Tonette, Antonella, Antonia, Toni, Antonina • Estruscan/Roman • *Roman family name but with confused origins*

Anwyl, Annwyl • British/Welsh • *beloved, darling, dear*

Aparición • Roman Catholic • *Christ's appearance to the disciples after Easter's resurrection*

Arantxa, Arancha, Aranzazu • Basque • *place name meaning thorn bush*

Arlene, Arleen, Arline, Marlene, Charlene • American English • *unknown origin*

Arlette • Germanic/Norman • *uncertain roots but possibly eagle*

Armelle, Artmael • Breton Celtic • *a female chief who is as steady as a rock*

Aisling, Aishling • Irish Gaelic • *a dream, vision or premonition*

Assumpta, Assunta, Asunción • Latin • *the assumption of the Virgin*

Mary into heaven
Aubree • Germanic/Anglo-Saxon/
Latin • *she who has the power of the*
faeries
Audra, Audrey, Audrie, Audry,
Audrina • Anglo-Saxon • *strength*
and noble of character
Autumn, Autumnus • Latin • *a*
season of the year
Ava, Avaline, Aveline, Avelina,
Evelyn, Eveline, Avila, Avis, Avice •
Greek • *desired*
Aveline, Eibhlín, Ailbhilin, Ellin,
Eileen • French/Irish Gaelic •
desired by others
Avery • Norman/Anglo-Saxon •
supernatural, faerie favours
Avis, Aveza • Germanic/Norman •
unknown root
'Azza • Arabic • *pride and power*

Becca, Beck, Becky, Bekki,
Rébecca, Bex • Biblical/Jewish/
Aramaic • *unknown origins; many*
suggestions, from cattle stall to snare
Bérénice, Bernice, Binnie, Bearnas,
Berenike, Pherenike • Greek/
Macedonian • *personal name:*
bringer of victory
Billie • Germanic/Norman • *her*
helmet gives her magical protection
and the will to win
Bodil, Bothild, Botilda • Norse •
compensation for the battle
Borghild • Norwegian • *fortified for*
the battle
Branwen, Bronwen, Brangwen •
British/Welsh • *raven or beast that*
is holy, sacred and white
Brandy, Brandyewijn • Dutch/
Anglo-Saxon • *distilled wine or the*
hill filled with a shrub called broom
Brenna, Braonan • American

English/Irish Gaelic • *descendant*
of Braonan; meaning moist, droplet
of water
Briar, Briony, Bryony, Bryonia •
Anglo-Saxon/Greek • *a thorny plant*
or shrub
Brie, Bracia, Bree • Latin/Australian
English • *marshland rather than soft*
cheese
Brónach, Bronagh • Irish Gaelic •
sad and sorrowful

Cameron • Gaelic • *crooked nose*
Cassandra, Cassie, Kassie, Cass,
Cassy, Cassidy • Greek mythology
Cecilia, Cécile, Cecily, Cecelia,
Cissie, Cissey, Sessy, Sissi, Sissy,
Cecille, Cecilie, Cacille, Cacilia,
Caecilia, Cicely • Latin/English • *old*
Roman family name Caecilius, from
the Latin, meaning blind
Chantal, Chantelle, Shantell •
French • *in honour of St Jeanne-*
Françoise, a woman of great
charity and virtue who married the
Baron de Chantal; when he died
she adopted a severe religious life
following St Francis of Sales
Chardonnay • modern • *French/*
English • a variety of grape that
makes the wine Chardonnay
Charna, Cherna, Charnke,
Charnele, Charnelle, Chernke,
Chernele • Jewish/Yiddish • *dark,*
black
Chausika • Swahili • *of the night*
Cherith, Cheryth • Biblical • *a dry*
riverbed at a place called Cherith
Chloe, Chloris, Cloris, Khloris,
Khloe • Greek • *another name for*
the Goddess of Fertility, Demeter or
Ceres
Ciara • Irish Gaelic • *black one*

Cindy, Cynthia, Lucinda, Cendrillon, Sindy, Cinderella • French • *cinders from the fire*

Claudia, Claudine, Claude, Claudinia, Claudette, Klavdia • Latin • *from the old Roman family name Claudius, with no confirmed origins*

Clelia, Cloelia • Latin • *a heroine, part true, part fantasy, she was a hostage who escaped back to Rome by swimming the River Tiber*

Clematis, Klematis, Clem, Clemmie • Greek • *climbing plant or vine, meaning twig or branch*

Clodagh • Irish Gaelic • *a river in County Tipperary*

Clothilde • Germanic • *famed through war and battles*

Cruz • Roman Catholic • *cross, meaning Mary, Christ's mother, in agony at the foot of the cross; her son's crucifixion*

Crystal, Chrystalle, Chrystall, Krystallos, Krystal, Kristel, Krystle • Greek • *ice*

Cyd, Syd, Sidney • Anglo-Saxon • *an ait, a small island in a river or a wide river meadow*

Daiyu • Chinese • *black jade*

Damayanti • Sanskrit • *she has a hold over men, she can sedate them*

Dana, Ana • Irish Gaelic • *name of an ancient Celtic fertility goddess, especially in Ireland*

Danae • Greek mythology • *her great-grandfather founded the Greek tribe of Danai or Argives; she was raped by Zeus/Jupiter when he appeared to her as a shower of gold, and she gave birth to the hero Perseus*

Dareen, Darrene • American/English • *unknown origins*

Dassa, Dassah, Hadassah, Esther • Hebrew/Persian/Jewish • *Myrtle, Star and Persian Goddess of Fertility, Love and War, Ishtar*

Delilah, Delila • Biblical • *uncertain origins*

Denise, Denese, Denice, Deneze, Deniece, Dionysia • Greek • *Dionysus, God of Wine, Orgies and Partying*

Desdemona, Dysdaimon, Mona • Greek/Latin • *unfortunate stars*

Destiny, Destinata, Destry, Destinie, Destiney, Destinee • Latin/Norman • *power of fate*

Dolores, Deloris, Delores, Doloris, Lola, Lolita, Dolly • Roman Catholic • *Our Lady of the Seven Sorrows of the Virgin*

Domitilla, Domitius • Latin • *a Roman imperial family name with no known roots*

Donla, Dunnflaith • *brown lady*

Drew • Biblical/Greek/Scots English • *a real sexy person*

Drusilla, Drausus, Drasus • Latin • *from the old Roman family name with no known origins*

Durga • Sanskrit • *out of bounds, off limits, inaccessible*

Dusty, Dustie, Dustee • Norse • *Thor, God of Thunder's stone*

Ebba • Germanic • *boar or pig*

Ernestine, Ernestina, Earnestine, Earnestina • *serious in all things and will fight to the death; means business to the point of obsession*

Ebony, Ebenos, Ebenius, Ebenos • Greek/Latin/American English • *a very black wood*

Edith, Eden, Edun, Edon, Edie, Edyth, Edythe, Eadgyth • Anglo-Saxon • *prosperity, riches and strife or war, possibly she who gains her wealth through the booty of war*

Edwina, Edwardina • Anglo-Saxon • *a person who guards her riches, blessed with wealth*

Ehrentraud, Arntraut • Germanic • *with strength goes honour, or she has the strength of an eagle*

Eiddwen, Eiddunwen • British/Welsh • *fond, passionate, desire, holy, white, fair*

Eileen, Aileen, Eibhlín, Eilín • Norman French • *desired by others*

Eimear, Émer, Eimh • Irish Gaelic • *vague origins but comes from the word for swift, the bird, describing a person who is fast and quick*

Eleri • British/Welsh • *unknown root; might be a river name*

Eléanor, Alienor, Ellenor, Elinor, Elenor, Nell, Ellen, Nellie, Nelly, Eleanora, Eléonore • Germanic/Frankish/Provençal • *prefix means foreign or stranger, the suffix is unknown*

Ellen, Helen, Elin, Elen, Ella, Elena, Nell, Nelly, Nellie, Ellena, Ellenor • modern English • *shortened form of Helen and Eleanor*

Elkan, Elkie, Elkanah • Jewish/Hebrew • *possessed by God*

Ellie, Elly, Eilidh, Ailie • Germanic/Frankish/Provençal • *short for Eleanor*

Elfleda, Aethelflaed • Anglo-Saxon • *supernatural strength or power*

Elvina, Alvina • Anglo-Saxon • *elfin, noble or faerie friend*

Emeny, Emonie, Ismene • Germanic/Greek mythology • *uncertain roots*

Émer, Eimear, Eimer, Eimhir • Irish • *vague origins, perhaps chastity and purity, beauty and wisdom*

Emma, Ermintrude, Emmaline, Emmeline, Emmie, Emmy • Germanic/Frankish • *entire, the whole, everything*

Encarnación, Incarnatio • Roman Catholic • *incarnation of Jesus Christ*

Enid • British/Welsh • *unknown root*

Erica, Ericka, Erika • Norse • *one ruler or king alone, no other*

Ermengard, Ermgard, Irmgard, Irmengard, Irmingard • Germanic • *this entire enclosure is mine*

Ermengild, Ermengildo, Irmengild • French/Visigothic • *a total sacrifice*

Ermenhilde, Ermenhild, Irmhild, Irmhilde • Germanic • *a whole load of muscle!*

Ermintrude, Trude, Trudy • Germanic/Frankish • *you are my entire world, my beloved*

Ernesta, Ernestina, Erna, Ernestina • German • *serious in all things and will fight to the death; means business to the point of obsession*

Esther, Esta, Hester, Haddasah, Eistir, Ester • Hebrew/Persian/Jewish • *Myrtle, Star and Persian Goddess of Fertility, Love and War, Ishtar*

Étaín, Éadaoin, Eaden • Irish Gaelic • *the jealous Celtic sun goddess*

Evelyn, Éibhleann, Aibhilin • Irish Gaelic/English • *desired by others*

Evette, Yvette • English/French • *yew tree*

Evonne, Yvonne • English/French • *yew tree*

Fay, Fae, Faye • English • *fairy or prescient*

Faoiltiarna, Wiltierna • Irish Gaelic • *mistress of the wolves*

Fauziya • Swahili • *victorious*

Fayza • Arabic • *champion, a winning woman*

Fiedhelm, Fedelma, Fidelma • Irish Gaelic • *unknown origins but given to a beautiful Irish Boudicca*

Fenfang • Chinese • *perfumed, aromatic*

Fern, Fearn • Anglo-Saxon • *the plant that repels evil spirits*

Fíona, Fionn, Ffion, Ffion, Fina • Irish Gaelic • *vine*

Fortunata, Fortuna, Fortunatus • Latin • *fortunate, lucky, fated*

Freya, Froja, Frouwa, Friday, Frøya, Freia, Freyja • Norse • *lady referring to the Goddess of Love, Freya*

Friday • Norse/English • *Freya's day, the Goddess of Love and Beauty*

Fulvia, Fulvius • Latin • *an old Roman family name meaning dark, dusky, exotic*

Galia • Jewish/Hebrew • *wave*

Gemma, Jemma • Italian • *precious jewel*

Genevieve, Jennifer, Genoveffa, Ginevra • Celtic • *a female chief or leader of the tribe of people*

Gerd, Gerda, Gärd, Garo • Norse • *Goddess of Fertility; protection as in a fort or castle*

Gertrude, Gert, Gertie, Gerde, Gertrud, Gerda, Gertraud, Gertraut, Gertrudis • Germanic • *she is a dear woman with strength, superlative with a spear*

Gertrun • Germanic • *magic spear*

Ghadīr • Arabic • *stream, brook, watercourse*

Giachetta • Biblical • *female version of James!*

Gilda • Germanic • *sacrifice*

Gillian, Gill, Jill, Gillyflower, Gillaine, Jillian, Jilly, Gilly • Latin • *from Julius, a Roman name with no known root*

Gina, Giorgina, Luigina, Ginette • Italian • *suffix for other name but on its own it is said to mean 'pure'*

Giuletta, Giulia • Latin/Italian • *from Julius, an old Roman name no known origins*

Gladys, Gwladys, Gwladus • British Welsh/Latin • *uncertain origins but said to be a local form of Claudia, from the old Roman family name Claudius*

Gobnat, Gobbán, Gobnait • Irish Gaelic • *female blacksmith*

Greer, Grier • Greek/Scots English • *from a Scottish surname, Gregor, meaning watchful*

Greta, Gretta, Greet, Gretchen, Margaretta, Margareta, Grete, Margarette, Margarethe • Greek/Norman/English • *pearl*

Griet, Margriet • North Germanic • *pearl*

Griselda, Grizelda, Grizel, Grishild • Germanic • *grey battle*

Gudrun, Guro • Norse • *magical, enchanted, a witch or wise woman*

Gunnborg • Norse • *a fort or castle ready for attack*

Gunna • Norse • *strife*

Gytha, Gyth, Gudrid • Anglo-Saxon/Norse • *discord or beautiful god*

Hadassah, Dassah, Esther •
Hebrew/Persian/Jewish • *Myrtle,
Star and Persian Goddess of Fertility,
Love and War, Ishtar*
Hāgar, Hājar • Arabic • *uncertain
origins*
Hannelore • Germanic • *combo of
Hannah and Eleanor*
Hazel, Haesel • Anglo-Saxon • *the
hazel tree, for the Celts a magic tree*
Hecate • Greek • *Goddess of Magic
and Enchantment*
Hedda, Hedwig • Germanic •
contentious and warlike
**Hedwig, Edwige, Hedda, Haduwig,
Edvige, Hedvig** • Germanic •
contentious and warlike
Heledd, Hyledd • British Welsh/
Celtic mythology • *not entirely sure
of its root but it is the name of a
princess whose name is at the heart
of a lament for her brother's death*
Helmina, Wilhelmina, Helmine
• Germanic • *her helmet gives her
magical protection and the will to
win*
Héloïse, Éloise • Germanic/
Frankish • *uncertain origins*
Hertha • Norse • *Norse Goddess of
Fertility*
Hester, Esther, Hettie, Hetty •
English • *Myrtle, Star and Persian
Goddess of Fertility, Love and War,
Ishtar*
Hilda, Hylda, Hilde, Elda •
Germanic • *battleaxe*
Hildegard, Hildegarde • Germanic
• *battlefield*
Hildegund, Hildegunde •
Germanic • *battle and strife*
Hiltraud, Hiltrud • Germanic •
strength in battle
Hind, Hinde • Arabic • *unknown*

origin
Hjördis, Hjorrdis • Norse • *warrior
goddess great with the sword!*
Honeysuckle • English • *a climbing
vine with fragrant flowers*
Hope, Hopa • Anglo-Saxon •
*Christians' belief in the resurrection
and life everlasting*
Horatia • Etruscan • *Roman family
name with no certain root*
**Hortense, Hortensia, Hortensius,
Hortus** • French/Latin • *old Roman
family name meaning garden*
Hualing • Chinese • *flourishing fu-
ling (herb used in oriental medicine)*
Huidai • Chinese • *sagacious black*
**Hyacinth, Jacinth, Jacinthe,
Jacintha, Hyakinthos** • Greek/
English • *love and passion*

Íde, Ita • Irish • *unknown origins;
possibly someone who thirsts*
Ilene, Eileen • Norman French/
modern English • *desired by others*
Imelda • Germanic/Visigothic • *the
whole complete battle*
Imke, Imma, Irma • Germanic •
whole, entire
Inderjit • Sanskrit • *victory over
Indra*
**Inge, Inga, Ingeborg, Ingrid,
Ingfrid, Ingetraud, Ingegerd,
Ingegärd, Inger** • Norse • *protected
by Ing, the God of Fertility*
Ingrid • Norse • *a beautiful woman
blessed by the God of Fertility, Ing*
Iolanda, Yolanda • Germanic/
Frankish • *unknown origin*
**Irma, Erma, Ermen, Irmgard,
Irmtraud, Irmen, Irmengard,
Ermengard, Irmgard, Irmingard,
Irmentrud, Ermentrud, Irmentraud**
• all and nothing less

Isadora, Isidoro, Izzy • Greek/
Egyptian • *Greek/Egyptian* • *a gift
from the goddess Isis, deity of magic
and life*
Ismene • Greek mythology • *Greek
tragedy!*
Ivy, Ifig • Anglo-Saxon • *ivy: the
climbing plant known as the survivor*

**Jacalyn, Jacqueline, Jackalyn,
Jaclyn** • Biblical/Latin/English •
*supplanter, a cuckoo in the nest!
Edging out someone to take their
place against their will*
Jacinta, Hyacinth, Jacinthe •
Greek/Spanish/French/English •
love and passion
**Jacqueline, Jackalyn, Jacalyn,
Jacqualine, Jacqueline, Jacquelyn,
Jacquelyne, Jacquiline, Jacaline,
Jacuelline, Jacqueline, Jacklyn,
Jaclyn, Jacki, Jackie, Jacky,
Jacqui, Jacquie, Jaqui, Jaki, Jakki,
Jacquelyn, Jacquelynn** • Biblical/
Latin/French • *supplanter, a cuckoo
in the nest! Edging out someone to
take their place against their will*
Jacquetta, Giachetta • Biblical/
Latin/Italian • *supplanter, a cuckoo
in the nest! Edging out someone to
take their place against their will*
Jade, Ijada, Jada • Spanish • *stone of
the bowels*
**Jaime, Jame, Jamesina, Jamie,
Jamey, Jamee, Jami, Jaimie,
Jaimee** • Biblical/Latin/Spanish
• *supplanter, a cuckoo in the nest!
Edging out someone to take their
place against their will*
Jaleesa • African American • *no
known origins*
Janaki • Sanskrit • *vague origins*
Jasmine, Jasmyn, Jazmin, Jazmine,

**Yasmīn, Yasmine, Jasmina,
Yasmina, Jaslyn, Jaslynne** •
Persian/Norman • *evergreen shrub
or vine with glorious fragrance*
Jaya • Sanskrit • *victory*
Jayanti • Sanskrit • *all-conquering*
Jayashree • Sanskrit • *Goddess of
Victory*
Jetta, Jaiet, Gagates • Latin/
Norman • *jet which is fossilised
wood or coal: a black stone from
Gagai (a city in Lycia, Asia Minor,
now Turkey)*
Jewel, Jouel, Iocus • Latin/Norman
• *rare stone that is a plaything, a
delight to the eyes*
Jinana • Arabic • *a woman as
beautiful and mystical as the Garden
of Eden*
**Jill, Jillian, Gillian, Gill, Jilly, Gilly,
Jillie** • *from Julius, a Roman name;
no known foundation*
Jingfei • Chinese • *forever fragrant*
Jocasta • literary • *Greek* • *mother
of Oedipus, tragic figure in classical
mythology*
Jordan, Hayarden, Jordana •
Hebrew/Jewish • *flowing down*
Ju • Chinese • *chrysanthemum*
**Julia, Juli, Julie, Giulia, Julietta,
Guilietta, Juliet, Juliette, Guiliette,
Juliana, Julianus, Julianna,
Julianne, Julián, Juliane, Julieann,
Julien, Julieanne, Julienne Jools,
Julia, Jules, Juleen, Julianne** • Latin
• *a Roman name with unknown
origins*

Kalpana • Sanskrit • *filled with
fantasy*
Kanta • Sanskrit • *you are desirable
because you are so lovely*
Karma • Sanskrit • *action, seen as*

bringing upon oneself inevitable results, good or bad, either in this life or in a reincarnation

Kiera, Keira • Norse • *a person who lives in marshes covered in shrubs and brushwood*

Kennedy, Cinnéidigh • Irish Gaelic • *ugly head*

Kestrel, Cresserelle, Cressele • Norman/English • *bird of prey; from the Norman French: a rattle*

Keturah • Biblical/Hebrew/Jewish • *incense, the strong perfume from frankincense used to purify in sacred places*

Kinga, Kinegunde, Kinge • Germanic • *in the face of strife she is brave and courageous*

Kriemhild, Kriemhilde • Germanic • *the mask of battle*

Leila, Laila, Layla, Leyla • Arabic • *a beautiful dark woman, as enchanting as the night, intoxicating to the senses*

Lamyā • Arabic • *a woman with fulsome brown lips*

Lana, Alana, Alanah, Lanna, Svetlana • American English • *vague origins but likely to mean a rock*

Lanying • Chinese • *lustrous indigo*

Laoise, Leesha, Luigseach • Irish Gaelic • *unsure origins but most possibly Lug, goddess of light; or someone from County Laoise*

Lara, Larissa, Larrisah • Russian/Greek • *unsure meaning; perhaps someone from a town near Thessaloniki, in northern Greece*

Larch, Larche, Larix • American English/German/Latin • *sacred tree to the shaman*

Larissa, Lara, Larry • Russian/Greek • *uncertain meaning; perhaps someone from a town near Thessaloniki, in northern Greece*

Lawāhiz • Arabic • *shy glances, whispered secrets*

Layla • Arabic • *a beautiful dark woman, as enchanting as the night, intoxicating to the senses*

Leda • Greek mythology • *Queen of Sparta who was raped by Zeus/Jupiter in the shape of a swan*

Leela, Lila • Sanskrit • *very sexy*

Leila, Laila, Layla, Leyla, Lela, Lila • Arabic • *a beautiful dark woman, as enchanting as the night, intoxicating to the senses*

Leonora, Eleonora, Léonore, Elenonore, Eleanore, Lenora, Lennora, Lennorah, Lenorah, Lena • Germanic/Frankish/Provençal • *prefix means foreign or stranger; suffix is unknown*

Life, Liffey • Irish Legend • *she who gave her name to a river*

Lifen • Chinese • *beautiful fragrance*

Lilian, Lilly, Lily, Lili, Lillian, Lilium, Lily, Lillie, Lilly, Lili, Lilli • Latin/Norman • *flower that is associated with purity and resurrection*

Lilith, Lily • Biblical/Jewish/Hebrew • *screech owl, nightmare or night monster*

Lin • Chinese • *beautiful jade*

Liqiu • Chinese • *beautiful autumn*

Lois • Biblical • *uncertain origins*

Lola, Dolores • Roman Catholic • *Our Lady of the Seven Sorrows of the Virgin*

Lolicia, Lola, Delicia • American English/Roman Catholic

Lolita, Lola, Lolita • Roman Catholic • *Our Lady of the Seven*

Sorrows of the Virgin
Lone, Abelone, Magdelone •
Danish • *Mary Magdelene aka Mary of Magdala, woman healed of evil spirits*
Lottelore • modern • *combo of Lotte (Charlotte) and Lore (Eleanore)*
Lourdes, Lurdes • Roman Catholic • *a French place of pilgrimage where a young girl had visions of the Virgin*
Lubna • Arabic • *storax tree that has sweet, honey-like sap, used to make perfume and incense. A fragrant, perfumed, honey-tasting woman as intoxicating as incense*
Lucretia, Lucrece, Lucrezia, Lucretius • *Roman family name; no known origins*
Ludovica • Germanic • *she finds her fame in war*
Luisa, Louisa, Luise, Lulu, Lou • Spanish/Frankish • *famous in war or battle*
Lulu, Luisa, Luise, Louise • German/Frankish • *famous in war or battle*

Madeleine, Madelaine, Magdalene, Magdala, Madelene, Madlyn, Madelyn, Madalene, Madaline, Madoline, Magdalen, Maddie, Maddy, Maddalena • Biblical/French • *Mary Magdelene aka Mary of Magdala, woman healed of evil spirits*
Madison, Maddison, Mady, Maddie • American/English • *son of Maud or Matilda, the battleaxe*
Maeve, Meadhbh, Mave, Meave, Medh, Mab, Medb • Irish mythology • *intoxicating and seductive*
Malfada • Spanish/Visigothic • *no certain root*

Magali, Magalie • Provençal • *pearl*
Magda, Magdalene, Magadelena, Lena • Biblical/Slavic/German • *Mary Magdelene aka Mary of Magdala, woman healed of evil spirits*
Maggie, Margaret, Magaidh • Scots Gaelic • *Greek/Latin/Norman* • *pearl*
Mahalia, Mahalah, Mahali • Biblical/Jewish/Hebrew/Aramaic • *unsure; either tender or marrow – perhaps tender down to her marrow!*
Maia, Maya, Mya • Latin • *Roman Goddess of Youth, Life, Rebirth, Love and Sexuality*
Maisie, Margaret, Mairéad, Maisy • Greek/Scots Gaelic/English • *pearl*
Maitland, Maltalent, Mautalent • Anglo-Saxon/Norman • *bad-tempered or from Mautalant, a barren place in France*
Malati • Sanskrit • *she is like the jasmine, she is even more beautiful at night*
Mallory, Malerie, Mallery • Norman • *unhappy or unfortunate one*
Mara, Naomi • Biblical/Jewish/ Hebrew • *bitter*
Marcella, Marcelle, Marcelline, Marceline, Marcelina, Marcela, Marcellina, Marcellus, Marsaili • Latin • *named after Mars, God of Sex and War*
Marcia, Marsha, Marcie, Marcy, Marci • Latin • *named after Mars, God of Sex and War*
Margaret, Margeurite, Margarita, Margarites, Margaron, Pearl, Marina, Margery, Marjory, Marjorie, Magarette, Margaretta, Meg, Peg, Madge, Marge, Maggie, Meg, Meggie, Peggy,

Peggie, Peggi, Margie, May, Daisy, Mairéad, Mairghead, Mared, Marged, Marget, Mererid, Margaretha, Margareta, Margarethe, Margrit, Margret, Meta, Margriet, Margrethe, Marit, Merete, Mereta, Mette, Margeurite, Margarita, Margarida, Margherita, Margareta, Malgorzata, Marketa, Marketta, Margrieta, Margarita, Margaretha, Margherita, Margrethe, Margit, Maighread, Maretta, Mared, Marged • Greek • *pearl*

Margot, Margaux, Marguerite, Margarete, Margit • Greek/Latin/ Norman • *pearl*

Margery, Marjorie, Marjorie, Margery, Marjory, Marjie, Margaret, Margery, Margie, Marjy, Marji, Marga, Marge, Marsaili • Greek/English

Marietta, Mariella, María, Mairéad, Margaret, Mariette, Maretta • Biblical/Italian • *Mary Magdelene aka Mary of Magdala, woman healed of evil spirits*

Marina, Marinus, Marius, Marna • Latin • *Roman family name; clouded meaning but associated with someone of or from the sea*

Maris, Stella Maris • modern name • *uncertain root but from Maria or Mary, meaning Star of the Sea*

Marjolaine • French • *marjoram, the herb*

Marla, Marlene, Magdalene • modern • *Mary Magdelene aka Mary of Magdala, woman healed of evil spirits*

Marlene, Maria, Magdalena • German • *Mary Magdelene aka Mary of Magdala, woman healed of*

evil spirits

Marna, Marnie • Swedish/Latin • *Roman family name; clouded meaning but associated with someone of or from the sea*

Marsha • Anglo-Saxon • *a person who lives on marshy ground or fenland*

Martine, Martina, Mari, Martie, Marty, Martinus • Latin/English • *named after Mars, God of Sex and War*

Martirio • Roman Catholic/Spanish • *to be a martyr*

Matilda, Mahthild, Mehthild, Mathilda, Tilda, Mattie, Matty, Tilly, Tillie, Mechtild, Mechthilde, Mechtilde, Machteld, Matilde, Mathilde, Mathilda, Matilde, Matylda, Martta, Matild, Mafalda, Matilde • Germanic • *mighty in battle*

Maud, Matilda, Mahauld, Maauld, Maude, Mallt • Dutch/Flemish • *mighty in battle*

Maura, Mavra • Latin • *Moor, as in Arab*

May, Mae, Maybelle, Maybella • Anglo-Saxon • *the magical hawthorn tree, which is also known as may*

Meadhbh, Medb, Maeve, Mave, Meave • *intoxicating woman; she who makes men drunk*

Meg • English/Greek • *short name for Margaret, meaning pearl*

Medea, Medesthai • Greek mythology • *a Colchian princess in 'Jason and the Golden Fleece'; means to contemplate and reflect*

Meg, Margaret, Mag, Magg, Maggie, Megan, Meggie • Greek/ Latin/English • *pearl*

Megan, Meg, Meghan, Meaghan, Meagan, Marged, Margaret • Greek/Gaelic • *pearl*

Mélanie, Melania, Melaina, Melany, Melony, Mellony, Meloney, Melloney, Melas • Latin/Greek/Norman • *black, dark*

Melinda, Melanie, Lucinda • modern • *combo of Mélanie and Lucinda*

Meredith, Meredydd • British/Welsh • *unknown prefix plus lord*

Merete, Margareta, Mereta, Mette, Meta • Greek/Latin/Danish • *pearl*

Merle, Meriel, Merula • Norman/Latin • *blackbird*

Michal • Biblical/Jewish/Hebrew • *brook*

Millicent, Milesende, Amalswinth, Millie, Milly, Mills • Germanic/Frankish/Norman • *strength, labour, work*

Mingzhu • Chinese • *bright pearl*

Minnie, Wilhelmina • Germanic/Norman • *her helmet gives her magical protection and the will to win*

Miriam, Maryam, Mary, Maria, Maiamne, Myriam, Mirjam • Biblical/Jewish/Hebrew • *uncertain origins but is the root of Mary and Maria*

Misty, Mistie • English • *obscure or vague*

Mohini • Sanskrit • *a woman who is enchanting and bewitching*

Monica, Monere, Monique, Monika • Latin/Phoenician • *cautious counsel, to advise or warn*

Morgan, Morgana • British/Welsh • *vague beginning but ends with ending, completion, full circle*

Muna • Arabic • *sexy, desirable and gives out hope and optimism*

Munira • Arabic • *radiant, bright, sends out a light*

Myra, Myrrha, Mary, Miranda, Mairéad • Latin • *anagram of Mary, meaning myrrh; the embalming spice*

Najwa, Nagwa • Arabic • *secrets abound, a woman who is discreet and confidential, keeper of secrets*

Nan, Nancy, Nanette, Ann • Biblical/Jewish/Hebrew • *pet form of Ann, of uncertain origins: God has favoured me*

Nancy, Nan, Ann, Annis, Agnès, Nancie, Nanci, Nance • Biblical/Jewish/Hebrew • *pet form of Ann, of uncertain origins: God has favoured me*

Nanette, Nan • Biblical/Jewish/Hebrew/French • *pet form of Ann, of uncertain origins: God has favoured me*

Nanna • Norse • *daring one!*

Narelle, Narellan • Australian Aborigine • *no known roots except a town named the same in New South Wales!*

Nastasia, Anastasia • Greek/Russian • *short form of Anastasia: resurrection*

Natalia, Natalya, Natalie, Natasha • Latin/Russian • *the birth of Jesus Christ or reborn with faith*

Natalie, Nathalie, Natalia • Latin/French • *the birth of Jesus Christ or reborn with faith*

Natasha, Natalia, Noel • Latin/Russian • *the birth of Jesus Christ or reborn with faith*

Nell, Nella, Nellie, Nelly, Eleanor, Ellen, Helen • *English short name for Eleanor, Ellen or Helen*

Nessa, Neassa, Neasa, Ness • Irish Gaelic • *unknown meaning but the name of a character in Irish legend*

Netta, Nettie • Gaelic/English • *confused origins; passionate in all she does, a champion*

Ngaire, Nyree • New Zealand Maori • *unknown origins*

Nigella • *black as pitch or passionate, dead sexy, really desirable; maybe a commitment phobe or refusing monogamy*

Nihād • Arabic • *ground that resembles a female's breasts and contours*

Nikita, Anitketos • Greek/Russian

Nirvana • Sanskrit • *extinction, disappearance of the individual soul into the universal*

Nyree, Ngaire • New Zealand English • *unknown origins*

Opal, Opel, Upala, Opaline • Sanskrit/English • *precious stone, said by many to be unlucky unless you are a Scorpio*

Oprah, Orpah, Ophrah • American English • *uncertain origin*

Oriana, Aurum, Oriane • Spanish/ Norman • *uncertain roots but may mean gold*

Orna, Odharnait • Irish Gaelic • *sallow complexion*

Ottavia • Latin/Italian • *personal name of Octavius, linked to number eight*

Padma • Sanskrit • *lotus flower, energy centres of the chakra*

Padmavati • Sanskrit • *full of lotus flowers*

Padmini • Sanskrit • *lotus pond or lake*

Pandora, Dora, Pandoran • Greek mythology • *all and every gift;*

alluding to Pandora's box that she was told never to open, when she did, she allowed everything evil and bad out, leaving the fairy Hope as the only thing left inside

Parthenope, Parthenosops • Greek mythology • *maiden as in the goddess Athene in her form and face; one of the Sirens, who lured men to her with their enchanting, bewitching voices was named Parthenope*

Patience, Pati • Latin • *to suffer, a virtue*

Peg, Peggy, Peggi, Margaret, Meg, Pegeen, Peigín, Peig, Peigi • Greek/Latin/Norman

Pearl, Penelope, Pen, Penelops, Penny, Penni • Greek • *uncertain origin but 'duck' is one suggestion*

Peninnah, Pen, Pearl, Perle, Peninna, Penina • Biblical/Hebrew/ Jewish/Latin • *coral or pearl, beautiful pink underwater mineral found in warm water*

Pernilla, Pella, Pernille, Petronel, Petronilla • Latin/Greek/Swedish • *a stone or someone who lives in the country*

Petronel, Petronella, Petronilla, Petronius • Latin • *a Roman family name Petronius that could be connected to St Peter*

Petra, Peta, Piera, Peta, Petra • Greek • *the rock or stone*

Phoenix • Latin/Greek • *mythical bird that represents rebirth or reincarnation*

Phyllis, Phillida, Phyllis, Phyllidos, Phyllidis, Phyllida, Phyllicia, Phylicia • Greek mythology • *a Thracian queen, Phyllis died for love and transformed herself into an almond tree; her name means*

leaves or leaf and she is a symbol of undying love and friendship
Pierce, Pearce, Perse, Pierette, Peta • Greek • *the rock or stone*
Portia, Porcia, Porcius, Porcus, Porsha • Latin • *Roman family name of Porcus, meaning pig*
Psyche, Psykhe • Greek • *butterfly, spirit and soul*

Qiu • Chinese • *autumn*
Qiuyue • Chinese • *autumn moon*
Quan • Chinese • *thermal spring*

Raisa • Slavic • *paradise, heaven*
Rajani Rajni • Sanskrit • *something of the night... as dark as night*
Rakeisha • African • *no known root*
Rati • Sanskrit • *she desires; gives sexual pleasure and carnal knowledge*
Raven, Rafn, Raefn, Ravenna • Anglo-Saxon/Norse • *Odin's winged friend, the Raven*
Rébecca, Rebekah, Beathag, Becca, Becks, Bex, Becky, Becki, Rella, Rebekka, Reba • Biblical/Jewish/Hebrew/Aramaic • *shadowy or vague origins, possibly connected to 'cattle stall' but doubtful*
Renée, Reenie, Rena, Renatus, Renata, Serena, Rina • Latin • *reborn; resurrected*
Regina, Queenie, Raine, Régine, Raghnailt, Ragnhild • Latin/Roman Catholic • *queen (of heaven)*
Renata, Renée, René, Renate • Latin • *reborn*
Ricarda • Germanic • *strong, brave and powerful*
Richelle • Germanic/French • *strong, brave and powerful*
Rio • Portuguese/Spanish • *river*

Rocio • Roman Catholic • *Our Lady of the Dews, or tears shed for the wickedness of the world*
Roswithe, Roswitha • Germanic • *famous and strong*
Runa • Norse • *a woman who has magical powers she uses through the runes or secret spells*
Ruqayya • Arabic • *talisman, lucky charm, magic spell; moving upwards, advancing/ascending*
Ruth, Ruthi, Ruthie, Rut, Rutt, Roo • Biblical/Jewish/English • *unknown roots but in English: compassion*

Sabina, Sabine • Latin • *from the Sabine women who were kidnapped by the Romans*
Sabrina • Celtic mythology • *from the river goddess who lived in the River Severn*
Salud • Roman Catholic • *Our Lady of Salvation*
Samsara • Sanskrit • *just passing through, referring to life being just part of a cycle*
Sandhya • Sanskrit • *twilight of the gods, devout, ritualistic*
Sappho • literary Greek • *poetess Sappho, noted for her verse honouring lesbian passion*
Sarāb • Arabic • *a mirage; not as she seems from a distance*
Saroja • Sanskrit • *born in a lake, like a lotus*
Sarojini • Sanskrit • *lotus pond or lake; having lotuses*
Satin, Zaituni, Tsingtung • Chinese/Arabic/French/English/Latin • *soft, sleek, silky, shiny fabric*
Seanach • English/Norman French • *old, wise and venerable*
Selma, Zelma, Selima • German/

Scandinavian • *unknown roots*

Sévérine, Severina, Severa • Latin • *Roman family name, austere, severe*

Shahīra • Arabic • *destiny for fame and fortune*

Shakonda • African American • *unknown origin*

Shakti • Sanskrit • *she possesses the power of the gods*

Shandy, Shandi, Shandigaff • American English • *from the drink Shandigaff, with no known roots*

Shane • Irish Gaelic/English • *supplanter, a cuckoo in the nest! Edging out someone to take their place against their will*

Shanice • American English • *combo of Shane and Janice*

Shanta • Sanskrit • *she who finds inner peace through yoga or meditation*

Shanti • Sanskrit • *she who finds tranquillity and serenity through yoga*

Sharada • Sanskrit • *autumn*

Shaughan, Shaun, Shaughn, Shawn, Lashawn • Irish Gaelic/English • *supplanter, a cuckoo in the nest!*

Sieghilde, Siedlind, Siedlinde, Sigi • Germanic • *conqueror in battle; winner takes all*

Siegrun, Sigrun, Sigi • *she who uses the runes or magic to gain power over her enemies*

Simran • English • *no known roots*

Sindy, Cindy, Sinda • French • *cinders from the fire*

Sissel, Cecily • Scandinavian/English • *old Roman family name Caecilius, from the Latin, meaning blind*

Siv • Norse • *bride or wife, name of Thor's golden-haired missus*

Siwan, Joan • British/Welsh • *sea trout*

Sorrel, Sorrell, Sorell, Sorel, Sur • Norman/German/Frankish • *the herb sorrel with its sour leaves*

Solange, Sollemnia, Sollemna • Latin • *solemn*

Stacey, Stacy, Stace, Eustacia, Stacie, Staci • English/Greek • *confused roots; could mean juicy, tasty grapes!*

Stella, Stella Maris • Latin • *a star and Star of the Seas (often used to describe the Virgin Mary)*

Su'ād • Arabic • *origin not known*

Suhād, Suhair • Arabic • *insomnia*

Sybil, Sybille, Sybilla, Sibylla, Sibilia, Sibella, Sibéal, Cybille, Sibilla, Sibella, Cybil, Cybill • Greek mythology • *a woman with the power to predict; a devotee of Apollo, the sun god*

Sydney, Sid, Sidney • Anglo-Saxon • *an ait, a small island in a river or a wide river meadow*

Tacey, Tace, Tacita • Latin/English • *to be silent*

Tanya, Tania, Tanja • Latin • *Sabine Roman family name with no known roots*

Tansy, Tanesie, Athanasia • Greek/Norman • *herb: tansy, giving immortality*

Tasha, Natasha • Latin • *the birth of Jesus Christ or reborn with faith*

Tatiana, Tanya, Tatyana, Tatianus, Tatius • Latin/Russian • *Sabine Roman family name, Tatius, of vague origins*

Teresa, Theresa, Terri, Tessa, Tes, Teresia, Theresia, Treeza, Thérèse, Resi • Italian/Spanish/Portuguese •

unknown root
Tessa, Tess, Theresa, Tessie, Tessy
• Italian/Spanish/Portuguese •
unknown root; pet name for Teresa
Thelma, Thelema • Greek • *to wish*
or have the will
Thera, Theresa • Greek • *vague*
origins; could be short for Theresa or
Greek isle of Thera
Thessaly, Thessalie • Greek/Illyrian
• *an area and city of northern*
Greece; unknown root
Thora • *follower of Thor*
Thurayya, Surayya • Arabic • *coping*
with sorrow and sadness
Tilda, Matilda, Tilde, Mathilde •
Germanic • *mighty in battle*
Tilly, Tillie, Tilli, Tili • Germanic •
mighty in battle
Tita • Latin • *old Roman name,*
unknown origins
Toni, Tonia, Tonia, Tonya, Antonia,
Antoinette • Estruscan/Roman
• *Roman family name but with*
confused origins
Torborg, Thorbjorg • Norse •
fortified place belonging to the god
Thor
Tordis • Norse • *goddess connected*
to Thor
Tori, Tory, Toria • Norse/Danish •
Thor
Tori, Tory, Toria • English • *short*
form of Victoria
Treasa, Trean • Irish Gaelic • *a*
woman of intense, immense strength
Trista, Trysta • American English/
British Welsh • *rowdy, rebellious,*
blue, melancholic, chaotic
Tuesday • Anglo-Saxon/Norse •
Tiw's day, equivalent to Mars
Tulip, Tiwlip • English • *flower of*
enchantment: tulip

Ulla • Norse • *willpower and*
determination
Ulrike, Ulrika, Ulla • Germanic/
Anglo-Saxon • *power and riches;*
wolf power
'Umniya • Arabic • *your wish is my*
desire

Valérie, Valeria, Valère, Val •
French/Latin • *old Roman name*
Valerius, meaning healthy, robust
and strong
Velma • modern English/Greek • *to*
wish or have the will
Victoria, Vicky, Vickie, Vicki, Vikki,
Tory, Toria, Vita, Victoire, Viktoria,
Vittoria, Bhictoria • Latin/English •
conqueror, winner
Vigdis • Norse/Norwegian •
Goddess of War
Vijayalakshhmi, Vijayashree •
Sanskrit • *Goddess of Victory*
Vita, Victoria • Latin • *life; also short*
name for Victoria
Vivienne, Vivien, Viv, Vi, Vivi,
Vivienne, Vivianne, Béibhinn
• Latin/Norman • *Roman name*
Vivianus meaning life, including
resurrection

Walburg, Walburga • Germanic •
she rules over a stronghold or fort
Waltraud, Waltrud, Waltrude •
Germanic • *rules with great strength*
Wenqian • Chinese • *madder red*
Wilhelmina, Mina, Minnie, Billie,
Wilma • Germanic/Norman • *her*
helmet gives her magical protection
and the will to win
Willa • Anglo-Saxon • *a person with*
tremendous willpower, powerful in
every way
Wilma, Wilhelmina, Billie,

Wilmette, Wilmetta • Anglo-Saxon
Winta • Ethiopian • *desire*

Xena • Greek • *stranger, foreigner*
Xifeng • Chinese • *western phoenix*

Yola, Yolanda, Yolande, Jolenta
• Germanic/Frankish/Norman •
uncertain origin
Ysuelt, Isolde • French/British
Welsh • *a beautiful Irish princess*
Yvette, Yves, Eve, Yvonne, Yvon •
French/Germanic • *yew tree*

Zelah • Biblical/Hebrew/Jewish •
*literal meaning is 'side'; one of the
14 cities of the tribe of Benjamin*
Zelda, Griselda, Grizelda •
Germanic • *grey battle*
Zelma, Selma • German/
Scandinavian • *unknown roots*
Zena, Zina, Xena • Russian/Greek •
stranger, foreigner
Zane, Zhane • American English
• *unknown roots of British surname*
Zillah • Biblical/Hebrew/Jewish •
shade
Zuleika; Zulēkha • Arabic/Jewish •
unknown origins

SAGITTARIUS

23rd November to 21st December

Planet: Jupiter

Day: Thursday

Stone: topaz

Metal: tin

Colours: imperial colours: roman red, royal blue, rich purple

Design: bold large designs

Trees: exotic trees that grow in other lands, e.g. Chilean pine, monkey puzzle, birch, mulberry, laurel

Flora: carnation, dahlia, anemone

Celebrity Sagittarians: Louisa May Alcott • Woody Allen • Jane Austen • Ludwig van Beethoven • Busby Berkeley • William Blake • Maria Callas • Thomas Carlyle • Andrew Carnegie • David Carradine • Edith Cavell • Sir Winston Churchill • Arthur C Clarke • Richard Crenna • Jamie Lee Curtis • Sammy Davis Jr • Walt Disney • Kirk Douglas • Deanna Durbin • Dick Van Dyke • George Eliot • Friedrich Engels • Jane Fonda • James Galway • J Paul Getty • Robert Goulet • Randolph Hearst • Jimi Hendrix • Billy Idol • Andrew Johnson • Don Johnson • Billie Jean King • Toulouse Lautrec • Bruce Lee • Charles 'Lucky' Luciano • Mary Martin • Harpo Marx • Bette Midler • John Milton • Rita Moreno • Jim Morrison • Sinead O'Connor • Christina Onassis • Donny Osmond • Brad Pitt • Carlo Ponti • Lee Remick • Keith Richards • Edward G Robinson • Jan Sibelius • Frank Sinatra • Alexandr Solzhenitsyn • Steven Spielberg • Lee Trevino • Tina Turner • Mark Twain • Liv Ullmann • Robert Ulrich • Eli Wallach.

Planetary Influences: see Jupiter at the back of this book (page 463)

Boys

Abbán, Abbot • Irish Gaelic • *the head of a monastery*

Abbondio, Abundius, Abundans • Latin • *abundant*

'Abd-al-Fattāh • Arabic • *servant of the opener of the gates of prosperity*

'Abd-al-Hakīm • Arabic • *servant of the wise, Allah*

'Abd-al-Hamīd • Arabic • *servant of the praiseworthy, Allah*

'Abd-al-Jawād • Arabic • *servant of the magnanimous, Allah*

'Abd-al-Karīm • Arabic • *servant of the generous, Allah*

Abid • Arabic • *worshipper*

Abraham, Abe, Avraham, Avrom, Abe, Avhamon • Hebrew/Aramaic • *father of the tribes or nations*

Achilles, Achilleus, Achille, Achilleo, Aquiles, Akhilleus • Greek • *from the River Akehloos*

Achim, Akim, Joachim, Akim, Yakim • Hebrew/Jewish • *made and created by God*

Adelard, Adelhard • Germanic • *what a strong looking and noble boy*

Ādil • Arabic • *just and fair*

Adrian, Adrien, Adriano, Hadrianus • Latin • *a man from Hadria, after which the Adriatic Sea is named*

Aeneas, Aineas, Ainein, Angus • Greek • *singing praises*

Aiden, Aidan, Áedán, Aodhán, Aoghan, Aodhagán, Edan, Eden, Aeddan • Irish Gaelic • *fire god*

Aiguo • Chinese • *patriotic, I love the land of my birth*

Ailill • Irish • *elf*

Ainsley, Ainslie, Ainslee, Ainslie • English • *a person from the village of Annesley or Ansley*

Aitor • Basque • *founder of the Basques, local hero*

'Alā • Arabic • *excellent and supreme*

Alaric, Aliric • Germanic • *a foreign power or powerful, ruling stranger, perhaps invader*

Albion • Latin/Celtic • *possibly meaning white or rocky cliff, white cliffs of Dover*

Aldo, Adal • Germanic • *noblesse oblige*

Alfonso, Alphonse, Alonso, Alonzo • Spanish/Visigothic • *royal at the ready*

Algot • Norse • *elf and gothic*

Alfonso, Alphonse, Adalfuns, Alphonsus, Anluan, Fonzie, Fonsie, Fonso • Spanish/Visigothic • *ready for battle, noble fighter, proactive!*

Aloysius, Alois, Alwisi, Alaois • Provençal/Latin/Germanic • *all-wise, all-seeing*

Alvin, Aelfwine, Athelwine • Anglo-Saxon • *elfin, noble or faerie friend*

Amadeus, Amédée, Gottlieb, Amedeo • Latin/Germanic • *love God or God of Love!*

Ambrose, Ambroise, Ambrosius, Ambrois, Ambroix, Ambrogio, Ambrosio, Ambrosios, Ambros, Emrys, Ambros, Ambrogio, Ambrozy, Ambroz • Latin • *immortal, eternal*

Amias • French/Biblical/Hebrew • *someone from Amiens in Picardie or love God*

Amilcare • Phoenician/Italian • *friend of the god Melkar*

Amīr • Arabic • *ruler, prince, caliph or prosperous, wealthy*

Armitabh • Sanskrit • *eternal splendour*

Amjad, Amgad • Arabic • *glorious*

Amos • Biblical/Jewish/Hebrew • *to carry the Lord like St Christopher*

Amrit • Sanskrit • *immortal, divine foods*

Angelo, Ángel, Angelos • Greek/Latin • *messenger of God*

Angus, Aonghas, Aengus, Angie, Angaidh, Gus • Scots Gaelic • *Celtic god, there is only one choice*

Aniello, Agnellus • little lamb, patron saint of Naples

Annibale, Hannibal, Hannbaal • winning the favour of the chief or the lord

Aodh, Áed • Irish Gaelic • *fire, Celtic sun god*

Anthony, Antony, Tony, Antain, Antaine, Anton, Antoine, Antonio, Antoni, Antonin, Antoninus, Ante, Antun, Antal, Antanas, Anthos, Antwan, Antonino, Nino, Ninny, Anthony, Antoine, Anton, Antonio, Antonius • Etruscan/Roman • *Roman family name*

Antshel, Anshel, Amshel • Jewish/Yiddish • *angel*

Aquilina, Akilina • Latin • *like an eagle*

Arkadi, Arkadios • Greek • *a man from Arcadia*

Are, Ari • Norse • *eagle*

Arfon • British/Welsh • *area of Caernarfon and Gwynedd*

Arnold, Arnaud, Arnd, Arndt, Arnaldo, Amwald • Germanic • *eagle power*

Arne • Norse • *eagle*

Arran • cosmetic Scots • *an island in the Firth of Clyde, part of Buteshire*

Armani, Armanno, Hariman • Lombardic/Italian/Germanic • *freeman*

Arnold, Arnald, Arnaud, Arnwald, Arn, Arnie • Germanic/Frankish • *he rules like an eagle*

Art • Irish Gaelic • *champion*

Asa • Biblical/Hebrew/Jewish • *doctor, one who heals*

Åsa, Ase, Ass • Norse • *god, deity*

As'ad • Arabic • *happy and fortunate*

Asdrubale, Asrubaal • Phoenician/Italian • *give aid to the lord or receive it*

Asher • Jewish/Hebrew • *auspicious, born happy under a lucky star*

Ashish • Sanskrit • *prayer, wish or blessing*

Ashraf • Arabic • *honourable and distinguished*

Åsmund, Assmund • protected by the gods

Athan, Athanase, Athanasius, Afanasi, Athanasios, Athanatos • Latin/Greek • *eternal life*

Atholl, Athfodla • Gaelic • *'New Ireland' area of Perthshire*

Atilla, Attlius, Attilio • Latin/Etruscan • *family name from Rome*

Augustine, Augustus, Austin • *great, the max, magnificent, nobody does it better*

Augustus, Auguste, Gus, Augustín, Augustine, Agostino, Augusto, Avgust, Agustin, Aghaistin, Aibhistin, Augustijn, Agustin, Agusti, Agostinho, Avgustin, Tauno, Agoston, Augustinas, Augere • Latin • *great, the max, magnificent, nobody does it better*

Aurelius, Aurèle, Aurel, Aureus, Aurelio • Latin • *Roman family name meaning golden*

Austin, Awstin, Awstyn, Austen,

Austyn, Augustinius, Augustine
• English/Latin • *the tops! The very
best, el supremo*
Ayman • Arabic • *blessed be, wealthy*
Azriel • Jewish/Hebrew • *God helps*

Baptiste, Baptist, Bautista • Biblical
• *John the Baptist*
Barak • Jewish/Hebrew • *a bolt of
lightning*
Baron • English/Norman • *noble man*
Barrington, Bearain • Norman/
Anglo-Saxon • *a person from
Barentin, France or the village of
Barrington*
**Bartholomew, Barton, Bart,
Barthélemy, Bartholomaus,
Bartolomé** • Biblical/Jewish/
Hebrew • *son of Tolmai from Galilee*
Baruch • Biblical/Jewish/Hebrew •
blessed
Bāsim • Arabic • *smiling!*
Bastien, Sébastien, Sebastián •
Greek • *venerable, wise*
Beatus, Beat • Swiss • *blessed*
Bellarmino • Roman Catholic/Jesuit
• *named after Italian saint, Roberto
Bellarmino*
**Benedict, Bennett, Benneit,
Benedikt, Bendt, Bent, Benoît,
Benito, Benet, Bento, Benedetto,
Venedikt, Benedykt, Pentii,
Benedek, Bendikts, Beynish,
Benes, Benedictus, Benneit** • Latin
• *blessed*
Benson, Bensington • English • *son
of Benedict*
Berthold, Barthold, Bertil •
German • *splendid, powerful ruler*
**Bertram, Bertie, Bert, Bertrand,
Beltrán, Burt, Albert** • German •
bright
Bharvesh • Sanskrit • *Lord or King*

of the World, linked to Shiva
Bingwen • Chinese •
clever/cultivated
Blythe, Blithe, Bly • English • *I'm
HAPPY!*
**Bob, Bobbie, Bobby, Robbie,
Robert** • American/English/
Germanic • *bright, famous and
clever*
Bodo • Gemanic • *messenger, glad
tidings*
Boleslav • Russian • *distinctly large
and rather glorious*
Bonaventura • Italian • *good luck,
be fortunate*
**Boniface, Bonifacio, Bonifacius,
Bonifaz** • Latin • *good fate*
Bonito, Bonitus • Latin • *goodness,
that's me*
Boone • Norman/English • *a man
from Bohon, France*
Börries, Liborius • German/Celtic •
to be free!
**Brad, Bradford, Bradley, Bradleigh,
Braeden, Braden, Brayden** • Anglo-
Saxon • *a man from the broad
meadow, ford, farm or clearing*
**Brendan, Brendon, Breandán,
Brendanus** • Latin • *prince, heir*
Brent, Brenton • British/Welsh •
holy river or hill
Brett, Bret • Celtic • *a man from
Brittany*
Brian, Bryan, Bryant, Bryon • Irish
Gaelic • *high or royal born, noble*
Broderick • British/Welsh • *son of
Rhydderch*
Brooklyn • Dutch • *name of a New
York borough*
Bruce • Norman/English • *someone
from Bruis*
Brutus • Latin • *old Roman family
name*

Bryson • American/English • *son of Brice*

Burgess • Anglo-Saxon • *a man who is on a town council*

Cadfael • British/Welsh • *prince of warriors, battle prince*

Cadwgan, Cadwgawn, Cadogan • British/Welsh • *a man who has won honour and glory in battle*

Caesar, César, Kaiser, Tsar • Latin • *leader*

Cai, Kay • British/Welsh • *rejoice!*

Callisto, Kallistos • Greek • *most fair, simply the best*

Camille, Camillo, Camillus, Camilo • Latin/French • *Roman family name*

Carlos, Carolus, Charles • Spanish/Latin • *freeman*

Carlton • English • *the place of the free men*

Carson • American/English • *a Christian, follower of Jesus Christ*

Ceallach, Kelly • Irish Gaelic • *fair-haired or monk, church, monastery*

Cecil, Cesil • Latin/English • *old Roman family name Caecilius*

Chance • American/English • *take a chance; fortunate*

Chaoxiang • Chinese • *fortunate, hopeful*

Charles, Carl, Karl, Carlo, Carlos, Séarlas, Teàrlach, Siarl, Karel, Carel, Charel, Carles, Karol, Carol, Kaarle, Karoly, Karolis, Charlie, Charley • Germanic • *a freeman*

Chas, Chaz, Chuck, Chuckie, Chukkie • American/English • *little Charles*

Charlton, Chas, Chaz, Chuck, Chuckie, Chukkie • English • *the place where the free men live*

Chuanli • Chinese • *propagating prosperity*

Christopher, Chris, Christian, Crìsdean, Karsten, Christiaan, Carsten, Christer, Chretien, Cristiano, Krysztian, Krisztian, Christie, Christy, Kristy, Kristopher, Christopha, Kristopha, Críostoír, Christoph, Christofoor, Kristafoor, Kristoffer, Christophe, Cristobál, Cristofol, Cristovao, Cristoforo, Krzysztof, Krystof, Hristo, Risto, Kristof, Kristaps, Kit, Kester • Greek • *the man who bears Jesus Christ*

Christhard • German • *as brave and strong as Christ*

Christian, Carsten, Christer, Kristian, Criosd, Crìsdean • Latin • *follower of Christ*

Christmas, Noël • English/French • *the nativity of Jesus Christ*

Cillian, Killian, Kilian • Irish Gaelic • *fight or church*

Cinnéidigh, Kennedy • Irish Gaelic • *ugly head*

Ciriaco, Cyriacus, Kyriakos • Latin/Greek • *lord*

Clarence • English/Latin • *Dux Clarentiae, a royal title*

Clitus, Kleio, Clio, Kleitos • Latin/Greek • *famous, splendid*

Clovis • Germanic/Frankish • *a famed warrior or fighter*

Comhghán • Irish Celtic • *twins!*

Conn • Irish Celtic • *chief, leader*

Conrad, Konrad, Corrado • Germanic • *one who gives forthright and candid advice*

Corin, Quirinus, Quirino • Latin • *an ancient Roman deity connected to Romulus*

Cornelius, Cornell, Corneille • Latin • *Roman family name, connected to*

Cornucopia and the horn of plenty
Courtney, Curt, Kurt, Curtis,
Courtenay • Norman • *the barony of*
Courtenay
Coy, McKay, McCoy • American/
English • *the real McCoy; son of*
Aodh, Celtic sun god
Creighton, Crichton, Criochiune •
Scots Gaelic/English
Cuthbert, Bert, Cuddy, Cuddie,
Cuithbeart • Anglo-Saxon • *a man*
well known for what he does, his
personality or wit
Cynddelw • British/Welsh • *he who*
worships holy and sacred images,
pagan or Christian
Cyprian, Cyprianus • Latin • *the*
man who comes from Cyprus, the isle
of Venus or Aphrodite

Dallas, Dalfhas • Scots Gaelic/
American/English • *the village of*
Dallas in Moray, north Britain
Dalmazio, Dalmatius, Dalmacio •
Latin • *a person from Dalmatia in*
the Adriatic
Damodar • Indian • *a rope round his*
belly, to prevent mischief!
Daniel, Dan, Danny, Danyal,
Deiniol, Daniele, Daniil, Taneli,
Dannie • Biblical/Hebrew/Jewish •
God is my judge
D'Arcy, Darcy • Norman • *a man*
from the barony of D'Arcy
Darell, Darrell, Darryll, Darryl,
Darell, Darrell, Darrel, Darryll,
Daryl, Darryl • Norman/American/
English • *a chap from D'airelle, a*
barony in Normandy
David, Dave, Davy, Dewi, Dafydd,
Dai, Davie, Davey, Dàibhidh,
Davide, Taavi, Daw, Dawson,
Dawūd, Dewi, Dewydd, David, Dai

• Biblical/Hebrew • *vague origins but*
possibly from a baby word meaning
darling one
Davis, Davies • American/English •
in honour of Jefferson Davis, leader
of the Dixie states
Dayaram • Sanskrit • *as kind*
and tender as Rama, the perfect
man/divinity
Dean, Dino, Deane, Dene, Denu,
Decanus, Dane • Anglo-Saxon
• *a man who served as dean in a*
Christian church or cathedral
Deforest, Deforrest • American/
English • *surname of American Civil*
War novelist John DeForest
Demid, Diomedes • Greek •
wisdom of Zeus/Jupiter
Dennis, Denis, Denys, Den,
Dionysios, Denny, Dioniso,
Dionizy, Denes, Dionysius •
Greek/French • *named after the god*
Dionysius
Derek, Dereck, Derrick, Deryck,
Del, Dirk, Theodoric • German/
Dutch • *God's gift*
Desmond, Deasún, Des,
Deasmhumhnach • Irish Gaelic •
a man from south Munster (around
Cork)
Devereux • Norman • *someone from*
the barony of Evreux in Eure
Devdan • Sanskrit • *gift of the gods*
Dewey, Dewy • British/Welsh/
American/English • *possibly the*
English spelling of Dewi, which
means David, darling one
Didier, Desiderius • Latin • *longing*
for
Dietmar, Theodemar, Theodemaris
• Germanic • *famous people or*
person
Dieudonné • French • *God-given*

Dilip • Sanskrit • *patron of Delhi, the city*

Dilwyn • British/Welsh • *fair, blonde, white, blessed, sacred, holy*

Dion, Dionis, Diodoros, Diogenes • French/Latin • *gift from Zeus or Jupiter*

Dionysus, Bacchus • Greek • *Dionysus, God of Wine, Orgies and Partying*

Dominic, Dominick, Dom, Dominique, Domingo, Dominicus, Dominus • Latin/Roman Catholic • *Lord, as in St Dominic, founder of the Dominican order*

Dónal, Domhnall, Donall • Irish Gaelic • *ruler of the world*

Donald, Don, Donny, Donnie, Donnell, Dolly, Dhomhnuill, Domhnall • Scots Gaelic • *world ruler*

Donat, Donato, Donatus, Donatien, Donatianus • given by God

Doran, Deoradhain, Deoradh • traveller, such as pilgrim or stranger

Dorotheos, Dorofei • Greek • *gift of God*

Dositheos, Dosifei • Greek • *God-given*

Duke, Marmaduke • Irish Gaelic/ American English • *noble name*

Duncan, Donnchadh • Celtic • *brown chief or noble leader*

Dustin, Dusty, Thorstein • Norse • *Thor, God of Thunder's stone*

Duyi • Chinese • *independent and at one*

Earl, Earle, Erle, Iarll • American/ English • *a noble man*

Ebun • Nigerian • *gift*

Edgar, Edgard, Eadgar • Anglo-Saxon • *he who wins riches and titles through battle*

Edric • Anglo-Saxon • *a powerful, rich ruler*

Edward, Ed, Eddie, Eideard, Eudard, Edvard, Édouard, Eduardo, Duarte, Edoardo, Edvard, Eduard, Eetu, Ned, Ted, Neddy, Teddy, Ewart, Eadbhárd, Eadweard • Anglo-Saxon • *a person who guards his riches, blessed with wealth*

Efisio, Ephesius, Ephesus • Sardinian • *a person from Ephesus in Asia Minor*

Egbert, Bert • Anglo-Saxon • *by the edge of his sword he famously rules*

Ehrenfried, Arnfried • Germanic • *peace with honour or person who, like the eagle, has power, but uses it as a deterrent*

Ehrenreich • Germanic • *honour-able and rich*

Eli • Hebrew/Jewish • *God's height, probably tall*

Elias, Eli • Biblical/Greek • *Yahweh is God*

Eliezer, Eleazar, Eli • Jewish/Hebrew • *God's help*

Elijah, Eliezer, Elisha, Eli, Eliyahu, Eli • Jewish/Hebrew • *Yahweh is God*

Elisud, Elus, Ellis • British/Welsh • *a kind, benevolent man*

Elliott, Eliott, Elliot, Elias, Elijah • English • *Yahweh is God*

Elpidio, Elpidius, Elpidios • Latin/ Greek • *hope*

Elwyn, Alyn • British/Welsh • *white, fair, blessed, sacred and holy*

Emmanuel, Emanuel, Manny, Immanuel • Hebrew/Jewish • *God is with us or amongst us*

Emerson • English • *son of Emery*

Emery, Amauri, Emauri, Amalric

• Germanic/Frankish • *he gains power over others by his vitality and courage*

Emett, Emmett • Germanic/Frankish • *from the female name Emma; the real deal*

Emidio • Latin • *vague origin; patron saint of Ascoli Piceno*

Emrys, Ambrose • British/Welsh • *immortal, eternal*

Enoch • Biblical/Hebrew/Jewish • *experienced and wise*

Erland, Orland • Norse • *a stranger or traveller from another land*

Ermete, Hermes • Greek • *messenger of the gods*

Eugene, Gene, Eugenios, Eugen, Eugenio • Greek • *well bred and high born*

Eustace, Eustakhios, Euistathios, Eustache, Eustaquio • Greek/French • *confused roots; could mean juicy, tasty grapes!*

Evan, Iefan, Ieuan, Ifan • British/Welsh • *from John, Johannes; God is gracious or gift of God*

Ewald, Ewawalt • Germanic • *a wise and just ruler; powerful leader, lawful ruler, judge*

Ezekiel, Zeke • Biblical/Jewish/Hebrew • *God gives me strength*

Ezio, Aetius, Aetios • Latin • *Roman family name meaning eagle*

Fabián, Fabianus, Fabius, Fabien • Latin • *old Roman family name*

Fabio, Fabius • Latin • *Roman family name who were powerful during the republic*

Fabrizio, Fabrice, Fabricius, Fabricio • Italian/Etruscan • *Roman family name; one noted for his incorruptibility*

Fādi • Arabic • *redeemer, saviour, God*

Fahīm • Arabic • *a man of deep understanding and wisdom*

Fang • Chinese • *upright, honest, fair*

Farūq, Farouk • Arabic • *clever, intuitive and wise*

Fathi • Arabic • *conqueror or freedom giver*

Fawzi • Arabic • *victorious and triumphant, reaching the pinnacle*

Faysal, Feisal • Arabic • *a man or judge who knows the difference between good and bad, right and wrong*

Feliciano, Felcius, Felicianus, Felix • Latin • *what a happy chappie!*

Ferapont, Therapon • Greek • *he who worships*

Ferdinand, Ferdinando, Hernán, Ferdi, Ferdie, Fernand • Spanish/Visigothic • *ready, prepared to travel*

Fergus, Fearghas, Ferrer • Irish/Scots Gaelic • *vital, dynamic man*

Fernando, Ferdinando, Hernando, Fernán, Hernán • Spanish • *a man at peace wherever he is; always ready and prepared to travel*

Fergus, Fearghas • Scots Gaelic • *a dynamic man*

Fife, Fyfe • Gaelic • *someone from the kingdom of Fife; Fif was a Pictish hero*

Fikri • Arabic • *intellectual and contemplative*

Filat, Feofilakt, Theophylaktos • Greek • *protected by God*

Filiberto • Germanic • *very bright, royal house of Savoy name*

Fingal, Fionnghall, Fingall • Gaelic • *blonde, fair stranger or traveller or Viking settler*

Finn • Scandinavian • *a man from Finland/Suomi*

Fitzgerald, Fitz • Norman/English • *son of Gerald*

Fitzroy, Fitz • Norman/English • *often the bastard son of the king*

Flaithrí, Florry, Flurry • Scots Gaelic • *prince, king*

Flavio, Flavien, Flavianus, Flavius • Latin • *old Roman family name*

Flinders, Flanders • English • *a Flemish person from Flanders*

Foka, Phocas • Greek • *someone from Phocaea in Asia Minor*

Foma, Thomas • Russian/Biblical • *twin*

Fortunato, Fortunatus • Latin • *fortunate*

Francis, Francisco, Fran, Franciscus, Frank, France, François, Francesco, Franz • Latin • *to be French, someone from France*

Frank, Franklin, Frankie • Germanic • *a loyal and free man or from the Frankish tribe*

Franz • German/Italian • *to be French, someone from France*

Frode, Frodi, Frod • Scandinavian • *a knowledgeable man, well informed*

Fry, Frig, Freo, Frio • Anglo-Saxon/ Norse • *either freeman or a small man*

Fu • Chinese • *rich and wealthy*

Fuhua • *fortunes flourishing and growing*

Fürchtegott • German • *fear God*

Gabriel, Gabby, Gaby, Gabriele • Biblical/Hebrew/Jewish • *man of God*

Gaétan, Gaetano, Caietanus • Latin • *a man from Caieta in Latium*

Gallagher, Gallchobhar • Irish

Gaelic • *foreign ally, helpful stranger*

Gamaliel • Jewish/Hebrew • *benefit of God*

Ganesh • Sanskrit • *Lord of the Hosts*

Gennadi • Russian • *roots unknown; name of Orthodox saint*

Garrison, Gary, Garry • American/ English • *someone from Garriston in North Riding of Yorkshire*

Gaston • Geographic • *a man from Gascony*

Gavino, Gabinus, Gabino • Sardinian/Latin • *a man from Gabium*

Geb, Gudeif • Norse/Russian • *he who lives his life like a god or saint; heir of God*

Geoffrey, Jeffrey, Jeff, Geoffroi, Geoff, Godofredo, Sieffre • Germanic/Frankish/Lombardic • *a stranger in your own land or foreigner who pledges allegiance*

Gerasim, Gerasimos • Greek • *saint of the Eastern Orthodox Church; honoured old man*

Gesualdo • Germanic • *I pledge to rule*

German, Germanus • Latin • *brother in God*

Ghālib • Arabic • *conqueror and victorious*

Ghassān • Arabic • *youth*

Gilbert, Gib, Gibb, Gilberto • Germanic/Frankish/Roman Catholic • *he who pledges or sacrifices his life for greater things*

Giulio • Latin • *old Roman family name*

Gjord, Gyrd, Jul • Norse • *God of Peace*

Gladwin • Anglo-Saxon • *an optimistic, positive friend*

Gobind • Sikh • *name of one of the pantheon of Sikh gurus*

Godfrey, Godefroy, Gofraidh, Godfrid, Godfred • Germanic/Frankish • *God of Peace*

Godwin, Godwine, Win • Anglo-Saxon • *God is my friend*

Gonzogue • *patron of young people*

Gottfried, Götz • Germanic • *God of Peace, God bring me peace*

Gotthard • Germanic • *God give me strength*

Gotthelf • Germanic • *God help me*

Gotthold, Gottwald • Germanic • *wonderful (lovely) God*

Gottlieb, Theophilus • Germanic • *love God*

Gottlob • Germanic • *praise God*

Gottschalk • Germanic • *God or the Lord's servant*

Grant, Grand, Grande • Anglo-Saxon/Norman • *a large, portly person*

Granville, Grenville • Norman • *large village or town*

Gerlach • Germanic • *playful and sporting swordsman*

German, Germanus • Latin • *brother in God*

Gruffudd, Griff, Griffith, Griffinus, Griffin, Grippiud, Gripiud, Gutun, Gutyn, Guto • Prince of Lords

Guaire • Irish Gaelic • *proud and noble, upstanding*

Guangli • Chinese • *lighting up virtue and propriety*

Gui • Chinese • *honourable*

Gwyn, Gwynn, Wyn • British/Welsh • *white, holy, sacred and blond*

Gwynfor • British/Welsh • *a large, grand man who is sacred, holy, blessed and fair*

Gwythyr, Gwydyr, Victor • British Welsh/Latin • *victorious!*

Hādi • Arabic • *mentor, guru, reflective and spiritual*

Hāfiz • Arabic • *devoted scholar, guardian, foster*

Hakeem, Hakīm • Arabic • *wise and sagacious*

Halfdan, Halvdan • Norse • *a man who is half Danish*

Hamdi • Arabic • *praise be, grateful*

Handel, Hans, Hans, Hansel, Johannes • Germanic • *God is gracious or gift of God*

Hāni • Arabic • *happy, gay*

Hannibal, Haanbaal • Phoenician • *I give the Lord grace and favour or he gives it to me*

Hari • Sanskrit • *pet name for Vishnu or Krishna, preservation of the universe*

Harinder • Sikh • *Hari (Vishnu) and Indra, the supreme god*

Haytham • Arabic • *young eagle*

Heddwyn • British/Welsh • *tranquil and peaceful white, fair and sacred*

He • Chinese • *yellow river*

Helge, Heilag, Helje • Scandinavian • *Middle Ages personal name meaning wealthy*

Henning • Scandinavian • *short form of Henrik and Johannes*

Herbert, Bert, Herebeorht, Herb, Herbie, Heribert • German • *a famous army that carries all before it; a shining light*

Hermenigild, Hermengildo, Emengildo • Spanish/Visigothic • *a total sacrifice*

Hernán, Fernando, Hernando • Spanish • *a man at peace wherever he is; always ready and prepared to travel*

Hesketh, Hesskeid • Norse • *where the horses race, a Viking hippodrome*

Hieronymus, Hieronymos, Jérôme
• Latin/Greek • *I bear a holy name*

Hikmat • Arabic • *wise*

Hilary, Hillary, Hilare, Hilario, Ilar •
Latin • *as in hilarious!*

Hillel • Jewish/Hebrew • *praise him!*

Hippolyte, Hippolytos, Hipolito •
Greek • *a free spirit (horse!)*

Honore, Honoratus, Honorius,
Ynyr • Latin • *an honoured man*

Hopcyn, Hopkin, Hob, Robert •
British/Welsh • *famous and bright*

Horace, Horatius, Horatio •
Etruscan • *Roman family name with
no certain root*

Horatio, Horatius, Horace •
Etruscan • *Roman family name with
no certain root*

Hosea • African American •
salvation

Howard, Howerd, Haward •
Scandinavian • *high or noble
guardian or defender*

Huan • Chinese • *happy*

Hubert, Hugbert, Huppert,
Hupprecht, Hobart • Germanic •
brilliant heart and famed mind

Hui • Chinese • *magnificent*

Hywel, Hywell, Howell • British/
Welsh • *conspicuous by his eminence*

Ian, Iain, John • Scots Gaelic/
Biblical • *God is gracious or gift of
God*

Ianto, Ifan, Ieuan, Iohannes, John,
Iefan, Ioan • British/Welsh • *God is
gracious or gift of God*

Ibrāhīm, Abraham • Arabic • *father
of the tribes or nations*

Igal • Biblical/Hebrew/Jewish •
redeemer

Ignazio, Ignatius, Ignus, Ignace,
Ignaz, Egnatius, Ignati, Ignacio
• Latin/Estruscan • *Roman family
name*

Ihāb • Arabic • *gift, promise*

Ihsān • Arabic • *charitable, giver*

Ilario, Hilarius, Hilaris, Illari, Illarion
• Latin • *cheerful, merry, hilarious!*

Ilya, Elias, Elijah • Greek/Biblical •
meaning Yahweh is God

Ingemar, Ingmar • Norse • *famous,
well known to God*

Inigo • Spanish • *Roman family
name*

Innes, Aonghas, Inis • Scots Gaelic
• *an island or man from Innes in
Moray*

Iosif, Osip, Joseph • Biblical/Jewish/
Hebrew • *God will add another*

Ipati, Hypatios, Hypatos • Greek •
most high, el supremo

Isaac, Zak, Zac, Zack, Ike, Izaak,
Isak • Biblical • *unsure roots; probably the hireling or the laugh of a
baby*

Isaiah, Izzy, Isaïe • Biblical/Jewish/
Hebrew • *God is salvation*

'Isām • Arabic • *protection, keeper
of the faith*

Iser, Iserl, Issur • Jewish/Yiddish •
he who strives with God

Ishmael, Ismā'īl • Arabic • *receiver
of the divine spirit; listen to God*

Israel, Jacob • Biblical/Jewish/
Hebrew • *he who strives with God*

Italo, Italus • Latin • *father of
Romulus and Remus, founders of
Rome*

Ithel, Iudhael • British/Welsh • *a
generous but common man who
behaves like a goodly prince or lord;
philanthropist*

Ivan, John, Ewan • Russian • *God
is gracious or gift of God*

Ivory • African American • *tusks*

and teeth of certain animals like the
elephant

**Jack, John, Jankin, Jan, Jehan,
James, Jacques, Jock, Jake, Jak,
Jac, Jackie, Jackson, Jacky, Jackin**
• English • *God is gracious or gift of
God*
Jada • Biblical/Hebrew/Jewish • *he
knows*
Jalāl, Galāl • Arabic • *great and
glorious*
Jagannath • Sanskrit • *Lord of the
World, Vishnu, as in sacred Puri*
Jagdish • Sanskrit • *ruler of the
world, Brahma, Vishnu and Shiva*
Jagjit • Sanskrit • *conqueror of the
world*
Jahangir • Persian • *he's got the
whole world in his hands*
Jakada • Hausa West Africa • *the
messenger*
Jake, Jack • English • *God is
gracious or gift of God*
Jan, John, Johannes • Germanic/
Slavic • *God is gracious or gift of God*
Japheth, Yapheth • Biblical/Jewish/
Hebrew • *growth, development,
expansion*
Jayakrishna • Sanskrit • *victorious
Krishna*
Jayashanka • Sanskrit • *victorious
Shiva*
Jean, Jehan, Gene • French • *God is
gracious or gift of God*
Jed, Jedidiah, Ged • Biblical/
Hebrew/Jewish • *beloved of God*
Jenkin, Jankin, Siencyn • British/
Welsh • *God is gracious or gift of
God*
Jens, Jons, Johann • Scandinavian •
God is gracious or gift of God
Jeffrey, Geoffrey, Jeff, Geoff,

Jefferson, Jeffery, Jeffry, Jep •
Anglo-Saxon • *a stranger in your
own land or foreigner who pledges
allegiance*
**Jeremiah, Jeremy, Jerry, Jem,
Gerry, Jeremias** • Biblical/Hebrew/
Jewish • *appointed by God*
Jeremy, Jem, Jeremiah • Biblical/
English • *appointed by God*
Jenson, John, Jan • English • *son
of Jan or John*
**Jérôme, Hieronymos, Jerry,
Jerrie, Jeri, Jerónimo, Geronimo,
Hierosonoma** • Greek • *I bear a
holy name*
Jesse, Jess, Jessie, Jessi, Jessye •
Biblical/Hebrew/Jewish • *gift*
Jesús, Joshua • Aramaic/Jewish •
saviour
Jlanyu • Chinese • *building the
universe*
Jiang • Chinese • *Yangtze River*
Jing • Chinese • *a boy born in the
capital city Beijing or regional capital*
**Joachim, Jo, Johoiachin, Joaquin,
Jochim, Jochem, Jochen, Joakim,
Jokum** • Biblical • *created by God*
Jobst, Jodocus, Iodoc • Latin/
Breton Celtic • *lord*
**Jocelyn, Jocelyne, Joscelyne,
Joselyn, Josceline, Joslyn, Joss,
Gautzelin, Joscelin** • Norman •
*someone from the Germanic tribe
of the Gauts*
Jody, Jude • American/English •
*uncertain root: possibly from Jude:
praise*
Joël, Yahel • Biblical/Hebrew/Jewish
• *God*
**John, Iohannes, Johannes,
Ioannes, Johannan, Johanan, Eóin,
Seán, Ian, Iain, Seathan, Ieuan,
Siôn, Johann, Johannes, Jan, Jens,**

Johan, Jons, Jon, Jan, Johan, Jean, Juan, Joan, Joao, Giovanni, Gianni, Ioannis, Iannis, Ivan, Juhani, Jussi, Hannu, Janos, Janis, Johnnie, Johnny, Jack, Hank, Jonathan, Johnathan, Jonny, Jon, Johnson, Juwan, Johnston, Johnstone, Jones • Biblical/English/Latin • *God is gracious or gift of God*

Jonathan, Jon, Jonn, Johnny, Johnnie, Jonathen, Jonathon • Biblical • *God has given*

Joseph, Jo, Joey, Jose, Josef, Yosef, Joe, Jo, Seosamh, Ioseph, Josef, Jozef, Josep, Giuseppe, Iosif, Josip, Jooseppi • Biblical/Hebrew/Jewish

Joshua, Josh • Biblical/Hebrew/ Jewish • *God is my salvation*

Josiah, Josh • Biblical/Hebrew/ Jewish • *God heals*

Jozsef, Osip, Jazeps, Juozapas • Biblical/Jewish/Hebrew • *God will add another*

Juan, John • Biblical/Greek/Spanish • *God is gracious or gift of God*

Judah, Judas • Biblical/Hebrew/ Jewish • *praise*

Jude, Judas • Biblical/Greek • *praise*

Judge, Dayan • Norman/Latin/ Hebrew/Jewish • *a rabbinic judge or legal judge*

Julián, Jules, Julianus, Julius, Julyan, Jolyon, Julien, Julio, Jools • Latin • *a Roman name*

Junior, Junia • Biblical • *youth*

Just, Juste, Justus • Latin • *just, fair and honest*

Justin, Justyn, Justinus, Justus, Iestyn • Latin • *a Roman name*

Kajetan, Caitanus, Gaetano, Kayetan • Latin • *man from Caieta*

Kalyan • *most beautiful and*

fortunate

Kapiton, Capito • Latin • *big-headed*

Karam, Karīm • Arabic • *generous, magnimous, philanthropic*

Karanja • Kenyan • *he who guides*

Karl, Charles, Karlmann • Germanic • *freeman*

Kasi • Sanskrit • *radiant; Varanasi or Benares, sacred city on the Ganges*

Keith • British/Welsh • *wood, copse or thicket, or a man from East Lothian*

Kemp, Kemper, Kempa, Kempe • Anglo-Saxon/English • *a warrior champion at sports*

Kendrick, Kenrick, Cenric, Ceneric, Cynwrig, Maceanrig, Cyneric • British/Welsh/Scots Gaelic • *a sacred place high on a hill, or son of Henry or royal power*

Kent, Kenton, Kenntun, Cenatun, Cynetun • British/Welsh • *someone from the British kingdom (now county) and tribe of the Cantii*

Kenya • English • *someone from the African land of Kenya*

Kerry, Ceri • English/British/Welsh • *after the Celtic Goddess of Poetry*

Khalipha, Caliph • Arabic • *successor, heir*

Khwaja • Persian • *the master*

Kirill, Kyrillos, Cyril • Greek • *belongs to the Lord*

Kishore • Sanskrit • *colt, a young horse*

Kyle, Caol • Gaelic • *narrow in geographical terms; a region in Ayrshire*

Lachlan, Lachlann, Lochlann, Lochlan, Lachie, Lockie, Loughlin, Lochlainn, Laughlin • Scots Gaelic • *a man from the land of the lochs or*

Norway
Ladislas, Ladislaw, Ladislaus, Wadislaw, Vladislav, Laszlo, Volodslav • Latin/Slavic • *glorious ruler, rules with glory*
Lakshman, Laxman • Sanskrit • *the mark of God; most*
Lamont, Lagman, Logmad • Norse • *a man of the law; legal person*
Laoiseach, Laois, Louis, Lewis, Leix • Irish • *a man from County Leix*
Laurence, Lawrence, Larry, Laurentius, Laurentum, Laurie, Lawrie, Labhrás, Labhrainn, Lorenz, Laurens, Lars, Laurent, Lorencio, Llorenc, Laurenco, Lorenzo, Lawson, Lavrentios, Lavrenti, Laurencjusz, Wawrzyniec, Vavrinec, Lovrenc, Lauri, Lasse, Lassi, Lorinc, Laz, Lenz, Lavrenti • Latin • *a man from Laurentum, the capital of the Latins*
Lazarus, Laz, Lazare, Eleazar, Lazaros, Lazar • Biblical/Greek/Aramaic/Hebrew • *God is my helper*
Leberecht • Protestant German • *live your life properly, give it to God*
Lemuel • Hebrew/Jewish • *devoted to God*
Lewis, Lewie, Lou, Louis, Lew • Anglo-Saxon/Germanic Frankish • *someone who gains fame through waging war and conflict; a hero, he who vanquishes and is revered*
Liang • Chinese • *bright, luminous, radiant*
Liaqat • Persian • *dignified, noble, wise and clever*
Licio, Lycius • Latin • *man from Lycia in Asia Minor*
Lindsay, Lindissi • Anglo-Saxon • *Old Saxon kingdom whose root means Lelli's island*

Llywarch, Lugumarcos • British/Welsh • *the horse god or God of the Horses*
Logan • Scots Gaelic • *a family name or someone from Logan in Ayrshire*
Lorin, Loren, Lorrin, Laurence • Latin • *man from Laurentum, the capital of the Latins*
Lorne, Latharna, Lorn • Canadian/English • *Scottish place name Lorne, Argyll*
Lothar • Germanic/Frankish • *famous, royal army*
Louie, Louis, Lewie, Lewi, Lou, Luthais, Ludwig, Lodewijk, Ludvig, Lovis, Luis, Lluis, Luigi, Lodovico, Lutz, Ludwig, Ludvig, Ludwik, Luthais • Germanic/Frankish • *a person who gains fame through waging war; a hero who vanquishes the enemy and is revered by his people*
Loyal, Leial, Legalis • Norman/Latin • *keep it legal*
Lucas, Luka, Luke, Luca, Loukas • East European/Greek • *man from Loucania, a Greek colony in southern Italy*
Ludger, Luitger • Friesian • *place name derived from the famous monk*
Ludovic, Ludovik, Ludovicus, Hludwig, Maoldomhnaich, Ludo, Ludwig, Lutz • Germanic • *famous in war*
Luke, Lucas, Loukas, Lukas, Luc, Lluc, Lluch, Lukasz, Luukas, Lukacs, Luka • Greek • *man from Loucania, a Greek colony in southern Italy*
Lyle, De L'isle • Norman/Gaelic • *someone from the isles or marshy land*

Macey, Macciscum, Maccius •
Norman/Latin • *someone from
Massey, Normandy*

**Madison, Madde, Madeleine,
Maud** • American English • *son of
Maud or Matilda, the battleaxe*

Madog, Madoc, Aodh • British/
Welsh • *fiery and fortunate*

**Magnus, Maghnus, Manus, Måns,
Mogens, Mànas** • Latin • *a great
man*

Mahavir • Sanskrit • *great hero,
founder of the Jain religion*

Mahendra, Mahinder, Mohinder
• Sanskrit • *Great Indra, first great
Buddhist missionary*

Mahesh • Sanskrit • *great ruler*

Māhir • Arabic • *clever, dexterous,
skilful*

Mainchín, Mannix • Irish • *monk*

**Maitland, Maltalent, Mautalent,
Mautalant** • Anglo-Saxon/Norman
• *bad-tempered or from Mautalant,
a barren place in France*

Majdi, Magdi • Arabic

**Makarios, Macaire, Macario,
Makari** • Greek • *blessed one*

Makram • Arabic • *giving, generous
and magnificent*

Malachi, Malachy, Maoileachlainn
• Biblical/Irish Gaelic • *my
messenger or follower of St Seachnall
or St Secundinus*

Malcolm, Maelcoluim, Maelcoluim
• Scots Gaelic • *follower of St
Columba, the Dove*

Manāl • Arabic • *materially
prosperous*

Manār • Arabic • *light of goodness*

Manlio, Manlius • Latin • *Roman
family name famous for republican
leanings*

Mansūr • Arabic • *victor, conqueror*

Manuel, Emmanuel • Biblical/
Spanish • *God is with us or amongst
us*

Maoilíosa • Irish Gaelic • *follower
of Jesus Christ*

Mario, Marius • Latin • *from Roman
family name and male version of
Mary*

Marius • Latin • *Roman family
name; clouded meaning*

**Marmaduke, Maelmaedoc,
Maedoc, Maolmaodhog, Duke** •
Irish Gaelic/English • *follower of
Madog*

Marvin, Mervyn • British Welsh/
English • *he's a lord or eminent being
down to his marrow*

Mas'ūd • Arabic • *fortuitous,
auspicious*

**Mathias, Matthias, Matthaeus,
Matthäus, Mattathia** • Biblical/
Greek/Jewish/Aramaic/Latin • *gift
of God*

**Matthew, Matt, Mathew,
Mattathia, Maitiu, Matthias,
Maitias, Mata, Matha, Matthäus,
Matthijs, Mads, Mathies, Mats,
Mathieu, Mateo, Mateu, Mateus,
Matteo, Mattia, Matvei, Mateusz,
Maciej, Matej, Matyas, Matija,
Matti, Matyas, Mate, Mattanah,
Mattaniah, Mattathah, Mattatha,
Mattathiah, Mattathias** • Biblical/
Hebrew/Jewish/English • *gift of God*

**Maurice, Moris, Morris, Mo,
Maurus, Moritz, Maurizio,
Mauricius, Mavriki, Mauricio,
Maurits,** • Latin • *a dark swarthy
person as in a Moor from Arabia*

Mauro • Latin • *a Moor as in Arab;
early followers of St Benedictine*

**Maxim, Max, Maximus, Maxime,
Massimo, Maksim, Maximo,**

Macsen • Latin • *the greatest!*

Melvin, Melvyn, Mel, Melvin, Melville, Melvyn, Malleville • *a man from a bad place*

Mengyao • Chinese • *a parent's wish for a wise child*

Merfyn, Mervin, Mervyn, Marvin, Mervyn • British/Welsh • *he's a lord or eminent being down to his marrow*

Methodius, Mefodi • Greek • *following the path or road, spiritual as much as a traveller*

Meurig, Mauricius, Mouric, Meuric, Maurice • British/Welsh • *a dark swarthy person as in a Moor from Arabia*

Michael, Micah, Micheal, Meical, Mihangel, Machiel, Mikael, Mikkel, Michel, Miguel, Miquel, Michele, Mikhail, Michal, Mihovil, Mihajlo, Mihael, Mikko, Mihaly, Mike, Mick, Micky, Mikey, Mickey, Meical • Biblical/Hebrew/Jewish/English • *who is like God?*

Michelangelo • Bibilical • *angel*

Midhat • Arabic • *tribute*

Mihangel, Michael • British/Welsh • *Michael the Archangel*

Milan, Milano • Czech/Italian • *grace and favour or someone who comes from Milan, Italy*

Mingli • Chinese • *lighting up propriety*

Misha, Micha, Mikhail • Russian • *he who is like God*

Mitchell, Michael, Michel, Mitch • Norman/English • *he who is like God*

Montague, Montaigu, Monty • Norman/Latin • *a person from the pointed hill, particularly Montaigu, La Manche, Normandy*

Montgomery, Montgomeric, Monty • Germanic/Norman • *the powerful man from the hill country*

Morgan, Morgannwg, Morcant • British/Welsh • *vague beginning but ends with ending, completion, full circle*

Morris, Maurice, Mo, Miuris • English/Latin • *a dark swarthy person as in a Moor from Arabia*

Moses, Moshe, Moïse, Moss, Moses, Mostyn, Monty • Biblical/Hebrew/Egyptian • *born of God*

Mubārak • Arabic • *fortunate, blessed*

Muhammed • Arabic • *sacred qualities, scrupulous*

Mujtaba • Arabic • *the chosen one*

Munīr • Arabic • *shining, dazzling, glorious*

Murray, Moray, Muireach • Scots Gaelic • *a person from Moray*

Mus'ad • Arabic • *born lucky!*

Mu'tasim • Arabic • *trust in God or the Lord*

Nabīl • Arabic • *royal born or noble birth*

Nadīm • Arabic • *best friend, companion you share your social life with*

Nā'il • Arabic • *he who cannot lose, always comes up smelling of roses*

Nājib, Nāgib • Arabic • *cultured, cultivated, in a class of his own*

Naldo • Spanish/Visigothic • *wise, powerful and strong*

Nanda • Sanskrit • *joy, happiness, child (especially son), many riches*

Nathan, Nat, Jonathan, Nathen • Biblical/Hebrew/Jewish • *God has given*

Nathaniel, Nat, Nathanael,

Natanaele • Biblical/Greek/English • *God has given*

Naveed • Persian • *glad tidings, invite to the wedding or something just as jolly*

Nazaire, Nazarius, Nazario • Latin • *Nazareth, Jesus Christ's home town*

Neo • African • *gift*

Nestor, Nestore • Greek • *personal name of King of Pylos in legend, one of the Greeks (bearing gifts!) at Troy*

Niaz • Persian • *prayer, gift, sacrifice*

Nikita, Aniketos • Greek/Russian • *unconquered; name of Orthodox saint*

Nino, Giannino • Latin/Spanish • *the boy, referring to the Christ Child*

Noam • Jewish/Hebrew • *joy, pleasure and happiness*

Noble, Nobilis • American English/Norman Latin • *someone who has noble qualities even if not born aristocratic*

Nolasco • Latin • *personal name honouring the man who rescued the Christians from the Moslems during the Crusade*

Norman, Nordman, Tormod • Germanic • *a man from the north; Norseman or Viking*

Norris, Norreis • Germanic/Frankish • *a person who has migrated from the north to Normandy; Norseman or Viking*

Obadiah, Abdullah • Biblical/Hebrew/Jewish • *servant of God*

Obed • Hebrew/Jewish • *God's servant*

Octavian, Octavianus, Octavius, Octavus, Octavio • Latin • *a Roman family name*

Oleg, Helgi • Norse • *prosperous, the chap who created Kiev, Ukraine*

Olijimi • Nigerian • *God gave me this*

Oliver, Olivier, Olivarius, Ollie, Oleifr, Noll • Germanic/Frankish/Norse • *olive tree, prosperity or abundance*

Onofre • Egyptian • *a man who opens up to God*

Osbert, Osbeorht • Anglo-Saxon • *illuminated by God, famous for his devotion*

Oswald, Osweald, Oz, Ozzy, Osvaldo • Anglo-Saxon • *my ruler is God or God rules*

Oswin, Oswine, Oz • Anglo-Saxon • *God is my friend*

Otis, Ote, Ode • Germanic/Frankish • *wealthy, prosperous*

Otmar, Ottmar, Ottomar • Germanic • *famed riches*

Otto • Germanic • *riches, a royal and imperial name*

Ozzy, Oz, Ozzie • Anglo-Saxon • *shortened version of any name beginning with Os, meaning God*

Pacey, Pacciacum, Passy, Paccius • Latin/Gaulish • *a man called Paccius or from the town of Passy*

Paderau • modern Welsh • *a rosary*

Pajonga • Sierra Leonese • *walk tall, tall man*

Palmer • English • *a pilgrim who had been to the Holy Land and returned with a palm branch*

Palmiro, Palmiere • Latin/Spanish • *a pilgrim who brought back a palm from the Holy Land*

Paris, Parisii • Latin/Celtic • *member of the Parisii tribe, origins unknown*

Parthalán, Párthlán, Pártlán, Partnán, Bartholomew, Berkely, Barclay • Latin/Irish • *first ever* citizen of Ireland after the Biblical flood; Biblical meaning son of Tolmai from Galilee

Parvaiz • Persian • *lucky, auspicious, successful*

Patrice, Patrick • Latin/French • Latin/Irish Gaelic • *patrician*

Patrick, Pàdraig, Pat, Paddy, Patsy, Páraic, Patrice, Patricio, Patrizio, Porick, Podge, Pàra, Pàdair, Pàidean, Padrig, Paddy, Patrick, Pat, Patrice • Latin/Irish Gaelic • *patrician*

Paul, Paulus, Pol, Pål, Poul, Pall, Pauwel, Påvel, Pablo, Pau, Paulo, Paolo, Pavlos, Pavao, Pavle, Paavo, Paulius, Pablo • Latin • *Roman family name*

Paulino, Pablo, Paulus • Spanish/ Italian • *Roman family name*

Paco, Francis, Francisco • Spanish • *to be French, someone from France*

Pepe, Pepito, Joseph, José • Spanish • *God is my salvation*

Percival, Parsifal, Parzifal, Perceval, Peredur, Percy, Perce, Perce, Pearce, Pierce, Percy, Piers, Perceval, Perce • Celtic/Norman • *Celtic name of Peredur; Peredur's valley*

Percy, Piers, Percival, Perci, Persiacum, Persius, Perse, Percehaie, Percerhaie • Latin/ Gaulish • *Pierce's hedge*

Peregrine, Peregrinus, Perry, Pellegrino • Latin • *stranger, wanderer, foreigner*

Persis • Biblical/Greek • *a Persian woman*

Piaras, Piers, Pierce, Pearce • Irish Gaelic/English • *Pierce's hedge*

Philip, Phil, Phillipos, Phileinhippos, Pip, Pilib, Filib, **Philipp, Filip, Philippe, Phillip, Felipe, Felip, Filipe, Filippo, Filip, Vilppu, Fulop, Filipes, Philipp, Pino** • Greek • *friend or lover of horses*

Phineas, Fineas, Panhsj, Phinehas, Pinchas • Hebrew/Jewish/Biblical • *a person from Nubia, now southern Egypt or northern Sudan, or from the snake's mouth*

Pompeo, Pompeius • Latin • *Roman family name*

Pontius, Ponzio, Poncio • Latin • *family name; origin unknown*

Porfirio, Porphyrios, Porphyrius, Porphyra, Porfirio • Greek • *the colour purple*

Prakash • Sanskrit • *a famous, radiant person*

Pramod • Sanskrit • *joy, happiness, pleasure*

Prasad • Sanskrit • *by the grace of God, gifts from the deity to the worshippers*

Pravin • Sanskrit • *dexterous, clever and skilful*

Preston, Preosttun • Anglo-Saxon • *priest's town*

Prince, Princeps • Latin/English • *royal title*

Proinséas, Francis • Irish/Latin • *to be French, someone from France*

Prosper, Prosperus, Prospero • Latin • *a person who prospers*

Qāsim • Arabic • *giver*

Quentin, Quintinus, Quintus, Quintin, Quinton, Cwentun • Latin • *Roman family name*

Qi • Chinese • *enlightened, wonderment and intellectual*

Qingshan • Chinese • *celebrating goodness*

Quirinius • Latin • *governor*

Qusay • Arabic • *vague origin but could mean someone who comes from a long way away*

Radwan • Arabic • *pleasure and enjoyment*

Raghīd • Arabic • *freedom loving and devil-may-care*

Raghnall, Raonull, Rannal, Ronald • Norse • *wise, decisive chief or an oracle of the gods or kings*

Raj, Raju • Sanskrit • *king, royal*

Rajendra • Sanskrit • *mighty king, mighty ruler*

Rajesh, Raj • Sanskrit • *above the law, above the king, divine*

Ramadān • Arabic • *ninth month of the Muslim calendar: the hot month*

Rameshwar, Ramnath • Sanskrit • *Lord Rama*

Ramiro • Spanish/Visigothic • *a man famous for his advice and counselling*

Raphael, Rafael, Rafa, Rapha, Raffaele • Biblical/Jewish/Hebrew • *God has healed*

Rashād, Rashīd • Arabic • *spiritual or religious wisdom*

Reagan, Regan, Riagain • Irish Gaelic/English • *descendant of Riagain, the impulsive or impatient one*

Rearden, Ríordan, Rordan, Ríoghbhardán • English/Irish Gaelic • *wee poet king*

Régis • French/Provençal • *the ruler*

Reinhold, Reinwald, Reine • Germanic • *splendid, wonderful adviser*

Reinmar, Reine • Germanic • *famous adviser, speaker*

Remus, Remo • Latin • *with Romulus, founder of Rome*

Reuben, Reuven, Rube, Rubén • Biblical/Hebrew/Jewish • *behold, a son!*

Rhys, Reece, Rees • British/Welsh • *enthusiasm*

Ríordan, Rearden, Ríoghbhardán • Irish • *poet king or king of the poets*

Riscu • African • *prosperity*

Roald, Hrod • Norse • *famous ruler, famous chief*

Robert, Rob, Robbie, Rodberht, Reodbeorht, Bob, Rob, Bobby, Robin, Roibéard, Raibeart, Rupprecht, Robrecht, Rupert, Robbert, Roberto, Roopertti, Roberts, Rabbie, Rab, Rigoberto • Germanic • *famous and bright*

Robhartach, Rob • Irish Gaelic • *bringer or broker of prosperity and wealth*

Robin, Robben, Robert • Germanic • *famous and bright*

Rodney, Rod, Roddy • Anglo-Saxon • *famous island; a person from there*

Rohan • Sanskrit • *ascension, healing, medicine*

Roland, Rodland, Rowland, Roly, Rowley, Rolie, Rolland, Roldan, Rolant • Germanic • *famed throughout land*

Roman, Romanus, Romain, Romano • Latin/Czech/Polish/Romanian • *to be Roman*

Romeo, Romaeus • Latin • *a pilgrim who has visited Rome*

Romulus, Romolo • Latin • *someone from Rome; one of the founders of Rome*

Rory, Ruaidhrí, Ruairidh, Roderick, Roy, Ruadh • Gaelic • *fiery temper or red-headed*

Rosendo • Visigothic • *a man on the path to fame*

Roshan • Persian/Urdu • *splendid,*

glorious, famous

Rostislav • Slavic • *to seize or grab victory*

Ru • Chinese • *Confucian scholar*

Rupert, Ruprecht, Robert • Germanic/Dutch • *famous and bright*

Rurik, Hrodrik, Roderick • Norse • *famous ruler, the name of the man who founded Russia's Novogorod, the Big New City*

Rushdi • Arabic • *old head on young shoulders; ahead of his years*

Ruslan • literary invention/Russian • *meaning unknown; name was used by Aleksandr Pushkin in his poem 'Ruslan and Ludmila'*

Sacheverell, Sautechevreuil, Sachie • Norman • *surname from place name Saute Chevreuil, meaning roebuck leap*

Sachdev • Sanskrit • *truth of God, totally honest*

Sa'd • Arabic • *good luck and good fortune*

Safdar • Arabic • *a man who breaks ranks; loose cannon*

Safwat • Arabic • *choice and best*

Sa'īd • Arabic • *happy-go-lucky*

Sage, Sauge, Sapius • Anglo-Saxon

Salāh • Arabic • *righteous and devout religiously*

Sālih • Arabic • *devout, devoted*

Salvatore, Salvator, Salvador, Sal • Latin • *saviour*

Samant • Sanskrit • *universal, the whole thing*

Samuel, Shemuel, Shaulmeel, Sam, Sammy, Sawyl • Biblical/Hebrew/Jewish • *name of God, God has heard, listen to God*

Sancho, Sanctus • Latin/Spanish • *holy*

Sanjay • Sanskrit • *victorious, triumphant*

Santos • Roman Catholic • *saints*

Saul • Biblical/Hebrew/Latin • *asked for, prayed for, yearned for*

Seanán, Shannon , Senan • Irish Gaelic • *wise, mature and ancient*

Seathan, Jean, Jehan • Scots Gaelic/French/Biblical/English/Latin • *God is gracious or gift of God*

Sebastián, Sebastianus, Sebastos, Sébastien, Sebastiano, Sevastyan • Latin/Greek • *a man from Sebaste in Asia Minor (now Turkey)*

Selig, Zelig, Asher • Jewish/Yiddish/Hebrew • *happy and fortunate*

Selwyn, Selewyn, Selewine, Silvanus, Silas, Selwin • Anglo-Saxon • *prosperous, high-flying friend*

Serafino • Jewish/Hebrew • *the burning ones*

Serge, Sergio, Sergius • Latin/Etruscan • *old Roman family name*

Sergei, Serzha • Russian/Etruscan • *old Roman name; vague roots*

Seth • Biblical/Hebrew • *appointed to a certain place*

Seth, Set • Egyptian/Greek • *dazzling God of Chaos and Deserts*

Severiano, Severus, Severo, Severinus, Sören, Severinus, Severino, Seve • Latin • *Roman family name*

Seymour • Norman • *baronial name from Saint-Maur in Normandy*

Shah • Muslim/Persian/Sufi • *king, god, lord, emperor, divine mystic*

Shahjahan • Muslim/Persian • *king of the world*

Shamshad • Persian • *tall as a box tree*

Sharīf • Arabic • *eminent in his field*

Shirong • Chinese • *reward as a result of learning*

Shripati • Sanskrit • *Lord of Good Fortune and Luck*

Siegbert • Germanic • *quick, famous victory*

Sigmund, Siegmund, Sigismund • Germanic • *a personal name meaning victorious and protector*

Siegwald, Sigiswald, Sigurd, Sjur, Sjurd • Germanic/Norse • *protector, victory*

Simcha • Jewish/Hebrew/Ashkenazic • *joy*

Simeon • English/Biblical/Hebrew • *he has heard*

Simón, Siomon, Sim, Simidh, Sieman, Simao, Simone, Semyon, Szymon, Simo, Sim, Simmie • Biblical/Hebrew/Jewish • *hearkening, hearing*

Sinclair • Norman • *baronial name from Saint-Clair who received earldoms in Caithness and Orkney*

Slava • Slavic • *glory*

Somerled, Sumarlid, Summerlad, Somhairle, Sorley • Scots Gaelic/Norse • *summer traveller (southern hemisphere)*

Somhairle • Irish Gaelic/Norse • *summer traveller (southern hemisphere)*

Srikant • Sanskrit • *beloved of Sri, Goddess of Light, Beauty and Wealth*

Sriram • Sanskrit • *devotee or worshipper of the Lord Rama*

Stanilas, Stanislaus, Stanislaw, Aneislis, Stanislav • Slavic • *glory to the court, glorious courtier or politician*

Stian, Stigand, Kris, Stig • *wanderer*

Storm • American English • *thunderstorm*

Subhash • Sanskrit • *eloquent and articulate*

Sudhir • Sanskrit • *wise and strong*

Sumanjit • Sanskrit • *he who conquerors the demon Sumana*

Sumantra • Sanskrit • *a person who is well versed in the classics*

Surendra, Surinder • Sanskrit • *the most powerful of the gods*

Suresh • Sanskrit • *ruler of the gods*

Sushil • Sanskrit • *a hail and hearty chap*

Svyatoslav, Syvantoslav • Slavic • *sacred glory*

Tad, Tadhg, Thaddeus, Tig, Tim, Taddeo, Teague, Teigue, Tadeo • Irish Gaelic • *poet, wise man, philosopher*

Tāha • Arabic • *opening letters of the 20th sura in the Koran*

Tam, Tammy, Thomas, Tommy, Tom • Greek/Aramaic • *twin*

Tāmir • Arabic • *rich in dates and figs and all good things*

Tammaro • Germanic • *clever; famous mind*

Taqi • Arabic • *God-fearing*

Tara • Sanskrit • *shining light for the saviour; carrying the Lord*

Taras, Tarasio • Greek • *man from Tarentum in northern Italy*

Tarquin, Tarquinius • Etruscan • *Roman family name with no known root*

Tavish, Tamhas, Thomas • Scots Gaelic/English • *twin*

Tawfiq • Arabic • *prosperity and luck*

Tengfei • Chinese • *soaring high*

Teodosio • Greek • *God-given*

Texas, Tex, Teyas • Native American • *friend, and of course someone from Texas, the biggest state in the US of A*

Thaddeus, Labbaeus, Theodoras, Theodotos, Thad, Tad • Biblical/

Aramaic/Greek • *given by God or God's gift*

Theo, Théodore, Theobald, Theodor, Teodoro • Greek • *God*

Théodore, Theo, Ted, Teddy, Theodor, Theodoor, Teodor, Teodoro, Feodor, Fyodr, Teuvo, Tivador, Todor, Teodors, Theodoric, Tiobad, Ted, Teddy, Edward, Theodos, Theodosios, Teodosio, Todos, Theodoros • Greek • *God-given or giving to God or God's gift*

Theophilus, Theosphilos, Theo, Théophile, Teofilo • Biblical/Greek • *God's friend or friend of God*

Thomas, Thos, Tom, Tommy, Tomás, Tamhas, Tomos, Tommaso, Foma, Tomasz, Toma, Tomaz, Tuomo, Toms, Didymos • Biblical/Aramaic/Greek • *twin*

Tiernan, Tighearnan, Tighearnach, Tierney • Irish Gaelic • *lord or chief*

Timothy, Tim, Tadhg, Timmy, Timotheus, Timotheos, Timetheo, Timmy, Tiger, Timothee, Timo, Timoteo, Timofei • Biblical/Latin/Greek • *honour God*

Tingfeng • Chinese • *thunderbolt or lightning peak*

Tingzhe • Chinese • *judgement or wisdom is required*

Tirso, Thyrsos • Oriental • *follower of Dionysus (Bacchus)*

Titus, Tito, Tiziano, Titianus, Titian • Latin • *old Roman name, unknown origins*

Tobias, Tobiah, Tobijah, Toby • Biblical/Hebrew/Greek • *God is good*

Tochukwa • Nigerian • *praise God*

Tony, Anthony, Tone, Tönjes, Antonius, Tonio • Estruscan/Roman • *Roman family name but with confused origins*

Tor, Thor, Tord • Norse • *the god Thor*

Tore, Ture • Norse • *a man like the god Thor*

Tormod, Torrmod • Norse • *a man with the courage of Thor, the God of Thunder*

Torvald, Thorwald • Norse • *ruler with the power of Thor*

Tory, Torir, Thor, Thori, Thorir • Norse/Danish • *Thor*

Toussaint • French • *tous les saints; a child who has the blessings of all the saints*

Tracy, Thraciusacum, Tracey • Latin/Gaulic • *a person from a place in Normandy called Tracy!*

Traugott • Germanic • *trust in God*

Trent, Trenton • British/Welsh • *after the River Trent in the English Midlands; its root meaning is to travel or journey*

Trenton, Trent • American English • *means the settlement by the Trent, or after William Trent, the British Quaker founder of the New Jersey city*

Trond, Tron • Norse • *a man from Trondelag in Norway*

Troy, Trey, Troyes • French • *someone from the French city of Troyes, or, more powerful, in memory of the Troy (in modern-day Turkey) of Greek mythology*

Tristan, Trystan, Tristram, Tristam, Trystram, Tristram, Dristan, Drystan • British/Welsh • *rowdy, rebellious, blue, melancholic, chaotic*

Tucker, Tucian • Anglo-Saxon/American English • *surname originally meaning to tease and torment*

Tullio, Tullius • Latin • *a Roman family name*

Tycho, Tychon • Greek • *hitting the mark, honest and true*

Tyson, Ty, Tison • Greek/Norman • *girl's name for Dionysius, God of Wine or meaning a hot-tempered person*

Ulric, Wulfric, Ulrick, Ulrich, Utz • Germanic/Anglo-Saxon • *power and riches*

'Umar, Omar • Arabic • *to flourish and to make the complex simple*

Urban, Urbanus • Latin • *a person who lives in the city*

Uriah, Urias, Uriel • Biblical/Jewish/Hebrew • *God is light*

Urien, Orbogen • British/Welsh • *born with a silver spoon in his mouth; privileged*

Urowo • Kenyan • *tall*

Uzziah, Uziah • Biblical/Jewish/Hebrew • *power of Yahweh*

Uzziel, Uziel • Biblical/Jewish/Hebrew • *power of God*

Val, Valentin, Valentine, Valentinius, Valens, Velten, Valentino, Valentinus, Ualan, Uailean, Folant • Latin • *flourishing, blooming, blossoming*

Valéry, Val • Germanic • *foreign power*

Vanya, Ivan • Russian • *God is gracious or gift of God*

Varfolomel, Bartholomew • Biblical • *son of Tolmai from Galilee*

Vasu • Sanskrit • *simply the best!*

Venkat • Sanskrit • *sacred mountain near Madras*

Victor, Vic, Viktor, Vittore, Vittorio • Latin • *conqueror, winner*

Vidkun, Vidkunn • Norse • *lateral thinking, wise, experienced*

Vijay • Sanskrit • *prizes or booty from victory*

Vikram, Vik • Sanskrit • *hero*

Vinay • Sanskrit • *education, intelligence, learning*

Vincent, Vince, Vincens, Vincentis, Vinnie, Uinseann, Vinzenz, Vicente, Vicenc, Vincenzo, Wincenty, Vincenc, Vinko, Vincentas, Vinzenz, Vincente • Latin • *to conquer*

Vinod • Sanskrit • *recreation, leisure, pleasure and sport*

Vishnu • Sanskrit • *joint conqueror of demon Vrtra*

Vladimir, Volodya, Valdemar, Waldemar • Slavic • *great, famous leader or ruler*

Vladislav • Slavic • *glorious leader or ruler*

Volkmar • Germanic • *famous people*

Vyacheslav, Wenceslas • Slavic/Latin • *greater and even greater glory*

Wahīb • Arabic • *philanthropist, giver, donor, benefactor*

Wā'il • Arabic • *reverts to the faith (Islam)*

Waldemar, Waldo, Wald, Walker, Wealcere, Wealcan, Woldemar • Germanic • *famous ruler*

Wallace, Wallis, Waleis, Wally • Anglo-Saxon • *foreigner*

Warren, Warin, Varenne • Germanic/Norman • *a person from La Varenne, Normandy, or a war guard*

Washington, Wassingtun • Anglo-Saxon • *the village or tribe of Wassa*

Weimin • Chinese • *honour the people with greatness*

Weishing • Chinese • *born great*

Weizhe • Chinese • *sagacious and wise*

Wenceslas, Ventieslav, Wenzel
• Slavic • *greater and even greater glory*

Wendell, Wendel • Germanic • *a member of the Slav tribe living between the Elbe and Oder*

Wynfor, Wyn • British/Welsh • *white, blonde, holy, blessed*

Wynne, Wyn, Wine, Wynn • British Welsh/Anglo-Saxon • *a friend and/ or one who is blessed and sacred*

Xue • Chinese • *studious, knowledge*

Yahya, John • Arabic/Biblical • *God is gracious or gift of God*

Yashpal • Sanskrit • *cherishes splendour*

Yasīn • Arabic • *opening letters of the 36th sura of the Koran*

Yāsir, Yusri • Arabic • *wealthy, prosperous*

Ye • Chinese • *bright*

Yefim, Euphemios • Russian/Greek • *eloquent, articulate speaker*

Yehiel, Jehiel • Biblical/Hebrew/ Jewish • *God lives*

Yeremiah • Ugandan • *exalted*

Yevgeni, Eugenios, Eugene • Russian • *well bred and high born*

Yilma • Ethiopian • *may he prosper*

Yongliang • Chinese • *forever light and bright*

Yongrui • Chinese • *eternally or forever lucky*

Yosef, Joseph, Yusūf • Jewish/ Hebrew/Arabic • *God is my salvation*

Yuan, Juan, John • Manx Gaelic • *God is gracious or gift of God*

Yuanjun • Chinese • *master or child of the Yuan river*

Yusra • Arabic • *rich, well endowed*

Yusūf, Joseph • Arabic/Biblical • *God is my salvation*

Zadok • Biblical/Jewish/Hebrew • *just or righteous*

Zāhir • Arabic • *radiant, bright, luminous*

Zamir • Arabic • *ideas, mental thoughts*

Zayd • Arabic • *growth, increase*

Zeb, Zebedee, Zebulun • Biblical/ Hebrew/Greek • *gift of Jehovah*

Zebadiah, Zabdi, Zabadiah, Zebedee • Biblical/Hebrew/Jewish • *living with, to dwell, Yahweh has given*

Zabulun, Zabulon, Zebulon, Zabal • Biblical/Hebrew/Jewish • *exaltation*

Zed, Zedekiah • Biblical/Jewish/ Hebrew • *justice of Yahweh*

Zedong • Chinese • *east of the marshes*

Zeke, Ezekiel • Biblical/Jewish/ Hebrew • *God gives me strength*

Zelig, Selig • Jewish/Yiddish • *happy and counting my blessings*

Zengguang • Chinese • *growing brightness*

Zeno, Zenon • Greek • *Zeus or Jupiter*

Zenodoros • Greek • *gift of Zeus or Jupiter*

Ziyād • Arabic • *to grow and build*

Girls

Abigail, Abbie, Abby, Abbey, Abbigail, Abbiegail, Abbygail, Abigayle, Abi • Biblical/Jewish/ Hebrew • *my father is joy, father is exaltation*

Abilene, Abbie, Abby, Abbey, Abi, Lena • Biblical/Jewish/Hebrew • *an area of Palestine or the Holy Land, meaning grass or grasses*

Abishag, Avishag • Biblical/Jewish/ Hebrew • *wise and educated*

Adelheid, Adalheid, Aleida, Aleit, Alke, Elke • Germanic • *noble woman, carries herself well*

Adeltraud • Germanic • *strong and noble*

Adélaide • Germanic • *noble, kind and caring*

Adèle, Adelle, Addie, Addi, Addy, Adeline, Adelina, Aline Adela, Adella, Alette • French • *noble*

Adria, Adrianne, Adrienne, Adrianna, Adriana • Latin • *a person from Hadria after which the Adriatic Sea is named*

Adrienne, Adriana • Latin • *a person from Hadria after which the Adriatic Sea is named*

Aegle, Aglaia • Greek • *splendid radiance*

Aeronwen • British/Welsh • *white, sacred and fair*

Africa • Latin • *the dark continent*

Agatha, Agathe, Aggie, Agata, Ágot, Águeda, Agathos • Greek • *good and honourable*

Agnès, Aggie, Aigneis, Inés, Agnese, Agnessa, Agnieszka, Anezka, Aune, Agnese, Agne, Annis, Annys, Annice, Aigneis,

Agnethe, Agnetis, Agnete, Ågot • Greek • *pure and holy*

Agrippina, Agrafena • Latin/ Estruscan • *family name of old Roman family*

Áine • Irish • *as bright, as radiant as the Queen of the Faeries*

Aingeal • Irish • *angel*

'Āisha, Aishah, Ayesha • Arabic • *alive; Mohammed's third and fave wife*

Alba • Latin/Germanic • *white or elfin*

Alberta, Albertina • French/ Germanic/Anglo-Saxon • *bright and noble*

Albina, Bina, Albus, Albius • Latin • *Roman family*

Alethea, Althea, Aletheia • Greek • *truth*

Alfreda, Freddie, Fred • Anglo-Saxon • *supernatural, faerie counsel, help*

Alice, Alicia, Alesha, Alisia, Alys, Alisha, Alissa, Alesha, Alisa, Alissa, Ailish, Alis, Alys • Norman • *noble, kind and caring*

Alina, Allina • Arabic • *noble and lovely*

Aline, Adeline, Alainn • French/ Gaelic • *noble*

Aloisa, Aloisia • Latin/Germanic • *all-seeing wisdom*

Alison, Allie, Ally, Aly, Alysoun, Aliyah, Aaliyah, Allison, Allyson • Norman • *noble, kind and caring*

Aliza, Freyde • Jewish/Hebrew • *joyful and gay*

Allegra • Italian • *happy, jolly, frisky*

Allina, Alina • French • *noble*

Aloisia • Provençal/Latin/Germanic • *all-wise, all-seeing*

Amal • Arabic • *hope, expection, anticipation*

Amrit • Sanskrit • *divine, immortal, good enough to eat*

Anais, Ana, Anya • Biblical/Catalan/Provençal • *God has favoured me*

Anastasis, Anastasia • Greek/Russian • *resurrection*

Angel, Ángela, Angelina, Angeline, Angie, Ange, Angelos • Greek • *messenger of God*

Angela, Angelita • Latin • *Greek/Latin • messenger of God*

Ángeles • Spanish/Roman Catholic • *Our Lady of the Angels*

Angelica, Angélique, Angelika • Latin • *a girl of the angels*

Angosto • Spanish/Galician/Roman Catholic • *Our Lady of Angosto, a place where the Virgin appeared*

Anita, Ana • Spanish/ Biblical • *God has favoured me*

Ann, Anne, Anna, Annabel, Annette, Annetta, Anouk, Anni, Annelie, Anneli, Annella, Annabell, Annabella, Annabelle, Belle, Annie, Anna, Anneke, Anke, Anoushka, Anouska, Arabella, Arabel Anna, Ana • Biblical/Jewish/Hebrew • *God has favoured me*

Annalisa, Annaliesa, Annalise, Annelise, Annelies, Anneli • German • *combo of Anne and Elisabeth; God has favoured me plus God is my oath*

Anneka, Anika, Annika, Anna, Anniken • German/Dutch • *God has favoured me*

Annemarie, Annmarie, Annamarie, Annamaria • modern • *combo of Anne and Maria; God has favoured me*

Annunziata, Nunzia, Anunciación, Anunciata • Roman Catholic • *announcing the birth of Jesus to Mary*

Antonia, Anthonia • Estruscan/Roman • *Roman family name but with confused origins*

Antoinette, Toinette, Tonette, Antonella, Antonia, Toni, Antonina • Estruscan/Roman • *Roman family name but with confused origins*

Anuradha • Sanskrit • *Stream of Oblations, 28th asterism of Hindu astrology*

Anwen, Annwen • British/Welsh • *blessed and beautiful*

Aphra, Afra • Latin • *a woman from Africa, the dark continent*

Araceli • Spanish/Latin American • *the sky is an altar to God*

Aranrhod • British/Welsh • *huge, big, round, plump and humped!*

Aretha, Arete • Greek/American English • *excellent*

Ariadne, Arianna, Ariana, Arianne • Greek/Cretean • *most holy*

Arlette • Germanic/Norman • *uncertain roots but possibly eagle*

Armani • Lombardic/Italian/Germanic • *freeman*

Åsa, Ase • Norse • *God*

Asha • Sanskrit • *hope*

Ashanti • Ghanaian • *tribe from Ghana*

Aslög, Asslaug, Åslaug • Swedish • *God-consecrated*

Asmã • Arabic • *prestigious*

Atalanta, Atlanta • mythological/American English • *capital of American state of Georgia*

Athene, Athena, Athina, Athenai • Greek • *Greek Goddess of Wisdom and protector of the city of Athens*

Atholl, Athol, Athole • Gaelic • *'New Ireland' area of Perthshire*

Audra, Audrey, Audrie, Audry, Audrina • Anglo-Saxon • *strength*

and noble of character
Augusta, Augustina, Augustine, Agustina, August • Latin • *great, the max, magnificent, expansive, nobody does it better*
Aurelia, Auriol • Latin • *Latin* • *Roman family name meaning golden*
Aurelie • Latin/French • *Roman family name meaning golden*
'Ayda • Arabic • *opportunity, beneficient*

Bahīja, Bahīga • Arabic • *joyful, beautiful woman*
Bahiyya • Arabic • *a beautiful, radiant, dazzling woman*
Bala • Sanskrit • *young*
Bano • Persian • *lady, princess, bride*
Barbara, Babette, Babs, Barbra, Barb, Barbie, Baibín, Báirbre, Varvara, Varya, Barbro, Barbora • Greek • *a foreign woman*
Basma • Arabic • *this woman melts your heart with her smile*
Bathsheba, Sheba, Bathsheeva • Biblical/Jewish/Hebrew • *daughter of the oath*
Bay, Baie, Baca, Bacca • Latin/Norman • *bay tree*
Beata, Beate • Swiss • *blessed*
Beatrice, Beatrix, Bea, Bee, Beattie, Beatriz, Beitiris, Betrys, Viatrix, Viator, Beatus, Begoña • Spanish • *honouring the Virgin as patron of Bilbao*
Belaynesh • Ethiopian • *you are above all*
Bertha, Berthe, Berta • Germanic • *bright and famous*
Bess, Bessie, Bet, Beth, Elizabeth, Elisabeth, Bethan, Betsy, Betty, Bette, Bettina, Buffy, Beitidh, Elisheba • Hebrew/Greek • *God is*

my oath or God is my abundance
Bethany, Beth • Biblical/Jewish/Hebrew • *village outside Jerusalem where Jesus stayed in Holy Week before travelling to Jerusalem for Palm Sunday; it means house of figs or dates*
Bethlehem, Belem • Biblical/Jewish/Hebrew • *where Jesus was born*
Bethan, Beth • British/Welsh • *God is my oath or God is my abundance*
Bina, Albina, Devorah, Deborah, Binah, Bine, Binke • Jewish/Hebrew/Yiddish • *bee or understanding*
Blodwen, Blodwyn, Blod • British/Welsh • *sacred, holy flowers*
Bobbie, Roberta • Germanic • *famous and bright*
Bodil, Bothild, Botilda • Norse • *compensation for the battle*
Breanna, Brianna, Breanne • Irish Celtic • *high or royal born, noble*
Bridget, Briget, Bridgid, Brigid, Biddy, Bride, Bridy, Bridie, Bridey, Brigitte, Britt, Brighid, Birgit, Brigette, Birgitta, Brigitta, Bedelia, Bríd, Breda, Breeda, Bree, Bríghe, Brídín, Bree, Bri, Brighida, Berit, Britta, Birgitte, Birthe, Birte, Ffraid • Irish Gaelic • *the exalted one*
Brittany, Britney • Latin • *the Celtic-speaking province of north-west France, so-called due to the influx of Celts from Cornwall when the Romans invaded, and who trans-ferred Britannia, their name for the island, across to this part of France*
Brooklyn, Lyn, Breukelen • Dutch • *a district of New York City when it was New Amsterdam under Dutch control, meaning broken land*

Bushra • Arabic • *happy news, glad tidings and fine omen*

Calista, Callie, Callie, Calixta, Calixtus • Latin • *cup as in a Christian chalice or holy grail*

Camilla, Milla, Millie, Milly, Camille, Camila • Latin/French • *Roman family name*

Canna • Latin/Australian English • *reed; bright flowers that grow in warm climes like Oz*

Carla, Carlene, Charlene, Charlotte, Carlotta, Charlotta, Carleen, Carlin, Carlina, Carlyn, Carlynne, Carline, Carolina, Caroline, Carly, Karly, Carley, Carola, Carlie, Carli, Carolyn, Caro, Carrie, Carol, Carole, Caryl, Caryll, Sharlene, Charlie, Charley, Lotte, Lottie, Tottie • Italian/English/Germanic • *a freeman*

Carmel, Carmella, Carmelina, Camelita, Carmen, Carmine, Carmela • Roman Catholic • *Our Lady of Carmel, the mountain where early Christians lived as hermits and later became the Carmelite order of monks*

Casilda • Spanish • *unsure origins; an 11th-century Moorish saint, she lived in Toledo*

Cecilia, Cécile, Cecily, Cecelia, Cissie, Cissey, Sessy, Sissi, Sissy, Cecille, Cecilie, Cacille, Cacilia, Caecilia, Cicely • Latin/English • *old Roman family name Caecilius*

Celia, Célie, Caelia, Caelum, Celina • Latin • *Roman family name meaning heaven*

Céleste, Celestine, Celestina, Celia, Celine, Marcelline, Caelius, Caelia, Caelestis • Roman family name meaning heaven

Céline, Caelina, Marceline, Marcelline, Caelius, Celina • Latin/French • *Roman family name meaning heaven*

Ceridwen, Ceridwynn, Ceri • British/Welsh • *Goddess of Poetry*

Chalice • Latin • *cup as in a Christian chalice or holy grail*

Chantal, Chantelle, Shantell • French • *in honour of St Jeanne-Françoise, a woman of great charity and virtue who married the Baron de Chantal; when he died she adopted a severe religious life following St Francis of Sales*

Charisma, Karrisma, Kharisma • Greek • *spiritual blessings*

Charline, Charlene, Sharlene, Shalene • French/American English/Australian/Germanic • *a freeman*

Charlotte, Carlotta, Karlotte, Karlotta, Séarlait • French/Germanic • *a freeman*

Charmaine, Charmian, Kharmion • created name • *combo of charm and Lorraine*

Cherie, Cheri, Cherie, Cheree, Sheree, Querida • French • *darling*

Chevonne, Siobhán, Shivaun • English/American/Irish Gaelic • *God is gracious or gift of God*

Cheyenne, Sahiyena • French Canadian • *an Indian tribe from Dakota*

Chiara, Clare, Claire, Clara, Ciara, Kiarah, Kiara, Kiera, Clair, Clarette, Clarinda, Clarrie, Clarus • Latin/Italian • *bright, famous, crystal-clear*

Christine, Christiana, Chris, Chrissy, Christianne, Christina, Cristina, Kristina, Chriselda,

Chrissie, Christa, Christabel, Christabella, Christabelle, Cristobel, Christobel, Christelle, Christella, Christel, Christene, Christeen, Cristina, Cairistine, Cairistióna, Crystin • Scots Gaelic/Latin • *follower of Christ*

Christian, Christiane, Christiana, Anna, Christie, Christy, Kristy, Christina, Chris, Tina, Cristiona, Cairistióna, Stineag, Cairistine, Crystin, Kristin, Kristina, Kerstin, Kirsten, Krzystyna, Kirsti, Kirsty, Krisztiana, Krisztina • Scots Gaelic/Latin • *follower of Christ*

Cilla, Priscilla, Pricus, Prissy • Biblical/Latin • *Roman family name meaning ancient, old*

Ciorstaidh, Ciostag, Kirsty, Kirstie, Chirsty, Curstaidh, Curstag • Scots Gaelic/Scandinavian

Clare, Claire, Clara, Chiara, Klara, Kiara, Clara, Kiarah • Latin/English • *bright, famous, crystal-clear*

Clarice, Claritia • Latin/French/English • *bright, famous, crystal-clear*

Clarissa, Clarisa, Clarice, Clarrisse, Clarisse, Claris, Clarissa, Cáitir • Latin • *bright, famous, crystal-clear*

Claudia, Claudine, Claude, Claudinia, Claudette, Klavdia • Latin • *from the old Roman family name Claudius*

Cleopatra, Cleo, Clio, Kleos, Kleio, Kleopatra • Greek/Ptolemaic • *glory to father*

Clothilde • Germanic • *famed through war and battles*

Consilia, Conseja • Roman Catholic • *Mary of Good Counsel and Advice*

Cordelia, Cordellia, Cordula, Cordis • literary invention • *possibly from Latin for heart; by William Shakespeare for the virtuous daughter in* King Lear

Cornelia • Latin • *Roman family name, connected to cornucopia and the horn of plenty*

Courtney • Norman • *the barony of Courtenay*

Crescentia, Kreszenz • Latin/Bavarian • *growing, glourishing as in the waxing crescent moon; a positive omen*

Cynthia, Kynthia, Kynthos, Cyndy, Cindy, Sindy, Cinzia, Chintzia • Greek • *Mount Kynthos on the island of Delos (the birthplace of Artemis, Goddess of the Moon and the Hunt)*

Dahlia, Dale, Dalia, Dalya, Dahl, Dale • Swedish • *named after botanist Anders Dahl from Sweden*

Dallas, Dallas, Dalfhas • Scots Gaelic/American/English • *the village of Dallas in Moray, north Britain*

Damask, Damas • Arabic • *the city of Damascus, Syria and the damask rose*

Daniella, Danielle, Danya, Daniele, Daniela • Biblical/Hebrew/Jewish • *God is my judge*

Danya, Donya • American English /Biblical/Hebrew/Jewish • *God is my judge*

Daphne, Laurel, Lorel, Lorer • Greek • *the laurel tree*

Darcy • Norman • *a woman from the barony of D'Arcy*

Daryl, Daryll • Norman/American/English • *someone from D'airelle, a barony in Normandy*

Davina, Davida, Davena, Davinia • Biblical/Hebrew • *vague origins but*

possibly from a baby word meaning darling one

Delphine, Delfina, Delphina • Latin • *a woman from Delphi, the place of the oracle of the gods*

Della, Adela • French • *noble*

Demelza • Cornish/Kernow • *a place name in Cornwall*

Dena, Dina • Anglo-Saxon • *someone who served as dean in a Christian church or cathedral*

Denise, Denese, Denice, Deneze, Deniece, Dionysia • Greek • *Dionysus, God of Wine, Orgies and Partying*

Deòiridh, Dorcas • Gaelic • *pilgrim*

Devon, Devonne • British/Welsh • *the tribe of the Dumnonos, who worshipped the Celtic god of the same name*

Dilwen • British/Welsh • *white, fair, true, genuine and sacred*

Dilys, Dylis, Dyllis • British/Welsh • *loyal, true and genuine*

Disgleirio • British/Welsh • *bright, glittering, dazzling*

Dinah, Dina • Biblical/Hebrew/ Jewish • *judgement*

Diorbhail, DEvorgilla • Scots Gaelic • *true testimony*

Ditanny, Diktamnon • Greek/ Cretan • *the name of a medicinal plant on Mount Dikte in Crete*

Diyā • Arabic • *bright and breezy*

Dixie • American English/Cajun • *someone from the American South/ Confederate states*

Dolina, Dolag, Donella • Scots Gaelic • *world ruler*

Dolly, Dorothy, Dolores, Dora • English/Greek • *gift from God*

Dominica, Dominique, Dominga • Latin/Roman Catholic • *Lord,*

as in St Dominic, founder of the Dominican order

Domitilla, Domitius • Latin • *a Roman imperial family name*

Donatella, Donatus • Latin • *given by God*

Donella, Donna • Scots Gaelic • *world ruler*

Dora, Isedore, Isadora, Theodora, Doria, Dorinda, Dory • Greek • *gift*

Doreen, Dorean, Dorene, Dorine • Greek/Irish • *gift*

Dorian, Dorienne, Dorean • literary name • *dor is Greek for gift. Oscar Wilde's invention for* The Portrait of Dorian Gray; *most likely from the Dorian women of southern mainland Greece*

Doris, Dorris • Greek • *a tribe of Greece, the Dorian women from Doros, southern mainland Greece, from the name son of or gift to the Hellenes*

Dorothea, Dorothy, Dorothee, Dorothie, Dot, Dottie, Dotty, Dodie, Dolly, Dorofei, Dorotheos, Dorete, Dee • Greek • *gift from God*

Dreda, Etheldreda • Anglo-Saxon • *noble and strong*

Drusilla, Drausus, Drasus • Latin • *from the old Roman family name*

Du'ā • Arabic • *prayer and worship*

Dusty, Dustie, Dustee • Norse • *Thor, God of Thunder's stone*

Earla, Erla, Earlina, Erline, Earline, Earlene, Earleen • American/ English • *a noble woman*

Edith, Eden, Edun, Edon, Edie, Edyth, Edythe, Eadgyth • Anglo-Saxon • *prosperity, riches and strife or war, possibly she who gains her wealth through the booty of war*

Edna, Eden, Ednah, Eithne •
Jewish/Hebrew • *pleasure and
delight*

Edwina, Edwardina • Anglo-Saxon
• *a person who guards her riches,
blessed with wealth*

Eglantine, Aiglent • English •
sweetbriar

Ehrentraud, Arntraut • Germanic •
*with strength goes honour or she has
the strength of an eagle*

Electra, Ellettra • Greek • *brilliant*

Elaine, Helen • Greek/French
• *sunbeam, ray of sun, coming
from the name for the Greeks, the
Hellen(es)*

**Eleanor, Alienor, Ellenor, Elinor,
Elenor, Nell, Ellen, Nellie, Nelly,
Eleanora, Eléonore** • Germanic/
Frankish/Provençal • *prefix means
foreign or stranger; the suffix is unknown*

Elke, Adelheide • Germanic • *noble
woman, carries herself well*

**Ellen, Helen, Elin, Elen, Ella, Elena,
Nell, Nelly, Nellie, Ellena, Ellenor** •
modern English • *shortened form of
Helen and Eleanor*

**Elizabeth, Elisabeth, Elisheba,
Elise, Eliza, Elisa, Elsa, Liza, Lisa,
Liz, Beth, Bet, Bess, Lisbet, Lisbeth,
Lysbeth, Elsie, Bessie, Bessy, Betty,
Betsy, Tetty, Libby, Lizzie, Lizzy,
Buffy, Eilis, Ealasaid, Elisabet,
Elisabete, Elisabetta, Elisavet,
Yelizaveta, Elzbieta, Alzbeta,
Elizabeta, Erzsebet, Elspeth, Eliza**
• Biblical/Hebrew/Jewish • *God is
my oath*

Elita, Elire • American English • *elite
person, upper class, VIP*

Ella, Ellen • Germanic • *foreigner,
stranger*

Ellie, Elly, Eilidh, Ailie • Germanic/

Frankish/Provençal • *short for
Eleanor*

Élodie, Elodia • Germanic/
Visigothic • *foreign wealth*

**Elspeth, Elsbeth, Elspie, Elsie,
Elspet, Elizabeth** • Scots English/
Biblical • *God is my oath*

**Eluned, Eiluned, Luned, Lunet,
Lunete, Eilun** • British/Welsh • *icon,
image*

Elvina, Alvina • Anglo-Saxon • *elfin,
noble or faerie friend*

Elvira • Germanic/Visigothic • *true
wealth, foreign*

Élise, Elyse, Elysia, Alicia, Elisabeth
• Biblical/French • *God is my oath*

Emelia, Amelia, Emilia • Latin/
Italian • *old Roman family name
meaning rival, competitor*

Émer, Eimear, Eimer, Eimhir • Irish
Gaelic • *vague origins, perhaps chastity and purity, beauty and wisdom*

Emily, Aemilia, Aemilius, Émilie
• Latin • *old Roman family name
meaning rival, competitor*

**Emma, Ermintrude, Emmaline,
Emmeline, Emmie, Emmy** •
Germanic/Frankish • *entire, the
whole, everything*

Ethel • Anglo-Saxon • *noble*

Eudocia, Eudoxia, Eudokia •
Biblical/Greek/Latin • *of fine
appearance and comfortable, easy
to be with*

Eudora, Dora, Doron • Greek • *a
good gift*

**Eugenia, Eugenios, Eugenius,
Eugenie** • Greek • *well bred and
high born*

Evangeline, Evangelina • Greek/
Latin/French • *good tidings from the
gospel*

Eydl, Edel • Jewish/Yiddish • *noble*

Fabia, Fabienne, Fabiola • Latin • *old Roman family name*

Fadīla • Arabic • *a moral, ethical, virtuous woman*

Fakhriyya • Arabic • *this woman is glorious and expects nothing for nothing; everything is unconditional*

Faith • English • *she who trusts in God, faithful follower*

Fanny, Frances • English/Latin • *to be French, someone from France*

Felicia, Felice, Felis, Feliz, Fenicia, Phoenicia, Felicie • Latin • *happy-go-lucky*

Felicity, Flick, Felcitas, Felicita, Felicidad • Latin • *good fortune*

Fifi, Joséphine • French/Biblical/Hebrew/Jewish • *short name for Joséphine, meaning God is my salvation*

Fikriyya • Arabic • *pensive, contemplative, intelligent, intellectual*

Flavia, Favius, Flavie • Latin • *old Roman family name meaning yellow-haired*

Fortunata, Fortuna, Fortunatus • Latin • *fortunate, lucky, fated*

Franca • French • *a girl from France*

Frances, Proinséas • English/Latin • *to be French, someone from France*

Francesca, France, Francene, Fran, Frances, Fanny, Françoise, Franceen, Franziska, Frankie, Francine, Francisca • Italian/Latin • *to be French, someone from France*

Frauke • German • *a lady from northern Germany*

Freyde, Freud, Freude • Jewish/Yiddish • *joy unconfined*

Fulvia, Fulvius • Latin • *an old Roman family name*

Gabrielle, Gabriella, Gabi, Gaby, Gabby, Gabriel, Gabriele, Gabriela • Biblical/Hebrew/Jewish • *woman of God*

Gae, Gay, Gaye • English • *bright, jolly, cherry, sanguine*

Gail, Gael, Abigail, Gaelle, Gaile, Gale, Gayle • Biblical/Jewish/Hebrew • *shortened Abigail, my father is joy, father is exaltation*

Genette, Jeanette • Biblical/English/Latin • *God is gracious or gift of God*

Geneva, Geneve, Ginevra • French • *after the Swiss city or can be variant of Jennifer or short form of Geneviève*

Ghislain, Ghislaine, Giselle, Gisil • Germanic/Frankish • *to pledge or promise something or someone to confirm an alliance*

Gigi • French • *pet name for Giselle; to pledge or promise something or someone to confirm an alliance*

Gillian, Gill, Jill, Gillyflower, Gillaine, Jillian, Jilly, Gilly • Latin • *from Julius, a Roman name*

Ginny, Virginia, Jane, Jaine, Jane, Ginnie, Jinny • Biblical/English/Latin • *pet name for Virginia or Jane; God is gracious or gift of God*

Gioconda, Jucunda • Latin • *happy, jovial, jocund*

Giovanna • Biblical/English/Latin • *LADY John! God is gracious or gift of God*

Giselle, Gisil, Gisella, Gisela, Gigi • Germanic/Frankish • *pledge, to pledge or promise something or someone to confirm an alliance*

Gislög, Gisillaug, Gislaug • Norse • *sacred hostage*

Gita • Sanskrit • *everyone sings her praises*

Giuletta, Giulia • Latin/Italian • *from Julius, an old Roman name*

Giuseppina • Biblical/Italian • *LADY Joseph! God shall add another son*

Gladys, Gwladys, Gwladus • British Welsh/Latin • *uncertain origins but said to be a local form of Claudia, from the old Roman family name Claudius*

Glenda, Gwenda • British/Welsh • *good, clean, pure and holy*

Glenys, Glynis, Glennis, Glenis, Glenice, Glenise, Glennys, Glynnis • British/Welsh • *pure and holy*

Gloria, Gloriana, Glory • Latin • *glorious!*

Godiva • Anglo-Saxon/Latin • *God's gift*

Goretti • Roman Catholic • *named after Maria Goretti, patron saint of youth*

Gormlaith, Gormflaith • Irish Gaelic • *a splendid, illustrious woman or princess*

Gro, Groa, Gruach • Norse/Celtic • *evolving/old woman*

Guadalupe • Roman Catholic • *site of a convent with the famous image of the Virgin Mary*

Gudrun, Guro • Norse • *magical, enchanted, a witch or wise woman*

Gumersinda • Spanish/Visigothic • *the path of man or woman*

Gwenda • British/Welsh • *a good, holy, pure woman*

Gypsy • Roman/Egyptian • *meaning an Egyptian, thought to be travellers from Asia*

Gytha, Gyth, Gudrid • Anglo-Saxon/Norse • *discord or beautiful God*

Hafza • Arabic • *devoted to the Koran*

Hannah, Hanna, Hanā • Arabic • *blissful, happy woman filled with wellbeing*

Hannah, Hanne, Johanna, Hanna • Biblical/Jewish/Hebrew • *God has favoured me*

Hannelore • Germanic • *combo of Hannah and Eleanor*

Hansine • Germanic • *God is gracious or gift of God*

Happy, Merry, Happie, Merrie • Norse/English • *prosperity, abundance, good fortune*

Harriet, Henriette, Henrietta, Hattie, Hennie, Hettie • German/French/English • *a famous army that carries all before it; a shining light*

Heaven, Heofon • American English/Anglo-Saxon • *where God is and good people go after this life*

Hebe, Hebos • Greek • *the goddess of youth*

Heidi, Adelheid, Adélaide, Heide • Germanic • *noble woman, carries herself well*

Heike • Germanic • *a famous army that carries all before it; a shining light*

Helen, Helena, Hélène, Elena, Elen, Elin • Greek/English • *ray of sunshine, sunbeam, sunny; another analogy is it means torch of the moon*

Helga, Heilag, Hella • Norse • *successful, prosperity, wealth*

Henrietta, Henriette, Enriqueta • German/French/Spanish • *a famous army that carries all before it; a shining light*

Heulog • British/Welsh • *sunny*

Heulwen • British/Welsh • *sunshine*

Hiba • Arabic • *a gift or prize from God*

Hikmat • Arabic • *wisdom*

Hilary, Hillary, Hilarie, Hilly, Hilario, Illaria • Latin • *hilarious!*

Hilda, Hylda, Hilde, Elda • Germanic • *battleaxe*

Hildebrande • Germanic • *flaming sword into battle*

Honesty, Honesta, Honestas, Honor, Honour • Norman/Latin • *truthful, fair and frank*

Honor, Honour, Honora, Honorah, Honoria, Honoré, Honorine, Honorina, Norine, Noreen • Norman/Latin • *an honoured woman*

Hope, Hopa • Anglo-Saxon • *Christians' belief in the resurrection and life everlasting*

Horatia • Etruscan • *Roman family name with no certain root*

Hualing • Chinese • *flourishing fu-ling (herb used in Oriental medicine)*

Huan • Chinese • *happiness*

Huguette, Huette • Germanic/Frankish/French • *heart, mind and spirit*

Huidai • Chinese • *sagacious black*

Huda • Arabic • *a woman who is wise and judicious counsellor or adviser; agony aunt*

Ibtisām • Arabic • *a woman wreathed in smiles and laughter*

Idony, Idone, Idunn, Idonea • Norse • *Goddess of the Apples of Eternal Youth*

Ihāb • Arabic • *a gift from God*

Ihsān • Arabic • *charity, generosity*

Ilayne, Elaine • Greek/modern English • *sunbeam, ray of sun, coming from the name for the Greeks, the Hellen(es)*

Ilona, Helen • Hungarian • *sunbeam, ray of sun, coming from the name for the Greeks, the Hellen(es)*

Ilse, Ilsa, Elisabeth • Germanic/Biblical

Imān • Arabic • *faith, belief*

In'ām • Arabic • *a gift given or bestowed by God*

Inderjit • Sanskrit • *victory over Indra*

Indira • Sanskrit • *she is so beautiful, radiant, filled with splendour*

Inés, Inez, Agnès • Spanish/Greek • *pure and holy*

Iona, Nonie • Latin/Gaelic • *sacred island in Hebrides in north Britain*

Ione, Nonie • English • *Ionian islands*

Isabel, Isobel, Isa, Isabella, Isabelle, Isobelle, Isobella, Izzy, Izzie, Sibéal, Iseabail, Ishbel, Isbel, Elizabeth • Spanish/Biblical/Hebrew/Jewish • *God is my oath*

Isaura • Latin • *a woman from Isauria in Asia Minor (Turkey)*

Isla • Scots • *name of Hebridean island in north Britain*

Jalīla, Galīla • Arabic • *exalted on high*

Jana, Yana, Jan • Biblical/English/Latin • *God is gracious or gift of God*

Jancis, Jancie • English literary • *combo of Frances and Jan from the novel* Precious Bane *by Mary Webb*

Jane, Jeanne, Jehanne, Jaine, Jayne, Jain, Jean, Joan, Janie, Janey, Joanna, Jaynie, Síne, Siân, Johanna, Hanne, Hansine, Johanne, Janja, Jannja, Sheena Jensine, Jonna, Jeanne, Juanna, Juana, Giovanna, Gianna, Hana, Jana, Janeen, Janelle, Jaynia •

Biblical/French/Latin • *God is gracious or gift of God*
Janet, Jannet, Janett, Janette, Jan, Janetta, Janeta, Seònaid, Shona, Seona • Biblical/English/Latin • *God is gracious or gift of God*
Janice, Janis, Janise, Jannice, Jan • Biblical/French/Latin • *God is gracious or gift of God*
Jan, Janna • Biblical/English • *God is gracious or gift of God*
Jaswinder • Sikh • *the thunderbolt*
Jean, Joan, Jane, Jeanne, Jehanne, Jehanna, Jeane, Jeana, Gina, Jeanna, Jeane, Jeanetta, Jeanette, Jeanie, Jeanine, Jeannette, Jeanne, Jeanett, Jenette, Jennet, Jenet, Ginett, Ginnette, Ginetta, Ginnetta, Jeannie, Jeannine, Jeannique, Jannike • Biblical/French • *God is gracious or gift of God*
Jerrie, Jerry, Geri, Gerry • Biblical/English • *appointed by God*
Jessica, Jesca, Jessika, Jess, Jessie, Jesse, Jessye, Teasag, Iscah • Biblical/literary • *William Shakespeare's invention from the Biblical name Jesca or Iscah*
Jetta, Jaiet, Gagates • Latin/Norman • *jet, fossilised wood or coal: a black stone from Gagai (a city in Lycia, Asia Minor, now Turkey)*
Jinana • Arabic • *a woman as beautiful and mystical as the Garden of Eden*
Jill, Jillian, Gillian, Gill, Jilly, Gilly, Jillie • *from Julius, a Roman name*
Jo, Joe, Joanna, Joanne, Jody, Josephine, Josie, Josey • Biblical/Greek • *God is gracious or gift of God*
Joan, Ionna, Iohanna, Joanna,

Johanna, Joanne, Johanne, Joanie, Joni, Siobhàn, Chevanne, Siubhan, Jane, Shevaune, Chevaune, Shona, Shevanne, Joann, Seonag • Biblical/Norman • *God is gracious or gift of God*
Jocelyn, Joselyn, Jocelyne, Joscelyn, Josceline, Joslyn, Joss, Céline, Gautzeline, Joscel, Joscein, Joscelyn • Norman • *someone from the Germanic tribe of the Gauts*
Jody, Jodene, Jodie, Jodi, Jude, Judith • Biblical/Hebrew/Jewish • *praise*
Johanna, Johna, Johannah, Johanne, Joanna, Joanne, Jo, Jannike • Biblical/Latin • *God is gracious or gift of God*
Jonina • Biblical/modern English • *God is gracious or gift of God*
Josefa, Yosefa • Biblical/Hebrew/Jewish • *God will provide me with another son*
Joséphine, Josefine, Josephina, Josefina, Jo, Josie, Jozie, Josette, Fifi, Posy, Josefa, Jozefa, Josée, Josiane, Seosaimhín, Josianne, Josiane • Biblical/French • *God will provide me with another son*
Joy, Joie, Gaudia • Latin/French • *joyful in the Lord*
Joyce, Josce, Josse, Joducos, Joducus, Iodoc, Joss • Breton Celtic • *lord*
Ju • Chinese • *chrysanthemum*
Juanita, Janita, Janita • Spanish • *God is gracious or gift of God*
Judith, Judi, Judy, Judie, Jutte, Jutta, Julitta • Biblical/Hebrew/Jewish • *praise*
Julia, Juli, Julie, Giulia, Julietta, Guilietta, Juliet, Juliette, Guiliette, Juliana, Julianus, Julianna,

Julianne, Julián, Juliane, Julieann, Julien, Julieanne, Julienne Jools, Julia, Jules, Juleen, Julianne • Latin • *a Roman name*

Julitta, Julitt, Julip, Judith • Biblical/Latin • *praise*

Juniper, Jennifer, Rothem, Juniperus • Biblical/Hebrew/Jewish/Latin • *desert shrub that was used to build the Temple of Solomon*

Justina, Justine • Latin • *a Roman name*

Jutte, Jutta, Jude, Judith • Biblical/Germanic • *praise*

Jyoti • Sanskrit • *light of mind, light of freedom, light of paradise*

Karama • Arabic • *a generous spirit*

Karīma • Arabic • *a woman with a noble personality and generous to boot!*

Karla, Carla • Scandinavian/English/Germanic • *a freeman*

Karlene, Karleen, Carlene, Carleen • American English • *a freeman*

Karlotte, Karlotta, Carlottam Charlotte • German/Scandinavian • *a freeman*

Karola, Carolyn, Karoline, Karolina, Carolina, Carola, Karoline • Scandinavian/English/Germanic • *a freeman*

Kelly, Kelley, Kellie, Ceallach • Irish Gaelic • *bright-headed, quick-tempered*

Kenda, Kendala, Kendall • Anglo-Saxon/British/Welsh • *someone who worships Celtic deities, or a place in Westmorland, Kendal, named after river Kent*

Kendra, Kendrick • British/Welsh/Scots Gaelic • *a sacred place high on a hill, or son of Henry or royal power*

Kirsten, Christine, Kristine, Kerstin • Danish/Norwegian/English/ Latin • *follower of Christ*

Kirstie, Kirstin, Kirsty, Kirstie, Christine, Chirsty, Ciorstaidh, Ciorstag, Curstaidh, Curstag • Scots English/Latin • *follower of Christ*

Klara, Clara • German/Latin • *bright, famous, crystal-clear*

Kris, Kristina, Kristina, Kristen • Swedish/Czech/Latin • *follower of Christ*

Krista, Christa • German/Latin • *follower of Christ*

Kristie, Christie, Kirstie, Kristina, Kristy • American English/Latin • *follower of Christ*

Kristina, Kristine, Christine, Christina, Kristeen, Kristene, Kerstin, Kirsten, Tina • Swedish/Czech/Latin • *follower of Christ*

Kumari • Sanskrit • *daughter or princess*

Kyla • Gaelic • *narrow in geographical terms; a region in Ayrshire*

Laetitia, Latisha, Leticia, Lettice, Tish, Tisha • Latin • *overcome with joy and happiness*

Lakshmi • Sanskrit • *lucky girl in matters of luck, money and beauty*

Lalita • Sanskrit • *this girl is as playful as a kitten; affectionate and amorous*

Lara, Larissa, Larrisah • Russian/Greek • *unsure meaning; perhaps someone from a town near Thessaloniki, in northern Greece*

Larch, Larche, Larix • American English/German/Latin • *sacred tree to the shaman*

Larissa, Lara, Larry • Russian/Greek • *unsure meaning; perhaps someone*

from a town near Thessaloniki, in northern Greece
Laura, Laurel, Laureen, Laurene, Laurelle, Laurie, Laure, Laurette, Lora, Lowri • Latin • *laurel tree, sacred to those who are victorious and honoured*
Lauren, Lauryn, Loren, Lorenna, Laurenna, Laurie, Lori • Latin • *man from Laurentum, the capital of the Latins*
Lauretta, Loretta, Lorette • Latin/Italian • *laurel tree, sacred to those who are victorious and honoured*
Lena, Yelena, Helen • Greek/Russian • *ray of sunshine, sunbeam, sunny*
Leonora, Eleonora, Léonore, Elenonore, Eleanore, Lenora, Lennora, Lennorah, Lenorah, Lena • Germanic/Frankish/Provençal • *prefix means foreign or stranger; the suffix is unknown*
Lettice, Leticia, Laetitia, Letitia, Letizia, Letty, Lettie • Latin/English • *overcome with joy and happiness*
Libby, Elizabeth • English • *God is my oath*
Liberty, Liberta, Libertas • English/Norman/Latin • *freedom*
Liese, Elisabeth • German • *God is my oath*
Lili, Lilli, Elisabeth • German • *God is my oath*
Lindsey, Linsey, Linsy, Linzi, Linzie, Lynsey • Anglo-Saxon • *old Saxon kingdom whose root means Lelli's island*
Linnéa, Linnaea • Swedish • *name honouring botanist Carl von Linne*
Liqiu • Chinese • *beautiful autumn*
Lisa, Liza, Elyse, Lise, Liese, Élise, Elisabeth • French/German • *God*

is my oath
Lisette, Lise, Elisabeth, Lysette, Lise, Lys, Liz, Lis, Elisbet, Liza, Eliza, Lisa, Lizzie, Lizzy, Lizi, Elizabeth • English/French • *God is my oath*
Livia, Livius • Latin • *Roman family name Livius*
Logan • Scots • *Scottish surname based on place in Ayrshire*
Lone, Abelone, Magdelone • Danish • *Mary Magdelene aka Mary of Magdala, woman healed of evil spirits*
Loreen, Lorene • Latin/Gaelic • *laurel tree, sacred to those who are victorious and honoured*
Lorelle, Laura • Latin/French • *laurel tree, sacred to those who are victorious and honoured*
Loretta, Lauretta, Loreto • Roman Catholic/Italian • *laurel tree, sacred to those who are victorious and honoured*
Lorna, Lorne, Latharna • English/Scots Gaelic • *Scottish place name Lorne, Argyll*
Lorraine, Lotharingia, Lorrain, Lorrayne, Lori, Lorri • Germanic/Lotharigian • *land of the people of Lothar and his famous army*
Lottie, Lotte, Charlotte • French/Germanic • *a freeman*
Lottelore • modern • *combo of Lotte (Charlotte) and Lore (Eleanore)*
Louise, Lou, Lulu, Lodwig, Louisa, Lovisa, Lovise, Liùsaidh • Frankish • *famous in war or battle*
Louella, Luella, Lou • Latin/Italian • *famous in war or battle*
Lourdes, Lurdes • Roman Catholic • *a French place of pilgrimage where a young girl had visions of the Virgin*
Lowri, Laura • British/Welsh/Latin

• laurel tree, sacred to those who are victorious and honoured
Lucretia, Lucrece, Lucrezia, Lucretius • Latin • Roman family name
Ludovica • Germanic • she finds her fame in war
Luisa, Louisa, Luise, Lulu, Lou • Spanish/Frankish • famous in war or battle
Lulu, Luisa, Luise, Louise • German/Frankish • famous in war or battle
Lydia, Lydie • Greek • woman from Lydia

Macey, Masey, Macie, Macy, Maci, Macciacum • Norman/Latin • someone from Massey, Normandy
Madeleine, Madelaine, Magdalene, Magdala, Madelene, Madlyn, Madelyn, Madalene, Madaline, Madoline, Magdalen, Maddie, Maddy, Maddalena • Biblical/French • Mary Magdelene aka Mary of Magdala, woman healed of evil spirits
Madonna, Madge • American Italian • my lady
Magda, Magdalene, Magadelena, Lena • Biblical/Slavic/German • Mary Magdelene aka Mary of Magdala, woman healed of evil spirits
Mahāsin • Arabic • charming and admirable qualities
Maia, Maya, Mya • Latin • Roman Goddess of Youth, Life, Rebirth, Love and Sexuality
Maitland, Maltalent, Mautalent • Anglo-Saxon/Norman • bad-tempered or from Mautalant, a barren place in France

Malak • Arabic • angel
Manara • Arabic • she sends out a radiant light like a pharo (lighthouse)
Manuela • Biblical/Spanish • God is with us or amongst us
Maoilosa • Irish Gaelic • follower of Jesus Christ
Marietta, Mariella, María, Mairéad, Margaret, Mariette, Maretta • Biblical/Italian • Mary Magdelene aka Mary of Magdala, woman healed of evil spirits
Marina, Marinus, Marius, Marna • Latin • Roman family name; clouded meaning
Marla, Marlene, Magdalene • modern • Mary Magdelene aka Mary of Magdala, woman healed of evil spirits
Marlene, Maria, Magdalena • German • Mary Magdelene aka Mary of Magdala, woman healed of evil spirits
Marna, Marnie • Swedish/Latin • Roman family name; clouded meaning
Marva, Marvalee • American English • he's a lord or eminent being down to his marrow
Maura, Mavra • Latin • Moor, as in Arab
Maxine, Max, Maxie • Latin • the greatest!
Maysa, Mayyas • Arabic • a woman with a graceful but proud gait
Mehetabel, Mehitabel • Biblical/Jewish/Hebrew • God makes happy
Meihui • Chinese • beautiful wisdom
Meredith, Meredydd • British/Welsh • unknown prefix plus lord
Merry, Merrily, Merilee, Marylee, Marilee • American English • to be merry
Michaela, Mikayla, Mica, Micah-

Biblical/Hebrew/Jewish/English • who is like God?

Michele, Michelle, Michel Chelle, Shell, Micheline • Biblical/Hebrew/Jewish/English

Milla, Camilla, Camille • Latin/French • *Roman family name*

Minerva • Latin • *Goddess of Wisdom, Roman equivalent to Athene*

Mirabelle, Mirabella, Mirabellis, Mirari, Mirabilis • Latin/French • *wonderful, glorious*

Miranda, Randa, Randy, Randie, Amanda • literary invention/Latin • *William Shakespeare invented this name for his heroine in* The Tempest: *admire, wonder at or in awe of her loveliness*

Mireille, Mireio, Miriam, Mary, Miranda, Mireio, Mirella • Provençal • *to admire*

Mona, Muadhnait, Monos, Muadh • Irish Gaelic • *noble*

Montserrat • Catalan • *the Lady of Montserrat, a Benedictine monastery near Barcelona*

Morag, Mór, Móirín, Moreen • Irish Scots Gaelic • *great, large, huge*

Morven, Morvern, Mhorbhairne, Morbheinn • Scots • *area of north Argyll or big peak*

Muna • Arabic • *sexy, desirable and gives out hope and optimism*

Munira • Arabic • *radiant, bright, sends out a light*

Nabīla • Arabic • *upper-crust woman*

Nadia, Nadya, Nadezhda, Nadine Nadezhda, Nadya • Russian • *hope*

Nadine, Nadia • Russian/French • *hope*

Nan, Nancy, Nanette, Ann • Biblical/Jewish/Hebrew • *pet form of Ann, of uncertain origins: God has favoured me*

Nancy, Nan, Ann, Annis, Agnès, Nancie, Nanci, Nance • Biblical/Jewish/Hebrew • *pet form of Ann, of uncertain origins: God has favoured me*

Nanda, Ferdinanda, Hernanda • Spanish/Italian • *short form of Ferdinanda or Hernanda*

Nanette, Nan • Biblical/Jewish/Hebrew/French • *pet form of Ann, of uncertain origins: God has favoured me*

Nanna • Norse • *daring one!*

Naomh • Irish Gaelic • *holy, saintly*

Narelle, Narellan • Australian Aborigine • *clouded meaning but a town in New South Wales*

Nazaret, Nazareth • Roman Catholic • *Jesus Christ's native village*

Nawāl • Arabic • *a gift bestowed or given*

Nell, Nella, Nellie, Nelly, Eleanor, Ellen, Helen • *English short name for Eleanor, Ellen or Helen*

Nerina, Nerine, Nereus • Greek/Latin • *Roman family name Nero or Nerio*

Neroli • Italian • *an aromatic oil based on bitter orange, founded by Princess Anne Marie de la Tremoille of Neroli*

Nesta, Nester, Nostos, Agnes • British Welsh/Greek • *pure and holy*

Ngaio • New Zealand Maori • *a clever tribe or people*

Nia, Niamh, Neve • British/Welsh/Irish • *beautiful and bright*

Niamh, Neve, Nia • Irish Gaelic •

beautiful and bright

Nigella • *black as pitch or passionate, dead sexy, really desirable; maybe a commitment phobe*

Ni'mat • Arabic • *a woman who is good to have around*

Nona, Nonus, Nonie, Non, Anona • Latin • *the number nine or ninth*

Nóra, Honora, Norah, Nonie • Irish Gaelic/Latin • *an honoured woman*

Noreen, Nóirín, Norene, Norine, Honoria • Irish Gaelic/Latin • *an honoured woman*

Norma • artistic Italian • *Felice Romani invented the name for Bellini's opera*

Normina • *a man from the north; Norseman or Viking*

Nuha • Arabic • *a woman who is clever, intellectual and cerebrally bright*

Nura, Nūr • Arabic • *this woman will light up your life and she has unique features too*

Nyamekye • Ghanaian • *given by God*

Odette, Odet, Oda • Germanic/ Frankish • *prosperity and good fortune*

Olympe, Olympia • Greek • *a woman from Olympus, the mountain of the gods*

Odile, Odila, Ottilie, Ottoline • Germanic • *prosperous and wealthy*

Oksana, Oxana • Russian • *praise God*

Olga, Helgi • Norse • *prosperous*

Olive, Olivia, Oliff, Oliffe, Oliva • Latin • *olive tree, a symbol of peace and abundance*

Olivia, Olive, Oliva • literary invention/Latin • *William Shakespeare*

named Olivia as the rich heiress in The Tempest

Ottilie, Odile, Odila • Germanic • *prosperous and wealthy*

Ottoline • Germanic • *prosperous and wealthy*

Pamela, Pam, Pammy, Pamella • poetic invention • *Sir Philip Sidney and Elizabeth I created the name*

Paris, Parisii • Latin/Celtic • *member of the Parisii tribe, origins unknown*

Patrice, Patricia • Latin/French • *Latin/Irish Gaelic • patrician*

Patricia, Patrice, Pat, Tricia, Trisha, Trish, Patty, Pattie, Patti, Patsy, Patrizia • Latin/Irish Gaelic • *patrician*

Patty, Pattie, Patricia, Martha, Patti • English • *pet name for Patricia and Martha*

Paudeen, Páidín • Irish Gaelic/ English • *pet name for Patricia*

Perdita, Perdie, Purdee, Purdy, Perditus • Latin/literary invention • *William Shakespeare invented the name from the Latin 'lost' as one of his characters in* The Winter's Tale

Persis • Biblical/Greek • *a Persian woman*

Philippa, Phil, Philippina • Greek • *friend or lover of horses*

Pilar • Roman Catholic • *Our Lady of the Pillar; appearance of the Virgin on a pillar at Zaragossa*

Pippa, Philippa • Greek • *friend or lover of horses*

Pixie • English • *playful sprite, mischievous, naughty*

Portia, Porcia, Porcius, Porcus, Porsha • Latin • *Roman family name of Porcus, meaning pig*

Posy, Posey, Josephine, Poesy •

Biblical/English • *God will provide me with another son*

Patribha • Sanskrit • *clever, radiant, imaginative and precocious*

Prudence, Pru, Prue, Prudentia, Prudentius • Latin • *provident*

Psyche, Psykhe • Greek • *butterfly, spirit and soul*

Qiaohui • Chinese • *dexterous and sagacious*

Qingling • Chinese • *celebrating understanding*

Qingzhao • Chinese • *clear understanding, crystal illumination*

Qiu • Chinese • *autumn*

Qiuyue • Chinese • *autumn moon*

Radwa • Arabic • *an area in the holy city of Mecca*

Raffaella, Rafaela • Biblical • *archangel*

Raghda • Arabic • *a carefree woman who enjoys life*

Ragna • Norse • *advice from the gods*

Raisa • Slavic • *paradise, heaven*

Ravenna • Italian • *an Italian city, someone from Ravenna, the capital of Roman mosaic*

Rāwiya • Arabic • *a narrator of classical Arabic poetry and prose and beautiful speaker*

Reagan, Regan, Riagain • Irish Gaelic/English • *descendant of Riagain, the impulsive or impatient one*

Renxiang • Chinese • *lucky fragrance*

Rhea, Silvia • Latin/Roman mythology • *mother of Romulus and Remus, founders of Rome*

Rhona, Rona • Scots • *name of*

Hebridean island off northern Britain

Rida • Arabic • *one who has God's (Allah's) approval*

Robbin, Robbie, Roberta • Germanic • *famous and bright*

Roberta, Robbie • Germanic • *famous and bright*

Robyn, Robin • Germanic • *famous and bright*

Rong • Chinese • *macho woman; tomboy*

Roni, Veronica, Ronnie • Latin/English • *shortened Veronica; true image*

Ros, Roz, Rosalind, Rosamund • English • *shortened for any name beginning with Ros*

Rosalind, Rosaleen, Rosalyn, Roslind, Rosaline, Rosalin, Rosalynne, Rosalynn • Germanic/Frankish • *horse, tender and soft, passive and weak*

Rosamund, Rosmund, Rosamunda, Rosamond, Roschen • Germanic • *horse protector*

Roxy • American English • *flashy, glitzy but just a little nouvelle riche!*

Sadie, Sarah, Sara, Sarai • English • *pet form of Sarah, princess*

Sage, Sauge, Sapius • English/Norman/American English • *the herb sage that promotes wisdom and is good for the liver*

Sally, Sal, Sarah • English • *another name for Sarah, princess*

Samantha, Sam, Sammy, Sammi • Biblical/Hebrew/Jewish • *the name of God, God has heard, listen to God*

Sandhya • Sanskrit • *twilight of the gods, devout, ritualistic*

Saoirse, Seersha • Irish Gaelic • *freedom, liberation*

Sarabeth • American English • *combo of Sara and (Eliza)beth*

Sarah, Sara, Zara, Sally, Sadie, Sari • Biblical/Jewish/Hebrew • *princess*

Sarita, Sarah • Biblical/Spanish • *princess*

Saraswati • Sanskrit • *filled with waters of knowledge of the arts, learning and academia*

Sayidana • Swahili • *our princess*

Sebastienne • Latin/French • *a man from Sebaste in Asia Minor (now Turkey)*

Seanach • English/Norman French • *old, wise and venerable*

Seraphina, Seraphim, Serafina, Fina, Serafima • Jewish/Hebrew • *the burning ones*

Sévérine, Severina, Severa • Latin • *Roman family name*

Shahīra • Arabic • *destiny for fame and fortune*

Shahnaz • Persian • *the glory of kings*

Shakti • Sanskrit • *she possesses the power of the gods*

Shan • Chinese • *a woman who bears herself elegantly; like royalty or a model*

Shannon, Shantelle, Shan, Seanain, Seanán • Irish • *wise, mature and ancient*

Shana, Shanae, Shania, Shanee, Siani, Siân • American English/British Welsh • *God is gracious or gift of God*

Sharada • Sanskrit • *autumn*

Sharifa • Arabic • *a woman who is eminent in her field and honourable to the nth degree*

Sharon, Sharron, Sharona, Sharonda • Biblical • *a place called Sharon on the coastal plain of the Holy Land; and for the shrub the Rose of Sharon*

Sindy, Cindy, Sinda • French • *cinders from the fire*

Sinéad, Janet, Jeanette, Seònaid, Shona, Seona • English/Scots Gaelic • *God is gracious or gift of God*

Siobhán, Joan, Jehanne, Shevaun, Chevonne, Chevaun, Chevaunne, Shevaunne, Jehanne, Joan • English/Norman French/Biblical/Irish Gaelic • *God is gracious or gift of God*

Sioned, Janet • English/British Welsh • *God is gracious or gift of God*

Sissy, Sisi, Sissey, Sissie, Elisabeth • Jewish/Hebrew/Bavarian • *God is my oath*

Sissel, Cecily • Scandinavian/English • *old Roman family name Caecilius, from the Latin, meaning blind*

Sky, Skye • Gaelic • *take your pick, the sky as in heaven or Skye as in the island in Scotland*

Skylar, Schuyler • Dutch/American English • *scholar, school teacher*

Slava • Slavic • *glorious*

Sofia, Sophia, Sofya, Sofie, Sophie, Sofie, Sophy • Greek • *wisdom*

Sonia, Sonya, Sonje • Greek • *wisdom*

Sorcha, Sarah, Sally • Irish Gaelic • *brightness*

Sprite, Spiritus, Esprit • American English • *a mischievous spirit*

Sri • Sanskrit • *a royal personage who radiates the light of goodness, beauty and wealth*

Sroel, Israel • Jewish/Yiddish • *he who strives with God*

Steffanie, Stéphanie, Steph, Steffi, Stefanie, Steff • Greek • *a crown or garland*

Stéphanie, Steff, Steph, Steffie, Steffy, Stevie, Stefanie, Steffany, Stephania, Stephana, Stefania, Estefania, Stevie • Greek • *a crown or garland*

Sultana • Arabic • *empress, queen*

Sujata • Sanskrit • *excellent character or born of nobility*

Sukie, Sukey, Susan • English • *pet form of Susan*

Sumati • Sanskrit • *good thoughts, devout in prayer*

Sunita • Sanskrit • *she's a good girl who gives wise advice*

Sunny, Sunnie • English • *cheery, cheerful, full of joy; a sunny disposition*

Susie, Susan, Suzie, Susi • English • *short form Susan or Susannah*

Suyin • Chinese • *straight talking*

Suranne • English • *combo of Sarah and Anne*

Svea • Swedish • *patriotic name for Sweden*

Talia, Talya, Natalya, Thalia • Latin/Russian • *the birth of Jesus Christ or reborn with faith*

Tallulah, Talulla, Tuilelaith • Irish Gaelic/English • *abundance, lady and princess*

Tamsin, Thomasina, Tammy, Tammie, Tamzin • Biblical/Aramaic/Greek • *twin*

Tanya, Tania, Tanja • Latin • *Sabine Roman family name*

Tara, Teamhair, Tarra, Taree • Irish Gaelic • *a hill that was the seat of the high kings of Ireland*

Tasha, Natasha • Latin • *the birth of*

Jesus Christ or reborn with faith

Tatiana, Tanya, Tatyana, Tatianus, Tatius • Latin/Russian • *Sabine Roman family name, Tatius, of vague origins*

Teàrlag • Irish Gaelic • *a woman who takes the initiative, starts things*

Tempe, Temnein • Greek • *a valley in Greece; the legendary home of the Muses, the nine goddesses of the arts and sciences*

Tempest, Tempeste, Tempestas • Latin/Norman/English • *nickname for a person with a wild temperament*

Teresa, Theresa, Terri, Tessa, Tes, Teresia, Theresia, Treeza, Thérèse, Resi • Italian/Spanish/Portuguese • *Roman*

Terri, Terry, Theresa, Terryl • Latin/Irish Gaelic • *from the Roman family name Terentius and Irish for someone who takes the initiative*

Tessa, Tess, Theresa, Tessie, Tessy • Italian/Spanish/Portuguese • *unknown root; pet name for Teresa*

Tetty, Tettie, Elizabeth • English • *pet name for Elizabeth*

Thalia, Talia, Thallein • Greek • *one of the nine Muses; the Goddess of Comedy whose name means to prosper comedically*

Thanā • Arabic • *a woman ready to praise and be praised; everything she does deserves praise*

Thea, Dorothea • Greek • *short name for Dorothea*

Thecia, Theokleia • Greek • *glory of God*

Theodora, Dora, Teodora, Feodora • Greek • *God-given or giving to God or God's gift*

Theodosia, Dosy, Theodosis •

Greek • *God-given*

Theokleia, Thecia, Tekla • Greek • *glory of God*

Thera, Theresa • Greek • *vague origins; could be short for Theresa or Greek isle of Thera*

Thessaly, Thessalie • Greek/Illyrian • *an area and city of northern Greece; unknown root*

Thora • Norse • *follower of Thor*

Thursday • Anglo-Saxon/Norse • *Thor's day; Thor is equivalent to Jupiter*

Tia, Laetitia, Lucretia, Tiana, Tiara • Spanish/Portuguese • *aunty or short form of any name ending in -tia*

Tierney, Tighearnach, Tighearnaigh • Irish Gaelic • *lord or chief*

Tiffany, Theophania, Theosphainein • English/Greek • *Epiphany: God will appear*

Tikvah, Tikva • Biblical/Jewish/Hebrew • *hope*

Tita • Latin • *old Roman name, unknown origins*

Toni, Tonia, Tonia, Tonya, Antonia, Antoinette • Etruscan/Roman • *Roman family name but with confused origins*

Topaz • Persian/Greek/Latin • *the Sagittarian gemstone*

Topaz • Biblical/Hebrew/Greek • *God is good*

Torborg, Thorbjorg • Norse • *fortified place belonging to the god Thor*

Tordis • Norse • *goddess connected to Thor*

Tori, Tory, Toria • Norse/Danish • *Thor*

Tottie, Charlotte, Lottie, Totty, Lotte, Carlotta • English • *short form of Charlotte*

Tova, Tofa, Turid, Tove, Tufa • Norse • *the god Thor made me beautiful*

Tracey, Trace, Tracie, Tracy • Latin/Gaulic • *a person from a place in Normandy called Tracy!*

Trinity, Trinidad • Roman Catholic • *the Holy Trinity*

Trista, Trysta • American English/British Welsh • *rowdy, rebellious, blue, melancholic, chaotic*

Trixie, Trix, Trix, Beatrix, Beatrice • *blessed through life*

Tuilelaith, Talulla, Talullah • Irish Gaelic • *a lady of abundance*

Uhuti • Swahili • *my sister*

Ujana • Kiswahili • *youth*

Ulrike, Ulrika, Ulla • Germanic/Anglo-Saxon • *from riches comes power; power and riches*

Uma • Sanskrit • *turmeric or flax; messenger of the gods*

Valetta, Etta, Valletta • Italian • *combo of Val and -etta; capital of Malta*

Vanessa, Nessa, Venessa • literary invention/Dutch • *created by Jonathan Swift from his lover's Dutch surname, Vanhomrigh*

Venetia, Venice, Venezia • Italian • *someone from Venice, celebrating the city of Venezia*

Vera, Verus • Slavic • *a woman with faith*

Verona, Veronica • Italian/English • *someone from the city of Verona*

Veronica, Verona, Bérénice, Ronnie, Ronni, Roni, Veraicon, Véronique, Veronika, Vroni • Latin • *true image: vera icon*

Victoria, Vicky, Vickie, Vicki, Vikki,

Tory, Toria, Vita, Victoire, Viktoria, Vittoria, Bhictoria • Latin/English • *conqueror, winner*

Virtudes • Roman Catholic/Spanish • *seven Christian virtues*

Visitacion • Roman Catholic/Spanish • *the Virgin Mary visits her sister Elisabeth*

Wallis, Wally • Anglo-Saxon • *foreigner*

Wanda, Wenda, Wendelin • , Germanic/Polish/Slavic • *a member of the Slav tribe living between the Elbe and Oder*

Wendy, Wenda, Wendi, Gwendolen • literary invention • *JM Barrie created it for his book* Peter Pan *from his own nursery name Fwendy-Wendy meaning friend*

Wahiba • Arabic • *a generous woman who gives her all*

Wenqian • Chinese • *madder red*

Xena • Greek • *stranger, foreigner*

Xenia • Greek • *hospitality and a welcome to or from a stranger or foreigner*

Xiaohui • Chinese • *little wisdom*

Yanlin • Chinese • *Beijing, Chinese capital*

Yelena, Helen, Helena • Russian/Greek • *ray of sunshine, sunbeam, sunny*

Yelisaveta, Elisabeth • Hebrew/Jewish • *God is my oath*

Yevgenia, Eugenios • Russian/Greek • *well bred and high born*

Ying • Chinese • *a clever girl*

Yusra • *a woman who attracts wealth, prosperity and good things*

Zelah • Biblical/Hebrew/Jewish • *literal meaning is 'side'; one of the 14 cities of the tribe of Benjamin*

Zeinab, Zaynab • Arabic • *a glorious, admired sweet-smelling plant*

Zena, Zina, Alexina • Russian/Greek • *descended from Zeus*

Zena, Zina, Xena • Russian/Greek • *stranger, foreigner*

Zenobia, Zenobios, Zenbios, Zenovial • Greek • *Zeus, Jupiter, life*

Zhu • Chinese • *bamboo: a lucky plant; symbol of happiness, wealth and health*

Zina, Zinaida • Greek • *descended from Zeus*

Zinnia • German • *a flower from Mexico named after botanist J G Zinn*

Zinovia Zina, Zenais, Zenovia, Zenobia • Greek • *life of Zeus*

Ziska, Zissi, Franziska • German • *to be French, someone from France*

Zongying • Chinese • *heroine the others look up to; a role model*

Zula • South African/Zulu • *someone from the Zulu tribe*

Capricorn and Aquarius – Saturn

Some years back, in fact many years ago, a renowned astrologer and good friend, Liz Greene, came to the conclusion that without Saturn we would all just be a pile of rubbery skin messing up the floor.

What did she mean? Why did she say it? First and foremost Saturn and Capricorn, like Scorpio and Pluto, tend to get a bad press due to people who don't know astrology and should keep quiet.

Saturn, to the ancients, was the outermost star and was just about as far as you could go in the limits of the universe. In medieval cosmic teachings he was the planet of death, of time and fate – and if anything might go wrong or did go wrong it was nearly always placed at Saturn's door. He was the most malevolent of malefics.

This kind of cosmic character assassination continues to this day. Many enlightened astrologers, though, led by Liz and me, started to look at this old devil in a new angelic light.

Personally speaking, I have Saturn rising in the 12th house, which in old battered 'fate and fortune' books meant imprisonment of some kind. That's enough to set young astrological nerves jangling but it was not entirely wrong; you simply had to look at the dynamic of the 12th house and the role of Saturn – the ringed planet – in an alternative or more modern way. Think about it: Saturn imprisoned himself behind his own rings, which is why his keywords of limitation and restriction ring so true. This can be interpreted in a Capricorn's reserved and cautious personality.

Emotional imprisonment is one interpretation which can lead to a lack of confidence, depression and self-doubt, and that's without taking into account the nebulous 12th house!

The psychological life challenge for strong Saturn types can be summed up in the same way as Sir Edmund Hillary must have felt when first arriving at Camp Himalaya on Mount Everest. Although one is physical and the other emotional, it doesn't mean that the guts required is any the less daunting – they can both give pain and attainment.

Back to Saturn's 'skin': Liz's words shed a fresh intelligence. Liz talked about a pile of skin, because Saturn represents, amongst other things, structure, foundation and support, so without a skeleton for our skin to hang onto, it really would be just be a pile of latex!

That same Saturn structure or skeletal framework is required for any plan or enterprise. Without Saturn's blueprint or customary concern with cost and feasibility, any venture is doomed to fail. A career cannot have a hope of withstanding the blasts of modern-day living and the precariousness of economic and climactical conditions of the 21st century unless everything is planned meticulously and the number crunching adds up.

In the mid-1990s on national British and American television, I made a stark warning-cum-forecast based on Saturn's transits to come. I gave a dire warning that unless the human race looked after Mother Earth, now and in the future, then prophesies of the Biblical kind – plagues, famines and anything else nature could throw at us – would become a stark reality. Shall I rest my ecological case now?

So what can a Saturnian name bring or add to the life of its bearer? Putting it simply: structure, prestige and seriousness. A Mars or Uranian name might be exciting and exhilarating, and a Jupiter or Venus signature excessive and entertaining, but a Saturnian sobriquet will keep the bearer calm and collected and introduce cool reality to any harem-scarem situation or personality.

Do not shy away from a Saturn name: he is as much a patron, father figure or wise teacher as an autocrat, strict pensioner or austere boss.

If you want to instil ambition into your child, then give them a moniker to help them get somewhere in life, with a self-made self-assuredness (even if it is sandwiched between first and surname). Armed with Saturn's shield it can help the bearer become a success.

A combo of Saturn and Jupiter will help set the tone that this kid means business.

As a devotee and teacher of feng shui, I know that yin/yang and a balance of the elements are crucial to get the best out of life's natural forces, which can be harmonious when placed fortuitously in a name.

Add a touch of Moon and Venus to Saturn to ensure your babe doesn't become emotionally starved or so reserved that love stumbles as it tries to find a way into their little heart.

Saturn is the old head on young shoulders and intellectually mature; the message a Saturn name sends out is 'Please take me seriously' and those who matter will do just that.

Because Saturn is governor of two signs (as a result of him originally being the last stop on our solar system's metro line), it is a necessity for all to understand the extreme difference between Saturn/Capricorn and Saturn/Aquarius. Capricorn is conventional, traditional, trustworthy and reliable. Aquarius is unconventional, rebellious, wayward and charismatic.

If Capricorn Saturn tends to concern itself with what people think, Aquarius Saturn does not give a toss: 'To hell with what others say, I am here to please myself, no one else.' While Capricorn wants to keep thoughts and ideas orderly and controlled and ready for when the 'time is right', Aquarius wants to be shocking and outrageous, wilful and upset the apple cart.

Saturn/Aquarius despises authority; Saturn/Capricorn is authority.

If you want to give your child a head start in life that will set the trend for a person who is ready to take on the world and carve out their own destiny, then christen them with a Saturn name and then you will get a little bit of both Capricorn and Aquarius. It is worth getting a baby's natal chart cast to see where or if other planets fall in either Saturn sign.

A Sun, Moon or Ascendant in Capricorn will enhance the diligent traits, whereas Sun, Moon or Ascendant in Aquarius will increase the more ingenious nature of the Uranian side of the sign.

Now for the really good stuff: the virtues of this age-old planet have the advantage of helping his children live a life of fulfilment and satisfaction, which might not come until their more mature years – but when it does they will love making up for lost time.

To prevent the young Saturnian missing out on youth, add a Mercury (the planet of youth) initial or name to their autograph. Give Saturn the same respect you would an ancestor or someone older and undoubtedly wiser and more experienced and you will win a faithful friend.

But here is my big Saturn secret: the greatest gift you can give a Capricorn or Aquarian child is an exquisite sense of timing and humour. Tears of laughter then create a great comedic player; this planet has a twinkle in his wry, dry eye with the laconic delivery of Jack Benny, Les Dawson, Jackie Mason: Jewish humour is all about the best of Saturn.

With Saturn at the helm of a name, at least your kid has a chance of keeping a semblance of order in their life and on the highway to success and making a name for themselves.

Although this planet has rulership over a dichotomous duo, Capricorn and Aquarius, by crafting the two correctly in a name your child can be the architect of and in control of their own destiny. What's in a name? Everything.

Aquarius – Uranus

There is a certain cachet to be labelled an eccentric, even when you're not. Try it next time you meet the most normal and unoriginal of people. Use the phrase 'Oooooh, you are camp!' and just watch a smile smother their face revealing sheer delight, because although they know they are ridiculously normal it thrills that they might just be a little bit different.

If you meet a real oddball it often leaves the stormin' normal fazed, concerned or even fearful that they might be different, as they think they're normal! The truth is that people who really are avant-garde and unconventional rarely know it themselves and to be labelled as such will bring a very different reaction to the normal, possibly one of shock-horror!

Uranian Aquarians produce a disco-ball full of razzle-dazzle. They can be described as off-the-wall. The thin dividing line between genius and madness is trudged daily by Uranians. You notice I didn't write 'Aquarians' for one good reason: they might be Saturn-types, which is the complete opposite of the Uranian Aquarian.

To give a child a Uranian name will invite excitement and the unusual to their lives, and introduce charisma and magnetism to their persona. But be warned: like any Uranian Aquarian, if the name is completely outlandish your child will be perceived as being perverse or en route to being seen as a wild child, even if they are the most shy and ordinary youngster on this earth.

As the parent or guardian, ask yourself this when you are choosing your baby's name: are you actually plonking a bonkers moniker on your child because it gives vent to your own frustrations or boredom? We all have to live up to a name that is not chosen but is given to us, so it is a wise mum and/or dad who realises that their choice will either be their child's cross to bear or a source of eternal pride.

Until your youngster is past the dreaded age of 12–15, they will find it hard to deal with the responsibility of having a name foisted on them by parents who name their baby as nonchalantly as they would a cat or dog. It is the child who has to walk into school and face the other children (who can be the cruellest of human beings) and that would be a terrifying experience if you're called, say, Talula Does the Hula from Hawaii. The name a child is given will only start to work once they are free of the yoke of parents and then they have either grown used to it and like the idea of being different or have learned to live with it by shortening it to something more acceptable. So Talula Does the Hula from Hawaii might simply call herself Kay.

As the planet of freedom, independence and individuality, Uranus is everything associated with the dawning of the Age of Aquarius. This planet was only discovered during the time of the French Revolution in the late 18th century so by association this unruly star despises authority, and, with a reputation as the cosmic iconoclast, will do all in his chaotic power to destroy order and blitz conservatism.

Inside even the safest and most stable Aquarian there breeds revolution ready to revolt and shock. I write from experience, for with a natal Aquarian New Moon plus Uranus at the zenith of my chart conjunct the Midheaven and square Saturn (the traditional Aquarian ruler) conjunct the Ascendant, I often have to hold myself in check so that I don't do things simply to shock the establishment. Having said that, that is usually my tactic: to burst the bubble of someone who is very pleased with themselves! I go to extremes because I want to provoke a reaction as I itch for confrontation to combat pomposity. Aquarians are often the catalyst others need to get their own lives together but they should only do it if they have control over their own lives. Thankfully most of the time I do; the blessings of Saturn rising!

Russell was undoubtedly an unusual name when I was born in the 1950s, and although the etymology of Russell bears no resemblance to my stature or look, it did have a strong Uranian/Aquarian tone because of when I was given the label. The vibration certainly caused sniggers when I first went to school.

The mocking from my classmates when I was introduced to a school or class became predictable because it is the way people, especially children, react to something new: they fear it and don't understand it. 'The only thing we have to fear is fear itself' said Franklin D. Roosevelt, and wouldn't you just know it he was a Sun Aquarian himself, which just goes to show why he instinctively knew this.

I worry greatly – well, my Saturn does – when celebrities tag children with weird names that can cause the developing youngster to provoke a negative response from others. When the kid is old enough then perhaps their Pluto will wreak revenge on their parents' tombstones with an epitaph that reads 'This idiot called me Talula Does the Hula from Hawaii and turned me into a laughing stock.' A Uranian Aquarian will take it in their stride and be more concerned about how you spell it. I go mad if someone spells 'Russell' with just one 'l' – see what I mean?

By the way, you might think I made up the name Talula Does the Hula from Hawaii but oh no. Get ready for a reality check: it was actually the name given to a young girl in New Zealand. Other names given to Kiwi kids have been Fish and Chips, Yeah Detroit, Keenan Got Lucy and Sex Fruit which were, thankfully, for the child's sake, blocked by registration officials; others were allowed, though, including Number 16 Bus Shelter and even Violence – how wicked is that? And I mean wicked as in evil. Back to Talula, who by the age of nine had had enough and took action. At the end of the case the judge said this, which sums up everything I believe: 'The court is profoundly concerned about the very poor judgement which this child's parents have shown in choosing this name... It makes a fool of the child and sets her up with a social disability and handicap, unnecessarily.' And from the child who was the victim? The girl had been so embarrassed at the name that she had never told her closest friends what it was. She told people to call her Kay instead.

This is the crazy world of the planet Uranus; it zaps from one extreme to another, but sometimes it can go just far too far – fanatical and wilful to a degree with no thought, and I mean no thought, for those who bear the consequences of others' actions.

Uranians will love to be noticed by their name and that's fine if they can handle their handle. When choosing your child's name, be kind, as they cannot change it until they are old enough to be out of your jurisdiction and able to choose for themselves.

You could face rage, resentment and rebellion, even revenge. Foisting a Uranian name can give a child the okay to behave without thought for others, and you have invited them to become a law unto themselves. What's in a Uranian name? Everything to woe betide the parents who do it without consulting the stars. Uranus requires discipline and control without denting or compromising the natural brilliance of the young individual. It is always about balance: a little bit of Saturn for self-control, Venus for charm or Mars for focus. It is worth reading all the planets in this guide to see what they can each offer.

Motivating the Uranian mind is good, so some Mercury or Jupiter will promote and advance the genius within. A child inspired will be a prodigy, way ahead of his or her time and able to put other kids in the shade. But it can attract opposition from more dimwitted dunces. Introduce Uranus into a name and it will always predict controversy somewhere along the line.

My middle name is D'Ammerall. You might think that is Uranian and it is because it is so, so different. But in personal terms it is Saturn/Moon Capricorn/Cancer. Why was I given it? Because it is a name given to the oldest child of each generation; part of my family's ancestral heritage. Russell is a fiery name but because of the decade I was christened, it reeks of Uranus because it was unusual for its time. And Grant is très French and très, très Jupiter.

All of this you need to know to weigh things up for yourself. Everyone is different even if they share the same name. This fine book will give you all you need to know about astrological names, but you also must be ready to understand that if a name isn't in vogue then it will be classed as Uranian merely because of that fact. And you need to take into account your family traditions, middle names, how the child will carry it and so on. This is something you will have to judge for yourself.

In the distant past the solar system originally stopped at Saturn; Uranus, Neptune and Pluto weren't discovered until centuries later. Known as the Trans-Saturnians they were less personal and more generational. Each has their own unique peculiarity. The Uranus/Aquarius peculiarity is that it creates a child ahead of its time but who's perceived as a kid who is weird as much as wonderful.

It will convert the ordinary child into a superstar so long as they don't become a supernova that burns out and becomes a black hole courtesy of its parents. Uranus needs support from Saturn and Mercury to discipline the mind without it crossing that thin dividing line between genius and madness. And if you don't want to cause your child to be the subject of ridicule because you gave them a name that is a supplement for your ego, then choose very carefully.

It's common practice for Uranian/Aquarians to choose a nom-de-plume; this can be the unwritten clause in the imaginary contract between child and parents to allow them to do what they must do – it is their safety valve in what could become, over time, a volatile situation.

So don't be surprised if you have named your baby anything remotely Uranian/Aquarian if the minute your maturing young-ster can think for themselves they go for a name change. This is your chance to support them in their own choice, you owe them that much at least – my life motto is 'do as you would be done by' or in one word: 'respect'.

Pisces – Neptune

With Neptune you are entering a phantasmagorical world. What is fact and what is fiction? The distortion of the facts can turn reality into fiction, which is one reason why this planet can cast a doubt in the mind of the most bright and logical thinker. It is hard to fathom most questions that a Neptunian Pisces can pose. It is best described as not being able to see the wood from the trees; the fog of doubt or secrecy that descends when Neptunians feel at their most insecure, anxiety that can lead to paranoia and neurosis. Because they have often been rock bottom and have got many a T-shirt to prove it, their triumph is being able to help others who have a problem distinguishing fantasy and reality and have sometimes taken measures to combat it by escaping the harshness of it all by resorting to drink or drugs. But they are not always victims; on the contrary, Neptune/Pisceans can be the salvation of so many people who have wanted to give up. They are Mother Teresas or Florence Nightingales in the making.

Neptune/Pisceans are not masters of disguise for nothing; they can switch the masks of comedy and tragedy in a flash. If they think someone is getting a mite too close for comfort and might, just might, be discovering their true side, they can alter their course or mood in a twinkling.

This planet and the sign it rules, Pisces, is one of tender feeling, of acute sensitivity and rivulets of emotion that can flow at the beginning, middle and end of any black-and-white movie. They have been known to burst into tears at the sound of music or join in with The Sound of Music, which will move them much more than sex. This placement wants fantasy, sparkles and disco balls everywhere, tinting their world with razzle-dazzle.

Hollywood and the movie industry reached its zenith when

Neptune was transiting Leo (the planet of glamour sashaying through the sign of showbiz). So if you cast a name on your baby with Neptune and Sun/Leo vibrations you are inviting celebrity, fame and fortune.

Sex can be a problem for Neptunians because this is an idealistic placing and so therefore, with their fevered, fantasy-filled imagination, the actual act itself is never quite as good as the build-up, and it's messy to boot. This is why many Neptune/Pisces types prefer blue movies and any other means of escapism as the actual intimate act is okay but foreplay is their thing as they are very sensual beings. When it comes to any kind of climax they are great at fake. They will make their partners think the earth moved, but the Neptunian was possibly thinking of someone or somewhere else at the time.

Little is for real, even less is tangible; positively this can mean a wonderful artiste is born, a patron of the arts and a lover of all things from dance to acting – for this is the Neptune Pisces role; they can portray their feelings through performance. You know, I wonder if Norma Desmond had plenty of Pisces and a powerfully aspected Neptune hovering over Sunset Boulevard? Could be as Norma was a name made-up for an opera and isn't, what you might think, the female version of Norman – see, Neptune is working already.

This is one of the most compassionate and caring of astrologicals because Neptunian/Pisceans can feel the pain, the agony and the distress of others. If you prick, do I not bleed? Disillusionment is part of their make-up. This is an area they share with the other Pisces ruler, Jupiter, exaggerating the circumstances of a situation. Making a drama out of a crisis if it saves lives is par for the cause, because they can justify their actions if a human or animal life is at stake – this is the sign of the saint and very often the martyr.

Part of the understanding of fantasy is manifested in a love of all that is glamorous, sophisticated and refined – the adoration of candlelight, soft music, the sensuous feel of satin and silks, the pungent smell of aromatic perfumes and oils – all of this makes the Neptunian royalty in the art of seduction. That is why foreplay is so important in anything, whether it's a good story so you can build up to a climax, you see it is never all about sex.

The Neptune/Piscean's life quest should begin with Once Upon A Time and always end with And They Lived Happily Ever After. So romance is not just a part of their escapism but they want to see it working in their own lives too. Living in a world of their own is often used as j'accuse against this impressionable sign and planet. They have a capacity to believe whatever they want to believe, even if it is not true; their propensity for covering up and self-pretence is an art in itself. That is why they don't often go out to deceive others, it is themselves they want to deceive first and foremost. They have won gold medals for the sport of sticking their head in the sand.

This planet and sign excel in doing the most wonderful things for others; selflessness and self-sacrifice occur at regular intervals and it is they who volunteer for charities and take up vocations in the caring services or public sector. I have seen first-hand how Pisces/Neptune are either victims, addicts who suffer whether for their art or the wickedness of the world, or the helpers and lifesavers who transcend the negative and blossom into someone divine and out-of-this-world.

To be given a Neptune name can be a burden if the child has a proclivity towards daydreaming, but lace it with some strict Saturn and your babe will become less gullible and susceptible, which is a big problem if they get in with the wrong crowd. Being taken in by people who are corrupt or users and abusers is all too easy for the unfocused Neptune/Pisces – the vicious circle was invented for them. Once they slip into vice it won't be easy to pull them out, unless a) they want to or b) they never drifted into it in the first place.

Following a spiritual and even aesthetic path is something every Neptunian should do – a yearly pilgrimage or sacred retreat for whatever religion they follow. All Pisceans, whether Neptune or Jupiter types, need a faith. It becomes their support network, the hope they need when all seems lost. The belief in a higher being works wonders for their morale and confidence: if as a parent you are atheist or agnostic you really must take this into consideration with your naming ceremony.

Worrying for worry's sake and being able to block out the truth if it hurts or isn't acceptable is a negative, so regular reality checks from friends and family are a must. Neptune/Pisces is the most psychic and spiritual of placements. Plant a Neptune name on a child and you will have waved a magic wand bringing out an innate love of the supernatural, the mystical and fairy world.

Their multi-coloured, vivid imagination should be channelled into something that will show their talent isn't just a passing phase but that they are very, very gifted. Add a Mercury name or initial to help give structure to their artistic inspirations.

Neptune/Pisces personalities are enchanting; in fact you will believe that you have Princess Aurora and Prince Charming living in your midst. But that can, in turn, spill over into dramas when school days come as most kids aren't nearly as sensitive as your Neptune child. Although some Pisceans are cold fish this can be a defence mechanism to avoid getting hurt. The addition of something Mars Aries/Scorpio will toughen them up.

This can be a most complex placement, a vague and confusing disposition that is offset by remarkable altruism and courage in the face of adversity, especially if it comes to easing the pain and misfortune of others. The best of Neptune/Pisceans are remarkable people: positive, spiritual and compassionate, someone who really does feel your pain and the pain of the world deep down, and most importantly wants to do something to ease it.

Aries and Scorpio – Mars

You are in total macho territory with Mars. This uber testosterone planet is mucho manly and head-up the I and Me factor. Nothing ventured, nothing gained and fortune favours the brave are both Mars maxims.

Because Mars is the first planet of the zodiac as governor of the first sign of the zodiac, being second best doesn't even figure in this Olympian who wants the gold medal or nothing at all.

Mars names boost confidence, enable assertion of the individual's rights and courage against all the odds. But this can easily turn to being self-centred, aggressive and a bully.

Because no-nonsense Mars delivers sex appeal in sex-loads, when we hook up with Mars he can offer more pelvis thrusts than any Tom Jones (Welsh singer or bawdy novel will do!) ever! He can't, indeed won't, believe that the object of his desires won't reciprocate or fancy him. He adores the classy, sassy side of Venus but to be honest, negative Mars will enter any port in a storm if lust gets the better of him, and it often does.

Lady Chatterley (top class Venus) and her lover (rough class Mars) is a classic version of Mars and Venus on top of Olympus, when they were often caught in flagrante and as a result of their love-making out popped Cupid (Eros), the mischievous archer of amour.

Just like the Sun needs the Moon, so Mars needs Venus. To judge the love temperature properly when name-choosing, a combination of a Mars and Venus for boy or girl is just fine and dandy: you will produce your own wee Romeo or Juliet.

This is when the dual names come in handy, for you can have your cake and eat it – Marie Antoinette, she lost her head but lived a life of Mars/Venus with her Swedish lover, a warrior from northern realms who came to the court of King Louis.

You see how easy it is to be drawn into sex and love with this astral aphrodisiac concocted by these two sex stars.

Back to Mars: what can he stand and deliver for you in a name?

Mars is still co-ruler of Scorpio along with Pluto but his influence is much stronger and more powerful in his own singular sign of Aries. Remember, Mars does not like to be second best; winner takes all for him.

With a Mars Aries name you will channel the energy, spirit, flair, dynamism and vitality of your child into thinking for him- or herself and stand up for themselves too. This is no namby-pamby name, though too much Mars can cause conflict and discord within the family, schoolroom, sports club or play group, in fact anywhere wee (or even big) Martians frequent.

Avoiding your Aries/Scorpio boy or girl getting in with the wrong crowd is an imperative simply because, just like animals, in the primeval world of Mars there is a pecking order and to get to the top means foul means will predominate if fair doesn't work.

All magnificent Martian energy needs to be focused – once given via name to a child it will help with a single-minded attitude that aims to get to the top – the arrow pointing out at one o'clock at the top of the Martian glyph is there for a reason. Numero Uno and don't you forget it!

The difficult years will be the teens because Martians will be at their most stroppy, indignant and uncontrollable. If they can find a release in sports, competition or the armed forces, all well and good; if not, like a Tom Cat or She Devil they will want to show who is boss and be the leader of a gang. Females of the Mars species are dangerous as they can goad and dare men to prove themselves by doing things they perhaps wouldn't usually do.

Martian and Aries named girls who use their name vibration well will shatter through any man-made glass ceiling and make it perfectly clear that they are a match for any male, and indeed they are: I wouldn't argue with that. They will use their super sex appeal and resort to feminine wiles whenever they need to call in the big guns! Mars Aries can make a name for themselves and excel in anything where they have known competitors, which brings out the best in their incredible spirit. Mars Scorpios are even more versatile: they can excel in secret ventures before their rivals have woken up to the fact they even have someone fighting for supremacy.

Martians can be a champion at anything they take on. They hate to lose and refuse to give up on any fight or challenge; even though fatigued and on a hiding to nothing they always believe they can snatch victory from the jaws of defeat.

What Scorpio Martians spring to mind? Think Lucretia Borgia who got her wicked way by mastering (should that be mistressing?) the art of poison. Hillary Rodham Clinton – dogged, determined and darn right bloody-minded, refusing to throw in the towel in the Democratic elections. Margaret Thatcher with Mars and Pluto as her ruling planets as she had Scorpio rising. No-one can say they didn't pick up the gauntlet and hang on in the battle until the final trump. In Maggie's case she chose the Falklands war as the springboard to electoral success.

This underlines the difference between Aries (a male sign) and Scorpio (a female sign). Mars Scorpio is endowed with the same high-octane fight power as Mars Aries; they just tend to do it more furtively.

A fundamental difference between Aries and Scorpio is jealousy. The Mars Aries is too busy fighting the good fight to resort to envy, jealousy or revenge – but the Mars Scorpio sees a Machiavellian approach by being manipulative, often through seduction and sex, as being the kind of cat-and-mouse, cloak-and-dagger game they like: it's so much easier than physical fighting. Psychological battles can be just as lethal.

So if you are going to name your little tinker in honour of Mars/Scorpio be aware you will make a more secretive, wily baby than your Mars Aries kid who tells all in a candid, frank and naïve way.

Nevertheless, the positive side of Mars Scorpio is no defeatist but they can become an obsessive. Not nearly as intense as a Pluto Scorpio as their still, dark waters run very deep; what you see ain't necessarily what you get.

Sex is never far from the thoughts of any person with a Mars moniker once he or she has burst through the constraints of adolescence or pangs of puberty.

You will release the brave and fearless within your child. But if you want to cool the ardour of the red planet, a little bit of Saturn will help but in small doses because his rings can also cause frustrations, inhibitions and hang-ups. A Moon middle name or initial will add feelings to this sensationally sexy sign and Neptune will add romance and glamour. So rather than a wham-bam approach to intimacy they will be sensitive to the other person's requirements.

But perhaps Mercury is the very best planet to add to the Martian name because Mercury is the planet of thought, meaning they are more likely to think before they act.

To summarise, a Mars named child will do everything to make you proud but they will need discipline and control but most of all direction; give them this and your Mars boy or girl will be a person with spirit and become the apple of your eye and in time, someone who can successfully power their way into the hearts of many.

Taurus and Libra – Venus

Don't think that a Venus nomenclature is strictly for girls, because it isn't. A Venus name introduced onto a baby boy will enable her to get to work most positively by influencing his personality and adding an innate charm, diplomacy and affection. The same goes for a girl but that is more obvious to folks.

Too much Venus (if that's possible) can make someone tarty and so unbelievably sweet that, like too much saccharine, it can leave a bitter taste. Just enough honey is delicious; a little sugar can boost the flagging soul and spirit. Getting the right balance (very much Venus Libra territory) is crucial to ensure that sugar and spice and all things nice strike the perfect Venus vibration.

Venus/Taurus versus Venus/Libra boils down to the elemental difference of air and earth. There is a distinct difference between the airiness of Libra and the earthiness of Taurus in comparison with Mercury in the air of Gemini and earth of Virgo.

If Gemini is a playful, blithe spirit, then Libra is the cooling breeze that rushes off the oceans when the city is stifling, suffocating, hot and humid – it refreshes the mind and body and spirit.

Virgo Mercury is a cerebral earth placement looking at life with a practical, pragmatic eye, looking into everything to see what makes it tick. Whereas Taurus Venus is very basic; ribald, prosaic and bawdy – just like Shakespeare (who was Sun Taurus), then his character Sir John Falstaff would have most surely been Taurean too, judging by his character.

A Libra Venus name brings cute, sugar candy, whereas a Venus Taurus will enrich the wine, women and song approach.

Venus in either Taurus or Libra is not only stupefied by love but is also turned on by pretty things; baubles, bangles and beads. If Venus/Libra cherishes look, style and colour of her sapphire birthstone, so Venus Taurus wants to know the carat, weight, worth and how much to insure her emerald stone for.

Now you can see that if you put a Venus and/or Libra moniker on a baby he/she will want to look pretty, be pretty and see beauty in others but will hate anything or anyone ugly or grotesque. They will be attracted to the adoration of music and the arts and elegant fashion and colour coordination.

Stick a Venus Taurus tag on baby to increase their love of gorgeous and sumptuous things, especially their possessions. A Venus Libra name will up the ante in their love of gorgeous and sumptuous people, especially if they are beautiful too.

Add Mars Aries/Scorpio to a Venus baby and you will produce a child that is so appealing but extremely forward in the legend of the birds and the bees! An Aquarius Uranus name will add ingenuity to an already gifted astrological.

If you want a baby that is going to bring out the very best of Venus Libra/Taurus, then understand that too much Venus can make for a greedy, ungrateful child. Not only inclined to expect something for nothing but later in life failing to grasp the meaning of how to grow old gracefully.

To temper the vanity of Venus, bring in a middle name that emphasises Mercury in his Gemini or Virgo guise. His influence will give the Libra or Taurus child a chance to think about matters as not just being skin deep or superficial. Venus would be so much wiser, happier and more successful if they appreciated that they have in their name the epitome of all that's good and if they live up to it they can give love and receive it in return.

The name given to your Venus baby is just one side of the ritual. Add a caring Moon initial and careful Mercury or Saturn letters and you start to create someone who is an all-rounder in the humanity stakes.

To create a popular person in years to come, in the early stages nurse your child by immersing them in the Venusian realms of the arts, love and beauty. You can do this by choosing a Venus Libra/Taurus name.

Judge it right and they will never be without love or money in their life. Now that is a comforting thought for your old age.

Gemini and Virgo – Mercury

There are similarities as well as differences between Mercury Gemini and Mercury Virgo names. Let's deal with the planet first. As the winged messenger of the gods, this wee planet hidden between the Sun and Venus is never more than 28 degrees away from the Sun. This means that whatever your Sun-sign is, Olympus's little lad will either be in the same sign as your birthday sign, the one before or the one after. So if you are Sun Aquarius, Mercury will be in Aquarius or Capricorn or Pisces: so the way you think – he rules mental faculties – will be very close to the way you want to creatively live your life.

Mercury zodiac names enhance either the positive or negative aspects of the planet. The positive side of Hermes (his Roman name) channels the negotiator, the broadcaster, the upwardly mobile, the traveller, the teacher, the student, the communicator in us all, and on the reverse side: the liar, the cheat, the swindler, the con-artist, the superficial, the shallow and the one-trick pony. Astronomically Mercury has one side always in sunlight and the other side in the dark. This is ideally symbolic of both his characters and gives authenticity to the old saying 'It takes a thief to catch a thief' – in other words he has the kind of mind that knows what people of a similar nature or placement are thinking.

To give your little person a Mercury name will bring out the beauty or the beast in this planet, so look to see what aspects there are to Mercury in your child's chart if you can. Negative aspects to Neptune for instance will tend to bring out the more sly and slippery side, whereas positive aspects will bring out the majesty of all that is artistic with a Technicolor or even psychic imagery. The same goes for rays to Pluto; this can make for a great forensic investigator on a positive level, but negatively secretive and a double agent. No matter, self-examination and an interest in psychology are brought to the fore. This is good if the child is born under Libra or Aries as it will add depth to their name vibration.

Although small, this little planet offers a great deal, including intelligence, and because it is a dual planet, it can give as much of the positive as the negative: as he is volatile and mercurial, one breath of airy Gemini can swing him both ways rather like a weathervane.

One difference between Gemini Mercury and Virgo Mercury is the element. Gemini is air and Virgo is earth.

Over the 50 years I have been an astrologer, I have come to the opinion that the Gemini is searching for knowledge, the eternal student and very observational. Active and outgoing, they are great talkers and must have kissed the Blarney Stone at birth. Gemini names therefore respond to a desire to reach out, to see, to touch, to learn, to hear; Gemini activates the five senses and sometimes even the sixth, dependent upon the planetary aspects connected to Mercury. If you have a child you want to be a teacher or author or broadcaster, then look to names that bring out this extra-dimensional Gemini ability intrigued by curiosity and wanting to find out more.

Virgo names are more down-to-earth (an obvious statement), but not nearly as earthy as Taurus or Capricorn. Although still a Mercury sign, this placement tends to be more practical and pragmatic, and has a desire to learn to the point of perfection. Whereas the Mercury/Gemini can easily go on flights of fancy and make do with what little info they've got, Virgo wants to know absolutely everything and won't be content with half measures. Let's take the old adage that travel broadens the mind: for Mercury/Virgo this means finding out about the culture, language and country before they go, whereas Gemini Mercury will go and pick up the lingo, local habits and so on as they go along.

If you want to bring out the more learned Virgo trait in a name, then go for Mercury with the earthy element as it will bring out the librarian, researcher or factual writer. The airy Gemini will become adept at putting the facts gathered by their Virgo sibling into a novel or creative writing of some kind. So it depends whether you want them to go on a flight of fancy or keep their feet firmly on the ground.

With both elemental placements, negative Gemini can be flippertigibbit; here today and gone tomorrow, never finishing what they start and like a butterfly flitting from one thing to another, lacking concentration and with a suspect memory. Unless something is interesting to a Mercurian, especially with the Gemini vibe, their boredom threshold will be zilch.

The mentally challenged Virgo Mercurian will be the exact opposite: too pedantic, worrisome and anxious about trivia, minutiae, an inability to see the bigger picture, cynical, sarcastic and concerned about the punctuation and grammar of a sentence rather than what it actually says. The identity given to a baby weighed down by too much Virgo needs a name to help them chill out, so a little Moon, Venus and Jupiter in their full moniker will be extra helpful to coax out the funny side of life and help them get over things that are just not important.

The Mercury maxim can be summed up in the lyrics of the song – It's not how you start, it's how you finish. Gemini types often leave things halfway because they are bored, Virgos pull things apart and can't put them back together again.

Let's conclude on a high. Name your babe with a positive Mercury moniker and you'll have a natural communicator who will become a high-flyer thanks to their mental and cerebral expertise and a brilliance that borders on ingenuity. Whatever trade or industry they choose to pursue their commercial skills and mercantile potential through word of mouth and knowledge and inventiveness can take them right to the top. They are born negotiators.

Mercury Gemini can use their mind in anything from PR to media to writing. Mercury Virgo can rationalize, systematize and organize, making a fine PA or editor or analyst.

Alternatively, the Mercury/Gemini is super agile enough to become a champion tennis player, actor, dancer or computer boffin. Whereas Mercury/Virgo runs the tournament, is producer or stage manager, writes the script or keeps log books for the computer programmer – which of course they do brilliantly.

On all fronts this name can bring out a mind that will be your baby's fortune.

Cancer – Moon

Everyone knows their Sun sign as it is when you celebrate your birthday, the day when you were born. But don't forget the Moon, the cosmic partner of the Sun. The Moon is just as important as the Sun in anyone's birth chart. If the Sun rules golden Leo then the Moon rules silvery Cancer.

The Moon represents our feelings, emotions and sensitivity.

A Moon name for anyone will soften and tenderize the more masculine side of the Sun.

But too much Moon could mean the individual can find it hard to motivate their warmer, sunnier side. Unless your baby is a Cancerian, thereby ruled by the Moon, it is easier to live their Sun sign and it expresses itself in sensitive, warm, kind and caring ways. Strong Moon people want to protect, nurture and look after others.

It is a thin dividing line between caring for others and being cared for, and Cancer/Moon folks need a chance to explore their individuality more than any other sign. That way they won't become too dependent, overly needy and a lifelong child. Moon/Cancerians need to declare independence early enough in their lives to escape relying on the security of someone else telling them what they should do and if it is all right to do it.

The name of a Cancerian baby should allow them to channel their wonderful soft, caring nature, but to toughen up too so that leaving home, when the big day arrives, isn't such a shock. Cutting claustrophobic family ties is healthy and you as parents owe it to your child to let them know that this will happen one day: don't cosset them so much or they will feel guilty about making the final break. You can't lead your life through your child and if you try it can lead to a serious emotional breakdown between you and your treasured offspring.

'Belonging' is very important to any Cancerian, whether to family, home, town, community, school or club. The name given to a Moon/Cancerian is paramount to allow the Moon to flow and reflect the positive it picks up from the other planets (it has no light of its own). This you can do by choosing some glorious non-Lunar middle names. Obvious girlie names to allow the Moon to glow are the fabulous Selina and Phoebe: what could be more fine or better for a Cancerian girl?

The name given to a Cancerian boy is more important so that they don't become too attached to the person/people who brought them up. Cancer as a sign is easily handled by a female born under this sign but a man can attach himself far more tenaciously to the person or place he first remembers. That's when familiarity can breed contempt for the Moon/Cancerian male's chance to develop as a person.

The positive Cancerian male is in touch with his feminine side without it overwhelming him. Too much Moon for a man will mean he runs back to Mother, or whoever represents that maternal thread, the minute something goes wrong.

So you as parents must be careful that the name given doesn't turn your kid inward. We all know that some mums and dads can be very manipulative and won't want their baby boy being taken away from them. Throughout my 50 years in astrology, you would not believe the many screwed-up Cancerian males who have come to me for advice as a result of finding a partner, a wife, girlfriend or even boyfriend who is just like their mum! This can be too much of a negative emotional trip for both.

Same goes for the dads who don't want to lose their little girl, their little princess (ugh!). Just take a look at that great film *The Father of the Bride* – the Spencer Tracy, Joan Bennett, and Elizabeth Taylor version says it all.

A predominance of Cancer/Moon should be tempered with the healthy independence of the Sun or Mars as part of the baby's name or, if you can cope, the ingenious individualistic Uranus!

If you can find out where the Moon is positioned in your child's chart if your baby isn't a Cancerian, you will be able see what needs to be done to entice the full glory of the Moon out into the open. Do whatever is necessary to ensure that the clingy side of this sign is used for the good. For instance, Lunar people never really know when something has finished; they still hold on thinking there might be a chance it isn't. This can be particularly self-destructive in a relationship context.

The name of your Cancerian babe should enable them in later life to let go, move on and never allow history to repeat itself in exactly the same way. Memories and dreams should be used selectively: take the good but leave the nightmares behind. Too much Moon prolongs the agony when it is time to look forward, not back. Just enough Moon will give you a caring, sharing, soft and tender, sympathetic and compassionate being – now that's something to be encouraged.

Leo – Sun

Any baby born under the Sun sign of Leo (approx 23rd July to 21st August) will excel in a royal name, reserved for this most magisterial of all signs; creative, big-hearted and a joy to behold by one and all. Does that sound over the top? Well, not really, for it is a fact that Leo parents nearly always love their children more than your average sign and the pleasure goes on forever.

The good news is that you don't have to be a Leo to be the proud possessor of a Leo Sun name. Because we all have the Sun in one of the zodiac signs we can use that to our advantage or detriment. So with Sun in Aquarius, where the sunbeams aren't quite as rich and radiant in February as they are in August, you might want to warm them up with a warm, summery Leo middle name. It's that easy.

Too much Sun Leo can also make for an egoist, megalomaniac and narcissistic, in which case temper the royal name with softer elements such as a middle name or a joint name from the friendly Gemini or Libran list. That will heighten a desire to compromise and discuss options.

A Sun/Leo name will make a baby incredibly unrelenting to other folk's wishes, including the parents. But it does give a child spirit, style and a creative talent and potential they can craft into something wonderful.

With the introduction of a Saturn or Mercury middle name, the vast but raw Sun Leo talent can be taken and moulded into something practical, versatile, useful and highly successful.

As parents, finding the right name will be an advantage as it should and must resonate with the gift your Sun Leo has been born with. Through play and enjoyment the minute you see where your baby is at their most comfortable that is the time to strike with extra tuition, lessons or games/sports and set down the marker of a hero(ine) or champion in the making.

Does your youngster want to dance, paint or just be the centre of attention?

In these early years it is up to you as their mum or dad to concentrate on establishing their ego in ways that are creative, loving and enterprising. More than most signs you must constantly heap praise on Sun Leos as they were born to take applause. But it must be the right amount; too much and you will create a diva and, worse, a child who believes they are talented when they are not, which can lead to disappointment that might scar them where it hurts, their pride.

I cringe when I watch *The X Factor*, one of the most successful shows on television. When some sad soul sings their heart out believing they are good. They are then pulverized by the smarter-than-smart panel all trying to make their name with soul-destroying remarks.

Okay, so the entrants know what they are in for and they don't have to take part. But hold on a minute, did they only enter because people around them told them they had a wonderful voice? And said, 'You are so much better than those people on *The X Factor*, why don't you enter?' Their Leo Sun ego has been flattered so much (the Achilles heel of this placement) that they enter the lion's den in the sincere belief that they are talented. But isn't it the fault of their friends or family who have deluded them into thinking they are a star in the making and given them false hope?

The musical Gypsy also throws out another warning for Leo parents. You cannot and must not live your life through your child. Every day, from Miss America pageants to local sporting events, parents get more hung-up than their child protégé. Leo/Sun babies need to feel whatever they have done, they have done their best. Your disappointments must not become theirs.

Besides, if you push them in the wrong direction you might miss the fact that they are 'a star' in something they want to do, and can do quite naturally. But instead you've already made your mind up that they are going to have what you never had – but what if they don't want it? Don't squash their potential, encourage it – and if you don't understand it find someone who does and let them release the creativity locked inside.

You are lucky enough to have one of the most loving, beautiful, gifted babies in the zodiac kingdom; now honour your heir with a name that befits their special undeveloped talents, then sit back and just watch them flourish.

Scorpio – Pluto

Give a child a Pluto/Scorpio name and you conjure up an aura wrapped in mystery, tied in an enigma and hidden in a riddle: someone who intrigues as much as does the Mona Lisa's enigmatic smile.

There is something in a name from the catalogue of this deep, dark, intense placement that will have you and everyone else coming back for more. It is a tempting thought that Adam and Eve might well have been perfectly happy in the Garden of Eden until the snake (Pluto/Scorpio) slithered down the tree and introduced them to the kind of erotic intimacy that would have never entered their mind before.

But that is the essence of Pluto/Scorpio, they control the situation in the most below-the-belt way, unleashing the basest and most primeval of feelings and carnal urges. And yet, this is the same sign that has the will and strength of character to be pure and chaste and follow a vow of celibacy. Because the Pluto/Scorpio energy is about control, self-control and control of others, being in control will hasten whomever you name under the Pluto banner towards the kind of intimate and psychological tests and challenges most signs would find hard to contemplate.

Renaissance, obsession, rebirth, jealousy, regeneration, envy, revenge – these are just some of the words that you graft onto a child with a Pluto/Scorpio moniker, so beware. Alongside a powerful Plutonic name, temper it with a softer, sensitive and more compassionate name from Neptune; although this will enhance the secretiveness of the wee being it will make them sensitive to finer feelings. A Venus and/or Mercury addition will give the added extra of being a normal human being even though you know you are cradling Superman or Wonder Woman.

There is far from anything wrong with a Pluto/Scorpio name.

I say this because when writing the Capricorn/Saturn chapter it occurred to me that some people stand back with half-opened mouths when Saturn appears in an astrological forecast. Why? Capricorn's ruler is there to give structure. But Scorpio receives a similar reaction. People's obvious reaction to a Highwayman's Stand is one of fear, fearful of what might happen. But it is precisely that and the danger of it all that turns Scorpio/Pluto on. It's the same with sex, another satisfying Scorpio/Pluto preoccupation. It's not the actual act, it's the psychology of it all.

Of course, you are playing with fire with a name from the underworld duo, but the release is that Scorpio is very much a water sign and if things get too scorching with Pluto and Hades the hot-as-hell fire, it can always been extinguished with a splash of the Moon or Neptune.

To gift a child a Pluto name will require careful handling, so when you invoke the Pluto vibration expect the more-than-average bouts of trying to control others, manipulating and being taken over by titanic feelings of passion that can present problems in themselves. Teaching the Pluto/Scorpio kid to share isn't such a bad start; that's Venus's governorship.

Get them to understand their actions and channel the laser-like Pluto ability to transform nothing into something, to use their concentrated energy to create rather than destroy something wonderful from a broken-down wreck that to everyone else is irretrievable. A Mercury middle name will help facilitate their mind and then you will have created a force for the good.

With Scorpio there are two planets to consider, which is why a name chosen from this list does need care and consideration, for you are tempting fate. Scorpios are devoted, loyal and faithful to those who give the same in return, but you do have to prove yourself to a Scorpio. The best way is to always keep their secrets and confidences.

But Pluto/Scorpio is an all-or-nothing combo, no half measures. You'd better realise early on that your child is going to see something through and will resemble a terrier pup more than an ordinary babe. There is a danger that however young it is easy for them to become obsessed by something or someone. Later on it might be a cause célèbre or a lost cause, so you must help your little one to brave the unknown waters of his or her deepest challenge by knowing when something has reached its natural end and move on.

The positive outcome is when they get behind something and it works, it can be life-changing for everyone. You don't get the word Plutocrat for doing nothing; this is someone determined to reach the heights of success and power. A workaholic (enter Saturn), uncompromisingly aiming for the top come hell (there's that word again) or high water – how's that for a fantastic Pluto/Scorpio finale?

With Scorpio being a water sign, this sign will have a natural and well-developed instinct to be able to sniff out weak or flaky people and like the scorpion there is a natural desire to stamp them out – like anything they finish, they don't let it linger, they let the end be quick.

Pluto can be ruthless and the more negative types will get where they want through foul means rather than fair. That's why you need fair-minded Venus or at the very least a bewigged Jupiter in his most justly guise.

But used positively Pluto/Scorpios can create wonderful transformations in their lives. There is no death but rebirth, for this sign believes that for every ending there is a new beginning. There is no other placement like this in astrology. Fate, kismet and destiny are top of this astro-combo's vocabulary. This gives them a kind of inner knowledge and that sense of 'knowing' stays with them all life long. Very often Pluto/Scorpio babies have had a brush with the afterlife via a difficult birth.

But what you or I may fear, Pluto people take in their stride. Their fate rests in their own hands and the outcome relies on their own initiative for it is meant to be. Therefore it has to be, the inevitable cannot be avoided: that is their fate. Regrets don't figure in a Pluto/Scorpio's thinking.

When success does come, Pluto/Scorpio takes pride in the fact they were architects of their own destiny – and then they don't have to share the spoils. Remember what I said about the early years, to learn to share will in itself bring generous reprisals and friends and allies for ever more. Pluto invented the phrase 'keep your friends close and your enemies even closer' – suspicious of all. Once you jump the high bar of friendship – and it won't come easy – you will have a powerful friend for life.

Saint or sinner, at least with a Pluto/Scorpio child you won't know whether you're watching Rosemary's Baby or the life of the Dalai Lama. But it doesn't matter, for at that age this child wants you to show the way. They can overcome the greatest of odds and challenges psychologically or physically that result from bad parenting; they will not be easily if ever defeated.

You only have control over them for the briefest of times so make the most of it, bring out the three faces of Pluto/Scorpio: snake, eagle or dove – all are symbols of Pluto and Scorpio.

You have given birth to a wee powerhouse and now it's up to you to make them a force for the good.

Sagittarius and Pisces – Jupiter

Whether a boy or girl, to bear a Jupiter name or at least to include a little bit of Jupiter in some part of their full name (is there such a thing as 'little' when Jupiter is invoked!) will imbue good humour, good fortune and good vibrations.

The biggest planet in our solar system is the Lord of Luck and Opportunity, and luck can work in a number of ways. It's the planet of luck, but of course it depends how you define luck in the first place: it is said that good luck is when preparation meets opportunity. Another is when you are 'saved' from a situation that looks fantastic and wonderful and then your luck comes shining through when you don't get the break you were desperate for but only find out later that Jupiter saved you from making a huge mistake – a narrow escape.

The negative side of Jupiter is having great expectations, building hopes too high or going beyond realistic bounds. But the positive benefits outweigh the inflated downfalls. It does depend on what you see as positive – a wonderful sense of humour can attract the right people, those with influence and power. This is one reason why Jupiter is exalted in Cancer (this means the positive Jupiterian traits work well in league with the sign of the Moon). The famous belly-laughs, optimism that lifts the name-bearer out of the slough of Saturn despondency, giving them insightful judgement and the wisdom of Solomon. This is earned through experience or learning; Jupiter is the planet of the higher mind, and naturally the higher octave of Mercury – these two educational planets work well together.

To bring out the best in Jupiter, a sprinkling of Mercury brightness and wit combined with the solemn but controlling Saturn immunizes a person against being too carefree and cavalier. In one of my many television series I was on location in Rome specifically to investigate the energy and dynamic of Jupiter. We arrived at the Temple of Jupiter and it came to me in a flash that negative Jupiter and Sagittarius was the X factor – Xcessive, Xtravagant and Xaggerative. I won't debunk my own description of this grandiose planet. If I did I would be going against my own astrologicals: I was born with Jupiter in Pisces (his traditional sign) conjunct Mars and Venus and trine Uranus and Midheaven – you'd have to go a long way to find someone who can be the face of Jupiter on earth! Even my surname Grant, which comes from Grand, describes me to a 'T'.

When I devised my Astro-Tarot pack and the usual Major Arcana was sent to the artist, the Jupiter card came back with my face and figure on it, because Kay Smith, the artist, without even knowing about astrology, saw me as Jupiter.

Although the good outweighs the bad, the king of the gods, the leader of Olympian pantheon, had a lightning batch of thunderbolts that he could and would nonchalantly hurl down from the summit to mortals who aspired to being gods down below. Mere mortals, for Jupiter people can often have the Divine Complex. This means they firmly believe they can do no wrong and even if they do they are sure they are a protected species and will be saved from destruction at the last minute. There is nothing too bad about that until they become bombastic, above the law, patronising and arrogant, truly believing they know better than their peers or superiors. That's when pride comes before a fall.

Jupiter is the planet of good fortune but also inflation, so when the ego gets inflated, others (especially Saturn and Pluto types) want to prick it.

But what is the main difference between Jupiter/Sagittarius and Jupiter/Pisces? They both share the mutable quality which gives them flexibility and the ability to see the positive – one of my favourite descriptions is: 'The optimist [Jupiter/Sagittarius/Pisces] sees the donut; the pessimist [Saturn/Capricorn] sees the hole.'

I would say that as a rule of thumb if you give your child a religious name of any description, then you are giving them a real boost of faith-restoring Jupiter. Jupiter is the planet of belief, worship and religion, and that can mean self-belief as much as belief in a higher being. This is good for the child's mind, body and spirit.

Jupiter in Pisces can be fortunate through Piscean/Neptunian pursuits – the arts, romance, glamour and enchantment. Jupiter in Sagittarius name-bearers will find fortune through finance, and positions with status in life such as politicians and education. Both Jupiter types will find opportunity through travel, with Pisces often journeying over water, with Sagittarius all other ways. So exotic names from other cultures will favour the child whose aspirations, even via the parent at the beginning, is to see the world or settle down in a place many miles from where they were born.

Negative Jupiters in either sign must watch their natural cravings for rich and luxurious lifestyles. For me it is food and comfort in my home and even more so in hotel suites. I remember my friend Lulu, the famous Glaswegian pop star, saying to me, 'Never take a job unless they can guarantee that your travel plans and hotel suite [note she said suite, not room] are as comfortable as your own home, otherwise what's the point in leaving it?'

If necessity (Saturn) is the mother of invention (Uranus), then Jupiter should follow the maxim of always leaving the table a little hungry – leave the meal table, business negotiations and anything else with a little room for manoeuvre and never completely full.

Who once said the expectation of making a journey is better than the arrival? How clever and how true. If we could be like Dr Who and snap our fingers and our Tardis would transport us to another place, would we like that? Well, probably yes, there would be no delays or crowds – but what about the enjoyment of reaching the destination? As I like my comforts, I would go for snapping my fingers and arriving in a split-second on my balcony looking out over glacial lakes and snow-capped mountains. I am Jupiter in essence whereas the Saturnian crowd of no gain without pain might prefer to get the no-frills-cheap-flight and have more money to spend when they get to journey's end.

Let's sum this planet up: if you name your child or even yourself with a Jupiter/Sagittarius name, you will bring out quite naturally a positive mental attitude that will put you at the top of every social list at a party. Every time someone says your name they invoke your personal wow factor and drop-dead gorgeous personality. But remember: moderation in everything is the golden rule and knowing when to stop can be tempered with some Mercury and Saturn middle names.

Jupiter brings much popularity whether in fiery Sagittarius or mouth-watering Pisces.

In Pisces there is a faith and spirituality – the Good Samaritan, philanthropist, kind-natured, generous to a fault and very big-hearted. Negatively, there is everything from biting off more than they can chew to expecting everyone to be as honest, true and sincere as they are.

The golden Jupiter rule is don't do Jupiter in Sagittarius by ramming your opinions down other people's throats; practise what you preach or you will labelled a hypocrite, bigot or unscrupulous. Self-publicity and opportunism can be labelled as negative; I don't really see this as true so long as you always give credit where it's due. A positive Jupiter person knows when to shut up and say enough is enough. Leave 'em wanting more.

Notes